P9-CEG-011

Beyond Tiananmen

To Professor Tang Hai-tao
Professor Yuan Hai-ying
two of my most influential teachers.
With gratitude and respect.

蘇葆立

May 2005

Beyond Tiananmen

The Politics of U.S.-China Relations, 1989–2000

Robert L. Suettinger

BROOKINGS INSTITUTION PRESS
Washington, D.C.

1775 Massachusetts Avenue, N.W., Washington, D.C. 20036
www.brookings.edu

Library of Congress Cataloging-in-Publication data

Suettinger, Robert L.
Beyond Tiananmen: the politics of U.S.-China relations, 1989-2000 /
Robert L. Suettinger.
p. cm.
Includes bibliographical references (p.) and index.
ISBN 0-8157-8206-3 (alk. paper)
1. United States—Foreign relations—China. 2. China—Foreign relations—United States. 3. China—History—Tiananmen Square Incident, 1989—Influence. 4. United States—Foreign relations—1989–1993. 5. United States—Foreign relations—1993-2001. I. Title.

E183.8.C5S865 2003
327.73051'09'049—dc21 2003006186

9 8 7 6 5 4 3 2 1

The paper used in this publication meets minimum requirements of the American National Standard for Information Sciences—Permanence of Paper for Printed Library Materials: ANSI Z39.48-1992.

Typeset in Sabon

Composition by Stephen D. McDougal
Mechanicsville, Maryland

Printed by R. R. Donnelley
Harrisonburg, Virginia

To Michel Oksenberg (1938–2001)
Teacher, mentor, colleague, friend, and inspiration

Contents

Foreword

The transformation of U.S.-China relations is one of the most complex and consequential developments of the twentieth century, and it has major implications for the twenty-first. Therefore the bumpy road of China's integration into the international community has been a frequent subject of work by individual Brookings scholars and authors, as well as by our Foreign Policy Studies program and our Center for Northeast Asia Policy Studies. This book by Robert L. Suettinger is a timely and distinguished contribution to that ongoing part of the Brookings agenda.

The U.S.-China relationship was frozen for more than twenty years after the Chinese Communists came to power on the mainland in 1949. The turning point came when President Richard M. Nixon and Chairman Mao Zedong recognized they had a common adversary in the Soviet Union. Nixon's historic trip to China in 1972 led to a period of euphoria and goodwill, allowing the two sides to achieve even a degree of accommodation on the difficult question of Taiwan's status. As China moved into a period of reform and opening to the outside world under Deng Xiaoping, the bilateral relationship flourished. Rapid growth in trade, tourism, and many other exchanges were undergirded by the belief on both sides in a "strategic relationship" of joint opposition to the Soviet Union.

Then came the showdown and slaughter on Tiananmen Square in 1989. Students and ordinary citizens of Beijing had taken over the symbolic center of Beijing that spring, demanding dialogue, democracy, and freedom. Day after day, Americans and others around the world watched as hundreds of thousands of Chinese demonstrated peacefully, their student leaders imploring the government for basic political rights. When units of the People's Liberation Army stormed into the city late on June 3, 1989, and regained control the next day at enormous cost in lives, the U.S.-China relationship was damaged in a way from which it has yet, fourteen years later, fully to recover. Since then, cycles of normalization and engagement, alternating with anger, recrimination, and distrust, have characterized bilateral ties. The fall of communist regimes in eastern Europe and then in the Soviet Union itself made it patently obvious that the Sino-American relationship had lost its original strategic rationale, making restoration of amicable ties that much more difficult to achieve.

It is from that tragic and tempestuous episode that Bob picks up the story, drawing from his perspective as a veteran analyst in the Central Intelligence Agency and the State Department. His twenty-five-year career culminated in an appointment to serve as director of Asian Affairs on the National Security Council from March 1994 until October 1997, followed by a tour of duty as national intelligence officer for East Asia on the National Intelligence Council.

Bob traces the course of relations from Tiananmen through the end of the Clinton administration, when the U.S. Congress granted "permanent normal trade relations" status to China. He chronicles the Taiwan crisis of 1995–96, Jiang Zemin's rise to dominance in the PRC's policy process, and China's involvement in the campaign finance and spying scandals of 1997–99. He also analyzes the role of economics and trade and sketches what he sees as the prospects for U.S.-China relations in the decades ahead.

One of the virtues of this book, which was funded in part by a grant from the Smith Richardson Foundation, is the justice Bob does to the sometimes neglected connection between domestic politics and foreign policy. As someone with decades of experience working inside the government, Bob brings to his reconstruction and analysis of events an intuitive understanding of how state-to-state relations often hinge on human and highly personal factors, such as the pique or insecurity of individual leaders, rather than on abstract calculations of national interests and goals. With its solid grounding in the real world of policymaking and diplomacy, this book is a model of the kind of research that we at Brookings are proud to support and publish.

April 2003
Washington, D.C.

STROBE TALBOTT
President

Acknowledgments

I have drawn on a wide variety of materials in primary and secondary sources, as well as the work of a growing and talented field of sinologists in the United States and America watchers in China. For this project, I have benefited immensely from access to and extended conversations with key participants in the policy process, people who considered, made, and implemented important decisions for the U.S. government on its approach to China. Among them are Michael Armacost, Jeffrey A. Bader, Samuel R. Berger, Kurt Campbell, William Clark, W. Bowman Cutter, William A. Danvers, Carl Ford, Charles W. Freeman Jr., Sandra J. Kristoff, W. Anthony Lake, Deborah M. Lehr, Kenneth Lieberthal, James R. Lilley, Winston Lord, Joseph Massey, Michel Oksenberg, Douglas Paal, Daniel Poneman, Stanley O. Roth, J. Stapleton Roy, Brent Scowcroft, Susan Shirk, and Richard Solomon. I am indebted to numerous scholars and officials in the United States and China who advised and informed me about aspects of bilateral relations during this period but are not able or willing to be acknowledged by name.

No book is the product of a single individual's work, and I acknowledge the gracious advice and assistance from people who have aided me with research or read critically various portions of the manuscript. Adrianne Moore helped out in early research on Tiananmen-related information. Thomas J. Christensen, Paul Heer, David Michael Lampton, and J. Stapleton Roy reviewed the entire manuscript, while Bates Gill, Billy Huff, John Kamm, Mickey Kantor, Dimon Liu, James Mulvenon, Alan Romberg, Lee Sands, Anne Thurston, and Bruce Wells reviewed and commented on various chapters. James Steinberg reviewed the manuscript twice, commenting on substantive issues and correcting specific facts, as he was an active participant in the policy process on China. Michael Armacost and Richard Haass were enormously supportive in guiding and encouraging the project in its early stages. The staff in the Brookings Press was remarkably helpful. Theresa Walker edited the final manuscript, Susan Woolen supervised the cover design process, Vicki Chamlee proofread the book, and Enid Zafran prepared the index. Janet Walker, managing editor, also contributed to the editing of the final manuscript.

I greatly appreciate the help I received from the Smith Richardson Foundation staff, especially Samantha Ravich, Allan Song, and Marin Strmecki.

Last but certainly not least, I thank my wife, Sue-Jean, my children, and other family members for their faith and support in the long and difficult process of writing a first book.

CHAPTER ONE

Introduction

It has been fourteen years since soldiers of the Chinese People's Liberation Army (PLA) raced into the center of Beijing from their suburban encampments, ordered to recover "at any cost" the capital city's most important symbolic landmark, Tiananmen Square, from student demonstrators who had occupied it for seven weeks. Fourteen years since the terror, the noise, the fires, the shooting, the bloodshed, the screams of rage and fear. Fourteen years since the collapse of the Communist Party's leadership cohesion and what remained of its moral authority, causing it to resort to force and intimidation to maintain its grip on power. Fourteen years since the United States and other Western countries recoiled from China in horror and disgust, expelling it from the company of modern civilized nations through sanctions of various kinds. Fourteen years since the relationship between the United States and China went instantly from amity and strategic cooperation to hostility, distrust, and misunderstanding.

Time has healed many of the wounds of those terrible days of June 1989. The dead have been laid to rest, if not accounted for or forgotten; the wounded have been treated and healed. Most of those arrested and imprisoned in the massive roundup that followed June 4 have completed their sentences and been released. The universities that were cauldrons of unrest and dissatisfaction then are thriving now, with improved equipment and better living conditions attracting China's best and brightest. Students have turned from the youthful pursuit of democratic ideals to the pursuit of advanced degrees and lucrative jobs in China's growing private sector, much of it foreign funded.

Most of the Communist Party elders who decided that military force was the only solution to the problem of the democracy activists in Tiananmen

Square have died. Many of the students who emerged as leaders of the 1989 democracy movement and the hunger strike are in exile in the United States, having escaped during the early phases of the crackdown or having been released from prison on "medical parole." Most of the soldiers who took part in the attack on the city of Beijing have left the PLA. Many of the officers who were promoted for their leadership in "quelling the turmoil" have subsequently been retired or demoted. The Communist Party leadership "core" under General Secretary and State President Jiang Zemin—brought in after June 4—has been one of modern China's most stable and successful leadership groups, its rule uninterrupted by major internal strife or political upheaval.

Tiananmen Square has been repaired—the bullet holes filled, paving stones cleaned and later replaced for the celebration of the fiftieth anniversary of the founding of the People's Republic of China in 1999. It is again the people's square, with casual strollers, schoolchildren, kite-flyers, and tourists in abundance. People's Armed Police and other security forces still patrol in groups of two and three, on the lookout for practitioners of Falun Gong—a form of breathing exercise and spiritual awareness banned by the still-nervous communist government—rather than democracy activists. Traffic clogs the streets around the square, with bicyclists making more rapid progress in their separate lanes than the hordes of tiny red and yellow taxis, tourist buses, and private automobiles crawling through the midday rush hours. There is no sign, no memorial of what happened there in 1989.

The city of Beijing itself has been transformed in these fourteen years. The streets down which the students marched and the tanks raced now are lined with new hotels, shopping centers, and modern office buildings, and many are adorned with neon signs advertising Western corporations and foreign products—McDonald's, IBM, Intel, Coca-Cola. A new "central business district" of multistory office towers has sprung up near the intersection of Jianguomen Dajie and the Second Ring Road, where heavily armed troops faced east in 1989, seemingly fearing attack from other military units. Shoppers no longer pick through piles of shriveled cabbages piled along dusty streets, as they did then, but walk through air-conditioned grocery stores and shopping malls looking for well-packaged foods, designer fashions, sporting goods, and consumer electronics. China has become one of the most dynamic economies in the world, and Beijing is its showcase capital city. Having won the bid to host the 2008 Olympics, the city is even more eager to show its new look, new economy, and new style to the rest of the world.

Amid all the change—the forgetting, if you will, of Tiananmen—the relationship between the United States of America and the People's Republic of China has remained one of wary distrust that occasionally deteriorates into enmity. There has been little forgetting and less forgiving of what the two countries accused each other of in 1989. Although the two governments have improved their cooperation and even achieved a degree of amicability in the wake of the September 11, 2001, terrorist attacks on New York and Washington, these changes nevertheless seem tenuous, unsupported by improved trust or understanding. There is still plenty of rancor on both sides.

The United States regularly castigates China for a broad array of human rights abuses, with the State Department issuing in February 2002 the longest and most critical report about China in its annual series on human rights practices worldwide. China responds with charges of hypocrisy, racism, and "demonization" against the United States and issues its own critiques of American legal and moral shortcomings.

—Beijing charges the United States with "interference" in its domestic affairs, not only in supporting democracy activists in 1989 but in seeking to use various sanctions since then to leverage improvements in China's treatment of religious and political dissidents. It suspects the U.S. Central Intelligence Agency is supporting Falun Gong. In Washington, many believe China sought to use illegal contributions to some candidates in the 1996 election campaign to distort American politics and policies. Business lobbyists and academics who seem sympathetic to China's positions sometimes are portrayed as disloyal to the United States.

—Many Americans believe that China's pressure on Taiwan—where the government of the Republic of China retreated after it lost the Chinese civil war in 1949—actually emanates from a post-Tiananmen fear of the American style of democracy that Taiwan has instituted successfully since the early 1990s. For its part, China accuses the United States of deliberately violating its agreements on sovereignty and arms sales to Taiwan in order to keep China from achieving unification.

—Despite a rapidly growing trade relationship between the two countries, Washington criticizes China's trade practices regularly as "mercantilist," and a special commission has been appointed by the U.S. Congress to monitor the relationship between the bilateral trade flows and the modernization of China's defense industries. Many in China believe the United States is determined to prevent China from becoming the world's largest economy.

—Washington charges China with selling the technology, know-how, and materials to make nuclear and chemical weapons, as well as ballistic missiles, to unstable or "rogue" states, such as Pakistan and Iran. China counters that Washington is the world's largest arms dealer and is only trying to prevent China's emergence as a competitor.

—Despite the easing of bilateral strains in light of their opposition to international terrorism, China and the United States remained locked in strategic distrust at the start of the twenty-first century, based largely on misperceptions. Many in China, including in the leadership, believe the United States has an insatiable lust to be the world's dominant power and will go to great lengths to prevent China from becoming a global force. They refer to the United States as "hegemonic," similar to the kingdom of Qin in the second century B.C., which forcefully conquered and incorporated the various kingdoms of China into a unified state. Some Americans see China as a modern counterpart of nineteenth-century Germany or Japan—an ambitious, aggressive emerging state that will upset the international balance of power and force a conflict. Strategic thinkers and military planners on both sides plot future conflict scenarios with the other side as the principal enemy.

—Perhaps most important, the United States and China have developed negative stereotypes of each other, contributing to all the above problems. Despite warm and even improving people-to-people relations, polls since 1989 have consistently shown most Americans consider China an "unfriendly" country that violates the rights of its citizens. Although polls in China are not independent or systematic, there is a clear growth in the manifestation of anti-American sentiment, particularly among students and intellectuals.

Axioms and Assumptions

How did this situation develop? What are the causes of the hostility and what are the political factors in both countries that sustain it? What does this situation portend for future relations between China and the United States? Are the two sides heading for war? Or can efforts be undertaken to ameliorate the suspicions and hostility, and if so, how?

This book is about relations between the United States and the People's Republic of China from the calamitous events of June 4, 1989, to the last days of the presidency of William Jefferson Clinton in the year 2000. It takes as its starting point the events of Tiananmen, as I believe those events marked a critical turning point in the bilateral relationship. Before that time, the relationship was founded on a more or less shared set of strategic perceptions about the nature of the threat from the Soviet Union and on a "realist" viewpoint that Soviet power needed to be balanced by cooperation between its principal opponents. Although the relationship grew and flourished in many other ways after the visit to China by President Richard Nixon in 1972 and the issuing of the "Shanghai communiqué" establishing the ground rules for Sino-American cooperation, the strategic underpinning remained a constant in the relationship. After Tiananmen, when American perceptions of China were radically changed, and after the fall of first the Soviet "bloc" in eastern Europe and then the Soviet Union itself, that constant disappeared, or at least lost credibility. Justifying a close, cooperative relationship thus became far more difficult for both sides, while all the other problems and disagreements in the relationship became far more apparent and difficult to manage.

Equally important, after Tiananmen, the bilateral relationship lost its insulation from domestic politics. In the United States, President George H. W. Bush found his China policy directly challenged by congressional Democrats, as President Bill Clinton's was by congressional Republicans. Although Deng Xiaoping's primacy over foreign policy was hardly challenged, even after Tiananmen, President Jiang Zemin's stewardship of the U.S.-China-Taiwan relationship became an issue in his efforts to consolidate his power and authority within the Chinese leadership as Deng faded from the scene. In both countries, bureaucratic maneuvering and broader sociopolitical changes also affected the conduct of foreign policy, particularly bilateral relations. And both countries experienced periods of intense popular suspicion and even revulsion that political decisionmakers could not ignore.

The principal focus of this book is decisionmaking—that very human process by which ideas, beliefs, strategies, theories, prejudices, pressures, tradeoffs, and choices become identifiable foreign policies. It is a complex and confusing process, often misunderstood, especially by those who look only at the policy outcomes. Readers will find no grand theory to explain American or Chinese actions or to put them in a lucid strategic context. Quite the contrary. This book consists of a series of narratives about policymaking, by which the complexity and confusion of the process of making decisions are laid out in somewhat greater detail—from an "insider's" perspective, in part. From April 1989 until the end of 1998, I served in positions within the U.S. government—on the National Intelligence Council and the National Security Council—that enabled me to observe the policy process at close hand. While I would by no means depict my position as a major "policy player," I was a participant on occasion and familiar with the events and individuals that shaped the relationship during that period. Moreover, before that time, I had been an analyst and observer of China's domestic politics and leadership for many years. My purposes for writing this book are, first, to tell the stories as completely as I can and, second, to create some doubts about the theories, suppositions, and unspoken assumptions that underlie "strategic analyses" on both sides of the goals and intentions of the other.

There are two fundamental propositions underlying the following chapters. First, foreign policies are not the product of pristine calculations of national interests by trained experts with all the facts at their disposal. Rather policies are the result of a profoundly political process in which differing, sometimes competing, domestic interests, bureaucracies, and individuals affect the outcome. Although some of the key players are well-informed experts, they are often working with incorrect or incomplete information, as well as inaccurate assumptions and cultural prejudices. Second and related, "strategic" assessments that extrapolate historical or ideological trends and project future policies and behavior are likely to be wrong, as they seldom take account of the domestic politics of decisionmaking or the effect of unpredictable events that often drive the process. Unlike a number of contemporary observers of bilateral relations, I believe that conflict between the United States and China is *not* inevitable; there is no ineluctable war between the two countries just waiting for the strategic paths to reach their convergence. There is, in fact, considerable prospect and opportunity for cooperation and improvement in what is likely to be the single most important bilateral relationship of the twenty-first century. However, the routine misperception of each other's goals and policies, one of the legacies of Tiananmen, is leading to increasing hostility and distrust that could eventually have tragic consequences. It is my hope that this work might contribute to an understanding of policy decisions as outcomes of complex processes rather than the results of grand strategic trends. To that end, I am looking at the decisions of the relationship in a comparative context, as outcomes of internal political processes in both countries.

Comparing Contrasting Systems

One can scarcely do justice in an introductory chapter to the enormous differences between the political systems of the United States of America and the People's Republic of China. Aside from a few common titles and descriptors, there is little the two states have in common in global influence, regional aspirations, strategic goals, ideology, or political structure.

The United States is a global power, with interests and capabilities in virtually every region of the world, and extensive international commitments and responsibilities. China is a major player in international relations but not a power in the sense of being able to affect outcomes, build coalitions, or project its will far beyond its borders.

Strategically, the United States is the world's most powerful nation militarily, whether considered from the perspective of conventional or nuclear forces. Its leaders appear determined to keep it that way by thwarting the efforts of any other country to match American capabilities and ensuring that America plays a major role in all international organizations. China is a defensive power, concerned about recovering lost territory (especially Taiwan) and seeking to deter the United States from interfering in that recovery process.

In the Asia-Pacific region, the United States is a status quo power, seeking to maintain the equilibrium and tenuous stability that have enabled the region to become so economically prosperous. China is a moderately discontented regional power, angry about American support for Taiwan, dissatisfied with some of the American-determined geopolitical relationships on its borders, and resentful of American leadership pretensions and of what it perceives as overbearing American behavior.

Ideologically, the United States sees itself as a model and defender of political democracy and individual freedom, sees private property, capitalism as the engines of progress, and free trade as the desired state of economic relations between nations. China is in an uncertain ideological condition, having cast aside radical Marxism and the egalitarian ideals of Mao Zedong, but having only a vague sense of what its chosen ideology—"socialism with Chinese characteristics"—really means.

Structurally, the two countries are vastly different. The United States is a federal republic with power divided among three coequal branches and a complex set of relationships to be factored into the policymaking process. Power relationships are defined structurally by the U.S. Constitution, and two major political parties compete for positions in the executive and legislative branches and are accountable to the public through regular elections. The Chinese system is a nondemocratic one-party regime, with all powers focused in the Communist Party of China (CPC), which directs all aspects of the executive, most of the legislative, and a large degree of the judicial functions of the state. The Communist Party is a classic Leninist political party, with a Central Committee consisting of 300 to 400 members "representing" the more than 60 million Communist Party members who dominate many aspects of social and economic activity and nearly all political life. The Central Committee is controlled by the twenty-plus-member Political Bureau (or Politburo), which is headed by a Standing Committee of five to nine individuals. The general secretary of the party and one or two others constitute the "core" of the leadership.[1]

The principal problem in doing any kind of analysis of the PRC political system—and particularly the decisionmaking process—is its lack of transparency. The normative ideal for Chinese decisionmaking is called "democratic centralism," wherein participants are free to express their views and disagree with one another, but once a decision is made and announced, all are expected to set aside their personal views and support the decision of the collective. The formation of alliances or factions to support a particular issue or set of issues is prohibited and cause for removal from power. Interest groups and the populace at large are not considered to have a legitimate right to try and influence the collective's decision. Thus for historical and ideological reasons, the Communist Party of China has never welcomed scrutiny of its operations and has cloaked most of its activities and decisions in tight secrecy. That has sharply limited the quantity and quality of reporting and analysis on the policymaking process in China.

In the United States, by contrast, there is often too much information available about the policymaking process, some of it contradictory, representing various interests or groups that have a stake in the outcome. Moreover, the significant influences on the process are continually shifting, rendering consistent tracking of the process more difficult and increasing uncertainty about how and why decisions are actually made.

Foreign policymaking is a subset of the political processes in both countries, founded on the evident premises that foreign affairs require a high degree of expertise and specialized knowledge and entail a high degree of attention from the chief executive authority. There are more points in common than might be expected, given the differences in government structure and philosophy. Neither country entrusts both the policymaking and policy implementation responsibilities fully to their foreign affairs bureaucracies, and ultimate decisionmaking authority rests with the chief executive and a small group of formal and informal advisers. In the United States, this includes the statutorily constituted National Security Council and the more informal system of interagency working groups, the Deputies Committee and Principals Committee, as well as informal coordination among the national security adviser, secretary of state, secretary of defense, the president's chief of staff, and the president. Decisions are often reached in face-to-face meetings of senior officials, then conveyed to the president in written form for final approval. In China, the policy process involves the heads of relevant ministries, the "foreign affairs leading small group," the personal staffs and members of the Politburo Standing Committee, and finally, the general secretary. More often than not, decisionmaking information is circulated in the form of decision papers, which go through an extensive process of revision and approval from the highest levels before being put into execution.[2]

In both countries, the foreign policy decisionmaking process is often event driven; that is, many important decisions are made in response to an action—or news of action—taken by another country rather than because of a strategy or proactive plan of action. This places a premium on the quality of those agencies or private organizations responsible for collecting and analyzing relevant information, principally the news media, diplomatic corps, and intelligence services.

In the United States, the major sources of news for decisionmakers are private corporate organizations, including the major American and British wire services, and the key national newspapers (*Washington Post, New York Times, Wall Street Journal,* and a few others), with network and cable television news providing coverage of breaking news or information with a strong visual impact. The Foreign Broadcast Information Service—part of the Central Intelligence Agency—provides transcriptions and translations of articles from foreign newspapers, television, and radio broadcasts.

China's *Xinhua* (New China) News Agency provides the bulk of foreign affairs information not only for China's many national and local newspapers but also for the foreign affairs bureaucracies, such as the Ministry of Foreign Affairs, as well as the key members of the leadership. Xinhua provides the Chinese leadership a broad range of materials translated from various foreign newspapers and wire services, in the form of "reference materials," or *cankao ziliao*, with special attention to news about China. In recent years, the Internet has expanded manyfold the information available to all Chinese with access to a computer and telecommunications. Although the government attempts to block many Western press sources, a wide variety of news and information—not produced by Xinhua—is available through a proliferation of official and quasi-official websites.[3]

The diplomatic corps of both countries, as well as their intelligence services, provide a broad variety of factual and analytical reports to their capitals to help inform and advise the decisionmaking process. Most of this information is classified to protect the sources and methods by which it is collected and to maintain the security of the decisionmaking process from public scrutiny. Classification levels are generally similar: confidential, secret, and top secret in the United States (with further restrictions provided by specific "compartments" that require special permission for access); *mimi* (secret), *jimi* (extreme secret), and *juemi* (absolute secret) in China. In the United States, the "intelligence community" consists of various agencies involved in the collection and processing of sensitive information, including the Central Intelligence Agency, Defense Intelligence Agency, National Security Agency (signals intelligence), National Imagery and Mapping Agency, the State Department's Bureau of Intelligence and Research, smaller intelligence units within the principal service arms and the regional commands, and on certain issues, the Federal Bureau of Investigation. China's intelligence services include the Ministry of State Security, Ministry of Public Security, the Second and Third departments of the General Staff of the People's Liberation Army (PLA), the Liaison Department of the PLA's General Political Department, and the International Liaison Department of the Central Committee.

A Note on Sources

Given the high importance that is attached to national security considerations in both countries, the information sources, decision processes, and even the personnel composition of key policymaking bodies are generally shrouded from public scrutiny. The problem is magnified for China by the lack of transparency in all matters related to politics and policy and by the reticence of even retired senior officials to include sensitive political or foreign policy issues in their memoirs. I have chosen deliberately to avoid the use of or extensive reference to classified information from the United States or China. There are no Freedom of Information Act documents contained in this book, nor are there internal (*neibu*) reports from China.[4] This was done both for the sake of maintaining consistency and because I consider that intelligence information is generally overrated in discussions of policy processes. Most intelligence information available to the public—whether through leaks or authorized disclosures—is only part of the full story and often deludes the reader into thinking it is more important than it was in the actual process of formulating policy.

Over the course of a twenty-four-year career in the U.S. government, I became familiar with both the intelligence and policy processes by observing and participating in them. Moreover, I was fortunate to have been able to interview a number of American policymakers and get their candid—if not always completely accurate or objective—views on the policies and decisions of their time. In hopes of maintaining confidentiality and accuracy, I have sought authorization from them to use their words and ideas. American journalists and scholars also have done extensive research on the policy process, and I have benefited greatly from the work of others in this area.

Unfortunately, I have not had comparable access to the Chinese policy process. After the American bombing of the Chinese embassy in Belgrade in 1999, whatever prospect I might have had for interviewing Chinese officials on the record disappeared entirely.[5] Chinese scholars are not encouraged to dig deeply into their own policy process to discover different perspectives or interests or how decisions are made. Although some of them show considerable sophistication in their understanding of the complexity of the American policy process, they seldom provide comparable insight about how politics affect the foreign policy process in their own country. Their books on U.S.-China policy issues tend to be orthodox commendations of the Chinese government's decisions. Neither do Chinese newspapers report the "inside scoop" on policy decisions, for obvious reasons.

That leaves only informed analysis of the available Chinese public record, along with the assessments of journalists and scholars from the United States,

Europe, Japan, Taiwan, and Hong Kong about China's domestic politics. While these are often very good, they are also sometimes ill-informed, biased, inaccurate, and speculative. Certain Hong Kong newspapers and journals, for example, report what can only be categorized as "speculative fiction" about domestic politics in China. Sorting through these materials to discern what is dependable and usably accurate can be a frustrating process and one that leaves large prospects for controversy and error. Obviously, I take full responsibility for whatever inaccuracies and mistakes may be contained in the following account. My use of various source materials of unverifiable authenticity should not be construed as validation based on my experience as an intelligence analyst. I have made judgments of what is credible and sensible based on my own personal appraisal, not that of the U.S. government. Questionable sources are still questionable, as are my analytical judgments when based upon them.

Despite these drawbacks and shortcomings, I have tried to present in the following chapters what I believe to be the most important domestic political dimensions of Chinese government decisions about the bilateral relationship. Sometimes these dimensions have to do with interpersonal politics at the topmost level, sometimes with bureaucratic differences, sometimes with the changing tides of unmeasurable public opinion. Again, my purpose is to tell the stories as completely and candidly as possible, rather than to provide the larger, more theoretical explanations. I have tried to cover the politics in both countries in the same chapters in the hope that the presentation of contrasting stimuli and reactions to the same events will convey a sense of the differing manners in which the two countries develop and implement policies toward each other.

CHAPTER TWO

Getting to Tiananmen

I visited Tiananmen on June 4, 1999, the tenth anniversary of the clearing of the square by troops of the People's Liberation Army (PLA). It looked like any other early summer day in Beijing—gray smog blanketed the city, magnifying the oppressive heat and humidity, flattening the vivid contrasts of China's capital. Traffic crawled along Chang'an Boulevard, Beijing's "Main Street." At the edges of Tiananmen Square, the area still teemed with its usual activity. Pedestrians walked leisurely along broad sidewalks in groups of two or three, stepping around piles of new paving bricks and the holes into which they were to be placed by slow-moving workers. Students, tourists, shoppers, and strollers edged around fenced-off construction areas in front of the Forbidden City, which, like the square itself, was undergoing a facelift in advance of the October 1 celebration of the fiftieth anniversary of the founding of the People's Republic of China (PRC).

Ten years after the tragedy, there were few clues of what had happened in 1989. The regime went to extraordinary lengths to ensure that there was no commemoration, no demonstration, no disturbance in or about Tiananmen. The square was closed for refurbishment. The massive one-hundred-acre public area that encompasses the Monument of the People's Heroes (Martyrs' Monument)—across from the Great Hall of the People—and the Mao Zedong Memorial Hall was fenced off by an eight-foot wall of blue-green corrugated metal and cyclone fencing, topped by barbed wire. Although originally scheduled to be completed by May, the renovation was extended through the June 4 date as a precaution against disturbances. Security in the Tiananmen area was exceptionally tight. Every fifty to seventy-five yards, uniformed but unarmed People's Armed Police (military police) patrolled in groups of three, watching for any untoward activity. Their presence was complemented by hundreds of nonuniformed security officers, conspicuous by their use of handheld radios.

Their efforts proved successful. Although two Chinese reportedly made individual efforts to remind others of the Tiananmen tragedy—one with leaflets, another with a slogan on an umbrella—they were quickly arrested and taken away by the security officials. The police confronted more foreign reporters than would-be demonstrators.[1] And although enough Chinese made their views known outside the square to make clear that the issue remained a festering sore for the government, June 4, 1999, passed quietly in Beijing.

Slightly more than three weeks later, the fencing and construction materials were removed, and the square was reopened. People flocked there by the thousands, strolling aimlessly in small groups, playing games, talking quietly in pairs, and enjoying the almost festive atmosphere. Even as late as 11 p.m., several thousand people were still there, ignoring the police, almost as if staking the people's claim to their cherished square. The following night, as if rising to the challenge, several hundred armed police troops efficiently and relentlessly cleared the crowds out of the square using crisply executed block and sweep methods unknown ten years previously. No reason for the maneuvers was evident—the crowds were not unruly or threatening; perhaps it was just practice. But it was a chilling reminder of the relationship between the rulers and the ruled in post-1989 China. The Tiananmen incident may have been ten years in the past, but it was not forgotten.

The Seeds of Crisis

It is a central premise of this book that the current state of U.S.-China relations cannot be understood without reference to Tiananmen and what happened there in 1989, or what each side thought happened there. People in the United States thought they saw an incipient democratic revolution, a youthful exercise in people's power brutally and unnecessarily crushed by an overwhelmingly superior military force, ordered into action by a cynical Communist Party in fear of losing its power. The leaders of China's Communist Party saw a conspiracy between "a very small number of political careerists" and "various political forces and reactionary organizations abroad," who created "turmoil" and a "counterrevolutionary rebellion" aimed at "toppling the Chinese Communist Party and subverting the socialist People's Republic."[2] It is beyond the scope of this book to provide a comprehensive examination of what happened at Tiananmen. That can never be done as long as the government of the PRC sticks with the "official" story of events and maintains a lock on the records of what happened.[3] But the purpose of chapters 2 and 3 is to review the principal events of the tumultuous period from the death of former general secretary Hu Yaobang on April 15 through the June 4 crackdown and the repression that followed, with an eye to understanding how they affected the decisions that were made about bilateral relations in both Washington and Beijing.

On June 9, 1989—five days after the PLA had charged into Beijing and, at enormous cost, regained control of Tiananmen Square—Military Commission Chairman and Chinese "strongman" Deng Xiaoping attended a reception at the Huairen Hall in Zhongnanhai, the leadership compound adjacent to the Forbidden City, in honor of the martial law units that had "suppressed the rebellion." In a rambling and defensive speech, Deng tried briefly to come to grips with the causes of Tiananmen. "This storm was bound to come sooner or later. This is determined by the major international climate and China's own minor climate. It was bound to happen and is independent of man's will. It was just a matter of time and scale."[4] Deng was, perhaps, overly modest in this appraisal. There was indeed a certain inevitability to Tiananmen, an inescapability that haunts participants and observers to this day. But the causes of the crisis lay primarily within China's "minor climate," for which Deng was mainly responsible. If one accepts the idea that the protagonists of Tiananmen were idealistic students opposed to corruption on the one side and elderly, conservative Communist Party leaders on the other, with the PLA deciding the outcome, then Deng brought on the contest by his policies and determined the outcome by his tragic decisions.

The Growth of Student Activism

In 1977, Deng returned to power after having been purged by Mao Zedong and his radical left-wing supporters in 1975. Almost immediately, he began a process of sweeping change of China's goals, policies, methods of governance, and international relationships that can hardly be overstated in terms of their impact on the people of China. Principal among these was the landmark declaration at the Third Plenary Session of the Eleventh Central Committee in December 1978 that the principal task of the Communist Party was no longer to wage class struggle but to develop China's economy, overcome its backwardness, and improve the living standards of the Chinese people. That decision also marked a personal triumph for Deng, who became China's "paramount leader" thereafter, even though others held the principal titles within the Communist Party and the government.[5] The party plenum also coincided with the final negotiations—after months of haggling—for the establishment of formal diplomatic relations between the United States and China, a process in which Deng made the critical decisions and concessions that sealed the deal.[6]

The party plenum was followed by a period of remarkable policy change that saw the decollectivization of agriculture (that is, the abolition of the commune system), the establishment of special economic zones (Shenzhen, Zhuhai, and Shantou in Guangdong Province, Xiamen in Fujian), and the more active encouragement of foreign investment and trade. Peasants were given production contracts for thirty years for particular plots of land and the right to decide how to utilize it. Rural and township enterprises were encouraged, as were other forms of entrepreneurship, and prices began to be decontrolled on a growing list of commodities and manufactured products. The results of these reforms were striking: agricultural production grew sharply, and rural incomes began to advance strongly as peasants took advantage of new opportunities to sell specialized products at near-free market prices. In the urban areas, enterprises began to pay workers bonuses for making profits, and monetary incentives encouraged individual efforts to exceed quotas. Individuals were permitted to establish small-scale services (repair and maintenance, food preparation, and other tasks). These changes created strains and discontent within the ministries managing urban industries and in the party's ideological circles, where their sharp departure from Marxist-Leninist orthodoxy and Maoist practice was viewed as dangerous.

At the insistence of Deng and General Secretary Hu Yaobang, the Maoist practice of disparaging and discriminating against intellectuals was terminated, and they were encouraged to contribute their ideas to the process of economic reform. Economists, historians, philosophers, scientists, educators, and party officials were urged to "liberate their thinking," abandon "forbidden zones" of party orthodoxy, and be open to new ideas on how to better modernize and develop the Chinese economy. Competitive entrance examinations for China's major universities were reinstituted, and students and researchers were permitted to apply to study at foreign universities and bring foreign research materials and practices into Chinese institutions of higher learning.

All this led to an upsurge in support for party reformers and a new intellectual and literary efflorescence. It led also to a growing expression of discontent about some of the excesses of the past—particularly the 1966–76 Cultural Revolution—and with remaining leaders of the party who had risen during that period. In the last two months of 1978, Democracy Wall sprang up in Beijing's Xidan market area. On the concrete and brick wall that separated West Changan Boulevard from a local bus yard, ordinary citizens began to put up "big-character posters" (*dazibao*) exposing corruption, injustice, and malfeasance within the Communist Party, the central government, and numerous provincial and local governments.[7] Deng benefited from this opening of literary and critical commentary, some of which attacked his remaining detractors within the leadership.[8] But the activity did not stop there. Taking advantage of the rare relaxation of controls over free speech, some intellectuals and workers began to advocate a more rapid democratization of the Chinese Communist Party and Chinese society. Some, such as Beijing Zoo electrician Wei Jingsheng and others, even began to attack Deng for his antidemocratic leadership style and aggressive pursuit of his personal political agenda.[9]

Prodded by conservative members of the upper leadership, Deng reacted to the growing critiques of Communist Party rule in March 1979 by issuing guidelines bounding the public expression of opinion or political view. These guidelines, known as the "four upholds" or the "four cardinal principles," required that political reformers and other public commentary should uphold the socialist road, the "people's democratic dictatorship" (that is, the party's right to monopolize power by claiming to exercise it on behalf of the people), the primacy of the Communist Party, and the relevance of "Marxism-Leninism–Mao Zedong Thought" as China's guiding ideology. Gradually through the spring and summer of 1979, Democracy Wall activities were more carefully monitored, censored, restricted, and finally shut down. Although Hu Yaobang and others continued through party channels to advocate more "liberation of thinking," Deng's intolerance for criticism of the party and himself—as being conducive to "instability"—was a harbinger of future events.

By the late 1980s, China's intellectuals were seething with discontent. Although well aware that Deng's reforms had brought significant improvements in the lives of the vast majority of Chinese people, they were extremely frustrated by a number of all-too-visible problems. As one American observer put it, official corruption had become an epidemic of many forms: "bribery, nepotism, smuggling, trading of favors, eating and drinking on the public dole, taking goods home to 'test' them, 'borrowing' money and not returning it . . . The mode of corruption that provoked the most comment and anger, however, was called *guandao* ('official profiteering'). In *guandao* an official or a member of his family buys commodities at low, state-fixed prices and then sells them—with huge, unearned markups—on the free market."[10] Only the highest-level officials or their children had the access to commodities to enable them to profit from *guandao*. And the children were profiting mightily, another fact well known among China's intelligentsia. Called "princelings" or "golden youth," the sons and daughters of China's top leaders mostly eschewed political office; rather, they used the perceived clout of their parents and went into private enterprise, often with foreign firms. They lived extravagantly and flaunted their wealth with fancy cars, clothes, and other Western consumer items.

Discontent was also growing over the increasingly obvious shortcomings in China's political and economic systems, especially when weighed against the situation in Hong Kong, Singapore, and Taiwan. Students and intellectuals often concluded that China's obvious backwardness in comparison to these other Chinese societies was caused by the communist system rather than other social or economic factors.[11] But there was resentment against some foreign countries—particularly over unfair pricing or labor practices or the suborning of corruption—and xenophobic sentiments burst forth on several occasions among university students.[12]

Intellectuals felt increasingly disadvantaged when they compared their lot to that of corrupt party officials, private entrepreneurs, and employees of foreign-invested firms (Chinese firms invested in by foreign companies). Confined mostly to working in universities or government-sponsored research institutes, they often found their fixed salaries insufficient to make ends meet in a time of rising inflation. Moreover, their working conditions (and student living conditions) were dismal. With scarce budgetary resources being distributed to more urgent modernization projects, universities and research institutes—many of which had been closed and damaged during the Cultural Revolution—were run down, poorly equipped, underheated, and overcrowded. Faculty and student living quarters were wretched.

By far the main cause of discontent, however, was the intellectually stultifying political climate. Although officially cleared from their Cultural Revolution stigmatization by Hu Yaobang in the late 1970s, students and older intellectuals were still the object of party distrust and occasional public criticism.[13] Although overseas study and foreign contacts were permitted, those who took advantage of these opportunities found themselves the objects of suspicion and job discrimination when they returned. The party pledged there would be no more ideological forbidden zones, but those who pushed the boundaries in movies, plays, and literature sometimes found themselves pilloried for violating the four cardinal principles when they did so. Although Western ideas were welcomed in economics and science and technology, those who propounded Western philosophy, political science, or sociology were attacked for succumbing to "bourgeois liberalism" in repeated campaigns in the 1980s.

Thus, while Deng maintained his reputation in the West as a reformer, albeit a rather antidemocratic one, in China he was increasingly seen by students and intellectuals as an autocrat, dedicated to maintaining his power, allied with the gerontocrats of China's past rather than the democrats of its future. Hu Yaobang, by contrast, retained the loyalty of students and intellectuals. Although he did not have much formal education, Hu ardently supported education and the restoration of the role of intellectuals as necessary for China's successful modernization. Despite Deng's caution, Hu pressed hard for "liberation of thought" on critically evaluating Mao and the Cultural Revolution. He supported somewhat greater political reform despite opposition from Deng and other party elders. He took a tolerant approach to literary works critical of the party and curtailed the 1983 campaign against "spiritual pollution" as too disruptive and potentially offensive to foreign investors.[14] He defended dissident intellectuals (such as Fang Lizhi, Liu Binyan, and Wang Ruowang) who came under attack from party conservatives, and he even deflected Deng's demands that they be expelled from the party.[15] Relations between the two men soured all through 1986, and their differences ultimately led to a showdown.

Deng's Failure to Reform the Party

Hu's disagreements with Deng set in motion a train of events that led to the tragedy at Tiananmen. Many commentators have observed that Deng espoused only economic reform, not political reform. Like many shorthand assessments of complex realities, this judgment is somewhat misleading on both counts. Although he had plenty of experience as an economic manager, Deng was no economist. He had no comprehensive theories on how the Chinese economy should be transformed but left to others the task of developing the detailed policies and the theoretical justifications for his ideas. Deng was driven by the need for political restoration of a properly configured and efficiently operating Leninist party structure. What needed to be reformed was Mao Zedong's distortion of that system through his personality cult, excessive focus on ideological theory, mass mobilization campaigns, and destruction of bureaucratic normalcy. Deng saw clearly the enormous damage that Mao's system had done to China's economy and society, the Communist Party, the army and the government, and the very legitimacy of the regime in the eyes of the Chinese people. Deng seemed to recognize that Western capitalism had accomplished a great deal and that China, by contrast, had fallen behind.

Deng was a flexible pragmatist, a problem solver. He saw modernization as China's paramount requirement and the Communist Party as the only effective instrument for achieving that goal. Reform of the party, for Deng, meant not transforming it into a social democratic party to compete with other political parties in a pluralistic democracy but honing and sharpening it to be an effective instrument of control and economic modernization. That required, primarily, casting aside the ideological encrustations of doctrinaire Maoism, restructuring the party and government apparatus to meet more modern requirements, putting the right people in the right positions, and avoiding a "one-man rule," "lifetime tenure," and overconcentration of powers within the party.[16]

It is essential to note, however, that although he was generally referred to in the West as "China's paramount leader," Deng was far more constrained in his exercise of power, both by his choice and by the choice of others. China's leadership after the death of Mao Zedong in 1976 and the purge of his principal followers, the so-called Gang of Four, was an uneasy amalgam of elderly party veterans, Cultural Revolution beneficiaries, and PLA veterans. The Politburo and its Standing Committee were chosen at the Eleventh Central Committee in August 1977, before Deng's restoration. Many of its members had acquiesced in Deng's ouster by Mao and his radical followers and were uneasy about the prospect of his return to power. Party Chairman Hua Guofeng was particularly uncomfortable and sought to block Deng's restoration. Chen Yun, Li Xiannian, and the elderly Marshal Ye Jianying supported Deng's return, during which process Deng pledged not to take revenge on those who had supported his purge in 1975.[17]

So Deng returned to power in late 1977 subordinate to Hua, beholden to party elders, and constrained from undertaking the sweeping purge of personnel he might have preferred. To strengthen his position, he oversaw the rehabilitation of numerous other party elders who had been purged during the Cultural Revolution—men such as former Beijing mayor Peng Zhen—and added them and other new leaders to the Politburo, rather than seeing former antagonists removed. Eventually, Deng was able to make the personnel changes he needed. He neutralized Hua Guofeng, forced several Cultural Revolution holdovers to resign from the Politburo, appointed Hu Yaobang as party general secretary and Zhao Ziyang as premier of the State Council, and brought in many younger members to the Central Committee. Deng eschewed promotion to higher positions, holding on only to the post of chairman of the Central Military Commission (CMC) of the party.[18] But he needed the support of other party elders—several probably considered themselves his political equal—to reconstruct the party apparatus and improve its performance. And he needed Hu, Zhao, and other younger leaders to provide the intellectual energy to bring about successful economic modernization. It became clear early on that the differences between party elders and younger reformers were becoming sharper and more numerous. Serious disagreements arose over ideology, evaluating Mao's contributions, expanding or limiting economic growth, setting up special economic zones where foreign investment would be permitted and favored, and especially over personnel changes. Thus Deng became the power broker, the one to whom different factional groupings within the leadership had to turn to have their positions considered.

Deng's lack of a clear vision for China's economic and political future became more problematic as he vacillated between the conservative economic theories of Chen Yun and his associates in the state economic planning bureaucracy and the liberalizing intellectual predilections of Hu Yaobang and his supporters in the party organization department and among the intelligentsia.[19] By the mid-1980s, it had become evident that elderly conservatives in the party were determined to undermine Hu's authority. For his part, Hu was eager to enforce the party's regulations on mandatory retirement for elderly cadres. He was also pushing hard for political reform of the party structure and the relationship between party and government to better support the economic reform policies that had begun to show results but were often hampered by ideologically inflexible middle-level officials and corruption. Deng, trying to balance between increasingly polarized elements within the leadership, supported the party elders in their demands that discussion of reform be limited to internal party administration rather than encompassing calls for a multiparty system. Deng's shift may have reflected his conservative impulses on party primacy, or he may have been concerned that his role as a balancer would have been diminished had conservatives been completely defeated on the issue. He may also have been annoyed by Hu's most costly mistake, which was taking his role as designated successor seriously and urging Deng to retire, as Deng had so often promised or threatened to do.[20] Chosen successors have not led charmed lives in Chinese Comunist Party history. Mao Zedong overthrew two—Liu Shaoqi and Lin Biao—and Deng ousted a third, Hua Guofeng, after Mao's death. Increasingly frustrated at having to refer all party reform proposals through a recalcitrant Deng, Hu ignored the warning signs and pressed ahead, even though he did not enjoy Deng's full support.

At the Sixth Plenum in September 1986, the battle was joined over a resolution on party work, which included language supporting political and economic reform but also a renewal of the campaign to oppose "bourgeois liberalization." Hu and his allies were pitted directly against party elders, and Deng sided with the elders, saying, "Exponents of liberalization want to lead us down the road to capitalism . . . the struggle against liberalization will have to be carried out not only now but for the next ten to twenty years."[21] Hu withheld the text of Deng's speech from circulation, in effect, slowing the emergence of the debate.[22] But it grew sharper quickly and led eventually to large-scale student demonstrations in Anhui Province, Shanghai, and finally in December, Beijing. In a prelude to Tiananmen in 1989, the students called for less party control of student organizations, more freedom of the press, human rights, and democracy. "The students' calls for freedom of speech and democratic reforms were meant to hasten along the political reforms supported by Hu Yaobang" and opposed by the party elders.[23]

Deng demanded that Hu crack down on the demonstrators and expel key liberal intellectuals from the party. Hu refused and held up both press criticism of the demonstrations and police efforts to end them. On December 30, Deng called Hu, Zhao Ziyang, Li Peng, and others to his home and criticized them directly for failing to take a "clear-cut stand" against the disturbances. He belittled concerns that a crackdown might have a negative effect on international opinion, citing foreign acquiescence in the arrest of Wei Jingsheng, and said bloodshed might be necessary to avoid "chaos."[24]

On January 2, 1987, after refusing to use police to break up another student demonstration, Hu informed Deng of his intention to resign as party general secretary. Fearing a trap, Deng moved swiftly on his own.

> January 4, 1987, was a Sunday. Deng Xiaoping summoned Zhao Ziyang, Peng Zhen, Wang Zhen, Bo Yibo, and Yang Shangkun to his home to make the arrangements to dismiss Hu Yaobang before he could resign. The upshot was that Zhao Ziyang was named to replace him. Supposedly this was a decision of members of the Politburo Standing Committee residing in Beijing. In reality, Deng Xiaoping and Zhao Ziyang were the only members of the Standing Committee present. Three of the five members were absent: Hu Yaobang was not even invited, Li Xiannian was in Shanghai, and Chen Yun didn't show. It was a palace coup d'état.[25]

At an "enlarged" meeting of the Politburo Standing Committee on January 16—at which party elders not otherwise permitted even to attend Politburo meetings were granted voting privileges—Hu's resignation as general secretary was demanded and given. Chinese television reported that Hu resigned after making "a self-criticism of his mistakes on major issues of political principles in violation of the party's principle of collective leadership."[26] Hu was permitted (as Hua Guofeng before him) to remain on the Politburo, but he was effectively stripped of all power and was replaced as general secretary by Zhao Ziyang. Although Zhao was considered a reformer like Hu, his appointment was a typical Deng compromise, one that preserved Deng's role as balancer. Zhao had to share his authority as premier (although he held the title until October 1987) with the far more conservative Li Peng, with whom he had already clashed on economic policy. Hu was obligated to undertake an extensive and humiliating process of self-criticism, with occasional larger leadership sessions where party elders berated him.[27] Student demonstrators, sensing quickly that the tide had turned against them, returned to their campuses.

As general secretary, Zhao continued to focus his efforts on economic modernization and reform and had comparatively little interest in the ideological issues that had preoccupied Hu. He nonetheless encountered the same problems that had dogged earlier efforts to promote significant change in China's economic structure—entrenched bureaucrats, ideological resistance, corruption, and the now enhanced authority of conservative party elders. With Deng's cooperation, Zhao undertook further reforms of Central Committee operations and personnel at the Thirteenth Central Committee Plenum in October 1987: ninety-six elderly full members of the Central Committee were dropped, Deng and several other elders retired from the Politburo and its Standing Committee, and a new voting method for Central Committee membership (more nominees than positions) resulted in the failure of several conservative ideologues active in the ouster of Hu Yaobang to be elected to the Central Committee.[28] The changes were not entirely effective, however, as many of the elders still retained influence on Deng and the Politburo through the Central Advisory Commission. Deng retained his principal power position as chairman of the Military Commission and continued to dominate the system through informal channels.

Zhao had wanted his ally, Tian Jiyun, to succeed him as premier but was unable to persuade Deng, who wanted Wan Li to get the post. The elders backed Li Peng, and Deng eventually appointed him as a compromise candidate.[29] Li shared the elders' distaste for radical reform or dismantling the state-controlled economy in favor of a free market system, which Zhao favored. The issue came to a head over proposals for how to reform China's state-controlled price structure. Some favored a rapid decontrol of prices for food, commodities, fuel, and other products—a "shock treatment" that would cause initial pain and dislocation but more rapid progress in other areas thereafter. Others preferred a more gradual approach, with the state gradually lifting price controls sector by sector. Another group favored an even more radical solution involving a reduction in public ownership and the growth of private property. Finally, conservative state planners favored an overall program of economic retrenchment, taking money out of the economy and cooling inflationary pressure.

In the spring of 1988, Deng suddenly pronounced himself in favor of rapid price reform, even if mistakes were made in implementing it. Zhao, although lukewarm to the idea, put together a plan of implementation and presented it to party leaders in August. The plan envisioned elimination of price controls within four to five years and currency devaluation to encourage exports. Details of the plan were leaked, however, and set off panic buying of foodstuffs and other commodities in some urban areas, as well as runs on several banks. Prices skyrocketed, bringing down on Zhao the renewed wrath of conservative elders, who called for his dismissal.[30] Deng retreated ahead of Zhao, letting him take the blame for the problems, and transferred more authority for economic decisionmaking to Li Peng and Yao Yilin.

The View from Afar—George H. W. Bush and China

By early 1989, China was rife with discontent, in the leadership, among prominent intellectuals, and in the society at large. Relatively little of the discontent was evident outside of China, however. The leadership kept differences and divisions well hidden, intellectuals were considered perennially fractious and unhappy, and the economic dislocations of the summer seemed to be easing. Some American scholars were aware of the increasingly tense atmosphere in China, as were several officials at the U.S. embassy in Beijing. But none of them conveyed a sense that a crisis was near.

The newly elected U.S. president, George H. W. Bush, was anxious to broaden America's strategic relationship with China, and he expressed some concern about indications of a thaw in Sino-Soviet relations. His foreign policy advisers seemed unworried about internal Chinese political problems or potential social unrest when they began making arrangements for a visit to China shortly after Bush was inaugurated on January 20, 1989.[31]

Bush and his Republican running mate, Indiana senator Dan Quayle, had been elected in November 1988, defeating the Democratic Party ticket of Michael Dukakis (former governor of Massachusetts) and Texas senator Lloyd S. Bentsen by more than 7 million popular votes and carrying forty of fifty states to win the electoral college by 426-111. The campaign had been a bitter one, with "attack ads" on television often distorting the main issues of the campaign, which included taxes, a rising federal deficit, health care, education, and Bush's role as vice president during some of the scandals of the Reagan administration. Foreign policy, as usual, was not a major issue in the campaign, although Bush was credited with more experience in that area, given his record as former Central Intelligence Agency (CIA) director, U.S. ambassador to the United Nations, and head of the U.S. Liaison Office in China. Bush was an indifferent campaigner and brought little support to other Republican candidates. He was thus faced in 1989 with a Congress overwhelmingly dominated by Democrats (55-45 in the Senate, 259-174 in the House of Representatives).

Bush was determined to be a "hands-on" president on foreign policy issues, and he assembled a solid team of experienced and capable people to lead the major foreign policy agencies.[32] James A. Baker III, a savvy Texas lawyer and longtime friend who had managed Bush's election campaign, was named secretary of state and was confirmed easily. Bush's first choice for secretary of defense, Texas senator John Tower, was defeated in an extraordinarily ugly partisan confirmation hearing that delved into his personal life. He was replaced by Congressman Richard B. Cheney, who won easy confirmation. William Webster, former director of the Federal Bureau of Investigation, was chosen to head the CIA, which had been tarnished by scandal during the Reagan administration. For his national security adviser, Bush chose General Brent Scowcroft, a calm, seasoned national security manager who had filled the same position under President Gerald Ford.

Bush had served in 1974–75 as head of the U.S. Liaison Office in Beijing—the unofficial representative office for the United States—while the two governments worked out the complex details of formal diplomatic recognition, particularly U.S. relations with Taiwan. Bush's experience gave him not only a deeper understanding of Chinese affairs than any previous president but also a large number of Chinese friends and an undeniable affection for the Chinese people. Bush supplemented that with a keen appreciation of the strategic importance of China in the ongoing cold war between the United States and the Soviet Union (USSR). At the beginning of his presidency, he was eager to re-establish contact with Deng Xiaoping and other Chinese leaders in order to bolster bilateral relations and steal a march on Soviet leader Mikhail Gorbachev, who had announced a May visit to Beijing to normalize long-strained relations.

The death of Japan's emperor Hirohito on January 7 and his scheduled state funeral on February 24 provided the administration with the justification it needed to travel on to China to seek reassurances from the Chinese about the Sino-Soviet-U.S. strategic relationship. In a hurried advance for the trip, Douglas Paal—then-director of Asian affairs at the National Security Council—heard privately from one embassy officer that Beijing was "ready to blow up," but other reporting, including political analysis from the embassy, was not so alarmist.[33] Paal and others had worked hard on short notice to put together a high-visibility "working" visit to Beijing and found the Chinese leadership eager to accord Bush the highest respect. After all, the visit of a newly elected president and "friend of China" so early in his administration augured well for continuing improvements in an already warm bilateral relationship.

The intersection of domestic and foreign policies, however, caused what was expected to be a warm and positive visit to turn sour. The precipitating event was the president's "return" banquet, scheduled for the last day of his visit, February 28, as a way of reciprocating the Chinese leadership's hospitality. The gala event at the Sheraton Great Wall Hotel was to be a Texas-style barbecue, with a guest list of 500 people, including not just Communist Party leaders but people from "all walks of life." Ever since President Ronald

Reagan's bold meeting with Russian dissidents during a visit to Moscow in 1988, an unspoken expectation had arisen in the United States that more attention would be paid to human rights and promotion of democracy in dealings with China and the USSR. Responding to this hope, Ambassador Winston Lord—a strong believer in human rights and democracy issues—approved the addition of Chinese dissident Fang Lizhi's name to the guest list that he forwarded to the State Department a week or two before the president's arrival. Knowing Fang's history and reputation, he highlighted his name in a cable to the department, which vetted the list with the National Security Council and Defense Department.[34]

Deputy Assistant Secretary of State for East Asia and the Pacific J. Stapleton Roy approved the list and the approach taken, which he expected would not be seen as unduly provocative: "There was a common understanding, based on the experience from the Reagan Administration, that there had to be some recognition during the Bush visit, of the existence of people like Fang Lizhi in China. The problem was to find a way to do it. The Soviet method of having Fang Lizhi to the [Ambassador's] residence was considered undoable, because the Chinese would have blocked it. And that's why the invitation to the banquet was decided on, because it was considered to be the necessary symbolic gesture, but one which should have been viewable in context by the Chinese government, since it was only one of many hundreds of invitations being issued."[35]

The embassy received no formal reply from the White House to the proposed list. Lord inquired a second time, but only when the advance team came out, less than a week before the president's scheduled arrival, did the guest list get cleared, including Fang Lizhi. That was just in time for the invitations to be sent out.

But Fang was not just another dissident—he was practically a declared enemy of Deng Xiaoping. A mild-mannered, respected astrophysicist and cosmologist who had been punished during the anti-rightist campaign of the 1950s and during the Cultural Revolution, Fang came to Deng's attention in the mid-1980s, when he began to publish articles critical of Marxism-Leninism as a "scientific" theory. Despite his ideological heterodoxy, Fang became influential among younger intellectuals around Hu Yaobang and Zhao Ziyang. As his bold promotion of democracy and rejection of socialism became more pronounced, Fang became a hero to university students, and his lectures were widely circulated. Fang also traveled to the United States in 1986 and returned with even more enthusiasm for democracy and the freedom it provided for scientific inquiry. The first student demonstrations in 1986 began at the university where Fang taught, the University of Science and Technology in Hefei, Anhui.[36] In December, Deng attacked Fang directly: "I have read Fang Lizhi's speeches. He does not sound like a Communist Party member at all. Why do we keep people like him in the Party? He should be expelled, not just persuaded to quit."[37]

Despite his expulsion from the party (which he welcomed), Fang remained influential. He traveled internationally until late 1988, when the government suspended his overseas travel privileges after a trip to Australia, where he criticized unnamed children of "senior party officials" for corruption. Deng evidently took this accusation personally, and a libel suit was threatened but never pressed. Fang also remained active among university students. After being removed from his university post, Fang worked at the Beijing Observatory. On January 6, 1989, Fang issued an open letter to Deng, calling on him to free Wei Jingsheng and other "political prisoners" and subsequently sought support from other intellectuals for similar petitions. All these activities meant that Fang remained a high-profile figure for the party leadership and a very troubling one.

As soon as Washington's approved guest list was passed on to the Ministry of Foreign Affairs in Beijing, the Chinese immediately expressed concern about Fang, first quietly and informally, then more forcefully in planning meetings for the visit. Two days before Bush's February 26 arrival, Lord was called into Vice Foreign Minister Zhu Qizhen's office and told that the leadership would not attend the return banquet if Fang remained on the guest list. Lord tried to explain that Fang was being invited as a prominent scientist, not as a dissident, that he would be seated far from the head table—nowhere near the leadership—and would not have a private meeting with Bush. But the Chinese were adamant and repeated the warning the day before the president's arrival. Lord reported these events by "Flash" priority cables to the president's party, warning them of a potential leadership boycott if Fang did attend and a public relations nightmare if he were disinvited.[38]

When they arrived on Saturday morning, Scowcroft and other senior officials went immediately into consultation with the Chinese. As Scowcroft recalled:

> The first night we were in Beijing . . . I stayed up most of the night discussing Fang Lizhi. And the position that I took was, "Look, it may have been a mistake to invite him, and if I had understood the situation before, he wouldn't have been invited. But he has been now, and you will make the situation worse, both for you and for us, if he were to be uninvited, because everybody knows he's been invited now." And the Chinese position was, "We want to honor President Bush and all of the leadership promised to come to the party, and we cannot come if Fang Lizhi is at the party."[39]

No resolution was reached, however, and the Americans thought the Chinese might decide to let the situation ride, trusting in their assurances that Fang would be far from the leadership tables.

The Chinese finally resolved the issue in a peculiarly clumsy way. In a scene with no small degree of comic bravado, security authorities set out to physically prevent Fang from attending the banquet by arresting his driver, impounding his car, stopping a taxi that had picked him up, preventing public buses from stopping for him, telling him his invitation was invalid, then giving him erroneous directions when he set out walking to the U.S. embassy to check on it.[40] Fang never made it to the Sheraton for the banquet, but he was not prevented from giving a press conference later, where he related the events of the evening, to the embarrassment of both the Chinese and American governments. Bush protested the Chinese action at a farewell meeting with Vice Premier Wu Xueqian the following day, prompting a waspish reply from the Foreign Ministry spokesman, who accused the Americans of inviting Fang "without consulting the Chinese side," which it "resented."[41]

The Fang incident not only cast a cloud over the otherwise successful Bush visit to China, but it also created frictions within the administration. After the presidential party returned to Washington, National Security Adviser Scowcroft, in an off-the-record press backgrounder, characterized the Fang invitation as a mistake by the embassy and said Chinese sensitivities about the invitation were "not conveyed to top Bush advisors."[42] Although no names were mentioned, Lord saw himself as the target of Scowcroft's criticism and was outraged at the implicit accusations that the embassy had "screwed up the President's trip." "So I went over a cable to Scowcroft, but I waited, kept re-drafting it . . . to tone it down and make it professional . . . I sent it purposely through [private] channels to the Situation Room [at the White House] to Scowcroft and only for Scowcroft. We also sent a copy to Vienna, where Baker was." The cable criticized the backgrounder, saying that it made the White House look weak to the Chinese and others in Asia, would alienate congressional support, would discourage reformers, and undercut not only his own position but also that of his successor. The White House never replied or even acknowledged receipt of Lord's message, which only heightened his anger.[43]

Brent Scowcroft, looking back on the trip later, was impressed by the cohesiveness of the leadership grouping that met with Bush. "It was a very collegial atmosphere," he recalled. "And at the dinner the President gave, all the leadership turned out. Factionalism was not apparent at that time."[44] Hints more obvious in hindsight were dropped, of course. The Fang Lizhi imbroglio revealed serious political strain. Yang Shangkun warned that the U.S. Congress was pushing too hard on human rights issues, and Zhao Ziyang

appeared to be pleading for U.S. support for government reformers rather than noisy dissidents in his talks with the president.[45] But Deng told Bush what he wanted to hear—that the impending improvement in Sino-Soviet relations was more form than substance, that the USSR was still China's most serious threat, while the United States was a potential "partner" for China. And he referred to Bush repeatedly as a *lao pengyou*, "old friend."[46] The Americans left satisfied with a visit that reinforced the strategic relationship, not realizing that it had less than two months remaining.

Hu's Last Hurrah

Hu Yaobang, like many a tragic hero from Chinese fiction and opera, found revenge in death for his 1987 mistreatment. He had been planning a comeback, some said, and was buoyed by continuing public support and proposals that his case be reviewed by the National People's Congress or the Chinese People's Political Consultative Congress (the powerless body formed in 1949 to promote cooperation between the ruling Communist Party and the preliberation "democratic parties"). Hu was preparing a speech on education that would inaugurate his return to action in the Politburo. But before he could deliver it at a Politburo session on April 8, 1989, he collapsed with a massive heart attack. Hu died in the Beijing hospital dedicated to providing health care for senior party and military cadres on April 15, at the age of seventy-three.[47] His death would rock China to its foundations.

Reaction was immediate but small scale. The same afternoon that Hu's death was announced, students at Beijing University (*Beijing Daxue*, often abbreviated *Beida*, even in English) hung up more than a hundred big-character posters commemorating Hu and lamenting his fall from power in 1987. Some of the posters had a hard edge to them, saying "Those who should have died still live," in a clear reference to party elders. Others expressed regret that they had not protested more strenuously when Hu was ousted. Some called for a committee to organize a formal mourning period.[48] A small number of workers from the Ministry of Textiles placed a wreath at the base of the Monument to the Martyrs of the People (Martyrs' Monument) in front of the Great Hall of the People in Tiananmen Square.[49] Party authorities, who had published a surprisingly generous appraisal of Hu in the official obituary, did not respond. The date of Hu's official funeral was set for April 22.

To understand the speed with which events then transpired, it is necessary to recognize that, when Hu died, students and intellectuals had already been making plans for public demonstrations on another occasion, the celebration

of the seventieth anniversary of China's May Fourth Movement.[50] Discontented students and intellectuals had been preparing for several weeks to use the commemoration of May Fourth to protest against corruption and the lack of democracy within the Communist Party. Among the leaders of those planning commemorations was Wang Dan, a twenty-two-year-old history student who had organized an informal "Democracy Salon" at Beida. Also prominent was Fang Lizhi, who did not regard Hu as all that important but later noted, "In China, a leader's death provides an excuse for people to assemble . . . [And] it's only when people can assemble that something can be achieved."[51] Fang was not active in the demonstrations that followed, but his views were well known to the students. Although much of the grief and respect shown for Hu was genuine, there was also an element of opportunism—taking advantage of the party's tolerance for displays of respect and grief for senior leaders to convey a less welcome political message.

After a day in which white flowers and other symbols of mourning for Hu brought by ordinary citizens piled up at the Martyrs' Monument, students began their first organized efforts to assemble for protest on April 16, when they marched from Beida and People's University to Tiananmen to emplace a large memorial wreath at the Martyrs' Monument. The following day, they marched again, twice, and in larger numbers and stayed longer in the square, leaving behind a large banner calling Hu the "soul of China." They also began making public demands on the regime, calling for a reappraisal of Hu's ouster and various political reforms, such as freedom of the press.[52] American print journalists stationed in Beijing reported the story immediately and noted strong antiregime sentiments among some of the students, but their editors consigned the stories to inner pages.

Late in the evening of April 18, the students got everyone's attention by demonstrating in front of Zhongnanhai, the restricted-access compound that houses most of China's senior leaders and the offices of many of the party's most important bureaucracies. After attempting to present a petition at the Great Hall of the People, which was received after dark by three nameless representatives of the National People's Congress, about 3,000 demonstrators moved across Chang'an Boulevard and west to Xinhuamen (Gate of New China), the ceremonial front gate of Zhongnanhai, where they resumed megaphone speeches and chanting slogans, such as "Long live freedom! Long live democracy!" Some pushing and shoving occurred when students attempted to get inside the gate—lightly guarded by PLA soldiers of the Central Guards Unit—to present their petition. The crowds did not disperse until 4:30 the next morning, when Public Security Bureau personnel moved them away from the gate and warned them that activities of the past two days in commemoration for Hu Yaobang would no longer be permitted. No arrests were made, however. The story, described as a "brazen challenge to the Government," broke onto the front pages of major American newspapers, but only the Cable News Network (CNN) covered the story on the evening news in the United States.[53]

On April 19, the confrontation between protesters and the government escalated into violence, as club-swinging police broke up another demonstration in front of Zhongnanhai late in the evening. Earlier in the day, as many as 30,000 people gathered at the Martyrs' Monument to hear increasingly strident calls for a restoration of Hu Yaobang's reputation, freedom of the press, and "public disclosure of the income and assets of China's leaders and [their] children."[54] A smaller crowd again moved to Xinhuamen late in the evening and began calling for Premier Li Peng—already a symbol of everything wrong with the leadership—to come out for a "dialogue." Others called for his resignation, ridiculing him as a modern-day "Ci Xi," China's infamous empress dowager of the Qing Dynasty. Still others chanted, for the first time, "Down with the Communist Party."[55] Wu'er Kaixi (Uerkesh Daolet), a Uighur student activist from Xinjiang studying at Beijing Normal College (*Beijing Shifan Daxue*, known as *Beishida*), persuaded many demonstrators to conduct a sit-in, then lectured them on the need for courage as well as organization.[56] The authorities cracked down after midnight, dispersing the students with nightsticks and leather belts, injuring several of them. They also used loudspeakers to attack student leaders for "insulting Party and government leaders" and "shouting reactionary slogans."[57]

Angered and more determined than ever, students spent the following day indoors (although some 10,000 did brave a driving rain to gather in Tiananmen), organizing themselves for April 22, the day of Hu's official funeral ceremony. Less noted by press commentary, several Beijing workers also announced the formal organization of the Beijing Autonomous Workers Federation. Independent labor unions were, of course, feared and prohibited in China, as in other communist countries. The All-China Federation of Trade Unions was the officially designated representative organ of the workers, even though it hardly ever met and had little means of communicating with real workers. The new federation issued its first statement in support of the students.[58] On April 21, Wu'er Kaixi announced the formation of the Beijing Autonomous Students Federation at a mass rally of 60,000 students at Beishida.[59]

Party and government leaders were meeting to consider how to deal with the situation—the demonstrations outside of Zhongnanhai clearly had alarmed them. The *Tiananmen Papers* records numerous phone calls and bits of conversation (collected after the demonstrations had been put down) that reflected the growing concern of the entire leadership. Li Peng pressed Zhao for a Politburo meeting but was fended off. On his own initiative, Li formed a sub-Politburo group to monitor the situation. Deng Xiaoping ordered 9,000 soldiers of the Thirty-Eighth Army to be brought into the city to reinforce the police.[60] All were concerned about demonstrations disrupting the memorial service for Hu Yaobang, scheduled for 10:00 a.m. on April 22.

On April 21, Beijing municipal authorities declared Tiananmen Square closed to pedestrian and motor traffic as of two hours before Hu's funeral. Demonstrations were strictly prohibited. A commentary in the party's official newspaper, *People's Daily* (*Renmin Ribao*), warned "a small number of people doing these unlawful activities" not to mistake the regime's forbearance for weakness.[61] But students literally stole a march on the government, arriving at Tiananmen just after midnight the night before. "When troops finally appeared early that morning, there were already over 100,000 students in the Square, and there was nothing commanders could do other than cordon off the entrance to the Great Hall."[62] The contrast between the crowds inside and outside the Great Hall of the People could not have been starker. Inside, the party elite, gray-suited, elderly, tired, and sick (many of the party elders needed attendants to help them stand and walk), were paying false homage to one they had rejected and purged. Zhao Ziyang read the brief eulogy stiffly, with no mention of Hu's ouster or a re-evaluation of his record. Outside in the square, a massive youthful crowd of students and workers were shouting slogans and singing China's national anthem and the "Internationale," communism's official anthem. Later in the afternoon, three students went to the top of the steps of the Great Hall and knelt in an attitude of supplication, holding above their heads a petition with their demands for dialogue with the government. It reminded witnesses of petitions being presented to China's emperors. But no one came out to receive it. The gap between the two sides deepened, as each felt insulted by the other.

The days following brought something of a lull in activity. Zhao Ziyang left for a scheduled visit to North Korea on April 23, having first secured the approval of Deng, Li Peng, and others to his three-point plan for dealing with the students: prevent further demonstrations and get students back to class; punish lawbreakers; and use methods of persuasion rather than repression. He placed Li Peng in charge while he was away, enjoining him to keep Deng informed of the situation.[63] For their part, the students focused on organization—more poster and petition writing, meetings of student organizations on each of Beijing's thirteen university campuses, and caucuses among student representatives. Relatively little is known about the details of these activities, apart from some post facto articles of questionable accuracy published by the regime after everything was over.[64] On April 24, all university student organizations declared a boycott of classes.

What did the students want? What were their goals? These questions caused considerable controversy, even among the students. The PRC government has always maintained that, though the majority of the students had good intentions, the leadership of a "small handful" was directly planning to overthrow the Communist Party to establish a Western-style political system. There is little reliable information to support such a claim and little reason to take it as other than a post facto justification for the regime's actions. Other commentators have taken a position defending the students, insisting they came out of the mainstream of Chinese democratic development and did not seek the overthrow of existing authorities.[65] Most reports in American media at the time, print and electronic, generally referred to the students as a "democracy movement." That established an almost immediate rapport with an American audience and unfortunately conveyed an inaccurate understanding of what they represented.[66] "I believe we tried to put a 'made in the U.S.A.' democracy stamp on it," said one TV reporter in a Barone Center report.[67] At times, the students contributed to this misunderstanding by waving banners or wearing T-shirts with well-known English phrases from the Declaration of Independence or the Gettysburg Address. This was good footage but not necessarily representative of most students' views.

In general, it seems that the students, in the early stages, wanted freedom of speech (broadly defined), democracy (dimly understood), and honest, accountable government (an improvement over the current regime). But they appeared more united in their view of what they did not like than what they did. They did not like the treatment accorded Hu Yaobang in 1987 and wanted his reputation restored. They did not like their system of education or their job prospects and wanted better treatment for intellectuals and more money for education. They did not like the obvious corruption of party officials at all levels and the flaunting of illicit wealth and influence by the children of high-level officials and wanted those guilty held accountable. They did not like oppressive party controls over their rights to organize themselves, speak in public, and publish their opinions, and they wanted the kinds of freedoms enjoyed by Western democracies, promised but not delivered by their own system.

In looking back on the students' and other protesters' goals, organization, and decisions, there was a chaotic element that must be borne in mind. A broad range of ideas, prejudices, aspirations, and fears was evident in China's universities, with little disciplined organization to centralize or focus the energies that operated. Leadership was in many cases ad hoc and changed frequently. Similarly, ideas presented in petitions and manifestos varied widely.

Slogans, tactics, and spontaneous responses to the crowds, security apparatus, and foreign media gave student activities an aura of excitement and genuineness but also lent themselves to a variety of interpretations. American reporters, many of whom spoke no Chinese, saw the student movement through its English-speaking participants and interpreted its goals as the establishment of an American-style democratic system. At least in the print media, journalists carefully listed the demands presented by student organizations at different times, but the headlines still hailed the students as a "prodemocracy movement." So did the TV reporters who became more evident as the story grew.

Observers behind the closed doors of the Great Hall of the People and in Zhongnanhai interpreted the different voices of the student movement according to their own ideological background, fears, and prejudices. They focused on the sarcasm directed at Li Peng, the symbolic acts of protest (such as the smashing of "little bottles," or *xiao ping*, a homophone for Deng's name), and some of the slogans calling for an end to Communist Party rule. The initial reaction of the leadership was harsh, though not necessarily forceful. Beijing municipal leaders, particularly Mayor Chen Xitong and Party Secretary Li Ximing, pressed for a crackdown early, however, possibly fearing being held accountable for deteriorating public order in the capital and the possibility that the movement would spread. They insisted that the student movement was a "planned, organized turmoil" and made their views and interpretations of student activity known to the leadership.[68] In response, Li Peng called a Politburo meeting on the evening of April 24, a meeting Zhao Ziyang could not attend, as he had already left for Pyongyang. Li Ximing and Chen Xitong reported on the situation in Beijing, while the vice minister of the State Education Commission, He Dongchang, commented on the rapid growth of student demonstrations in twenty other Chinese cities. The meeting decided to form a leadership "small group to halt the turmoil," which was headed by Li Peng.[69]

Deng's Miscalculation

In light of his reaction to Democracy Wall in 1979 and student protests in 1986, there could have been little doubt how Deng would react to this latest challenge, especially if it was described to him in terms that highlighted the threats presented by students to the party's domination and to himself. Information that became available in May—leaked to Hong Kong newspapers but considered accurate—makes clear that Deng was outraged by the student activities, but he spread the blame around, particularly to Hu Yaobang. Deng was briefed on the morning of April 25 by Li Peng, Yang Shangkun, and other members of the Politburo Standing Committee about the situation in Beijing, as well as violent incidents in Xi'an and Changsha. Li Peng made a point of telling Deng he was the focus of student wrath. "The spear is now pointed directly at you," he said. The briefers stressed the importance of "exposing" those "few people with ulterior motives" who were fomenting the turmoil.[70] Deng minced no words in reply:

> This is not an ordinary student demonstration, but turmoil (*dongluan*). So we must have a clear-cut stand and implement effective measures to quickly oppose and stop this unrest. We cannot let them have their way. Those people who have been influenced by the liberal elements of Yugoslavia, Poland, Hungary and the Soviet Union have arisen to create turmoil. Their motive is to overthrow the leadership of the Communist Party and to forfeit the future of the country . . . A dialogue can be held, but we cannot tolerate incorrect behavior. We must do our best to avoid bloodshed, but we should foresee that it might not be possible to completely avoid bloodshed. . . . The turmoil this time is definitely national in scope, and we must not underestimate it. We must issue a forceful editorial and make use of the law. . . . We must prepare ourselves to enter into a nation-wide struggle, and resolutely crush the turmoil. . . . Now the character of the student movement has changed. We need to quickly use a sharp knife to cut the tangled weeds in order to avoid even greater turmoil.[71]

Deng's harsh evaluation was reflected and expanded in an editorial prepared for publication in the *People's Daily* on April 26. It was read on the television news the night before. In language reminiscent of the Cultural Revolution, the editorial attacked the "extremely small number of people with ulterior motives" who led the students astray, who "spread all kinds of rumors to poison and confuse people's minds. . ., [who] vilified, hurled invectives at, and attacked party and state leaders." It accused them of trying to "seize power" in the universities, instigating student strikes and preventing students from going to class, and distributing "reactionary" handbills. "Their purpose was to sow dissension among the people, plunge the whole country into chaos and sabotage the political situation of stability and unity. This is a planned conspiracy and a disturbance. Its essence is to, once and for all, negate the leadership of the Communist Party of China and the socialist system." The editorial called for the entire party and government to "oppose the disturbance," prevent "illegal organizations" from being formed, and investigate rumormongers. It called for a prohibition on demonstrations, liaison activities by protestors, and interruption of classes. Claiming the students' demands for an end to corruption and promotion of democracy were the party's demands as well, it called on all to take action to stop the disturbances.[72] Zhao Ziyang had been notified and concurred with the Standing Committee's decision to publish an editorial and with the draft of the editorial.

The reaction of the students began with shock and fear. They gathered in dormitories and courtyards that same evening to discuss the editorial. They congregated in front of the makeshift offices of their new and independent Beijing Autonomous Students Federation, waiting to hear how their leaders would react. And as they listened to their representatives, student emotions turned to indignation and defiance. All day on April 26, student representatives met to plan a response. At the end of their meeting, they announced at a press conference that there would be a major protest demonstration over the editorial on April 27, beginning at 8:00 a.m. The government used all available means to discourage the effort. Beijing municipality publicly reissued regulations banning demonstrations. Faculty members pleaded with student leaders not to push harder. Party-organized student organizations and Youth League officials claimed the demonstration was canceled, and progovernment students warned of extensive police and military preparations to quell any demonstration.[73] Fearful students prepared for violence, tear gas, and possible death. Some wrote emotional farewells to their fellow students, others wrote wills and put them up as wall posters on campuses.

Early on the morning of April 27, thousands of students gathered at the entrance gates of Qinghua University, Beijing University, Beijing Normal University, and other colleges and prepared for an hours-long effort to reach Tiananmen. Arrayed before them were police lines several rows deep, determined to prevent them from leaving the campuses. Standing alongside were thousands of ordinary citizens, spectators at a public contest. But they were not neutral—their sympathy for the students was overwhelming, manifested in everything from providing food and drink to shouting at police to let them through to joining in lines to push against the barriers. Police were unarmed and did not use nightsticks or other weapons to attack the marchers. Student numbers were overwhelming. The police lines bent, then broke, to the wild cheers of spectators. The scene repeated itself numerous times as students and citizens made the long trek from university campuses to Tiananmen Square.

The different march groups linked up west of Tiananmen and overwhelmed the last police barricades at Xidan and Liubukou. By the time they reached Tiananmen, the number of marchers was estimated at 150,000 and their roadside supporters at half a million.[74] The PLA troops guarding the square were hurriedly withdrawn to avoid a direct clash, and student demonstrators, having won their symbolic victory, returned triumphantly to their campuses. Print media in the United States called it a "stunning humiliation" and a "stinging rebuke" for the Chinese government and spoke of its "impotence" in dealing with the "biggest display of dissatisfaction in 40 years of Communist rule."[75] Across millions of American television sets, CNN reported the events with riveting footage of the crowds and confrontation. Beijing CNN correspondent Mike Chinoy's "strong sense of identification with these young protestors" came through clearly in his coverage.[76] China's mass movement was going global.

The following day, the regime appeared to offer several partial compromises. First was an offer to hold a "dialogue," but with certain conditions, namely, that only officially sanctioned student organizations could attend the dialogue and that they had to end the boycott of classes. Independent student organizations were slow to respond and were highly dissatisfied with the proposal and the conduct of the first session of the dialogue on April 30. They were particularly annoyed by the behavior of the government negotiators—State Council Spokesman Yuan Mu and Vice Minister of the Education Commission He Dongchang—who were considered overbearing and arrogant in the first meeting. A far more important concession by the government was a statement by Hu Qili, Politburo Standing Committee member and ally of Zhao responsible for propaganda and media issues, who told China's tightly controlled newspapers on April 28 that they could report on the "actual state of affairs" regarding the student movement. That resulted in at least partial television coverage of the "dialogue" and a relatively balanced appraisal in China's official newspapers. Least noticed of the government's concessions was an offer by top Beijing officials Chen Xitong and Li Ximing to disclose their assets. Western journalists covering the dialogue focused principally on the student demands and student reaction, downplaying what were rather striking retreats by the government, especially in light of the hard tone of the editorial and the implicit threats it conveyed.

Independent student groups decided by April 30 to reject the dialogue as it was developing, and they formulated a twelve-point proposal for the government to consider. Wang Dan delivered the proposal personally to the State Council on May 1. Among the proposal's points were that the dialogue should be "between equals," that student representatives should be chosen by the students, that government representatives should be from the Politburo Standing Committee, that outside observers—including foreign journalists—be permitted and that sessions be broadcast live, and that a communiqué be issued on the results of the dialogue. The petition demanded that the government respond by noon on May 3 or there would be a demonstration on May 4. At the appointed time, government spokesman Yuan Mu publicly rejected the petition, calling it an ultimatum designed to threaten the government.[77]

Cracks in the Leadership

By far the most important development that took place that week, one largely unreported in the press, was Zhao Ziyang's April 30 return from North Korea and his decision to become more actively involved in the controversy. Exactly what happened, what leadership meetings took place, and what Zhao and his advisers decided are difficult to determine from the contradictory and heavily biased accounts that have appeared subsequently. With Zhao still under virtual house arrest and unwilling to engage in self-criticism for his actions, we have only the regime's post facto explanation of what transpired in the leadership during this period as well as the testimony of some of Zhao's associates who escaped from China. Even the Andrew Nathan and E. Perry Link reports, the *Tiananmen Papers*, provide only a partial account of internal leadership dynamics at the time.

The official verdict on Zhao was that he "tolerated and connived at" the activities of the students. After his return, he was said to have adopted a "changeable attitude" toward the party's verdict as delivered in the April 26 editorial.[78] But the Nathan and Link volume makes clear that there was no consensus in the Politburo, or even within its Standing Committee, on how to deal with the students. From the beginning, the notion of students being led astray by a small group of evildoers was not fully accepted. Zhao, Qiao Shi, Hu Qili, and others repeatedly affirmed that the students were patriotic and well meaning, and that several of their critiques of the party had merit. The right approach for the leadership, therefore, was to establish a dialogue with them, try to persuade them to be patient, and use appropriate methods to express their views. Ideological conservatives, such as Li Peng, Song Ping, Li Tieying, Chen Xitong, and others, were more critical of the students, but they did not have a cogent proposal to counter the idea of dialogue. Yang Shangkun and even Deng were ambivalent, admitting that dialogue was possible and even desirable. Even before Zhao returned from North Korea, the Politburo Standing Committee had agreed to hold a dialogue with students, but opinions were sharply divided.[79]

Did Zhao manipulate the students into supporting ideas that he favored and attacking leaders he disliked, as Deng had done with Democracy Wall in 1978? This, too, is implied by the official criticisms but again is difficult to square with available evidence. Philosophically, Zhao was considered a reformer, but his focus was mainly on economic affairs. He was less "liberal" in his approach to heterodox political ideas than Hu Yaobang had been. In fact, he had strongly supported a concept called "new authoritarianism," which posited that backward and predominantly rural China was not yet ready for a democratic transition but needed a strong authoritarian leader to manage the economic reform process.[80] Although some of his small circle of advisers may have had contacts with student groups, most of them were middle-aged intellectuals who may have shared some of their younger counterparts' discontent but did not necessarily have close and regular contacts with them. Moreover, Zhao was not a favorite among students, as his sons were considered to have used their father's connections to make lucrative deals in Hong Kong.

Did Zhao fear losing his position as Hu Yaobang had?And did he therefore decide to use the demonstrations to cast his opponents and detractors in a bad light? Hong Kong media—which sometimes tend toward the sensational in their assessments of internal Chinese politics—had speculated that Zhao was under intense attack from party elders, including Chen Yun, Bo Yibo, and Li Xiannian, for his economic policies and for permitting again a more open discourse on ideology and economics among China's intellectuals. The elders had suggested that Zhao be relieved of his post, an idea Deng supposedly rejected.[81] This is plausible but again seems a rather forced explanation. Zhao must have known the elders could not bring him down unless Deng agreed, and he probably had no reason to believe he had completely lost Deng's support. Playing political games with a mass movement—particularly one as volatile and unpredictable as the students of 1989 appeared to be—seems a highly risky, even desperate, gamble for one whose political instincts were as cautious as Zhao's. In analytical hindsight, Zhao's actions seemed those of a conciliator, a populist leader who wanted reforms to continue without the kind of interruption a major crackdown on students would have brought about. He comes across in the *Tiananmen Papers*, as Nathan observes, as "a liberal and a democrat" but unwilling to challenge Deng on fundamental political and procedural principles.[82]

There is no doubt, however, that two speeches he gave in early May were widely interpreted as being at odds with the tough sentiments expressed in the April 26 editorial. Students recognized the disparity, foreign reporters saw it, other party leaders saw it. With heavy domestic and foreign media coverage, and with foreknowledge of the active demonstration planned for Tiananmen Square on the May 4 anniversary, Zhao took a deliberately conciliatory stance. Speaking on May 3 to a forum marking the seventieth anniversary of the original May 4 demonstrations, Zhao focused positively on youth as China's hope and treasure. He did not threaten or bluster but praised the patriotism of Chinese students since 1919, their ardent support for science and democracy, and their optimism about the future. He counseled them to avoid turmoil and support the Communist Party and socialism. Zhao's speech carefully hit all the Dengist notes but balanced them with a sense of shared purpose clearly aimed at the students of 1989, not 1919.[83] It seemed based on a belief that a more peaceable approach was more likely to get them back to classes than the threats of the April 26 editorial, which had so clearly failed.

Zhao's remarks to a May 4 meeting of the Asian Development Bank (ADB) were more controversial. In his brief speech, Zhao appeared to be trying to reassure nervous foreign bankers and investors that China was not on the verge of a political meltdown. "Though demonstrations are still underway in Beijing and some other big cities in the country, I still believe there will be no big riots and the demonstrations will gradually calm down." In terms clearly in contrast with the April 26 editorial, Zhao said student demonstrations "should also be handled through legal and democratic means in an orderly and reasonable atmosphere. . . [and] urged that consultations and dialogues be pursued with students, workers, intellectuals, non-Communist parties and leading personages from all walks of life." He stressed, "Sober-mindedness, reason, restraint, order, and devotion to democracy and legality are most essential for resolving the problems."[84]

With perfect hindsight, many Western observers look back on Zhao's speeches as a watershed event that touched off a power struggle in the leadership, which paralyzed the government's efforts to deal with the student movement in early May, when it was still relatively small and disorganized. Journalists, in particular, seemed bemused by the leadership's lack of action during this period and attributed it to a power struggle. As one reporter put it, "It's only in retrospect that we go back and read those speeches and see how clear the split was. At the time we didn't know if Zhao was representing everyone in the government by giving a more conciliatory line. As it turned out, he was not."[85]

Zhao probably *was* reflecting a consensus view within the Politburo on handling the student movement cautiously—or at least within the Standing Committee (which consisted of Zhao, Li Peng, Hu Qili, Qiao Shi, and Yao Yilin). At a Standing Committee meeting on May 1, the divisions were clear: Li and Yao favored the restoration of order and stability first, dialogue and reform later. They did not prevail.[86] Zhao and Li clashed again—over revising the April 26 *People's Daily* editorial—shortly after the ADB speech, according to the *Tiananmen Papers*.[87] Party elders, who were no longer in the formal authority structure, were consulted and in some cases participated in Standing Committee meetings. Yang Shangkun played the key role, not only as respected elder but also because of his authority within the Military Commission and because of his influence with Deng. According to Xu Jiatun, formerly the ranking Communist Party official in Hong Kong who defected after Tiananmen, Zhao's consultations with other central and provincial leaders led him to believe that many others were reluctant to start a crackdown, but he worried about crossing Deng's hard-line views. Zhao asked Xu to prevail on Yang Shangkun (with whom Xu had long-standing close ties) to try and persuade Deng to change his mind. Zhao would work on Li Peng and Yao Yilin. Xu found Yang sympathetic to Zhao's position but not confident he could get "the old man" (*laoyezi*) to listen.[88]

Meanwhile, besides the huge demonstration in Tiananmen on May 4, large demonstrations were reported in Shanghai and several large provincial capitals.[89] In Beijing, Chinese journalists protested outside of the Xinhua News Agency headquarters, carrying banners that read "Don't Believe What We Write, We Print Lies." Intellectuals also formed an "autonomous federation" of their own in early May and drafted a manifesto, which they submitted to the government. Probably most worrisome to the government, independent unions of Beijing workers began actively supporting student demonstrators.[90] Events were moving rapidly toward a crisis. But it would be a "foreign intervention" that would take them over the top.

CHAPTER THREE

Escalation, Denouement, and Aftermath

After the May 4 demonstrations, things quieted down considerably in Beijing. Students mostly remained on campus, debating their next steps. Many wanted to end the boycott and return to classes. Final examinations were coming up, and they were tired of long marches in sweltering heat. Student leaders, however, energized by the success of their April 27 and May 4 marches, insisted the boycott be continued and looked for ways to expand their movement and keep pressure on the government. Moreover, they were concerned that the movement would disintegrate if not faced with new activities and challenges. The scheduled May 17 visit to China of Mikhail Gorbachev, general secretary of the Communist Party of the Soviet Union, provided an ideal target of opportunity.

Waiting for Gorbachev, Raising the Stakes

Gorbachev's visit had been agreed on the previous fall, after months of careful negotiation. China's troubled relations with the USSR dated to ideological disputes between Mao and Soviet leaders, and reached their lowest level in 1969, when large-scale combat between Soviet and Chinese troops broke out along their common border. Resultant military tensions were largely responsible for Mao's decision to try and mend relations with the United States. Mao's death in 1976 did not lead to an easing of the relationship, however, and was followed by the Soviet invasion of Afghanistan in 1980, which Beijing saw as threatening. Joint U.S.-Chinese arming of anti-Soviet guerrillas in Afghanistan and joint surveillance of Soviet military programs from Chinese territory helped cement the strategic relationship between the United States and China, as well as sustain Sino-Soviet hostility and mistrust. Gorbachev's succession to the post of general secretary after the death of Konstantin Chernenko in 1985 brought about sweeping changes in Soviet foreign and domestic policy. In the mid-1980s, Soviet troops began to pull out of Afghanistan and reduced their deployments in Mongolia and along the Sino-Soviet border.

Deng Xiaoping, seeing an opportunity to reduce Chinese military expenditures and strike a better balance in the triangular relationship with Moscow and Washington, pushed for a formal easing of Sino-Soviet relations. Gorbachev's agreement to travel to Beijing in May to normalize party-to-party relations was a major step forward—a milestone for Deng and for China. It had the additional benefit of bringing about President George Bush's trip to Beijing in February; China was being courted by both superpowers. Chinese leaders wanted the world to witness this important event and therefore had authorized American television networks to cover the summit as fully as possible, including the setting up of portable satellite dishes and microwave links for live broadcasting. These journalists, however, would soon have a far different story to tell.

Gorbachev was well known to Chinese students and popular for his advocacy of political restructuring (*perestroika*) and openness (*glasnost*). They saw him as the embodiment of reform, having replaced a tottering gerontocracy and brought in younger, more energetic talent. Thousands of Beijing University (Beida) students signed an open letter asking Gorbachev to speak on campus, a request the regime naturally rebuffed. Chinese government leaders were less than enthusiastic about Gorbachev's advocacy of reform and "new thinking" about foreign policy.

During early May, Chinese party leaders had been busily engaged in finalizing preparations for the Gorbachev visit and considering how to handle the situation with the students. Zhao called a Politburo Standing Committee meeting on May 8, during which he proposed measures to accommodate student demands by appointing special commissions to investigate financial improprieties of high-ranking officials and their children, passing new laws on press freedom and public demonstrations, cleaning up government organizations, and promoting the rule of law. But the meeting bogged down in wrangling by conservatives over student motives and methods. Zhao deferred the discussion for a full Politburo meeting on May 10. That meeting also was inconclusive but took note of the fact that protests had spread to virtually every province in the country. It was decided, however, to continue the dialogue with workers, students, and journalists.[1]

On May 12, however, students made a decision that was to alter the entire dynamic of China's politics, both private and public. During a spirited discussion at Beida on the next steps to be taken, Chai Ling—a twenty-two-year-old student from Beijing Normal University (Beishida) and the only woman among the leaders of the Beijing Autonomous Students Federation (BASF)—made an impassioned plea to mount a hunger strike before Gorbachev's visit. Her language was inspirational to the assembled student representatives but a grim portent of what was to come. "We, the children, are ready to die! We, the children, are ready to use our lives to pursue truth! We, the children, are ready to sacrifice ourselves!"[2] The BASF then passed a resolution that, unless the government agreed to negotiate with them as equals and acknowledge that they were a "patriotic" movement, they would begin a hunger strike the following day. Four hundred students pledged to begin the fast.

After lunch on May 13, the students left Beishida and trooped into Tiananmen Square without resistance, setting up their fasting headquarters at the base of the Martyrs' Monument about 4:30 p.m. Thus began the most dramatic phase of the protest movement, in which miscalculations and misunderstandings by the students and the government would have the most far-reaching implications. The hunger strikers presented striking imagery—dressed in white, with headbands inscribed with the Chinese characters for "no choice but to fast," many carrying placards with patriotic slogans and poems (some in English). Bystanders cheered them on their route, and a crowd estimated at 20,000 surrounded them at the Martyrs' Monument to hear them pledge. "I hereby swear that of my own free will, and in order to promote the democratization of China, I will engage in a fast, will abide by the rules of the Hunger Strike Group, and will not give up until our purpose is achieved."[3] Within hours, the number of hunger strikers had grown to more than 3,000.

Also within hours, a group of high-ranking government officials led by Yan Mingfu (director of the party's United Front Bureau) arrived to negotiate with student representatives about the terms under which they would be willing to withdraw from the square before Gorbachev's arrival. Although Zhao had earlier appointed Chen Xitong and Li Ximing to meet with students, they were heartily disliked and unwelcome, whereas Yan, an associate of Zhao, was considered a more sympathetic interlocutor. His mission took on a particular urgency, as Zhao had purportedly promised Deng that morning that the students would not disrupt the welcoming ceremonies for Gorbachev.[4] According to Li Xiaowen's account, there were three distinct organizations representing the students (the Dialogue League, the Hunger Strike Group, and the BASF) and a few middle-aged intellectuals acting as middlemen. Despite considerable confusion, an oral agreement was reached that the government would start a dialogue with the students "as soon as possible" in exchange for the students leaving Tiananmen Square on May 14.[5]

The following day, Yan returned with more senior leaders, including Education Commission head Li Tieying, to negotiate the terms of the dialogue. Although both sides evidently agreed the formal sessions would begin in the afternoon, government negotiators were dismayed to find out that their interlocutors did not know if they could persuade the hunger strikers to leave. For their part, student representatives were skeptical that any meaningful dialogue would continue once they no longer occupied the square. The dialogue was repeatedly interrupted by angry students and eventually was broken off late in the evening. An attempt by several prominent intellectuals to mediate between the government and hunger strikers failed when the strikers' demands escalated drastically. Among their demands: that Li Peng and Zhao Ziyang should visit them in the square to declare their movement patriotic. The scholars' efforts to convince the hunger strikers to leave the square brought immediate accusations that they were "spineless lobbyists" for the government. Chai Ling and her husband, Feng Congde, accused other students and middle-aged intellectuals of "selling" the movement, and they all took the hunger strike oath again.[6] On the evening before Gorbachev's arrival, Zhao's "multi-level, multi-channel dialogue" had failed completely.

The occupation of Tiananmen continued, abetted by the government's own media. Thanks to decisions by Zhao and Hu Qili to allow fuller coverage of domestic events—including the demonstrations—and the growing sympathy of Chinese reporters for the student cause, the hunger strike was given heavy coverage in the normally controlled central media. Television images of fasting students surrounded by worried medical personnel, radio interviews with emotional youths vowing to give their lives for democracy, and lengthy print stories about growing public support for the students had a riveting effect on the populace of Beijing. They came out by the thousands to see, encourage, and implore the government to meet the students' "reasonable" demands. Government offices were deserted, transportation snarled as people from all over Beijing headed for Tiananmen. By midday on May 15, more than 150,000 people filled the square, all in a surprisingly festive mood. Although banners appeared attacking Li Peng or calling on Deng to resign, most people were there to celebrate freedom and cheer on the students.

Tiananmen also became an international media event, thanks to the government's desire to have the Sino-Soviet reconciliation take place in full view of American television cameras. Dan Rather of CBS, Bernard Shaw of CNN, and others arrived with large teams of reporters to cover the Gorbachev visit, and they ended up devoting far more time to the extraordinary events in Tiananmen Square. Gorbachev's visit became a sideshow, in part because the Chinese government could not deliver Gorbachev to the media sites, because of enormous crowds. Gorbachev's arrival ceremony on May 15 had to be conducted at the airport rather than the square. Visits to the Martyrs' Monument and the Forbidden City had to be canceled. Even Gorbachev's meetings with senior PRC leaders had to be adjusted so that he could enter through the back door of the Great Hall of the People rather than the front. As if the embarrassment of being unable to control the streets in front of the central government headquarters were not enough, Gorbachev himself offered an attractive and obvious contrast to the Chinese leadership: young, outgoing, media-savvy, a dedicated reformer, open-minded—all the things China's leaders were not. Crowds in the square displayed banners that highlighted the irony. "I'm 58, you're 85."[7]

American journalists covering the summit got caught up instead in the spirit of Tiananmen Square—and they were enthralled at something that seemed even more historic than Sino-Soviet rapprochement. In ways that magnified the shock of the later crackdown, American journalists—especially TV journalists, and those who "parachuted" in with no language expertise, historical context, or knowledge of the Chinese government—became overwhelmingly sympathetic to the student movement. "'It was not possible to be dispassionate,' admitted Charles Kuralt, who was in Beijing for CBS News. 'The most cynical journalists could not help but be caught up.'"[8] Said CNN's Mike Chinoy, "The mere act of coming to Tiananmen Square was a liberating experience . . . I could feel the air of freedom."[9] A Canadian journalist admitted, "We were totally involved . . . with the students . . . We lost our objectivity for a while. I certainly did. It was hard to be objective with a government that seemed . . . run by a group of thugs who had no real right to kill their children."[10]

Watching it all on television, knowing that socialism was declining rapidly in eastern Europe at the time, caught up in the hopes of idealistic and attractive youth, Americans dared to hope that China's students would find a way to bring democracy to their country. As one observer mused later, "The coverage presented a wildly optimistic picture of the protesters' chances of victory. For American television viewers, setting up these false expectations would prove disillusioning but ultimately harmless. For the protesters, however, it may have been fatal. The American media's enthusiasm for the story may well have given the Chinese students a dangerously inflated sense of their own power—and of their immunity to the sort of vicious countermeasures that were eventually imposed."[11] It also reinforced the party elders' view that the student movement was being fomented by foreigners in order to bring down the government.

While American television focused on the square, inside the walls of Zhongnanhai, what remained of the leadership's cohesion was rapidly unraveling. "The failure to bring the occupation of Tiananmen to an end before

Gorbachev's arrival fatally undermined Zhao Ziyang's position in the leadership."[12] Even during the Soviet leader's visit, Zhao's supporters entreated students and older intellectuals alike to decamp from Tiananmen, actions that subsequently were held against both them and Zhao. Demonstrators took this as a sign that China's leaders were split over how to deal with the movement, but students were not sufficiently convinced of the value of supporting one faction or another to take clear action. And so the square remained full of people, taunting the leadership, heightening its embarrassment.[13]

Zhao's comments to Gorbachev on the afternoon of May 16, broadcast on Chinese television that evening, may have been the last straw, from Deng's perspective. In the morning, Deng had met with Gorbachev for two hours, saying that his meeting with Zhao in the afternoon would constitute the official reestablishment of relations between the communist parties of the USSR and China. Zhao told Gorbachev, however, that his meeting with Deng was actually the crucial one. He then went on to discuss what was no particular surprise to most China watchers but was not officially admitted, that Deng was the principal decisionmaker in the Communist Party of China, despite being retired.

> As recognized at home and abroad, Comrade Deng Xiaoping has been the leader of our party since the third plenary session of the Eleventh CPC Central Committee [December 1978]. Comrade Deng Xiaoping stepped down from the Central Committee and the Standing Committee of the Politburo of his own accord at the Thirteenth CPC Congress [in September 1987]. However, all the comrades in our party hold that in the interests of the party we still need Comrade Deng Xiaoping, his wisdom and his experience. This is of vital importance to our party. Therefore, the first plenary session of the Thirteenth CPC Congress made the solemn decision that we still need Comrade Deng Xiaoping at the helm when it comes to most important questions. Since the 13th CPC Congress, we have always made reports to and asked for opinions from Comrade Deng Xiaoping while dealing with most important issues. Comrade Deng Xiaoping also fully supports our work and the decisions we have made collectively.[14]

Although most American journalists ignored or missed the significance of Zhao's revelation, the Chinese interpreted it as an oblique attack on Deng: it implied that the problems about which the students were complaining were the results of Deng's decisions, it referred to him in ways that evoked the memory of Mao Zedong at his most dictatorial, and it suggested that Deng was in favor of the conciliatory approach being taken toward the demonstrations. The very fact that Zhao's remarks were published in the party propaganda organs was evidence that the center had lost control of information altogether. Foreign media were beaming out to the world stunning images of the party's helplessness and embarrassment, while domestic media were openly siding with students calling for the regime's humiliation. On the pages of China's major newspapers, Gorbachev's visit was relegated to a lower quadrant, while banner headlines shouted, "One Million from All Walks of Life Demonstrate in Support of Hunger-Striking Students."[15]

Now the regime was desperate, finally providing the concessions the students had been demanding. Yan Mingfu, at Zhao's behest, pleaded with the students again to leave the square, publicly indicating that the government would affirm the patriotism and correctness of the student movement (thereby negating the April 26 editorial).[16] In public remarks in a meeting with Gorbachev, Li Peng said, "People in socialist countries should also enjoy freedom, democracy and human rights. China is prepared to improve these aspects of its political reform."[17] But out of the public glare, the regime was in open disarray. At an emergency Politburo Standing Committee meeting the evening of May 16, Zhao and Li Peng quarreled bitterly about what was to be done, with Zhao urging retreat from the April 26 editorial's judgment about the "turmoil" and Li Peng insisting the editorial's principal judgments were "all Comrade Deng Xiaoping's original words. They cannot be changed."[18]

The following morning, May 17, in a rancorous Politburo Standing Committee meeting held at Deng's home, Li Peng forcefully laid the blame for the situation on Zhao. "I think Comrade Ziyang must bear the main responsibility for the escalation of the student movement, as well as for the fact that the situation has gotten so hard to control," he began, and continued with a recitation of Zhao's errors since his return from Pyongyang.[19] Yao Yilin criticized Zhao for trying to shift responsibility to Deng in his remarks to Gorbachev. Yang Shangkun put it bluntly, "Our backs are to the wall. If we retreat any further we're done for . . . This movement could . . . unleash forces that can't be controlled." Deng insisted that the real problem was what to do to end the demonstrations. "Beijing can't keep going like this . . . If things keep going like this, we could even end up under house arrest . . . I've concluded that we should bring in the People's Liberation Army and declare martial law in Beijing . . . I am solemnly proposing this today to the Standing Committee of the Politburo and hope that you will consider it." Zhao responded he had "problems" with the recommendation but would abide by party discipline. Deng also ordered Li Peng to meet with student representatives.[20]

Later that day, the Politburo Standing Committee deadlocked on Deng's recommendation, with Li Peng and Yao Yilin voting to support the imposition of martial law, Zhao and Hu Qili opposing it, and Qiao Shi abstaining. Yang Shangkun and Bo Yibo expressed support for Deng's proposal but had no voting rights. Yang said he would refer the issue back to Deng Xiaoping and the elders and "get a resolution as soon as possible." Zhao asked to resign, saying he could not carry on and implement decisions he disagreed with. Yang and Bo rejected the idea.[21]

Zhao then held a meeting with his closest advisers, who leaked the story of the Standing Committee meeting to some of the demonstrators. According to later accounts by the regime, that led to even angrier protests the following day and banners praising Zhao. Early in the morning of May 18, Zhao took the highly unusual step of visiting with students in a hospital near Tiananmen (hunger strikers had begun to collapse by the second day and were rushed to the hospital by specially organized ambulance squads). He was accompanied by Li Peng and several other members of the Politburo Standing Committee—probably as much to keep an eye on Zhao as to show solicitude to the students. Afterward, he immediately went back to his office and drafted a letter of resignation, saying he could not implement the decision on martial law. Yang Shangkun talked him out of sending it, but Zhao nonetheless refused to attend the meeting with Deng and the elders.[22]

Passing the Point of No Return

At 8:30 in the morning on May 18, Deng, Chen Yun, Li Xiannian, Peng Zhen, Deng Yingchao, Yang Shangkun, Bo Yibo, and Wang Zhen met with the Politburo Standing Committee—minus Zhao—and three senior People's Liberation Army (PLA) officers representing the Military Commission. Deng put the situation starkly: "Beijing can't go on like this; we have to have martial law." One by one, the elders and Standing Committee members supported Deng's proposal, with varying enthusiasm and critiques of Zhao Ziyang for allowing the situation to develop to such a point. The meeting decided to place certain districts under martial law as of midnight on May 21 and to inform party, government, and military officials on the evening of May 19. Yang Shangkun was given the responsibility for preparing the PLA deployment plans.[23]

Nonetheless, the regime undertook one last effort to bring the demonstrations to a halt short of using force. Premier Li Peng—the most reviled of China's leaders, with whom the students had been demanding a dialogue, as well as his resignation—met with a selected group of hunger strikers at 11:00 a.m. that same morning inside the Great Hall of the People. The meeting was filmed and broadcast later in the evening on Chinese Central Television

(CCTV). The symbolism was striking. Li and his State Council cohorts were dressed in Mao suits (usually an indicator of conservative perspective), Wang Dan wore a leather jacket and a headband, Wu'er Kaixi wore pajamas and an oxygen mask, which he claimed he needed because of weakness from his hunger strike. Li was brusque and dismissive but was interrupted by Wu'er Kaixi and others in a striking show of effrontery. Li and the government demanded that the students call off the hunger strike first and allow order to be restored; Wu'er insisted that the April 26 editorial had to be retracted and a genuine dialogue established. Even then, he hinted that the students might not agree to give up the demonstrations. It was a dialogue of the deaf, done for symbolic purposes on both sides.[24]

Wu'er Kaixi's claim that the demonstrations were beyond the immediate control of the student representatives in the dialogue session had become a reality by May 18. Although the ostensible reason for the gathering in Tiananmen was to show support for the hunger-striking students, in fact the demonstrations had grown well beyond that stage, approaching a general strike. Conservative estimates put the crowd in Tiananmen on May 18 at 1 million. Many came with delegations from their work units, carrying banners that not only expressed support for the students but also attacked individuals in their own government. "Dump Li Peng! Deng Xiaoping, retire!" Banners and petitions representing the Ministry of Foreign Affairs, the Youth League, the Xinhua News Agency, the Party School, and even units of the People's Liberation Army called for increased democracy in China's governance.[25] After temporizing and providing sideline support for student demonstrators, some of China's most prominent intellectuals came out fully in support of the hunger strikers on May 16, forming a Beijing Union of Intellectuals (others refer to it as the Beijing Intellectuals Autonomous Federation) and issuing a sweeping denunciation of China's "tyrannical" government. Even more disconcerting from the government's point of view, Beijing workers—who had been supportive of the hunger strike since its inception but remained on the sidelines—officially announced the formation of the Beijing Autonomous Workers Federation on May 18 and set up a headquarters area on Tiananmen Square. They also issued a series of incendiary handbills and threatened to call a one-day general strike if the government did not meet student demands.[26]

Early in the morning of May 19, Zhao Ziyang made his first and last visit to the students in Tiananmen Square. With Li Peng in tow, but apparently without the permission of the rest of the leadership, Zhao boarded a bus full of recuperating hunger strikers at about 4:45 a.m. and spoke to them briefly, exhorting them one last time to end the hunger strike. With tears in his eyes, Zhao told the students:

> We have come too late. I am sorry, fellow students. No matter how you have criticized us, I think you have the right to do so. We do not come here to ask you to excuse us . . .Your fasting has entered its seventh day. This simply cannot go on. . . . The most important thing to do now is to immediately terminate this fasting. . . . When you end your fast, the government will never close the door to dialogues, never. If you have questions, we will solve them. Despite what you say and the fact that we are a little late, we are getting closer to solving the problems . . . But things are complicated, and there must be a process to resolve these problems.[27]

Whether Zhao was acting out of genuine concern for the students, as Orville Schell and others believe, or was trying to generate a politically significant constituency from among student demonstrators is not known. Certainly some of Zhao's followers seemed to be trying to generate support for Zhao among the students to stave off his political collapse. But the early morning visit probably accelerated his opponents' timetable. As Melanie Manion put it, Zhao "made the protest movement even more threatening to hardliners: at the top was a leader who had formed a tacit coalition with the protesters. It was a bold and probably foolish gamble."[28] The gamble worked, at least in part. Later that day, student leaders agreed to end the hunger strike phase of their protest but to continue their occupation of Tiananmen Square as a "sit-in." But it was too late. Li Peng called a meeting of the Politburo Standing Committee to advance the timetable for announcing martial law by one day. Zhao refused a request from Yang Shangkun to show leadership unity and absented himself from the meeting, claiming illness. Sometime later, he was placed under house arrest.

Late in the evening of May 19, in a meeting held at the headquarters of the Beijing Military Region, Beijing party chief Li Ximing, Li Peng, and Yang Shangkun addressed a large group of party, government, and military officials. Li Peng described a situation of a capital city badly out of control and called for "resolute and effective measures to curb turmoil in a clear-cut manner, to restore normal order in society, and to maintain stability and unity."[29] Although he reverted to the language of the April 26 editorial in describing the "turmoil," Li went out of his way to reassure students that the government's agreement to hold a dialogue was still valid. Curiously, he made only oblique mention of the military being called on to aid in restoring order and never mentioned the words "martial law." The following day, however, Beijing municipality announced the imposition of martial law as of 10:00 a.m., May 20. Demonstrations were banned in Beijing municipality, journalists were prohibited from the martial law area, and police and martial law troops were authorized to use necessary force to handle resistance.[30]

From the beginning, however, things did not go according to plan. Early calls—evidently by Deng—to bring the Thirty-Eighth Army into Beijing to augment the People's Armed Police and the Beijing Garrison Command had been frustrated by the resistance of its commander, Xu Qinxian, to using the army against Chinese citizens.[31] Xu was immediately replaced. Judging by a speech made on May 24 by Yang Shangkun, others also questioned whether Deng had exercised the proper command authority in ordering troop movements on his own before May 20.[32] Nonetheless, Deng's order brought the following units into designated areas outside the city: from the Beijing Military Region, division-strength units of the Twenty-Fourth, Twenty-Seventh, Twenty-Eighth, Thirty-Eighth, Sixty-Third, and Sixty-Fifth group armies; from the Shenyang Military Region, the Thirty-Ninth and Fortieth group armies; and from Jinan Military Region, the Fifty-Fourth and Sixty-Seventh group armies, bringing the total PLA strength around the city to more than 180,000.[33] Later, units from the Fifteenth and Twentieth group armies also arrived.

But word of the pending imposition of martial law leaked to demonstrators well before the meeting that formally announced it, enabling messengers and roving motorcycle patrols to warn citizens in advance. The reaction was nearly universal—outrage at the government and a determination to do everything possible to prevent the orders from being carried out. Barricades were hastily put up at several major intersections on the way to Tiananmen. Citizens stayed outside in the thousands, warily watching for signs of government military action.

On May 20, when PLA units began moving from their suburban encampments toward the center of the city, they were surrounded and blocked by thousands of ordinary citizens. Workers, elderly men, and women lay down in front of the military vehicles while others climbed aboard transport trucks to plead with the soldiers not to move against the hunger strikers. Students drained the gas tanks and deflated the tires of some military vehicles. Others were stopped by barricades made of buses and other vehicles. Thousands of citizens congregated at railway stations in order to deal with any troops that might try to enter the city by train. Clearly unprepared for this kind of resistance and possibly with their own doubts about their orders, many of the troops returned to their encampments in confusion. In an astonishing display of mass public defiance, millions of citizens again moved into Tiananmen Square to surround demonstrators with a wall of protection. The students at the center of the square were jubilant and defiant at this unexpected support. The regime was initially shocked and perplexed but used the opportunity provided by their forced immobility to improve indoctrination of the mostly peasant soldiers, who had little idea of what was happening in Tiananmen.[34]

Although initial efforts to implement martial law did not go smoothly, the regime's efforts to control information at and about Tiananmen started early and were somewhat more effective. From the American perspective, China's decision to sever the satellite linkages that had enabled the major networks to deliver real-time coverage of events in the square was the most dramatic and important development. On May 20, an hour before the official commencement of martial law, "two officials of the Ministry of Posts and Telecommunications walked into the CNN workspace on the ninth floor of the Sheraton and ordered CNN to cease its live transmissions from Beijing in an hour . . . 'Gorbachev is gone. Your task is over.'"[35] Other networks' live feeds were similarly cut, but only CNN was able to report it live. Subsequently, most of the high-profile news teams left Beijing, leaving CNN as the principal news source. CNN couriered videotapes out through Hong Kong or reported live by telephone without pictures.

Far more important, for its own purposes, was the regime's effort to restore control over Chinese media channels, which also began on May 20. Some observers have concluded that many, but not all, Chinese journalists were inclined to support the students during the period from early May to the imposition of martial law.[36] To be sure, they had maintained some objectivity and reported government statements and news accurately as well. But the straightforward accounts of student activities in Tiananmen, full reporting of the "dialogue," and fearless portrayal of antigovernment banners and slogans in the *People's Daily* and on national television clearly helped bring the citizens of Beijing out onto the street in support of the students. Regime charges that the coverage contributed to demonstrations in many other parts of the country probably are accurate. If the regime was to quell the demonstrations, it had to first restore control of the press. Beginning on May 20, discipline began to be restored, if slowly. The loosening of restrictions on press freedoms instituted by Zhao and Hu Qili earlier in the month was rescinded, and press and television reporters were exhorted to return to their previous role as "mouthpieces for the party." This did not happen all at once. Journalists were reluctant to give up the freedom they had enjoyed. But within days after the declaration of martial law, newspapers and television again were reporting the news as the government saw fit to portray it.[37]

The slowness with which the government reestablished controls once it became clear that martial law would be stymied reflected the confusion within party, army, and government bureaucracies. With conflicting signals emanating from the top for at least two weeks, even officials loyal to the government were not certain how to carry out routine duties, much less orders as troubling as imposing martial law. Those government cadre who were not out showing support for student demonstrators or taking time off because of traffic tie-ups probably were reluctant to take firm measures without some form of assurance they would not be held accountable for them later.

On May 21, two members of the Standing Committee of the National People's Congress (NPC), China's rubber-stamp legislative body, prepared a petition calling for a special session to be convened to review the legality of (and, they hoped, rescind) the martial law order. Within three days, they had gathered forty-six signatures—enough under NPC guidelines to justify the convening of an emergency meeting.[38] But the petition was never acted upon. The chairman of the NPC Standing Committee, Wan Li, was at that time visiting the United States and in fact was received at the White House by President George Bush, who urged him and the PRC government to exercise "restraint" in handling the demonstrations. Wan had evidently been asked by Zhao to return to China to support and preside over such a meeting. Li Peng countermanded the order through the Politburo Standing Committee. A clearly anxious Wan cut short his visit and flew back to China on May 23, but rather than jump into the political controversy in Beijing, Wan landed in Shanghai and checked into a guest house, pleading illness. Although considered close to Zhao in his support for reform, Wan was also an associate—and bridge partner—of Deng.[39] Like many others confronted with the choice between ideals and political reality, Wan opted for reality.

Probably more troubling to Deng and other so-called hardliners was evidence of disagreement within PLA ranks about whether martial law was appropriate. On May 21, students gained access to two of China's prestigious "Old Marshals," Nie Rongzhen and Xu Xiangqian, and received assurances from them that martial law troops would not attack students in the square.[40] Several other senior retired PLA leaders issued a strongly worded open letter, widely quoted in the American press: "The army must absolutely not shoot the people. In order to prevent the situation from worsening, the army must not enter the city of Beijing."[41] It was evident that, before Tiananmen Square could be recovered, a great deal of work needed to be done to restore control of the government first.

Deng moved on two fronts, calling on the PLA high command and the Old Guard of the Party. Although some Western accounts of events at the time indicated that Deng was forced to call military officials to a conclave in Wuhan, in central China, to secure their obedience, it is more likely that such meetings took place in the secure leadership compound in Zhongnanhai or in the party compound in the Western Hills outside of Beijing. Nor is there much evidence of hesitation by China's regional military leaders in sending selected units to Beijing to become part of the Martial Law Command. Within days of the May 20 order, 150,000 to 200,000 soldiers from all over China were setting up camps outside the city.[42] In the "enlarged" Central Military Commission meeting on May 24, Yang Shangkun made a tough speech, highly critical of Zhao Ziyang and insistent upon the maintenance of military discipline. "If any troops do not obey orders, I will punish those responsible according to the military law."[43]

Along with regional military leaders, Deng also summoned the party secretaries and local government heads of China's twenty-nine provinces and centrally administered municipalities to Beijing to explain the imposition of martial law and to elicit their support. Many were anxious about student demonstrations—and some riots—in their own regions and wanted assurance that a crackdown in Beijing would not precipitate more violent protests.

Finally, and probably with misgivings, Deng was forced to rely on the support of the party elders whose retirement he had so carefully arranged over the past five years. Former president Li Xiannian had flown to Beijing from Shanghai to express his support for Deng. Chen Yun also arrived in Beijing to throw his weight behind Deng's efforts to restore order. Former NPC chairman Peng Zhen; Advisory Commission vice chairman Bo Yibo; former vice president Wang Zhen; former premier Zhou Enlai's widow, Deng Yingchao; and of course, Yang Shangkun all rallied in support of Deng.

According to the *Tiananmen Papers*, the elders met as a group on May 21 to consider what to do about the party's fractured leadership. They agreed that Zhao and Hu Qili had to go but were somewhat tentative about who should replace Zhao as general secretary. Deng asked Chen Yun for his advice. After a general description of the qualifications needed for the job, Chen came to the point. "Comrade [Li] Xiannian has pointed out to me that Comrade Jiang Zemin from Shanghai is a suitable candidate. Every time I've gone down to Shanghai he always sees me, and he strikes me as a modest person with strong Party discipline and broad knowledge." Li also extolled Jiang's virtues, including his strong action against a reformist newspaper in April, as well as his intelligence and knowledge of economics. "And he's got a good public image—in the prime of life, full of energy. I like the idea of him as general secretary." Other elders mentioned other possibilities—Deng expressing a preference of Li Ruihuan; Yang for Qiao Shi. Deng proposed they should think more about it.[44] In the meantime, he had Yang Shangkun send Jiang back to Shanghai to "persuade" Wan Li (chairman of the National People's Congress Standing Committee, who had just cut short his trip to Washington) not to return to Beijing to provide support for Zhao Ziyang.

On May 22, in an apparently enlarged Politburo Standing Committee meeting, Zhao was formally suspended from all his positions after being roundly criticized by several elders in attendance. The "two headquarters" problem resolved, the party and government were more prepared for a showdown.[45]

Six days later, the elders convened again, evidently at Deng's home. This time, Deng took the lead. "After long and careful comparison, the Shanghai Party Secretary, Comrade Jiang Zemin, does indeed seem a proper choice. I think he's up to the task. Comrades Chen Yun, [Li] Xiannian and I all lean toward Comrade Jiang Zemin for general secretary." Deng also proposed Li Ruihuan to be a member of the Politburo Standing Committee. Chen Yun proposed Song Ping be added. The others all concurred. Deng and Chen having made their trade-offs, the new leadership group was set.[46] In his biography of Jiang Zemin, Bruce Gilley claims Deng selected Jiang as general secretary on May 22, after consultations with Li Xiannian and Chen Yun, then offered him the job the following day. Jiang asked for a few days to consult with family and colleagues, then accepted after persuading Wan Li to stay in Shanghai until political affairs in Beijing sorted themselves out.[47] The account in the *Tiananmen Papers* is somewhat more credible, in that Jiang is offered the post after he passes the test of neutralizing Wan Li. Jiang returned to Beijing on May 30, and Deng explained to Li Peng and Yao Yilin the following day China needed a new leading group that would not be too "rigid, conservative, . . . or mediocre." Deng also lectured them on the need to maintain the "reform and opening" policy and that they were not to try and undermine Jiang.[48]

While the party and government were slowly getting organized and prepared, the student movement was deteriorating. After the emotional high point reached on the two days following the declaration of martial law, when Beijing's citizens prevented PLA troops from entering the city and protesters in Tiananmen Square numbered over a million, the student organizations fell to squabbling over goals, tactics, organization, personnel, and logistics of the "People's Republic of Tiananmen Square," as reporters dubbed it. Initial efforts to coordinate protest activities led to the formation of the "Capital Joint Liaison Group," which included representatives of students, workers, intellectuals, and Beijing citizens. But although it worked diligently to focus the efforts of the sprawling "democracy movement" and to develop a position to negotiate with the government, the group was hampered by the disorganization of its constituent elements, particularly within the student movement.[49]

As the threat of immediate military action subsided, students began to contemplate staging a tactical retreat from confrontation at Tiananmen and returning to classes. Wang Dan and Wu'er Kaixi pushed this option more forcefully as evidence mounted that hard-line elements in the leadership were gaining influence and more troops were reported in Beijing's suburbs. They were not successful in persuading others in Tiananmen, in part because the composition of both the protest and its leadership was changing. With the hunger strike over, many of the original student demonstrators were returning to campus to rest, recover, and prepare for final examinations. Others were repelled by the deteriorating sanitation conditions in the square and several days of high heat and torrential rain. "By the end of May, the Square had become a smelly squatters' camp. Heaps of garbage baked in the hot sun. Makeshift latrines—municipal buses with their seats removed—stank terribly. Many Beijing students had already drifted back to campus."[50] They were replaced by students from outside Beijing who had traveled to the capital to join in the revolution, were in no hurry to leave, and wanted to hold out for more government concessions. They formed the Tiananmen Square United Action Headquarters on May 24 and elected the volatile Chai Ling as supreme commander in chief. Chai and her husband argued for defending the square "at all costs," so as not to squander the gains that had already been achieved. Wu'er withdrew (or was expelled) from the student leadership.[51] Western reporters were offended increasingly by the officious behavior of student leaders, who surrounded themselves with bodyguards and withdrew from contact with foreign journalists.

Crowds of supporters began to diminish within three days of the declaration of martial law, in part because the threat of PLA action seemed to have disappeared, in part because government work units began restoring discipline and threatening punishment for those who provided support to the "turmoil." Although moral support for the students' cause and disdain for the central government probably did not diminish in intensity, fewer citizens felt obligated to trek to the square to demonstrate their solidarity. Increasingly, those in attendance at Tiananmen were unemployed youth—so-called hooligans (*liumang*)—or workers with a radical agenda for political change. They formed "dare-to-die" brigades to provide security for student leaders and "flying tiger squads" of motorcyclists to courier information and supplies. The danger presented by these outside elements was demonstrated on May 23, when three unemployed workers from Hunan Province threw paint at the portrait of Chairman Mao that hung on Tiananmen Gate. Students, wanting to avoid giving the regime an ideological pretext for taking military action, captured the perpetrators and turned them over to public security authorities (they eventually received very heavy sentences).

Finally, by May 27, the student movement seemed to have run out of steam. Estimates of the number of protesters occupying the square had fallen to about 15,000. Even Chai Ling reluctantly agreed that the time had come to withdraw from Tiananmen. Discussions of how to accomplish the retreat brought the student movement to the brink of dissolution. With dissident intellectuals Chen Ziming and Wang Juntao trying to act as intermediaries, the Beijing Autonomous Students Federation under Wang Dan and the Tiananmen Square United Action Headquarters split irrevocably over the date and conditions of a withdrawal. Wang Dan resigned from the BASF, as Wu'er Kaixi had before him. Under pressure from more radical provincial students, Chai Ling reversed herself. The final position was that the students would withdraw from the square on May 30 only if a special session of the National People's Congress was called within the next few days. Otherwise, they would stay in the square until June 20, the next scheduled regular meeting of the NPC Standing Committee.[52]

The die was cast. Provincial students cleaned up the garbage in the square, replaced the squalid latrines, put up new tents (received from Hong Kong), and settled in for a long stay. Chai broke down on May 28, resigned her position as commander in chief, and evidently left the square, turning leadership of the students over to one of the provincial activists. In a chilling but emotional interview with an Australian journalist, not translated or aired until long after the events, she gave a clue to her own sense of the outcome. "What we are actually hoping for is bloodshed," she said in the tearful monologue. "Only when the square is awash with blood will the people of China open their eyes!"[53]

The movement received an additional breath of new life on May 29 from the Central Academy of Fine Arts, which assembled a twenty-seven-foot statue—the Goddess of Democracy—directly across the square from the portrait of Chairman Mao. Bearing a striking resemblance to the American Statue of Liberty, the Goddess further galvanized the protest movement and brought it additional international support. At least 100,000 people came out to Tiananmen the following day to see the new challenge to the government. Even American reporters covering the event found the imagery worrisome. As CNN's Mike Chinoy later put it: "However riveting the image and however great the TV pictures, it was extraordinarily provocative. It was almost as if the students were taunting the authorities, daring them to act . . . To no one's surprise, the official media exploded in an orgy of condemnation."[54] Tragically, the symbol of students' hopes was probably the last straw for the government. Any chance of averting a violent showdown was now gone.

Denouement

Deng and the PRC government were ready to take action. Internal rifts had been patched over and consensus restored by removing dissonant elements from the leadership. Doubts about the correct course of action had been overcome by the united position of the party's most senior and respected elders. Military units from outside the capital had been brought in to buttress local troops, and all had been isolated, indoctrinated, and trained for their mission. Central control over television and the press had been restored, and the media now disseminated a consistent and hard-line message. Loudspeakers around Tiananmen drowned out the megaphones of the various student groups.

According to the *Tiananmen Papers,* the final decision to clear Tiananmen Square was made by the elders and the rump Politburo Standing Committee (Jiang Zemin evidently had not yet taken up his position) on June 2. Meeting in Deng's home, they heard an extraordinarily provocative report that had been prepared by Chen Xitong and Li Ximing of the Beijing Municipal Party Committee. In it, the demonstrators were no longer portrayed as misguided youth led by a "small handful" of evil elements. Now they were depicted as "terrorists" and "hooligans" involved in a "counterrevolutionary riot," instigated in no small part by "anti-communist, anti-China" elements from the United States, Taiwan, and Hong Kong.[55] Tiananmen Square had become the "command center for a final showdown with the Party and government," Li Peng told them. The student federations were under the influence of the United States and the Kuomintang Party in Taiwan. "It is becoming clear that the turmoil has been generated by a coalition of foreign and domestic reactionary forces and that their goals are to overthrow the Communist Party and to subvert the socialist system."[56] Ideologically outraged, the elders put themselves on record in resolute opposition to capitalism and called for quick action to recover Tiananmen. Yang Shangkun assured them the PLA troops were indoctrinated, disciplined, and ready to obey the Central Committee's orders to "clear the Square in a peaceful way." Deng ordered Yang to carry out the clearing in two days.[57]

It is not possible—using available sources—to fully and accurately describe the final decision process or the events of the night of June 3–4, 1989. Up until now, the PRC government has chosen not to provide a detailed explanation. The public reports it released, including the "press conference" held on June 7, 1989, and the pamphlet, "The Truth about the Beijing Turmoil," published in 1990, were primarily propaganda exercises aimed at justifying its actions and refuting Western press accounts of a "massacre." They are neither comprehensive nor, in all probability, accurate, especially about the numbers of casualties inflicted on the citizens of Beijing. Western press reporters were able to provide coverage of some of the events of the crackdown but were generally far from the most intense "action" or had partly obscured perspectives on the key events.[58] U.S. diplomats who dodged bullets and visited hospitals to look for American citizens who may have been caught up in the crackdown reported horrifying casualties and "lots of people killed" but could not provide a comprehensive overview of the scale of violence. Eyewitness accounts by students and others vary in detail but provide, at best, individual snapshots of actions witnessed in terror and flight. At worst, some of them are fabrications designed to exaggerate the brutality of the crackdown.

Since 1989, commentators about what happened on June 4 tend to be categorized on the basis of the noun used to describe the PLA action. Critics of the PRC seem to prefer the term "massacre," with its heavy emotive connotations. The regime calls it the "quelling of a rebellion" or a "clearing action." Western observers looking for more value-neutral terms talk about the Tiananmen "incident," or "crackdown," "event," or "tragedy." In fact, it was all of those and more. If one takes a dictionary definition of the term—"massacre: the indiscriminate, merciless killing of a number of human beings"[59]—then what happened the night of June 4 was indeed a massacre. Even conservative estimates of the number of civilian casualties put the number in the hundreds. And eyewitness accounts leave little doubt that, in some parts of Beijing, firing by PLA soldiers at unarmed civilians was indiscriminate and often deliberately cruel.

But more important than the what of Tiananmen is the how and why. On June 3, late in the afternoon, the Central Military Commission issued the order to martial law units on the outskirts of Beijing to "clear the Square" (*qingchang*) by dawn of the following day. Deadly force was authorized to overcome obstruction and opposition, and units likely were warned to expect violent resistance from "hooligans" and "ruffians" who were reported to be in control of key parts of the city. The decision to use lethal force probably was predicated on the ineffectiveness of other measures. Early in the morning of June 3—in what may have been as much a provocation as an effort to use nondeadly force—a group of several thousand young, unarmed soldiers of the Twenty-Fourth Army jogged toward Tiananmen Square. Before they got there, they were intercepted by angry citizens who pushed and shoved them into an embarrassing retreat. Weapons were discovered on buses accompanying the soldiers, and some apparently were confiscated by the civilians.[60]

That incident may have provided the excuse needed to justify a full-scale armed assault on downtown Beijing. At the afternoon meeting, Li Peng said, "We must be merciless with the tiny minority of riot elements. The PLA martial law troops, the People's Armed Police, and Public Security *are authorized to use any means necessary* to deal with people who interfere with the mission." Yang relayed a two-part message from Deng: "Solve the problem by dawn tomorrow"; and "No bloodshed within Tiananmen Square." Troops were to "carry away thousands of students on their backs," if necessary, but not to shoot them. The broadcast media were to persuade the students to leave the square.[61] To old men protected and isolated behind guarded walls, the orders probably seemed sensible. On the streets of Beijing, they were impossible.

At about 7:00 p.m. on June 3, all Beijing media began to broadcast the same message to the citizens. "Stay in your homes, stay off the street, do not go to Tiananmen Square." It was ignored. "Flying tiger" motorcycle sentries reported preliminary troop movements, enabling the strengthening of existing blockades (mostly municipal buses) on major routes to Tiananmen and the emplacement of new ones. Crowds swelled on the streets, hoping to stop military units as they had done two weeks earlier.

Sometime before 10:00 p.m., PLA units moving in earnest toward central Beijing from all points of the compass encountered civilian resistance. Although several units ran into civilian blockades north and east of the city, the heaviest fighting and highest casualties are believed to have taken place on the route leading into town from the west. At Muxidi, a residential housing area about four miles west of Tiananmen where elaborate roadblocks had been set up, troops from the Thirty-Eighth Army began firing above the heads of citizens blocking their path. When that had no effect, they began firing directly into the crowds at close range. The crowds exploded in rage, hurling bricks and Molotov cocktails at PLA units. Photographs of long lines of burned out military trucks and armored personnel carriers attest to the ferocity of the engagement. Enraged soldiers in some cases left their units to chase down fleeing civilians, shooting many of them in the back. Some were caught by angry crowds and brutally killed. The same column moved on toward Tiananmen, meeting similar large-scale resistance at the intersections of Xidan Street and Liubukou, less than a mile from the square. Again, frenzied PLA soldiers opened fire directly at crowds in the street and sprayed surrounding buildings indiscriminately with gunfire, killing many ordinary citizens who were obeying the government's orders to stay at home.[62]

By about 1:00 a.m. on the morning of June 4, various PLA units began arriving at Tiananmen Square, surrounding it and preparing for the final clearing operation. The remaining students, estimated to number 3,000 to 5,000, huddled around the Martyr's Monument, some angry and defiant, others fearful but resigned. Chai Ling was back among them, although Wu'er Kaixi and Wang Dan were not. A Taiwan-born rock singer, Hou Dejian, and three other Beijing intellectuals—Liu Xiaobo, Zhou Duo, and Gao Xin—were also at the monument, having begun their own hunger strike on June 2. Sensing that the situation was now desperate and hoping to avoid a bloodbath, they volunteered to try and negotiate a voluntary and peaceful withdrawal of the remaining students from the square. Many of the students were opposed, including Chai Ling. At about 3:30 a.m., Hou and Gao took a Red Cross–marked ambulance to the northeast corner of the square and negotiated with the troop commander there to permit the demonstrators to depart. After consulting with his headquarters, the commander assented. The agreement was that an exit would be permitted in the southeast corner of the square, but that the students would have to leave before the final clearing operation began. All during the process, weapons firing from other parts of the city could still be heard, and soldiers surrounding the square seemed to have worked themselves up into a preattack furor. At about 4:00, all the lights in the square suddenly went out, heightening the sense of fear among the students.

Hou and the other intellectuals returned to the monument to persuade the remaining students to accept the deal, which turned out not to be an easy process, involving a voice vote in the darkness. They also collected and destroyed at least one machine gun and other handmade weapons they found among the students. At about 4:40, the lights came back on, and government loudspeakers announced that the clearing operation was about to begin. At 5:00, PLA troops began to close in on the Martyrs' Monument, leaving the agreed-upon gap in their lines in the southeast corner near Qianmen. Most, but not all, of the students walked out quickly, carrying their banners, but were harassed toward the end by troops completing the task of recapturing Tiananmen Square. By 5:30, that part of the operation was over.[63] Beijing authorities subsequently used the withdrawal, and Hou's account of it, to validate their claim that "no one" died in Tiananmen Square during the crackdown.[64]

The killing, however, did not end with the capture of Tiananmen Square. For the next three days, Beijing became a virtual civil war zone, with scores of violent incidents and many more deaths, some of them close enough to Tiananmen Square to render the government's claim meaningless. Troop convoys raced through the streets, often firing their weapons in the air. Western reporters, mostly restricted to the downtown hotels, reported rumors of interunit combat and artillery firing and "tens of thousands" of casualties.[65] The regime would initially claim that about 300 people were killed and over 7,000 were injured during the operation. Of these, civilian casualties were claimed to be about 200 killed (only 23 of them students) and about 2,000 wounded.[66] Although these figures have never been accepted by any observers or nongovernment participants, much less by the foreign press, they have remained generally consistent over time.[67]

In an enormously unequal contest, the victor was foreordained. On June 6, the Politburo Standing Committee and several of the elders gathered to review the situation. They congratulated themselves for taking resolute action, denounced foreign countries (and especially the United States) for exaggerating casualty figures and condemning China, and commiserated with the PLA for their suffering. Then they called for a further crackdown. Deng set the stage: "Of all China's problems, the one that trumps everything is the need for stability. We have to jump on anything that might bring instability; we can't give ground on this point, can't bend at all. And we can't care what foreigners say. . . . In the future, whenever it might be necessary, we will use severe measures to stamp out the first signs of turmoil as soon as they appear. This will show that we won't put up with foreign interference and will protect our national sovereignty." Li Xiannian followed up with a call for a "super tough" crackdown, but Deng advised caution, moderation toward ordinary students and demonstrators, and observance of appropriate laws. But he made it clear that there were to be no more demonstrations. "We can't just allow people to demonstrate whenever they want to."[68]

On June 9, Deng, Li Peng, and the rest of the leadership appeared on television in a meeting congratulating martial law troops on the successful quelling of the "counterrevolutionary rebellion." In a tough and combative speech, Deng defended his reform policies against those who evidently blamed them for precipitating the crisis in the first place. He also blasted "bourgeois liberalization" (that is, foreign, especially American, influence) for causing the problems and misleading many party members. Deng credited first the elderly veteran party members, then the PLA for saving the situation. "What is most advantageous to us is that we have a large group of veteran comrades who are still alive. They have experienced many storms and they know what is at stake. They support the use of resolute action to counter the rebellion." And "The People's Army is truly a great wall of iron and steel of the party and state. . . . No matter how heavy our losses, the army, under the leadership of the party, will always remain the defender of the country, the defender of socialism, and the defender of the public interest."[69]

As Deng looked around the room at the other attendees, he could hardly have been optimistic about the prospects for returning to a course of economic reform. Seated to his left were Li Xiannian (age eighty), Yang Shangkun (eighty-two), Peng Zhen (eighty-seven), Wan Li (seventy-three), and Bo Yibo (eighty-one); to his right: Li Peng, Wang Zhen (eighty-one), Yao Yilin (seventy-two), and Qiao Shi (sixty-five). Chen Yun was not in attendance but sent his congratulations.[70] All the former Politburo and Secretariat members who had enthusiastically pushed economic and political reform in the past—Zhao Ziyang, Hu Qili, Rui Xingwen, and Yan Mingfu—were absent and soon would be officially purged from the party leadership. Deng was now faced with a profoundly different leadership lineup, one he could not dominate as easily as before, one that had fewer policy disagreements for him to broker, one that would not automatically turn to him for guidance, and one that might see him as responsible for the worst political setback for the party's cause since Mao and the Cultural Revolution.

American Reaction

President Bush and his administration seem to have been caught off guard by the rapid downward spiral of events. Coming as it did within months of his inauguration, the crisis hit before the administration had mapped out a full foreign policy design for Asia and before it had assembled a full team of Asia experts. There was no assistant secretary of state for Asian affairs—Richard Solomon was not nominated until mid-April and only confirmed after Tiananmen in June. William Clark was acting. There was no assistant secretary of defense for international security affairs, and the deputy assistant secretary in charge of East Asia, Carl Ford, had just taken up his duties in April. The senior director for Asian affairs on the National Security Council, Karl Jackson, was not a China expert, although Douglas Paal, his deputy, was highly knowledgeable. There was no national intelligence officer for East Asia on the National Intelligence Council, Carl Ford having moved over to defense. The U.S. ambassador to Beijing, James R. Lilley, arrived on May 3, in the midst of the crisis, replacing Ambassador Winston Lord, in whom the White House had little faith. In the circumstances, National Security Adviser Brent Scowcroft considered himself the key policymaker regarding China.[71] But none of the top policymakers had a particularly good idea of what was taking place in China early in 1989. Neither State Department cables, nor intelligence reporting, nor the increasing volume of U.S. media reporting on China had given them a very clear idea of the nature of the sociopolitical changes ongoing in China or the struggles that were going on within the leadership.

President Bush had a strong personal interest in China and U.S. policy toward China and made it clear from the outset that he would be very active in promoting U.S.-PRC relations.[72] Bush also was a firm believer in personal diplomacy at the chief-of-state level and wanted badly to establish a good working relationship with Deng Xiaoping early in his administration. Thus the February trip to Beijing. Bush's orientation toward China, like Scowcroft's, was predominantly strategic in origin and based on their mutual concern about the military intentions and capabilities of the Soviet Union. But Bush also believed that U.S.-China relations, especially the growing economic interaction between the two countries, was important for the development of a more open and democratic system in China.[73] Bush's hardheaded and pragmatic secretary of state, James Baker, did not share his boss's fondness for China. He saw China issues as political liabilities, even before Tiananmen and far more so afterward. Knowing that China policy was likely to be tightly managed by the White House in any case, Baker kept aloof from most China issues.[74]

As the situation deteriorated in Beijing during May, the Bush administration watched with growing anxiety and confusion. Scowcroft and others found it surprising that Deng would tolerate the takeover of the center of the capital by unruly students. They believed Zhao had fallen afoul of others in the Politburo but did not know how to factor in the populist element that appeared nightly on television. Lilley, driving down to the square on May 3 to see for himself whether the student movement was as momentous as Winston Lord had described it, recalled that he had very uneasy feelings about how it would turn out.[75] Intelligence reporting did not fill in enough of the blanks to enable Washington observers to measure the depth of the crisis, so they were constantly trying to catch up with rapidly moving events. It was not until after Gorbachev's visit that a special task force was established in the State Department, manned twenty-four hours a day, with an open telephone line to Embassy Beijing to keep up with the latest developments.[76]

Only when Li Peng declared martial law on May 19 did the State Department issue its first statement on the situation in China. "The United States supports freedom of speech, association and peaceful assembly in China as in the rest of the world. We regret that military action has been ordered with the aim of restricting those freedoms," said department spokesman Dennis Harter. From Bush's vacation home in Kennebunkport, Maine, White House spokesman Marlin Fitzwater took a slightly different tack, saying the situation appeared "confused," but that both sides should continue to exercise "restraint."[77] In a press conference the following day, Bush expressed support for student demonstrators, but he urged them to follow a nonviolent course. "We do support freedom of speech, freedom of assembly, freedom of the press and clearly we support democracy. I don't want to be gratuitous in giving advice, but I would encourage restraint. I do not want to see bloodshed. . . . And I would urge the Government to be as forthcoming as possible in order to see more democratization and to see a peaceful resolution of this matter."[78]

Privately, Bush officials were becoming more alarmed. They knew the martial law order could not be carried out against a million people in the square. But neither would it be rescinded. On May 20, Ambassador Lilley flew back to Beijing from Shanghai—where he had been welcoming the long-awaited visit of the USS *Blue Ridge*, flagship of the Pacific Fleet and strategic countermove to Gorbachev's visit—and rebuffed a White House request that he accompany Wan Li on his visit to Washington. He quickly established teams of embassy officers to be on the street day and night to report on events. Richard Solomon, although not yet confirmed as assistant secretary, kept up with the reporting and privately advised Baker that things were likely to get "nasty" in Beijing.[79]

Although Bush administration figures were as surprised as anyone at the massive show of defiance by crowds in Beijing after the declaration of martial law, they were increasingly pessimistic about the likely outcome. As the crowds began to dwindle after May 24, official Washington began to prepare for the worst. Intelligence reported increasing numbers of PLA troops getting into position on the outskirts of Beijing and began sketching out the likelihood of an attack on the square. The embassy received conflicting information but sent in at least one "false alarm" late in May that the PLA was about to move.[80] Publicly, however, the administration kept its counsel. As Douglas Paal explained it, "We knew this was going to be bloody. These are bloody-minded people. So we were never as shocked as the public was."[81]

In Congress, complaints were already being heard that the administration was not saying more. During the last week of May, both houses debated a concurrent resolution on supporting democracy in China (H. Con. Res. 136). Senate Majority Leader George S. Mitchell, during the debate, criticized President Bush for being too cautious and neutral in his support for the Tiananmen demonstrators. "The President's statements have been so balanced and neutral that they appear to be primarily concerned about not offending the Chinese leadership."[82] House Foreign Relations Committee East Asia Subcommittee Chair Steven Solarz also urged a stronger U.S. warning to China. "It is important for the Chinese to know that our relationship with them in the future will be determined in no small measure by how they resolve this crisis. . . . If they should attempt to resolve it by using force, by incarcerating demonstrators, possibly even by killing thousands of their fellow citizens, by incarcerating tens of thousands of others, then I have to say . . . that it would inevitably have significantly adverse consequences for the relationship between our two countries."[83] The resolution passed the Senate 89-0, putting the president on notice that a crackdown on the demonstrations would be met by congressional action.

Meanwhile, President Bush met with visiting National People's Congress Standing Committee Chairman Wan Li on May 23, urging him strongly in a private session in the White House residence that China must exercise restraint. Wan was the wrong messenger in the wrong place, but the administration was not certain who was in charge at that point, and Wan was the only Chinese official available. Under conflicting pressures from Beijing, Wan cut short his trip and returned to house arrest in Shanghai, eventually going along with the majority in the Politburo and supporting the violent crackdown. Although he may have conveyed Bush's message back through embassy channels, he certainly had no opportunity to do so in person.

The events of early morning, June 4, in Beijing were reported the afternoon of Saturday, June 3, in Washington, owing to the twelve-hour time difference. The administration's response was quick, but careful, given the lack of detail about what was going on. Late in the afternoon, President Bush issued a statement from Kennebunkport (prepared for him by the State Department task force). "I deeply deplore the decision to use force against peaceful demonstrators and the consequent loss of life. We have been urging and continue to urge non-violence, restraint and dialogue. Tragically, another course has been chosen. Again, I urge a return to non-violent means for dealing with the current situation."[84] Scowcroft indicated he and the president were "alarmed and disappointed," as they had believed the regime was on the verge of winning without violence. Secretary Baker, in a CNN interview Saturday evening, noted that violence had been used by both sides and refused to be drawn out on what steps would be taken to punish China. The department issued a travel advisory for China, warning tourists to avoid Beijing.[85]

Congressional reaction was swift and far less cautious than the administration's response. In public statements, various congressional leaders called for punitive actions to be taken immediately, including a cutoff of military cooperation and technology transfer, the imposition of punitive tariffs on Chinese goods, the cessation of U.S. support for World Bank loans to China, withdrawal of the American ambassador to Beijing, and cancellation of Peace Corps assignments to China. Representative Mickey Edwards (R–Okla.) probably expressed the view of many on the Hill, both about events in China and the administration's response. "Diplomatic messages of disapproval are a pretty puny reaction to the murdering of innocent civilians whose only crime is to want the same freedoms we in the West take for granted. We need to do something besides talk."[86] Jesse Helms, ranking Republican on the Senate Foreign Relations Committee, called for a full review of the entire bilateral relationship.

On Sunday morning, June 5, Acting Assistant Secretary of State for East Asian and Pacific Affairs William Clark chaired an emergency policy working group meeting in a seventh-floor conference room at the State Department, where the Tiananmen task force was located. In attendance were policy and legal specialists from various executive branch policy agencies and members of the intelligence community, many of whom had been regular participants in the task force. After a briefing on the latest reports from Beijing, including very high casualty estimates, the meeting got down to its main business, drawing up a list of possible actions the U.S. government could take in response to Tiananmen. Most of the proposals raised were not momentous, and State Department lawyers reminded participants of what sanctions could and could not be applied in different circumstances. The meeting proposed suspension of scheduled meetings of the Joint Commission on Commerce and Trade (JCCT) and the Joint Commission on Science and Technology, meetings that, while symbolically important, did not have significant impact.[87]

Carl Ford, deputy assistant secretary of defense for international security affairs, having discussed matters with Defense Secretary Cheney and Undersecretary Paul Wolfowitz, recommended the defense relationship take the brunt of the punitive cutbacks. He said the military-to-military relationship should be suspended so that other aspects of the relationship could be sustained. He indicated that the PLA had been the obvious perpetrator of outrageous behavior during and after the crackdown, so it was natural to break off ties, perhaps indefinitely.[88] Ford also proposed suspension of four military technology programs:

—Grumman Aircraft Corporation's $502 million program to upgrade the avionics in China's F-8 (MiG-21) fighter aircraft was the most significant. The program, code-named Peace Pearl, was intended to replace outdated navigation and flight control systems in fifty-five F-8 fighters, and it remained controversial with some congressional critics.

—The sale of four MK-46 torpedoes (worth about $8.5 million);

—A plan to assist China in improving artillery production (about $28.5 million); and

—The sale of counterartillery radar sets (valued at $62.5 million).[89]

The following day, President Bush held a news conference, where he announced the suspension of military contacts and technology transfers worth approximately $600 million, a "sympathetic review of requests" by Chinese students studying in the United States to extend their stays to avoid going back to China, the offer of humanitarian aid and medical assistance to those wounded in the crackdown, and "a review of other aspects of our bilateral relationship as events in China continue to unfold." Bush spent more time fending off questions and demands from Congress that he take more drastic steps, such as suspending trade and investment or prohibiting high-tech exports. Bush defended his preliminary steps as consistent with "both our long-term interests and recognition of a complex internal situation in China."[90]

Privately, however, Bush was working hard to re-establish contact with the Chinese leadership, even though he was not certain whom to contact or how to do so. He tried calling Deng on the telephone but could not get through. He summoned the Chinese ambassador, Han Xu, to the White House to express his displeasure with events and to try and find out more about who was in charge. He spoke with Richard M. Nixon, who advised him not to disrupt the relationship.[91] Clearly looking for any opportunity to keep the relationship from deteriorating further, Bush was repelled and constrained by the brutal revenge taking that was going under the auspices of martial law in Beijing, graphically depicted every night on U.S. television. On June 9, in another press conference, Bush ruled out the restoration of "totally normal" relations "unless there is a recognition of the validity of the students' aspirations."[92]

China: The Aftermath of a Pyrrhic Victory

While the Bush administration was deciding on sanctions against the PLA, the PLA was still dealing with the unsettled situation in Beijing municipality and with reaction to the crackdown in other parts of the country.[93] China's capital was awash in rage, grief, and shock at what the PLA and the Communist Party leadership had done. The regime's reaction had been, in all likelihood, deliberately excessive. "The force used on June 4 promised to end the movement immediately, certainly, and once and for all. . . . The excessive use of force demonstrated that the potential costs of protest were prohibitive: the regime was willing to sanction the killing of protesters in the streets."[94] Besides fear and intimidation, the public reaction to Tiananmen represented a thorough disillusionment with the Communist Party and its leadership. While the legitimacy of a government cannot be measured, the esteem in which it is held by those it governs is difficult to recover once it has been lost. Without a doubt, the legitimacy of the Communist Party after June 4 had never been lower.

Equally damaged by Tiananmen was the reputation of the People's Liberation Army, which carried out the party's orders brutally. Long accustomed to being the object of public affection and adulation, the military now found itself the object of hatred and derision. Serious morale problems afflicted the PLA during and after the martial law action. Perhaps as many as 3,500 soldiers were disciplined subsequently, most of them for refusal to obey orders.[95] While its senior leadership might have enjoyed a significant increase in influence over the party as a result of ensuring its survival, that hardly compensated for the resentment and distrust generated elsewhere in society by the way it carried out its orders to recapture Tiananmen Square or the way it flaunted its authority in the early phases of martial law.

The party's actions immediately after order was restored in Beijing ensured that the bad feelings generated by the quelling of the Tiananmen demonstrations were magnified manyfold. Gathering all the coercive authority available through the massive military and police presence and its firm control of propaganda, the regime set about punishing those it held responsible for its loss of face and loss of control in April and May. Kind words and reassurances for the students were quickly replaced by denunciations, most-wanted lists, and intensive investigations. All the unofficial groups that formed during May—the Beijing Autonomous Students Federation, Beijing Autonomous Workers Federation, Beijing Citizens Association—were banned outright, and their leaders were urged to turn themselves in. Chinese television broadcast film of the arrests of so-called ruffians. Many of them appeared to have been badly beaten. Democracy activists were rounded up by the hundreds and jailed simply because they were known to be activists, not because they were connected to demonstrations at Tiananmen. In a chilling throwback to the Cultural Revolution, party leaders put out public notices that people should inform authorities if they had knowledge of any of their neighbors or coworkers having been involved in demonstrations.[96] By June 17, Beijing announced that trials of "thugs" connected with Tiananmen had commenced, and death sentences were handed down and carried out in Beijing and Shanghai. Thousands of others were charged with "counterrevolutionary" offenses or with "disturbing social order." Many were given quick or no trials and sent to prison or labor reform camps.

Part of the crackdown was a matter of getting foreign news services out of China, where they had seriously compromised the regime's ability to control the information available to its citizens. The task was complicated by the fact that most U.S. news agencies and networks had expanded their Beijing operations by adding reporters and camera crews in the aftermath of June 4. China's response, according to U.S. ambassador James Lilley, was to "close the door and beat the dog"—get the foreigners out so they could punish the demonstrators without fear of interference or embarrassing attention.[97] Although there is no definitive proof of it, several observers believe the Chinese may have wanted to precipitate foreign flight from Beijing immediately after the crackdown. Deliberate and extensive gunfire at the Jian Guo Men Wai diplomatic compound on June 7 was the final act that set in motion U.S. plans to evacuate American nationals from Beijing. Responding to orders from the secretary of state, Ambassador Lilley and his staff spent the next several days in an exhausting but ultimately successful effort to get hundreds of Americans—including many embassy family members—out of the city.

Although the regime denied any intent to force foreigners out of China and accused the United States of overreacting to the situation, there were other indications that at least some in the Chinese military held foreigners accountable for the events leading up to Tiananmen. Martial law authorities focused intently on preventing foreign journalists from moving around in

Beijing. Two American correspondents were expelled from the country, others were arrested, and some were beaten. Accusations that the Voice of America had interfered in China's domestic affairs became a staple of the regime's explanation of what had happened.

The crackdown, in its earliest and most violent stages, accomplished its likely goals. Chinese citizens, despite the rage and grief of many, cooperated in restoring a semblance of public order to the city. Transportation was resumed, stores and factories reopened, life returned slowly to normal. Tiananmen Square remained closed to the public while cleanup and repairs were accomplished. The media kept up a steady barrage of news designed to intimidate—expanded most-wanted lists, reports of widespread arrests of "hooligans," television accounts of trials and executions.

A Reluctant Guest

On June 5, 1989, after the initial phase of the bloodletting in Tiananmen was over, and before the public crackdown on student dissidents had yet swung into high gear, Fang Lizhi, along with his wife, Li Shuxian, and their son, Fang Zhe, paid a visit to the U.S. embassy compound on North Xiushui Street. There they met for nearly four hours with the acting deputy chief of mission, Ray Burghardt, and the public affairs officer, McKinney Russell, discussing political refuge and asylum. Knowing that he was likely to be arrested and punished, even though his role in the Tiananmen events was minimal, Fang was concerned for the safety of his family, as well as his own. Hoping to discourage a potentially messy asylum case, the two officers outlined the problems Fang might cause by seeking refuge in the embassy and offered to facilitate his travel to the United States instead. Confused and discouraged, Fang and his family retreated to the Jianguo Hotel, a few blocks from the embassy, where they stayed with an American journalist and a longtime friend and discussed their plight.[98]

In Washington, the State Department reacted to the embassy's handling of Fang with anger and dismay. Believing that Fang's arrest after having been denied refuge at the embassy would precipitate a damaging public outcry, Secretary Baker and Undersecretary Robert Kimmitt instructed Acting Assistant Secretary William Clark to have the embassy recontact Fang and authorize refuge for him and his family. Hoping to keep the situation low key, Clark telephoned Ambassador Lilley and urged him to "send somebody out to tell him that if he'd like to come to the Embassy, he can."[99] Lilley immediately dispatched Burghardt and Russell to the Jianguo Hotel, where they invited Fang to be the "guest of President Bush" and spirited him and his family out the back door of the hotel and into a minivan, which drove them past PLA guards to the ambassador's residence. Fang and his family took up residence on the first floor there, afraid even to turn on a light for fear of attracting attention. Somewhat later, they moved to a makeshift flat behind the residence itself.[100]

The story of Fang's being picked up at the hotel and escorted to some form of official American protection was soon learned by the Chinese, although they did not seem to realize at first exactly where he was. On June 8, Chinese media, predictably, accused the United States of interference in Chinese domestic affairs and violation of international law. In conjunction with their accusations that American media had exacerbated the situation to undermine China's government, propagandists probably saw Fang's sojourn in the U.S. embassy as a golden opportunity to keep shifting the blame for Tiananmen to external sources, namely, the United States. Within days, arrest warrants for Fang and his wife were publicized, charging them with "crimes of counterrevolutionary propaganda and instigation."[101] In his press conference on June 8, President Bush had admitted that Fang was indeed in U.S. hands but denied any violation of law. "It is awful hard for the United States, when a man presents himself—a person who is a dissident—and says that his life is threatened, to turn him back," Bush explained.[102]

Fang Lizhi had little to do with the demonstrations at Tiananmen. Although he supported the cause of student demonstrators in Tiananmen, he avoided going to the square to show support for fear his presence would taint their cause with the regime. He did, however, give interviews to Western journalists in which he commented favorably on the growing enthusiasm for democracy. There is little doubt that he would have faced arrest and possible prosecution, since even more moderate democratic reformers like Chen Ziming and Wang Juntao were soon on the government's most-wanted lists. But Fang's flight to the U.S. embassy and the unusual circumstances of his being granted protection (not political asylum, as the State Department was careful to point out) probably increased Chinese suspicions of American collusion in Tiananmen and certainly heightened Beijing's antipathy for Fang and unwillingness to negotiate an arrangement for his release.

Fang was a major issue in U.S.-China relations for the next year. Widely admired in the United States for his staunch advocacy of democracy, there was no way the Bush administration could release him into Chinese custody, where he faced certain imprisonment and possible physical abuse; that option was never seriously considered. The United States sought some guarantee of his freedom from arrest or safe passage out of China. For Beijing, the issue was equally important, symbolically and politically. Fang's presence—unassailable under international law—in the American embassy smacked of the extraterritorial privileges that foreign missions had once claimed in China and incited genuine resentment in the leadership. Moreover, he had already been indicted as a "counterrevolutionary criminal," and there was no way the regime could grant amnesty or safe passage for him without compromising its fierce crackdown on all forms of dissidence.

Thus, although Ambassador Lilley referred to the Fang issue as an "irritant" in the bilateral relationship, he in fact had become a major stumbling block, affecting all other efforts to improve the relationship, owing to the sharply conflicting demands of domestic politics on both sides.[103] There were numerous other problems in the relationship in the summer of 1989—economic sanctions, the evacuation of American citizens, nonproliferation, the future of military-to-military relations, student exchanges, and trade, to name a few. But none would prove more difficult to resolve than Fang Lizhi's unexpected long-term visit to the ambassador's residence. It even led to further tensions in and of itself, as when the regime posted additional armed guards outside the embassy compound, probably out of fear the United States would try to spirit Fang out of the country.[104]

China's Post-Tiananmen Leadership

On June 24, the Communist Party showed it had recovered control of the capital and of itself well enough to hold a Central Committee meeting to display its new leadership. At the two-day party plenum, Zhao Ziyang was officially ousted from all his positions (although he was not expelled from the party), Hu Qili was dropped from the Politburo and its Standing Committee, and Yan Mingfu and Rui Xingwen, two Zhao associates who attempted to negotiate with students in mid-May, were dropped from the party secretariat. Three new members were added to the Standing Committee: Li Ruihuan, age fifty-four, formerly mayor of Tianjin; Song Ping, an economic planning expert associated with Chen Yun; and the new general secretary of the party, Jiang Zemin. Public reaction to Jiang's appointment was mixed—some saw his appointment as representing an effort to reassure foreign investors and those favoring reform. Others, especially in Shanghai where he was well known and not widely respected, viewed Jiang's appointment with resignation or dismay. Few had any doubts that Deng Xiaoping would remain in charge. As the *New York Times* put it, "Whoever is the Communist Party General Secretary will owe his position to the support of Mr. Deng, whose virtually unquestioned personal authority has been amply demonstrated by recent events."[105]

What was less visible to Western observers, however, was the degree to which Tiananmen had shattered the party's unity and weakened Deng's authority. Nathan and Link's *Tiananmen Papers* has excerpts of some of the speeches made by senior Communist Party veterans at the Fourth Plenum. Taking advantage of an opportunity to comment on the party's formal charges against Zhao, several of these senior officials obliquely attacked the entire reform movement, which had been founded by Deng.[106] Deng's insistence in his post-Tiananmen speeches that the reform and opening policy must be maintained reflected his understanding that his policies would come under renewed attack and that the new leadership might not be able to hold the line. Making things even worse, Zhao Ziyang refused to admit that he had made any mistakes. His speech at the plenum, expected to be a self-criticism, instead was a stout defense of his actions and decisions. Calmly but firmly, he refuted point by point Li Peng's charges that he had "supported the turmoil and split the party." Although the resolution criticizing him was passed, Zhao was not expelled from the party, and his refusal to accept the party's judgment left his case open. It also left him, rather than Deng, clearly identified as the party's strongest advocate of reform.[107]

Li Peng appeared to most outside observers to be the big winner in the aftermath of Tiananmen. The *New York Times*, for example, proclaimed that Li "has emerged as the victor in a bitter and complex struggle for power and influence with Zhao Ziyang. . . . Mr. Li is now the most visible and powerful of the younger generation of leaders in China."[108] Given the fact that he was the one chosen to announce the imposition of martial law, was clearly behind efforts to bring down Zhao Ziyang, and was known to be unenthusiastic about economic reform, Li had been universally reviled by Tiananmen protesters. From the first days of demonstrations after Hu Yaobang's death, Li's ouster was a consistent demand of Beijing crowds, and he was regularly ridiculed in student publications and posters. His survival was not only the symbolic proof of the complete failure of the demonstrators but reinforced the image of conservative strength within the new leading group.

Li came by his conservative credentials naturally. Born in Sichuan Province in 1928, his father was a Communist Party cadre who was captured and executed by the Kuomintang in 1931. Li was raised by his mother, with generous help for his education from former premier Zhou Enlai and his wife, Deng Yingchao. Although most of his higher education was in the communist base camp in remote Yanan (Shaanxi Province), Li focused his studies on engineering. In 1948, he was sent to study at the Moscow Power Institute, where he remained until 1954, learning fluent Russian in the process. After his return to China, he worked his way up through the various strands of the electrical power bureaucracy, eventually heading Beijing's Municipal Electrical Power Administration. His connection to Zhou Enlai (some considered him almost an adopted son to Zhou, who had no children of his own) enabled him to escape persecution during the Cultural Revolution.

After Deng returned to power in 1977, Li moved rapidly up the bureaucratic ladder to vice minister of Power Industry in 1979, then vice premier of the State Council and minister in charge of the State Education Commission in 1983. At a special party delegates meeting in 1985, Li was added to the Politburo as a full member. Li became acting premier of the State Council after Zhao Ziyang was moved over to be general secretary of the Communist Party upon Hu Yaobang's ouster in early 1987, and he was promoted to the Politburo Standing Committee in October. At that time, Li was also placed in charge of the Central Committee's "leading small group" for foreign affairs.[109] In 1988, he replaced Zhao as the principal official in charge of economic policy and immediately began trying to retrench on some of Zhao's inflationary reform measures. Already one of the party's most powerful and influential figures, Li's authority was strengthened by the addition of Song Ping to the Politburo Standing Committee after Tiananmen.

Jiang Zemin was the most prominent of the newly appointed leaders. Little was known of him outside of China, and even within China, opinions were mixed. Born in Yangzhou, Jiangsu Province, in August 1926, Jiang's early education was interrupted by Japan's invasion and occupation of eastern China, but he completed high school and was admitted to Nanjing Central University (which later merged with Shanghai's prestigious Jiaotong University), where he majored in science. According to various biographies, Jiang joined the underground Communist Party at the university but did not play an active role.[110] After graduation and the establishment of the People's Republic of China in 1949, Jiang worked in various industrial enterprises, drawing favorable attention from Wang Daohan, then an up-and-coming party leader in Shanghai. Jiang became a manager in China's "machine-building" sector and was rewarded with a year of study in Moscow in 1955. Subsequently, he worked at the Changchun (Jilin Province) No. 1 Automobile Factory, where he was known as an amiable and diligent cadre who got the work done without threatening anyone and who had a slightly eccentric air about him.[111]

Jiang returned to Shanghai in 1962 and worked in various industrial enterprises in the region for the next five years. During the Cultural Revolution, when Mao's rampaging Red Guards arrested and humiliated many party and government officials, Jiang was suspended from his work but was not jailed or otherwise punished. Other members of his family were not so lucky—one of his uncles reportedly was killed by Red Guards, and both Jiang's sons were "sent down" to the countryside and not permitted to return to take up educational opportunities until after 1979.

In 1970, having been rehabilitated relatively early, Jiang was assigned to Beijing, where he worked in the Foreign Affairs Bureau of the First Ministry of Machine-Building, and managed to steer clear of the political perturbations that accompanied Mao's death in 1976 and the purge of his radical followers, the Gang of Four, in October of that year. The Gang of Four—Mao's wife Jiang Qing, Politburo Standing Committee member and PLA General Political Department Director Zhang Chunqiao, Politburo Standing Committee Member and Party Vice Chairman Wang Hongwen, and Politburo propaganda overseer Yao Wenyuan—had extensive influence throughout China, and the party purge that followed their ouster was broad and deep. Among the localities where the radical Maoism associated with the Gang was strongest was Shanghai, where all four had close ties and many followers. After 1976, Shanghai municipality was extensively purged and reorganized, and Jiang was part of the team brought in from Beijing (under his mentor, Wang Daohan) to ensure the city continued to operate while it was being re-educated.[112] His earliest experience with economic reform came in 1979, when he was assigned to the State Foreign Investment Control Commission, which was then setting up and managing the special economic zones (SEZs) in Guangdong and Fujian Provinces. Jiang began a rapid rise in 1982, when he was selected to become a member of the Twelfth Central Committee. This was followed by appointment as minister of electronics in 1983, where he was credited with improving China's backward and poor-quality electrical technology.[113]

In 1985, Jiang was selected to replace Wang Daohan as mayor of Shanghai. In the rapidly changing circumstances of China under reform and with intense debates and disputes swirling in the central and local governments, it is not surprising that Jiang vacillated in his policy views. He eagerly embraced the economic reform programs promoted by Zhao Ziyang and Hu Yaobang and worked hard to ensure that the negative effects—particularly soaring inflation in the mid-1980s—were minimized. In late 1986 and early 1987, however, when student demonstrations against corruption and a lack of democracy roiled Shanghai campuses, Jiang showed himself to be a staunch political conservative. Ignoring Hu Yaobang's recommendations for a conciliatory approach, Jiang cracked down hard on campus protests, ordering expulsion from school and, if necessary, arrests of demonstrators. After Hu Yaobang was sacked, Jiang's tough approach was lauded in Beijing.[114] At the Communist Party's Thirteenth Congress in October 1987, Jiang was added to the Politburo. After that he took over the more important post of Shanghai party secretary, turning over mayoral duties to Zhu Rongji.

Jiang and Zhu made a formidable team, and although very different from each other in political style, capabilities, and interests, they worked together successfully in Shanghai, contributing to that city's remarkable economic recovery and growth. During the period before the Tiananmen crisis in Beijing, Shanghai also was beset with student activism and street protests. Jiang earned the enmity of China's intellectuals and students by closing down the *World Economic Herald*—a Shanghai newspaper that had become celebrated for its outspoken espousal of economic and political reform—in late April 1989 and suspending its editor, Qin Benli. But unlike leaders in Beijing, Jiang sent representatives to negotiate with students about allowing transportation and other business to continue during the protests. And after martial law was declared on May 19, Jiang reportedly spent the entire evening among crowds of angry protesters on Shanghai's Bund, assuring them that the Shanghai municipal government, at least, considered them patriotic and well meaning and was open to honest dialogue. Jiang publicly supported the martial law proclamation but made clear to Shanghai officials that the preferred solution to the problems was not confrontation and violence but dialogue and patience.[115]

Shortly afterward, he was called to Beijing, where Deng informed him he was to be promoted to the topmost party position. Although Jiang was probably in Beijing at the time of the PLA's attack on demonstrators, he held no formal or informal position in the hierarchy at the time and probably had no input into the decision. Shanghai exploded in anger at news of the violence in Beijing, but its potent and competent police force was able to keep the situation under control without calling on the PLA for assistance. There was violence at the fringes of the demonstrations, and many arrests were made, but Shanghai handled the situation far more deftly than Beijing.[116]

The available information suggests that the selection of Jiang Zemin was made by Deng, with strong inputs from elders Chen Yun and Li Xiannian, who became acquainted with Jiang when he worked in Shanghai. Jiang had demonstrated loyalty and a tough approach to dissent, was educated and worldly, did not appear to have strong ambitions or policy preferences, had not engaged in faction building, and was satisfactory to other elders. He was supportive of economic reform but had not linked his career with either Hu Yaobang or Zhao Ziyang; he had conservative and technocratic credentials but no strong ties to Li Peng. In other words, he had accumulated neither the supporters nor the enemies of other prominent leaders in the ranks of potential successors. Having just overseen the purges of his two previous handpicked successors, Deng may have been looking for something of a blank slate, someone he could train to carry on his legacy. As Deng said to Li Peng, "If we present a lineup which the people think is a rigid, conservative leading body or a mediocre leading body which cannot reflect China's future, there will still be a lot of trouble in the future. . . . We must establish credibility among the people."[117]

Deng in Eclipse?

What Deng may not have foreseen, however, is how much his own position was weakened by the events surrounding June 4. Evidence is intangible and the conclusion is intuitive rather than completely deductive. Deng was not in obvious disgrace, and many American observers, such as Ambassador Lilley and others in the Bush administration, saw Deng's hand continuing throughout 1989 to guide China's policies, particularly toward the United States. But in China's power-focused political system, where authority is informal and personal, a leader's influence stems from a combination of elder support, bureaucratic backing, military approval, ideological propriety, policy success, and public reputation. Deng had enjoyed all of these before Tiananmen and called on most of these elements of power to bring the challenge to the Communist Party's rule to an end. But he also squandered these resources by using them to such a violent and appalling end.

Deng's resort to the People's Liberation Army as the final guarantor of the party's survival had enormous significance for both the party and the PLA itself. While it did not permanently compromise Mao Zedong's long-standing injunction that "the Party must control the gun; the gun must never be allowed to control the Party," Deng's reliance on the army to put down the Tiananmen demonstrations probably did create an uncomfortable sense of obligation for civilian party leaders and reduced their ability to resist PLA requests for budgetary support. Deng's reliance on Yang Shangkun to carry out his wishes within the military greatly strengthened Yang in relation to other leaders. The enormity of ordering the "people's army" to fire on the people created severe morale problems within the PLA and probably reduced Deng's esteem among the officer corps.

By actively seeking the support of Chen Yun, Li Xiannian, Peng Zhen, Wang Zhen, and other elders, Deng, in effect, was weakening his own authority and strengthening theirs. He had expended considerable political capital in moving China's conservative gerontocrats back away from the front lines, while at the same time preserving his own powers as balancer and first among equals. When it became clear that his own powers were insufficient to guarantee party legitimacy and consensus, he called on the old veterans to support his position. That support came at a high cost, namely, the reemergence of the elders into a more active policy advisory role—recognized by Deng and the entire party leadership.

By turning on his own chosen successors, Deng implicitly acknowledged the criticisms—mostly grounded in conservative Marxist dogma—that the reform programs Hu and Zhao had pursued with such vigor did indeed weaken China's ideological orthodoxy and needed to be slowed down, if not rolled back. Deng's purge of the reformers thus brought ideological conservatism back to life. Moreover, he compromised his reputation for integrity as well as his repeated commitment to establishing an orderly succession.

Deng's programmatic support for economic reform was doubly compromised by the Tiananmen protests. On the one hand, the economic reforms had brought significant economic dislocation and dissatisfaction, which had animated many of the protests. On the other hand, the diminution of party authority that accompanied economic reform made it far more difficult to quell the street protests once they had begun.

Finally, and most difficult to quantify, Tiananmen cost Deng much of his public support. While that is not essential to exercise power within the PRC, it is important to ensuring the party's legitimacy and to maximizing compliance with party directives. In the immediate aftermath of Tiananmen, demonstrable public support for the party—and the man who led it—plummeted to unprecedented lows. During the demonstrations Deng's leadership had been disparaged and incessant calls were made for him to step down. Although many Chinese initially were reluctant to accept that Deng had given the orders for the crackdown, his appearance on June 9 with martial law troops removed any doubts of his responsibility. Despite the leadership's persistent defense of Tiananmen as necessary, and even a "good thing," the public in China will never view it as anything but a shameful episode for which responsibility—or blame—will ultimately have to be ascribed publicly. The weight of that responsibility—that guilt—reduced Deng's authority and his reputation.

After his June 9 meeting with martial law troops, Deng made no public appearances for three months. He did not even show up for the Central Committee that anointed Jiang Zemin as the "core" of the next generation of Chinese leaders on June 24. Inevitably, speculation was aroused about his health, power, and relations with the regime's new leadership. There were even rumors that he had died.[118] In all likelihood, Deng was exhausted by the ordeal of Tiananmen. At age eighty-five, he had been forced by the sudden leadership vacuum at the center of the Communist Party to do many of the things he had hoped to avoid when he went into semiretirement, such as chairing meetings, negotiating policy and personnel decisions, and planning military action. It is entirely possible that the stress and long hours dealing with the fast-moving crisis overwhelmed Deng's already failing health, forcing him to spend a long time recuperating.

A Secret Journey

With Americans fleeing China by the planeload and Beijing in the tightening grip of open repression, Bush was clearly conflicted about how to proceed. Innately cautious and worried about his "friend" Deng Xiaoping, Bush continued to try and contact Deng, finally resorting to a personal letter he transmitted through Chinese ambassador Han Xu. The letter is a remarkable communication. Beginning with affirmations of his friendship for China, respect for Deng, and "reverence for Chinese history, culture and tradition," Bush implored Deng to understand that American public opinion demanded he take punitive actions and asked him to show "clemency" toward the students.[119] The Chinese reply was pro forma, arriving on June 12. It probably was written by a low-level official in the Foreign Ministry, used stock phraseology to describe Tiananmen, and suggested that if the United States was interested in improving the relationship, it would need to stop taking actions that "hurt the feelings or the interests" of the Chinese side.[120] On June 21, Scowcroft went to the Chinese embassy to meet with Han and explain that the president wished to talk concretely about whether the relationship could be improved and wished to send a high-level secret envoy to begin these discussions. The Chinese quickly approved—sending word on June 24 that they wished the relationship to continue and that a secret envoy would be welcomed.[121]

The planning for the trip was very tightly held. After receiving the Chinese reply, Bush chose Scowcroft to be the envoy for obvious reasons: closeness to the president, familiarity with the key issues and with the Chinese, and secrecy. At Baker's insistence, Deputy Secretary of State Lawrence Eagleburger was added to represent the department at a suitably high level.[122] Neither Baker nor Eagleburger was fond of the idea of a secret envoy but went along with the president. Baker did not tell his undersecretary for political affairs, Robert Kimmitt, about the trip, even though Kimmitt had been handling the details of the relationship for several months. To avoid sending cables through State Department channels, Ambassador Lilley was ordered by telephone to return to the White House for consultations and to lie to his staff about where he was going. Upon arrival in Washington, he did not contact Assistant Secretary Richard Solomon—newly approved by the Senate to head the department's Bureau of East Asia and Pacific Affairs—and "sneaked around" both the department and the city, avoiding both official and press contacts.[123]

The final planning meeting was in the Oval Office, attended by Bush, Baker, Eagleburger, Bob Gates (Scowcroft's deputy), and Lilley. They agreed on the broad outlines of the message to be delivered, which was that the president was committed to preserving the important strategic relationship between the United States and China but shared the shock and outrage of the American people over what had been done to peaceful student demonstrators. Bush wanted the Chinese to know that he had taken the actions he had after Tiananmen because domestic pressure required it and he had to fend off harsher sanctions from Congress. China needed to understand it had to do its part to repair the relationship, mainly by showing clemency to the students. Bush was particularly offended by the Chinese television pictures of badly beaten prisoners being led off for execution, which was causing a furor in the United States, and recommended the mission call for a halt to the intimidation campaign. Lilley counseled the best that could be hoped for was a reduction of Chinese publicity for the revenge taking; there was no way to stop the regime from punishing those who had humiliated it.[124] But Bush had already made up his mind—and no one disagreed, including Lilley—that the relationship was worth the risk to try and restore.

With anger over China still high in Washington, elaborate precautions were taken to ensure the secrecy of the Scowcroft-Eagleburger trip. The C-141 Starlifter that carried the delegation had all its U.S. Air Force markings removed. The flight left in the early hours of the morning from Andrews Air Force Base, having filed a flight plan for Okinawa, and refueled in midair to save time and avoid having to land at a U.S. base where the party might be recognized. The crew, who had changed into civilian attire before landing, got a scare when uninformed Chinese air defense forces scrambled a fighter aircraft to intercept the transport, only being waved off after reassurances from Yang Shangkun that the aircraft had official clearance to land.[125]

On July 1, the sleek black aircraft landed at Beijing's international airport and taxied to the old terminal, now unused, and was parked in a secluded area. Only three passengers disembarked: Scowcroft, Eagleburger, and Scowcroft's executive assistant. No U.S. embassy officers were on the tarmac to greet them—no embassy officers even knew they were coming. Only Ambassador Lilley knew about the trip, and he was in South Korea visiting his wife (who had been evacuated from Beijing with all embassy staff families after the Tiananmen violence) and participating in the elaborate charade by not greeting the delegation. The Scowcroft party quickly boarded Chinese limousines and sped off into Beijing, arriving about half an hour later at Diaoyutai (Fishing Terrace), China's elaborate and isolated complex for foreign visitors.

The morning of July 2, Scowcroft and Eagleburger met first with Deng Xiaoping at Zhongnanhai, about a ten-minute drive from the guesthouse. Although some observers thought Deng had looked shaky during his television appearance on June 9, Scowcroft thought he looked fine in early July and was as sharp as ever. Deng was accompanied by Premier Li Peng, Foreign Minister Wu Xueqian, and Vice Foreign Minister Qian Qichen. After the obligatory photographs, which the Chinese agreed would not be publicized, they got down to tough talk, with Deng taking the lead. He acknowledged that Bush was a good friend and "trustworthy" but criticized his handling of Tiananmen, saying the United States had become "too deeply involved."[126] He accused the United States of siding with those who were trying to overthrow the Chinese government and warned that bilateral relations had reached a "dangerous state." He attacked U.S. media for exaggerating the violence of Tiananmen and for interfering in Chinese internal affairs, and he criticized the U.S. Congress for acting on the basis of rumors and emotions. He vowed that China would punish those who instigated the "counterrevolutionary rebellion" and said no foreign country should try to interfere. Deng said he considered Bush a friend, and he hoped the president considered him one as well, but that the problem was one that mere friendship could not resolve. The United States had created the problem, he said; it was up to Washington to "untie the knot."[127]

Scowcroft responded that although what happened at Tiananmen may have begun as an internal affair, the regime's response had created serious international repercussions that the president could not ignore. He told Deng that the bilateral strategic relationship had been valuable to both sides, but that President Bush shared the dismay of all Americans at what had happened in Tiananmen Square and had taken some necessary actions in response. He hoped to work cooperatively with Deng and others in the Chinese leadership to repair the relationship over time. But he faced serious opposition in Congress, as evidenced by near-unanimous votes in Congress on broadening the sanctions against China, and would need some help from China if he were to be able to turn things around. China needed to be sensitive to the negative impact its actions were having on world opinion, he insisted.[128]

Deng's reply was icy. China had fought a revolution for more than twenty years at the cost of many lives, he said. Now it was an independent country, and no foreign nation could interfere any longer in its internal affairs. China would watch what the United States did. Although Scowcroft was a friend, Deng said he disagreed with everything the president's national security adviser had said. With that, he got up and left the room.

Li Peng took up the cudgels after Deng's departure. With his characteristic combination of sarcasm and cold disdain, he denied the accuracy of U.S. media reports about Tiananmen. He said only 310 people had been killed, not the thousands rumored in the Western press, and only 36 of them were students. He claimed China had shown great forbearance—more than the United States had during antiwar protests in the 1960s and 1970s—and insisted the demonstrators were trying to overthrow the government. He then took the Americans to lunch and pointedly dropped the subject of Tiananmen, focusing instead on a review of global strategic issues.[129]

It was a classic "dialogue of the deaf," one that would be repeated numerous times throughout the Bush administration. Although he believed that the trip was useful and important in keeping lines of communication open and having both sides review their positions, Scowcroft was aware of the depth of the problems. "It was clear to me that the clash of cultures had created a wide divide between us. The resentment by the Chinese of foreign 'interference' was omnipresent. They were focused on security and stability. We were interested in freedom and human rights."[130] More than that, both sides were still extremely angry with each other. Scowcroft and Eagleburger tried to use diplomatic phraseology to convey to Chinese leaders how revolted and shocked the president, Congress, and the American people were at the events surrounding Tiananmen. Deng and Li worried less about diplomatic nicety in expressing their anger—and that of the rest of the Chinese leadership—over the behavior of American media, over the punitive sanctions adopted by Bush and the U.S. Congress, over the students' adoption of American slogans and symbols during their protest, and over the obvious support of many Americans for the students' cause. Washington expected Beijing to understand and appreciate the complexity of its domestic political situation and make accommodations to buttress and justify the relationship. Beijing expected Washington to understand that it believed it had no alternative to the violent crackdown. Neither, in fact, had a thorough understanding of the other's domestic political situation, and neither trusted the other to be telling the truth.

Scowcroft and Eagleburger left in the afternoon of July 2, slightly more than twenty-four hours after they arrived, again using special security to avoid publicity. Both were cautious in their reports to their bosses about how the trip had gone. Baker related that Eagleburger had called the Chinese "inscrutable as ever," but that he thought some of them, at least, had gotten the American message that relations could not be improved while they were killing their own people.[131] Scowcroft was similarly low key in his appraisal of the trip, saying several Chinese had later told him they appreciated the gesture of friendship and understanding at a difficult time. He made no claims that the message was received, or that the Chinese moderated their conduct of the post-Tiananmen crackdown, or that they became in any way more relaxed about the relationship.[132]

Because the secrecy of the trip held for several more months, it is difficult to evaluate its significance at the time. Ambassador Lilley believed that "Scowcroft made his points" and that the public executions were somewhat scaled back.[133] More important, he conveyed a message that, despite public pressure and congressional calls for more punishment and sanctions, the relationship was personally important to the president, and he was looking for opportunities to repair it. Less charitable observers charged later that visiting China only strengthened "hard-liners" and showed American weakness. But in fact, it is unlikely the July trip had much effect on China's domestic or international policies, owing to the continuance of leadership turmoil and insecurity in Beijing.

One of the less publicized goals of the Scowcroft-Eagleburger trip was to ascertain the state of the Chinese leadership. President Bush had worried publicly and privately about who was in charge in Beijing, especially whether Deng Xiaoping was still China's principal leader. The Scowcroft meeting with Deng was thus, in part, reassuring that the man whom all considered to be the leader most favorably disposed toward the United States was still in charge and healthy. In retrospect, however, Scowcroft was struck by Deng's insistence that he would not be the principal interlocutor for the Americans. Although his health seemed satisfactory, Deng went out of his way to make the point that he was only meeting Scowcroft as a "friend," that he was no longer a decisionmaker, and that the Americans would have to deal with Li Peng and the new leadership to resolve the many new problems that confronted U.S.-China relations. When he departed Beijing, Scowcroft had only an inkling of how difficult that process would be.[134]

Congress, the White House, and American Anger

While Scowcroft was in Beijing trying to restore and ameliorate the relationship, the U.S. Congress was moving in exactly the opposite direction. Reflecting growing public outrage at the widening crackdown, Congress was calling for tighter and more punitive sanctions against China. Hoping to head off legislative restrictions on how to deal with China, Secretary of State Baker testified before the House Foreign Relations Committee on June 20. He augmented executive branch sanctions already in place by pledging that all official contacts with China above the assistant secretary level would be suspended, canceling a commerce secretary trip scheduled for July, and by promising to recommend the suspension of all new international financial institution lending to China. Baker entreated Congress to moderate its anger and support the president, whose actions had been "measured," "carefully targeted," and designed to preserve a geopolitically important relationship and to keep options open for the future.[135]

Congressional response was mixed. At least some in the Republican Party—with editorial support from major publications—initially expressed support for the president's measured response. But as U.S. and foreign media devoted more coverage to the brutal crackdown that followed Tiananmen—the televised arrests and trials of protesters, the quick executions of several "hooligans," the wanted posters and manhunts for student leaders, and the stilted propaganda denunciations of the United States for conniving in the demonstrations—the mood in Congress changed to anger and a desire to punish China. Led initially by Democratic Party leaders—Senate Majority Leader Mitchell, House Majority Leader Richard Gephardt, and Steven J. Solarz, House Foreign Affairs Asia-Pacific subcommittee chairman—bipartisan support grew quickly for measures to impose harsher penalties on China for its actions.

The most readily available vehicle for congressional action was the foreign aid authorization bill, which came up for consideration in both houses in late June. Historically a magnet for members pushing particular foreign policy issues, the authorization bill permits the executive branch departments to spend the money allocated to them in the appropriations bill—within certain limits established by Congress. The foreign aid authorization bill has often been the venue for major executive-legislative branch struggles over foreign policy, with the State Department and presidency trying to water down amendments that restrict its flexibility or structure its handling of certain issues. Although little of the $23 billion allocated for foreign aid over two years was to go to China, Solarz and others used the power of amendment to the authorization bill to put together a package of much tougher sanctions against China.

Among the amendments offered during hearings on the foreign aid authorization bill in late June were proposals for a recall of the U.S. ambassador, suspension of Overseas Private Investment Corporation (OPIC) assistance to U.S. firms doing business in China, and cancellation of Trade Development Program (TDP) initiatives. Other members called for a ban on sales of all high-technology goods on the munitions list (including satellites and police equipment), suspension of China's most favored nation trade status, and increased U.S. efforts to block the World Bank, International Monetary Fund (IMF), and other lending by international financial institutions to China.[136] Congressional leaders initially pledged to work with the White House to draw up a comprehensive sanctions package but found few takers in the White House. Marlin Fitzwater told reporters, "The White House is no part of this deal . . . Those people are aware of the President's position," which was opposed to new restrictions on China.[137]

The final version of the amendment put into law the restrictions President Bush had already imposed on China—munitions list bans and suspension of technology transfers—and added a suspension of OPIC guarantees for private investment in China, a ban on TDP activity in China, and tighter restrictions on dual-use nuclear technology for China. The amendment passed the House by a vote of 418-0 on June 30—a veto-proof margin.[138] The Senate passed a similar bill in July, 81-10. Thus the stage was set for the increasingly rancorous and destructive battle between Congress and the executive branch over China policy—a battle that would last through the Bush presidency and beyond.

The events of June 4 dealt an enormous setback to bilateral relations between the United States and China—a setback from which, in some ways, they have never recovered. Indeed, one could say that the Tiananmen crackdown set the U.S.-China relationship on an entirely different course, one that is far more contentious and hostile than at any time since the late 1950s. The extent of the American reaction is remarkable. Even years later—after nearly all the leaders who ordered the PLA into action have died, retired, or been purged; after China has moved in a completely different direction socially, politically, and economically; after most people in China have apparently forgiven, if not forgotten, those terrible events—the United States maintains Tiananmen as an ongoing issue in the bilateral relationship through economic sanctions, frequent criticism of human rights abuses that trace to 1989, and regular commemoration of the event. An evaluation of Tiananmen on American policy toward China needs to look at several different levels of political decisionmaking.

As Richard Madsen points out in his post-Tiananmen study, *China and the American Dream: A Moral Inquiry*, "Tiananmen . . . troubled Americans far out of proportion to its direct cost in human life and suffering. . . . The tragedy in China was so upsetting for many Americans because it contradicted widely cherished American understandings about the meanings of their democratic values."[139] It was, Madsen claims, a drama with the wrong ending—goodness and justice did not triumph at the end, but rather, innocent and idealistic students were suppressed and killed by a cynical and corrupt tyranny. A yearning for freedom and democracy, for the dignity of the individual—ideals on which many believe America was founded—was brutally denied, not only by the use of military force, but by the revenge taking and police-state crackdown that followed. This extraordinarily cruel and unjust action was ordered by a leader whom many in the United States had come to admire. Deng Xiaoping was not idealized in the way Mao Zedong was—for a time—by the American left. But he was considered an admirable figure by many (he was named man of the year twice by *Time* magazine) for his outspoken advocacy of economic reform and for working to undo Mao's tragic legacy. Moreover, he was considered by some, at least, to be moderately pro-American—one of the chief supporters of an enduring strategic relationship in opposition to the Soviet menace.[140]

Other analysts of the huge impact of Tiananmen on American opinion have focused on the behavior and reporting of the American news media as being in part responsible for the widespread outrage that followed June 4. Beyond a doubt, serious questions remain about the objectivity and accuracy of American news accounts—particularly television journalism—in the lead-up to Tiananmen. Many reporters have been candidly critical of how their disproportionate sympathy with, and admiration for, the student demonstrators distorted their reporting of the demonstrations. Many admitted, in the Barone Center Study, for example, that they found the Chinese government's response repellent even before the troops were brought in.

After martial law was declared and the television access of most U.S. networks was cut off, smaller staffs and camera crews were left to report on the follow-up, getting film out of China not through live satellite feeds but via videotapes taken to Hong Kong by couriers. And although they were not present at the points west of Tiananmen where the violence was most extreme, nor did they witness directly the clearing of the square itself, nonetheless the footage they broadcast back to the United States was dramatic and compelling. The sight of bleeding students being carried to hospitals on makeshift bicycle ambulances, the felling of the Goddess of Democracy (broadcast by CCTV), and the riveting CNN video of June 5 with the lone student blocking the passage of several PLA tanks had an enormous emotional impact on U.S. television audiences.

Given the restrictions under which American reporters were operating at the time—enormous demand for information, restricted access to Tiananmen Square and other areas under martial law, and virtually no contact with Chinese officials—it is not surprising that they fell victim to hoaxes, exaggerations, rumor spreading, and disinformation, which they reported, often uncritically, to the American public.[141] Overblown estimates of the number of people killed in the square—based on little evidence or hearsay—and false accounts of pitched battles between martial law units were unfortunate but understandable in the circumstances. And at least the more responsible of the print journalists made efforts to correct the record when more accurate information became available.

The reason why most Americans consider Tiananmen a "massacre" with many hundreds if not thousands killed is largely because of China's refusal to publicize a credible accounting of what happened. The government sticks with a version prepared for propaganda purposes. In other words, it has perpetrated a cover-up, which in post-Watergate America is reprehensible indeed. The Chinese government has never provided any reliable information to corroborate its claim of "about 300" killed and 2,000 wounded. No formal accounting of the names of civilians killed during the Tiananmen crackdown has ever been made public, although authorities promised one. Others who have reviewed available information cannot specify a casualty figure, although they reject the regime figures as far too low. A year after the event, for example, *New York Times* reporter Nicholas Kristof seemed to accept that death estimates "exceeding 1,000" were not supported by any available evidence.[142]

Whatever its origin, the turnabout in American public opinion about China after Tiananmen was startling. While 65 to 72 percent of Americans viewed China favorably before June 4, only 16 to 34 percent did so afterward, according to State Department estimates. Unfavorable views of China rose to a figure higher than 55 percent.[143]

The more lasting damage to U.S.-China relations, however, was probably done in the perceptions of that small percentage of Americans for whom foreign affairs are of consistent interest and importance. For them, the television imagery and gruesome stories of what happened after June 4 reinforced what had already been growing concerns about the nature and behavior of China's government, the disparity between China's on-again, off-again economic reform efforts and the consistently negative attitude of the regime toward political reform, and the failure of China's government to recognize and improve the human rights of its citizens. This small, relatively elite audience—largely urbanized, well educated, East Coast, and liberal—turned on China quickly and unequivocally after June 4. Allied in their outrage with American conservatives—who despised and distrusted China's government for its continued allegiance to communist ideals, repression of religion, and draconian birth control policies—they achieved considerable influence within the U.S. Congress, played on the emotions of Tiananmen, and became a political force demanding change in the basic pattern of the U.S.-China relationship, which had persisted since the Nixon administration.

Given rapidly unfolding changes in eastern Europe and the Soviet Union, the fading out of the cold war, and the American "triumphalism" that had become evident during the later years of the Reagan administration, patience with Beijing already was wearing thin for many American foreign policy elites well before June 4. China's strategic importance was less acknowledged, mercantilist trade policies less forgivable, repression of human rights and democracy less acceptable, proliferation of nuclear materials and missiles (such as the sale to Saudi Arabia of CSS-2 intercontinental ballistic missiles [ICBMs] in 1987) less tolerable. The Tiananmen massacre and subsequent crackdown, which fueled enormous public outrage, for them was not a sharp break with the past but rather the last straw that broke an already weakened consensus on maintaining China policy.

CHAPTER FOUR

The Slow Road to Recovery, 1989–92

When he finally did return to public visibility on September 16, 1989, meeting with Chinese American physicist T. D. Lee, Deng Xiaoping appeared to be in good shape and claimed he had spent much of the summer "swimming." That means he was probably at Beidaihe, where he no doubt met on several occasions with other vacationing leaders.[1] In talking about Tiananmen, Deng told Lee that China's leaders had not been sufficiently vigilant against corruption, a major complaint of student demonstrators and a theme he had stressed even before Tiananmen. He admitted that "mistakes" were made in handling the demonstrations. He also indicated that the economic reforms and opening to the outside would continue. When he reported the conversation to President George Bush several weeks later, Lee said that Deng and Jiang Zemin had "made statements to me that I regard as the first step toward reconciliation."[2]

Deng had also told Lee—asking him to keep it a secret—that he had made a decision to retire from the last official post he held, that of chairman of the Central Military Commission (CMC) of the Communist Party of China. Deng recounted to Lee that he had informed Jiang and Li Peng and others of that decision on September 4, because the notion of the stability of the state resting on the health of "one or two persons" was still troubling him, as it had during the last days of Mao Zedong. "Recently the story circulated in Hong Kong that I had been assassinated or that I was seriously ill, and that rumor caused fluctuations in the stock market there. This shows that it would be better for me to retire soon," Deng told Lee. "When a man gets old, he becomes stubborn and fragile . . . I am old now, and although my mind is fine, I am likely to lose my senses in the future."[3] We do not know the reasons why Deng chose to retire at that time, and his own explanations put the issue in the best light—that he was doing so for the good of the party.

It may also be, however, that Deng realized he was out of synch with what the rest of the leadership was doing, domestically and internationally. Or he may have wished to put his chosen successors in a position to be tested by the responsibilities of power, without relying on the People's Liberation Army (PLA) to back up every decision. In any case, Deng's request to resign the Military Commission post was approved at the Fifth Plenum of the Central Committee, held November 6–9, 1989. In what seemed to be a political victory, Deng was able to have Jiang Zemin formally installed as CMC chairman, giving him the perquisites and powers of the military position that Deng had used to anchor his own authority within the party. Although Jiang had no military experience or ties within the armed forces, observers speculated that PLA officers would accept his authority—at least so long as Deng was supporting him.

But in a move that Deng and Jiang no doubt later regretted, the plenum also approved Deng's recommendation that Yang Shangkun be elevated to the position of first vice chairman of the Military Commission, and that his half-brother Yang Baibing (also an active supporter of the Tiananmen operation) be named executive secretary of the commission. With Jiang widely perceived as weak and dependent, that put the Yang brothers into the key positions to control the military and the propaganda operations of the PLA and arguably placed Yang in a position to claim Deng's mantle as the most influential party elder. Press accounts indicated that Chinese intellectuals were troubled by the appointment, since it put Tiananmen hardliners in charge of the army and the government.[4]

Finally, it is possible that Deng's retirement was intended to be a signal to the other party elders that they should resume their retreat from positions of influence within the party. In his September 4 remarks, Deng mentioned that the Central Advisory Commission (CAC)—which Deng had set up in 1982 to provide a transition for elderly leaders into retirement—would be completely disestablished at the party congress scheduled for 1992. Since the CAC was headed by Chen Yun, Deng's remarks were seen as confirming the tensions between the two elders.[5]

Elderly Politicians, Old Policies

Although in much worse health than Deng, Chen (then eighty-four) appeared to be enjoying more influence on China's policies in 1989 than he had for many years. A central party leader since 1943, Chen was a staunch believer in a centralized economic system, and as such, had objected to Mao Zedong's policies of mass mobilization economic development (for example, the Great Leap Forward) and to Deng Xiaoping's promotion of market economics and foreign investment (for example, the special economic zones). He had supported the efforts of other elders to weaken Hu Yaobang and Zhao Ziyang in the mid-1980s. Chen also had strong ties within the party and government administrative apparatus, including the State Planning Commission, the Central Discipline Inspection Commission, and the Central Advisory Commission, of which he was chairman. Chen numbered among his protégés or strong supporters three members of the Politburo Standing Committee—Li Peng, Yao Yilin, and Song Ping.

China's array of post-Tiananmen policies represented a throwback to an earlier era. Domestically, Beijing continued to press its crackdown on dissent, arresting thousands for political crimes, such as "counterrevolutionary incitement," or for disturbing social order. American human rights activist John Kamm, who has specialized in trying to get China to account for "counterrevolutionary" criminals dating from this period, estimates that between 1,500 and 2,000 individuals were arrested and tried for counterrevolution in connection with the June 4 disturbances, and that 10,000 to 15,000 more were arrested and tried for "disturbing the social order" (chiefly disrupting traffic) and "beating, smashing, looting and burning." About 300 people were executed, mostly for crimes causing injury or death but also for some property crimes as well. Thousands more were detained and sent to labor reform camps, which entailed a maximum three-year period of incarceration.[6]

Although Deng told T. D. Lee that the regime would not "just blame the demonstrators" but would try to correct its own mistakes as well, the party began a classic repression campaign within two weeks of June 4, focusing on those party members who had supported the demonstrations.[7] The Central Discipline Commission announced on June 24 that an investigation would be conducted of all party members' activities during what it called "the turmoils." "Those party members who deviated from the correct political stand . . . should be strictly punished with the disciplines, including expelling them from the party."[8] Individual party organizations sent security teams to universities, think tanks, government bureaucracies, and other work units, with instructions to find out who participated and especially organized participation in antigovernment demonstrations, who made antigovernment statements, and so on. As had been done so often in the past, people were pressured to inform on one another, declare their support for the crackdown, and admit their own mistakes. The campaign was particularly heavy in Beijing's universities, the Chinese Academy of Social Sciences, and other academic or scientific units that had been active in the demonstrations. Part of the intensity of the campaign was in reaction to the fact that most of the student leaders identified in wanted posters on June 13 still had not been captured weeks after the crackdown had begun.

The efforts to root out organizers and participants in prodemocracy demonstrations were accompanied by a virulent campaign to malign the ideas that had been espoused during the democracy movement. Following an intense purge of media personnel who had supported the Tiananmen demonstrators, PLA and conservative propaganda specialists were tasked with bringing the media back under firm party control and directing the counterattack. Veterans of the mid-1980s ideological campaigns against "spiritual pollution" and "bourgeois liberalization"—such as Deng Liqun—returned to prominence within the propaganda apparatus and used it to attack Zhao Ziyang and his supporters, student leaders and intellectuals, and foreign ideas and practices for contributing to the "turmoil" of June 4.

The first priority of Beijing's new propaganda assault seemed to be shifting the blame for the Tiananmen protests from the Communist Party and its leadership to foreign forces. Starting with repeated accusations that Western media deliberately exaggerated the violence and the casualties at Tiananmen (which they did but not deliberately), Beijing propagandists moved on to charge Voice of America (VOA) and other foreign broadcast media with "spreading rumors" and attempting to undermine China's efforts to restore order. In ever more shrill tones, Chinese media accused the West of trying to interfere in China's internal affairs by supporting democracy, defending the rights of demonstrators, and criticizing Beijing's crackdown. Even Deng believed some of these accusations, telling a visiting Japanese delegation in December, "Western countries, particularly the United States, set all their propaganda machines in motion . . . to encourage and support the so-called democrats or opposition in China, who were in fact the scum of the Chinese nation. That is how the turmoil came about."[9]

The next step was charging that the students were motivated not by anger at the leadership's corruption and inefficiency, but because their minds were poisoned by "bourgeois liberalization"—shorthand for Western values, such as democracy and freedom. Those values were conveyed through a deliberate Western effort to undermine socialism in China and bring about its "peaceful evolution" from a socialist to a capitalist society. Beijing leaders probably saw the efforts of Hong Kong citizens helping fugitive dissidents to escape into exile there (a well-organized "underground railroad" called Operation Yellow Bird) as further evidence of the West's complicity in the plot to undermine China.

Even though he attacked and clearly distrusted Western interference during and after Tiananmen, Deng insisted in meetings with foreign visitors that his program of reform and opening up to the outside world would continue.

Before long, however, central planners and conservative propagandists expanded their criticism of Zhao's economic mistakes to include some of the fundamental principles of Deng's own reform program, attacking marketization—that is, the encouragement of private enterprise and structural reform of state-owned enterprises—as examples of "capitalist reform."[10] A fierce debate had already been raging in the party press over whether certain reforms should be "surnamed [that is, labeled] 'capitalist' or 'socialist.'" By the end of 1989, as conservative propagandists continued to dominate China's media, it appeared increasingly clear that Deng—once reviled by Mao as a "capitalist roader"—and his policies were under growing attack.[11]

Despite his popular reputation as the architect of China's economic reforms, Deng was no match for Chen Yun as an economist. In some ways like Mao and his experiments with social engineering (such as the high-speed development of the commune system in the mid-1950s), Deng seemed to believe that willpower and concerted action could overcome economic difficulties. For example, although he seemed unaware of the complexities of reforming China's antiquated price control system, Deng in 1988 had called for "boldness" in implementing price reform, which led Zhao Ziyang to put together hastily a package that not only failed to resolve price problems but brought about panic buying, bank runs, and serious inflation that cost Zhao his control of economic policy.

What Deng understood clearly, however, was that the party's legitimacy and reputation, its mandate to rule, would have to be based on its ability to bring about economic prosperity for an increasing number of people. That was the message of the landmark Third Plenum of the Eleventh Central Committee of December 1978. Such a program required extensive reform of traditional socialist economic organization and methods, as well as opening China up to Western capitalist markets, technology, management, and innovation. Both Hu Yaobang and Zhao Ziyang had enthusiastically embraced Deng's philosophy and worked to bring about reforms against significant opposition from China's entrenched industrial bureaucrats and hidebound ideological satraps. When Deng purged them, and particularly after he permitted Zhao to be the scapegoat for Tiananmen, Deng undermined his own reform program, by putting its critics in charge of the economy and ideology and by effectively silencing many who understood and supported reform.

Li Peng and Yao Yilin, beginning in 1988, had put together a program of economic retrenchment, which was called "curing and rectification" to correct and balance the problems that had emerged during the previous three years. They set about reversing Hu and Zhao's programs of encouraging rapid growth, decentralizing economic decisionmaking authority, freeing rural markets, attracting foreign investment in special economic zones, reforming the price system, freeing farmers to grow the crops they wished and establish rural enterprises, and restructuring the massive state-owned industrial sector. Li and Yao instead promoted slow, stable growth, recentralization, the primacy of planning over markets, minimizing foreign involvement, restoring price controls and agricultural quotas, and perfecting the state sector. Deng, a classic balancer of conflicting opinions, had sought to define an "organic synthesis" of the "socialist market economy," but the balance between planning and market forces in determining economic policy after 1989 remained a matter of nearly open dispute. Li Peng oversaw the simultaneous preparation of China's Eighth Five-Year Plan and a Ten-Year Economic Program in late 1990, both of which envisioned slow growth (6 percent) and predominant central planning.[12] Deng counseled that a such a low growth rate would result in the loss of popular support for the party, but his advice went largely unheeded.[13]

In these circumstances, with the United States being blamed publicly and privately for instigating Tiananmen, with economic policy in retreat from reform and opening up, and with Deng under oblique attack, it is not surprising that U.S.-China relations did not pick up any momentum. The leaders principally responsible for China's domestic and foreign policies were bitterly hostile toward the United States, while those who supported improved ties were in political limbo or on the defensive. On the Chinese side, domestic politics set the tone for the relationship, and the tone was cold. At an ambassadorial conference called by the Ministry of Foreign Affairs in early July 1989, Deng's guidance for riding out the storm of foreign opinion was passed on to the beleaguered diplomats: "Observe matters coolly, keep our own counsel, keep our feet firm, calmly meet our responsibilities, keep in touch with friends, keep a count in our hearts." With respect to the United States, he added, "A soft attitude cannot stabilize the relationship. If we are a little tougher, we can force a turn for the better."[14]

Bush Perseveres against Growing Congressional Hostility

Although genuinely troubled by the excesses of the post-Tiananmen crackdown, President Bush was strongly motivated—out of strategic considerations and because of his personal experience as head of the U.S. Liaison Office, where he established good relationships with a number of senior Chinese leaders—to try and restore the relationship. Bush also seemed to favor a "realist" approach to international relations that subordinated ethical, humanitarian, and ideological considerations to a concept of the national interest.[15] He repeatedly referred to America's national interest in public statements and press conferences after Tiananmen. For example, as Congress was considering more punitive sanctions than Bush had imposed, Bush held a press conference on June 27, 1989, at which he said, "If you look at the world and you understand the dynamics of the Pacific area, good relationships with China are in the national interest of the United States. Now, it's hard to have them. It's impossible at this moment to have what I would say normalized relations, for very obvious reasons. But I am going to do my level best to find a way to see improvement there."[16]

After the Scowcroft-Eagleburger mission, Bush wrote again to Deng, appealing this time more directly for him to undertake measures that would ease the growing hostility in the United States and provide "some kind of opening" to repair ties. He recommended an amnesty, for example. Deng stonewalled him with a "polite" reply that included a demand that Bush "'stop permitting the criminals in the United States [meaning the Chinese dissidents and students there] to carry out their activities against the Chinese Government.'"[17] By this time, Bush was worried that he would not be able to maintain the relationship in its existing state, much less improve it. Congress had passed—by overwhelming margins—additional sanctions against China in late June and early July, including them in the Foreign Relations Authorization Act (H.R. 1487). Congress continued to press for tougher sanctions through the summer, with growing support from public opinion, from Chinese student groups in the United States, and from the international media. The president tried to do everything possible to eliminate the most objectionable elements of the sanctions legislation and build implementing language designed to maximize the flexibility of the executive branch in dealing with China.

But there was more to the divergence over China policy than mere disagreements over how angry to get at the Beijing leadership. Much larger principles of international relations and American governance were involved. Many members of Congress instinctively distrusted realpolitik justifications for U.S. policy and subscribed to a more "idealist" perspective more closely wedded to the American experience—distrustful of foreign entanglements and guided by "American values," such as freedom, democracy, and human rights. The trampling of those values by the Chinese government genuinely outraged many members of Congress and led to the demand for punishment of China. Arguments that punishment should be mitigated because of China's strategic importance in the U.S. competition with the Soviet Union were rejected by many on the grounds that the USSR, under Gorbachev, was becoming less of a strategic threat, and China's cooperation in dealing with Moscow was unreliable and unnecessary. Others saw Beijing's insufficiently controlled sales of missile and nuclear weapons–related equipment and technology to unstable or hostile Middle Eastern regimes as inimical to American interests and in ways not offset by Chinese support for U.S. opposition to the USSR.

George Bush clearly favored a strengthening of presidential powers in the conduct of American foreign policy. But he also determined to ease the struggle with the Democratic Party–controlled Congress. As national security adviser, Brent Scowcroft made what he considered were conciliatory gestures toward Congress, including the establishment of a Congressional Liaison office within the National Security Council, under the capable direction of Virginia Lampley.[18] Before Tiananmen, Scowcroft, at least, believed that a high degree of comity existed between Congress and the White House on foreign policy in general and China policy in particular. "Congress was fine, pre-Tiananmen. The love affair with China, which I think began with Nixon's trip, by and large lasted until Tiananmen Square . . . Because Russia, you know, was still the big bugaboo, so China was seen as a more-or-less friendly associate."[19]

After Tiananmen, however, Scowcroft realized quickly that Congress was going to become a major problem. Besides the resolutions and statements condemning China and the Bush administration's response to China, and punitive amendments to the Foreign Relations Authorization Act, Congress began considering measures clearly designed to supplant executive authority. On June 21, Representative Nancy Pelosi—a Democrat representing San Francisco, California—introduced in the House the Emergency Chinese Adjustment of Status Facilitation Act of 1989 (H.R. 2712). Seemingly innocuous at first, the bill became the setting for a major showdown between Congress and the Bush administration over control of China policy.

Initially, the bill was intended to make it easier for Chinese students in the United States to extend their visas, to apply for a change in their nonimmigrant status, and to work in the United States, without having to return to China for a two-year period, as required by U.S. immigration law. Its purpose was to prevent Chinese students in the United States (estimated to number about 40,000 at that time) from being forced to return to China, where they might have been subjected to punishment or discrimination because they had participated in demonstrations against the Tiananmen crackdown while they were in the United States. Strongly supported by Chinese student organizations in the United States, the bill proposed easing of tight Immigration and Naturalization Service (INS) restrictions on Chinese nonimmigrant visa holders so that they could remain in the United States if they feared persecution upon return to China.

Given the extensive sympathy in the United States for Chinese students, the bill was a high priority for Congress and moved quickly through the legislative process. Before the end of July, it had picked up 259 cosponsors in the House and had moved through hearings in the Subcommittee on Immigration, Refugees, and International Law of the House Judiciary Committee.

After amendments and markup, it passed the House by voice vote on July 31 and moved on to the Senate, where it was sponsored by Majority Leader George Mitchell and Senator Edward Kennedy (D-Mass.). After a period of stall because of contradictory amendments and necessary conference action, the House passed the Senate-amended version on November 19 by a vote of 403-0, while the Senate passed the measure by unanimous voice vote the following day and presented it to the president on November 21.[20] The administration expressed repeated objections to the legislation, primarily on the grounds that China might react by canceling the entire program of joint academic exchanges, including the Fulbright program. Chinese students in the United States generally supported the legislation and declared that administration pledges issued after Tiananmen were not sufficient protection from potential Chinese government retaliation.[21] The administration's efforts to find friends in Congress to help head off the legislation were unsuccessful. Observed Brent Scowroft later, "Then we knew we had a big problem."[22]

On November 30, despite the overwhelming congressional support for what had become known as the Pelosi bill, President Bush vetoed H.R. 2712 on the grounds that it constituted "congressional micromanagement of foreign policy."[23] At the same time, he ordered the attorney general to afford Chinese students in the United States the same protections as had been mandated in the bill, namely, "irrevocable waiver of the 2-year home country residence requirement . . . assurance of continued lawful immigration status [for those] who were lawfully in the United States on June 5, 1989, . . . authorization for employment," and notice of expiration, rather than deportation proceedings, for those whose nonimmigrant status had expired. Bush insisted that his actions "accomplish the laudable objectives of the Congress in passing H.R. 2712 while preserving my ability to manage foreign relations."[24] Bush's veto was widely condemned on the Hill and set the executive and legislative branches on course for a major collision.

Fitful Reconciliation—Help from Nixon and Kissinger

Bush may have been influenced in his veto of the Pelosi bill by a belief that there had been some progress in easing of tensions in the bilateral relationship. Bush's repeated efforts to communicate with the Chinese gradually began to break down the wall of hostility and distrust that Tiananmen had produced. He continued to write letters to Deng Xiaoping, delivering them through various channels, including the Chinese embassy. Secretary of State James Baker met Qian Qichen at the Paris Conference on Cambodia in July, and again at the UN General Assembly opening in September, but found him cold and defensive.[25] Bush also sent personal envoys, such as his brother,

Prescott Bush, and former secretary of state Al Haig, not necessarily to carry specific messages but to make appearances and show concern.

In late October, former president Richard M. Nixon visited Beijing for formal talks with Chinese leaders. He had planned the trip well before Tiananmen and decided to go ahead with it despite the obvious difficulties. He spoke in detail to President Bush about his mission before he left and had written to Deng as well, warning that he would be delivering a tough message. Anxious to show the Chinese people that the Chinese leadership still enjoyed the respect of international leaders and to maintain a communications link with Washington, Deng assented to the visit. Accompanied only by former Carter administration NSC staffer and noted China scholar Michel Oksenberg and a personal aide, Nixon arrived on October 28 for what he hoped would be a low-key but high-impact visit. Nixon knew well the political sensitivities in the United States and the Chinese eagerness for favorable publicity. Having been burned repeatedly by negative press in the United States, Nixon set out strict guidelines for press coverage of his meetings—photographers would be allowed but not for greetings or banquets (that is, no photographs of handshakes or toasts). Although the Chinese agreed to the guidelines, Nixon and Oksenberg were repeatedly chagrined at Chinese efforts to evade them to provide more favorable domestic coverage.[26]

In a report delivered to Congress after his return, Nixon described his remarkable access. "In six days in Beijing from October 28 to November 2, I had over twenty hours of one-on-one discussions with eight major Chinese leaders, including Chairman Deng Xiaoping, Premier Li Peng, General Secretary Jiang Zemin, President Yang Shangkun, the sophisticated Foreign Minister Qian Qichen, the very able Minister of Education Li Tieying, the brilliant Minister of Propaganda Li Ruihuan, and the extraordinarily competent Mayor of Shanghai Zhu Rongji."[27] By all accounts, he spoke to them bluntly about the "tragedy" of Tiananmen and about the anger against China in the United States. In remarks released to the public, Deng accused the United States of being "involved too deeply in the turmoil and counterrevolutionary rebellion that occurred in Beijing not long ago," and he insisted that "China was the real victim, and it is unjust to reprove China for it."[28] In private, however, Deng was more conciliatory than his colleagues and generally agreed to a package deal for the release of Fang Lizhi in exchange for a visit by Jiang to the United States. Nixon also secured the Chinese agreement to an easing of the tight PLA guarding of the U.S. embassy compounds, which had become obtrusive and menacing to American personnel.

Nixon left China with what he thought was a workable approach—that of a sequenced series of steps by both sides that would lead eventually to the release of Fang Lizhi and the resumption of a more "normal" relationship.

He even believed he could bring Congress along on such an effort. As he said in his report to Congress and a much longer report he delivered to President Bush, Nixon proposed the administration take the first step in the form of resuming contact at a high level with the Chinese leadership. According to Oksenberg, his initial suggestion was for Treasury Secretary Nicholas Brady to make a trip to Beijing, but he acquiesced, evidently in a private meeting at the White House, in a (second) Scowcroft mission.[29]

Henry Kissinger, Nixon's national security adviser and secretary of state, paid a visit to Beijing shortly after Nixon left. He conveyed the same message from Bush that the others did: the president sincerely wanted to improve the overall relationship, but in the face of strong opposition in the United States, could not do so unless China indicated that it would ease the crackdown and take account of U.S. concerns about human rights. Although he continued to resist the notion that the United States accepted any responsibility for Tiananmen, Kissinger hinted that a deal was in the offing when he told his hosts that "both countries should take steps together to put relations onto a smoother path."[30] Deng sent a letter back through Kissinger reaffirming the "package" solution, which included a resolution of the Fang Lizhi situation in conjunction with a visit to the United States by Jiang Zemin.[31] Bush assented to a Jiang visit but only after the Fang Lizhi situation was cleared up. He offered to send an envoy to China, ostensibly to brief on his summit with Gorbachev in Malta but in fact to work more on a package deal for improving relations.

The deal was fairly straightforward but difficult for both sides to deliver. As Ambassador Lilley put it, "The basic thing was: We wanted Fang Lizhi out. We wanted martial law lifted, and we wanted amnesty for some of the people at Tiananmen." There was also a desire to get the Chinese to cease efforts to sell medium-range missiles to troublesome countries in the Middle East. The Chinese wanted an easing of restrictions on World Bank loans, Bush administration waivers so China could launch American-origin communications satellites on their booster rockets, and some lifting of sanctions.[32] Douglas Paal, NSC Asia director, thought there was a domestic dimension as well. "He [Deng] was looking for something . . . to show the rest of them why it was worth relenting from their hard-ass public position in dealing with Americans."[33]

To make the deal come together, the president sent Brent Scowcroft and Lawrence Eagleburger on a second mission to Beijing. Although secrecy was not considered as essential on this trip as on the earlier one, it was hoped the visit would be "low profile." The U.S. Air Force plane still left at 2:30 a.m., however, and Scowcroft decided to postpone announcing the trip until after their arrival on Sunday, December 10. Scowcroft later conceded this decision was a mistake, as the U.S. media reported the trip as a "surprise visit" and an "unexpected policy shift." Because Scowcroft did not reveal the real agenda for the trip, the American media focused on the symbolic aspects, which seemed to favor the Chinese. More seriously, he did not follow Nixon's example of controlling press coverage of his meetings with Chinese leaders.

The Chinese press—reflecting the wishes of the party leadership—was again eager to showcase symbolic aspects of the trip to demonstrate to Chinese and foreign audiences that China was emerging from isolation and being visited by important foreign guests. So they happily provided Western journalists with photographs of a serious-faced Scowcroft raising a glass of wine with a beaming Qian Qichen. As Scowcroft recalled in his book, the Chinese suddenly let the photojournalists in just as he had begun his toast. "It was an awkward situation for me. I could go through with the ceremony and be seen as toasting those the press was labeling 'the butchers of Tiananmen Square,' or refuse to toast and put in jeopardy the whole purpose of the trip. I chose the former and became, to my deep chagrin, an instant celebrity—in the most negative sense of that term."[34] The picture appeared on the front page of nearly every major newspaper in the world the following day.

Worse still, Xinhua released selected portions of Scowcroft's toast. "My colleagues and I have come as friends, to resume our important dialogue on international questions of vital interest to both our nations . . . We also come today to bring new impetus and vigor into our bilateral relationship and seek new areas of agreement—economic, political and strategic. . . . Speaking as a friend, I would not be honest if I did not acknowledge that we have profound areas of disagreement—on the events at Tiananmen, on the sweeping changes in Eastern Europe. . . . In both our societies there are voices of those who seek to redirect or frustrate our cooperation. We both must take bold measures to overcome these negative forces. . . . We extend our hand in friendship and hope you will do the same."[35] In the best of times, Scowcroft's toast might have seemed a bit obsequious. It was not the best of times.

American opinion makers in the media and Congress exploded with outrage. The *Washington Post* attacked the trip in editorials three times in one week and added several critical op-ed articles. The *New York Times* accused the president of "hailing the butchers of Beijing."[36] Republican commentator George Will called Bush "a Pekingese [lapdog] curled around the ankles of China's tyrants."[37] Winston Lord castigated the Scowcroft mission in a *Washington Post* op-ed article, saying it "both erased any pretense of official indignation [over Tiananmen] and weakened the true foundations of Sino-American relations."[38] Bush quickly came to the aid of his beleaguered national security adviser: "I do not want to isolate the Chinese people; I don't want to hurt the Chinese people. We have certain sanctions. I hope I needn't reiterate my concerns about the events that took place in Tiananmen Square. I think we were positioned in the forefront of human rights concerns, and I think the Chinese know that they still have to address themselves to the problems that were inherent in this episode. But I don't want to see that China remains totally isolated. I don't want to take any further steps that are going to hurt the Chinese people."[39]

The situation took a turn for the worse on December 18, when CNN broke the story of the July trip to Beijing by Scowcroft and Eagleburger. Thereafter, on top of indignation at dealing with Beijing at all were added critiques of "secret" diplomacy, of "hasty" trips to "kowtow" to Beijing, of lying and duplicity about the suspension of high-level contacts (that is, the Baker statement of June 20), and "betrayal" of American ideals. Congressional Democratic Party leaders poured scorn on the visit, the policy, and the president personally, and promised new legislative efforts to reverse his conciliatory approach. Even the chairman of the House Republican Policy Committee, Representative Mickey Edwards, called the trips "absurd, an outrage," and charged that Bush had "lost his moral compass on this issue."[40]

Bush responded testily, saying critics should "stay tuned" for positive results of the Scowcroft mission.[41] Press Spokesman Marlin Fitzwater, Secretary Baker, and others were left the task of explaining the secrecy of the missions, the difference between "misleading" Congress and "lying to" Congress about preserving secrecy, and other less delicate issues. The president, of course, was hinting that the Scowcroft mission had achieved an understanding with the Chinese about a sequencing of events designed to make progress in bilateral relations.[42] Although not set down in any document agreed to by both sides, the process began playing out immediately after Scowcroft and Eagleburger left Beijing as the following events show:

—The Chinese Foreign Ministry, responding to U.S. concerns about possible M-9 and M-11 missile sales to Syria and Libya, announced on December 12 that, except for the 1987 sale of CSS-2 ICBMs to Saudi Arabia, "China has never sold, nor is planning to sell missiles to any Middle East country."[43]

—On December 19, President Bush announced he would authorize licenses for three communications satellites built by Hughes Aircraft Co.—two for AUSSAT, an Australian firm; and one for AsiaSat, a Sino-British consortium—to be launched by Chinese carrier rockets in 1991 and 1992. Although satellite launches were prohibited expressly by U.S. law before and after the announcement, the president made use of the law's granting him the right to waive the export prohibition on the grounds of "national interest."[44] He also announced that he would waive—again on grounds of "national interest"—congressionally imposed limitations on Export-Import Bank lending for China. (Congress had approved but not yet sent to him legislation—H.R. 1487—mandating the sanctions he had imposed in June, with additional conditions).

—On January 10, 1990, China announced that it would lift martial law in Beijing municipality the following day. Although the gesture was largely symbolic—PLA soldiers were replaced by paramilitary People's Armed Police troops, maintaining the same heavy security presence as before—it did represent a positive response to Scowcroft's entreaty that China had to "help out" the president in order to make more progress. It was welcomed by the White House and State Department as one of a number of "positive steps" that had recently been taken but was rejected as "meaningless" by congressional and media critics.[45]

—On January 11, State Department spokesperson Margaret Tutwiler announced that the United States would support World Bank lending to China on a case-by-case basis for "humanitarian, basic human needs-type loans." This was a "partial reversal" of a policy that had been in effect since Tiananmen of opposing World Bank lending to China (project loans would still be opposed).[46]

—On January 18, Beijing announced it had released 573 persons who had been detained after the Tiananmen demonstrations. This was by no means the amnesty that the administration had been seeking, as the number represented the total released over several months and was only a small percentage of the thousands that had been arrested in the wake of the "counterrevolutionary turmoil." It appeared rather to be a cynical effort to influence foreign opinion, particularly in the United States, where Congress was to take up efforts to override the president's veto of the Pelosi bill. The Chinese refused to give the names of those released or the dates of their release, saying only that they were "lawbreakers" who had shown "repentance." Moreover, in the weeks before the announcement, more than 800 who had been detained in 1989 were formally sentenced to jail terms.[47]

Symbolically most important, the president fought hard to sustain his veto of the Pelosi bill. After the holiday recess, Congress had returned to Washington in the mood for a fight on China policy. The second Scowcroft-Eagleburger visit to Beijing, followed by the public revelation of the July visit, set off a renewed burst of anger over Bush's soft handling of China. Republicans in Congress, including House Minority Leader Robert H. Michel and Minority Whip Newt Gingrich counseled the president not to fight the inevitable veto override. Gingrich called the effort to sustain the veto, led by White House Chief of Staff John Sununu, "inexplicable" and criticized the president's overall approach both to China and to Congress.[48] Realizing there was little chance of gaining the one-third majority of the House needed to block an override, the administration focused on the Senate. Even there,

Scowcroft admitted, prospects were bleak. "We did a [preliminary] head count in the Senate, and we had five—five of the thirty-four [votes] we needed. And Pete Wilson, who then was a Senator from California, got up out of a sick-bed and flew back to vote against us. Rock-ribbed Republican Pete Wilson. It was really, really tough."[49]

But with presidential popularity high after the forceful overthrow of Panamanian dictator Manuel Noriega and with the inherent strength a veto gives the president, Sununu and others decided to push ahead, lobbying Republican senators intensely to support their party and support the president. Opposition was fierce. Editorials in the most influential newspapers supported an override. Former ambassador to China Winston Lord testified against the veto before the Senate Finance Committee. Few Republican congressmen supported the president on January 24, when the House of Representatives overrode his veto by a 390-25 margin. The administration, in response, issued a report on how successfully it had protected the interests of Chinese students in the United States. The president met with Senate Republican leaders and telephoned others. Vice President Dan Quayle called numerous Republican senators, as did Secretary of State Baker, Chief of Staff Sununu, and former President Nixon. They insisted the Chinese decision to lift martial law in Beijing, to permit VOA reporters to return to China, to discuss further academic exchanges, and to release more than 500 prisoners were ample evidence that Bush's China policy was working and should be supported.

In the end, and by the barest of margins, Bush's veto of the Pelosi bill was sustained (62 senators favored override, 37 were against). Pugnaciously, despite the nearly unanimous House vote to override and the thin four-vote margin over the one-third needed to prevent override in the Senate, Bush claimed the vote was an endorsement of his China policy. "The thing I like about it, given the mournful predictions of some a couple of weeks ago, is that it gives me the confidence that I'm going to go forward the way I think is correct here . . . I'm very, very pleased with the result."[50] If anything, however, the bruising battle stiffened opposition in Congress to his policy of engagement with China. It also sharpened partisanship in Congress and damaged Bush's reputation. "This was a victory for President Bush and the Chinese leadership that was responsible for Tiananmen Square," sniped Senator Edward Kennedy, equating the two. "It was a defeat for human rights."[51] Majority Leader Bob Dole countered, however, that it was "not a public trial of George Bush's China policy," but an opportunity to "bash George Bush, embarrass George Bush, set some Republican up for a difficult vote."[52]

In reality, however, President Bush no doubt realized that any efforts to improve relations that required congressional approval would be nearly impossible to carry out. He may also have noted that China's steps were small and nearly meaningless as far as real improvement in its human rights policies. Whatever the reason, the president took no further steps forward and in fact took public steps backward, signing the State Department Authorization Bill (P.L. 101-246)—which codified the economic sanctions applied to China after Tiananmen—and publicly denying permission for a Chinese company (China Aero-Technology Import-Export Corporation) to invest in MAMCO, a Seattle-based aircraft parts manufacturer.[53]

China reacted quickly and harshly, calling Ambassador Lilley to the Foreign Ministry, where Vice Minister Liu Huaqiu expressed China's "utmost indignation" over the sanctions legislation, which he claimed "willfully trampled on the basic norms governing international relations." Liu insisted that the *lifting* of post-Tiananmen sanctions was a "necessary condition for the return of normal bilateral relations."[54] Days later, the Chinese government issued new regulations on overseas study for Chinese students, requiring applicants to have had five years of work experience before going abroad for study. Deputy Secretary of State Lawrence Eagleburger, testifying before a fiercely hostile Senate Foreign Relations Committee on February 7, while still defending the Bush policy toward China, admitted that "not enough had been done" by China in improving its human rights record.[55] The brief period of cooperation in trying to improve bilateral relations had hit an impasse on both sides.

Eastern European Events and China's Domestic Politics

It is broadly accepted conventional wisdom that the downfall of eastern European communist regimes, which took place at such breathtaking speed in the latter half of 1989, contributed greatly to the decline of support in the United States for a "strategic" relationship with China. With the communist bloc in disarray and the Soviet Union in serious economic and political difficulties, the notion of maintaining close relations with China to keep it from returning to the Soviet orbit seemed increasingly anachronistic to American opinion makers. George Bush's single-minded focus on the need for "strategic" ties with China rang hollow as the threat from the Soviet Union receded.

Less understood, perhaps, is the impact the successive dissolution of socialist governments and disestablishment of communist parties had on the domestic political situation in China. Still reeling from the shock of Tiananmen and the obvious unpopularity of the Communist Party, Chinese officials must have looked at the events in eastern Europe in the summer and fall of 1989 with shock and dread. On the same day as PLA soldiers raced into Tiananmen, Polish citizens voted overwhelmingly for noncommunist legislators in their parliament, the first of several elections that peaceably removed the Polish

Communist Party from power the following year. One month later, Mikhail Gorbachev told a Warsaw Pact meeting that each nation should pursue its own solution to national problems, that there was no "universal model of socialism, " and that Russian troops would begin to be withdrawn. Without the fear of Soviet intervention in their domestic affairs, eastern Europeans rushed to free themselves of oppressive one-party dictatorships. Hungary's legislature changed its constitution to allow opposition parties, abolished the leading role of the Socialist Party, and dropped "People's Republic" from its name in October. In November, East Germany's communist government bowed to public pressure and opened all border crossings to West Germany, which brought about the fall of the Berlin Wall and the eventual replacement of the Communist Party government. Also in November, the Czech government resigned after public outrage at the violent breakup of antigovernment demonstrations. As happened in Hungary, the Communist Party's "leading role" was disestablished, and by the end of the year, Czechoslovakia had a new government under Vaclav Havel. During the same time period, Bulgaria's Communist Party government resigned and the party surrendered its dominant role.[56]

Many Chinese leaders viewed these events with alarm and consternation, but not because they expected that they would soon fuel similar protests in China. They had reason to feel confident that they had silenced prodemocracy demonstrations of any significant scale. If anything, the travails of eastern European parties reinforced the view of Deng and others that they could not compromise with prodemocracy activists and that their decision to send in troops in June was basically correct. China's well-controlled media simply stopped reporting on what was happening in Berlin, Prague, Sofia, and Warsaw. That did not prevent people in China from finding out what was going on, but it limited the impact of the news. What China's leaders probably found more disquieting, however, was evidence that the West was actively supporting the protests, economically and politically. President Bush's travel to Poland and Hungary in July was not seen as unrelated to changes in the governments and policies of those two countries. The Paris G-7 summit declaration of support for political reform, including debt relief, also stood in stark contrast to its condemnation of China's crackdown and its unanimous recommendation that World Bank loans to China be postponed. These actions and the continuing turmoil in eastern Europe no doubt heightened leadership fears and doubts about foreign plotting against socialism in China.

But it was the violent and brutal collapse of the Nicolae Ceausescu regime in Romania that probably had the strongest impact on China. China had not been especially close to any of the eastern European bloc countries while they were under Moscow's thumb, but it had developed relatively warm relations with Romania. Beijing had encouraged Ceausescu's independence from Moscow during the Brezhnev era, and while there may have been some doubts about the propriety of Ceausescu's increasingly nepotistic rule in Romania, Chinese leaders appreciated his tough-minded refusal to undertake the domestic political reforms that Gorbachev was proposing. Ceausescu had even found words to praise China's crackdown on dissent after Tiananmen, and Beijing reciprocated by sending Qiao Shi to the Romanian Communist Party Congress in August 1989, at which Ceausescu was re-elected general secretary.[57]

Although Beijing did not publicly praise the Romanian dictator when he ordered his troops to open fire on human rights demonstrators in Timisoara, China's leaders were probably disturbed by the speed with which events then unfolded in late December, 1989—the revolt of Romanian military, Ceausescu's attempted flight, capture, trial, and execution. It was not only concern about the grim fate for their last European ally. The domestic implications were chilling—that even support from the security apparatus might not be enough and that popular vengeance against the party leadership was a potential outcome of demonstrations. The regime ordered a tightening of security at major Beijing universities, arrested protesters in front of a government TV building, and put security forces on alert to quell possible worker protests.[58] Concern about the army's role in Ceausescu's downfall led to heightened indoctrination within military units. Aside from a few posters at Beijing University and phone calls of celebration and support to the Romanian embassy, however, Chinese students took no action in response to the Romanian crisis.

Although specific evidence is elusive, it seems likely that events in eastern Europe contributed to the party leadership's unwillingness to undertake any further efforts at easing its crackdown internally or cooperating with the United States externally. Given the still restive situation on university campuses and in urban factories, a stagnant economy, a serious intraparty dispute about reform and opening, and strained leadership relations, the less risky course was to maintain iron-fisted control, regardless of foreign consequences. The regime took the safer course—a hard line on everything. According to Gilley, "Within the party, . . . Ceausescus's sudden and violent death sparked a clear hard-line response. The party leadership now asserted its opposition to even moderate political reform, which was blamed for precipitating the changes in Eastern Europe."[59]

Inside China, the collapse of east European communism played into an already serious rift between those who believed that major reform of the Communist Party's philosophy and style of governing needed to continue, and those who believed that the reforms had brought in dangerous ideas from the West and needed to be halted. The debate had simmered since 1978, when Deng Xiaoping engineered a change in the party's work focus from ideological purification—Mao's goal—to the practical improvement of China's economy and the standard of living of the Chinese people. Deng's approach—rendered in common Chinese numerological fashion—was called "one center and two basic points." "Economic construction is the core of national work; on the one hand, we pursue reform and the open-door policy; on the other, we uphold the 'Four Cardinal Principles.'"[60]

Although Deng's pragmatic viewpoint was welcomed by most party members and was greeted with relief by people weary of Mao's constant mass campaigns, it was not always easy to put into practice, and the habit of filtering all policy ideas through Marxist-Leninist-Maoist orthodoxy was one that led to nearly constant debate and disagreement. Many of the party elders were highly wary of the Western-style economic reforms that Deng and his followers proposed, such as free markets, foreign investment zones, private enterprise, and bankruptcy for failed state enterprises. They believed that planned economy theories were fundamentally sound and just needed to be practiced more rigorously to prove their value. They feared the potential chaos of uncontrolled markets and the economic leverage that foreign countries could get were they permitted to invest in China. For them, the capitalist West was implacably hostile to China and socialism and would take every opportunity to undermine and subvert them. Understanding ideological debates in China is a difficult task for non-Marxist observers. It is hard enough to understand equating "leftists" with "conservatives" (the latter preferring to conserve Mao's basically left-leaning system of social engineering) and "rightists" with "reformers." Moreover, it is difficult to assess how seriously to take apparent ideological arguments, since they are sometimes the accepted political cover for interpersonal or factional clashes within the leadership. Worse still, because open ideological disagreements have not been permitted in China's party-controlled press, fundamental disputes are often disguised as debates over philosophical points, historical figures, or artistic trends. The authors of such articles frequently use pen names and seldom directly attack their target by name. While obscure to foreign observers, these arcane disputes have been a central feature of leadership contests in China.

In the post-Tiananmen period, and especially after the dissolution of socialist regimes in eastern Europe, China's ideological debate was somewhat more direct, asking whether the reforms carried out or considered by the disgraced Zhao Ziyang were "surnamed socialist" or "surnamed capitalist" and whether Zhao had been sufficiently wary of the perils of "bourgeois liberalization." It did not take much imagination, however, to understand that criticism of Zhao and Hu Yaobang could be construed as criticism of Deng Xiaoping.

It is extremely difficult to trace in detail the effect of ideological disputes on specific policy initiatives, given the many factors that affect policy outcomes. This is especially true with foreign policy, which has been more or less insulated from the turbulence of Chinese domestic politics. Generally speaking, ideological disputes tend to freeze policy initiatives in place, sustain a status quo approach, and generate ideologically "safe" positions on important issues. As far as the United States was concerned, the ideologically safe position was one of limited cooperation, accompanied by harsh rhetoric and an insistence that the United States make the key concessions in bilateral disputes. The brief interlude of step-by-step improvement of U.S.-China relations was thus a casualty of east European unrest. Scowcroft speculated later that "when Ceausescu fell, I think the Chinese . . . said, 'We can't afford to let up at all.' Because the roadmap [for restoring relations] just stopped. No explanation."[61] Nixon also knew it was over as soon as Ceausescu fell, telling Michel Oksenberg, "There goes everything we tried to work for in China."[62] The Bush administration acknowledged in March that it was "deeply disappointed" in China's response to the Scowcroft-Eagleburger efforts to improve relations and indicated no new initiatives were likely any time soon.[63]

Fang Lizhi Again and the MFN Debate

In April, however, Ambassador Lilley was called to the Foreign Ministry and asked to resume discussions on the release of Fang Lizhi. Although the deliberations and process for that decision are unknown, most observers—including Lilley—believed the growing threat of a revocation of China's most favored nation (MFN) trade status by the U.S. Congress played a large part in reviving negotiations for Fang's release.[64] China's MFN status also became a dominant issue in how the United States dealt with China for the ensuing decade.

Most favored nation treatment (now referred to as *normal trade relations* status) essentially means that the exports of a country receiving MFN treatment will not be subjected to discriminatory tariffs or exclusionary rules different from those of any other country, or in other words, treatment will be equal to that provided the most favored nation.[65] The United States routinely provided MFN treatment to all its trade partners after 1934. In 1951, Congress passed the Trade Agreements Extension Act of 1951 (P.L. 82-50), which required the president to suspend MFN status for the Soviet Union and all communist bloc countries, which then included the People's Republic of China. President Harry S. Truman suspended MFN for China in September of that year. In 1974, Congress passed the Trade Act of 1974 (much amended since then), Title IV of which provided conditions under which so-called nonmarket economies could qualify for MFN treatment. They were the successful negotiation of a bilateral trade agreement approved by Congress and compliance with freedom-of-emigration provisions of the Jackson-Vanik amendment (sec. 402) of the Trade Act. Those provisions were aimed at easing Soviet proscriptions against certain citizens (most notably Jews) emigrating to another country. The president may formally certify that the country in question does not block emigration or may waive the requirement for full compliance under certain conditions.

The MFN treatment for a nonmarket economy can continue in force if the trade agreement is renewed under satisfactory conditions every three years and if the president recommends by midyear that the waiver authority be maintained. Extension is automatic unless Congress enacts a joint resolution of disapproval.[66] President Jimmy Carter—having completed a trade agreement with China in July 1979—extended Jackson-Vanik waivers to China after Congress approved the trade agreement, and China was granted MFN status on February 1, 1980. It was automatically renewed every year through 1989.

Following their failure to override President Bush's veto of the Pelosi bill, members of Congress interested in punishing China for Tiananmen and its aftermath met with Chinese students and human rights groups to consider other legislative means to offset the Bush administration approach. From meetings held in early January between congressional staffers and Chinese student representatives, the idea gradually took shape that the most effective way to pressure China was to move against its MFN status.[67] Congresswoman Nancy Pelosi initiated an informal congressional "working group" in March that began considering the possibilities for changing China's MFN treatment.

At first, activists recommended outright revocation. Subsequently, however, a "compromise" position, involving the establishment of *conditions* under which MFN would be renewed in the future, gained support. Several bills calling for each approach were introduced into the House and Senate in 1990. One, introduced by Representative Donald Pease of Ohio, was actually passed by the House in October, but was not taken up by the Senate and so expired.[68] But as James Mann points out, the problem with a conditioned approach to MFN was that there were many different ideas of what conditions should be applied.[69] Some representatives favored conditions pertaining to the treatment of Tibet, some wanted amnesty for Tiananmen demonstrators, some a cessation of prison labor exports, some wanted a reduction in religious persecution, others stressed abortion and China's one-child policy, while still others wanted conditions added that would stop China's sale of nuclear materials or missile technology to other nations or force it to cut off its support for Khmer Rouge guerrillas in Cambodia. The Pease bill, which passed the House by a vote of 384-30, proposed that MFN not be extended unless the president submitted a report to Congress stating that China had released all Tiananmen prisoners and had made "progress in reversing gross violations of human rights; terminating martial law (including in Tibet); easing restrictions on freedom of the press and on broadcasts by Voice of America; terminating harassment of Chinese citizens in the United States; removing obstacles to study and travel abroad for students and other citizens; taking appropriate action to observe internationally recognized human rights, including an end to religious persecution there and in Tibet; and adhering to the Joint Declaration on Hong Kong that was entered into between the United Kingdom and it in 1984." The bill also included a "sense of the Congress" section (Title II) that recommended a code of conduct for American businesses operating in China.[70]

Although the administration offered no support for such legislation, the approach gained some public support, including from former ambassador Winston Lord, who testified in favor of conditioned MFN as early as May 1990. The formal resolution of disapproval of the president's decision to extend MFN passed the House in October, but only by a vote of 247-174, well short of the two-thirds majority needed to override a promised Bush veto. The Senate, therefore, did not take up the proposal.

According to Ambassador Lilley, he and others negotiating the conditions for Fang Lizhi's release stressed the congressional threat to China's trade privileges as an incentive to get the Chinese to relent on Fang. Bush's message to the Chinese was that he might well lose the MFN extension vote if China did not do something to help him out. The point was essentially the same one Scowcroft and Eagleburger had made in their July visit of 1989, but this time there was something more tangible than positively influencing American public opinion at stake—dollars and cents. Revocation of MFN would have meant an increase of punitive duties on more than 95 percent of China's exports to the United States (over $18 billion in 1989, with a trade surplus of more than $6.2 billion).[71] In a period when Beijing's austerity program and popular discontent with government policies had led to a drop in economic growth and a reduction in international loans to China, the decline in competitiveness in their biggest market would have been a serious blow for China's economy. As the June 3 date for announcing MFN and the first anniversary of Tiananmen approached, Bush temporized while Congress seethed, looking for ways to punish China's intransigence.

There is, of course, no available public record of Beijing's deliberations on what to do about this issue or about China's larger diplomatic and economic isolation. There is some evidence to support the notion that Beijing made a deliberate decision to trade Tiananmen prisoners for an attenuation of sanctions. The first indication was the January "release" of more than 500 prisoners, which was discounted in Washington. On May 11, perhaps in an effort to improve its image and prospects for MFN renewal, Beijing released 211 Tiananmen prisoners. After Bush's announcement on June 3 that he would renew MFN, it released another 97.

But Fang Lizhi was different. Fang had become a symbolic figure—the embodiment of democratic opposition. To release him without subjecting him to Chinese justice would gladden democratic activists and embolden others to continue their resistance. Fang was the ward of America, the proof of its interference in China's domestic affairs. To release him in the face of American economic threats would be to perpetuate those threats and would be read as a sign that China was buckling in the face of American economic pressure, which might even bring about further pressure. Moreover, Fang was Deng's bête noire, his antagonist. To release him would be a great loss of face for Deng and for the entire leadership. These and other arguments simmered as the terms of Fang's release were negotiated, although the extent of disagreements among the leadership only became evident later.

Fang did not make things any easier. He refused to plead guilty or confess to any of the charges against him. He had to be persuaded to accept some of the minor conditions for his release that the United States was negotiating in his behalf, such as claiming to need medical attention overseas, not going directly to the United States after his release, and agreeing not to engage in "anti-China" activities.

But finally, on June 25, China granted Fang Lizhi permission to leave China for "medical treatment" and after showing "signs of repentance," Fang and his wife, Li Shuxian, boarded a U.S. Air Force transport plane that took them to England, where Fang had been offered an appointment by the Royal Society to pursue his research and teach at Cambridge University.[72] In a brief press statement, Bush's press secretary, Marlin Fitzwater, said, "This humanitarian action is a farsighted, significant step that will improve the atmosphere for progress in our bilateral relations."[73] Fang, although he had written a letter to the authorities, was hardly repentant, certainly was not ill, and had no intention of staying in England. By mid-July, he announced he would be moving to the United States, publicly denied he was in any way in need of medical treatment, promised to continue supporting the democratic movement in China, and accused President Bush of having a "double standard" on democracy in China, compared to that for eastern Europe.[74]

Although the resolution of the Fang Lizhi case did give both sides the opportunity to work on the relationship free of its most immediately contentious issue, neither side was ready to take another step forward. In China, Deng was not able to sustain an initiative, while Li Peng, as head of the Foreign Affairs Small Group, seemed to take the view that China did not need the United States. He and Foreign Minister Qian became more actively engaged in repairing relations with other countries to ease China's isolation. Qian and others traveled widely, promoting China's visibility and taking the initiative in solving long-standing disputes with countries on its borders. China established formal diplomatic relations with Saudi Arabia, Indonesia, and Singapore in 1990, and laid the groundwork for further improvements in relations with South Korea, India, and the USSR.

The release of Fang did not provide any "bounce" or encouragement for policymakers in Washington. For many of them, China had lost its appeal and was now considered merely a supporting player in international affairs. For the president and his national security adviser, China had become little more than a source of domestic political pain, its strategic significance diminished by its incapacity, the meltdown of communism in eastern Europe, and the president's improved relationship with Gorbachev. Secretary of State Baker had little regard for China and left the problems for Deputy Secretary Eagleburger to work. He took special delight in flying over China—without stopping—to visit places like Mongolia and the USSR.[75] For Assistant Secretary of State Richard Solomon, finding a peace accord in Cambodia became his principal task, and China helped to build a consensus among the permanent members of the Security Council. But for other observers, China was the arms supplier and principal supporter for the detested Khmer Rouge—yet another example of the Chinese government being on the wrong side of an issue.

The Gulf War—Short-Term Gain, Long-Term Strain

Saddam Hussein's decision to invade Kuwait on August 2, 1990, provided an opportunity for the United States and China to cooperate on an international crisis of importance to both sides. Assistant Secretary of State Richard Solomon flew immediately to Beijing for consultations, which proved fruitful. Both countries agreed that Iraq's action contravened acceptable norms of international behavior and joined quickly in passing a United Nations Security Council (UNSC) resolution calling on Baghdad to withdraw immediately or face mandatory sanctions. China also imposed an arms embargo on Iraq on August 5 and supported a UN ban on trade with Iraq on the following day. When President Bush ordered U.S. warships to the Persian Gulf to enforce the embargo, however, China (and other countries) balked. As it considered its next steps, China's ideologically based approach to the United States came to the fore, and cooperation became more difficult. Although it ultimately voted in favor of a UNSC resolution in late August to authorize enforcement of the blockade, China began to push its own agenda in the deliberations.

According to Chen You-wei, who worked for China's Foreign Ministry during this period,[76] Jiang Zemin called the Politburo Standing Committee into session three times during August to discuss the Persian Gulf. Jiang turned almost exclusively to Foreign Minister Qian Qichen and the Ministry of Foreign Affairs to analyze the issue and provide policy guidance. Qian's assessment reflected the suspicion of U.S. motives that characterized China's response to virtually all U.S. initiatives: the United States was not resisting Iraq's aggression in principle but was pursuing a "hegemonistic"[77] goal of controlling Persian Gulf oil resources; China would not support U.S. military activities in support of the embargo, nor would it support a joint UN force; China did not think the United States could fight a desert war effectively and would not mind seeing the United States get entrapped in the region; and the United States would need China's help to extricate itself from the conflict, which might benefit China. While Chen's "insider" account cannot be verified from other sources, it is plausible and fits with China's behavior at the time.

Aside from its "principled" and long-standing opposition to the use of force by coalitions of other nations to resolve disputes, China seemed to be maneuvering to enhance its own reputation at the United Nations. It was interested in working with the five permanent members of the UN Security Council (China, France, the Soviet Union/Russia, the United Kingdom, and the United States) and cooperated fully with the "P-5 Committee" to craft language for the UNSC resolutions on Iraq and the Cambodia Peace Plan, announced at the end of August. Within the P-5, China tried to maximize its credentials as a third world nation better able to represent some of the smaller Middle Eastern countries. It may have hoped its contribution toward a peaceful resolution of the problem would put it in position to press the European Union (EU) and the United States for reduction of post-Tiananmen sanctions.[78]

More important, if less tangibly, Beijing was trying to restore its self-image through the affirmation of its importance as a major power and conferral of respect on its dignitaries and diplomats. Publicity for these events was important to shore up the regime's tattered image within China. Western interpretations that China was simply looking for the lifting of sanctions against international lending are not incorrect—without doubt, the lack of World Bank, Japanese, EU, and U.S. financing of development projects in China contributed to its economic malaise. But the desire to show TV pictures of Chinese leaders—some of whom were reviled domestically—being celebrated internationally cannot be underestimated. Through diplomacy, the leadership was trying to accelerate the process of restoring its legitimacy.

Certainly that factor must have influenced the rather odd behavior of Foreign Minister Qian in November of 1990. American expectations of China at that point were minimal. As Secretary Baker put it, "By 1990, given the overwhelmingly hostile climate toward China in the aftermath of the Tiananmen Square massacre, any significant overtures to thaw the Sino-American relationship were neither justified nor possible. We were not willing simply to write off China, however. As a result, the emphasis in our policy shifted toward multilateral opportunities, where we could deal with the Chinese in a larger and less controversial context on issues of mutual interest."[79] The principal goal was to dissuade China from vetoing any of the UN resolutions that provided necessary cover for the Middle Eastern nations participating in the U.S.-led coalition to force Iraq out of Kuwait. Washington had already put together the coalition and was making the military preparations. Working patiently with Russian, French, and Chinese dilatory tactics had been frustrating but necessary. By November, the final UN resolution was ready—one that set an actual deadline for Iraqi troops to be withdrawn from Kuwait and authorized the use of force if they were not. The Bush administration wanted it not only for international affirmation and to persuade Saddam Hussein of the gravity of American resolve, but also to use against congressional critics who vigorously opposed the use of force in the Persian Gulf.

On November 7, Baker met Qian in Cairo and received a preliminary indication that China would not block passage of a resolution authorizing the use of force. But Qian's language was cryptic, both in his ninety-minute meeting with Baker and with the press later. "I think all the resolutions adopted by the United Nations are intended to increase the pressure on Iraq so as to achieve a peaceful settlement," Qian told eager journalists. Some observers interpreted what he said as leaving open the possibility that China would vote for the resolution.[80] Li Peng drew Ambassador Lilley aside privately two or three days later and clarified the situation, "As a matter of principle, we will never vote for the use of force resolution. This is a matter of principle to us. We are not going to do it. Please explain this to your people." Lilley passed the message on to Baker, who evidently ignored it.[81]

On November 19, Baker called Qian from his hotel room in Paris to try and persuade him to vote for the resolution. He read the U.S. draft resolution over the phone and asked how China was going to vote. Qian demurred, having not even raised the issue within the leadership small group. Evidently as a deal sweetener, Baker invited Qian to visit Washington on November 30, after the Security Council session, saying the president would be leaving for a Latin American tour the following day.[82] Qian happily accepted, probably thinking that he would be meeting President Bush. On November 24, Qian met with Soviet Foreign Minister Eduard Shevardnadze in Xinjiang but remained publicly noncommittal on China's vote on the UN resolution.

American diplomats still held out the hope that China would support the resolution.

On November 26, the day his visit to Washington was announced (although not a meeting with Bush), Qian publicly labeled as "groundless" reports that China would support the resolution. But he also indicated China would not veto it. Curiously, observers in the press and the State Department seemed to ignore the possibility of an abstention and continued to call Qian's position "ambiguous."[83] That same day, an American diplomat met with the head of the Ministry of Foreign Affairs Information Department, Liu Huaqiu, and informed him that only a vote in support would get a meeting with the president. An abstention would mean no Washington trip. After consulting with Beijing—where there was opposition to his going to Washington to "kowtow"—Qian eventually responded that if there was no Washington trip, he would not attend the Security Council session.[84] On November 27, State Department Deputy Spokesman Richard Boucher announced that Qian would be meeting with Baker but as a "contact," not as a formal exchange, which had been banned after Tiananmen. The game of sliding invitations had now become a game of diplomatic chicken.

On November 29, with Baker in the chair at the UN Security Council meeting, Qian abstained on the vote, saying China "has difficulty voting in favor of this draft resolution" owing to its threat to resort to armed force.[85] The final tally was twelve votes in favor, two opposed, and one abstention. Despite the overwhelming Security Council vote and lack of a Chinese veto, Baker was furious, feeling he had been misled by Qian.[86] He therefore had the chief of the Office of Chinese and Mongolian Affairs, Kent Wiedemann, inform the Chinese embassy that Qian's visit was to be described as a "private visit," not even a contact. Baker told Qian at dinner on November 30 that, although he had tried, he could not get him on the president's schedule. Qian, in his turn, was outraged. After consulting with Beijing, he had Ambassador Zhu Qizhen call China Desk Chief Wiedemann after midnight to find out before 7:00 a.m. whether the president would see him. If not, he would not come to Washington. Zhu made a similar call to NSC Asia director Douglas Paal at 1:00 a.m., demanding to speak with Scowcroft. Scowcroft took the call about 3:00 a.m. and agreed that Qian could see Bush. He cleared the decision with the president three hours later. As he explained in his memoir, "I was only dimly aware of the understanding [with Secretary Baker] about the arrangements, but we did not need an international crisis in the wake of our UN success."[87]

So Qian got his photo opportunity with the president on December 1, which was displayed prominently in all the major Chinese newspapers. Significantly, the half-hour meeting was not held in the Oval Office but in the

Cabinet Room. But Baker got to set the agenda and prepared the talking points for the president's meetings. And he put American concerns at the very top, namely, human rights, missile proliferation, and intellectual property rights. He insisted the president make a strong presentation on human rights and that any follow-up meetings should be devoted to working on that issue and the problems of Chinese proliferation. He had already, in his own two-hour session with Qian, requested that Assistant Secretary of State for Human Rights and Humanitarian Issues Richard Schifter and Reginald Bartholomew, undersecretary for International Security Affairs, as well as Assistant U.S. Trade Representative Joseph Massey, should make separate trips to China to work on details of problem areas. Qian had assented. Bush again appealed to Qian that China had to "help him out" against congressional critics by making progress on human rights issues and indicated he would consider inviting Jiang Zemin to the United States in response.[88] In public, he indicated that there could be no progress in the bilateral relationship unless China improved its human rights record.

Both sides put the best face on the incident, each telling the public that the visit was evidence of the need for a more normal relationship, each telling insiders that there was resentment about the way the other side had handled things, each telling the other that it was principally responsible for taking steps to improve the relationship. And in setting out a preliminary road map for ensuing visits and issues to be discussed, Qian's meetings made some progress in restoring some communication. But they could hardly be considered a breakthrough. Behind the niceties of diplomacy, powerful domestic forces were pushing the two governments further apart.

As the massive buildup of U.S. forces in the Persian Gulf region continued, along with concomitant U.S. determination to use them to drive Iraqi forces from Kuwait, China's sense of alarm grew and its cooperation with the U.S.-led alliance decreased. After the air attacks on Baghdad began in mid-January, China stepped up its support for Soviet efforts to find a negotiated solution to the conflict, efforts that many American officials resented as pro-Iraqi interference. Chinese spokesmen began talking about "the two belligerent parties," suggesting a moral equivalence between Iraqi troops in Kuwait and American-led forces in Saudi Arabia. In early February, word leaked out that Deng Xiaoping had described the situation as "big hegemonists beating up small hegemonists."[89] Despite this increasing "tilt" toward Iraq, U.S. policy toward China did not change. As then-deputy assistant secretary of defense Carl Ford recalled it, China's actions "didn't seem to be an important issue" among Defense Department planners. They knew much of Iraq's armor and artillery had come from China, but "it wasn't that big a deal."[90] As far as the Middle East was concerned, China was a nonplayer.

For the PLA, however, what the U.S. military did in the Gulf War was a very big deal indeed; it was an enormous shock. The "revolution in military affairs" that had been taking place in the U. S. armed forces—so startlingly and vividly displayed first during the high-tech air war over Baghdad, then with the swift and methodical crushing of Iraqi ground forces after February 23—caught the Chinese off guard. U.S. technological superiority over Iraq's Chinese-made weapons was overwhelming and led to expressions of great concern in China's chain of command, about the inferiority of China's military technology and about the costs of equipping China's armed forces to be able to deal with the U.S. threat.[91] In the wake of the Gulf War, the PLA high command overhauled China's entire concept of warfare, adopting the development slogan of preparing to fight "modern local wars under high-tech conditions" and ordering weapons procurement, military education, training, and doctrinal programs to adjust to the new situation.[92] In most of its training exercises, the anticipated aggressor force, the expected enemy, was the United States.

Beijing also must have been concerned by the popular Chinese support shown for the American side in the Persian Gulf conflict. Books, television programs, and newspapers devoted a great deal of attention to the war—the high-tech wizardry of pinpoint bombing, stealth aircraft, electronic countermeasures, cruise missiles—much of it positive. China had officially condemned the Iraqi invasion of Kuwait, so wishing America well against Saddam Hussein was not prohibited. Some Chinese citizens even sent small contributions to Ambassador Lilley to support the American effort.

Whatever Chinese citizens' views of American operations in the Persian Gulf, China's leaders chose the most intense period of the conflict to deal with some of their most controversial dissident cases. Perhaps in a deliberate retort to the American request for amnesty for 150 Tiananmen prisoners, raised by Assistant Secretary Schifter in late December, China publicized the trial and sentencing of a number of student leaders and intellectuals from early January through early March 1991. The students, even leaders of the Tiananmen protests, usually received somewhat lighter sentences. Wang Dan and Guo Haifeng, for example, each were sentenced to four years in prison for "counterrevolutionary propaganda and incitement." Some others, including Liu Xiaobo, were released without trial. Heavier sentences were meted out to the students' intellectual mentors and advisers: Bao Zunxin, a Beida historian, received five years; 1979 democracy activist Ren Wanding was sentenced to seven; economist Chen Ziming and journalist Wang Juntao each got thirteen years for "counterrevolutionary activities," "incitement to subversion," and resisting martial law authorities. In April, China's supreme court chief justice told the National People's Congress that the trials of Tiananmen demonstrators were "basically completed."[93]

Suspicions that these trials were rushed to conclusion while the Bush administration's attention was focused on the Gulf War made the reaction from U.S. human rights groups and members of Congress that much more bitter. Editorialists and human rights organizations condemned China's court system and its human rights record. Li Peng, on a visit to Europe, provided additional ammunition for China's critics by portraying the armed crackdown as necessary and correct and justifying the government's refusal to account for civilian casualties—as had been promised in 1989—because the families of the victims did not wish to have their relatives associated with a "counterrevolutionary rebellion."[94] Meanwhile, U.S. intelligence agencies reported that China was seeking to sell advanced missile systems to Pakistan and other Middle Eastern countries and was providing nuclear assistance to Algeria, contrary to its 1984 pledge to sell nuclear-related equipment only to countries that permitted International Atomic Energy Agency inspections.[95] The Office of the U.S.Trade Representative (USTR), moreover, charged that China was increasing nontariff barriers to U.S. goods while promoting Chinese exports, causing the U.S. trade deficit to rise to $10.4 billion in 1990. It threatened punitive sanctions unless China took steps to improve market access for American companies.[96] The stage was set for another battle over MFN between the president and Congress.

Bush Fights, Then Retreats

When Secretary of State James Baker pressed Chinese Foreign Minister Qian, during his December 1990 meeting in the White House, to accept three U.S. officials for consultations, he was, in effect, signaling two important changes in the Bush administration's policy toward China. First, that the administration was moving from an approach focused on trying to restore strategic ties with the PRC regime to one designed to pressure Beijing into altering its behavior in certain important areas—namely, human rights, nonproliferation, and trade. Second, Baker was promoting a substantive agenda that was very similar to that of the U.S. Congress, although the means by which the administration would seek to achieve its goals were much different. Baker and others at the State Department were probably animated by the realization that Congress was gearing up to pass major legislation on China's MFN status in 1991, and with a slightly larger Democratic Party majority in the House as a result of the 1990 midterm elections, the administration was in for an even rougher time.

The 102d Congress came in determined to change the president's China policy. It intended to do so by manipulating the president's decision on China's most favored nation trade status. Congressional persistence in taking a contrarian stand on this issue is not altogether easy to grasp:

—China was not, for example, a constituency issue. Although some very vocal citizens pressed representatives and senators on various China issues, there was no evidence in the 1990 elections that China was an important campaign issue—certainly no contests turned on China policy questions.

—Nor was it a partisan issue. Some Democratic Party leaders in the House and Senate used the China issue to attack President Bush, but they did not broaden it into an overall condemnation of his foreign policy. Neither did they bargain China votes with the administration for other legislative issues. But a majority of congressional Republicans also voted against Bush on China questions, except when veto override issues came up, and they were called on to demonstrate party solidarity.

—Lobbying was intense on the MFN question and became more so as the struggle was repeated year after year. On the side of those wishing to curtail or condition MFN, for example, were ad hoc groups of Chinese students and well-established human rights organizations, such as Amnesty International, the Lawyers Committee for Human Rights, Asia Watch (later Human Rights Watch-Asia), the Campaign for Tibet, and others. Business groups—such as the American Chamber of Commerce, the Business Roundtable, and other representatives of large U.S. corporations operating in China—also became more involved in lobbying for extension of MFN for China, but they were not able, at least during the Bush administration, to prevent conditioning legislation from passing by overwhelming margins. Lobbying was important in framing the issue; in calling attention to new information on Chinese human rights, trade, and nonproliferation violations; and in providing policy analysis but was not crucial to the outcome of the voting.[97]

—Influential American media, such as the *New York Times* and *Washington Post*, were overwhelmingly critical of China in their editorial pages and supportive of conditioned extension of MFN from about March 1991 forward. Editorials and regular op-ed commentaries by syndicated columnists, such as A. M. Rosenthal and Leslie Gelb of the *New York Times*, and Jim Hoagland, Mary McGrory, Hobart Rowen, and David Broder at the *Washington Post* also supported taking stronger steps to "register the aversion most Americans feel to China's anti-democratic and anti-human rights policies, to its suspect arms and technology exports and to its disregard for normal trading rules."[98] Such views contributed to a climate of hostility and distrust toward China that affected both Congress and the administration, but there is no reason to believe these opinion makers were especially influential on legislation pertaining to China.

China, for many members of Congress, had come to be seen as the epitome of everything the United States opposed in international affairs: a tyrannical government, oppressing democracy at every turn; intolerant of religion, whether Christian or Buddhist; a mercantilist trade cheat, closing its own market while dumping low-cost, pirated, and prison labor–made goods in the United States to expand its trade surplus; an uncontrolled proliferator of weapons of mass destruction, selling dangerous technology and weapons to unstable governments that threatened U.S. interests; a rising military threat to U.S. allies and friends in the Asia-Pacific, expanding its military reach with ever-growing budgets; a murderer of unborn children, forcing abortions and sterilizations to meet family planning quotas. Whether those formulaic perceptions accorded with reality or not (and some clearly were exaggerations), they were strongly held by congressional leaders. And during the two or three years following Tiananmen, they were reinforced by events reported from China—arrests, executions, sales of nuclear materials, threats to stop buying American goods, and so on. Moreover, the Chinese leadership's stiff-necked resistance to admitting any of these flaws or accepting that any foreign country had the right to criticize them only inflamed the critics further. As a result, many members of Congress and their staffs were determined to take action—any action—against China or against the Bush administration, which they viewed as being perversely blind to China's faults.

As the June deadline approached for declaring whether the United States would extend MFN to China, Congress tried to block it. On May 2, Representative Nancy Pelosi submitted a bill (H.R. 2212, later known as the United States–China Act of 1991) that again would establish strict conditions for China to be accorded MFN treatment. (Majority Leader George Mitchell introduced a similar bill in the Senate on May 16). The bill began with the finding that "the Government of the People's Republic of China . . . continues to engage in flagrant violations of internationally recognized human rights, . . . is engaging in unfair trade practices against the United States . . ., [and] has not demonstrated its willingness and intention to participate as a full and responsible party in good faith efforts to control the proliferation of dangerous military technology and weapons."[99] Then the bill set out "additional objectives which the Government of China must meet in order to receive nondiscriminatory [MFN] treatment." The act prohibited the president from recommending a continuation of MFN unless he reported to Congress that China had accounted for all those arrested and sentenced for Tiananmen, released those still imprisoned, and made "overall significant progress" in several elements of its human rights, trade, and nonproliferation policies.

Among the actions China was called upon to take were ending all religious persecution, removing restrictions on freedom of the press, terminating prohibitions on peaceful assembly and demonstration, providing American exporters fair access to the Chinese market, and ceasing activities inconsistent with international control regimes for missile, nuclear, and chemical weapons.[100]

President Bush took his own preemptive action, telling first Republican legislators and then reporters on May 15 that he intended to renew MFN for China, evidently before his advisers were expecting it. His press spokesman later insisted that no "formal" decision had yet been made, but Bush left little room for doubt in his remarks to reporters. "I want to see MFN for China and I made a strong pitch for it [to the Members of Congress]. We do not want to isolate China."[101] Fitzwater implied the following day that the administration was not entirely opposed to "adding conditions or at least expressing our views about human rights progress in China."[102] Less than two weeks later, however, Bush announced he would attach no conditions on MFN. But he added an additional justification, indicating he had moved closer toward a values-oriented China policy, "It is right to export the ideals of freedom and democracy to China. . . . It comes down to the strength of our belief in the power of the democratic idea. If we pursue a policy that cultivates contacts with the Chinese people, promotes commerce to our benefit, we can help create a climate for democratic change."[103]

Another administration official told *Washington Post* reporter Don Oberdorfer that Bush's unconditional renewal was a "tactical" decision, made in the knowledge that he "eventually . . . may have to accept some conditions due to the strong views in Congress against an extension."[104] Senate Democratic Majority Leader George Mitchell immediately attacked Bush's decision as "without any moral or logical basis" and vowed Congress would fight to overturn it.[105]

But while it was maintaining an open-handed approach on MFN issues, the administration began turning up the pressure on China in other areas. On April 26, for example, USTR announced it was beginning a special 301 investigation of China's pirating of American pharmaceuticals, software, music, and books, under the newly expanded authority granted in the Omnibus Trade and Competitiveness Act of 1988.[106] The American software industry had been pressing for such an investigation, estimating that its losses to pirated Chinese software in 1988 amounted to over $300 million.[107] China was the first nation cited as a "priority foreign country" under the special 301 provisions, and USTR called for negotiations with the clearly implied threat that it would impose tariff increases of up to 100 percent on selected categories of China's exports to the United States, up to and above the estimated damage to U.S. trade by the piracy.

On April 30, presidential spokesman Marlin Fitzwater announced that the administration would prohibit licenses for the sale of U.S.-origin equipment for the *Dongfanghong-3*, a communications satellite being built in China. The suspension was in response to intelligence reports that China was preparing to sell M-9 600km-range missiles to Syria and M-11 intermediate-range ballistic missiles to Pakistan and had secretly built a nuclear reactor for Algeria.[108] Alarmed at the possibility that China might be expanding its already troublesome weapons-of-mass-destruction sales program, Secretary of State Baker sent Undersecretary of State for Political Affairs Robert Kimmitt and Undersecretary of State for International Security Affairs Reginald Bartholomew to Beijing in May and June with tough warnings. "We have made it clear that there would be potentially profound consequences for our bilateral relationship if they were to change the missile export policies that they might have represented to us," Baker was quoted as saying.[109]

Although initially harsh, China's response to the dispatch of two senior U.S. officials to Beijing began to thaw a relationship that had again fallen into a deep freeze. Chinese officials admitted to Kimmitt that Beijing had indeed agreed to sell "short-range, tactical missiles" to Pakistan, but insisted their range fell within the guidelines of the missile technology control regime (MTCR) (a dubious claim, since an earlier sales brochure advertised a payload of 800 kg).[110] They also told Kimmitt that the Algerian reactor was a small research reactor not intended for the production of weapons-grade fissile material and would eventually be placed under international safeguards. They told Bartholomew that China was considering adhering to the MTCR guidelines and was preparing to join the Non-Proliferation Treaty.[111] In August, Premier Li Peng told Japan's prime minister, Toshiki Kaifu (the first Western head of state to visit post-Tiananmen China), that Beijing had decided "in principle" to sign the NPT, a pledge the Bush administration immediately welcomed.

As the MFN debate in Congress heated up, China took some contradictory steps in response. On some occasions, they made crude threats: Ambassador Zhu Qizhen, for example, said that China would "use high tariffs to drive American companies out of its markets," costing the United States billions of dollars and thousands of jobs.[112] At the end of June, Premier Li Peng threatened the Boeing Company that it would lose all its contracts if MFN were not renewed.[113] Later, China sent two buying missions to the United States, which contracted for more that $1.2 billion worth of U.S. agricultural and manufactured products. Beijing also hired a Washington-based lobbying firm to help it present its case to members of Congress. In his book, *Inside Stories of the Diplomacy between Communist China and America*, former Chinese embassy official Chen You-wei claims China spent about $4 million for the Hill and Knowlton contract but only kept it for about six months, believing afterward it did not need professional help.[114]

Bush was facing two actions in Congress, one a resolution of disapproval of his MFN decision (H.R. 263, sponsored by Representative Gerald Solomon of New York), the other the Pelosi-sponsored United States–China Act (H.R. 2212), which set numerous conditions on renewal of MFN. As expected, both bills passed the House of Representatives on roll call votes, the MFN disapproval bill by 223-204, the MFN conditions by 313-112. As in the earlier Pelosi bill vote, the key battle was in the Senate, and the administration worked very hard to gain the thirty-four votes needed to block a veto override of HR 2212 (the Solomon bill was not taken up by the Senate).

Aside from the usual meetings and phone calls, Bush responded to a letter he had received from fifteen senators from both parties, asking him to "take appropriate action" against China to redress its unfair trade practices and to restrict missile sales to Pakistan. The principal drafter of the letter was Senator Max Baucus, a pro-MFN Democrat from Montana, who had discussed the letter in advance with the White House.[115] Bush's reply, timed just before the Senate took up the conditions bill in late July, pledged that the administration would impose tough new sanctions if China did not take substantial measures to improve its trade practices and said it would work to facilitate Taiwan's entry into the General Agreement on Tariffs and Trade (GATT). It was more vague on what it would do with respect to human rights and nonproliferation issues, leading Majority Leader Mitchell to dismiss the letter as "mostly rhetoric."[116] The Senate passed the conditioned MFN bill on July 23 by a margin of 55-44, well short of what would be needed to override the expected Bush veto. As the White House had hoped, the vote was nearly a party-line event, with only six Republicans voting for conditions and seven Democrats voting against. The bill then went to a conference committee, which delayed its final disposition by several months. Bush vetoed the measure in early 1992, and the Senate override failed by four votes.

Deng Retreats, Then Charges

In late 1990 and early 1991, Deng Xiaoping might have felt some sympathy for Mao Zedong, who had accused Deng and other party leaders of treating him like a "dead relative" in the period leading up to the Cultural Revolution. Deng was now in a comparable position. Although still active and in relatively good health, the retired elder was having trouble getting his views translated into action by the new leadership he had installed. Deng probably saw clearly the many dilemmas China was facing—nothing was going well.

—The economy, under a deliberate cooling off and austerity program, had slowed to about 5percent GDP growth (which Deng considered too low), foreign investment had declined markedly, price reform had been spiked, as had reforms of state-owned enterprises. Even the agricultural reforms that had begun the reform movement in the late 1970s were being called into question by Chen Yun and his fellow devotees of centralized planning, including Jiang Zemin. China's budget deficit increased 36 percent between 1989 and 1990, and provincial authorities were complaining bitterly about central efforts to increase its share of revenues from local enterprise taxes.[117]

—Although the post-Tiananmen crackdown had effectively squelched all popular resistance to the regime, the police seemed to be having an extraordinarily difficult time rounding up their "most-wanted" dissidents. Many of them, including Chai Ling, Wu'er Kaixi, Feng Congde, Li Lu, Yan Jiaqi, and Chen Yizi, hid in various parts of China for months, then escaped to Hong Kong through a well-funded underground railroad that worked in close cooperation with local police and some of China's most notorious criminal gangs.[118] At the leadership level, Zhao Ziyang refused adamantly to admit that he had made any errors in handling the demonstrations, thereby preventing the party from being able to close the books on the case. Chen Yun quietly leveled criticism against Deng for allowing "bourgeois liberalization" such free rein under Zhao and Hu.

—Efforts to root out demonstrators and "rectify" thinking even in some of the organizations most heavily involved in the protests, such as Beijing University and the Chinese Academy of Social Sciences, met with indifferent success. In sharp contrast to earlier political campaigns in which intellectuals were intimidated into informing on their colleagues, this time there was a sense of solidarity against the party apparatus, with the result that few punishments were meted out and mandatory study sessions were sullen and silent. Students packed off to rural areas or military boot camps before matriculation arrived on campus angry and resentful but not prepared to undertake mass protests again.[119] Within the Communist Party, although nearly 300,000 members were expelled or disciplined in the reregistration campaign that examined every member's behavior during the Tiananmen crisis, that number represented less than 1 percent of the party's 50 million members.[120]

—Not only did the failure and fall of communist parties throughout eastern Europe not abate, but the Soviet Union itself—under Gorbachev and other democratic reformers—became increasingly unsteady in defense of socialism, in Chinese eyes. Although uncertain about Gorbachev and still angry about his role in Tiananmen, China's leaders sent numerous officials—including Jiang Zemin—to Moscow to support the Soviet Communist Party and also to evaluate the leadership situation. They secretly hailed the strengthening of conservative forces. When Russian conservatives attempted to topple Gorbachev on August 19, 1991, Chinese leaders privately called it a "good deed" and quietly supported the conservatives. When Boris Yeltsin brought down the coup plotters two days later, declared the Communist Party illegal, and dissolved the Soviet Union, the Chinese leadership was aghast. But it recovered quickly, using events in Moscow to toughen its opposition to further party democratization. They blamed Gorbachev's "new thinking" and flirtation with the West for the crisis and strengthened China's own campaign against "peaceful evolution."[121]

According to Willy Wo-lap Lam, then a reporter and China watcher for Hong Kong's *South China Morning Post,* Deng remained convinced that a return to reform, not a return to stringent Stalinism, was the key to overcoming the malaise of socialism in China. Gorbachev's failures were manifold but included an inability to bring about an overall improvement in the Russian economy. China had made a good start, but now the effort seemed stalled. Deng recognized that the kinds of economic reforms Zhao Ziyang had carried out were still necessary, perhaps even more so. And so he favored a "quickening" of reform, meaning a faster overall growth rate for the economy as the surest means of satisfying the people's desire for prosperity and an improved standard of living. "Deng, however, had to wage a fierce battle against ideologues and central planners who insisted that the lesson to be drawn from the crumbling of the eastern bloc was that the public sector, or the socialist road, must be shored up." Rather than trying to choose between a market and a planned economy, Deng favored experimentation to try and implement the best attributes of both, an "organic synthesis of a planned economy and market adjustment."[122]

In private meetings in late 1990 and early 1991, Deng began to press more strongly for a return to a reform agenda. But he no longer had ready access to the power mechanisms he needed to get his message across to the larger audience in the party and government. The economic bureaucracies were solidly under the control of Li Peng and Yao Yilin, both of whom favored economic austerity, modest growth rates, and centralized control along lines laid out by Chen Yun. Propaganda was nominally under the supervision of Li Ruihuan, but he had little real influence over the media organs. Propaganda Department Director Wang Renzhi and Deputy Xu Weicheng, *People's Daily* editor in chief Gao Di, and conservative ideologue Deng Liqun fostered a hard-line atmosphere that challenged the ideological underpinnings of reforms in such a way as to prevent reform programs from recovering significant momentum. Deng was somewhat less isolated from the PLA chain of command, but the armed forces were not in a position to initiate economic reform, and their dependence on China's centralized defense industries left them unsympathetic to the kinds of reforms Deng favored. Jiang Zemin probably supported Deng's approach in general, but he was still learning the ropes as party general secretary and CMC chairman and was outflanked on economic policy matters by Li Peng. Intense debate over economic policies—especially the relationship between planning and market mechanisms—took place in late 1990, but Deng's ideas did not prevail. Jiang increasingly parroted Chen Yun's views in his public speeches on economic matters.[123]

As Mao had done when he was stifled in Beijing, Deng headed for the provinces to generate support for his ideas. His first stop in late January 1991 was Shanghai, where he raised the idea of permitting Shanghai—and particularly the new industrial zone of Pudong—the same kind of tax and foreign investment advantages that had been given to the special economic zones in Guangdong and Fujian Provinces. "We say that Shanghai opened up and developed late, now it must go all out!" Deng told Shanghai municipal leaders.[124] But Deng had more than that in mind. Though he was in Shanghai, he gave several speeches to municipal party leaders, railing against "ossified thinking," sloppiness, and excessive caution within the central leadership. Worse still, "no one is listening to me [in Beijing] now. I have no choice but to have my articles published in Shanghai."[125] Deng's ideas were incorporated into a series of four articles published in Shanghai's flagship newspaper, the *Liberation Daily*, under the byline of Huang Pu Ping (homophonic for Shanghai's principal river, the Huangpu, and the word for "commentary.") Unusually pointed, the articles called for a resurgence of reform, boldness in implementing market economic measures, "emancipation of minds," and rejection of sterile arguments over whether certain reforms were surnamed "capitalist" or "socialist," and for promotion of leading cadre who were intelligent, courageous, and dedicated to reform.[126] The articles created a furor in Beijing (even though they were not republished there), and Deng Liqun sent an investigation team to Shanghai to find out who wrote them.[127]

More important than the articles, however, was the support Deng gained in April by bringing Shanghai's strongly reformist mayor, Zhu Rongji, to Beijing to become a vice premier of the State Council. Besides his exceptional ability as an economic thinker and manager, Zhu was Jiang Zemin's associate and successor in Shanghai, and although the two were not considered close, they knew each other well and worked harmoniously. Typically, in the post-1989 political scene dominated by several elders, Zhu's elevation was matched by the appointment to vice premier of an economic conservative, Zou Jiahua, who had served as head of China's State Planning Commission. Foreign Minister Qian Qichen continued his rise in the government, being appointed a "state councillor," a rank just below vice premier. Deng also approved the partial rehabilitation in June of three officials who had been purged with Zhao Ziyang in 1989: former Politburo Standing Committee member Hu Qili and secretariat members Yan Mingfu and Rui Xingwen. Although the three were given posts far below their original level, observers viewed their restoration as an important signal that reform was returning to China's political and economic agenda.

Events in Moscow in August 1991 derailed the reformist comeback, however, as the leadership retreated into dogma and paranoia in the wake of the fall of the world's oldest communist party. Chinese party documents exaggerated the disruptions that followed in Russia—accusing Yeltsin of carrying out a "white terror" against Communist Party members—to reinforce the conclusion that China could not follow that same route.[128] Deng cautioned against overreacting to the situation but was disregarded. Instead, party ideologues suggested at an expanded Politburo meeting that included the elders that combating "peaceful evolution" plots by the West should become the "core" of the party's work. Deng and Yang Shangkun fought off that challenge, but even Jiang Zemin agreed with the ideologues that the regime could show no signs of loosening its grip by experimenting with any economic reforms. By the end of the year, Deng was under attack from "leftists" within the propaganda apparatus, his "year of reform" having come to naught.[129]

Again in early 1992, Deng left Beijing for the Spring Festival holiday, spending much of January and February inspecting the special economic zones in Guangdong Province, particularly Shenzhen (adjacent to Hong Kong) and Zhuhai (next to Macao). Although frail in health, Deng pursued a rigorous schedule of inspections, meetings, and speeches. But his purpose was more than inspection—it was to re-energize economic reform throughout the country. This time, Deng presented well-thought-out policy positions and ideological justifications. Moreover, he was better prepared to get his message out. Although no central media covered his trip, some Hong Kong newspapers did so and included plenty of direct quotes and photographs. Slowly but surely, the message made its way back to Beijing—Deng had thrown down the gauntlet.

Deng's purpose was to break the ideological and bureaucratic shackles that continued to hold back productivity, even in more advanced economic areas like Guangdong and Shanghai. He made clear he was tired of ideological foot-dragging and back stabbing about reform.

> We should be bolder in carrying out reforms and opening up to the outside world and in making experimentations; we should not act like a woman with bound feet . . . The achievements made in the construc-

tion of Shenzhen provide clear answers to people with various misgivings. The special economic zones are socialist, not capitalist. . . . Whether the emphasis is on planning or market is not the essential distinction between socialism and capitalism. Are negotiable securities and stock markets good stuff after all? Are they risky? Are they peculiar to capitalism? Can they be used in socialism? Try them out, but try them out resolutely. If they prove to be correct after one or two years, let's open them up . . . Localities with [appropriate economic] conditions should carry out development as quickly as they can . . . Low speed development is equal to stagnation or even retrogression.[130]

Deng lashed out at his critics, some by name, others by implication, and turned the tables on his detractors by kicking off a major campaign against "leftism." "The party must raise its guard against rightism, but its major task is to prevent leftism," he stressed on numerous occasions during his trip.[131] He called on those officials who could not honestly and enthusiastically support reforms to "get off the stage" and make room for those who could. Although Deng's ad hominem attacks did not get picked up by the media or the official party documents, they were widely known through the rumor mill and had a remarkable effect. They were a prominent signal that the political winds were changing and that those who had used ideology to stifle reform and creativity were now to be targets. They emboldened party reformers to resuscitate ideas and programs that Zhao Ziyang had been promoting before his purge. And they were a striking wake-up call to the leadership in Beijing.

Even after Deng returned to Beijing, the central propaganda organs were reluctant to publish anything more than unattributed excerpts of his speeches or even to acknowledge that he had made the trip. Deng went to work on Jiang Zemin, whom he had mildly praised during his travels. Pressed hard to finally declare which side he was on, Jiang the "weathervane" wisely chose to support Deng. Jiang first circulated Deng's speeches to Politburo members, then at a Politburo meeting on March 9, he summarized them and instructed that they be circulated to all levels of the party. He also criticized himself for not having supported reform and opposed "leftism" vigorously enough. Three days later, the party media organs proclaimed that the "basic line" of reform and opening up would be carried out more daringly, and would last for one hundred years, and that "leftism" constituted the main threat to the party's work.[132] Not coincidentally, Yao Yilin, conservative economist and Chen Yun's principal protégé on the Politburo Standing Committee, resigned from his position (ostensibly for health reasons) at that time, as did the prominent "leftist" minister of culture, He Jingzhi.

The cumulative effect of Deng's *nanxun,* or "southern tour,"[133] is hard to overestimate. Willy Wo-lap Lam called it "a gigantic triumph of the will. Almost single-handedly, [Deng] succeeded in giving the appearance of blotting out the disgrace of June 4 [1989]—and re-anchoring the nation onto a path of reform."[134] More than that, when disseminated to local officials, Deng's words legitimized and expanded a course of economic reform that led to China's emergence as one of the world's fastest-growing and fastest-changing economies. They energized local economic development in rural and urban areas and fostered private entrepreneurship on a vast scale. They renewed and accelerated the foreign trade boom in Guangdong and Shanghai and other urban areas of China's east coast. They encouraged an enormous increase in foreign investment, especially from Hong Kong and Taiwan. Of course, there were errors and excesses, and Vice Premier Zhu Rongji would spend two years dealing with the inflation, misplaced investment, excess capital construction, and unstable financial markets that accompanied the re-energizing of economic reform. Economic policy would continue to be controversial, as the leadership struggled to deal with an array of structural and financial problems. But the political and ideological challenges to the general course that Deng had set out in 1980—and that Zhao Ziyang and many others had worked to put into effect—were basically over.

Deng did not accomplish the hard work of developing economic policies and providing the depth of political support they needed by himself. He had—and needed—plenty of help. On the economic front, Zhu Rongji and a battery of reformist economists quickly prepared Central Directives 4 and 5 of 1992, which laid out the economic principles and concrete plans for putting Deng's ideas into practice. Politically, Deng again received timely assistance from the People's Liberation Army. In March, General Political Department Director Yang Baibing coined a slogan that the PLA would be the "protective imperial escort" (*baojia huhang*) for the party's reform efforts. The declaration served notice that the army would support Deng over others in the leadership. It was also an effort on the part of Yang and his brother Yang Shangkun to curry favor with the resurgent Deng Xiaoping.[135] Deng also received ample support from local officials, and to a certain degree, from the public, who saw clear benefits to be gained from a return to a more robust and productive economy with less interference from Beijing. Despite the damage to his reputation from the Tiananmen crackdown, Deng's southern tour showed others that he had maintained the support and affection of many ordinary Chinese.

Deng had, in effect, restored himself to his pre-1989 position as first among equals, the most influential of the party elders. None of the others had the energy, health, intellectual gifts, or broad political support that Deng had enjoyed, and none could offset the advantages he accrued by taking the initiative on his *nanxun*. Deng was aided by the actuarial tables, which began to catch up on the elders in 1992. Slowly but surely, the "longevity contest" that characterized China's elder politics began to sort itself out. In May, Nie Rongzhen—the "father of China's atomic bomb" and the last of the "Old Marshals"—died at the age of ninety-two. He was followed in June by former president Li Xiannian (eighty-two), who had been one of Jiang's other patrons, and in July by Deng Yingchao (eighty-eight), not herself a power player but an important symbol as the widow of Zhou Enlai and the adoptive mother of Li Peng. Former vice president Wang Zhen—reviled for his denunciation of students and his active promotion of campaigns against "bourgeois liberalization"—was reported in rapidly failing health, as was Chen Yun, Deng's chief rival.[136] Deng appeared to be serious in his wish to retire, but now he wanted to do so with his restored reputation intact.[137] For that to occur, he would need a Jiang Zemin beholden to him and strong enough to survive on his own once Deng left the scene.

Giving Up on China

Despite the frigidity of the bilateral relationship, both sides appeared anxious to find ways to make progress when newly appointed ambassador to Beijing J. Stapleton Roy arrived on post in August 1991.[138] He and National Security Council Director Douglas Paal had worked to ease Secretary Baker's misgivings about traveling to China. Paal was eager to solicit China's assistance in dealing with North Korea's nuclear weapons program, which intelligence reporting indicated was in a more advanced stage than had earlier been believed.[139] In September, Baker told Foreign Minister Qian that he and the president had agreed the time was ripe for him to make a trip to China, but only if positive results could be achieved, particularly in human rights and nonproliferation. Although Beijing was also eager for a high-level visit to ease their isolation, Qian responded with a vague message that there could be "some success," which Baker interpreted as sufficient to justify the trip, especially since he was going to South Korea and Japan at the same time.[140]

Nonetheless the stakes were high, and Baker was anxious for success in the human rights area. Congressional critics attacked the trip as a "pointless exercise," as it would give China the prestige of a Cabinet-level visit without having to give up much in return.[141] Two weeks before his arrival, China's State Council Information Office had issued a White Paper rebutting foreign criticism of China's human rights situation, and although it was basically a whitewash, some took it as a positive sign that China was at least beginning to conceive of the issues in Western terms.

When Baker arrived in Beijing on November 15, however, he ran into a brick wall. He might have foreordained his rough treatment by insisting that all leadership greetings and handshakes be conducted off camera, and that there be no welcoming banquet. Although he avoided the embarrassment back home of the Scowcroft-Eagleburger trip, he denied the Chinese what they wanted most, domestic publicity for a restored relationship. They responded to incivility with incivility.

In his first meeting with Qian Qichen, Baker heard strident demands that the United States end all sanctions against China and stop interfering in its internal affairs. In response, Baker presented a detailed list of concessions he wanted from China, including guarantees on assistance to the Algerian nuclear program, agreement to abide by MTCR guidelines on missile sales, pressure on North Korea to allow international inspection of its nuclear facilities at Yongbyon, and most important, visible progress on human rights. Baker told Qian, "I need concrete results—not promises, not meetings, not delays. When I get on my airplane, judgments will be formed immediately about the success or failure of this visit. If I am seen as having failed, the Congress will take China policy away from the President."[142] Qian, unmoved by the threat of congressional action to override the president's likely veto, gave nothing.

The following day, Baker met Li Peng for what was described to the press as a "businesslike" meeting.[143] In fact, it was a bitter argument, carried on by two men skilled at being tough in meetings. Douglas Paal described it as "the worst meeting I've ever been in in my life," while Ambassador J. Stapleton Roy said it was "the tensest and most confrontational meeting I ever sat in on in China."[144] The two men argued about Tiananmen, human rights in general, American policy, Taiwan, GATT, and virtually every other topic that was raised. By all accounts, Baker gave as good as he got, but he came away "appalled" by Li's "surreal performance," and thought the meeting a "disaster."[145] His meeting with President Yang Shangkun was nearly as bad, although a subsequent session with Jiang Zemin provided something of a respite from the tension.

On the last day of his visit, Baker and Qian had a "marathon" session. Baker began by reading a letter President Bush had given him to present to Deng Xiaoping, but since the Chinese refused to allow him to see Deng, he had to resort to passing on Bush's compliments secondhand. The letter reportedly entreated Deng to intervene personally to rescue a bilateral relationship that was seriously at risk. A five-hour discussion followed, in which every issue was reviewed in detail. In the end, patience and persistence paid off. Qian—who reportedly had consulted far into the night with others in the leadership—delivered what Ambassador Roy and others considered important concessions:

—On missile sales, the Chinese agreed orally to "observe the guidelines and parameters" of the MTCR, which American officials took to disallow both the sales of M-9s to Syria and M-11s to Pakistan. But the language was vague. In return, Baker agreed the United States would remove the May and June sanctions that had prohibited the licensing of high-speed computers and satellite technology for China.

—On other nuclear-related issues, the Chinese reiterated their earlier pledges on the Algerian nuclear facility and their support for the NPT and spoke of their support for a "nonnuclear" Korean Peninsula. They did not agree, however, to suspend exports of equipment for civilian nuclear power programs that might be dual use.

—On trade, China accepted the need to work together to prevent prison labor goods from reaching the United States and agreed to send a delegation to Washington to negotiate further on U.S. charges of massive piracy and intellectual property rights violations. They made no commitments on reducing the trade deficit, however.

—On human rights, Baker got next to nothing. The Chinese agreed to continue a formal human rights "dialogue" with Assistant Secretary of State Schifter; they provided a rough accounting of 733 prisoners on a list Baker had provided at an earlier meeting and agreed to release two "prominent" critics of the regime within a short period of time.[146] Adding insult to injury, the Chinese detained two prominent dissidents rather than allow them to meet with a member of Baker's traveling party.[147]

Not as steeped in the nuances of Chinese negotiating style as Ambassador Roy, Baker was bitterly disappointed, and he made little effort to conceal his dissatisfaction. He acquiesced in press characterizations of his trip as a "failure" and gave nearly apologetic briefings to Congress on his return. His distrust and dislike of the Chinese—already high—grew as a result of his trip, and he never had substantive meetings with them again. He left to subordinates the important work of formalizing and completing the agreements he had reached.

In effect, the domestic politics of both sides had again intervened to prevent any improvement in the bilateral relationship. In late 1991, Baker went to China with an agenda largely dictated by congressional pressure. To avoid press criticism, he skipped the symbolic gestures of goodwill the Chinese consider so important. And he took the criticism of his trip by domestic opinion makers as a fair evaluation of its results. The Chinese, locked in their own ideological debates and still dealing with the aftereffects of Tiananmen, could not give ground on sensitive human rights issues. They rejected U.S. concerns about weapons of mass destruction as hegemonic "pressure" and decided not to take firm action against activities by their military industries that were lucrative in the short term but damaging in the long. They viewed congressional protests about human rights as part of a plot to undermine their socialist regime through "peaceful evolution." They demonstrated no depth of understanding of U.S. domestic politics and ended up embarrassing and angering a key official who had hoped to make progress in restoring the relationship.

Politically in the United States, the Baker visit was a wash—no minds were changed, no policies revised. Administration officials, particularly in the USTR and the State Department, worked hard to follow through on the meager results of the trip. On November 26, seven months after she had designated China a "priority foreign country" for violating acceptable protections of U.S. intellectual property, USTR Carla Hills announced that, because of unsatisfactory negotiations with China on solving the problems, her office was drawing up a list of $1.5 billion in Chinese goods that would be subject to 100 percent tariffs. The list included luggage, clothing, shoes, toys, and watches. A thirty-day period of comment and challenge from American businesses followed, during which China responded by publicizing its own list of American goods to be subjected to increased tariffs—corn, aircraft, steel, chemicals, and cotton. American business executives—importers and exporters—were alarmed at the situation, which portended a nasty round of retaliation and counterretaliation, damaging commercial interests on both sides.[148]

On December 16, USTR declared a one-month extension on negotiations, following a request by China to put together one more round of negotiations. Vice Minister of Trade and Economic Cooperation Wu Yi came to Washington in early January with one last offer and a hope for "a little bit of sincerity."[149] Negotiations continued through the January 16, 1992, deadline, when an agreement was finally reached. Curiously, relatively few details of the agreement were released. The USTR insisted, "We have gotten what we needed on the patent protection . . . we feel very happy and satisfied."[150] American industry groups, such as the Intellectual Property Alliance and the Business Software Alliance, declared their satisfaction, and a more than $2 billion trade dispute disappeared overnight. What USTR got was promises that China would provide patent protection, join international copyright conventions—including on software—and honor internationally protected copyrights on computers, software, books, and recordings. In the circumstances, it was probably the best they could get, and some industry analysts have praised the agreement as a good start on improving China's primitive structure of legal protections for intellectual property rights (IPR).[151] But the issue would return to haunt USTR three years later, when it turned out that China's promises to cut back on piracy of U.S. music, movies, and software were empty.

The State Department, meanwhile, focused on firming up China's commitment to abide by the MTCR. Baker, edgy and distrustful of Qian Qichen's verbal agreement, was reluctant to lift officially the sanctions imposed the previous year on two Chinese corporations. American diplomats sparred with Chinese officials, at one point accusing them of trying to renege on Qian's agreement with Baker. The critical issue involved the inclusion of certain additional restrictions on missile-related technology contained in the annexes to the MTCR agreement. China agreed to abide by the "guidelines and parameters" (meaning range and payload) of the agreement but was more circumspect with respect to technology issues. Qian wrote a letter on February 1 that formally reiterated his agreement with Baker but did not resolve questions pertaining to China's willingness to abide by the MTCR annexes. Xinhua News Agency published the terse Chinese statement on February 19. "China will act in accordance with the existing Missile Technology Control Regime guidelines and parameters in its export of missiles and missile technology." The administration nonetheless agreed to lift the sanctions on February 22, a move immediately criticized by Congress. Senator Joseph Biden of Delaware—a persistent critic of China's proliferation record—called for a full Senate hearing on intelligence reports that suggested China was selling missile and nuclear-related technology to Iran, Syria, and Pakistan, despite Qian's commitments.[152]

Bush got personally involved one last time with China policy in early 1992, when he agreed to have a meeting with China's Premier Li Peng at the United Nations. The meeting, a summit of the heads of state of all members of the Security Council, was proposed by the United Kingdom's prime minister, John Major, for the purpose of discussing the UN's role in a post–cold war future and the need for better efforts to prevent the spread of nuclear weapons. Bush felt he "could not say no" to Major and felt obligated to accede to the Chinese request for a private session with Li. Sharing with critics of his China policy a strong aversion for the acerbic premier, Bush put off publicly announcing the meeting until a few days before the February 2 summit and tried to ensure that there were no embarrassing photo opportunities at the beginning of an election year. National Security Council staffer Douglas Paal told the Chinese no photographers were to be present during the initial handshake and greeting—and even had the Secret Service physically remove a member of Li's party who deployed a camera. The "official" photo showed a grim Bush between Scowcroft and Baker, across from a smiling Li Peng.[153]

Critics of the president, of course, claimed Bush handed the Chinese a "considerable gift" and completed the process of rehabilitating China's reputation after Tiananmen.[154] Clearly Li must have relished the opportunity to make the Americans uncomfortable in his presence one more time. But if he gained any personal prestige in China for meeting with Bush, it was short lived. While he was in New York, Deng was in Shenzhen, putting together the political and economic strategy that would turn Chinese politics around dramatically and cost Li no small amount of prestige and authority. At the National People's Congress meeting in April, Li was publicly humiliated by having his government work report corrected by delegates no fewer than 140 times after he delivered it and before it was finally approved.[155]

The standoff over MFN came to its inevitable conclusion when Congress—after a lengthy conference to iron out differences—sent the United States–China Act of 1991 to Bush on February 27, 1992. Bush promptly vetoed it, saying that, although he agreed with the goals of the bill, he disagreed strongly with the means chosen to try and achieve them. "If we present China's leaders with an ultimatum on MFN, the result will be weakened ties to the West and further repression . . . not . . . progress on human rights, arms control, or trade." Bush insisted his policy of "comprehensive engagement" and "targeting specific areas of concern with the appropriate policy instruments" had achieved progress that would be undone by the bill's restrictive provisions.[156] Ten days later, the House overrode the veto 357-61, but the Senate sustained it on March 18, falling short of the necessary two-thirds vote to override, 60-38. That did not end the struggle, however. The day after the president declared his intention to renew MFN for China, Representative Donald Pease submitted the "China Most Favored Nation Trade Status Bill" (H.R. 5318), again setting policy conditions (principally human rights but also nonproliferation and trade) on China's trade with the United States. Under accelerated rules in the House and Senate, the bill sped through committees and conferences and was presented to the president in late September, forcing him to veto it just a little more than a month before the election. The veto stood against efforts to override it, but in the end, represented not the president's strength but his vulnerability.

Jiang's First Victory

Jiang Zemin's role during this crucial period is not easy to track. Ever since his appointment in 1989, Jiang had maintained a fairly low profile, delivering careful speeches that reflected the consensus of the times, trying not to offend any of the elders, economic administrators, surviving reformists, and PLA generals who populated the topmost ranks of the party leadership. Deng at times had been obliquely critical of Jiang's performance, but now evidently decided to work closely with him to prepare for leadership changes at the upcoming Fourteenth Party Congress. Jiang had much to gain from such cooperation and probably knew it. With ideological and policy issues now clarified, the two men focused on the personnel decisions needed to ensure that the policies would be able to prevail in a still-uncertain political climate.

The most critical decisions involved the leadership of the PLA. Deng's effort to give Jiang a foothold in the military by making him chairman of the Central Military Commission had not worked particularly well. Jiang, who never actually had served in the military and who lacked military bearing, had difficulty gaining the respect of the much-decorated heroes of World War II and Korea who dominated the PLA. Moreover, President Yang Shangkun and his half-brother, Yang Baibing, seemed determined to turn the PLA into a "Yang Family Army," dominating promotions and political work and offering few opportunities for Jiang to enhance his authority within the armed forces.[157]

Yang Baibing was particularly resented among active and professional military cadre for focusing excessively on ideological indoctrination and for advancing the careers of carefully selected cronies. Some officers believed he had not absorbed the correct "lessons" from the U.S. victory in the Gulf War and was an indifferent supporter of military modernization. There were also concerns that his offer to "escort" Deng's reform program represented an inappropriate threat of interference in party affairs (even if Deng might have solicited it). Finally, there were reports that Yang was holding secret PLA senior staff meetings to prepare plans for maintaining order after Deng's death. Yang Shangkun, while loyal to Deng, appeared to be preparing to succeed him as the country's strongman in the event of Deng's incapacitation. He also had proposed that his brother be promoted to the Politburo Standing Committee at the upcoming party congress.[158]

The combination of career officer complaints, suspicion of Yang Shangkun's loyalty, and probably a dose of anger at Yang Baibing's *lèse-majesté* probably led Deng to take rather precipitous action. Less than a week before the Fourteenth Party Congress was to open in October 1992, Deng reportedly sent a letter to a specially convened Politburo meeting, recommending that Yang Baibing be dropped from the Central Military Commission and from the party secretariat but that he be elevated to the Political Bureau. Although an apparent promotion, it represented a clear separation of Yang Baibing from his power base and therefore his political emasculation. Knowing that Yang Shangkun had already requested to resign from his CMC and Politburo positions, Deng recommended that Admiral Liu Huaqing—a CMC vice chairman—be elevated to the Politburo Standing Committee. Liu, a Deng loyalist and respected senior general, was expected to "protect" Jiang's position in both the army and the party.

Deng's "recommendations," approved by the Politburo on October 10, apparently caught the Yangs by surprise, and they had no choice but to accept them. It was a classic Deng political maneuver, and it worked smoothly to protect Jiang Zemin's flank in the PLA and to deftly move the Yang brothers out of the military hierarchy without humiliating them or giving them cause for grievance. Deng and Jiang followed their minicoup with a major reorganization of the Central Military Commission, Ministry of National Defense, General Staff Department, and the regional military commands, shuffling a total of about 300 senior officers.[159]

The Fourteenth Party Congress, held in October 1992, was both Deng's last victory and Jiang's coming-of-age on the leadership scene. Deng made one brief ceremonial appearance but otherwise did not attend the congress. He was nonetheless widely perceived to have scored yet another political triumph in the restoration of a reform agenda and the appointment of younger and more capable officials to implement it. He also received a restoration of his status as China's paramount leader, even though he appeared subsequently to be interested in "nothing more than safeguarding his place in history."[160] Now that he had outmaneuvered his peers yet again and mobilized bureaucratic, ideological, and public opinion powers to regain his former dominance, he was prepared to retreat back to the second line, satisfied that no other elder could assume his role or—after his death—undermine his reputation.

Deng's reputation got a huge boost at the Fourteenth Party Congress and thereafter. "Deng Xiaoping thought" would henceforth become enshrined as ideological guidance for the party's work at virtually the same level as Mao Zedong thought once had been. Jiang, in his report to the party Congress, referred to Deng's thought as "scientific, penetrating, and brilliant."[161] It would be cited repeatedly in central guidance as the ultimate authority—a third volume of Deng's *Selected Works* would be published the following year. Credited already for three political comebacks, Deng should probably be credited with a fourth. Even though he had not suffered a political eclipse as dramatic as his earlier periods of disgrace, Deng's return to the top in 1992 was certainly evidence that, at eighty-eight years of age, he had not lost his political skills.

But Deng's most important achievements had to do with his helping Jiang consolidate his position in the party hierarchy. Despite his pique at Jiang's lackluster support for his economic program, Deng created the conditions for Jiang's successful domination of the leadership by helping him eliminate potential PLA and party elder interference in the political process. Although he would never enjoy the kind of unrivaled power that Deng and Mao had achieved, Jiang emerged from the Fourteenth Congress a stronger, more secure, and confident leader than he had been before it. Although he was still viewed by many as a "transitional" figure whose tenure was tied to Deng's longevity, Jiang was able to use the advantages he gained from the party congress to build up his power base and reputation.

Jiang's advantages were manifold:

—A more reformist Politburo Standing Committee. Conservative Chen Yun supporters Song Ping and Yao Yilin were dropped, replaced by Zhu Rongji and Hu Jintao, both with firm credentials in supporting economic reform. Liu Huaqing—a Deng loyalist and PLA professional—was added to maintain a military presence at the topmost level.

—A new Politburo. Aside from the four Standing Committee members and three former members of the previous Politburo who were held over, half of the twenty-two members elected were new. Seven of them had served in provincial party or government positions. As a group, they were younger, better-educated, and more professionally oriented than their predecessors. Qian Qichen was also added as a full member of the Politburo, bringing foreign policy expertise to the penultimate level of decisionmaking.

—Abolition of the Central Advisory Committee. Originally intended as an honorary retirement post for superannuated cadre, the CAC under Chen Yun had become more active and influential after Tiananmen, generally in support of highly conservative ideological causes.

—A more pliant military. The removal of the Yangs and the installation of a new chain of command effectively took the PLA out of the political limelight and focused its work more on needed professionalization of its officer corps and modernization of doctrine, equipment, and training. Although the armed forces would continue to expect and receive a higher proportion of national budgetary resources, Jiang no doubt considered that a small price to pay for, in effect, returning the PLA to its barracks.

—A revamped Central Committee. Although the Central Committee is neither a policymaking or power-wielding body, it did debate and discuss general political and economic policies and provided the public affirmation of central decisions that helped guide the 50-million-member Communist Party. Nearly half of the 319 members of the Fourteenth Central Committee were newcomers, more than 80 percent were college educated.[162] Among those dropped from membership were several of the hard-line propagandists whom Deng had criticized earlier in the year.

—A reconfirmation of the decision removing Zhao Ziyang as general secretary. Just before the congress, a Central Committee work conference had announced that the investigation of Zhao Ziyang's case had been concluded, and that the decision to strip him of his posts was upheld. Despite his disgrace, however, Zhao remained popular within the party because of a strong association with the course of reform and a charismatic personality. Had his reputation been restored, he might have staged a comeback, eclipsing Jiang.

The party's continued ambivalence about Zhao was demonstrated by the fact that, although his ouster was reaffirmed, he was not expelled from the party or subjected to criminal prosecution.[163]

—Relatively clear guidelines for economic work. The Fourteenth Congress report effectively ended the debates about the direction of economic policy that had blown up after Tiananmen. Although conservatives would continue to snipe at reform experiments and "leftist" commentaries would still be written and circulated, the basic reformist orientation of the party's work—and its focus on economic, rather than political, reform—was as clear as it had been since 1978. With a set of priorities on which the party had established a basic consensus, Jiang's leadership tasks were somewhat easier.

In his long speech to the assembled party congress delegates, the product of extensive drafting, consultation, and redrafting, Jiang focused primarily on economic issues, with the controversial ideological issues that had roiled the party for a decade as an important subtext. "To accelerate economic growth we must further emancipate our minds, speed up the reform and opening to the rest of the world, and not get bogged down in an abstract debate over what is socialist and what is capitalist," he insisted. He maintained a hard line against "leftism" in the party and hammered away at the appropriateness of using capitalist concepts and market mechanisms to advance a socialist economy. He also enthusiastically endorsed foreign participation in China's economic modernization, from the special economic zones to attracting foreign investment and capital to expanding foreign trade. But he rejected "absolutely" the appropriateness of a "Western, multiparty parliamentary system" for China.

Foreign policy issues gained scant attention. Jiang put the United States on notice—without naming it—that it could not expect to use human rights to pressure or coerce China, and he repeated the mantra that China would always oppose hegemonism in any form. He concluded his remarks on foreign policy with what seemed like advice for American policymakers, rather than for China. "The experience of history tells us that regardless of one's cause, if one encroaches on another nation's independence and sovereignty, intervenes in the internal affairs of another country, if the large bullies the small, the strong torments the weak, or the rich oppresses the poor, they will never win people's hearts. A just cause enjoys much support, while an unjust one will find little help; the power of justice can never be defeated."[164]

U.S. Politics in Command—The F-16 Sale to Taiwan

As is the norm with foreign policy concerns, China policy was not a significant issue in the presidential campaign of 1992. It was not an issue on which

Bush could trumpet his success as a "foreign policy president." By late 1992, even though the relationship had begun to show signs of improvement (an agreement on investigating prison labor export cases was signed in August, for example), Bush did not try to take credit. Just about every major foreign policy commentator in the principal media outlets—including Republican heavyweights Jeanne Kirkpatrick and William Safire—was insisting it was time for a new China policy. Democratic presidential candidate William Jefferson Clinton, governor of Arkansas, did not raise foreign policy issues often. His guiding campaign theme was what he perceived was Bush's lackluster performance in promoting American economic growth. He supported the Democratic Party congressional leadership, which advocated conditional MFN for China, but otherwise steered away from taking a strong position on most foreign policy issues. When he did speak on China-related issues, he accused Bush of not standing up for democracy in China but rather sending his aides to "toast China's leaders." Like others in the Democratic Party, he sometimes asked for advice on China policy from former Tiananmen dissidents, such as Chai Ling and Li Lu. He pledged that under his administration, America would never "coddle tyrants from Baghdad to Beijing."[165]

But it was not just the Clinton challenge, but the maverick candidacy of H. Ross Perot that beset Bush's candidacy for re-election. Most polls predicted Perot would take more votes away from Bush than from Clinton, and relatively small margins of votes conceivably could affect the outcomes in key states. As he looked for every advantage, Bush decided to make use of the president's considerable powers of dispensing government largesse. On July 30, well behind Clinton in the polls, Bush told reporters he was "taking a new look" at whether the United States should sell F-16s to Taiwan.[166] Hardly more than a month later, Bush appeared at the General Dynamics plant in Forth Worth, Texas, under a banner saying "Jobs for America. Thanks, Mr. President," to announce he had decided to sell 150 of the aircraft (worth about $4 billion) to Taiwan. "This F-16 is an example of what only America and Americans can do," Bush told the cheering crowds, several thousand of whose jobs he had just saved.[167] About the same time, the Pentagon announced its approval of the sale to Saudi Arabia of 72 F-15 fighters, worth about $5 billion and thousands of jobs at McDonnell-Douglas plants in Missouri and California.

Most commentators at the time saw it as cynical election-year politics, although some applauded the idea of increasing support to Taiwan. But the decision was far more complex than that, involving intrabureaucratic wrangling in Washington and a fundamental misreading of China's position and reaction. In the end, the decision did major damage to U.S.-China relations, exactly when prospects for improvement were good. The repercussions of the decision were long-lasting.

In his book, *About Face: A History of America's Curious Relationship with China, from Nixon to Clinton*, James Mann traces the various dimensions of the F-16 deal in detail.[168] He includes U.S. sanctions against military sales to China after Tiananmen (particularly the cancellation of the "Peace Pearl" F-8 upgrade program) as a factor in China's decision in early 1992 to buy a number of Sukhoi-27 high-performance aircraft from Russia. That led to increased lobbying by Taiwan and its friends in the United States for a change in U.S. policy on selling the F-16. For a decade, Taiwan had been asking for F-16s, fearing the erosion of its qualitative edge in air power as aging F-104 and F-5E fighters crashed with distressing regularity. The United States had consistently turned down the request, on the grounds that it would violate the August 17, 1982, communiqué with China that limited arms sales to Taiwan to "defensive" weapons systems, and that Taiwan's aircraft needs would be met by the so-called Indigenous Defense Fighter (IDF). The IDF, a limited-range upgrade of the F-5 being manufactured in Taiwan under American guidance, was behind in its production schedule, and its performance was not a match for the Su-27. As late as May 1992, at the annual meeting on arms sales between Taiwan defense officials and American counterparts, the request for F-16s had been turned down again.

Mann tracks the issues and their background and implications well, but the issues did not drive the decision. The president did. The decision chain actually started in July 1992 with President Bush deciding he wanted to go ahead with both the F-15 and F-16 sales and tasking the Defense Department to make it happen. First, DOD/ISA—at Secretary of Defense Cheney's instruction—made certain that Israel's concerns about the F-15 Strike Eagle sales to Saudi Arabia were dealt with appropriately. Although the Israeli government complained about the sale, it was well compensated. Besides $650 million worth of Apache and Blackhawk helicopters and Harpoon missiles being given to Israel, roughly $200 million in U.S. munitions were prepositioned in Israel, and the United States agreed to maintain $1.8 billion in military assistance and provide $10 billion in loan guarantees to the Israeli government.[169] It was a classic Bush-Baker kind of deal, complex but workable, although some observers told the *New York Times* reporter Tom Friedman that it both undermined longer-term prospects for Middle East peace (and Bush's own post–Persian Gulf War diplomacy) by bringing more arms into the region and injected the wrong kind of stimulus into the American economy.[170]

Instead of giving similar consideration to China for compromising the August 17 communiqué and other implicit agreements about arms sales to

Taiwan, Defense Department officials worked instead through the interagency system to provide a substantive justification for the sale on the grounds that Taiwan needed the equipment upgrade, that the F-16 A/B version was equivalent in performance to the IDF, and that China should not and would not overreact to the sale. The basic goal was to lessen bureaucratic objection to the deal, particularly from the State Department, by demonstrating that the sale did not violate the qualitative or quantitative restrictions of the August 17 communiqué.[171] Several interagency work groups were held in August at which the Defense Department presented its case to a rather skeptical audience of State Department, Commerce Department, and intelligence community representatives. The end result was a briefing to the national security adviser (not even a deputies or principals committee meeting) on the pros and cons of making the sale).[172] Given that the decision had already been made, few were surprised when the White House announced on September 3 that it approved the sale, citing Taiwan's need for replacement aircraft, especially as a counterweight to the Russian SU-27s, and insisting the sale did not violate the 1982 communiqué.[173]

Assistant Secretary of State for East Asia and the Pacific William Clark suggested to the White House that a "distinguished American" be sent to Beijing as a presidential envoy to offer some form of face-saving explanation and compensatory gestures to the Chinese. Unbeknown to him, the Chinese had already been notified. The day after Bush said he was "taking a new look" at the F-16 issue, NSC Senior Director Douglas Paal—at the president's behest—invited Ambassador Zhu Qizhen and visiting MFA North American and Oceanian Affairs Department Director General Yang Jiechi to the White House residence for a drink with the president. Zhu made a preliminary complaint about Bush's remarks on the F-16 issue, to which the president replied, "This is going ahead. It's political. Tell Deng Xiaoping that this is something I have to do."[174] The White House believed that this manner of private communication of bad news, preventing a later surprise, would mollify the Chinese and mute their reaction. But the NSC also approved Clark's idea of sending a presidential envoy and chose him for the job.

Beijing's reaction to the F-16 sale was compounded by the fact that, only two weeks before the F-16 announcement, USTR had announced a decision to impose $3.9 billion of punitive tariffs on China in response to the failure of negotiations to resolve a section 301 dispute over China's market access restrictions. The USTR gave China until October 10 to come up with a satisfactory agreement on lowering tariffs and removing nontariff barriers to American goods. (Although USTR may not have known at the time, the deadline was just before the opening of China's Fourteenth Party Congress, a sensitive time to be exerting external pressure.) The list of goods to be subjected to 100 percent tariffs included nearly everything China exported to the United States. To notch up the pressure, American officials added that failure to come to an agreement would result in U.S. efforts to block China's entry into the General Agreement on Tariffs and Trade.[175] The Chinese probably also were aware that another bill conditioning MFN to its own human rights performance was on its way to the president and that an overreaction to the sale might lead to the president allowing it to become law.

China's public reaction was one of controlled fury. On September 4, Vice Minister of Foreign Affairs Liu Huaqiu called in Ambassador Roy to deliver "the strongest protest" over the action. The Chinese press quoted extensively from his remarks, saying the sale proved "American promises cannot be believed," that it would "lead to a retrogression of Sino-American relations" and a decrease in international cooperation, and that the consequences would be on Washington's head.[176] National People's Congress delegates were quoted attacking American "lies and deceit." Subsequently, Beijing broke off bilateral discussions of both human rights and nonproliferation issues and dropped out of a U.S.-sponsored international forum to discuss how to restrict arms sales to the Middle East.[177]

When Assistant Secretary Clark arrived on September 7, he was treated with unusual discourtesy, and his explanation for the sale was publicly refuted by Vice Minister Liu Huaqiu almost immediately after he presented it. Clark did not go to Beijing empty-handed. After his explanation of the sale, which he claimed was not inconsistent with the 1982 communiqué, he offered four new initiatives for China to consider, being careful not to present them as compensation: a return of equipment stored in the United States from the aborted Peace Pearl program and $23 million as a "refund"; agreement to reopen military-to-military talks, including on technology transfer; agreement to resume the Joint Committee on Commerce and Trade talks, starting with a trip by the commerce secretary to China; and agreement to resume Joint Committee on Science and Technology talks.[178] These were serious concessions. As Clark put it, "We undid the things we did after Tiananmen."[179] But Beijing failed to appreciate them.

The Chinese undid some things, too, and they would have more far-reaching consequences than canceling a few dialogues. The first was to break the agreement they had reached with Secretary Baker about shipping missiles to Pakistan. In late November, U.S. intelligence reported that China appeared to have shipped an unknown number of missiles from an M-11 production plant to Pakistan—although no actual missiles were sighted.[180] Even though no "smoking gun" was discovered then or later, a strong supposition grew within the intelligence community that Beijing—and probably Deng Xiaoping—had decided that two could play at the game of violating vague agreements. If the United States felt it could violate a joint communiqué with impunity, then China could violate an MTCR pledge. Second, China—within a week of the F-16 announcement—very publicly signed an agreement to provide Iran with a nuclear power reactor. Both countries agreed it would fall under International Atomic Energy Agency safeguards, but the agreement was seen as contributing to Iran's efforts to develop its nuclear program. According to Ambassador Roy, Baker had reached an agreement with China during his November 1991 visit that such assistance would be limited. Now it was expanded. Roy concluded that the Chinese were "thumbing their nose at us."[181]

Most important, China appears to have made a decision, after the F-16 sale, to revise its approach to the Taiwan issue. Always the central and most controversial issue in U.S.-China relations, the U.S.-PRC-Taiwan relationship took on a new sense of urgency for Beijing. Evidently perceiving the F-16 sale, the U.S. agreement to press Taiwan's case for GATT admission, and the increased seniority of Taiwanese government visitors to the United States and U.S. visitors to Taiwan as portending a U.S. shift in policy toward the island, Beijing began to step up pressure on Washington. Henceforward, no arms sale would go uncontested, no visit unprotested, no hint of change in the procedures for U.S.-Taiwan relations unchallenged. Beijing had a grievance, and it would henceforth work to extract every ounce of leverage it could from what it called Bush's "mistaken decision" on selling F-16s.

Bush did undertake a few more initiatives to mollify the Chinese. On September 28, he vetoed the United States–China Act of 1992 (H.R. 5218) and saw his veto sustained by the Senate four days later. On October 10, the USTR signed a market access agreement with China that was, again, long on promise and short on details. While the Chinese pledge to remove most tariff and nontariff barriers to U.S. products appeared to offer the promise of much-improved access to the China market for U.S. corporations, and also a reduction in China's trade surplus, enforcement provisions were not clearly defined. For its part, the United States also agreed to reduce American restrictions on high-technology goods, such as computers and telecommunications equipment.

Bush and his senior aides had told the Chinese that he would work to preserve U.S.-China relations better than his Democratic rival, and he implied that he would "make it up" to Beijing after the election.[182] The Chinese had made little secret of their preference for Bush over Clinton, even though they may have felt betrayed by him over the F-16 deal. Whether Bush's gestures would have been successful in restoring the relationship to a normal course is a moot point, since Bush lost the November 3 presidential election to Bill Clinton. Now the Chinese were left to pick up the pieces and swallow their humiliation. There would be no new initiatives from Washington to undo the damage. Although Commerce Secretary Barbara Franklin did travel to China in December—a trip highly criticized back home—none of the other meetings Assistant Secretary Clark promised came to pass. Even the Franklin visit was offset, to a certain degree, by the November "unofficial" visit to Taiwan of USTR Carla Hills, the first U.S. cabinet-level official to travel to the island since 1979.

At the close of the Bush administration, U.S.-China relations were nearly as icy as they had been all the way through. Neither side had been able to generate the domestic political support to justify a serious initiative to restore relations. Neither side had any reason to trust what the other said or did. Both harbored growing ideological and emotional misgivings about the other's intentions. And both took actions for domestic political reasons that seriously damaged prospects for improving the situation. Both governments professed a sincere desire to improve the relationship, but neither could take the steps to bring it about. The Bush administration may have hoped the Franklin trip would set bilateral relations on a positive course well into the new year. But the Clinton administration brought so much of its own baggage to the relationship that leftover problems from the Bush administration—particularly the Taiwan issue—would go nearly unnoticed.

CHAPTER FIVE

New Politics, Old Problems, 1993–94

The period following Deng Xiaoping's trip to southern China in 1992 is one of the most extraordinary periods of economic growth ever seen in any country. China had undergone economic reform sporadically since 1979 and achieved important results, going from an extremely poor and inefficient command economy to a mixed planning and market economy. The country also saw sharp gains in agricultural and rural industrial productivity. But the period after Deng's *nanxun* amounts to little short of a takeoff into the upper ranks of the world's economies. The statistics are striking. Between 1991 and 1993:

—China's nominal GNP grew by nearly 60 percent;

—The overall value of China's foreign trade rose more than 44 percent;

—World Bank project lending committed to China more than doubled; and

—Foreign direct investment (FDI) in China jumped nearly 450 percent.[1]

But the numbers do not do justice to the extraordinary amount of economic activity that seemed to seize the Chinese government and people during this period. With conservative command economy planners in political retreat, reform economists who had been laying low since the purge of Zhao Ziyang were able to push forward Zhao's economic reform plans with renewed vigor. During 1992 and 1993, the central government achieved many of the price reform goals that had eluded Zhao (decontrolling prices on most agricultural products, industrial goods, and energy), began to set down guidelines for the reform of money-losing state-owned enterprises (SOEs), established a new tax system to improve central control over revenues, formally legitimized private enterprise, established dozens of new "economic development zones" with special incentives for export-related industries, started revising the state constitution to support economic reform, adopted new accounting standards, reformed the banking system so it could better implement macroeconomic control, revised China's foreign exchange system, and broadened standards for foreign participation in the Chinese economy.[2] Each of these measures involved not only making significant changes in philosophy, attitude, and action among thousands of Chinese bureaucrats but massive shifts in capital flows, budgetary allocations, and resource utilization.

It's the Economy, Comrade

The process of deconstructing China's failed economic system and the political-ideological structure that undergirded it was complex and extremely controversial. Deng and his reformist cohorts had to battle not only dogmatic Marxists and Maoists in the Communist Party but also the enormous tradition-bound bureaucracies at central and provincial levels that implemented and controlled the central planning process. Furthermore, Deng had only a vague notion of what he wanted to put in place of the central command economic structure. Fundamentally pragmatic, he was willing to accept the idea that the capitalist system, and particularly the market system of allocating economic resources and channeling economic activity, had much to offer China. And he believed that economic decisionmaking could and should devolve to lower levels. But there was no model to follow for how to blend the economic dynamics of a free market system with a Leninist, tightly controlled political structure. Furthermore, there were huge risks for the Communist Party, as had been amply demonstrated in the fall of eastern bloc countries, the dissolution of the Soviet Union, and Tiananmen. Western democracy, he insisted, was not right for China, and its excesses needed to be controlled.[3]

Reformers adopted a tentative approach, which they called "crossing the river by groping for the stones."[4] In practice, it was a process of trial and error, implementing various reform measures on an experimental basis in different localities. Sometimes the initiative for the reform came from the local area, sometimes it came from the think tanks that grew up around Hu Yaobang and Zhao Ziyang. If the reforms were successful in solving problems or raising production, they were gradually expanded to other areas of China. If they failed, they were abandoned. Often, even successful reforms created new problems that had to be addressed with further reforms.

The most important benefit for the provinces was the new freedom many areas—particularly along the east coast and inland borders of China and along the Yangzi River—were given to manage their own economic development. In 1992, thirty cities (beyond the original four special economic zones) were authorized to open up important sectors of their economies, including commerce, banking, and real estate, to foreign investment. Private sector development—particularly small-scale rural and township industrial enterprises—was also given new approval, with the result that new nonstate enterprises emerged in large numbers very quickly. Even existing successful state-operated firms were encouraged to become joint-stock companies and sell shares on China's embryonic stock markets in Shanghai and Shenzhen.[5] Central government bureaucracies that had formerly managed all industrial enterprises were downsized and restructured, freeing local businesses significantly from central control or even oversight. Encouraged by the seriousness of China's reform plans, business executives in Hong Kong (who had generally limited their engagement in the Chinese economy following Tiananmen) poured billions of dollars of new investment into China's newly opened cities, contracting for hotels, leisure facilities, and industrial parks in the new development zones.

The result was massive economic activity, fueled by a combination of foreign, local government, and private investment. Even outside of Guangdong (where Hong Kong's entrepreneurial culture had been prevalent for several years), a new spirit of enthusiasm and risk taking began to be felt. "The whole country is going into business" (*quan min jie shang*) became a popular slogan, and communist role models were overshadowed by popular admiration for bold new entrepreneurs who "jumped into the sea" (*xia hai*) of entrepreneurial commerce. Even some prominent former dissidents took up private enterprise. Mou Qizhong, a former political prisoner-turned-deal maker, was represented in late 1992 as China's "first millionaire,"[6] while newly released Tiananmen student leader Wang Dan told Western reporters in 1993, "If I have the chance to go into business, I won't hesitate."[7]

The rest of the world soon took notice, and the idea quickly took hold in the Western business press that China had reached an economic take-off stage for its enormous market. Starry-eyed and optimistic about the long-hoped-for emergence of the nearly limitless China market, Western corporations were easily persuaded they would be wise to invest big and gain access early. Motorola Corporation vice president Richard Younts told the *New York Times* at the opening of a $125 million plant in Tianjin in 1992, "We want to be ready when this market takes off, and everything we see indicates that will come about."[8] World Bank and IMF studies speculated that China was not only the fastest-growing economy in the world but had suddenly become one of the world's two or three largest economies.[9] World Bank economist and future treasury secretary Lawrence Summers rhapsodized, "It may well be when the history of the late twentieth century is written one hundred years from now, the most significant event will be the revolutionary changes in China, which will soon be Communist only in a rhetorical sense."[10]

Leadership Dances

The important changes that took place within the party in 1992 were soon reflected in the government structure as well, with Li Peng stepping back, and Jiang and Zhu stepping forward. In March 1993, China's National People's Congress (NPC) met to take up issues pertinent to China's rapidly reforming economic, legal, and political structure. Most closely watched were the government positions:

—Jiang Zemin replaced eighty-five-year-old Yang Shangkun as China's president (in Chinese, *guojia zhuxi*, or state chairman), completing Jiang's assumption of all the major positions in China: Communist Party general secretary, chairman of the Military Commission, and head of state.[11] Although the position of president does not command any significant bureaucratic authority, Jiang's "election" indicated that he continued to enjoy Deng's favor and would be given every institutional advantage to succeed him as first among equals. From a foreign affairs perspective, Jiang's ascension to the presidency was a significant boost to his international reputation. As head of state, he was now entitled to travel more often and meet with counterpart heads of state, rather than just Communist Party leaders—an endangered species outside of Asia after 1991. Given his clear enjoyment of the ceremonial aspects of leadership, Jiang was certain to take advantage of new opportunities to engage in foreign policy.

—Although he probably would have retired in any case, hard-line vice president Wang Zhen died in early March, and his replacement was chosen at the NPC meeting. In a gesture laden with symbolism, Rong Yiren—former Shanghai capitalist (his family dominated the prewar textile business) and chairman of China International Trust and Investment Corporation (CITIC)—was named to the position. Besides being a reward for his loyalty to Deng and the regime, Rong's appointment demonstrated that nonparty persons with capitalist backgrounds were fully rehabilitated and could hold high office (if they had the party's blessing), and that business experience was now a desirable qualification for national office.

—As expected, Li Peng was chosen to serve a second (and by constitutional requirement, final) term as premier of the State Council. But in a sign of his personal unpopularity and a new climate of reformism, more than one in ten of the delegates (320 of 2,903) either abstained or voted against his reelection. Zhu Rongji was confirmed as the ranking vice premier, with overwhelming support from the delegates. Other conservative candidates for vice premier, such as Politburo member Li Tieying, had even more negative votes than Li Peng. Although hardly a flowering of democratic accountability, the results were evidence of a new attitude of NPC delegates, who increasingly felt obligated to carry out their duties of supervising the State Council and somewhat freer to vote against the government on occasion without fear of retribution. Moreover, the results of the voting were publicized. In a post-NPC press conference broadcast by Chinese TV, a foreign reporter even asked Li about his negative vote tally but got no response.[12]

—Qiao Shi, Politburo Standing Committee member and head of the party's Political and Legal Affairs Leading Group, was chosen chairman of the NPC Standing Committee, replacing Wan Li. Although Qiao, sixty-eight, was the senior leader most involved in China's internal security apparatus and had deserted Zhao Ziyang when the general secretary was under fire in 1989, he still maintained a reputation as a moderate reformer. With active assistance from First Vice Chairman Tian Jiyun, Qiao would accelerate the pace of change within China's rubber-stamp parliament, making it more active legislatively (it enacted sixty-seven laws in 1993, many supporting reform of the economy), more representative of local constituencies, and more aggressive in its supervision of government work. Although there was no definable "liberal wing" of the Communist Party, Qiao and Tian appeared dedicated to expanding gradually the rule of law in China and pursuing systemic political reform.[13]

—Finally, Politburo Standing Committee member Li Ruihuan was appointed chairman of the Chinese People's Political Consultative Conference (CPPCC) in March. A vestige of Mao Zedong's desire for the appearance of public support from China's prerevolutionary noncommunist parties, the CPPCC, representing eight separate parties and patriotic organizations, meets annually in conjunction with the NPC to ratify its decisions and reports. The appointment of a reform-minded Li suggested to some analysts that an effort might be under way to breathe new life into the moribund and elderly nonparty organization, perhaps even to provide an additional forum for criticism and supervision of the Communist Party and government. Although Li did travel more in his capacity as CPPCC chairman, his organization did not have the will, personnel, or capacity to go much beyond its traditional role as mere "window dressing for democracy," a yearly showcase for the fiction that China was not completely a one-party dictatorship.[14]

Before the NPC session, the party had convened a Central Committee plenary meeting at which delegates approved the revision of China's five-year plan growth targets from 6 percent to 8 percent. Given Li's personal association with the austerity program of 1989–91 and the 6 percent growth target figure, the decision was viewed as yet another setback for the beleaguered premier. Humiliated by the high number of votes against his reelection as premier and the sharp change in the direction of the government's work, Li evidently suffered some kind of health crisis in April and disappeared from public view for seven weeks. Chinese press authorities denied at first the sixty-four-year-old Li was ill, then admitted he was suffering from a "bad cold." Western press rumors had it that Li had suffered a mild heart attack and was recovering in an army hospital.[15] Whether his illness was genuine or "political," Li reappeared in mid-June and began "gradually resuming" his duties as premier, while still taking care of his health, according to the Chinese press spokesman.[16]

However, Li's duties had been reduced during his illness. Jiang Zemin had already been selected in March to head the newly revived Central Committee Leading Group on Finance and Economics, with Li and Zhu Rongji as his deputies. During Li's illness, Jiang replaced Li as head of the Foreign Affairs Leading Group, responsible for guiding China's overall foreign policy. Jiang was already head of the Central Leading Group on Taiwan Affairs, responsible for coordination of policy toward Taiwan, having taken over that position from Yang Shangkun.[17] One of his apparent initiatives was an agreement by the heads of the two organizations responsible for cross-Strait relations (the "Straits Exchange Foundation" on the Taiwan side and the "Association for Relations across the Taiwan Strait" in the PRC) to meet in Singapore in April 1993.

Although Zhu Rongji was not publicly designated as "executive vice premier" or "first vice premier" in Li's absence, he continued his takeover of China's economic apparatus even after Li returned. In July, for example, Zhu was appointed governor of the People's Bank of China (PBOC—China's central bank), replacing a Li Peng crony who was blamed for major strains in China's economy caused by irresponsible banking practices. Zhu brought in three new vice governors to do the hard work of implementing major changes in bank procedures, while he took the top job as a guarantor of discipline and control. In the circumstances, Li Peng probably was not unhappy to have someone else held accountable for the wild performance of the Chinese economy.[18]

Despite great public and official enthusiasm for reform and opening and impressive statistical performance in many sectors, China's economy was in trouble by mid-1993. Long-delayed price reforms implemented that year caused fuel, food, and other important commodity prices to rise sharply—in some cases, by more than 100 percent. Even the government's probably understated numbers showed the overall cost of living rose nearly 15 percent in 1993 and more than 24 percent in 1994.[19] With fewer controls on spending, local governments and enterprises used new infusions of funds from foreign direct investment and central government coffers to buy foreign luxury goods, build lavish tourist hotels and empty industrial parks, and invest in the Shanghai or Shenzhen stock market rather than putting the money into developing production.

Worse still, local officials pressured local banks to make available additional funds (often disguised as interbank loans) to invest in the volatile real estate and stock markets or other dubious speculative schemes. Land for the real estate development projects was, of course, public land—often bought and sold illegally by high-level cadres or their families with connections. Stories of massive corruption by Communist Party officials spread widely and stirred up considerable public anger. The thirst for investment capital was so great that some local areas even issued IOUs, rather than cash, to pay peasants for their grain, causing some riots and destruction of government property. Overall money circulating in the economy rose 50 percent in 1992, while the value of China's currency against the U.S. and Hong Kong dollars fell by more than one-third in the swap markets.[20]

Zhu Rongji, who balanced a solid record of support for reform as mayor of Shanghai with a keen understanding of the need for effective centralized macroeconomic control mechanisms, issued a series of administrative regulations first to stop uncontrolled speculation with official credit. He forbade issuance of IOUs to farmers, insisted that bank lending practices be brought into line with government standards, and prohibited the issuance of unregulated securities. He then instituted a restructuring of the central banking system, strengthening the role of the People's Bank of China as a central bank, modeled somewhat on the U.S. Federal Reserve system. He also ordered a tightening of restrictions on interbank lending and the recall of a large number of improper interbank loans.[21] To take more money out of circulation, he mandated the purchase of government bonds by millions of urban workers and ordered a 20 percent cut in government spending. Other aspects of Zhu's reported sixteen-point austerity plan included a ban on foreign automobile imports and cancellation of approvals for many new economic development zones.[22]

To some observers, Zhu's measures looked like a return to a centralized planned economy, although Western commentators generally appeared to appreciate the necessity of taking rather drastic actions to rein in inflation and stock market speculation.[23] Local governments and speculators in China, particularly in the southeastern coastal regions, protested to their friends in Hong Kong and Beijing. Those protests, among other factors, reached the nearly deaf ears of Deng Xiaoping, who chose to intervene in the policy arena one last time. In September 1993, Deng reportedly called a meeting of senior leaders, including Jiang, to put a halt to austerity measures and to announce another round of rapid growth. His cause clearly was advanced by the publication in early November of the third volume of his *Selected Works*, which extolled again fast-paced economic liberalization. "Development at a slow pace is not socialism," Deng supposedly told party leaders just before the Third Plenum of the Fourteenth Central Committee, held November 11–14.[24] As he had so many times before, Deng appeared to be trying to rebalance the political system through simplistic pronouncements on economic issues. Others in the leadership, including a suddenly far healthier and belatedly reformist Li Peng, echoed Deng's remarks in advocating a high rate of growth.[25]

Although probably embarrassed by Deng's about-face and forced to back away from inflation-fighting policies that looked too much like retrenchment, Zhu still emerged from the Third Plenum with Central Committee approval of a codified fifty-point program for speeding up China's transition to a market economy. He retained control of the State Council economic bureaucracy, as well as of Communist Party leading groups in charge of agriculture, finance, and trade. Given the inevitable rise in indicators of an overheating economy in 1994, Zhu remained the one to whom the government would turn to bring the situation back under control. But while Zhu remained the most influential figure in China's most important political arena—the economy—he had been humiliated somewhat by the patriarch and seemed to be both out of sorts and out of favor by the end of the year. Li Peng's return to health and Jiang Zemin's indifferent support for Zhu's economic policies would have a deleterious effect on Zhu's political prospects and his ability to accomplish his goals.

Deng's intervention, however, was to be his last of any significance. Increasingly weakened by Parkinson's disease and other illnesses—though evidently not mentally incapacitated—Deng's withdrawal from political activity was probably not entirely voluntary. But at the age of eighty-nine, he no longer had the energy or stamina to assert his will regularly on increasingly complex policies. Television pictures of Deng at a spring festival reception in Shanghai in February 1994 showed a frail old man, supported by his daughters when standing, smiling vacantly, and waving shaky hands at well wishers.

Press commentators in Hong Kong and Taipei continued to report rumors on Deng's activities and opinions. Some American officials thought that he was still making key decisions about bilateral relations. Deng's family proclaimed his health was satisfactory. But it was unlikely that Deng was playing any more than an occasional advisory role by early 1994. The same was true of Chen Yun, who had also sunk into senescence. As rumors recurred about the state of Deng's health, the "third generation" of China's leadership began making its internal accommodations without him. Jiang, Zhu, Li Peng, and Qiao Shi began a complex process of maneuvering for position and influence, preparing for political life without Deng. In the meantime, they used his words, prestige, and authority for maintaining the course of economic reform and social stability. Dengism was alive and well. But Deng—like Mao in his dotage—had become a political wraith: feared, respected, perceived to be powerful, used by those who needed him but usually invisible and increasingly insubstantial.

Economic Reform and Foreign Policy

China's economic influence and performance in the early 1990s had a profound impact on China's self-image and view of the world but a somewhat less perceptible change on its foreign policy line and practice. The World Bank/International Monetary Fund report, which rated China's economy as the world's third largest in 1993, after the United States and Japan, generated elation and shock in China. But its main effect clearly was to enhance a sense of national pride and entitlement. "The main importance of this [IMF report] is geopolitical," said Paul Krugman, an economist at the Massachusetts Institute of Technology. "It's a reminder that China is a great power already, which is something many people haven't quite grasped yet."[26]

China had long entertained great power aspirations, and in certain respects—such as in the United Nations and its relations with some of its Asian neighbors—had become used to being so treated. Most Chinese seemed to believe that China merited consideration as a global power by virtue of its size, long history, and complex culture. But in many other ways, the Chinese perceived their country and believed it was perceived by others as poor and backward, a victim of great power politics more than a great power itself. The duality of Chinese nationalism—pride in China's achievements combined with hypersensitivity to its past humiliation—was heightened by its economic success.[27] Now that it was being recognized by international financial institutions and Western corporations as an economic global power—on a scale comparable to the United States and Japan—many Chinese began to believe China deserved to be treated with greater respect and deference. While this did not entail throwing its weight around economically or politically, this attitude did manifest itself in a somewhat more assertive approach to external pressure by China's leaders. More than ever, they "were convinced that China ought to stand equal with other great powers and that there was something profoundly wrong with a world that denied it this status."[28] No country was more anxiously looked to for that respect than the United States. But to put it mildly, China's view of the United States was ambivalent.

China's leaders supported and were supported by a significant change in attitude among China's intelligentsia during the mid-1990s. No longer allowed to discuss liberal Western democratic theory as freely as in the 1980s, and disenchanted by China's experience and by their observations of Russia and the eastern European postcommunist states, several of China's prominent thinkers turned toward a more conservative, traditional political philosophy. "Neo-conservatism" posited the need for a strong, authoritarian, traditional Chinese state to deal with the numerous problems involved in economic reform.[29] And it rejected Western-style democracy as being unable to deal with China's problems or accelerate its modernization. *Zhanlue yu Guanli (Strategy and Management*—a journal begun in 1992 with rumored support from the military) and several other conservative political journals published sophisticated and cogent critiques of Western liberal philosophy and persuasive inquiries into Chinese historical questions that attracted wide readership at the time.[30] *Looking at China through a Third Eye*, a best-seller in 1994, was a nationalistic, critical diatribe on the failings of Western liberal democracy to solve China's emerging economic and social problems, replete with sharp criticisms of the United States (chapter 1 is entitled "Don't Interfere in China.").[31]

Popular culture also helped reinforce the leadership's predisposition toward a tough approach to foreign affairs. Although the immediate aftermath of Tiananmen witnessed a crackdown on literature and the media, they were beginning to flourish again by early 1993. Part of the cause was economic—China's growing middle class had more leisure time and disposable income and consequently an interest in better-quality entertainment. Moreover, party leaders made a conscious decision—probably also dictated by necessity—that the publications business should be self-sustaining, not state operated. Finally, the "opening to the outside" promoted anew by Deng in his southern tour in 1992 brought a new wealth of entertainment possibilities from Hong Kong and Taiwan, particularly cable television. China's media industry was quick to catch on and catch up. The result was an explosion in popular entertainment—television game shows, rock music, talk radio, and escapist fiction. "By 1994 China had 561 publishing houses, about 8,000 periodicals, more than 2,100 newspapers and over 300 audio-visual publishing companies," all competing for the attention of the urban, as well as the rural audience.[32] Some of the popular entertainment had a strongly nationalistic, even an anti-American, flavor.

From Candidate to President—Clinton's Rocky Transition

William Jefferson Clinton was elected the forty-second president of the United States on November 3, 1992, defeating President George Bush and independent candidate H. Ross Perot with 43 percent of the popular vote. The first "baby boomer" president—born after the end of World War II—the former governor of Arkansas won on the strength of his own qualities (youthful, intelligent, articulate, and telegenic), Bush's listless campaign, dissatisfaction with twelve years of Republican control of the White House, serious economic and social problems, and Perot's quirky protest candidacy, which garnered 19 percent of the popular vote, pulling slightly more votes away from the Republican than the Democratic Party. Clinton's election strategy focused on maintaining traditional Democratic Party support among organized labor and African American voters, coupled with a strong appeal to independents, moderate Republicans, women, and older voters. The Democratic Party also promised to work for social change, better economic growth, and improved employment for American workers.

Clinton's campaign watch words, "It's the Economy, Stupid," reflected his own and his advisers' view that economic issues—jobs, inflation, welfare, Social Security, trade, and taxes—counted most for American voters. He took full campaign advantage of the public perceptions that the American economy was still suffering from a post–Gulf War recession (it had actually already begun a recovery) and that the enormous budget deficit required political action to resolve. He also managed to neutralize one of Bush's political assets—his knowledge and experience in foreign affairs—by accusing Bush of spending too much time but not enough money on foreign affairs and by attacking Bush's astute political realism as "coddling tyrants from Baghdad to Beijing."[33] He faulted Bush for not paying sufficient attention to "American values," such as democracy and human rights, and charged he was "out of the mainstream." But mostly, Clinton criticized the damage that Bush's handling of the U.S. economy did to foreign policy. "An anemic, debt-laden economy undermines our diplomacy, makes it harder for us to secure favorable trade agreements and compromises our ability to finance essential military actions."[34]

Clinton was not a novice in foreign affairs. He had majored in international relations at Georgetown University and remained interested in it during his two years at Oxford University in England, where he was a Rhodes scholar. But his deep involvement in the local politics of Arkansas had turned his interests elsewhere, and aside from a few Asian trade junkets (including several trips to Taiwan), he came into office with little experience—and some said, little interest—in foreign affairs. Nonetheless, Clinton announced a strong foreign policy team in late December. He chose Warren Christopher, a California-based lawyer who had served as deputy secretary of state to Cyrus Vance during the Carter administration, as secretary of state. Christopher had headed the team that helped Clinton choose Senator Albert W. Gore of Tennessee as his vice presidential running mate and was highly regarded as a skilled negotiator and problem solver, though not a broad foreign policy conceptualizer.

Clinton chose Les Aspin as secretary of defense. Aspin was elected to the House of Representatives from Wisconsin in 1970 and eventually became chairman of the powerful House Armed Services Committee. He had been a Ph.D. "whiz kid" in Secretary of Defense Robert McNamara's Pentagon. Considered brilliant, but rather folksy and disorganized, Aspin had thought a great deal about the post–cold war U.S. military and was expected to bring innovative approaches to bear.

Anthony Lake, a former foreign service officer who served in the Kissinger National Security Council (NSC) during the Nixon administration but quit in opposition to the 1970 U.S. incursion into Cambodia, became national security adviser (assistant to the president for national security affairs, or APNSA). Cerebral and self-effacing, Lake was head of Policy Planning at the State Department and a key adviser to Vance during the Carter administration. After that he taught at Mt. Holyoke College in Massachusetts and raised cattle on his 140-acre farm.

Other key members of the foreign policy team included James R. Woolsey as director of Central Intelligence (DCI); Madeleine Albright as ambassador to the United Nations, a position Clinton upgraded to Cabinet rank; and General Colin Powell as chairman of the Joint Chiefs of Staff (JCS). Woolsey was considered an expert on nuclear weapons and arms control issues and had served as undersecretary of the navy during the Carter administration. Albright was on the NSC during the Carter administration, then taught political science at Georgetown University, where she had a reputation as a strong advocate of democracy and human rights. Powell, a Bush holdover who had once been national security adviser, was not expected to stay long.

Rounding out the top positions in the National Security Council were Samuel R. (Sandy) Berger, a friend of Clinton's from Yale Law School days and Lake's deputy at Policy Planning, and Nancy R. Soderberg, former staff assistant to Senator Edward M. Kennedy, who had been active in the campaign.[35] Robert E. Rubin, a successful Wall Street stockbroker and cochairman of Goldman Sachs, was appointed "assistant to the president for economic policy" and chairman of the newly formed National Economic Council (NEC).[36] Press coverage of the foreign policy team noted the strong contingent of Carter administration officials (and its "dovish" wing, at that), the careful selection of women, in keeping with Clinton's promise to build a Cabinet that "looked like America," and the preference for team players, low-key personalities, and implementers rather than conceptualizers of policy. "By the nature of his . . . choices, Mr. Clinton has in effect assigned himself the main roles of chief policy architect, articulator and arbiter," *New York*

Times columnist Tom Friedman speculated.[37] That would operate satisfactorily on domestic political and economic issues, but given the president's lack of enthusiasm for foreign affairs, it was a structure that lacked clear and directed leadership from the top.[38]

Getting Organized

Activist and enthusiastic, the new policy team hit the ground running and occasionally stumbling. They were hampered first by organizational and personnel constraints. Structurally, they set to work quickly to maximize communication and coordination among the principal foreign policy bureaucracies. Christopher and Aspin were confirmed easily by the Senate on Inauguration Day, January 20. The NSC staff positions do not require Senate confirmation, so Lake also was in position by then. On January 20–21, Clinton issued two Presidential Decision Directives (PDDs), establishing the foreign policy decisionmaking structure for his administration and the documentary formats that were to be used.[39] More important, he expanded the formal membership of the National Security Council to include the secretary of the treasury, the U.S. permanent representative to the United Nations, the assistant to the president for national security affairs, the assistant to the president for economic policy, and the chief of staff to the president.[40] In practice, however, the formal National Security Council did not meet often.

Instead, Clinton continued the practice established by the Bush administration of having a three-tiered foreign policy decisionmaking process. At the highest level was the Principals Committee, which essentially was the National Security Council without the president and vice president, namely, the secretaries or heads of the relevant departments and agencies. Because Principals Committee meetings were called and chaired by the national security adviser, the NSC staff prepared the agenda and issued a written summary of the results of the meeting, as well as any recommendations for the president that may have been reached.[41] At the next level, the Deputies Committee operated similarly—called and chaired by the deputy assistant to the president for National Security Affairs (DAPNSA), attended by the number two officials of the relevant agencies. Often, but not always, the Deputies Committee recommendations fed into a Principals Committee. In both meetings, departments were generally allowed to bring a "plus one," usually an assistant secretary–level person with knowledge of the issue at hand. Unusually sensitive meetings sometimes dropped the "plus ones" out of concern for leaks. In general, depending on travel schedules, there was at least one Principals Committee or Deputies Committee meeting each week and very often more than that.

The basic level of policy formulation and coordination was the Interagency Work Group (IWG, usually pronounced "eye wig"), which replaced the Policy Coordinating Committee of the Bush administration. Although formulated and coordinated through the NSC, these meetings were often cochaired by State Department assistant secretaries and NSC senior directors and attended by deputy assistant secretary personnel as well as substantive desk officers and analysts from the relevant departments and agencies. Papers for the IWG were prepared by the office principally responsible for the issue, most often the relevant State Department desk, with inputs as needed from other agencies.[42]

Within a matter of a few months, Lake realized the formal committee and meeting structure did not always facilitate what he perceived to be his principal role as "coordinator" of policy, or honest broker. Despite his intentions—shared by Christopher—to avoid the kind of rivalry between national security adviser and secretary of state that had plagued the Nixon-Ford and Carter administrations, divergences of view came up early and often on controversial issues such as Bosnia and Haiti. Recognizing that both policy coordination and initiative often flow through informal channels, Lake, Christopher, and Aspin established events at which issues could be discussed and hashed out without formal agendas, position papers, and decision memorandums. One was a Wednesday morning breakfast at the White House, which included the secretaries of state and defense, the DCI, chairman of the Joint Chiefs of Staff, and UN ambassador, as well as APNSA.[43] Another was a weekly lunch, attended only by Lake, Christopher, and the secretary of defense. The agenda was agreed on in advance, and each would bring staff-prepared notes for the issues to be discussed, but the purpose was informal dialogue, not decisionmaking. Lake acknowledged that, on occasion, some decisions were vetted in advance of Principals Committee meetings. It was significant, however, that the president did not attend any of these sessions. Christopher tried to persuade him to meet informally with his foreign policy team but was, for the most part, not successful.[44]

Each of the three principal foreign policy decisionmakers struggled early with organizational difficulties. At the State Department, although most of the undersecretaries were confirmed by mid-February, several assistant secretaries were held up by Senator Jesse Helms, then-ranking Republican on the Senate Foreign Relations Committee. Helms used his prerogative of putting a "hold" on specific nominations as a means of leveraging the State Department on policy or personnel issues.

At NSC, Lake, Berger, and Soderberg faced difficulties in organizing a paper flow, determining who had what access to the president, and dividing up the enormous workload of substantive issues among themselves. They were further hampered by the absence of a detailed record of Bush administration foreign policy, owing to the fact that all records were transferred to archives for eventual storage in the Bush Presidential Library.[45] Most seriously, they had to start out implementing a presidential campaign promise to reduce by 25 percent the staff in the Executive Office of the President. "Our White House will be leaner but more effective, and designed to work both hard and smart for the changes we seek in America," Clinton told reporters on February 9.[46]

In practice, the personnel cut created an NSC staff that was constantly understaffed and overworked. "It was a good one-day headline and had terrible consequences ever after," Lake complained later.[47] The Asia Directorate, for example, had only two professional officers covering issues pertaining to China, Japan, the Korean Peninsula, Southeast Asia, and Oceania. Although somewhat less afflicted than other White House operations with an overabundance of young, inexperienced staffers, the Lake NSC also suffered somewhat from the problems of "newness, haste, hubris and naïveté" that typify early White House actions of most administrations.[48]

The NSC difficulties, however, paled in comparison with the Defense Department, where Secretary Aspin proved an inept administrator. He got on poorly with many senior military officers, who saw his casual style as lacking in bearing and seriousness. He tried to reorganize the Pentagon's policy offices, bringing in several nonmainstream academic experts, including Morton Halperin and Graham Allison, to prepare policy on some of Clinton's campaign agenda issues, such as peacekeeping and humanitarian assistance. They not only elicited significant congressional opposition (particularly Halperin, who had testified in support of Daniel Ellsberg in leaking the Pentagon Papers) but also won little support at the State Department or NSC. Aspin's style of management within his own department was disorganized and detached, resembling the way he had run the House Armed Services Committee. Finally, Aspin's handling of the question of lifting restrictions on homosexuals in the military—a Clinton campaign promise that blew up within days of his inauguration—was resented by most of the service chiefs and JCS Chairman Powell.[49] Undersecretary for Policy Frank Wisner and Assistant Secretary for Regional Security Charles W. "Chas" Freeman brought stability and professionalism to the more "traditional" issue areas of Pentagon policymaking, but they were hampered by the controversies that swirled around the Defense Department during Aspin's brief tenure as secretary.

Foreign Policy Priorities

From the first days of the new administration, Clinton's foreign policy agenda was to a large degree set by problems that had carried over from the

Bush administration. Vicious ethnic warfare in the former state of Yugoslavia, with its chilling reminders of Nazi concentration camps showing up on evening newscasts, shocked Americans and Europeans alike into calling for military action. Desperate Haitians took to the sea in boats to escape their brutal government and reach sanctuary in the United States. Iraq's Saddam Hussein, defeated but not deposed, stirred up trouble in the Middle East. And Bush's sudden military involvement in Somalia—turning a famine-alleviation mission into a search-and-destroy campaign against Somali warlords—worried military and civilian defense officials alike.

Besides dealing with immediate crises, the new foreign policy team was attempting to take stock of American international commitments and to define a new strategy for a post–cold war world. Within two weeks of inauguration, the NSC had commissioned twenty-nine policy review directives at three levels of urgency on issues ranging from those cited above to Russia, international trade, the North American Free Trade Agreement, peacekeeping, democratization, and regional affairs.[50] At the same time, they were trying to develop a coherent and activist foreign policy in the face of public attitudes toward foreign affairs that ranged from apathy to outright hostility and isolationism.

In late May, Undersecretary of State for Political Affairs Peter Tarnoff, speaking on a not-for-attribution basis, declared that the United States no longer had the economic resources to provide leadership in all international circumstances and that European allies and international organizations would have to play a larger role. His remarks—although never officially reported—were officially disavowed by the State Department press spokesman and by the White House press secretary, who said, "That person does not speak for the President, the Secretary of State, or the Administration."[51] The sharp rebuttals—which embarrassed Tarnoff but did not damage his career—were evidence of the organizational untidiness of the administration's foreign policy bureaucracy and the difficulty of harmonizing domestic economic considerations and foreign policy. *Washington Post* columnist Jim Hoagland fumed, "It is not clear today what this government means by leadership, how it proposes to exercise that definition abroad when it is reached or how other governments are expected to respond."[52] Others complained increasingly of the absence of "bold new thinking" to address the problems of a post-Soviet world.[53]

Winston Lord and China Policy

In light of major foreign policy problems in other regions of the world and intense focus on domestic issues—particularly a budget deficit reduction plan—China policy was low on the new administration's list of priorities in 1993. But what was said and done probably caused considerable consternation in Beijing. In his confirmation hearings in January, Warren Christopher warned of troubling changes. "A complex blend of new and old forces requires us to rethink our policy toward China . . . We cannot ignore continuing reports of Chinese exports of sensitive military technology to troubled areas, widespread violations of human rights, or abusive practices that have contributed to a $17 billion trade imbalance between our two nations. Our policy will seek to facilitate a *peaceful evolution* of China from communism to democracy by encouraging the forces of economic and political liberalization in that great country."[54] The use of a term so politically freighted in China no doubt created instant suspicion. To Chinese Communist Party leaders, "peaceful evolution" was just a polite term for slowly overthrowing socialism.

Christopher asked Winston Lord in January 1993 to serve as assistant secretary of state for East Asia and the Pacific. Lord was no stranger to Asian affairs—and particularly China policy. After his break with the Bush administration over the Scowcroft mission and the Pelosi bill, Lord had been active in promoting more punitive approaches to the government and supporting "progressive" forces in China, although he still supported strategic engagement. By 1991, his position "evolved" toward conditioning renewal of most favored nation (MFN) status on China's accounting for political prisoners, allowing more freedom of emigration, and ceasing the jamming of Voice of America (VOA) broadcasts—conditions he believed China could meet if it chose to do so.[55] During the 1992 presidential campaign, Lake invited Lord (with whom he had worked on Kissinger's NSC staff) to brief candidate Clinton on the China issue. Lord included in his discussion the issue of "moderate conditions" for MFN, following up subsequently with a paper.[56]

Although Lord's nomination was one of those held up by Senator Helms, he eventually won easy confirmation from the Senate Foreign Relations Committee. In his statement to the committee on March 31, Lord sketched out his overall approach to Asia in detail and reflected the new administration's efforts to balance strategic and moral considerations in policy toward China. "Our policy challenge . . . is to reconcile our need to deal with this important nation with our imperative to promote international values. We will seek cooperation with China on a range of issues. But Americans cannot forget Tiananmen Square." Clearly reflecting a view that the Beijing regime would not remain in power indefinitely, Lord described Chinese leaders as "gambling that open economics and closed politics will preserve their system of control," an approach he predicted would fail. He recommended that the United States "conduct a nuanced policy toward Beijing until a more humane system emerges" and pledged that, although Washington would not shun Beijing, it would "condemn repression and preserve links with progressive forces which are the foundations for our longer term ties."[57]

Although he had several other Asian issues he believed required careful attention, Lord focused heavily on China immediately after his confirmation. He chose his former deputy chief of mission from Beijing, Peter Tomsen, to serve as his principal deputy and persuaded Lake to hire his former economic counselor, Kent Wiedemann, as senior director for Asian affairs at the National Security Council.[58] He started a comprehensive China policy review directive, working with Wiedemann and the China desk at the State Department to develop a broad issues-based engagement approach. One of his most important tasks, however, was working with Congress to find a compromise on how to deal with MFN.

The Democratic Party platform on which Clinton had run promised "conditioning of favorable trade terms of China on respect for human rights in China and Tibet, greater market access for U.S. goods, and responsible conduct on weapons proliferation."[59] Clinton had reiterated the intention to link MFN and human rights at several points during the campaign. After his election, he appeared to shift toward more neutral ground, noting some progress had been made under the Bush administration, but he still saw a relationship—a means of leverage—between China's growing trade surplus with the United States and its vulnerability to pressure on other issues. Congressional leaders—and particularly Representative Nancy Pelosi in the House and Senator George Mitchell in the Senate, who had emerged as the China "issue leaders"—fully expected the president to follow through on his pledge of linking MFN with China's performance on human rights, nuclear and missile exports, and market access.

Working with Wiedemann, Berger, and Soderberg in the White House and quietly within the State Department at Christopher's behest, Lord contacted Mitchell's and Pelosi's offices not long after his confirmation and indicated the administration wanted to work with Congress on the MFN issue in 1993. Lord knew there were some in Congress who were proposing outright revocation of MFN, which the administration could not support. Other congressional proposals for conditioning MFN were far too stringent and not practicable. Lord became, in his own words, the "point man," "trying to work out conditions that were moderate from our standpoint but enough from their standpoint that they could deliver the House and the Senate, particularly the House" in support of renewing MFN for another year.[60]

On April 22, Mitchell and Pelosi announced they were introducing new legislation to condition China's MFN for the following year. The United States–China Act of 1993 (H.R. 1835) was very similar to the bill President Bush had vetoed (H.R. 5318) in 1992 and was intended to establish a clear congressional position. As Mitchell put it, "My hope is that the bill won't be necessary. My hope is that it will enable the administration to bring about the kind of changes that this legislation will impose only if no meaningful action is taken."[61]

The bill stipulated that the president

> may not recommend continuation of [MFN] for the People's Republic of China, unless the President reports . . . that the government of that country—
>
> (1) has taken appropriate actions to begin adhering to the provisions of the Universal Declaration of Human Rights in China and Tibet;
>
> (2) is allowing unrestricted emigration of the citizens who desire to leave China for reasons of political or religious persecution to join family members abroad . . . ;
>
> (3) has provided an acceptable accounting for and release of Chinese citizens detained, accused, or sentenced as a result of . . . demonstrations in Tiananmen Square on June 4, 1989 . . . ;
>
> (4) has taken effective, verifiable action to prevent export of products to the United States manufactured wholly or in part by convict, forced, or indentured labor . . . ;
>
> (5) has made *overall significant progress* in—
>
> (A) ceasing religious persecution and lifting restrictions on freedom of religious belief in the People's Republic of China and Tibet . . . ;
>
> (B) releasing leaders and members of religious groups detained, imprisoned, or under house arrest for expression of their religious beliefs;
>
> (C) ceasing unfair and discriminatory trade practices which restrict and unreasonably burden American business;
>
> (D) providing United States exporters fair access to Chinese markets, including lowering tariffs, removing nontariff barriers, and increasing the purchase of United States goods and services;
>
> (E) adhering to the guidelines and parameters of the Missile Technology Control Regime and the controls adopted by the Nuclear Suppliers Group and the Australian Group on Chemical and Biological Arms;
>
> (F) adhering to the Joint Declaration on Hong Kong that was entered into between the United Kingdom and the People's Republic of China;
>
> (G) cooperating with United States efforts to obtain an acceptable accounting of United States military personnel who are listed as prisoners of war or missing in action as a result of their service in . . . the Korean conflict or . . . the Vietnam conflict;

(H) ceasing the jamming of Voice of America broadcasts; and

(I) providing international human rights and humanitarian groups access to prisoners, trials, and places of detention.[62]

Reaching Out to Clinton

China's leaders scarcely needed any public encouragement in 1993 to take a tough stand against Clinton. They were still highly upset with the United States over Taiwan policy questions—particularly the sale of F-16s to Taiwan—and were even rumored to be considering withdrawing their ambassador. They were something less than charmed or encouraged by the election of the Arkansas governor as president in November. Although Chinese leaders had been unhappy with decisions President Bush had made in late 1992, they were even more concerned with the statements Clinton had made during the campaign and the signals they had received from him. Clinton's campaign platform had explicitly supported congressional plans to link China's MFN status to improvements in its human rights, trade, and nonproliferation practices.[63] Prominent student leaders Chai Ling and Li Lu had appeared on the podium at the Democratic National Convention, where they were cheered as heroes, and another student activist, Zhao Haiching, president of the Chinese Students Association, was known to have advised Clinton on China policy.[64] Although the Chinese government had not come out directly in support of George Bush's re-election, few American observers were in any doubt about its preference.

Nonetheless, Chinese leaders made carefully guarded efforts to reach out to Clinton after his election. They sent brief and somewhat belated congratulations to the president-elect on November 6. Vice Foreign Minister Liu Huaqiu traveled to Washington in mid-November for quiet consultations with congressional Democrats, including Senator David Boren of Oklahoma, chairman of the Senate Select Committee on Intelligence.[65] Boren and Senator Claiborne Pell (chairman of the Senate Foreign Relations Committee) subsequently traveled to Beijing in early December, where Jiang Zemin, Qiao Shi, and other senior leaders received them. They were given assurances that China would cooperate with American investigators trying to account for American fliers who might have crashed in China during the Vietnam War. They were also permitted to travel to Tibet, if only for one day.[66]

Representative Patricia Schroeder of Colorado led a small House delegation to Beijing at about the same time. Jiang chose the meeting with Schroeder to use for the first time a sixteen-character slogan that he hoped would exemplify the relationship: "Increase mutual trust, reduce troubles, develop cooperation, and avoid confrontation" (*zengjia xinren, jianshao mafan, fazhan hezuo, bimian duikang*).[67]

Both American delegations, however, warned the Chinese that the Clinton administration was more likely to be tough and probably would allow Congress to impose conditions on China's MFN status. They recommended that China make some goodwill gestures, such as an amnesty for Tiananmen political prisoners or permitting the International Committee of the Red Cross (ICRC) to visit Chinese jails.[68] Beijing's leaders did not respond to those entreaties but did make some gestures, perhaps to see if they would be noticed. Even before the delegations arrived, they had announced the purchase of 2 million tons of American wheat, after threatening to cut off all imports in the wake of the F-16 sale.[69] Neither delegation made mention of the sale. In January 1993, the regime announced the release from prison of 1979 Democracy Movement leader Wang Xizhe and Tiananmen activist Gao Shan. The State Department noted briefly that it "welcomed the releases."[70] In February, Wang Dan—a key student leader at Tiananmen who had been first on Beijing's wanted list in 1989—was released on parole, four months ahead of schedule. Several other dissidents were released at the same time. In March, Beijing released eighteen Catholic priests from long terms of imprisonment and indicated to visiting Americans that it was interested in a "reasonable" discussion of human rights.[71] In May, as Clinton's MFN decision approached, Beijing released Xu Wenli, another prominent dissenter from the Democracy Wall era. In each case, there was no official response from Washington.

Linkage and Tension—The Human Rights Question

Winston Lord and NSC Senior Director Kent Wiedemann traveled to Beijing in May for talks with the Chinese Ministry of Foreign Affairs officials. Press accounts indicate they presented a fourteen-point list of concerns the United States had with China's policies, a list that corresponded closely to the fourteen points in the Pelosi-Mitchell bill described above. The talks were contentious and hard-edged and reached virtually no agreement on how to proceed. Lord departed with a statement that "the Chinese certainly should be under no illusions now of the seriousness of the situation and the fact that conditions [to MFN] are very likely." He said there would have to be "dramatic progress" in human rights, trade, and nonproliferation if sanctions were to be avoided.[72] Chinese officials issued no official statement but told the Hong Kong press they were "prepared for the worst." "No conditions are acceptable to China," said one trade official.[73] Privately, Chinese officials expressed anger and frustration at the visit, because it was arranged at the last minute and because Lord provided no clear path for them to take to avoid the humiliation of conditioned MFN.[74] They sent back their own list of seven demands they wanted the United States to address. Subsequently, there were unsubstantiated reports that Jiang denounced the Lord visit at a Politburo meeting, calling the fourteen points a "coercive ultimatum."[75]

After a trip to Singapore, where they informed worried Asians that conditions were likely to be attached to China's MFN, Lord and Wiedemann returned to Washington to finalize preparations for the joint congressional-executive China policy pronouncement on MFN. They began the process of converting a congressional action into an executive branch decision, namely, an Executive Order, paring down the list of conditions and the standards by which Chinese behavior would be judged. In hindsight, NSC deputy Berger insisted they were aiming for a two-step, two-year process that would eventually "get to a point where we would have a human rights policy and a trade policy, but not linking one to the other." But the first step was getting the policy initiative restored to the executive branch, free of a number of extraneous issues—such as labor standards, abortion, and nonproliferation—that had attached themselves to congressional bills.[76] This was still a very closely held process, not handled within an Interagency Working Group context. The economic agencies of the U.S. government—Treasury, Commerce, the Office of the U.S. Trade Representative (USTR), and even the National Economic Council—were excluded from the policy formulation process. Lord insisted that including them "wasn't my mandate" from the White House. "We had to have a deal before the hot-heads on either side knew what it was about" and wanted very much to avoid leaks to the press.[77]

As the June 3 date required by law for the president to announce his decision on MFN drew near, Lord intensified his consultations on Capitol Hill and received critical support from key House Democrats for the approach of extending MFN for a one-year period via Executive Order and mandating revocation the following year if certain human rights standards were not achieved by the Chinese government. Besides leaving the initiative in the hands of the executive branch, Lord's proposal stripped out nonproliferation and trade balance issues from the Executive Order, leaving it strictly a human rights–related document. The State Department and some members of Congress praised the "spirit of cooperation" that underlay these efforts.[78] Although the briefings and consultations went on at precisely the same time as the president's all-important budget plan was coming up for a vote in the House, there was no evident political relationship between the two actions, and it was very clear the president was far more engaged in the budget vote than the China issue.

On May 28, 1993, the day after he won approval of his budget plan in the House by a two-vote margin, President Clinton called key members of Congress (pointedly, Senator Mitchell and Representative Pelosi), White House and State Department officials, business leaders, representatives of human rights organizations, and Chinese expatriate students to the White House for the announcement of his signing Executive Order 12850, "Conditions for Renewal of Most Favored Nation Status for the People's Republic of China." Still reflecting his elation over the House budget vote, he observed how the "annual battles between Congress and the Executive [over MFN] divided our foreign policy and weakened our approach over China. It is time that a unified American policy recognize both the value of China and the values of America. Starting today, the United States will speak with one voice on China policy. We no longer have an executive branch policy and a congressional policy. We have an American policy." Clinton noted how reform had begun to change the face of China in hopeful ways but that the United States still needed to express "our clear disapproval of its repressive policies." After briefly describing the seven conditions that would apply to the renewal of MFN in 1994, he went on to discuss issues that had been excluded from the Executive Order, particularly missile proliferation and trade balance problems, indicating that the administration intended to pursue a tougher policy toward China across the board.[79]

Not surprisingly, the Executive Order bore a strong resemblance to the Pelosi-Mitchell bill. It differed in that it gave the Chinese government, in effect, a year's grace period in which to revise its human rights policies. But for the president to recommend extension again in 1994, he needed a recommendation from the secretary of state that China had complied with the standards of freedom of emigration contained in the Trade Act of 1974 and with the 1992 Memorandum of Agreement on preventing Chinese prison labor exports to the United States. (These two conditions were mandatory).

China also had to have made "overall, significant progress" in the following areas:

—Adhering to the United Nations Universal Declaration of Human Rights;

—Releasing and accounting for persons imprisoned for expressing their political or religious beliefs, including specifically those involved in Tiananmen;

—Permitting international humanitarian and human rights organizations to have access to Chinese prisoners to ensure their humane treatment;

—"Protecting Tibet's distinctive religious and cultural heritage;" and

—Permitting international radio and television broadcasts into China (that is, ceasing the jamming of Voice of America).[80]

Reaction to the Executive Order linking MFN extension and China's human rights "performance" was mixed. Some in Congress wanted tougher sanctions or even outright and immediate revocation. Others, such as Robert Matsui of California and Lee Hamilton, chair of the House Foreign Affairs Committee, were wary of the president's approach and would have preferred unconditional renewal. But most were willing to go along with the president's criteria and approved his adoption of congressional standards for evaluating China's human rights record. Human rights organizations were appreciative but distrustful of China's ability to meet the conditions. Business interests expressed concern about possible Chinese retaliation and losing competitiveness in the world's potentially largest market. Editorial boards in New York and Washington praised the decision modestly. Sinologists and U.S. government China experts expressed skepticism, although a few indicated the president was moving in the right direction. "Clinton has bought time," observed Pei Minxin, an expatriate student who had joined the faculty at Princeton University, "but he has not dug his way out of his China problem."[81] Stapleton Roy, U.S. ambassador to Beijing, thought the Executive Order was "doable." He was reasonably pleased that the conditions were not as onerous as he had expected. "I thought they had defined them in a way that, properly interpreted, gave us a reasonable shot at trying to accomplish something. Although it was going to be very difficult."[82]

Beijing's reaction was stern but not harsh. The Ministry of Foreign Affairs issued a statement on May 29, charging that the Executive Order constituted an "open violation of the three joint communiqués and principles of the trade agreement between the two countries, and serious interference in the internal politics of China. The Chinese Government expresses its absolute opposition . . . and lodges a strong protest with the U.S. Government." "China cannot accept" the conditioning of its MFN status and believes "it can only seriously impair Sino-U.S. relations and their economic and trade cooperation, which eventually will hurt the vital interests of the United States." It concluded with a hope that the United States will "size up the situation, change its course and correct its erroneous practice."[83] Other Asian governments expressed views ranging from outright opposition to linkage to studied neutrality, with most opposing the principle of linking trade and human rights.

A Summer of Discontent

Had the MFN issue been the only issue in dispute, there might have been some hope for progress. But nearly the entire array of difficult bilateral issues came up during the first few months of the Clinton administration. In February, a trade delegation from the USTR had visited China and presented a very tough position on China's prospects for getting into the General Agreement on Tariffs and Trade (GATT), and on its need to live up to the market opening agreement it had signed with the Bush administration.[84] In March, the United States and several European nations sponsored a resolution critical of China in the Vienna meeting of the UN Human Rights Commission, one that China beat back through a procedural motion but which was embarrassing nonetheless.[85] In April, President Clinton met informally with the Dalai Lama in the White House, ignoring a sharp Chinese protest.[86]

After Lord's visit in early May, reports began to circulate in Hong Kong of serious military dissatisfaction with China's "passive" foreign policy in the face of American provocations. According to *Cheng Ming* magazine—which has a very uneven record for accurate reporting of "insider" politics in China—116 People's Liberation Army (PLA) generals wrote a letter to Deng Xiaoping and Jiang Zemin, complaining that China's policy of forbearance and compromise with the United States had "impaired the dignity of the Chinese people and damaged the image of the Chinese nation." They demanded the Chinese government "resolutely and forcefully to hit back at the rude acts of interference, subversion, and extortion by the U.S. hegemonists."[87] Although the details of the story are open to question, its broad circulation in different forms suggests it represented a political reality: "that since late 1992 the PLA has lobbied long and hard for a tougher response to perceived U.S. transgressions against China."[88]

As the Clinton administration's "human rights foreign policy" emerged, Beijing was facing the possible failure of the tactics it had taken toward human rights ever since Tiananmen. China had pursued an approach to human rights that was complex and nuanced, focused on keeping international pressure at bay through a combination of resistance and compromise. As one American observer saw it, China's "mix of policies was designed simultaneously to rally Third World support, especially in multilateral settings; to appeal to advocates of realpolitik in the West; and to construct policy dilemmas for human rights advocates."[89] Now, however, it appeared that, with George Bush defeated, the principal American practitioner of realpolitik was gone, and the new administration did not seem fully aware of the costs China could impose if the U.S. government revoked China's MFN status. In May, the Chinese upped the ante, issuing warnings of retaliation against U.S. corporations if MFN were lost, while at the same time appealing to Washington to recognize the importance of good trade relations to both sides.

But if the Chinese believed they could work with Washington to find a harmonious compromise, subsequent events caused them to reconsider. The issue that seemed to have the most negative impact on Chinese views of the United States involved Beijing's bid to host the Olympic Games in the year 2000. China first announced its intention to compete for the honor in January 1993 and began an international and domestic campaign of great intensity to persuade the International Olympic Committee (IOC) to approve its bid. Other contenders were Berlin, Brasilia, Istanbul, Manchester (England),

and Sydney. Banners appeared all over the capital, stickers in every taxi, advertisements in newspapers, and posters on every blank wall, saying "Beijing 2000" and "A More Open China Awaits the 2000 Olympics." Special efforts were made during the IOC selection committee visits to persuade them that China had the spirit and the capability to carry out all the tasks required of an Olympics host. Chinese officials promised to spend $7 billion on infrastructure development, including a fourth ring road and new highway to the airport, to eliminate Beijing's chronic coal-dust pollution, and to pay all athlete expenses, including travel. China even released its most controversial dissident—Wei Jingsheng—just a week before the IOC vote in September.[90] Tiananmen leader Wang Dan publicly supported Beijing's bid with an article in the *New York Times*. One Beijing official, in a moment of excessive candor, promised, "Neither now nor in the future will there emerge in Beijing organizations opposing Beijing's bid and the hosting of the 2000 Olympiad."[91]

These sentiments—along with the appointment of Beijing mayor and Tiananmen hard-liner Chen Xitong as chairman of China's Olympic Bid Committee—stirred up growing opposition outside of China, and especially in the United States. U.S. nongovernment organizations (NGOs), such as Human Rights Watch, began a concerted campaign to persuade the IOC not to approve China's bid and American corporations not to sponsor the games if it succeeded. Editorialists and pundits railed against Beijing, comparing it to Nazi Germany in using the 1936 Olympics as a showcase for its tyranny, and making the case that, because of its human rights record, China did not "deserve" the Olympics. Both houses of the U.S. Congress took up resolutions opposing the selection of Beijing and urging the U.S. IOC representatives to vote against it. The House passed the resolution on July 26 (287-99), while the Senate settled for a letter, signed by 60 of its members, sent directly to the IOC selection committee. Even some American IOC members found those actions inappropriate. The Chinese were outraged, denouncing the actions as "gross interference" and an "insult" to the Chinese people.[92]

When the IOC voted on September 23, China led in the first three rounds, then lost to Sydney by two votes after Manchester withdrew and its supporters switched their votes to the Australian bid. The Beijing Olympic Committee reacted appropriately and promised China would not boycott the 1996 Atlanta Olympics. But Chinese propagandists used the decision to heighten their campaign of opposing American pressure. And because of the intense publicity and sense of letdown after the results were announced, Chinese around the country expressed a strong sense of grievance at the United States. Not inclined to accept American criticism of China's human rights situation in the first place, Chinese citizens tended to share the government's view that the Olympic defeat had been carefully orchestrated to humiliate China.[93]

"This exercise of 'leverage,' more than any single event, convinced students, intellectuals, and ordinary Chinese alike that the United States opposed China, not [just] the Chinese government."[94]

Nonproliferation Battles

Structurally, U.S.-China disputes over the proliferation of weapons of mass destruction were similar to disagreements over human rights. Substantively, the two sides had a fundamentally different understanding of the nature of the problem. Strong and vocal constituencies in the United States demanded action, which usually consisted of congressionally mandated economic sanctions against those countries that sold weapons. Executive branch policy consisted of sequential efforts to impose and lift sanctions and a concerted effort to get the Chinese to accept and implement international standards for weapons sales. In the circumstances, it is not surprising that the results—or lack of them—were also similar.

Nonproliferation was one of the Clinton administration's highest-priority concerns, and the NSC was eager to get off to a strong start. For that reason, it held over key Bush administration officials who had developed expertise in the issue. Daniel Poneman, who had worked the issue in the Bush White House, stayed on and was given the new title of senior director for nonproliferation and export controls, while Robert Gallucci and Robert Einhorn remained, respectively, assistant secretary and deputy assistant secretary of state for political-military affairs, handling nonproliferation issues. Lynn Davis, formerly of RAND, a defense issues think tank, was confirmed in April as undersecretary of state for arms control and international security affairs, the position that was delegated the authority—from the president through the secretary—for making decisions on imposing nonproliferation sanctions.

Even before her confirmation, Davis was under pressure from Congress about China's nonproliferation activities. Not long after her confirmation, she was called on to testify before a Senate Foreign Relations Committee hearing, after CIA analysts had briefed the evidence on reported 1992 M-11 shipments. Davis and Gallucci were careful in their remarks about missile sales to Pakistan to remind senators that there was no definitive proof of the allegations, although they allowed that the "weight of the evidence" against China was significant.[95] Members were in no mood to split hairs on the rules of evidence, however, and demanded the administration take tough action to deal with China's behavior. In his press conference announcing the conditional extension of MFN, the president vowed to "take action" if the allegations were proved true.

As late as July, the administration was still reported to be divided between those who found the evidence conclusive and thought it should trigger sanctions, and those who believed a high standard of proof was necessary before invoking the costly sanctions required, which would have economic and political repercussions. Gordon Oehler, director of the CIA's Nonproliferation Center, told *Washington Times* reporters, "There is no question about what our views are," a remark that drew criticism from Einhorn, who insisted the judgment on M-11s was still a "work in progress."[96] The agency testimony also persuaded members that entire missiles were present in Pakistan (not just components), which required the imposition of so-called category I sanctions against China.[97]

Media commentary on this issue has usually portrayed the divisions as being between those committed to expunging weapons of mass destruction and punishing proliferators on the one side, and "business lobbyists" and China sympathizers on the other. As *Washington Post* commentator Lally Weymouth put it, "Most senior intelligence officials agree there is sufficient proof that China has shipped M-11 intermediate-range missiles to Pakistan, thereby violating . . . the Missile Technology Control Regime . . . To date, the Clinton administration has maintained that the evidence is strong—but not conclusive enough to act against China. American business interests are pushing Clinton toward a softer line on China: Businessmen point out that China will soon be a key market for U.S. exports."[98]

In fact, the issue was far more complex, involving congressional legislation and a Chinese government that were equally cumbersome and inflexible. The legislation was interpreted by the State Department to require, for example, that State Department officials pay no heed to the consequences of imposing the sanctions—for example, whether they would further U.S. nonproliferation goals or harm U.S. business interests—but simply enforce them if clear evidence of a violation of MTCR guidelines was discovered.[99] State Department and NSC officials in 1993 were fairly certain that the Chinese had shipped M-11 equipment to Pakistan, whether in retaliation for F-16 sales to Taiwan or for other reasons. Photographic evidence was not available, but other indications were plentiful and credible. But decisionmakers reviewing the issue—many of them lawyers—considered that a standard of "beyond reasonable doubt" was appropriate for deciding an issue with such important consequences and repercussions. And the evidence presented was not irrefutable.[100]

Moreover, past experience had shown that full imposition of sanctions against China would not prevent further M-11 shipments but probably cause more to be sold. Administration officials also knew that China probably would suspend whatever bilateral agreements were in place with regard to other nonproliferation issues, and all further progress would cease until the sanctions were lifted by the United States. China's record on nonproliferation issues was by no means admirable at that point, but the general trend had been one of improvement. China had signed the Non-Proliferation Treaty (NPT) in 1992 and had agreed to abide by the MTCR that same year. In 1993, it had signed the Chemical Weapons Convention, regulating the sale of dangerous compounds and reagents used to manufacture chemical or biological weapons. No one was eager to scrap that hard-won progress just to impose unilateral sanctions.

The only other option available to the Clinton administration to resolve the dilemma of imposing mandatory sanctions was to find that China had violated the MTCR but waive the sanctions under a "national security" clause available under the law. Given China's poor reputation in all other areas, that option was not considered feasible. The notion that the president would waive justifiable sanctions for a country that many in both Congress and the executive branch considered a gross human rights violator and conscious proliferator was simply too distasteful. Consultations with the Chinese were tried instead, with Undersecretary Davis traveling to Beijing in mid-July to ascertain whether the Chinese government was willing to provide information about the suspected shipment. Davis's mission was to present the Chinese with something of a Hobson's choice: either admit that it had shipped the missiles to Pakistan (for which it would be sanctionable) or face sanctions.[101] The Chinese chose not to play, dismissing all charges relating to M-11s as "unfounded" and refusing to discuss nonproliferation unless the United States agreed to talk about its own proliferation of weapons of mass destruction (namely, F-16 fighters) to Taiwan.

Faced with Chinese stone walling, intelligence community certainty, and the demands of U.S. law, the State Department—after lengthy deliberation internally and with approval from the NSC—decided on August 25 to impose category II sanctions on China for the shipment of undisclosed equipment to Pakistan in 1992. The sanctions amounted to a two-year ban on export licenses for American corporations selling advanced electronics and satellite technology to China, a trade worth upward of $500 million a year. The sanctions could be expanded to include Chinese exports to the United States if further investigation showed entire missiles had been shipped. American high-tech corporations complained, publicly and privately, that the restrictions would cost thousands of American jobs but would do little real damage to China.[102]

China's reaction, nonetheless, was shrill. It denied the accusations, berated a "wrong judgment" based on "inaccurate intelligence" and denounced the decision as a "naked hegemonic act." Vice Minister Liu Huaqiu called in the U.S. ambassador and threatened to reverse China's 1992 agreement to abide by the MTCR. "Now that the U.S. side has resumed these sanctions," Liu was reported to have said, "the Chinese government has been left with no alternatives but to reconsider its commitment."[103] While no one believed China would undertake new efforts to sell missiles, its reaction was seen as a step backward and contributed to the general deterioration of relations at the time.

China's October 5 detonation of a small nuclear weapon at its underground nuclear test site gave further evidence of the costs of the deterioration of the bilateral nonproliferation dialogue. While Beijing had indicated it would be prepared to sign the Comprehensive Test Ban Treaty in 1996, its decision to break the informal moratorium among the nuclear powers was seen as a response to U.S. sanctions and a reminder that it was capable of derailing larger American nonproliferation efforts. The most worrisome result of the Chinese test was a brief period of very public pressure to resume testing in France and the United States.

Given its desire to not lose whatever cooperation was available on nonproliferation issues, the State Department proposed to the Chinese a return to constructive dialogue, with a specific end goal in mind: China would promise not to export M-11 missiles to Pakistan, in return for which the United States would lift the August sanctions.[104] The impetus for this offer was the hope to have a nonproliferation "deliverable" for the November 1993 Clinton-Jiang summit at Blake Island. To sweeten the deal, the United States approved the license for a supercomputer for China's national weather service and offered to lift the sanctions on certain satellites to be launched on Chinese carrier rockets. In private sessions, the Chinese expressed mild interest in the proposal but insisted that the United States must drop the sanctions first, and China would consider a positive response afterward. The deadlock persisted for another year.

The Peculiar Voyage of the S.S. Yin He

On July 15, 1993, the Chinese containership *Yin He* (Milky Way), registered to the China Ocean Shipping Company (COSCO), made its way south along the Chinese coast on a voyage into controversy. Early in its journey, U.S. intelligence received a report that the 21,000-ton vessel—bound for Hong Kong, Singapore, Jakarta, and ports in the Middle East—was carrying a large quantity of chemicals used in the production of chemical and nerve gas weapons and banned by the Chemical Weapons Convention. According to the U.S. information, which reportedly was a cargo manifest, the suspect chemicals—thiodiglycol and thionyl chloride—were bound for the port of Bandar

Abbas, Iran, where they would possibly be used in that country's worrisome chemical weapons program.[105]

Reports of Chinese violating yet another nonproliferation agreement were greeted with alarm and anger in the White House. Shortly after receiving the report, Senior Director for Nonproliferation Daniel Poneman convened a classified videoconference to discuss the report and what to do about it with nonproliferation experts in the State Department, Defense Department, Joint Chiefs of Staff, and various parts of the intelligence community. A lawyer by training, Poneman questioned the intelligence experts in detail and repeatedly about the reliability of the reporting. Reassured of their strong confidence in the validity of the information, he reported the matter formally to Berger and Lake. After consultations with Christopher and Aspin, it was decided to have Embassy Beijing deliver a démarche to the Chinese Foreign Ministry in general terms (not revealing details or sources), asking them to investigate the allegations and order the ship back to its home port. Ambassador Roy delivered the démarche on July 23, and received the customary assurances that China did not violate international agreements.[106]

Later, as the *Yin He* left Singapore and headed into the Indian Ocean, it was closely shadowed by U.S. Navy vessels. The surveillance was neither unobtrusive nor gentle, and although no attempt was made to halt or board the ship, that possibility was raised with the Chinese government. It was rebuffed. Ambassador Roy told the Chinese that the ship would not be permitted to unload its cargo unless and until it was searched. On August 4, Assistant Foreign Minister Qin Huasun summoned him to the ministry to inform him that the government had thoroughly investigated the U.S. claims and found them to be without validity. The suspect chemicals were not aboard the *Yin He,* and China was willing to allow a neutral port inspection to verify the matter. U.S. intelligence officials dismissed Qin's statement as a "big bluff," and the surveillance continued. The U.S. Navy made clear it would not permit the vessel to dock at Bandar Abbas, and none of Iran's neighbors was willing to allow it to put into port for inspection.[107]

On August 7, the Chinese went public with the problem. Xinhua publicized the content of Qin Huasun's August 4 counterdémarche to Ambassador Roy, complaining about U.S. Navy harassment of the *Yin He*. In unusual detail, the news account cited the vice foreign minister's accusation that "arbitrary" U.S. actions had "prevented the Chinese ship from reaching her scheduled ports, . . . forced [it] to be adrift on the high sea, subjected to such extraordinary activities of interruption and coercion, including pursuit and photography by U.S. warships and military aircraft." The article claimed China had offered to have the ship inspected once it reached port, but the United States had refused. Qin rebutted the specific charges in the earlier

U.S. démarche and claimed the U.S. information was "fabricated." He was also cited as accusing the United States of "unjustifiable bullyism," tarnishing China's reputation, damaging its relations with other countries, endangering the ship's crew, and causing "great economic loss" to China.[108] Stung, the U.S. Navy and the State Department denied they were harassing the ship or pressuring any of the Persian Gulf states to refuse docking privileges.

For the next three weeks, the *Yin He* anchored at various points in the Persian Gulf, refused permission to dock by any of the emirates, while the diplomatic battle between Washington and Beijing escalated. Intelligence officials in the United States backgrounded the press on the "tens of tons" of dangerous chemicals aboard the ship, "bound for Iran's chemical weapons plants."[109] Warren Christopher insisted, "We're determined to inspect the ship" to make sure the chemicals were not "delivered into the wrong hands."[110] China published increasingly detailed rebuttals of American charges, and its leaders began to issue personal assurances that the chemicals were not aboard the ship.

Jiang Zemin told a visiting representative, Gary Ackerman, on August 13 that there were no illegal chemicals on the *Yin He*, but the message did not get through. He repeated the message for a larger congressional delegation on August 18, but the delegates hardly mentioned it to the press, intent as they were to report their own objections to China's human rights practices.[111] Stapleton Roy took note, however, and reported back through channels that Jiang's statements ought to be given credence, since an inspection proving him wrong would be extremely damaging to his reputation.[112] Washington was not interested in Jiang Zemin's reputation, however. Those who were driving the decisionmaking process were mostly nonproliferation specialists determined to make an example of China and cut into its all-too-active presence on the illicit or dual-use chemicals market. Anthony Lake recollected being skeptical, but he did not feel he would have been able to tell the intelligence community they would "take a pass" on the issue. It was too high profile and had proceeded too far; it had to be carried through. And the intelligence community remained certain of its information, dismissing Jiang's statements.[113]

After considerable wrangling over the particulars of an inspection, the *Yin He* finally docked at Dammam, Saudi Arabia, on August 27, and was boarded by a joint Chinese and Saudi Arabian inspection team (China refused to allow Americans aboard the ship but acquiesced in a sizable group of American chemical weapons experts being available in Dammam to advise the Saudis on what to look for). For an entire week, they searched every one of the 782 containers aboard the *Yin He*, checked all the ship's paperwork and logs, looking for the two dozen containers of thiodiglycol and thionyl chloride the Americans said was aboard or evidence that they had ever been aboard. There was no trace of the chemicals. On September 4, Chinese, Saudi, and American representatives signed a certification that no chemical weapons–related reagents were aboard the vessel.

China's chief representative on the inspection team, Foreign Ministry Deputy Department Director Sha Zukang, insisted, "The Chinese side has every reason to demand that the U.S. side apologize in public, compensate its loss and pledge not to create such incidents in the future." State Department spokesman Mike McCurry, however, only allowed that the "inconvenience" to the ship and the Chinese and Saudi governments was "unfortunate." "The dangers of proliferation require us to pursue effective means of resolving concerns when credible evidence of destabilizing transfers occurs."[114] Intelligence officials continued to insist that their evidence was rock solid and that the Chinese had had plenty of time to figure out a way to dispose of twenty-four containers of hazardous chemicals.[115]

In the Washington policy community, however, the intelligence agencies—and particularly the Central Intelligence Agency and the Nonproliferation Center—suffered a serious loss of credibility and prestige. Their mistake had caused a major international incident and considerable embarrassment to the president and secretary of state. Policymakers already highly sensitive to the double pressure of intelligence agencies and congressional committees seeming to act in coordination became more suspicious of policy "agendas" developed by intelligence information. Intelligence analysts already skeptical of policymakers they suspected did not want to hear bad news about China's nonproliferation activities found themselves even more "out in the cold," having sworn near-absolute confidence in information that turned out to be completely wrong.

What had happened? Theories abound—that the Chinese dumped the cargo in the sea, that it was all a setup designed to embarrass the intelligence community. The most plausible scenario, however, remains that the chemicals were scheduled to be shipped aboard the *Yin He* but did not arrive at the port in time for the ship's scheduled departure and so were left behind. In their eagerness to prove the Chinese guilty of something, intelligence analysts failed to account for time and tide and presented policymakers with "actionable intelligence" that was erroneous. When indicators showed up that should have led to questioning earlier data, they were not sufficiently analyzed and were too readily discounted.

Slowing the Slide?

Both sides now appeared to realize that the constant ratcheting up of tensions was bringing the relationship to a near crisis, and both took steps at about the same time to stabilize a deteriorating situation and calm internal schisms about where the relationship should be going. In Washington, Winston Lord at the State Department, Chas Freeman at the Defense Department, and Kent Wiedemann at the NSC all concurred that a new tactical approach was needed. In their view, the limitations on meeting with senior Chinese officials, or allowing American Cabinet-level officials to travel to China, were having a harmful effect on nearly every aspect of American policy, for the simple reason that lines of communication were not operating. Beginning in July, they had been preparing the groundwork for a presidential decision in support of what Lord initially called "enhanced engagement."[116] As Lord later described the policy, it was designed to allow the United States to address a growing number of discrete bilateral problems with China, including military issues, with "high-level meetings, much more intensified dialogue, negotiations, and visits back and forth with China."[117]

The new approach was discussed at Principals Committee meetings in July and August and was finalized as an "action" Memorandum for the President from the National Security Adviser, which he approved in mid-September. The key elements of the new engagement approach were the presidential summit at the Asia Pacific Economic Cooperation (APEC) forum and a series of visits to China by senior American officials, including Agriculture Secretary Mike Espy, Treasury Secretary Lloyd Bentsen, and Assistant Secretary of Defense Chas Freeman, who was to reopen the military-to-military channel, closed since Tiananmen. Lake briefed Ambassador Li Daoyu on the new policy in late September, and Secretary Christopher did the same for Foreign Minister Qian when they met in New York for the UN General Assembly meeting.[118] Most important, however, Christopher delivered a letter from President Clinton to President Jiang, inviting him to attend the first-ever "leaders meeting" of the APEC forum in November on Blake Island, Washington, and to have a private "summit" meeting at the same time.[119]

Although Beijing leaders appeared to welcome the change in the Americans' approach to the relationship, they remained skeptical and distrustful of American intentions. Moreover, the impact of the "new" American approach may have been offset by China's reaction to speeches made by Secretary of State Christopher and National Security Adviser Lake in late September. The two speeches, undertaken in response to growing criticism in the United States that the Clinton administration's foreign policy lacked focus, were intended to provide a strategic framework and unified set of goals for American foreign policy. Controversial in the United States, they were cause for alarm in China.

Christopher addressed isolationism and American leadership in his September 20 speech at Columbia University. "The United States chooses engagement . . . We must reject isolationism for the dangerous argument that it is. We must renew our commitment to internationalism, which has served us so well for 50 years . . . The end of the Cold War . . . has left the United States with a continuing responsibility—and a unique capacity—to provide leadership." Although he did not mention China in the speech, he replied to a questioner afterward, describing the bilateral relationship as being in a state of "testing and watching," particularly on human rights.[120]

Lake's speech the following day was broader in scope and marked the first time any senior U.S. policymaker had tried to set out a comprehensive vision of American policy goals in the post–cold war world. Lake insisted that engagement was not enough and that America needed to convey a sense of purpose and mission for its foreign policy. Lake's speech described an American strategy of "engagement and enlargement." Positing democracy and market economics as America's "core values," he declared the highest priority of U.S. doctrine in the post–cold war world should be "to strengthen the core of major market democracies, the bonds among them and their sense of common interest," and "to minimize the ability of states outside the circle of democracy and markets to threaten it."[121] From the Chinese perspective, Lake laid out a worrisome U.S. approach of aggressively pursuing its economic interests as a strategic imperative, expanding the number and importance of democracies around the world, and isolating what he called "backlash" states—those who threaten the "circle of democracy."[122] In discussing "backlash states," Lake lumped together Iran and Iraq, Burma, North Korea, and China. Although he later insisted he did not intend to equate China with Iran and Iraq, and did refer to China as a country that was "opting for liberalization," his speech was widely interpreted, in China and among American sinologists, to convey an antagonistic attitude toward Beijing.[123] "Our policy toward such states," he said, "must seek to isolate them diplomatically, militarily, economically, and technologically. It must stress intelligence, counterterrorism, and multilateral export controls. It also must apply global norms regarding weapons of mass destruction and ensure their enforcement."[124]

Lake's address seemed to put the otherwise unconnected U.S. actions over the summer into an understandable context and probably began tipping the balance of the debate in China about what U.S. strategic intentions toward China really were. According to Hong Kong press reports, military and conservative criticism of China's weak reaction to the *Yin He* incident and missile sanctions had led to another high-level meeting in early September, at which Jiang Zemin reiterated Deng's policy of "not seeking confrontation, not provoking confrontation, [but also] not avoiding confrontation and not fearing confrontation."[125] Deng's policy of continuing to try and work with the United States was maintained. But a harder edge began to appear more regularly. China's think tanks and strategic writers began talking more openly and frequently about America pursuing a policy of "containment" toward China. Curiously, the arguments were in some ways driven by economic rather than purely strategic perceptions. With China's GDP predicted to surpass that of the United States at some point in the twenty-first century, some Chinese commentators concluded that the United States would be forced to contain China to maintain its position as the world's strongest economy.

Thus the new engagement policy was confusing to Chinese and to American policy officials. The first visits went smoothly, and China appeared to welcome the new American approach. But a significant difference in the tone and attitude became evident between meetings run by the different agencies of the U.S. government. Agriculture Secretary Mike Espy talked about improving agricultural trade during his October visit, while Charlene Barshefsky, assistant U.S. trade representative, laid out American dissatisfaction with China's adherence to the market access agreement signed in 1992 and threatened punitive action against Chinese evasion of textile quotas. Assistant Secretary of Defense Chas Freeman's November trip brought the symbolic end of ostracism of the People's Liberation Army (PLA), with his cordial and substantive meetings with top military leaders.

But human rights remained the dominant issue in the relationship, and the State Department kept a tight grip on it. Although the Executive Order had made clear the importance of China's human rights performance for the future of the relationship, it contained no benchmarks or standards for how the required "overall, significant improvement" would be evaluated. Despite several attempts, the embassy could not obtain any guidance to pass along to the Chinese on what actions on their part would enable them to "get over the bar" on the Executive Order's conditions. Ambassador Roy attributed this drawback to a lack of attention to the issue and to divisions within the State Department between those who favored a strict reliance on human rights factors in determining the course of bilateral relations and those who viewed the relationship in a broader context.[126] Among the former was John Shattuck, assistant secretary of state for human rights and humanitarian affairs, who was the first visitor to China under the new "engagement" approach.

Shattuck had planned an early summer trip to Beijing to begin a dialogue on the Executive Order and China's human rights situation, but his travel was put off by China because of the deteriorating overall relationship and Shattuck's insistence on traveling to Tibet. When he finally was permitted to go in mid-October, he received a chilly reception from Qin Huasun, the assistant foreign minister responsible for handling human rights issues, and a carefully scripted and monitored trip to Tibet. He warned the Chinese as he left that "as things stand now," the president would not be able to extend

MFN, because there had been "little or no human rights progress in China since last June."[127]

The basis for making that judgment is unclear, but it was probably based on two criteria. One was the quantifiable elements of China's human rights situation, such as prisoners released or accounted for, new arrests, emigration cases pending, percentage of VOA broadcasts blocked, whether or not Chinese officials had met with ICRC representatives or Tibetan leaders, and so on. The other was subjective reporting on conditions in China from official and nonofficial American sources. Although the priority placed on human rights reporting had increased for State Department officers after Clinton's election, personnel resources were still thin. Only one officer, for example, worked full time on human rights issues at the U.S. embassy in Beijing.

First Summit

With the relationship continuing to be viewed with hostility and suspicion in many quarters in the PRC, Jiang approached his November 19 meeting with Clinton cautiously. Beijing had taken some steps to ease the atmospherics somewhat. In a meeting in Washington in early November, Vice Foreign Minister Liu Huaqiu told Undersecretary of State Peter Tarnoff that China was "seriously considering" a U.S. offer to lift the August sanctions on M-11 missile deliveries to Pakistan in return for a detailed and binding promise by Beijing not to ship such missiles or components in the future.[128] Qian Qichen announced on November 10 that China would give "positive consideration" to permitting the ICRC to visit Chinese prisons to evaluate conditions, one of the areas in which "overall significant progress" had been demanded. State acknowledged it was one of the criteria for judgment and noted that simply engaging in "serious" talks toward the goal of ICRC visits might be sufficient, since the ICRC's requirements were stringent and might not be quickly met. At the same time, however, Qian made clear China's rejection of the principle of linking human rights and trade. "This method is a means left over from the Cold War. It is a means to exert pressure, and therefore one cannot expect China to accept this," he told reporters.[129] For Jiang, the meeting with Clinton was a critical appearance. Still untested and considered a Deng puppet and a consensus seeker without strong views of his own, Jiang had a complex and nearly impossible agenda for the scheduled one-hour meeting. He had to show himself as a tough and determined leader, reflect the growing anger of the collective Chinese leadership at the shabby treatment of China by the United States, defend China's positions (especially on sensitive human rights issues), but at the same time encourage the American leader to take a more balanced, long-term approach to China and establish some personal rapport with him. He told reporters before departing on November 17, "I hope, through my meeting with President Clinton, that we will enhance mutual understanding, . . . handle Sino-U.S. relations from a long-term perspective, so as to put this relationship on a normal track and to have a new start."[130]

Clinton was under similar pressure. As the summit approached, the volume of media criticism of China on human rights grounds increased. Mary McGrory of the *Washington Post* charged China with "escalating its gross and egregious human rights practices," and Jim Hoagland recommended that Clinton squeeze Jiang's hand "hard enough to produce results" on the human rights and other agendas.[131] Wei Jingsheng sent out an op-ed article to U.S. newspapers charging Clinton with abandoning "policies of pressure in favor of a policy of persuasion . . . a misguided shift."[132] Asia Watch published a thirty-eight-page pamphlet entitled "China in 1993—One More Year of Political Repression." Christopher and Lord testified before separate congressional hearings that China had not made sufficient progress to date to qualify for MFN extension in 1994.[133] Nancy Pelosi and 269 other members of Congress wrote an open letter to Clinton, urging him to press Jiang harder on issues pertaining to Tibet, where there had been "no sign of improvement" since Clinton signed the Executive Order.[134] Pelosi, by then head of the Congressional Working Group on China, even advised Clinton not to smile or greet Jiang too effusively when they met at the summit.[135]

Clinton followed the advice, and the meeting between the two presidents at the APEC meeting in Blake Island on November 19, 1993, was somber and stiff. Jiang appeared nervous and seemed to address most of his remarks at the Chinese officials who accompanied him rather than at his American interlocutors. But Clinton also was clearly looking to convey to the American audience an image of seriousness of purpose and of disdain for China's human rights policies and so held his natural gregariousness in check—particularly when photographers were around.

American participants would later describe the meeting as "terrible." Jiang read endlessly from prepared talking points, complaining about American policy and responding to Clinton's question about China's economy with a long-winded lecture.[136] Clinton was unimpressed, and the American media amplified his displeasure by claiming he had been "stiffed" by the Chinese leader, who gave nothing on human rights. Jiang and his staff, however, were elated, not so much by the summit as by the exposure he got and the way he handled himself. Chinese media were full of praise for his "principled" approach, and senior military officers declared themselves "proud of and inspired by Comrade Jiang Zemin."[137] By their criteria, Jiang had been successful—he had been tough, delivered the right lines, gave away nothing, but had made the contact and got the photo op.

Negotiating MFN

There is no way of knowing how the MFN linkage story would have turned out had not the United States chosen to alter course and move toward delinkage in late 1993 and early 1994. Most American accounts of events give the Chinese more credit than they probably deserve for understanding and manipulating political dynamics in the United States. Some analyses, for example, assert that Beijing leaders knew Clinton would not "pull the trigger" and revoke MFN and that Beijing had a well-defined strategy to force Clinton to back down. That strategy, according to David Lampton, was to activate the American business community and threaten loss of China's enormous market if MFN were revoked, to make some large "teaser" purchases from prominent corporations, to release a few high-profile dissidents and promise more, and to work carefully and cooperatively on some important international issues, such as Cambodia and North Korea.[138] Chinese officials and academics are happy to claim retrospective credit for that sophisticated an understanding of how delinkage would work. But there is little in the record of China's actions and interactions with Washington during that period to suggest that fine a calculus of cause and consequence was in operation. The Chinese government probably was operating in accordance with its understanding of Deng's principles of international affairs—seek mutual respect, reject efforts to interfere in China's domestic affairs, keep economic lines open—and implementing them as flexibly as possible, "crossing the river by feeling the stones."

Following the Clinton-Jiang summit, the Chinese seemed to adopt a relatively optimistic and cooperative stance toward solving bilateral difficulties. Treasury Secretary Lloyd Bentsen visited Beijing in January to deal with implementation problems on a 1992 agreement to end export to the United States of products made by China's prison labor system.[139] Chinese observers, of course, took pains to point out that, while Americans complained about China's implementation of its laws against exporting prison labor products, the United States had no such laws of its own. But all in all, the visit went smoothly, and the two sides signed an additional Memorandum of Understanding allowing for more visits by U.S. Customs officials to suspected facilities and more effective reporting on such inspections. That appeared to be enough to satisfy one of the mandatory requirements of the Executive Order of 1993, but American officials were not willing to make such a statement, as it would be up to the secretary of state to decide the matter.

China took other steps to begin meeting some of the requirements of the Executive Order. In January, Chinese officials invited the International Committee of the Red Cross to Beijing for detailed discussion on the ICRC's standard "mandate" for making visits to political prisoners. Neither side revealed details of the discussions, but they agreed to meet again, and the visit was considered a positive indication of China's seriousness about addressing U.S. concerns. Jiang Zemin met with House Majority Leader Richard Gephardt and former president George Bush and indicated clearly that China was going to "make an effort" to address the Clinton administration's concerns, within China's "legal limits."[140] China released two prominent Tibetan dissidents in January and promised a U.S. human rights activist that more prisoners would be freed during the Spring Festival in February.

Ambassador Roy believed the United States needed to establish some specific goals for the Chinese to attain a judgment of "overall significant progress" and made his view known to *New York Times* reporter Patrick Tyler early in 1994 (as he had done through channels to Lord and Shattuck). While he did not present a view on the overall human rights situation, Roy said China had made "dramatic" progress in improving the lives of its citizens, which "should be taken into account" when the United States reviews its qualifications for MFN. Asked if China had met the standards for "overall significant progress," Roy was blunt. "I can't answer those questions, because the Administration is going to have to define what it views as significant progress," he told Tyler.[141]

Shattuck and others were furious at Roy for "undercutting" U.S. policy and demanded a transcript of the interview for a review. Representative Tom Lantos wrote a letter to Lord demanding to know if he agreed with Roy, while human rights activists talked of a plot to let China off lightly. Someone leaked a draft of the State Department's annual human rights report on China, which concluded that "China did not make significant progress in curbing widespread abuses last year."[142] The State Department investigated Roy's interview for more than a week, during which time the ambassador demanded to be exonerated or dismissed. Department spokesperson Christine Shelley finally tried to end the controversy by affirming Roy's experience and high reputation within the department, denying there was any difference between his position and the secretary's, then stating flatly that China had *not* made "the kind of progress that we're looking for in terms of conditions that have been set for a renewal of MFN . . . It's clear that there is still a long way to go."[143] Christopher repudiated Roy without naming him on a television program two days later, saying it was "not my position" that China's economic progress justified easing up on human rights issues.[144]

Christopher met Foreign Minister Qian again in Paris in late January and warned him sternly that China had not "made enough progress to justify my saying that there has been 'significant overall progress.'"[145] In response, Qian reiterated China's opposition to the linkage of MFN and human rights but also agreed China would review a list of 235 political prisoners that Shattuck had delivered to them in his October 1993 visit and invited him to return to Beijing in late February.[146] He also invited Christopher to pay his first visit to China as secretary of state, which was accepted in principle for early March.

In early 1994, China's economy—insufficiently cooled down because of Deng's intervention in 1993—roared ahead, dragging consumer prices with it. Although the causes and scale of the price increases were subjects of dispute among economists, there was general agreement that the government's decontrol of prices in 1993 was an important cause of serious inflation. The practical effects were felt early in 1994, particularly in urban areas, where prices for cooking oil, rice, and vegetables shot up by more than 50 percent. State-owned enterprises, most of which were already in the red, borrowed further from the banks to increase urban wages, thereby increasing the inflationary spiral and delaying efforts to reform both the banking and the state-owned industrial system. Nonetheless, urban discontent grew, and reports of industrial actions and even riots among laid-off and underpaid workers became more numerous.[147] Faced with a choice between implementing potentially disruptive economic reform measures and maintaining social stability, the regime opted for the latter, paying wage subsidies and reimposing price controls to head off unrest.

Chinese critics of the regime, as well as a few dissidents who had been released from detention, began to call for further reform and change to deal with the economic crisis. Wei Jingsheng, defying government warnings, gave interviews and essays to Western journalists calling for tougher U.S. pressure on human rights questions. Wang Dan announced he would undertake an investigation of human rights violations in China. Small groups of activists attempted to organize discontented workers and peasants in Beijing and Shanghai. Others openly petitioned the government for a redress of Tiananmen cases and for more active political reform. In a situation that must have looked a bit like the period before Tiananmen, the leadership was faced with a choice between its inclination to nip dissent in the bud and its desire to avoid MFN revocation on human rights grounds.[148] Although the domestic considerations likely would have prevailed in any case, Assistant Secretary Shattuck's visit in late February probably tipped the balance.

Stormy Visits

Shattuck arrived in Beijing on February 26. Before his trip, the department had released the final version of its annual report on human rights in China, which acknowledged that some progress had been made, but it judged that China's record on human rights "fell far short of internationally accepted norms."[149] China had released a handful of dissidents but had arrested others. In response to Wei Jingsheng's increasing activism and meetings with foreign journalists, Chinese authorities repeatedly had warned him that his activities were a violation of his parole agreement and he could be rearrested. Wei nonetheless sent word to the American embassy that he wanted to meet privately with Shattuck. Ambassador Roy advised against it, mainly on grounds that it might have a negative outcome for Wei, but he did not press the point. He instructed an embassy officer to set up the rendezvous for Sunday, February 27, in the lobby of the China World Hotel—unlikely to be missed or raided.

The meeting went off smoothly. Shattuck had not cleared the meeting with Christopher and did not report it immediately through channels after it took place.[150] Nor did he make a public statement about it. Although it seems clear the Ministry of Foreign Affairs (MFA) officials who met with Shattuck after his evening rendezvous were not aware of the meeting with Wei, Chinese security services observed but did not interrupt it. Had not Wei chosen to brief the Western press about the meeting, it is possible a blowup could have been avoided.[151]

During the week, Shattuck met with Chinese Foreign Ministry officials, who complained about the annual human rights report but also gave him a partial readout on his October prisoner list and discussed in detail all the other aspects of the Executive Order. The human rights dialogue—the main purpose of his visit—was businesslike and lengthy, though little real progress was made. Shattuck presented more detailed requirements for meeting the Executive Order criteria and added to the list of political prisoners the U.S. government wanted China to account for.

Shattuck was surprised after the first day of his official meetings (Monday, February 28) when Wei informed the American press of their private meeting, including his gratuitous advice to President Clinton to "be as tough as the Chinese" on human rights.[152] Chinese MFA officials also seemed surprised, but it was not until Wednesday that Roy was called into the ministry to explain. Two days later, March 4—the day Shattuck left China and Christopher left Washington for Australia, the first stop on his Asia trip—China's public security authorities got into the act, detaining Wei for about twenty-four hours, then freeing him. The delay and quick release suggest there may have been some bureaucratic disagreement about how to handle the issue. When rumors began to circulate that Christopher might also seek to meet with dissidents, perhaps even including Wei, the security services prevailed. Wei was quietly spirited out of Beijing for a "rest," and the Ministry of Public Security began detaining at least fifteen other prominent dissidents, including Wang Dan, they suspected might be interested in meeting with the secretary.[153] The detentions set off charges and countercharges between Washington and Beijing that would turn Christopher's trip into a nightmare.

Aboard his plane, Christopher told reporters on Friday that Wei's arrest was "unhelpful in creating what I would regard as a positive atmosphere for my visit." Earlier, President Clinton had sharp words for the Chinese action. "We strongly disapprove of what was done and it obviously is not helpful to our relations."[154] As the secretary continued to Australia and outrage built in the United States, opinions within Christopher's party began to fragment. Some suggested he cancel the Beijing stop. Winston Lord and others argued strongly against that option, saying it would "wreck the relationship" without accomplishing anything positive.[155] Christopher phoned back to congressional leaders, who supported continuing the trip but advocated being very tough. The traveling party chose a middle course of criticizing China harshly and publicly before their arrival, and like Secretary Baker in 1991, canceling Christopher's ceremonial appearances in Beijing.

In what one participant called "escalation by press conference," Christopher stepped up his criticism of China. "It would be hard to overestimate the strong distaste that we all feel over the recent detentions and hostile measures," he told reporters. "Certainly these actions will have a negative effect on my trip to China as well as on the subsequent review of the favored-nation trade question."[156] Beijing replied in kind, saying, "No foreign country, organization or individual has the right to make irresponsible remarks or interfere" in China's domestic affairs.[157] Although most of the dissidents detained had been released after interrogation, Wei remained out of town, and it was clear Beijing would take action to prevent any dissidents from seeing Christopher.

Christopher arrived in Beijing on the evening of March 11. He was met by a vice minister of foreign affairs with a "perfunctory" handshake. Security was tight, and reporters were jostled to keep them away from the plane. No arrival or welcoming speeches were made, and Christopher canceled both the sightseeing tour and the banquet on the following day to "set a tone focused on the purpose of his meetings."[158] Beijing obliged with a tone of its own on Saturday—hard-nosed and rancorous exchanges with Foreign Minister Qian in the morning and the sneering, contemptuous sarcasm of Premier Li Peng after lunch. Qian accused Shattuck of breaking Chinese law, while Li dared Washington to revoke MFN. "The U.S. will lose its share of the big China market," he blustered.[159] American journalists with the secretary's party picked up on the scent of a disaster-in-progress and reported back in excruciating detail. Although Lord had warned the secretary that the first day might be a bit rough, Christopher was shocked and angered at what he called "insolent" treatment by the Chinese, and he considered cutting the trip short. Back in Washington, the president was furious—at Christopher. "What the hell is Chris doing there now?" he reportedly grumbled to aides.[160]

On Sunday, March 13, Christopher met with about 300 American business executives at a breakfast sponsored by the Chamber of Commerce. There he heard a chorus of complaints about how U.S. policy toward China was endangering American business investment and potential market access in the world's fastest-growing economy. Ending a favorable trade relationship because of concerns over the treatment of prisoners would be a huge step backward, executives insisted; increased commerce and contact with the rest of the world would be a better way to modulate the government's treatment of its citizens. Christopher implored the business leaders to use their influence "to persuade the Chinese of our seriousness and also urge them to be pragmatic."[161] Christopher then moved on to a meeting with Jiang Zemin, who was characteristically more genial a host but no less firm in resisting what he called U.S. "interference" in Chinese domestic affairs with its linkage of trade and human rights.

Consistent with the pattern seen in earlier pummeling of American officials, Christopher's last day of meetings was the most successful. On Monday, Qian offered a few concessions: prominent dissident Wang Juntao would be released on medical parole, a preliminary accounting was provided of the 235 dissidents on Shattuck's list, experts' meetings were set up to discuss U.S. charges that China was still jamming Voice of America broadcasts, and talks with the Red Cross on prison visits would move forward. He also pledged to resolve the few remaining cases of Chinese who were not being permitted to emigrate to the United States to join relatives. In a predeparture press conference, a somber Christopher described these as "positive steps" but hardly a breakthrough. "We've begun to narrow the differences," he said, but pointedly declined to say whether China's progress to date was sufficient for him to report "overall, significant progress" had been made. "I'm really out of that business," he told reporters.[162]

Beijing's reasons for treating Christopher in so harsh a manner can only be speculated upon. China's spokesmen merely reiterated the party line, which was that the linkage of human rights considerations and MFN was inappropriate, that Christopher did not show "sincerity," and that the Shattuck meeting with Wei had violated Chinese law. It can probably best be understood as a calculated risk, driven by domestic and foreign policy concerns and the interaction between them, for some of the following reasons:

—For reasons that derive from China's modern history virtually all Chinese leaders respond with outraged defiance to anything seen as pressure or "bullying" by a foreign power. To be accused of knuckling under to such pressure is an extremely serious and damaging charge. It carries emotional connotations similar to an accusation of "appeasement" in the West. Qian and Jiang had already been targets of such criticism and could not show much flexibility.

—Li Peng, fully in character, was playing to a nationalistic domestic audience of party and military conservatives and re-establishing his authority within the foreign policy "small group."

—Worried by economic and social problems, the leadership chose to take action against known dissidents to remind them of the limits of its tolerance and to prove that seeking support from the United States was fruitless. After Christopher departed, Wei returned to Beijing in early April, when he was again seized by security authorities and held incommunicado. Most of the dissidents detained before the Christopher visit were released afterward, but Beijing was sending a signal domestically that another crackdown was possible.

—Finally, the leaders probably were genuinely affronted and worried by the Shattuck-Wei meeting, and they wanted Clinton to change his human rights–dominated China policy. Having failed to detect a willingness in Washington to engage in a give-and-take negotiation on the Executive Order and increasingly aware of political divisions in the United States over the Clinton policy, Beijing chose a tougher stance in hopes it would precipitate a change in the American approach. For reasons that had more to do with U.S. politics than Chinese perspicacity, it worked.

One other factor bears mentioning on China's policy toward the United States—the increasing incapacitation of Deng Xiaoping. Rumors about his failing health had proliferated in 1993, compounded by his unwillingness to be seen in public or meet with foreign visitors. By February 1994, when he was shown appearing dazed and senescent on Chinese television, it had become evident he was no longer a driving force in Chinese domestic or foreign policy. Although he would live for another three years, Deng's appearance alarmed many observers and set off a fresh round of speculation about succession as well as political jockeying among the leaders.[163] Probably aware of Deng's mortality and his own uncertain authority, Jiang Zemin began to take steps to firm up his own power base, particularly with the PLA. He oversaw the reshuffling of regional military commanders in January and promoted nineteen officers to full-general status in May—likely all with little help from Deng, although one of the officers he promoted was Wang Ruilin, head of Deng's private office.[164] Jiang's concern about succession, as well as the maintenance of public order, probably inclined him even more strongly toward conservative military officers' views on foreign policy and domestic issues. He knew that he still needed the military to underpin his own—and the Communist Party's—hold on power.

Deng's departure from any significant role in foreign policy decisionmaking also deprived the United States of an important voice of moderation and patience in developing the bilateral relationship. On numerous occasions after his return to power in 1979, Deng had played a critical role in breaking leadership deadlocks, making key concessions, or guaranteeing compromises that enabled Chinese and American diplomats to resolve knotty problems. With that voice muted by disease and inactivity, no one else was willing to take a risk for the relationship. In a 1996 conversation with Anthony Lake, Jiang claimed that Deng had "entrusted" to him (at a date not specified but probably early 1994) the responsibility for managing Sino-American relations.[165] But Jiang took no initiatives that could be detected at that critical period or that would have risked his stature within China's still conservative leadership.

Changing Direction

Back in Washington, the highly visible failure of Christopher's trip catalyzed simmering discontents with the substance of the Clinton administration's China policy and its management by the State Department. The print media were merciless, though not in accord on what had gone wrong. "Astonishing debacle" (Charles Krauthammer); "bungled diplomatic foray . . . policy disaster" (Jim Hoagland); "the administration is clearly in disarray" (Hobart Rowen).[166] Former secretaries of state Henry Kissinger, Cyrus Vance, and Lawrence Eagleburger criticized the policy of allowing a single dimension of U.S. interests—advancing human rights—to dominate the entire relationship. Sinologists and foreign policy mavens publicly lamented the amateurishness of the Clinton team's approach. Members of Congress criticized the State Department openly. Clearly, a very public and messy debate was opened up over the direction and methods of the administration's China policy.

The trip also kicked off a messy debate within the administration. In public, the president indicated he was "disappointed at the results of the meeting," but insisted he would hold to the policy and make the decision on MFN in June.[167] In private, however, he remained annoyed at the secretary. Angered and humiliated themselves, State Department officials looked to the White House for public words of support for Christopher's mission. None was forthcoming. Looking back on the experience some years later, Winston Lord was still angry: "The White House [was] deathly silent, Christopher is twisting in the wind, and it was obviously deliberate."[168] On March 22, Christopher published an op-ed article in the *Washington Post*, justifying the human rights–related policy approach and enumerating the positive accomplishments of his trip.[169] That same day, Lake convened a Principals Committee meeting in the Situation Room of the White House to take stock of the policy. The results of the meeting were leaked to the *New York Times* by the evening.

State Department officials—and others, to be sure—turned the issue into a "we versus they" struggle within the administration. "This is partly about who is going to be in charge of the China policy," one senior State Department official told the *New York Times* after the Principals Committee meeting. "The Secretary is trying to keep the Commerce and Treasury Departments from trying to make a run over taking over the policy. He wants to make sure State Department keeps a very strong control over the China relationship, that it's not tenable to have the economic agencies in open revolt against the policy."[170] What transpired in the wake of the Christopher visit was a natural outgrowth of the broadening of U.S. policy interests with respect to China that had taken place in the years since Tiananmen. With economic and defense ties growing rapidly and different constituencies eager to have their views represented in policy councils, the State Department was viewed as having too narrow a focus on human rights. And in the wake of the trip, it was becoming clear that the policy of pressuring China on human rights was doomed to fail, with heavy costs to be borne by other agencies. The economic agencies were not trying to "take over" China policy; they simply wanted to have their views better represented.

With the clear approval of the president, the NSC and the National Economic Council (NEC) began to be more active in managing policy toward China. First they had to get their own house in order. Like the State Department, the NSC was divided over China policy. Lake and Soderberg had actively supported the linking of MFN and human rights conditions, hoping to use what they perceived as China's dependence on the U.S. market as "leverage" to bring about improvement in China's human rights behavior. Sandy Berger had gone along, but perceived early on, and with increasing anxiety in the face of Chinese intransigence, that the policy was not workable. Carrying through on the threat to revoke MFN if conditions were not met was the equivalent of a "nuclear bomb" that would have terrible consequences for both sides.

On the NEC, Robert Rubin and W. Bowman (Bo) Cutter, his deputy for international economic policy, had entertained serious misgivings about the linkage between MFN and human rights from early on. Their concerns were manifold. From an economic perspective, they believed that the scale and breadth of the economic relationship between the United States and other large economies like China were not well understood by policymakers in either the State Department or the White House. They thought that tinkering with those relationships to achieve leverage on political issues was not good policy or good economics. Cutter also felt that neither the NEC nor any of the other "economic agencies" in the Cabinet had been properly consulted in the process of putting together the Executive Order of May 1993. "We were not involved in the vetting of that in any substantial way. It went by very fast, if it went by us at all. And we were surprised, shocked, angered by how it came out, and thought it was going to be a fairly fast disaster" for the president.[171] Owing to the press of other international economic issues—the president's budget agreement with Congress, the North American Free Trade Agreement, the Uruguay Round of the General Agreement on Tariffs and Trade, and trade tensions with Japan—they did not register their concerns with the president or with Lake and Berger. By the end of 1993, however, when the American business community had begun complaining openly about the linkage policy's potential costs, they started speaking out more openly. "I think probably everybody feels [trade and human rights] ought to be delinked," Rubin said in early 1994. "On the other hand, it has to be done in such a way that human rights concerns are satisfied."[172]

The NSC made some staff changes that played a role in the change of policy. Shortly after the Christopher trip, Stanley Roth, deputy assistant secretary of defense for East Asia and Pacific Affairs, exchanged positions with NSC senior director Kent Wiedemann. Formerly staff director of the East Asia and Pacific Subcommittee of the House Foreign Affairs Committee, Roth was recruited by Lake and Berger for his political savvy, as well as his broad expertise in Asian affairs. At Roth's suggestion, I was brought over from the National Intelligence Council, where I had served for five years as deputy national intelligence officer for East Asia, to help out with China policy. Sandy Kristoff was named special assistant to the president for Asia economic issues, which made her part of both the NSC and NEC. Roth and I were in agreement with Berger and others that the linkage policy was not working and should be dropped, but that it would be very difficult to resolve the policy dilemma posed by the Executive Order unless further efforts were made to get more cooperation from the Chinese.[173]

In late March, a small group of NSC and NEC staffers began meeting informally in the White House situation room, under the joint leadership of Berger and Cutter, to map out a plan for the end game on the Executive Order. They had three main tasks. The first order of business was to review the seven criteria for progress set out in the Executive Order, evaluate in detail the steps Beijing had taken to meet those criteria, and try to establish standards that would enable Secretary Christopher to make his judgment about "overall, significant progress" objectively. That entailed working closely with the China desk and John Shattuck's staff at the State Department, as well as the NSC's directorate for democracy and human rights senior director Mort Halperin (who had withdrawn his nomination for assistant secretary of defense after intense congressional opposition) and NSC director Eric Schwartz.

A second priority was to develop several steps China might take that would demonstrate further interest and intent to move toward compliance with the Executive Order and get Beijing to take them. That was not an easy task. First, Chinese leaders were still angry over the Christopher trip and wanted to reinforce the message that they would not be pressured into making public concessions. Qian claimed that because China was prepared to forgo MFN treatment, that the pressure was on Washington and that Clinton had "enmeshed himself in a web of his own spinning by setting the June 3 deadline for an MFN decision."[174] And the public security apparatus was operating to quell growing domestic dissidence, with little regard for foreign reaction. Wei Jingsheng was detained again on April 1 and taken off into administrative detention while his case was being investigated and charges were developed against him.[175] His secretary was also seized. A Hong Kong journalist was sentenced to twelve years for "spying," while a bank clerk who gave information on gold policy to a reporter was given fifteen years. The Ministry of Foreign Affairs, however, did want to demonstrate its willingness to continue working with Washington. Wang Juntao was released and permitted to travel to the United States for medical treatment. But much more was needed.

The third task was to try and develop a rough consensus on China policy, within the various bureaucracies and with Congress. The NEC staffers took the lead with Congress, looking for a support coalition that would include senators and House members from states heavily involved in trade with Asia—such as Senators Max Baucus (D-Mont.) and Diane Feinstein (D-Calif.) and Representative Robert Matsui (D-Calif.)—along with foreign affairs "centrists," such as Representative Lee Hamilton (D-Ind.) and Senator Richard Lugar (R-Ind.). It was hoped that support could be maintained from human rights activists, but it was recognized that a larger base was needed. Within the executive branch, it was acknowledged that several important agencies had equities in the U.S.-China relationship and that their views had not been adequately represented by the State Department, which had focused too heavily on human rights issues. Winston Lord had earlier established a senior steering group to coordinate interagency China policy, but it met too infrequently and with too large a cast of characters to bring about a workable consensus.

Moreover, creating consensus within the executive branch was complicated by the fact that the State Department had concluded that there was no longer a possibility for a judgment of "overall, significant progress" to be reached before June. The Beijing trip had convinced Christopher and his staff that there was no way the Chinese would do enough to meet even the vague standards of the Executive Order. Under pressure from human rights groups, many of whom began making public declarations that China had not made any progress,[176] State Department officials began to be concerned about their "credibility" if they were to make any judgment but a negative one. At the same time, most were increasingly aware of the high political and economic costs of revoking MFN altogether. With support from the human rights NGOs and from activists on Capitol Hill, such as Representative Pelosi, Winston Lord and others began publicly musing about possible "selective sanctions" or "targeted sanctions."[177] This idea, the germ of which was contained in the 1993 Pelosi-Mitchell bill, recommended that MFN treatment be denied only to the products of China's state-owned enterprise system, while those items produced by China's growing private sector would continue to enjoy low MFN tariffs.

While attractive conceptually, distinguishing items produced by state-owned enterprises from those made by private enterprise would have been impossible to implement. Huge numbers of U.S. inspectors would have to be added to the Customs Service, and their judgments would have been easily avoided by changing the names and registrations of Chinese enterprises, a common practice even without the additional incentive of avoiding punitive tariffs. Although the issue was discussed within both the Senior Steering Group on China and the smaller NSC-NEC forum, it was rejected early on as impractical. It did remain on the agenda for discussions with NGOs and members of Congress, however. Other proposals for "targeted sanctions" included raising tariffs on certain products known to be made largely by state-owned enterprises, such as textiles or machine tools. Yet another would have focused sanctions solely on the products of military industries.

The End Game on Linkage

The White House remained hopeful that China could be persuaded to take a few more steps that might get it "over the bar" for a favorable judgment on "overall, significant progress." Encouraged by Qian's April 6 statement that China would abide by the "Universal Declaration on Human Rights"[178]—one of the Executive Order conditions on which progress was required—Berger and Lake raised the idea of sending a special presidential envoy to China to see if more progress was available. Although skeptical of the efficacy of such a mission, Christopher agreed and in mid-April called Michael Armacost, former undersecretary of state for political affairs and ambassador to Japan during the Reagan-Bush years, to secure his agreement to undertake such a mission. Armacost agreed after concluding that the linkage policy, which he opposed, probably was going to be scrapped.[179]

At the California funeral of former president Richard Nixon on April 29, Lake met privately with Ambassador Li Daoyu and asked him to ascertain if Beijing would be willing to meet with a presidential envoy to work on further steps toward meeting the conditions of the Executive Agreement. By the time Vice Premier Zou Jiahua met with the president the following Monday, the Chinese had agreed to meet with an envoy. Armacost flew to Washington on Thursday, May 5, and was briefed by both the State Department and the NSC. He suggested that if he were to be represented as a presidential envoy, it might be useful for him to see the president, which he was able to do that evening. He found the president somewhat distracted but able to focus enough on his mission to leave the clear impression that the White House was leaning strongly toward delinking human rights and MFN, and that his mission was "to explore in a quiet, confidential way whether there were additional things the Chinese might be prepared to do to make it easier to manage this decision, which was politically difficult for the Administration."[180]

Armacost arrived in Beijing on May 8, via commercial air, and was met at the airport by Ambassador Roy. He spent the next two days in meetings—accompanied only by the ambassador and unencumbered by detailed talking points—with Vice Foreign Minister Liu Huaqiu, Foreign Minister Qian, and President Jiang. The meetings were private, relaxed, and cordial. Armacost laid out his case for more public and substantial gestures in exchange for dropping the linkage of MFN and human rights, but the Chinese were prepared to make only modest gestures—even though Armacost hinted at the possibility of further summit meetings. He got only the promise of release on parole for Chen Ziming, another of the "black hands" of Tiananmen; the clearance of two remaining high-profile emigration cases; and a repeat of assurances that VOA jamming would be discussed at the experts' level. Armacost and Roy reported the events of those meetings in detail by secure phone and cable, and at the conclusion of the trip, Armacost returned to his home in California.[181]

The White House by that time was focused almost equally on the substance of the decision—on which there was not yet a consensus—and on how best to present it so as to maximize domestic support, minimize criticism and embarrassment to the president (and others in the administration), and put the issue aside. Three factors weighed most heavily on the substance:

—The president's campaign commitment and base among human rights supporters;

—His commitment to improve the American economy by opening up international markets for U.S. goods, which American business leaders insisted required him to delink; and

—The growing recognition that U.S. long-term goals and commitments in the Asia-Pacific region required a stable relationship with China, which would be impossible if he commenced a trade war over human rights.

The president was besieged with contradictory opinions during the last weeks of May, and he tried to listen to all of them. The State Department was divided, with Shattuck reportedly favoring MFN revocation while Lord was arguing that larger Asian perspectives should be borne in mind.[182] Clinton met with congressional leaders from both parties and found widely variant views there as well. Mitchell and Pelosi, of course, favored sanctions, preferably targeted ones, while Republican leaders suggested the president admit his error and delink. He consulted former government officials and sought counsel with former president Jimmy Carter, who advised him to make a clean break. The leading newspapers provided op-ed articles and editorials filled with gratuitous criticism of his campaign promises, the policy process, personnel involved, problem at hand, and the Chinese government in general.

On May 23, the Principals Committee met on the issue, with the president in attendance. Christopher reported that the Chinese had met the two mandatory conditions on prison labor and free emigration. But on the five other categories in which "overall, significant progress" was required by the Executive Order, he said China had not satisfactorily met the standards. Beijing had stated its adherence to the Universal Declaration and provided partial accounting of Tiananmen prisoners; it had freed some dissidents, although it had arrested others. It had agreed to talk with the ICRC on prison visits and to VOA specialists about jamming but had not yet done so. Beijing had made no progress on easing conditions in Tibet. Christopher suggested that China's mixed record perhaps merited a response that was short of full revocation of MFN and suggested targeted sanctions against imports of goods produced by the PLA.[183]

Three days later, on May 26, after more telephone consultations and meetings with members of Congress, former president Carter, and numerous other domestic advisers, who suggested various last-minute adjustments of position, the president appeared in the White House pressroom to make his announcement, which by then was not a surprise. Although he appeared somewhat uncomfortable, he made the announcement clearly and carefully:

> The Chinese did not achieve overall significant progress in all the areas outlined in the executive order relating to human rights, even though

> clearly there was progress made in important areas . . . I have decided that the United States should renew Most Favored Nation trading status toward China . . . I am moving, therefore, to delink human rights from the annual extension of Most Favored Nation trading status for China. That linkage has been constructive during the past year. But I believe, based on our aggressive contacts with the Chinese in the past several months, that we have reached the end of the usefulness of that policy, and it is time to take a new path toward the achievement of our constant objectives. We need to place our relationship into a larger and more productive framework.[184]

Clinton also announced that he was maintaining other Tiananmen sanctions from the Bush administration, banning small-arms and ammunition imports from China, and undertaking a more aggressive program of support for human rights groups' activities and broadcasting into China, as well as developing a "code of conduct" for American businesses operating there. Following the president's brief remarks, Lake, Rubin, Lord, and Shattuck took further questions but added little to what the president had already said. There was little more to the policy than the delinkage. Proposals for more broadcasting, support for NGOs, and a code of conduct were all cover proposals, and little more. Shattuck had prepared a fact sheet about the president's new "vigorous" human rights advocacy with China, but the proposals on it had not been vetted within the bureaucracies involved and were not particularly well-supported anywhere.[185]

All in all, it was an unsatisfactory outcome for the president. In the following days, he was savaged by human rights groups, such as Asia Watch and Amnesty International. The usual pundits said the usual things but with more rhetorical punch, and Clinton's criticism of Bush for "coddling dictators" was repeated endlessly. "Sellout, cop-out, kowtow, surrender, cave-in, and smarmy reversal" were among the terms used to describe the outcome. "Foul-up, cock-up, adhocracy, flip-flop, bungled, disarray, and fudging" were applied to the process by which the outcome was reached. Pelosi and Mitchell denounced the president sharply, then gathered the rest of the House Democratic Party leadership (including House Majority Leader Gephardt and Majority Whip David Bonior) around them in June to sponsor legislative action to revoke MFN for China's military and state-owned industries.[186] Clinton found himself in the same situation with regard to congressional Democrats that Bush had been in. He probably did not appreciate the irony.

Implicit in the 1993 Executive Order, with its concern for using American economic leverage to force change in China's human rights policies—and the highly emotional and critical response to its failure and abandonment in

1994—was a false assumption, a mistaken judgment, and a misunderstanding of the relationship between actions and consequences.

—The false assumption was that China's trade surplus with the United States created a sense of obligation that any rational actor-policymaker would understand. The United States was more important to China's economic progress than China was to America's, it was thought, which gave Washington usable leverage. Threaten to reduce the economic benefits, and China would come to heel.

—The mistaken judgment was that China's leaders would only consider their economic interest when they were making a decision about human rights policies. But ideology, security, national pride, and the overwhelming need to maintain social stability probably outweighed economic factors in decisions on how to respond to U.S. demands. Beijing took small steps in a negotiator's fashion, looking for indications that the United States valued the relationship enough to make reciprocal steps. Washington appeared constantly to be moving the goalposts.

—The misunderstanding of the action-consequences relationship was a failure to consider the serious damage that might be done to American investors in China and American retailers of Chinese goods if MFN were actually cut off. Once those consequences began to be clarified, enthusiasm for following through on the threat evaporated quickly.

The president seemed instinctively to understand this situation. He did not deliberately choose trade over human rights, as so many of his critics charged. He wanted both and did not see a contradiction between them. He saw correctly that China was not a country that would be easily pressured. And he saw that the earlier policy was mistaken. The steps he took to correct that mistake, however, were directed at domestic goals and a domestic audience and had repercussions, in perpetuating partisan and executive-legislative disputes over China policy and in failing to impart new momentum to the bilateral relationship. As Stapleton Roy put it, "We could have, in fact, gotten very significant progress on human rights in China if we'd used the breaking of the linkage as momentum . . . [But] instead of declaring victory on the basis of what we did get, which was substantial, we declared defeat on the basis of what we didn't get, which was 'fundamental improvement' in all the areas."[187] Thus the confrontational approach toward human rights was perpetuated by a sense of anger that China had beaten the United States in that particular round, but others would follow.

As far as China's leaders were concerned, they had basically opted out of the process by mid-May, leaving Washington to make the decision with no further input. They refrained from making any comment on congressional discussions of "targeted" sanctions to be imposed only on PLA enterprises. When Clinton announced on May 26 that China had not made "overall significant progress" but that he nonetheless was renewing MFN without conditions, the official reaction was low key. "This decision will create favorable conditions for the further strengthening and expansion of trade and economic cooperation between the two sides and the improvement and growth of the overall relations between the two countries. The Chinese Government and people welcome this decision of President Clinton." The Foreign Ministry statement went on to complain about previous U.S. actions on MFN and expressed "regret" that the post-Tiananmen sanctions remained in place. Finally, it pledged China would make "major efforts" to improve relations and called on the United States to show "sincerity" in improving ties.[188] It was a spare statement, still containing tinges of resentment. There was certainly no gratitude for reversing a decision that Chinese leaders believed should never have been made in the first place. And if there were any recognition in Beijing of the difficulty of the political process Clinton went through to arrive at the decision, it was not reflected in any public way. Like leaders in Washington, China's foreign policy decisionmakers emerged from the MFN linkage imbroglio still surly, suspicious, and on guard for the next round of trouble. They did not have long to wait.

CHAPTER SIX

Crisis over Taiwan, 1995–96

Since 1949, the issue of Taiwan (the Republic of China [ROC]) has been one of the most persistent and intractable problems in developing, establishing, and maintaining relations between the People's Republic of China and the United States. From the Korean War through the Quemoy-Matsu crisis of 1958 to the vote for China's United Nations representation in 1971, the PRC and the United States have been in conflict over the status of Taiwan for more than fifty years. The PRC claimed sovereignty over Taiwan but did not exercise it owing to the interposition of American forces, operating under a U.S.-ROC defense treaty. Even after the United States broke the defense agreement and recognized the People's Republic of China as the "sole legal government of China" in 1979, it maintained the right—under the Taiwan Relations Act—to continue providing advanced weapons systems to Taiwan for its self-defense. Beijing acquiesced in a continuing "unofficial" relationship between Washington and Taipei for the sake of other benefits it derived from the normalized relationship with the United States and because it probably expected eventually to recover Taiwan without opposition. Deng Xiaoping announced a policy of "one country, two systems," toward Taiwan, providing considerable flexibility and continuity for the Kuomintang (KMT) government to ease its transition to being part of a reunified China. Under the terms of a third and final communiqué with the United States, signed in August 1982, Beijing believed it would see a gradual reduction and termination of American arms sales to Taiwan, which would also lead toward peaceful reunification.[1]

Taiwan Changes the Game Board

After Chiang Kai-shek's son, Chiang Ching-kuo, died in early 1988, Beijing grew increasingly alarmed at the policies and aspirations of his successor, Lee Teng-hui. A native-born Taiwanese (unlike most KMT leaders, who were transplanted mainlanders), educated in Japan and the United States, Lee set about reforming the KMT from the bottom up and top down. And although originally chosen as vice president because he seemed pliant and unambitious, he proved to be a formidable party politician. By the time he was elected president in his own right in 1991, Lee was restructuring the KMT so that it better represented the Taiwanese majority and was increasingly defining Taiwan as an entirely separate entity from the PRC, not part of "one China."

At the same time, Lee was also reaching out to the PRC, sending secret emissaries to arrange discussions of how to improve cross-Strait relations.[2] Eventually, both sides formed "unofficial" organizations to carry out the discussions more openly: the Straits Exchange Foundation (SEF) was founded in mid-1991 in Taipei, and Beijing followed with the Association for Relations across the Taiwan Strait (ARATS). Both organizations were headed by influential elders (ARATS by Jiang Zemin mentor Wang Daohan) and appeared to be making progress on developing a framework for negotiations on improving cross-Strait relations.[3] In April 1993, Wang and his Taiwanese counterpart, Koo Chen-fu, met in Singapore and agreed on some of the modalities of furthering a dialogue, although it was clear the Taiwan government was the more reluctant of the two parties to engage in substantive negotiations.[4] Taiwan's businesses were enthusiastic in their response to China's "reform and opening," pouring billions of dollars of investment into several special economic zones in China and expanding the textile, petrochemical, and even automobile industries across the Taiwan Strait.[5] Jiang Zemin, head of the Taiwan Affairs Leading Small Group, was no doubt pleased with the prospects.

But Lee Teng-hui was losing enthusiasm rapidly for ameliorating relations with the PRC. " I could not understand why there is such a high degree of optimism toward the changing relationship between the two sides of the Taiwan Straits,"[6] Lee was quoted in early 1993. Besides the fundamental disagreement over sovereignty, analysts said Lee had several other concerns. He did not want Taiwan's economic investment in China to become a means for the PRC to exert leverage on Taiwan. He was also aware that investment money flowing into the PRC was slowing investment in Taiwan's multibillion-dollar infrastructure development plan. Politically, he probably thought that moving too fast on improving cross-Strait relations might alienate supporters of Taiwan's growing pro-independence political party, the Democratic Progressive Party (DPP). Finally, he saw little reason to move Taiwan any closer to a China that was growing militarily and politically more powerful, yet showed no hint of the kind of political liberalization and democratization that was taking place in Taiwan.

Lee concluded that, for its security and self-respect, Taiwan needed to keep its distance from China and expand its international influence, its "international living space." So he began to pay more attention to widening Taiwan's circle of international contacts and broadening its political influence commensurate with its growing economic power (Taiwan was ranked the world's fourteenth largest economy in 1993, based on trade volume.)[7] Lee called his campaign "pragmatic diplomacy," and it involved seeking to expand contacts even with countries that had formal diplomatic relations with Beijing. In 1993, hoping for support from such countries, he called for Taiwan to be readmitted to the United Nations and to have access to other international organizations, regardless of Beijing's opposition.[8]

Beijing reacted negatively to Lee's efforts and tried to prevent them from being successful. Lee's attempt to change unilaterally the status quo in cross-Strait relations was hardly something that China's leaders would have wished for, being in a poor position to develop a creative approach on their own. From their perspective, policy toward Taiwan, which had been in place and mostly unchanging since 1979, was working satisfactorily. It had an overall framework—Deng Xiaoping's "one country, two systems"—with a long timetable. It had intermediate goals to ease tensions, namely, the "three communications" and the "four exchanges" (academic, cultural, economic, and sports).[9] The policy enabled both sides to develop their economies separately and jointly, expand people-to-people contacts, and minimize military deployments and exercises.[10] It brought enormous and much-needed investment to China's developing export industries and had the additional benefit of giving Taiwan's business leaders a stake in maintaining good cross-Strait relations.

Most of China's leaders did not understand the political process going on in Taiwan and had neither the incentive nor the desire to accommodate it. They were suspicious of Lee and his studied indifference to cross-Strait relations and preference for broadened international contacts. They charged that he was more sympathetic to the DPP than he let on publicly. The notion of "Taiwan independence," which Beijing also saw growing in importance during Lee's tenure, made the issue that much more sensitive. For Beijing, this was a "core" issue, one that involved the Chinese people's sense of history and destiny, the Communist Party's legitimacy, the pride of the People's Liberation Army (PLA), and the government's claim to sovereignty, as well as regional and global prestige. With firmly rooted principles, a sense of historical justification, a feeling of grievance against foreign intervention, and a growing public mood of nationalism supporting a firm stance, this was hardly a subject on which any leader—particularly one with Jiang Zemin's weak power base—could show much flexibility.

Finally, China's domestic political situation made it impractical to consider revising its Taiwan policy. Economic difficulties and dissension with the United States over human rights and most favored nation (MFN) status were already proving sufficiently difficult for a weak and insecure leadership. Deng's declining health had led to increased jockeying for position within the Politburo Standing Committee, in anticipation of succession. More important, altering Taiwan policy was something on which the PLA had to be consulted and involved in for reasons as follows:

—First, because the armed forces would be called on to carry out a costly and dangerous campaign to reclaim Taiwan should all else fail—and that was a job that realistic PLA planners could hardly look on with anticipation;

—Second, because Jiang and Deng and the rest of the party leadership were beholden to the army for saving their mandate to rule in 1989;

—Third, because the military, by tradition and ideological training, was the most nationalistic and xenophobic segment of the regime, and by habit one of its most outspoken;

—And fourth, because the PLA saw Taiwan as the key challenge for the future now that the Soviet threat had disappeared, and it would need additional budgetary resources to carry out its tasks.

Travel and Trouble

But while Beijing was not eager to change its approach to Taiwan, events were pushing in that direction. Lee and his vice president, Lien Chan, engaged in a high-profile round of "vacation diplomacy" in early 1994, traveling privately to Thailand, Singapore, Malaysia, and Indonesia, where they met unofficially or played golf with senior government officials. Both also traveled to Central America, Africa, and Europe, often asking permission to transit the United States en route. In July, Taiwan published a White Paper on relations with the PRC (a response to a tough PRC White Paper published in August 1993), rejecting Deng's "one country, two systems" formula for reunification and espousing a "'one China, two equal political entities' [approach] for defining the cross-straits relationship."[11]

In March 1994, the travel issue picked up greater political salience and controversy. President Lee had been invited to attend inauguration ceremonies for newly elected presidents of Costa Rica and South Africa, two of the few nations that maintained formal diplomatic relations with Taiwan. In light of his interest in expanding Taiwan's "international space," Lee was inclined to accept. The State Department's East Asia Bureau was determined to head off a diplomatic tussle over whether Lee would be permitted to make a rest stop in Hawaii or California en route to Central America. It drafted a blunt démarche for the director of the American Institute on Taiwan (AIT—the "unofficial" U.S. embassy) to present to Taiwan's foreign minister, advising that the president's itinerary should not include a stop on U.S. soil and certainly not an overnight rest stop and round of golf. Lee's "golf diplomacy" in Southeast Asia earlier in the year had aroused Beijing's ire, and China had already begun to warn U.S. officials against allowing Lee to visit the United States. When the cable came over to the National Security Council (NSC) for "crosshatch" clearance—standard procedure for such cables—as director of Asian affairs, I flagged it for Anthony Lake's attention, complaining it was too blunt and might cause an angry reaction in Taipei. Noting that Secretary Warren Christopher had already cleared the cable, Lake let it go without change.

When AIT director Lynn Pascoe presented the démarche to Taiwan's foreign minister, Fred Chien (Ch'ien Fu), he exploded in rage, calling American officials "a bunch of spineless jellyfish" for giving in preemptively to Beijing's complaints.[12] He had not calmed down by the time he met his next visitor, former AIT director and ambassador to Beijing James Lilley, who also found offensive the idea that the United States could not provide a courteous transit for the president of Taiwan. On return to the United States, he began advocating among Republican Party leaders that a better balance was needed in U.S. relations with Taiwan and the PRC.

After considerable follow-up negotiation, State Department officials agreed that Lee could make a refueling stop in Honolulu en route to Central America, although they held fast against an overnight rest stop. Fearing that enthusiastic Taiwan supporters would attract the media to Honolulu International Airport, they arranged for Lee's plane to be refueled at adjacent Hickham Air Force Base and asked the head of the Washington office of AIT, Natale Bellocchi, to receive Lee at the base VIP lounge. Taiwanese officials complained that the lounge was small and poorly furnished and inappropriate for hosting a president. On hearing about the accommodations from his chief Washington representative, Lee chose to remain on his chartered 747 when it landed to refuel at Hickham on May 4. Bellocchi went aboard to extend a welcome and found Lee angry and sarcastic and vowing not to accept "second class" status from the United States any more.[13] After his departure, the story quickly spread to the news media and began to be embellished, to the effect that Lee had not been allowed off the plane. Senior State Department officials, who had been unaware of the conditions at Hickham's VIP lounge, insisted the treatment was "courteous" and represented a "step forward," as no Taiwan president had ever visited the United States before.[14] Lilley criticized the treatment as "humiliating."

Members of Congress soon began to weigh in. Senator Paul Simon (D-Ill.) publicized a letter he had written to President Bill Clinton, in which he criticized "the cold shoulder we gave President Lee of Taiwan when his plane landed in Hawaii to refuel. Not only did we not give him any of the usual courtesies, we even made sure the base commander did not greet him." "We should no longer conduct policy toward Taiwan within the narrow limits of Beijing's tolerance," he continued, calling for Cabinet-level exchanges with Taiwan and support for its UN membership.[15] Senators Frank Murkowski (R-Alaska) and Hank Brown (R-Colo.) publicly invited Lee to visit the United States, and Brown inserted amendments in three separate appropriations bills in August to require the United States to approve a visa for Taiwan's president or other high-level officials to come to the United States for consultations. One such amendment was approved 94-0. In House and Senate conferences on the bills, however, the amendments were removed or converted to nonbinding "sense of the Congress" resolutions.[16] The language was then inserted into the Immigration and Nationality Technical Correction Act (H.R. 783), which contained a visa waiver program the administration was eager to continue. The president signed the bill in late October but noted he would instruct the secretary of state to continue to "weigh particularly carefully the foreign policy interests of the United States in considering any application by Taiwan's leaders to visit the United States," which included maintaining "the successful balance struck between our unofficial relations with Taiwan and our relations with the People's Republic of China."[17]

Misconstrued Review

Among the first Policy Review Directives proposed by the new Clinton administration in 1993 was a review of American policy toward Taiwan. Ever since the normalization of relations with the PRC and the requirement that the United States maintain only an "unofficial" relationship with the former Republic of China, strains and discontents had arisen over how to manage ties with an active and confident government, one of the world's largest trading economies and a budding democracy. Fifteen years after U.S.-PRC normalization, some of the routines and regulations to maintain the symbol and substance of unofficial relations had begun to pinch, and there was pressure to make adjustments from within the executive branch and from outside. Treasury Department officials complained they could not meet with Taiwan counterparts in their offices but had to meet them in restaurants to conduct their business. Taiwan's representative office in Washington was called the Coordinating Council on North American Affairs (CCNAA, which some callers mistook as an office of Alcoholics Anonymous), and its staff members could not set foot inside the State Department or any executive branch agency. Taiwan's foreign minister could travel to the United States but not to Washington. Taiwan's president, vice president, premier, and vice premier could not travel to the United States at all, even to visit with family members or receive honorary degrees from universities they had attended. None of these procedures were formally set down but had emerged in practice to maintain the image of "unofficiality." The policy review was intended to make appropriate revisions to reflect changing circumstances and Taiwan's growing economic importance to the United States. But the State Department's original draft of proposed changes was considered unsatisfactory by the NSC, and the review was put off in the face of more pressing problems with MFN and nonproliferation issues.

Following the delinkage of MFN and human rights in May 1994, the NSC and State Department again took up the Taiwan Policy Review with intent to complete it. Although obviously aware of growing congressional interest in improving U.S. ties with Taiwan, the Interagency Working Group moved cautiously on proposing changes, partly out of concern for Beijing's reaction, partly to keep Taiwan's expectations in check. Considerable attention was paid to how other countries structured their unofficial relations with Taiwan and managed them on a day-to-day basis. On September 7, after the president had approved an NSC memo outlining the proposed changes, they were briefed to Taiwan's chief representative, Ding Mou-shih; to the Chinese embassy; and subsequently to the press. Among the changes announced:

—The name of Taiwan's unofficial mission was changed to Taipei Economic and Cultural Representative Office (TECRO);

—Taiwan's officials could call on American counterparts in their offices, except for State Department and Executive Office of the President officials;

—American representatives could call upon the Taiwanese president, premier, and foreign minister in their offices;

—A regular subcabinet economic dialogue would be established to deal with important bilateral economic issues;

—Cabinet-level exchanges could take place occasionally in both capitals on economic and technical issues;

—The United States would support Taiwan's entry into the General Agreement on Tariffs and Trade (GATT) and other international organizations not requiring statehood for membership;

—Taiwan's top leadership would be permitted to make "transit stops" in the United States under approved conditions but were still not permitted to make lengthy personal or official visits.[18]

Although Winston Lord said only half in jest that both sides should be "ecstatic" about the review, believing it was carefully crafted to stay in the middle on their sovereignty dispute, both sides attacked it. Taipei's was the milder criticism: the changes "have not sufficiently addressed the needs arising from the close relationship between the United States and Taiwan," TECRO said in a brief statement.[19] China's reaction was much more negative. Vice Foreign Minister Liu Huaqiu called in Ambassador J. Stapleton Roy on September 11 to register a "strong protest" at the changes, which he called "gross interference" in China's internal affairs and a "serious infringement" of China's sovereignty. He characterized the U.S. change as a "serious retrogression" of American policy, which could bring about "grave consequences."[20] He also escalated the rhetoric by threatening that the issue could become "explosive" if not handled correctly.[21] Curiously, Washington seemed to miss the seriousness of Liu's words. Undersecretary of State Peter Tarnoff, who visited Beijing two days later, said after his talks he was confident "China now understands that the US has a consistent position that is not changing."[22]

PLA Plaints

Hong Kong press sources reported during this period a growing controversy within the leadership over Beijing's response to the United States. On the one hand, elderly "leftists" were taking advantage of the economic difficulties and increased tensions with the United States to attack Deng Xiaoping and his entire policy orientation.[23] More seriously, senior PLA leaders were reported to be giving hard-line speeches and writing protest letters to the Central Committee about the direction of China's foreign policy and even about Foreign Minister Qian's handling of it. Politburo Standing Committee member and Military Commission Vice Chairman Liu Huaqing reportedly told a PLA audience in April that China needed to send an "explicit and firm message to the United States: China will never tolerate foreign interference in its internal affairs and will never barter away its principles. China will not seek confrontation, but will not fear confrontation and will not evade any imposed confrontation."[24] Chief of Staff Zhang Wannian reportedly had made similar remarks at a Central Committee secretariat meeting earlier that month,[25] while Defense Minister Chi Haotian traveled frequently during the summer with Jiang and began taking on a more active diplomatic role.[26]

Hong Kong's *Hsin Pao* reported in July 1994 that eighty PLA generals—retired and active—had written a letter to the Central Committee in June, complaining about American "attempts to subvert, penetrate, interfere in and undermine China" and calling for China to "uphold its principles." Jiang met with some of the officers and praised their patriotism, assuring them that China would not shrink from confrontation should that become necessary. Also in June, military academicians and officers in PLA businesses affected by President Clinton's ban on imports of Chinese assault weapons reportedly called for Qian Qichen's resignation. Jiang reportedly defended Qian strongly at a Politburo meeting, in part by invoking Deng's praise of him.[27] In August, at a week-long high-level meeting of Taiwan specialists from the party, government, and military bureaucracies, recommendations were made about a staged escalation of military pressure on Taiwan over a twenty-year period. General Liu Huaqing spoke at the conference and indicated the proposals would be taken up to the highest decisionmaking levels.[28]

Jiang's handling of increasing PLA restiveness on foreign policy issues was deft but ultimately limited his policy flexibility. On the one hand, he used his position as chairman of the Central Military Commission prudently, seeking out senior military officials, praising and reassuring them. He referred to hostile external forces and exhorted the armed forces to "be prepared for danger in times of peace." He set PLA leaders a challenge to prepare for their greater national defense responsibilities by improving their party loyalty and ideological training and to pay special attention to the concept that "the Party commands the gun, the gun must never be allowed to command the Party."[29] Jiang was able to maintain the allegiance of the military through the party plenum in October and won more time to deal with the Taiwan issue.

On the other hand, Jiang and Qian also were able to bring some positive benefits to the PLA from easing relations with Washington. First was a relatively cost-free agreement with Washington in October 1994 over missile exports to Pakistan, a topic of high concern to the PLA. In exchange for a lifting of high-technology sanctions imposed in 1993, Qian reiterated a commitment to not sell to any other country missiles that exceed, or had the "inherent capability" to exceed, missile technology control regime (MTCR) guidelines.[30] The sequence of actions was critical for China. The United States agreed to lift the sanctions first, after which China repeated a commitment it had made earlier on M-11s. The agreement opened the way for American satellites again to be launched on Chinese carrier rockets, a lucrative business for the PLA and one that afforded limited access to sophisticated American space technology. Subsequently, the United States offered secretly to waive sanctions over whatever M-11s may have been delivered to Pakistan in return for a Chinese accounting of those sales, which U.S. intelligence agencies had never been able to prove definitively.[31] Not trusting Washington's record on applying and lifting sanctions was probably part of the reason Beijing did not rise to the offer, even though it was made before the Clinton-Jiang summit meeting at the Bogor, Indonesia, leaders meeting of the Asia Pacific Economic Cooperation (APEC) forum.

Second, Secretary of Defense William Perry made a high-profile visit to China in October, completely erasing the restrictions on high-level military contacts that had been in place since 1989. Perry carried with him a proposal for a joint U.S.-PRC commission on "defense conversion," helping China transform some of its inefficient state-owned military-industrial enterprises into businesses that could produce for the civilian economy. He also offered U.S. assistance in helping China develop more effective civilian air traffic control. In return, Perry encouraged more "transparency" on the part of PLA budget planners, so as to ease regional and American concerns about China's military intentions. PLA leaders appeared to be highly appreciative of the Perry visit, which not only accorded considerable deference to China's strategic perspective but also demonstrated respect for PLA leaders and an apparent recognition of the important role they played in China's political and economic affairs.[32]

Whatever goodwill may have been generated by the Perry visit was undone within two weeks, however, by an encounter in the East China Sea between Chinese aircraft and submarines and the American aircraft carrier *Kitty Hawk*. While patrolling off the coast of South Korea, the American carrier detected the presence of a Chinese submarine in its vicinity. Antisubmarine warfare aircraft and other planes from the *Kitty Hawk* engaged the Han class submarine and pursued it back toward the Chinese coast in a vigorous manner, dropping sonar buoys and simulating an attack. As the U.S. planes approached China's twelve-nautical-mile territorial waters boundary, Chinese aircraft were scrambled and approached within visual range. The American aircraft broke off the encounter and returned to the *Kitty Hawk*.[33]

Although no shots were fired nor any physical damage done—and the incident was gentle compared with some U.S.-Soviet encounters at sea—the Chinese were outraged. U.S. diplomats were quietly asked to provide "clarifications" of the situation, and American military attachés were informed that the PLA air force had issued a "shoot down" order to be carried out against any American aircraft approaching Chinese territory.[34] No formal protests were made, however, probably because of the PLA's embarrassment at not being able to provide effective protection to one of its own ships operating off its own coast.

The upshot was that Jiang and Qian probably were under some pressure to be "tough" on the Taiwan issue when they met with President Clinton on the margins of the APEC leaders meeting in Bogor, Indonesia, in November. Jiang's position had been bolstered by the promotion of two of his protégés at a late September Central Committee plenum: Huang Ju, major of Shanghai, was added to the Politburo, and Party Secretary Wu Bangguo was given a position on the central secretariat. But with Deng's health rumored to be deteriorating, Jiang needed to move cautiously to strengthen his position.[35]

The November 14 summit meeting marked a slight improvement in the relations between the two presidents. Jiang seemed more confident and outgoing than he had been at Blake Island. He deployed his sixteen-character maxim on developing good bilateral relations. He nonetheless still read from a prepared text toward the end of the discussion, focusing more intently on his subordinates than on his counterpart. Clinton seemed somewhat remote, distracted, perhaps, by the implications of the midterm elections held the week before, in which the Democratic Party had lost control of both houses of Congress.

The hour-long meeting moved through a set agenda of issues in a typically tedious fashion, with both leaders intoning prepared points, followed by translation, and little real exchange of views. The principal issues were the U.S.–North Korean nuclear agreement signed the previous month, China's possible entry into the GATT/WTO (the World Trade Organization was to be established in 1995), human rights, free trade aspirations within APEC, and finally, the Taiwan issue, raised by Jiang.[36] Jiang put down a firm marker, saying that China would not "sit idly by" if Taiwan were to pursue "Taiwan independence" with the assistance of foreign intervention. Clinton responded with the mantra that the United States would abide by the three communiqués and maintain a "one China" policy. The contrast between PRC and U.S. coverage of the meeting was striking. Xinhua devoted much of its coverage of the meeting to the Taiwan issue, while the NSC "senior official" briefing the press afterward mentioned it almost as an afterthought.[37]

Again, the summit meeting provided little additional momentum to the bilateral relationship, which remained in a state of tense dissatisfaction on the Chinese side and gloomy disregard on the American side. The optimism that had followed Commerce Secretary Ron Brown's late August visit to Beijing with a large contingent of American business executives had faded, replaced by a simmering trade dispute over China's failure to protect American intellectual property. The Office of the U.S. Trade Representative (USTR) threatened to draw up by the end of the year a list of $800 million worth of Chinese products to be sanctioned, eliciting the predictable threat of retaliation from the Chinese side. Transportation Secretary Federico Peña—the first

Cabinet member to visit Taiwan under the guidelines of the Taiwan Policy Review—was disinvited to China after he met with Taiwan president Lee Teng-hui in early December.[38]

Jiang's Gambit

Despite the deterioration in relations between Beijing and Washington, Jiang Zemin undertook an effort to ameliorate tensions with Taiwan early in 1995. On January 30, in a lunar New Year celebration speech to a group of non-party representatives, Jiang laid out an eight-point modification of Beijing's policy toward Taiwan. While in no way intended as a fundamental departure from Deng's "one country, two systems" approach to reunification, Jiang's address did attempt to present some new perspectives and possibilities to entice Lee Teng-hui into a more fruitful dialogue. Jiang offered negotiations to "end the state of hostility"; asserted political differences should not affect burgeoning economic cooperation and trade; reassured listeners that the PRC threat of force was not directed against Taiwan but against foreign meddling, because "Chinese should not fight fellow Chinese"; and proposed high-level summit meetings to resolve difficulties.[39] No doubt, Jiang's words were aimed as much at other PRC leaders as at Taiwan. It was nonetheless a risky move, as it depended for its success on complex and changing politics in Taiwan.

Taipei reacted slowly and cautiously to Jiang's initiative, which was barely noticed in the United States. Lee Teng-hui withheld a definitive reply while awaiting readouts from different constituencies on the island. Business executives seemed to think Jiang's offer was positive, while political pundits were skeptical, claiming Jiang's initiative was dictated by domestic politics rather than by a real desire to make progress in cross-Strait relations. They noted heightened concern about Deng Xiaoping's health and potential leadership instability in the event of his death as well as Jiang's uncertain grip on power. Taiwan's military was highly doubtful of Jiang's sincerity and claimed in late February that China was moving mobile missiles into Fujian Province as a means of intimidating Taiwan.[40] Taiwan conducted military exercises during March and April, although it claimed they were not related to the PRC actions.

Finally, on April 8, at a meeting of Taiwan's National Unification Council, Lee responded to Jiang Zemin's late January proposal. Although billed as an "olive branch" to Beijing, Lee's speech was a carefully crafted rebuttal of Jiang's eight points. Lee called on Beijing to renounce the use of force before negotiations on ending hostilities could begin, proposed unification talks "based on the reality that the two sides are governed respectively by two governments," and suggested he would be willing to meet Jiang in a "natural setting," such as a meeting of an international organization to which both sides belonged "on an equal footing."[41] The PRC reaction to Lee's speech was quick but relatively mild: Lee's proposals "lacked sincerity" and were "disappointing."[42]

Meanwhile, Lee Teng-hui was accelerating his efforts to expand Taiwan's international prestige. Lee wanted to go to Cornell University in Ithaca, New York, to attend a reunion event at his alma mater, where he had received a doctorate in agricultural economics in 1968. The U.S. restrictions on the travel of Taiwan's topmost leaders had prevented him from accepting an invitation to Cornell the previous year, and the Taiwan Policy Review of 1994 had not promised any change. But Lee and his supporters had begun a vigorous and effective lobbying campaign in the United States, spurred by publicity of the botched transit through Honolulu in May 1994. By March 1995, two resolutions were working their way through the U.S. Congress calling for Lee to be permitted to make the trip.

Congress and the Lee Teng-hui Visit

The 104th Congress, under the flamboyant leadership of House Speaker Newt Gingrich, took office in January 1995 and promptly mounted the most comprehensive and determined struggle for dominance between the legislative and executive branches of the U.S. government that had been seen in decades. The Republican Party had won a stunning victory in the 1994 midterm elections, picking up fifty-two seats in the House and eight in the Senate, winning control of both houses for the first time since the end of World War II. With an ambitious Contract with America as their master plan, congressional Republicans would challenge the Clinton presidency on nearly every domestic issue and several foreign policy questions, especially peacekeeping and national missile defense. The challenges were posed in a confrontational and inflexible manner that created a great deal of anger and animosity between the two parties and between the executive and legislative branches of government.[43]

The changes in key committee assignments that accompanied the Republican takeover were also to prove significant. Dedicated anticommunist Jesse Helms (R-N.C.) took over the chair of the Senate Foreign Relations Committee (SFRC), while Benjamin Gilman of New York—a Republican moderate strongly committed to human rights—became chairman of the House International Relations Committee (HIRC). Both made clear they expected the White House to consult more closely on foreign policy issues with Congress and that they would not shrink from opposing Clinton policies or proposing their own. Key opinion leaders on Taiwan—Senators Hank Brown (R-Colo.), Frank Murkowski (R-Alaska), and Joseph Lieberman (D-Conn.) in the Senate, Dana Rohrabacher (R-Calif.), Robert Torricelli (R-N. J.), Tom Lantos (D-Calif.), and others in the House—gave early indications of returning to the conflict over the Lee Teng-hui visit with a vengeance.

The Taiwan government encouraged and supported efforts by Capitol Hill to pressure the Clinton administration on Taiwan-related issues. Limited by the "unofficial" relationship with the U.S. government, Taiwan was under no constraints on its contacts with Capitol Hill, and it pursued them aggressively. TECRO officials established numerous close contacts with members of Congress and staffers, sponsoring visits to Taiwan and special events in Washington. Both of Taiwan's main political parties regularly sent delegations through Washington, with stops in congressional offices high on their list of priorities. Equally important, American lobbying firms were used frequently to promote Taiwan's public affairs, as well as its legislative agenda. A deal worth $4.5 million between the KMT-sponsored Taiwan Research Institute and the public relations firm Cassidy and Associates gained particular notoriety.[44]

Taipei's influence was not just a matter of lobbying. There was also widespread admiration for Taiwan's economic prowess and for the democratic development that had taken place under Lee Teng-hui. Moreover, the growing contrast between a thriving, open democracy in Taiwan and Beijing's closed, truculent, and repressive system drew most Americans almost automatically to support Taiwan in its competition with the PRC. Without a clear strategic interest to justify taking the side of Beijing, many members of Congress were unwilling to do so. And they were also unsympathetic to the executive branch doing so.

Executive-legislative skirmishing on Taiwan began almost immediately after the new Congress was sworn in. The HIRC chair, Benjamin Gilman, held hearings on January 12, at which both he and former secretary of state James A. Baker expressed support for a Lee Teng-hui visit to the United States. The Heritage Foundation, a conservative think tank influential among congressional Republicans, recommended approval of a Lee visit to Cornell as one of several steps that could improve U.S.-Taiwan relations without damaging U.S.-PRC ties.[45] House Speaker Gingrich took things a step further on February 2, when he not only supported a Lee visit but also said the people of Taiwan should have "the right of self-determination; they have every right to be in the United Nations."[46] In testimony on February 9, Assistant Secretary Winston Lord defended U.S. policy against sharp attacks from several House members on the question of a Lee visit to Cornell.[47]

On March 6, Frank Murkowski and thirty-five other members of Congress introduced a concurrent resolution—a nonbinding "sense of the Congress" resolution—in the Senate and House, recommending "that the President should promptly indicate that the United States will welcome a private visit by President Lee Teng-hui to his alma mater, Cornell University."[48] In a letter to President Clinton on March 15, Jesse Helms, chairman of the Senate Foreign Relations Committee, expressed what was a widely held view in Congress. Noting that provisions for Lee's visit had already been passed into law, Helms discounted PRC protests. "I find it hard to imagine that U.S. relations with Red China would . . . come to a standstill because of a weekend visit to the United States by Taiwan's President," he wrote.[49]

Winston Lord and Kent Wiedemann (who had moved back to the State Department from the Defense Department in early 1995), Stanley Roth, NSC senior director, and I were well aware of the growing pressure from Congress about the visa , having had numerous conversations about it with House and Senate staffers. We were also concerned that U.S.-PRC relations, after a brief pause following the Clinton-Jiang summit, were again headed sharply downward and could be exacerbated by a high-profile Lee visit. At the end of 1994, after months of fruitless negotiation, the USTR—with full White House and State Department support—had raised the amount it would impose in retaliatory tariffs against Chinese products to $2.8 billion unless China took action by February 1995 to close down illegal compact disk (CD) manufacturing plants. Anthony Lake described the action as a means of restoring U.S. "credibility" with the Chinese leadership, who were underestimating U.S. resolve, in his view.[50]

Also in February, the State Department's human rights report on China noted no significant progress since delinkage in any area of its inquiry. The State Department and the NSC agreed to press hard for passage of a resolution critical of China by the UN Human Rights Commission. That effort was successful in March in overcoming the usual Chinese effort to block consideration of the resolution, but the resolution was narrowly defeated. The renewed pressure on human rights had raised bilateral tensions significantly.[51] There were also simmering problems relating to China's naval activities in the Spratly Islands of the South China Sea and a nuclear reactor deal it was considering with Iran.

Contacts in Beijing had reinforced the strong—if somewhat overstated—view of anxieties among China's leaders about a Lee Teng-hui visit to the United States, even a private one. We were aware of the complicated state of cross-Strait relations and the growing strains within the Chinese leadership over Taiwan. But the opposition to a Lee visit was adamant and widely shared at all levels of the PRC government. Arguments we made that Americans did not understand or support keeping Lee out, and that allowing such a visit would not change the fundamentals of the U.S.-China relationship, fell on deaf ears. We also understood that Lee's travel plans were not a "sentimental journey" to his alma mater but rather a campaign kickoff for the presidential election in 1996, in which he was already the front runner. Stanley Roth had hopes he could come up with a plan for a golf outing in Hawaii that would give Lee the satisfaction of a respectful visit but also avoid public relations embarrassment for the United States. Ambassador Roy wanted to approve the Lee visit but also to assuage the PRC's unhappiness with a state visit to the United States for Jiang, which he believed would pay multiple benefits.[52] Neither could get higher-level approval for their proposals, and the administration remained largely passive in the face of growing public pressure to allow Lee to make a speech at Cornell's alumni reunion weekend in early June.

By early April, both House and Senate committees had unanimously moved respective versions of the Murkowski resolution on to full floor consideration. On May 2, the House passed its version of the Murkowski resolution by 396-0. The Senate took up the measure one week later, passing it by a margin of 97 to 1. While "sense of the Congress" resolutions are nonbinding and often are ignored by the executive branch, this one was different. In early April, Congressman Torricelli and ten others had introduced H.R. 1460, an amendment to the Taiwan Relations Act forbidding the secretary of state from excluding any elected Taiwanese official on the grounds of "adverse foreign policy consequences."[53] Even if the president vetoed such a piece of legislation, an override was likely.

A Presidential Retreat Leaves State Exposed

Clinton had been talking for some time about Taiwan with congressional moderates—members of the Democratic Leadership Council like Senator Chuck Robb (D-Va.) and Joseph Lieberman. He was sympathetic with their perspective. As governor of Arkansas, he had visited Taiwan four times, and he thought highly of the island's political and economic development. Moreover, he saw the issue in terms of the traditional American value of freedom of travel, rather than in China-Taiwan terms.[54] Lake was similarly in favor of finding small ways to move beyond the "anachronisms" that severely circumscribed U.S. official contacts with Taiwan. His main concern was that the administration was being "absolutely driven by the Congress" on Lee's visit. At the breakfast meeting with Christopher and Defense Secretary William Perry on May 17, the three agreed to try and find a way to allow Lee to visit yet minimize damage to U.S.-PRC relations.[55]

Knowing the matter was an urgent one and that the president would make the final call (even though the secretary of state has legal responsibility for visa decisions), NSC's Asia Directorate had already prepared an Action Memorandum for the president. Stanley Roth was traveling in Asia at the time, but we had discussed the issue and I knew his view. We believed that we should hold out until Congress forced the administration's hand. During that time we could try to persuade Taiwan to accept an extended transit, perhaps including golf, and to prepare Beijing to swallow the bitter medicine. We were under no illusions that this was a satisfactory option, but we also believed that the consequences of flip-flopping would be dire. I prepared a memo with two alternative recommendations: first (and preferred), to hold out against allowing Lee to visit Cornell; second, to work quietly with Taipei and Beijing for several days to structure a Cornell visit that would be manageable and appropriate, then make a public announcement. I submitted the memo on a priority basis on the same day as the Christopher-Lake-Perry breakfast.

The following morning, I was called over to Lake's West Wing office to discuss the memo. Only Lake and I, Sandy Berger, and Lake's assistant, Peter Bass, were present. Lake said he and Christopher and Perry had discussed the issue, and he wanted me to reverse the order of the recommendations in the Action Memorandum, giving preference to the granting of a visa. I argued briefly against this course, focusing on the adverse reaction likely from China and the small benefits to be derived for the United States. Berger, who had strongly opposed granting the visa, sat silent, frowning, believing the decision was a mistake.[56] Lake repeated the order. I asked to include with the Action Memorandum an annex on the likely PRC reaction as part of the decision package. Lake agreed.

Recasting the memorandum was easy enough, although in retrospect I wish I had placed more stress on the need to keep a lid on the decision. But I focused on the annex, on the grim consequences I expected to follow the visit: another deep freeze for U.S.-China relations, with major visits postponed and ongoing human rights and nonproliferation dialogues suspended; a longer-term decline in PRC-Taiwan relations, with the PRC resorting to military exercises and possibly even missile tests as a means of discouraging Taiwan's perceived movement toward "independence." The revised memorandum moved quickly through "the system" and was on the president's desk by the afternoon of May 19. He approved it immediately. White House spokesman Mike McCurry had told the press at noon that the visa issue was "under consideration." By that evening, the Taiwan press had the whole story.[57] We did not have several days to manage the process. We had none.

Tony Lake and Peter Tarnoff met with China's ambassador, Li Daoyu, on Saturday morning to convey the news to him. He did not take it graciously.

Kent Wiedemann and I met with the TECRO director, Benjamin Chao-chung Lu, at the same time to pass along the obviously more welcome news. We tried to ensure that he understood the distinct parameters of a private visit—no large press contingent, no flag-waving receptions at airports, no meetings with U.S. officials, no political rallies, no lengthy rest stops in other American cities. Lu smiled and promised full cooperation and communication.

On Monday, May 22, the State Department announced the president's decision to the press. The justification was that Lee's visit was completely private, would have no official content, and was therefore "consistent with U.S. policy of maintaining only unofficial relations with Taiwan." "Americans treasure the rights of freedom of speech and freedom of travel and believe others should enjoy these privileges as well," the briefer added. He also indicated that Lee's itinerary and other details of his trip would be discussed with Taiwanese authorities to make sure that "his activities here, with all due respect, are consistent with the understanding we have, which is this will be a private visit."[58]

The Last Straw

Although increasingly suspicious that the Taiwanese leader was promoting de facto independence, and probably annoyed at Lee's insouciance on reunification issues, Jiang and Foreign Minister Qian seemed to think in early 1995 that the United States understood the sensitivity of the Taiwan issue sufficiently that it would not grant Lee permission to visit the United States. Officials at all levels of the Ministry of Foreign Affairs had made the point repeatedly in conversations with American counterparts and had heard in response that the revised guidelines still prohibited a visa for Lee. Qian had heard directly from Christopher on April 17 that a Lee visit to Cornell would be "inconsistent with . . . an unofficial relationship."[59] What Qian and others chose to disregard were warnings from their American counterparts, and presumably from their embassy in Washington, that congressional pressure was becoming extremely strong.

Reluctance to deal with yet another problem in the relationship probably contributed to Beijing's static approach to Lee's travel plans, along with a recognition that their options for preventing it were limited. After some progress in late 1994, bilateral ties were again skidding downward in early 1995. American trade officials had threatened punitive tariffs on China for insufficient protection of American intellectual property and market access problems, just when China's economic boom was beset by inflation of nearly 22 percent.[60] U.S. Commerce Department and Ministry of Foreign Trade and Economic Cooperation (MOFTEC) leaders argued publicly about the size of China's trade deficit. Chinese space launch officials and American satellite manufacturers blamed each other for the January 26 explosion of a Chinese Long March rocket carrying a U.S.-made satellite. The United States vigorously pushed a resolution critical of China's human rights practices at the UN Human Rights Commission meeting in Geneva and nearly got it passed. Americans seemed to be reverting to pressure across the board in dealing with China.

Internal politics were also difficult in early 1995. Deng Xiaoping's daughter, Deng Rong (also known as Xiao Rong), alarmed the entire leadership by revealing to an American reporter in January that her father no longer was able to walk and was declining in health "day by day."[61] After near-public criticism by party officials and contrary assessments of the ninety-year-old patriarch's health by other family members, she partially recanted her comments a month later, but rumors about Deng's health and political succession swirled anew. The death of party elder Chen Yun in early April added to the uncertainty of the leadership picture, even though Chen had been inactive for at least a year.

As Deng's incapacitation became more apparent, maneuvering among other top leaders became a subject of considerable speculation. Western press observers discerned significant policy differences among members of the Politburo Standing Committee, noted that more than one-third of National People's Congress delegates voted against one of the party's candidates for vice premier in March, and speculated on the possible return of Zhao Ziyang and Yang Shangkun.[62] Forty-five prominent intellectuals and scientists circulated a petition appealing to the government to overturn the party's condemnation of the 1989 Tiananmen protests and release all political prisoners. Corruption probes were opened against Deng family members and political allies. In April, Beijing mayor and Politburo member Chen Xitong—one of the strongest proponents of the Tiananmen crackdown—was forced to resign from the Politburo after his involvement in a massive corruption scandal in Beijing was exposed. *South China Morning Post* correspondent Willy Lam observed, "So much energy of the top cadres is consumed with skullduggery and backstabbing, . . . one wonders how much time is left for policy-making."[63]

The Clinton administration unwittingly provided the beleaguered leadership with a unifying cause by announcing that it had decided to reverse course and permit Taiwan's president Lee Teng-hui to pay a "private" visit to Cornell University. Shocked and angry, the Foreign Ministry called in the American ambassador to register a "strong protest" and demanded that Washington rescind the decision or "pay the price."[64] But it was too late. Washington was not about to reverse itself. And opinion in China was about to take a sharp turn toward a much more negative and nationalistic approach toward both the United States and Taiwan. The PLA led the charge, immediately postponing Defense Minister Chi Haotian's planned trip to Washington in June and recalling the air force commander from his travels in the United States. On May 28, the Ministry of Foreign Affairs postponed MTCR discussions with State Department officials and called off experts' consultations on the peaceful use of nuclear energy. Despite U.S. explanations and reassurances about the policy, Beijing proceeded progressively to downgrade relations.

Lee's travel plans also created serious strains in U.S.-Taiwan relations. TECRO chief Benjamin Lu could not deliver on his pledge of full cooperation, probably because leaders in Taipei viewed the turn of events as proof of the Clinton administration's weakness and a vindication of their congressionally focused approach, and therefore treated coordination of plans with the State Department as a nuisance or afterthought. Resentment built up at the State Department and TECRO as every detail of the trip needed to be negotiated, and many had to be renegotiated when unwritten agreements were broken. They argued over the size of the press contingent, security detail, and official coterie; where Lee's aircraft would stop; what officials could meet him; and where Taiwan's flags could be displayed. The basic problem was that the State Department and Lee's office had diametrically different agendas for the trip to Cornell: Washington wanted to show it to be an unofficial trip that did no further harm to U.S.-China relations; Taipei wanted it to be an official-looking trip that made Lee appear presidential and respected in the United States. If it raised Sino-American tensions, that might have a positive outcome in bringing U.S. public opinion closer to Taiwan's side.[65]

On June 8, Lee arrived at Los Angeles airport, where he was greeted by hundreds of Taiwan supporters, waving flags and cheering as he stepped off the plane. Hundreds more greeted his arrival at the Ritz-Carlton Hotel, where he was met by the mayor of Los Angeles and several other California dignitaries. Although he did not speak at the reception, Lee's spokesman told the press the president hoped his visit would lead to further exchanges and closer friendship between the United States and the Republic of China. A similar scene greeted his arrival in Syracuse, where three U.S. senators (Helms, Murkowski, and New York's Republican senator Alfonse D'Amato) joined the local officials and crowds of flag-waving Taiwanese Americans in welcoming Lee. Any hope of maintaining the illusion of "unofficiality," however, disappeared the following evening, when Lee delivered the Spencer T. and Ann W. Olin Lecture at Cornell University's alumni reunion.

In discussions with Benjamin Lu, Kent Wiedemann and Winston Lord were assured that Lee's speech would be a warm retrospective on Lee's years at Cornell and a mild discussion of economic reform in Taiwan. It was also implied that a draft would be made available for review well in advance of delivery. The draft arrived the day before it was to be delivered, far too late for any changes to be proposed, much less accepted. And Lee's staff had already made copies available to the press. It was a classic campaign speech by a man proud of his record, proud of his country, and eager to extol its virtues and proper place in the world.

After a brief reference to his Cornell years, Lee launched into a passionate advocacy of "the Taiwan Experience." "Communism is dead or dying, and the peoples of many nations are anxious to try new methods of governing their societies that will better meet the basic needs that every human has . . . In my heart, I believe that the Taiwan Experience has something unique to offer the world in this search for a new direction." He described the "political and economic miracle" that had taken place in "the Republic of China on Taiwan" and contrasted it implicitly with the absence of democracy on the mainland. "The needs and wishes of my people have been my guiding light every step of the way. I only hope that the leaders in the mainland are able one day to be similarly guided, since then our achievements in Taiwan can most certainly help the process of economic liberalization and the cause of democracy in mainland China." Lee concluded with a strong plea for more contact and recognition from other countries and international organizations.[66]

Lee's speech effectively put an end to any prospect in Beijing of allowing the issue to die down. Offended by his repeated reference to the "Republic of China on Taiwan," his condescending offers to help the mainland find democracy, and his open pitch for international recognition, Beijing reacted quickly and angrily. The Taiwan Affairs Office quickly canceled the planned second round of high-level talks between Wang Daohan and Koo Chen-fu, blaming Lee for "attacking and cursing the mainland, agitating to split up the country and advertising 'two Chinas.'"[67] Beijing's propaganda apparatus began a personal vilification campaign against Lee, calling him a "pawn" and "tool" of the United States, bound to be disregarded by the Chinese nation. The defamation of Lee reached its peak in late July, when *People's Daily* and Xinhua published joint commentaries on Lee's speech on four consecutive days. Accusing him of trying to establish his own dictatorship, advocating Taiwan's independence, and endangering the people of Taiwan, the commentaries—clearly approved at the highest levels of the party—represented an elevation of the psychological pressure Beijing was prepared to apply to show their displeasure with Lee in advance of the presidential elections scheduled for March 1996. Given that the commentaries also coincided with the launching of six Chinese ballistic missiles into the Taiwan

Strait approximately eighty-five miles north of Taipei, it was clear that China had shifted to a policy of coercive diplomacy with respect to Taiwan.[68] It was a policy that eventually would lead to direct confrontation with the United States.

The decision to grant a visa to Lee also evidently tipped a fine balance within the Chinese leadership on policy toward the United States. Although internal repercussions were relatively mild—Jiang and Qian reportedly made self-criticisms at an enlarged meeting of the Politburo—the change in policy approach toward both the United States and Taiwan was far-reaching.[69] Within the Politburo Standing Committee, the Central Committee Foreign Affairs Small Group, and the Taiwan Affairs Small Group, voices calling for toughness and retaliation grew stronger, while the ones who had encouraged patience and cooperation with Washington were silent. There was little payoff to be seen in taking a stance that could be criticized as weak-kneed toward the "hegemonist" United States.

In an effort to assuage China's aggravation over the Lee visa and to signal the continuing importance of U.S.-China relations, President Clinton agreed to invite China's ambassador Li Daoyu to the White House for a brief early evening meeting on June 8, the day Lee Teng-hui was arriving in Los Angeles. Clinton almost never met privately with ambassadors, and there were hopes the Chinese would absorb the symbolic message and substantive reassurances that the Cornell visit did not mark a change in U.S. policy. Li, however, was angry and insolent, clenching his fists and pumping his legs to punctuate his brusque talking points, his official anger probably augmented by his own embarrassment. The following week, Li was called back to Beijing "for consultations," and rumors quickly spread that he was under attack in China for not warning the leadership about the Lee visa. In any case, his performance in the Oval Office did not win him, or his cause, much sympathy.

Within hours of Li's recall, U.S. ambassador Stapleton Roy left Beijing for onward assignment as ambassador to Indonesia. With none of the farewell calls that usually attend the end of an ambassadorial tour, Roy's departure was quiet, almost somber. The relationship he had worked so hard to rebuild from its low point when he arrived in 1991, was heading back downhill. His advice on how to improve the relationship had gone largely unheeded in Washington. He had watched in frustration as U.S. domestic politics repeatedly had misguided and damaged the bilateral relationship and what he considered larger U.S. strategic interests in the region. Unlike Li Daoyu, he had warned of the consequences of a high-profile Lee Teng-hui visit. Now he would watch from Jakarta as the relationship deteriorated further.

Party, Army, and Policy

From mid-May 1995 through the spring of 1996, China adopted a series of policies toward the outside world that appeared to represent a sharp break with its previous approach. It pushed more vigorously its territorial claims in the contested Spratly Islands in the South China Sea. It violated the implicit moratorium on nuclear testing with underground blasts at Lop Nur on May 15 and August 17. It heightened the pitch of belligerent press attacks on the United States for its purported strategy of containing China or treating it as a threat to Asian security. But most alarmingly, it began a campaign of extremely harsh rhetoric, threats, and military intimidation toward Taiwan in the aftermath of the Lee Teng-hui visit to the United States. Many observers attributed this turn to a general increase in the influence or power of the PLA in policy deliberation councils in Beijing. Few tried to detail how that influence was exerted, however, or to what ends. Of all the unknown factors in the shrouded decisionmaking process of the PRC, gauging the policy influence of the PLA is one of the most difficult.

Since the earliest days of China's communist revolution, the PLA, as the military arm of the Communist Party, has always been closely entwined with the political leadership. Most of the party's early leaders held some position or other within the military chain of command, and many army leaders were given positions on the Political Bureau of the party. Mao Zedong's dictum that "power grows out of the barrel of a gun" did not apply only to China's civil war. Even after the People's Republic was established in 1949, Mao continued to rely on the military to carry out his often radical programs of social engineering and political restructuring, and military men at times exercised great influence within the leadership. Deng, like Mao, recognized the importance of exercising direct party control over the military and also of having the personal support of key military leaders in his quest for dominance within the party leadership. After his restoration in 1977, he never needed or aspired to any power position within the civilian party structure but rather established himself as first among equals through his chairmanship of the party's Central Military Commission (CMC).

That position enabled Deng to sidestep the paralyzed political leadership during the Tiananmen crisis and bring to bear the military force needed to crush the demonstrations and restore control of the capital. It was a reminder that the party's authority was still dependent on the coercive capabilities of its security forces and armed forces and that it could not afford to disregard military interests or allow the PLA to move out of the party's direct control. Deng and other party leaders considered it necessary to reward the military for its loyalty, which they did in a number of ways. One was public praise and recognition, which failed to restore the army's reputation among the citizens of Beijing or the self-esteem of those who participated in the Tiananmen incident. Another was promotion and party recognition. At the Fourteenth Party Congress in October 1992, the proportion of military members on the Central Committee rose to almost one-quarter, with one-third of new members being PLA officers.[70] Although overall PLA representation on the Politburo declined, the addition of Liu Huaqing to the Standing Committee did maintain military influence at the highest levels of decisionmaking. Most important, however, budgetary resources devoted to PLA modernization—a high priority for all military leaders—began a pattern of double-digit growth in 1990 that has continued to the present day.[71] Between 1990 and 1995, China's announced military budget more than doubled.[72] Even considering the uncertainty about the accuracy of the figures and China's high inflation, there is no doubt that the party leadership was making up for several years of relative privation, when national defense spending received a lower priority in the budget.

Deng clearly wanted Jiang Zemin to establish and strengthen his leadership credentials through the CMC and ceded the chairmanship to him in November 1989. Directing the armed forces, however, is not simply a matter of institutional positions. Deng was able to exercise authority over the military, in part because he had valorous and high-level military experience as political commissar of the Second Field Army during China's civil war. He also had a quality of mental toughness that inspired military respect. Most important, he had a deep *guanxi* network in the armed forces; that is, he knew the top military leaders personally and had earned their esteem. Jiang had none of those advantages, and it was only Deng's firm support—and Yang Shangkun's—that enabled him to operate initially within the PLA's leading group.[73] Deng then helped Jiang rid himself of the threat of Yang and his half brother and persuaded Admiral Liu Huaqing and General Zhang Zhen—both at that point past retirement age—to serve as vice chairmen of the Military Commission in support of Jiang.

Jiang worked carefully with Liu and Zhang to bring about necessary changes in the composition and political loyalty of the PLA high command, breaking the grip of the Yangs. Then slowly but surely, through promotions and transfers, he brought into the CMC and the PLA hierarchy a group of younger officers who were beholden to him for their promotions and positions. And as Deng's health and influence weakened, Jiang continued to work carefully with Liu Huaqing to maintain the impression of firm military support for himself as the "core" of the party rather than any of the other potential claimants of Deng's mantle. He regularly visited PLA units in his capacity as CMC chairman, showing interest and concern for the lot of the common soldier, learning more about the issues of concern to them. He issued specific guidelines on improving political education in the military and inculcating the idea of the armed forces loyally "safeguarding" political power in China.[74] Jiang also ingratiated himself with the military leadership by addressing the political and economic issues that were of most concern to them and, where possible, adopting them as his own, or at least supporting them in higher party councils. Aside from national defense spending, PLA priorities included foreign weapons acquisition, loose constraints on PLA business operations, strict maintenance of internal stability, assertive nationalism, and perhaps most important of all, an uncompromising position on Taiwan.

On Taiwan, and the closely related issue of relations with the United States, however, Jiang and at least some of the PLA's senior cadre did not seem to be in full agreement in 1995. The difference in approach began to emerge as early as 1992, after the sale of American F-16s, and grew more serious as overall U.S.-China relations deteriorated in the first years of the Clinton administration. After Jiang's January 1995 "eight-point" proposal—which some in the PLA, according to Willy Lam, considered "dovish to the point of capitulation"—failed to generate a positive change in the cross-Strait dynamic and was followed by Lee's trip to Cornell, a major reevaluation of China's policy reportedly was undertaken within the Politburo Standing Committee.[75] Jiang no doubt found his options severely narrowed. He needed PLA support for his own political survival and faced greater opposition within the party over Taiwan policy if he did not act. Now the military was pressing through all its channels for a firmer stance toward both the United States and Taiwan. Liu Huaqing represented the military perspective in the Politburo Standing Committee. Liu and Zhang Zhen and other PLA leaders also had access to Jiang in the Central Military Commission. By one account, they delivered in a CMC meeting a letter to Jiang signed by numerous military officers advocating a tougher approach to Taiwan and calling for the Ministry of Foreign Affairs to be held accountable.[76]

Jiang may have been more attentive to PLA opinion even within the Central Committee's Taiwan Affairs Leading Small Group (TALSG), which he headed. The army had always been represented on the party's principal decisionmaking group on Taiwan, given that it was responsible for the ultimate task of reunification if all else failed. Yang Shangkun had headed the Leading Group from 1984 to 1992, aided by a career PLA officer, Yang Side, as secretary general of the TALSG and director of the Central Committee's Taiwan Work Office (TWO).[77] But Jiang had succeeded in "civilianizing" the group somewhat when he took over as its head in 1993, dropping Yang Side and adding United Front Work Department Director Wang Zhaoguo as secretary general.[78] Foreign Minister Qian Qichen and several other civilian officials with intelligence or trade responsibilities also were believed to be members. In response to the pressures of 1995, however, Jiang gave more responsibilities to its PLA representative, Xiong Guangkai, then director of the Intelligence Department of the PLA General Staff. He also may have begun inviting senior generals Liu Huaqing, Zhang Zhen, and PLA Chief of General Staff Zhang Wannian to attend meetings and staff out policy papers.[79]

The PRC statements on Taiwan took on a more militant and threatening cast beginning in mid-June, then escalated sharply in late July. This change cannot be attributed solely to PLA influence in policy councils, as many other individuals and organizations shared the Army's outrage over Lee's trip and the remarks he made at Cornell. Most likely, a full leadership meeting in Beijing set down new guidelines for the PRC's overall approach to Taiwan. Among its conclusions: there were no longer to be any "illusions" about Lee Teng-hui—he intended to "split the motherland" and move Taiwan toward independence, and he would be "taught a lesson" in return; the PRC would do all in its power to defeat his plans of enlarging Taiwan's "international space;" all cross-Strait contacts and discussions would be suspended indefinitely; the PRC would try to affect the domestic political dynamics on Taiwan by a campaign of political pressure; and the PLA would demonstrate its commitment to "defend Taiwan by force."[80]

Responsibility for the most visible form of pressure on Taiwan was given to the PLA, which had a unique and effective means of exerting it—the movement and disposition of military forces and the conduct of military exercises on Chinese territory contiguous to Taiwan. These exercises did not require significant civilian oversight, other than the approval of Jiang Zemin as CMC chairman. The first exercise, called East Sea No. 5, was conducted by the PLA navy and air force in the Taiwan Strait off Dongshan Island (about seventy-five miles southwest of Taiwan's Chin-men/Quemoy Island) on June 30.[81] It was a more or less routine exercise, not very large in scale, and probably entailed landing craft drills.[82]

On July 18, Xinhua announced the PLA would be conducting from July 21 to 28 "a training for launching a surface-to-surface guided missile into the open sea" in a ten-square-mile area roughly eighty-five miles north of Taiwan and informed foreign aircraft and vessels to stay out of the immediate vicinity of the closure area.[83] As intended, the announcement of such an unprecedented and provocative exercise caused an economic and political shock in Taiwan, where the stock market immediately tumbled and President Lee felt compelled to make a public appeal for calm.[84]

Washington's reaction was more muted—the State Department spokesman said, "We don't believe this test contributes to peace and stability in the area."[85] On July 21–22, China launched four M-9 missiles with dummy warheads from a military base near Leping, Jiangxi Province. One of them failed to reach the target area. Two days later, two medium-range DF-21 ballistic missiles (range of 1,100 miles) were launched from Tonghua, in Jilin Province.[86] Hong Kong press reports suggested that ground force troops and high-performance aircraft began moving into Fujian Province—across the strait from Taiwan—at about this same time. As the exercises concluded, Beijing media published authoritative attacks on Lee Teng-hui and his Cornell speech on four consecutive days. At the end of the month, two U.S. Air Force attachés posted in Hong Kong but traveling in Fujian to observe military activity were arrested for spying and expelled in early August. Winston Lord nonetheless maintained a low-key approach, stating in a press conference before leaving for Asia that the United States wanted to "strike a balance on this missile situation . . . We don't think that this [test] helps stability but we also don't want to inflate the situation or exaggerate it."[87]

Taiwan's armed forces responded with a naval live-fire exercise north of the island in late July. President Lee gave a defiant speech to Taiwan's National Assembly, calling for a speed-up in the construction of an "'effective deterrent and rapid-reaction' defense force that will offer the communist Chinese regime an idea of the possible costs and serious consequences of launching an armed invasion of Taiwan and keep it from acting recklessly."[88] He also announced the ROC armed forces would conduct a major exercise in September and October. Taiwan's stock market rebounded sharply after the PRC tests were completed.

Beijing responded to Lee's speech with more militant rhetoric at the August 1 celebration of the PLA's founding, with more attacks on Lee, and with the announcement of another missile exercise on August 11. This one reportedly had been planned as a routine exercise by PLA forces stationed in Fujian but was augmented with antiship missiles, live artillery fire, and extensive air and naval maneuvers in a 2,500-square-mile area about ninety to one hundred miles north of Taiwan. The purpose was to keep up pressure on Lee Teng-hui and demonstrate the PLA's willingness to use force to oppose "Taiwan independence."[89] Again, the reaction in Taiwan was a drop in the stock market and the value of Taiwan's currency against the dollar, which the Central Bank offset—at a substantial cost—with adjustments in interest rates and reserve requirements. Taiwanese politicians vowed to resist PRC intimidation and rallied popular support by accusing Beijing of trying to interfere in Taiwan's election process. Lee Teng-hui's popularity hit 80 percent, according to some polls. Washington again protested mildly that the tests were "not conducive to peace and stability" but otherwise focused on improving the overall U.S.-China relationship. It used stronger language to criticize China's August 17 nuclear test, its second in three months.

Crossed Purposes and Missed Signals

China policymakers in Washington had been caught off guard by the intensity of Beijing's reaction to the Lee visit and sought measures and opportunities to restore a sense of normalcy and progress. China's suspension of virtually all the elements of the American "engagement" policy created considerable consternation and put Washington on the defensive. Faced with Beijing's demand for "concrete measures" to restore the relationship, both the State Department and the National Security Council looked for initiatives to foster improvement. There were few options, however. As the repercussions of the Cornell visit spread, second-guessing and blame-laying began "inside the Beltway." Most of the fingers pointed at the administration for not arranging a better transit for Lee in 1994, not telling Beijing earlier about the Cornell decision, not offsetting the Lee visit with a Jiang summit invitation, not consulting with Congress more closely, and so on. Whatever the merit of these accusations, it was apparent in mid-1995 that the Clinton administration had not yet developed a coherent strategy for dealing with China. Instead, it reacted to events, looking to domestic political actors to provide direction for a multifaceted and complex problem. As a result, it had deteriorating relationships with Beijing and Taiwan, no sympathy from the rest of Asia, and a growing chorus of critics at home.

It also had a growing list of problems. In late June, U.S. press outlets began reporting that the Central Intelligence Agency had delivered to the administration reports strongly indicating that China, in apparent violation of the agreement reached with Washington the previous year, had delivered missile components to Iran and Pakistan.[90] Intelligence sources called the accumulating evidence, which included overhead imagery, communications intercepts, and human-source reporting, "incontrovertible," and some accused the Clinton administration of ignoring the evidence "for political reasons."[91] Critics stepped up attacks on China and on Clinton's foreign policy for failing to prevent the proliferation of weapons of mass destruction and called for sanctions to be imposed again. State demurred. "We have not yet determined whether or not China has violated U.S. sanctions [on missile sales to Pakistan] or the Missile Technology Control Regime [MTCR]," State Department spokesman Nicholas Burns said in response to questions about the missile deal. "We are treating [these reports] seriously."[92]

On June 27, news of another event buffeted the relationship. On June 19, PRC authorities in Xinjiang Province had arrested a naturalized American citizen named Harry Wu as he tried to cross into Chinese territory from Kazakhstan. The U.S. embassy was not informed of the arrest—which the State Department learned from Wu's family and a traveling companion—and its initial requests to meet with him were rebuffed. Wu was no ordinary Chinese American businessman traveling off-the-beaten-track, however. In the view of the human rights community in the United States and Europe, Harry Wu was a hero and a crusader, and when the story of his arrest broke in the United States a week later, it stirred new outrage against both China and the Clinton administration.[93]

Wu was born in Shanghai in 1937. As a university student, he got in trouble in 1957 for criticizing the Soviet invasion of Hungary in one of his classes. In 1960, he was branded a counterrevolutionary and sentenced to "reeducation through labor" (*laogai*) for his views. He spent the next nineteen years of his life in what he would later call "China's gulag"—the extensive system of labor reform camps, mines, and factories used to supplement the penal system and augment the state's labor pool for large public projects. Originally intended as a means of dealing with petty criminals efficiently and "reforming" their behavior through hard labor for the state, the *laogai* system degenerated into a convenient means for local officials to rid themselves of troublesome people—dissidents, religious figures, critics, and political adversaries—without being held accountable through the court system. During the Cultural Revolution, millions were sent to labor reform camps of one sort or another. Afterward, Wu and many others were released back into society, but the system remained intact, a source of enormous abuse—and profit for the Chinese state—that the world knew little about.

Wu emigrated to the United States in 1986 and after Tiananmen, began a one-man campaign to inform the world of the evils and excesses of the Chinese prison labor system. His first book, *Laogai: The Chinese Gulag*, published in 1992, was not only a personal recollection of life in the twelve different prison camps in which he had been incarcerated but also a detailed listing of nearly one thousand prison labor facilities and the products produced in them.[94] In post-Tiananmen Washington, Wu's charges that China was exporting products made by "slave labor" gained him a ready audience with members of Congress, human rights organizations, labor activists concerned with prison labor exports to the United States, and with the media. He became, in certain circles, something of a celebrity.

In the early 1990s, Wu returned to China and surreptitiously visited several *laogai* facilities to gather more information on the products they produced. CBS News sponsored two of the trips and used some of the handheld video footage Wu obtained—at great personal risk—in a documentary segment of *60 Minutes* that ultimately won an Emmy award. Wu followed up with accusations of Chinese enterprises being engaged in prison labor exports, which were investigated under the auspices of the bilateral Memorandum of Understanding reached in 1991. He also made charges that the Chinese prison system "harvested" the organs of executed prisoners for profitable transplants and that the World Bank was considering a loan for China that would actually go to a prison labor facility in Xinjiang.[95]

The publicity obviously brought Wu the enmity of the Chinese government, which put him on a blacklist of people not permitted to visit China. In early 1994, after receiving his U.S. citizenship, Wu changed his name to "Peter Hongda Wu" and received a U.S. passport in the name of Peter H. Wu. State Department officials warned him that further travels to China to gather information on the *laogai* system might subject him to charges by the Chinese government that he was traveling on questionable documents.[96] Wu traveled to China without incident in April 1994, then made plans for a more extensive trip in June 1995. When he crossed the Xinjiang-Kazakhstan border with an American colleague at Horgas on June 19, however, Wu was immediately arrested and held without charges.

The first reaction from the State Department was to try and ascertain the facts through the Chinese government. This precipitated a testy exchange between press spokesmen when it became apparent the Ministry of Foreign Affairs did not know what had happened to Wu. Informal word that Wu was being held in a hotel in the city of Karamay prompted Embassy Beijing to dispatch a consular officer to Urumqi, the capital of Xinjiang Autonomous Region. He then took a twelve-hour taxi trip to Karamay, only to find that Wu was not there.[97] Wu had been at the Karamay Guest House in Horgas, but by the time the embassy officer arrived, Wu had already been moved.[98] U.S. complaints that China was not being cooperative in honoring the bilateral consular agreement—which provides for notification of the arrest of a citizen and access by consular officials within a specified period—drew countercharges that the United States also had failed to honor the agreement for Chinese citizens, and that the U.S. consular officer failed to obtain permission to travel in western Xinjiang.

On July 8, Embassy Beijing was informed that Wu had been charged with "entering into China under false names, illegally obtaining China's state secrets and conducting criminal activities," namely, providing China's secrets to "foreign organizations and institutions" (that is, CBS News and the BBC).[99] Two days later, a U.S. consular official was permitted to speak with Wu under carefully guarded circumstances. The fact that Wu was charged and would be tried in Wuhan—the city where he had resided before leaving for the United States in 1985—suggested that China's security authorities were at least considering treating him still as a Chinese citizen. Chinese Foreign

Ministry officials, unaware of how celebrated a person Wu was in the United States, charged that his case was a deliberate distraction to avoid dealing with what they considered the principal issue, Taiwan.[100]

It was imperative for the American officials dealing with this issue—mainly in the State Department and the NSC—to reinforce the point that Wu should be given full recognition as an American citizen and that he should not be denied any of his legal rights under the Chinese system. In a way, the United States had to empower the Chinese Ministry of Foreign Affairs to deal with a situation that was not under its jurisdiction. This would require a combination of public pressure—to reinforce the point that Wu was a special case and a politically significant one—and private reassurances that other issues could be dealt with but only if the Wu case was properly handled. Despite public anger over what many Americans considered an "illegal" arrest, care had to be taken not to impugn China's legal system or claim any kind of extraterritorial special privileges for Americans traveling abroad. That would only play into the hands of the security apparatus hard-liners. The United States could not expect to get Wu released by publicly demanding it or threatening retaliation. A more subtle and careful approach was needed.

The public pressure was provided in full by Congress and the media, which lionized Wu and used his bravery and dedication to human rights to draw attention to the dark side of the PRC regime and its intolerance for dissent and criticism. The House and the Senate passed unanimous resolutions condemning Wu's arrest and enjoining the president to use every means available to have him returned to the United States. Members of Congress began to talk openly of linking Wu's detention with their votes on China's most favored nation trade status, which Clinton had ordered renewed on June 2, subject to disapproval by Congress. The usual bills of disapproval had been introduced into the House and Senate, and preliminary counts by State and NSC legislative affairs specialists were that the vote would be close.

Private communications with Chinese Ministry of Foreign Affairs officials in Beijing and Washington reinforced the public messages. Chinese chargé d'affaires Zhou Wenzhong was called in to the State Department on several occasions to meet with Undersecretary for Political Affairs Peter Tarnoff and assistant secretary Winston Lord to hear formal complaints about China's failure to abide by the consular agreement. Informally, lower-ranking officials meeting with Chinese diplomats told them that the Wu case would make it very difficult to achieve any progress on any other issues, including Taiwan. Whatever Wu may or may not have done, prosecution and conviction on flimsy espionage charges and lengthy imprisonment would have an enormously adverse affect on U.S. public opinion of China.

Henry Kissinger also provided a channel for private communication, as he had in the past. Heading a delegation from the "America-China Society," which included former secretary of state and national security adviser Al Haig, former deputy secretary of state John Whitehead, former U.S.trade representative Carla Hills, and American Insurance Group chairman Maurice (Hank) Greenberg, Kissinger met with President Jiang, Li Peng, and Qian Qichen in early July. He was treated to the full display of Beijing's anger over the Lee visit, including a finger-wagging lecture by Li Peng on how the Clinton administration had "shaken the foundation" of bilateral relations and "hurt the feelings of the entire Chinese people."[101] Kissinger was taken aback by the depth of Chinese anger and returned to Washington with a public message that the relationship was in "free fall" and that no one should expect Harry Wu to be released soon.[102] Privately, he met with President Clinton (along with Haig, Whitehead, and Greenberg) and repeated his public criticisms of allowing domestic political concerns to overwhelm strategic considerations in developing China policy. He advised strongly that the president should engage with the Chinese in "strategic" terms. "Even if you don't believe in it," he advised Clinton, "you should speak to them in the language of strategic dialogue. They expect it."[103]

During this same period, China specialists in the State Department and the NSC were working on proposals for other means by which bilateral relations could be ameliorated. On the positive side, we considered inviting Jiang Zemin to the United States for some kind of summit meeting with President Clinton and what kinds of actions we could expect in response. On the negative side, we felt obliged to rebut two linked charges from Beijing: that the visa for Lee Teng-hui had represented a fundamental shift in U.S. policy; or if it did not, then Washington should declare formally it would never to allow him to visit again (Lee had already been invited to attend a meeting in Alaska in September). The scheduled meeting between Christopher and Qian at the APEC ministerial meeting in Brunei at the end of July seemed to be an appropriate place to try and clear the air.

Working jointly, the State Department and the NSC developed a briefing for Christopher that would make clear that the Lee visa did not signal a change in U.S. policy. On whether he would be allowed to repeat the Cornell performance, an elaborate dodge was constructed. Rather than permitting unrestricted travel by Taiwan's top officials (which some in the United States believed would lead sooner or later to a Washington visit) or refusing further transits (which would have been politically unacceptable to Congress), it was decided to define the circumstances in which such visits would be approved. There would be four criteria of judgment: such visits were to be strictly for personal reasons, to include health and family considerations;

they were to be rigorously unofficial; applications were to be reviewed and approved on a case-by-case basis; and the State Department expected that such requests would be "rare."[104]

Separately, the NSC went to work on a letter from Clinton to Jiang, discussing larger issues in a post-Cornell situation.[105] The principal goals were reassurance that American policy had not changed, encouragement to reengage in solving difficult problems, and an effort to calm what had become a potentially dangerous rage against Taiwan. In consultation with the State Department China desk, the NSC's Asia Directorate prepared a draft Clinton-to-Jiang letter for Christopher to deliver to Foreign Minister Qian at the APEC ministerial. It contained several general, anodyne statements about hopes for improved relations and cooperation, along with the kernel of the "three noes," which became controversial later. That is, it restated what were standard and consistent policies of the United States but more directly than before and at the highest level. The letter reassured Jiang that the United States "does not support" efforts to create "two Chinas or one China, one Taiwan," does not support "Taiwan independence," or Taiwan's admission to the United Nations.

There is some controversy about whether the letter said the United States "does not support" or "opposes" Taiwan's independence.[106] After the "three noes" imbroglio came out in the open in 1998, some commentators charged that President Clinton's use of the term "opposes" Taiwan independence in his 1995 letter actually encouraged China's subsequent aggressive pressure against Taiwan. There is little to substantiate the facts or the interpretation of such charges.[107] There is ample evidence that the Chinese either missed or ignored the difference between "does not support" and "opposes" with respect to all three elements of the policy. Even as late as October, Jiang was quoted as saying, "We have attached importance to the repeated promises made recently by the US side to uphold the 'one China' policy, observe the three Sino-U.S. joint communiqués, *oppose* 'two Chinas or one China, one Taiwan', *oppose* Taiwan independence and *oppose* Taiwan's membership of the United Nations."[108] This suggests that Jiang and others were overstating the congruence between the U.S. position and their own, perhaps for domestic political reasons, perhaps to increase the pressure on Taiwan. In any case, the U.S. side reiterated the "does not support" position and emphasized in private to Chinese officials the importance of the distinction.

The Christopher-Qian meeting in Brunei on August 1 was cordial and businesslike but cool, and it changed little in the dynamic of the relationship. Each side's press coverage reflected different expectations and preparations for the meeting. The U.S. side reported the meeting was "positive and useful," mainly because the two agreed to have further discussions at a slightly lower level (Undersecretary for Political Affairs Peter Tarnoff and Vice Minister Li Zhaoxing). One of the subjects to be explored was the possibility of a Washington summit meeting between Jiang and Clinton, which Christopher had mentioned in the meeting. Xinhua reported that Qian emphasized the relationship was facing "serious difficulties," mainly because of the Taiwan problem. The Chinese press did not mention the summit proposal.

Christopher had made a major Asia policy speech on July 27, at which he laid out a comprehensive justification for U.S. policy in the Asia-Pacific region. He discussed U.S. engagement, focusing on relations with Japan, Korea, and Southeast Asia. China's concerns about a U.S. policy change toward Taiwan were "unwarranted," he said. Nonetheless, he recited the mantra of U.S. steadfastness in its "one China" policy, then went on to catalogue the "profound disagreements" between China and the United States, focusing on human rights and nonproliferation. He concluded with a recommendation that "China can take an immediate step to help restore a more positive atmosphere with the immediate release of American citizen Harry Wu."[109] Just before his meeting with Qian, Christopher told accompanying press, "It's very difficult for me to envision any circumstances under which President Jiang Zemin would be able to come to Washington to meet with the president if Harry Wu is still incarcerated."[110]

Christopher's remarks were only a hint of the disagreements going on within the Washington policy community over the possibility of a Jiang visit. The NSC Asia Directorate and the China desk at the State Department proposed the idea as a means of offsetting the negative effects of the Lee Teng-hui visit and encouraging the Chinese, and particularly Jiang, to be more forthcoming in efforts to resolve mounting problems, including the Harry Wu issue. Other parts of the White House, particularly those involved in domestic politics and congressional affairs, objected vehemently. Besides the president's dislike of the stodgy formality of state visits, there was a pervasive "you can't have those human rights violators in the White House" attitude that limited the range of planning.[111] With Harry Wu under interrogation in a Chinese jail, it was hard enough to generate interest in any kind of Chinese visit. A state visit, with all the pomp and circumstance and implied harmonious relations, was out of the question.

Two additional White House factors entered into the equation. First was the desire of Hillary Rodham Clinton to attend the Fourth World Conference on Women, scheduled to be held in Beijing in early September. The First Lady was eager to establish herself as a leader in the women's movement and to carry that movement to China as head of the American delegation to the UN-sponsored conference. But China's human rights record—further tarnished by its inept handling of the politics and logistics of the high-profile conclave—and the Harry Wu case stood in the way. Hoping that a wish to have the First Lady visit China would be an incentive for the Chinese to "do the right thing" and release Wu, the White House temporized in a very public way, postponing the decision on whether Hillary would attend the meeting.[112]

The second factor, which would become a major part of the China policy debate in 1997, was the freelance hostage-negotiation activities of Johnny Chien Chuen Chung, a Taiwanese American businessman from California. Sometime after July 28, I received a folder from the NSC documents distribution office assigning the Asia Directorate responsibility to respond to a memo to Tony Lake from a staffer named Janice Enright in the Office of the Deputy Chief of Staff to the President. The memo recounted a phone conversation she had had with the executive director of the Democratic National Committee (DNC), Bobby Watson, who had said that a DNC "trustee" (that is, heavy financial contributor) named Johnny Chung had asked for a presidential letter of recommendation to carry with him to China. Chung had said he would be meeting with Jiang Zemin and other senior Chinese officials in an effort to get Harry Wu released from prison.

I was appalled. I immediately called Watson to find out what had happened. It was not the first time I had dealt with DNC interlopers in sensitive foreign policy issues, nor was it the first time I had heard of Chung. Chung had called the NSC Asia Directorate a few times in early 1995, seeking a meeting with Stanley Roth. I demurred, as I did not think he had any unique insights to offer and seemed only concerned with pursuing his personal business interests. In April, I was asked by Deputy National Security Adviser Nancy Soderberg's office to evaluate whether it would be appropriate to give Chung photographs of the president with a delegation of Chinese Chung had brought to watch the taping of one of Clinton's weekly radio addresses. In my e-mail reply—later widely publicized—I referred to Chung as a "hustler" who should be treated with "a pinch of suspicion." I warned he appeared to be trying to set up a business operation that would trade photo opportunities with the president and First Lady—obtained through the DNC—for business deals in China.[113] I had hoped that the White House would have little more to do with him. But I was unaware of the easy access Chung had obtained through the First Lady's office and that it had continued.

I was only mildly relieved to learn from Watson that they had decided not to seek a presidential letter but only to supply Chung with a generic credentials letter from DNC chairman Donald L. Fowler, describing Chung as a "friend and great supporter of the DNC."[114] As I wrote in a memo to Lake on July 31, Chung could "conceivably do damage" to efforts to get Wu freed from Chinese prison. We had no idea what he was going to say, or to whom, or by what authority. Other efforts were afoot to free Wu, both through official contacts and through members of Congress, and I was concerned that Chung, if he gained high-level access, might confuse the process. But since he had already left for China, there was little that could be done to prevent him from making his pitch. "All we can do is hope the Chinese recognize Chung's credentials are thin and that his message should be treated with caution," I concluded.[115] Lake called me after he had read the memo to ask if we should contact the U.S. embassy to try to find Chung and wave him off. I recommended against such a course, believing it would draw unnecessary and potentially embarrassing attention to the case.

Chung's account of the events—some in testimony under oath before the House Governmental Affairs Committee—provides additional interesting details. Chung first got involved in the issue after he was called by Charles Parish, the U.S. embassy officer dispatched to Urumqi to find Wu in late June. At a DNC fund-raiser in California in mid-July, Chung had had an animated exchange with President Clinton, who supported Chung's plan to seek Wu's release. "Tell them they have no right to arrest U.S. citizens," Clinton reportedly told Chung. "We have enough problems between our two countries. We don't need any more." In Chung's mind, apparently, that was his mission directive. In China, Chung used his connections to arrange a meeting on August 18 with Liu Huaqiu, vice minister of foreign affairs, head of the State Council Foreign Affairs Office, and one of Jiang Zemin's principal advisers on relations with the United States. Liu Xiaoming, a Foreign Ministry staffer and eventually deputy chief of mission at China's embassy in Washington, also sat in.[116] They told him China would "do something" soon about Wu. Chung's access to the highest levels of Beijing's foreign policy decisionmaking apparatus is a testament to the enduring importance of *guanxi* in Chinese politics, although it is unlikely that Chung's views on the Harry Wu case carried much weight.

Congressional attention to China continued through July, as China's rhetorical and military pressure on Taiwan escalated. For the most part, it was angry attention, although Senators Diane Feinstein and Bennett Johnston traveled to China to seek Wu's release as a means of improving bilateral relations. To insulate the MFN issue from all the other problems, the administration encouraged and cooperated with Representative Douglas Bereuter (R-Nebr.), who chaired the East Asia Subcommittee of the House Foreign Affairs Committee, in developing a comprehensive "China policy" bill. The China Policy Act of 1995 (H.R. 2053) consisted of several "findings"—mostly negative—about PRC economic and political activities and a call for "intensified diplomatic initiatives" with the PRC to bring about Harry Wu's release, improvements in China's human rights practices, adherence to international conventions on nonproliferation, reduction in tensions with Taiwan and Southeast Asia, and defense policy transparency. It also mandated that Radio Free Asia commence broadcasting to China within ninety days.[117]

The White House quietly supported the bill on the premise that it would give Congress an opportunity to vent its anger by voting for the China Policy Act rather than against MFN extension. Legislative liaison officials were confident that the bill was unlikely to be taken up by the Senate. Bereuter's skillful management of the bill got it passed 416-10 on July 20, accompanied by torrents of criticism of China and the administration's China policy. On the same day, the bill to revoke China's MFN privileges was defeated, 321-107. Beijing's vituperation about the China Policy Act, which it predictably accused of being "gross interference" in China's internal affairs, probably obscured its understanding of the fact that the more important legislation, with far greater consequences, had been soundly defeated.

The State Department was determined to restore a sense of normalcy to the relationship, however much U.S. public opinion—and Chinese behavior—seemed to militate against it. What appeared to some U.S. observers as excessive deference to China was actually a conscious effort to keep an already volatile situation from becoming worse. That entailed responding in a low-key manner to some of China's provocative actions, such as the late July missile tests into the Taiwan Strait ("not helpful" to stability), the arrest and expulsion of two Hong Kong–based U.S. Air Force attachés caught "spying" on China's military exercises in early August (State faulted the Pentagon), the intelligence reports on M-11s in Pakistan, and the underground nuclear test on August 17 (not enough to justify new sanctions).

In late August, with Harry Wu still in prison and the relationship heading for crisis, Undersecretary Peter Tarnoff prepared to travel to Beijing in the face of what a Xinhua commentator on August 23 called the "lowest ebb" in bilateral relations since 1979. The commentary, couched in angry, polemical terms and with little regard for accuracy, railed at "the administration," American journalists, "hegemonists" with a "gloomy, Cold War mentality," and anti-China elements, advising them to wake up before "cold war II" emerged.[118] It was not the first or the last time a senior American visitor to Beijing would be greeted by a cold blast from the Propaganda Department.

The day before Tarnoff's arrival, however, Beijing announced that the Wuhan Municipal Intermediate People's Court had tried Wu Hongda (Harry Wu) on charges of "stealing, spying and illegally providing state secrets to overseas institutions, organizations and people, and of passing himself off as a government worker to carry out deceptive activities."[119] At the conclusion of the four-hour trial, it sentenced him to fifteen years in prison and simultaneous expulsion from China. Within hours of the sentencing, Wu was on an Air China flight to San Francisco. President Clinton welcomed Wu's release in a low-key statement by Mike McCurry from Wyoming, where the First Family was vacationing. But little else was done to highlight Wu's release.

Had a bargain been struck? Many in the press suspected as much, with the main evidence being McCurry's well-informed speculation, two days before the trial, that "they [the Chinese] will most likely put him on trial and convict him of something—from what we hear, short of espionage. Then the issue will be, what do they . . . propose, then, to do about it?"[120] But it was never a specifically agreed-upon deal. The U.S. position had always been, "Wu should be released for the sake of the relationship, but the United States will not interfere in China's legal processes." The Chinese position had been, "China's legal processes must be respected, and we understand the importance of the Wu issue." It was something of a "diplomatic gavotte," with both sides moving carefully and slowly because they were blindfolded. Neither side wanted to court criticism from powerful domestic forces in order to reach a formal agreement. So there were understandings that were never articulated, common expectations that were never formalized. But no deal.

In the end, it was a clever solution. Chinese security authorities got maximum publicity for the case, savaging Wu's reputation, citing his "confession" of distorting facts to discredit his television reports, warning any others of the perils of challenging the labor camp system. The fifteen-year suspended sentence would keep Wu from undertaking any further clandestine journeys to China. The White House got to announce on August 26 the First Lady's participation in the Fourth World Conference on Women, which it was extremely eager to do. But there was little progress achieved in improving bilateral relations. It removed one obstacle, but only a small one.

Tarnoff arrived in Beijing on Saturday, August 26. His main purpose was to follow up on a possible summit meeting between Clinton and Jiang. In three hours of discussions with Vice Minister Li Zhaoxing, Tarnoff made little progress. The Chinese, while interested in a Clinton-Jiang summit, were more interested in talking about the Taiwan issue, and their dissatisfaction with U.S. positions was signaled by the fact that Qian only met with Tarnoff for a half hour. Tarnoff told reporters he was encouraged by the talks, even though no progress had been made on any of the substantive issues raised. He said both sides recognized the value of engagement and that both would begin working on an agenda for the presidents' meeting, which he suggested would take place around the time of the celebration of the fiftieth anniversary of the United Nations, in October. The Ministry of Foreign Affairs spokesman noted that the talks were "useful" but said a restoration of relations was still dependent on "whether the U.S. side can take actions to honor its commitment" to "opposing 'two Chinas or one-China-one-Taiwan,' Taiwan independence, and Taiwan joining the UN."[121]

Struggling for a Summit

The Taiwan issue seemed to be fading in importance at the end of summer. At the annual August leadership retreat in the resort town of Beidaihe, discussions reportedly focused on the Ninth Five-Year Plan, an anticorruption drive, and personnel issues, although the Taiwan question did receive some consideration.[122] Jiang Zemin appears to have become intrigued at the possibilities for a significant improvement of relations and particularly the prospect of a summit meeting and state visit to Washington, D.C. The offer was no doubt attractive to Jiang for many reasons—his love of pomp and ceremony, the opportunity to outshine Lee Teng-hui, a chance to take the U.S.-China relationship out of a negative cycle, and simply the lure of Washington.

Meanwhile, the Foreign Ministry was facing difficulties in getting the Americans to make further progress on the Taiwan issue. Encouraged by the initial U.S. response to their insistence that it was up to the United States to mend the relationship by doing something "concrete," the Chinese had pushed hard to get a formal commitment that no more Lee Teng-hui visits would be permitted. They were concerned about a pending invitation to Lee to attend a September meeting of the U.S.-ROC Economic Council in Anchorage, Alaska. Even after Lee decided to decline the invitation in late July, the Chinese pressed for a promise that the Cornell visit would not be repeated. Washington focused on trying to restore the relationship to pre-visit levels and reassuring Beijing that U.S. policy toward China had not changed. Beijing's goals, however, seemed to be to publicly isolate Taiwan and force it off of what China perceived as a path toward independence.

The Ministry of Foreign Affairs tried to get a public affirmation of Clinton's and Christopher's informal assurances on future Taiwanese visits, but the State Department declined to be pinned down. After Taiwanese reporters began asking about negotiations over a "fourth communiqué" in September, the State Department's approach to further movement on Taiwan-related questions stiffened publicly. Spokesman Nicholas Burns, after being badgered about it persistently, indicated that the United States had done enough to assuage China's concerns about Taiwan. "I think that stage is over in the relationship . . . And we certainly hope that we can now go beyond this issue and get on to the nonproliferation issues which . . . are at the top of the agenda, as well as the economic and political issues that we have to deal with."[123]

Plans for the summit were not going well either, primarily because too few people in the Clinton administration saw much need for one. Many were still angry over what appeared to be China's deliberately provocative behavior, its arrogance and cynicism. That anger was most clearly demonstrated in the First Lady's participation in the Fourth United Nations Conference on Women, being held in Beijing, September 4–15. Shortly after the announcement of her attendance on August 26, the First Lady's aides declared that she would not be meeting with any Chinese leaders on her visit. Efforts to persuade them that even a brief courtesy call on Jiang Zemin's wife or a senior female Chinese official might aid the process of restoring bilateral relations fell on deaf ears. She would meet with Mongolian officials when she visited that country after the conference. But she wanted nothing to do with the Chinese government. The trip to Beijing was to be about women's issues, not diplomacy.

In her speech to the delegates on September 5, the First Lady was true to her promise not to single out certain countries for special criticism on women's rights issues. But in her deftly worded, powerful speech to a cheering audience of women who had braved Chinese security and a huge rainstorm to hear her, she left little doubt about her targets:

> Our goals for this conference . . . cannot be fully achieved unless all governments here and around the world accept their responsibility to protect and promote internationally recognized human rights. . . . It is time for us to say here in Beijing and the world to hear, that it is no longer acceptable to discuss women's rights as separate from human rights. . . . Even today there are those who are trying to silence our words. . . . It is a violation of human rights when women are denied the right to plan their own families, and that includes being forced to have abortions or being sterilized against their will. . . . It is indefensible that many women in non-governmental organizations who wished to participate in this conference have not been able to attend, or have been prohibited from fully taking part."[124]

The speech was well received by the delegates and by editorialists back home. The Chinese, however, were not impressed. "We have taken note that some people from some countries have made unwarranted remarks and criticisms against other countries. We would like to caution these people to pay more attention to the problems within their own countries," a Foreign Ministry spokesman told reporters after Clinton had left.[125]

As already noted, there was never any serious consideration given to the idea of inviting Jiang to Washington for a full state visit. Under the circumstances, with public anger at China spiking for human rights violations, nonproliferation problems, and the growing threat to Taiwan, no one in the White House thought such a visit—with a guard of honor, twenty-one-gun salute, state banquet, and all—was politically sustainable. So an "official working visit" was offered instead, first in meetings between Vice Foreign Minister Li Zhaoxing and Peter Tarnoff in Washington in mid-September, then in more detail at the late September meeting between Qian Qichen and Warren Christopher. Tarnoff and Christopher tried to explain that such a meeting—which could be called a "summit" but not a "state visit," entailed a long, substantive meeting with the president in the White House, usually a "working lunch," and other meetings around town. It was, in fact, the president's preferred style of meeting foreign heads of state. The focus would be on the substantive issues, not the protocol, or the "trappings," of a state visit.[126]

The Chinese, however, were having none of it. Their frame of reference was not how other foreign leaders were received by Clinton, but how other Chinese leaders had been received by American presidents. Deng Xiaoping had paid a state visit to President Jimmy Carter in 1979, and Li Xiannian—only a figurehead—had been given a state visit by President Ronald Reagan in 1985. Anything less than a full state visit for Jiang was unacceptable. Recognizing that a potentially embarrassing stalemate had arisen that could have damaged the relationship further, Christopher and Qian agreed on an easily available compromise—a private meeting in New York City during the late October celebration of the fiftieth anniversary of the establishment of the United Nations. Both sides went public with their complaints about the way the other side had handled the issue. White House spokesman Mike McCurry said bluntly that bilateral relations were not "at a sufficient state of progress to warrant a state visit," while Qian accused the White House of lacking "political will."[127]

Irritation levels increased as the October 24 date for the summit approached. After the Christopher-Qian meeting in New York on September 28, the State Department announced that China had agreed to cancel the sale of two nuclear reactors to Iran, a deal that had drawn a lot of fire in Washington. Although the "senior official" (probably Winston Lord) insisted that China had made the decision unilaterally, reporters were encouraged to interpret it as a gesture of goodwill toward the United States. The following day, Qian corrected the record, saying China had agreed only to "suspend for the time being" the reactor sale, not cancel it. He attributed the discrepancy to "inaccurate reports" of his meeting with Christopher.[128] Subsequently, the State Department spokesman told reporters that the Taiwan issue had barely come up in the Christopher-Qian talks and insisted that the relationship had "gotten away from a fixation on Taiwan."[129] This point was disputed by both Qian and Jiang in subsequent meetings with American reporters, where they continued to express dissatisfaction at the U.S. position, particularly on the Lee visit. Just before the summit itself, the Chinese side demanded a change of location when advance men discovered photographs of the

Tiananmen demonstrations in the New York Public Library, where the meeting had been scheduled to take place.

In spite of the dismal atmospherics preceding it, the meeting between President Clinton and President Jiang at the Lincoln Center on the afternoon of October 24 went remarkably well. The Lincoln Center locale had already been checked by the Secret Service, and last minute changes demanded by the Chinese were easily accommodated. Human rights demonstrators were kept far enough away from the center that their chants, while faintly audible, were not distracting inside the meeting room. Clinton was well aware of the importance of the meeting and prepared for it thoroughly and carefully. The premeeting briefing at the Waldorf-Astoria was longer than usual, and he asked numerous questions as he read the information memo on the meeting and edited his talking points.

Jiang arrived at the summit considerably strengthened back at home. The Fifth Plenum of the Fourteenth Central Committee had concluded on September 28 with a significant boost for Jiang's practical authority and his prestige. Besides approving the party's "proposal" for the Ninth Five-Year Plan, the plenum formalized Jiang's purge of his former rival, Beijing mayor Chen Xitong, expelling him from the Politburo and Central Committee and holding him for further judicial action.[130] The plenum also added four new members to the Central Military Commission leadership: Defense Minister Chi Haotian and Chief of Staff Zhang Wannian became vice chairmen; soon-to-be General Logistics Department head Wang Ke and Wang Ruilin (a General Political Department deputy who also headed Deng Xiaoping's private office) became CMC members. Observers noted that Jiang had succeeded in bringing into the CMC leadership individuals loyal to himself, isolating Deng's lieutenants Liu Huaqing and Zhang Zhen, whom he had reportedly tried to persuade to retire.[131] Finally, two weeks before his summit with Clinton, Jiang reviewed a massive military exercise in northern China, shown on Chinese television, which included an outing aboard a cruiser and a speech to the troops.[132]

The general secretary's renewed self-assurance and authority were reflected in his conduct of the summit. Jiang spoke confidently and without notes, making eye contact with Clinton and seeking to engage him personally in a genuine dialogue. He addressed controversial issues directly, occasionally easing the atmosphere with mildly humorous asides, some in English. The meeting plan was for a thirty-minute private session with a minimum of staff (Christopher, Lake, Lord, and myself as note taker, with an equal number on the Chinese side), to be followed by an hour-long meeting of the full delegation, which included on the American side representatives of several bureaucracies. But the chemistry between the two presidents was good, and the private talks lasted for almost an hour, leaving only a brief time for the larger, more formal discussion.

Jiang picked up on themes from Clinton's October 22 address to the commemorative meeting for the UN's fiftieth anniversary, offering to expand bilateral cooperation in fighting against international crime, narcotics trafficking, and terrorism, and working to improve the environment. He talked at length about China's economic development and its interest in participating in the international trading system. He also focused on Taiwan in some detail, trying to explain why it was such a painful issue for Beijing. Clinton raised the standard U.S. issues in a fairly standard format. Human rights was discussed in general, but details were left to a private exchange after the summit, when I presented a list of four priority prisoners—which included Wei Jingsheng—to a Chinese counterpart. But it was the first time the two had relaxed a bit in each other's company, and the dialogue was not entirely an exchange of scripted talking points. Clinton observed afterward that it was the first time he had begun to understand and appreciate Jiang as a politician.[133]

The summit restored a sense of procedural normalization to the relationship. Ambassador Li Daoyu returned shortly afterward to Washington, and the new U.S. ambassador, former senator James R. Sasser, took up his post in Beijing. "Engagement" was back on track, in the sense that high-level officials, including military leaders, began scheduling meetings with one another. Clinton and Jiang expressed the intention to meet again at the APEC leaders meeting in Osaka, Japan, in November. But the relationship had not recovered. It was still fragile, susceptible to buffeting by unpredictable events, and under attack by domestic forces in both countries. It would not take long for it to deteriorate again.

The sharpest shock came on November 22, less than a month after the Clinton-Jiang summit, when China announced it would bring to trial its most famous dissident, Wei Jingsheng, on charges of attempting to overthrow the Chinese government. After being held incommunicado since his arrest in April 1994, Wei was to be arraigned on December 13 by the Beijing Intermediate Court. Two former attorneys general of the United States, Richard Thornburgh and Nicholas Katzenbach, had offered to aid in his defense but were not permitted. The House of Representatives unanimously adopted a resolution (H. Con. Res. 117) calling for his "immediate and unconditional release," which was ignored by Beijing. Wei's trial lasted five hours and was closed to all but family members and observers selected by the regime. He made a twenty-minute speech in his own defense, claiming he was only trying to promote democracy in China, then was pronounced guilty by a three-judge panel and sentenced to fourteen years in prison.[134]

Reaction in the United States was immediate and heated. The White House, State Department, Congress, and virtually all major media condemned the verdict in strong terms and called for its reversal. Many of the commentators in the press focused their criticism equally on the president's China policy, calling for a tougher approach to a recalcitrant and contemptuous China, including the relinkage of trade and human rights. In the White House, there was a sense of personal affront, that the president "went out on a limb for the Chinese, and they sawed it off," one senior official told *New York Times* reporter David Sanger.[135]

Back to the Hard Line

On returning to China, Jiang and others in the leadership reviewed the situation. Clinton and his advisers had moved no further on the Taiwan issue in terms of pledging no further visits to the United States by high-level Taiwanese officials. In fact, in the wake of the summit, Winston Lord and others were saying that Taiwan was "just one of many issues" to be resolved.[136] For its part, Taiwan evidently had not made a decision to change course and try to improve relations with China. At a training exercise in early October, Lee Teng-hui had boasted that China "did not dare" to attack Taiwan because of the island's military prowess, and he continued to insist publicly that Taiwan had a right to seek expansion of its international influence.[137] Although details are sparse, Jiang and his advisers—particularly the senior PLA officers who had been advocating stronger action—seem to have decided by early November to take an even more vigorous approach to Taiwan, including:

—A direct effort to influence Taiwanese voters in the December 2 parliamentary elections and the March 21 presidential elections not to support Taiwan's independence, meaning especially the Democratic Progressive Party candidates;

—Establishment of a Headquarters for Operations Targeting Taiwan within the General Staff Department and a Nanjing War Zone headquarters, both under the command of Zhang Wannian, to carry out larger and more intense military exercises in the Taiwan Strait area and demonstrate the PLA's readiness and capability to "defend Taiwan by force"; and

—Intensified efforts to determine Washington's military capabilities and intentions vis-à-vis Taiwan and to warn it not to interfere.[138]

The mid-November visit to Beijing of American assistant secretary of defense for international security affairs Joseph Nye was yet another occasion for missed communications. Nye considered his mission one of relationship repair, continuing the process of returning U.S.-China relations to a more normal track, including in the crucial area of military-to-military exchanges and "strategic" dialogue. He reassured his Chinese interlocutors, including President Jiang, that the United States did not seek to "contain" China but rather to engage it. PLA officers, including Defense Minister Chi and Assistant to the Chief of Staff Xiong Guangkai, repeatedly stressed the dominant importance of the Taiwan issue, urging the United States not to interfere in what they called an "explosive" issue in the relationship.[139] They also probed repeatedly about what U.S. reaction would be if hostilities were to take place in the Taiwan Strait. Trying carefully to measure his words in line with his understanding of U.S. policy, Nye dodged the question, saying in essence, "We don't know and you don't know" how the United States would react.[140] He also reiterated the American position that disputes between Taiwan and the PRC should be settled peacefully and that the use of force by China would be a "serious mistake."[141]

Predisposed as they were to a view that the United States was a declining superpower unwilling to engage in combat that might entail heavy casualties, PLA leaders may have mistaken Nye's effort to maintain a balanced U.S. approach to the Taiwan issue as a sign of weakness or indecision. In the mood of anger and eagerness to "teach Lee Teng-hui a lesson" that prevailed among military officials at that time, there was probably nothing that Nye would have been authorized to say that could have turned the military away from the path they had chosen. Jiang had given the go-ahead in early November, and troops were already being moved into place for the PLA's next exercise-demonstration while Nye was in Beijing.

On November 25, just two weeks after a large-scale Taiwanese military exercise, less than a week after the APEC meeting at which Jiang met privately with Vice President Al Gore,[142] and one week before Taiwan's legislative elections, a massive PLA combined air, naval, and ground force armada carried out a mock amphibious attack on the island of Dongshan, on the Fujian coast about one hundred kilometers from Quemoy. Obviously intended to simulate an attack on Taiwan, the exercise featured offshore artillery bombardment, air strikes by China's most modern fighter-bombers, helicopter and landing craft assaults on a beach, and mop-up operations by armed police units. It was accompanied by an impressive propaganda blitz: extensive footage of the pyrotechnics was shown on Chinese television, while radio and other PRC media outlets, especially in Hong Kong, hammered home the message that the exercises were evidence that the PLA was capable of and prepared for taking action to prevent Taiwan's independence.[143]

Taiwanese voters—some of them, at least—evidently got the message. In the parliamentary elections held on December 2, the ruling Kuomintang Party saw its majority trimmed to 52 percent of the 164-seat Legislative Yuan, while the New Party, which openly campaigned for reunification with the mainland, gained fourteen seats. "Communist China's military exercises drew some votes for us from people who supported Taiwan independence before," a New Party spokesman said afterward. The pro-independence Democratic Progressive Party gained marginally at the KMT's expense, holding at about one-third of the popular vote and the same percentage in the legislature. It had been expected to make significant gains, however, and some of its more strident activists were defeated in close elections. While analysts in Taiwan quibbled over the impact of the PRC military exercises, all seemed to agree that it was a factor in the voting and would likely be so again in the March presidential contest.[144]

Beijing now appeared fully committed to a policy of threatening and pressuring Taiwan, while actively warning the United States to keep its hands off. Insofar as other U.S. interests were concerned, a similar hardening of attitude was to be expected, in some cases because the center ordered it, in others because of the absence of concern about negative U.S. reaction. Aside from the Wei trial, there were other indications of an overall crackdown on religious and political freedoms in China, including the arrest of Christian church leaders and the setting aside of the Dalai Lama's choice to fill Tibetan Buddhism's second-highest position, the Panchen Lama.[145] Confronted with an understandable international outcry and condemnation of these actions, Beijing responded caustically: Ministry spokesman Chen Jian referred to U.S. criticisms and affirmations that Washington would continue to press for Wei's release as "vicious actions" and "malicious interference in Chinese affairs."[146]

Tensions also escalated in the trade arena, as Chinese authorities failed (or refused) to carry out the terms of the agreement reached in February 1995 on improved enforcement of Chinese law against copyright infringement and CD piracy. The USTR catalogued a growing list of illegal CD manufacturers in central and southern China, some of which appeared to have connections to the military or high-level leaders' families. Beijing claimed that it had undertaken thousands of raids to curtail the trade in pirated music and computer software. But the USTR insisted the enforcement actions had focused only on distributors, not producers, and threatened to impose economic sanctions by February 1996 if its concerns were not addressed. It also suggested that failure to satisfactorily resolve the problem would affect U.S. support for China's bid to enter the World Trade Organization. China warned of unspecified retaliation in response, calling threatened U.S. special 301 punitive tariffs "unacceptable."[147]

But the main issue was still Taiwan, especially for the military. It is difficult, in retrospect, to see exactly what China's goals were during this period. Hindsight explanations from the mainland make the point that the objective was to heighten Taiwan's sensitivity to the issue of reunification and foil the plot of Taiwanese independence supposedly being carried out by Lee Teng-hui and the DPP.[148] Robert Ross claims that "China's objective was to coerce the United States to end the recent trend of its indirect yet increasingly significant support for Taiwan independence by adopting a new position on U.S.-Taiwan relations and Taiwan's role in international politics. China also aimed to coerce Taiwan into abandoning its effort to redefine the 'one-China' principle and Taiwan's status in international politics."[149]

Although these factors doubtless entered into the process of explaining and justifying the policy choices made, Suisheng Zhao's account of Beijing's motivations is somewhat more persuasive, as it focuses on domestic political interests, such as justifying requests for continuing increases in PLA budgets, arousing patriotism to buttress regime legitimacy, and enhancing central authority above regional interests. He also cites the frustration and anger over Lee Teng-hui's unwillingness to engage in serious cross-Strait discussions and his willful disregard of Beijing's opinions and prestige in formulating Taiwan's foreign policy.[150] Some have argued that Beijing's goals shifted in the wake of its "success" in affecting Taiwan's December elections, claiming that Beijing turned to an effort to prevent Lee from being elected in March. This seems unlikely, as Beijing was well aware that Lee held an insurmountable lead as he entered the final stage of his campaign.[151]

Aside from increasing the rhetorical attack on Lee Teng-hui and continuing preparations for military exercises, Beijing sought to weaken Taipei's relations with the United States and keep the United States off balance about the situation in the Taiwan Strait. Press commentators continued to stress that the United States was intent on "containing" China's growth and reunification, thereby prompting further denials from American defense officials. Chinese Defense Ministry leaders claimed the military-to-military relationship was being restored and agreed to reschedule Defense Minister Chi's postponed trip to Washington for sometime in the spring of 1996.

At the same time, PLA officers were warning Americans in secondary channels that China was prepared to go to war over Taiwan. Military intelligence officials told former assistant secretary of defense Charles Freeman in October 1995, for example, that China was planning more missile tests, including closure zones just off Taiwan's principal ports of Kaohsiung and Chilung. Freeman's response—that such tests would probably cause the United States to react militarily—was rejected by Chinese officers. Xiong Guangkai and others appeared to believe the U.S. military was averse to situations in which it might suffer casualties and would not respond militarily to China's actions in the Taiwan Strait. Freeman passed these comments on to American officials after his return from China in late October.[152]

The Path to Confrontation

The period between Thanksgiving and Christmas is often a slack period in the U.S. government. Large projects and issues are put aside as people prepare for the holidays. But Tony Lake was worried. The U.S.-China relationship was heading downhill again, partly because of the Wei trial and what it implied but mainly because of Chinese aggressiveness in the Taiwan Strait. The New York summit had not provided much "bounce" to the bilateral relationship, and the follow-up APEC summit meeting between Jiang and Gore had not furthered the dialogue. In late November, the Chinese had conducted a very large military exercise off Dongshan Island, and intelligence agencies were reporting plans for an even larger one before Taiwan's presidential elections. Lake was concerned that the Chinese leadership seemed to be discounting U.S. interests in the region, not factoring U.S. concerns into their decisions on Taiwan. He thought the U.S. reaction to China's missile tests had been too weak, but because he already was so actively engaged in the diplomacy on Bosnia, Haiti, and Northern Ireland, he did not wish to contest the issue with Christopher.[153]

After a staff meeting in early December, Lake invited me into his office and asked me to undertake two tasks, off-line and off "the system" (formal NSC records). First was a review of the terminology the United States used with the PRC on the Taiwan issue, including the three communiqués, the Taiwan Relations Act, and general discourse. He was particularly interested in how U.S. officials responded to "what if" questions about a military attack on Taiwan and was unhappy with the idea of "strategic ambiguity" that had become a shorthand description of the U.S. efforts to avoid making precise commitments on Taiwan's defense.[154]

The second task Lake had in mind was to begin developing a varied set of U.S. responses to different actions the PRC might take against Taiwan. I met privately to discuss this aim with the State Department's China desk director, Jeffrey Bader, and Brigadier General Robert "Doc" Fogelsong, then a deputy director for politico-military affairs in the Strategic Plans and Policy (J-5) Office of the Joint Chiefs of Staff. Although I had hoped to avoid bureaucratic channels, the project soon became known at the upper levels of the Pentagon, where objections were raised to nonmilitary officials being involved in "contingency planning," which was strictly the preserve of the Joint Chiefs. I readily relinquished the organizational and analytical task to Fogelsong but continued to participate informally in the process, making sure that nonmilitary actions—on the Chinese and the U.S. side—were considered in the analysis.

At the end of December, Senior Director for Asia Stanley Roth resigned from the NSC and was replaced by Sandra J. Kristoff, who had returned from a stint as coordinator for Asia-Pacific Economic Cooperation (APEC) at the State Department. With Lake, Kristoff oversaw a process of bringing the initiative for China policy back to the White House or at least strengthening the NSC's—and Lake's—oversight of China policy.[155] To help him get up to speed on China issues, Lake asked for a meeting of prominent China experts from various fields to advise him.

The first "policy breakfast" on China took place on January 4, 1996, in the situation room of the White House West Wing. Among the invitees were former Clinton administration officials Chas Freeman and Stanley Roth; former Bush staffer Douglas Paal; academic experts Michel Oksenberg, Kenneth Lieberthal, and Dick Solomon; human rights activists Holly Burkhalter and John Kamm; business executive Hank Greenberg; and several NSC staffers. Lake led a lively discussion of issues, covering the entire gamut of U.S.-PRC problems. The most startling moment of the meeting came when Freeman related the substance of conversations he had held with military leaders in Beijing during the late fall. The PLA leaders seemed to be of the view, Freeman said, that the United States would not come to Taiwan's assistance in the event of a Chinese attack on the island, because, as they said, "you care more about Los Angeles than you do about Taiwan." It was an implicit threat to use nuclear weapons against an American city, and Lake was incredulous, as were others. Freeman stuck by his story, reiterating the point that it should be taken not as a threat to the United States, but as an indicator of the unrealistic mind-set of senior PLA leaders and their fixation on Taiwan.[156]

The story had a larger impact on public perceptions after it was leaked to the *New York Times* in late January than it had within policymaking councils. The original source of the threat—presumed to be Xiong Guangkai, a deputy chief of the PLA General Staff, head of China's military intelligence, and a member of the Central Committee Leadership Small Group on Taiwan—was authoritative enough to make such a threat. But the context of his remarks did not lead the administration to conclude that plans were under way to conduct a missile attack on Taiwan, or that it was preparing to use its small force of nuclear missiles in a first-strike capacity. Xiong's remarks were considered empty bluster—possibly fueled by *maotai*, the fiery alcohol beloved by some PLA generals—or a calculated bluff. If it was the latter, it was going to be called. "If this was some sort of serious message, we had to make it clear that we were returning it unopened," Lake recalled in an interview later.[157]

In January, the NSC initiated an in-house review of China policy, which then became the focus of meetings of both the Principals and Deputies committees. The intent was not to change direction but rather to alter the perspective on China policy: from trying to resolve problems in the context of "engagement" to trying to manage—in cooperation with the Chinese—the inevitable problems in the relationship; from seeking to repair the relationship to preventing it from deteriorating further. For the first few months of 1996, Lake and Berger saw a series of potential crises.

—First was a growing realization that the Chinese were not close to being in compliance with the agreement reached in 1995 on the protection of American intellectual property rights (IPR). U.S. Trade Representative Mickey Kantor was eager to pressure the Chinese about the piracy of American software and was prepared to back it with sanctions against Chinese exports to the United States. Negotiations between the Chinese and USTR staffers Lee Sands and Deborah Lehr were going badly. Congress was aware of the issues and eager for the administration to get tough.

—The Taiwan issue was looking extremely grim, with military exercises replacing any kind of dialogue. After the November PLA exercises, the Central Intelligence Agency had set up a special task force to monitor Chinese military activities in the Taiwan Strait on an around-the-clock basis. Rhetoric and observable planning for military exercises suggested that the period just before the March 23 presidential elections in Taiwan would be extremely tense. Some military action by the PLA could not be ruled out. The Defense Department and Joint Chiefs of Staff were proceeding with contingency planning and found that U.S. forces in the Pacific had not planned fully for the kinds of PLA actions considered most likely.[158]

—Nonproliferation issues festered, as it appeared clear the Chinese were lax in their enforcement of agreements reached with the United States on ceasing missile cooperation and nuclear weapons development programs with Pakistan. Most troubling were reports that a Chinese corporation had sold 5,000 "ring magnets"—probably for use in uranium enrichment—to the A. Q. Khan Laboratory, long associated with Pakistan's suspect nuclear weapons program.[159]

—Human rights was shaping up to be a bruising issue again. With the bilateral human rights dialogue still suspended, the State Department was completing its annual human rights report on China, and it was expected to document a deteriorating situation. Congress and the NGO community had focused on the annual meeting of the UN Human Rights Commission, at which the United States had sponsored a resolution critical of China every year since 1991, always without success.

—Finally, the annual struggle with Capitol Hill over renewing China's most favored nation trade status was shaping up to be more difficult, owing to the sharp deterioration in the bilateral relationship and in China's observance of bilateral agreements.

Faced with growing pressures from Congress and the media to "get tough" with China, the administration chose to try a higher level of dialogue with China, namely, at the level of national security adviser. The decision was reached at a Principals Committee meeting on February 19.[160] To avoid the appearance of an NSC takeover of China policy, it was agreed that Christopher and Perry were also to intensify discussions with their counterparts as soon as possible. But the involvement of Lake was a new development. Part of the rationale was that as the assistant to the president for national security affairs, Lake could speak more directly on behalf of the president. He would be a "new" voice Lake had not met separately with Chinese leaders very often and could present a "strategic" view of the relationship different from the departmental views of Christopher and Perry. He would also speak confidentially and strongly to the Chinese about the risks their recent behavior could have for a more confrontational relationship with the United States. Not publicized at the time was a decision to hold a comparable "strategic dialogue" with the head of Taiwan's National Security Council, Ding Mou-shih.

Unfortunately, there was no counterpart for the national security adviser within the Chinese system. So it was decided to invite Vice Minister Liu Huaqiu, director of the State Council Foreign Affairs Office, for a private meeting with Lake during his scheduled visit to Washington in March. There was some reluctance in doing so, because while Liu lately had styled himself as "China's Tony Lake," neither his position nor his influence was considered comparable. But Lake had met him and was comfortable with his straightforward approach and knew that Liu would report directly and without embellishment to Qian Qichen (because most of his staff came from the Ministry of Foreign Affairs), Jiang Zemin, and Premier Li Peng.

The principal goal for meeting with Liu was to give the Chinese a straight readout of American strategy and policy goals; commitment to security in the Asia-Pacific region, including Taiwan; and expectations of China. They had shown evidence of misinterpreting American policy and goals, and it was hoped that a clear and extended private conversation would at least ensure that their decisions related to Taiwan and other subjects were not made out of ignorance of American positions or likely responses. We did not expect to hear new or creative commitments to improve the relationship. The invitation was tendered in late February and immediately accepted. Liu advanced his trip to Washington by a few days and agreed to meet with Lake on March 8. At the suggestion of Andrew Sens, NSC executive secretary, an off-site (out of Washington) location was chosen to ensure confidentiality and cordiality for the meeting. The Middleburg, Virginia, estate of Pamela

Harriman—then ambassador to France—was available, and Sens thought it ideal.

In the meantime, the sense of crisis surrounding Taiwan deepened, as military preparations and rhetoric escalated on both sides. In late February, the Joint Chiefs completed their review of China-related contingencies and scheduled a briefing for the president. General John Shalikashvili, chairman of the Joint Chiefs of Staff, presented the material in a late-afternoon meeting in the Oval Office. Lake; Berger; Christopher; Perry; the vice president's national security adviser, Leon Fuerth; and a few others were present. It was a sobering briefing, detailing extensive commitments of American air and naval forces—as well as nonmilitary actions, called "flexible deterrent options"—in response to a sliding scale of aggressive Chinese actions in the Taiwan Strait. The president, contemplating combat scenarios that escalated up to nuclear war, was silent and somber. "We've got to do all we can to avoid this," several participants recall him saying.[161]

In the awkward dance between the State Department and the NSC that preceded Liu Huaqiu's visit, political, rather than diplomatic, protocol played a critical role. Although Liu's meeting with Lake was to be the central event in his visit, Secretary Christopher was not to be cut out. It was decided—after much debate—that the secretary would host a dinner for Liu on the evening of March 7, with several of the undersecretaries and assistant secretaries who covered China issues also in attendance. Lake invited Liu to the West Wing for drinks before the dinner, at which he would give him a preliminary plan for their private discussions. After the meeting in Middleburg, Liu would return to Washington for meetings in the Chinese embassy, then would meet with Christopher and other administration officials and members of Congress the following week.

Missiles and Meetings

On March 5, 1996, Xinhua announced the PLA would again conduct "ground-to-ground missile launching training" in the Taiwan Strait, specifying two rectangular areas off the Taiwan port cities of Chilung and Kaohsiung. Foreign ships and aircraft were advised not to enter those areas from March 8 through March 15.[162] Because the closure areas extended to within about twenty miles of Chilung and less than thirty miles of Kaohsiung, the initial reaction in Taiwan was that the tests amounted to a virtual blockade of the island's principal ports. Closer examination revealed that shipping lanes would not really be impeded, especially since no PLA vessels were expected to try operating in the closure zones. International public reaction, nonetheless, was harsh toward Beijing and overwhelmingly supportive of Taipei. The missile tests were only the first of three exercises scheduled. A live-ammunition exercise with naval and air force participation was scheduled for March 12–20 in a large closure zone on the Fujian coast approximately sixty miles southwest of Kaohsiung, and a final amphibious assault on Taiwan-like terrain on Fujian's Pingtan Island was planned for March 18–25.

But the missile tests were the main news, and this time, the PLA had miscalculated. This time, the intimidation factor—in effect, using the missiles as terror weapons—was too obvious, too much like bullying. Beijing had pushed its advantage too far and found its moral high ground lost, its psychological advantage overcome by revulsion, resentment, and determination to resist. In Taiwan, the government disparaged Beijing's "crude threats" and vowed to carry through with election plans. The Taiwan stock market dropped about 3 percent in the two days following China's announcement, but a $7 billion market stabilization fund used by the government largely offset the nervousness. Taiwanese residents again rushed to banks to sell Taiwan's currency for dollars and gold, creating shortages of dollars in some locations. But again, Central Bank intervention held the currency stable.[163] Qian Qichen, at the annual session of the National People's Congress (NPC), reassured Taiwanese "compatriots" that they had no reason to panic over the missile tests, but that if the "independence seekers, with support from some international forces bent on splitting China, continue on their wrong path . . . , that would be a real disaster."[164] Although possibly meant to be conciliatory, his words were disregarded.

The initial American response to the PRC's announcement was frosty. The State Department spokesman called the planned tests an "irresponsible" effort to intimidate Taiwan's voters and warned there would be "consequences" if any Chinese missiles went off target.[165] In testimony before the Senate Armed Services Committee, Defense Secretary Perry called the tests a "bad mistake." Congressional Republicans, in a statement prepared before the Xinhua announcement but publicized afterward, took a much more forceful position. "The Communist government in Beijing must harbor no doubt that the United States will not tolerate the PRC's use of military force against Taiwan or interference with her air or sea access. To this end, the United States must stand ready to join Taiwan in her defense against any resort to force or other forms of coercion that would jeopardize her security."[166] As public reaction to China's "bullying" of Taiwan grew, the administration sharpened its reaction. A day later, on March 6, the State Department characterized the tests as "provocative" and "destabilizing" as well as unhelpful.

Just after midnight on the morning of March 8, China launched three M-9 missiles from mobile launchers in Jiangxi into the designated target zones—two landed off Kaohsiung and one off Chilung.[167] U.S. intelligence assets in the region monitored the launches and reported back to Washington,[168] where it was still March 7 and where Liu Huaqiu was just arriving for talks with Secretary Christopher and National Security Adviser Lake. Whether the PLA timed the missile tests in consideration of Liu Huaqiu's meetings in the United States is not known, although it seems unlikely. In any case, news of the launches was flashed at highest precedence to the White House. Telephone conversations between officials at the State Department, Defense Department, and the NSC began immediately, about what the news meant for Taiwan's security and for Liu's visit. It was quickly agreed that the tests seemed to pose no immediate threat to Taiwan, though careful monitoring needed to be maintained. As for the Liu visit, Lake and Christopher agreed to change the protocol arrangements—from a welcoming banquet to a working dinner, at which America's indignation at the missile launches would be conveyed at a very high level. Only Secretary Christopher and Assistant Secretary Winston Lord remained of the State Department invitees, the others were replaced by Secretary of Defense Perry and National Security Adviser Lake. Jeffrey Bader and I were attached as note takers.

The dinner, held in the Madison Room of the State Department, was dreadful: cold soup, undercooked vegetables, dry salmon. The discussion, however, was hot. Christopher led off with a stern but calmly delivered critique of China's approach to the Taiwan issue, in particular the missile launches, which he characterized as "reckless and provocative." He said there would be "grave consequences"—meaning American military involvement—if the exercises got out of hand. Liu countered with a spirited attack on Taiwan and U.S. support for Lee Teng-hui's "Taiwan independence" aspirations. He rejected American concerns about the missile tests, which he insisted were a matter of Chinese sovereignty and were "normal, routine" exercises.

Perry, visibly agitated, tried to convey to Liu that the missile launches were over the top from an American perspective: "dangerous, coercive, absolutely unnecessary, and risky." He recounted his experience as an army artilleryman and accused China of "bracketing" Taiwan with the two closure zones, as artillery spotters do before "firing for effect." He, too, said there would be "grave consequences" if Taiwan were to be hit by the missiles. Lake, relishing an unusual role as "good cop," told Liu the issue would be an important agenda item in their meeting the following day. After Liu left, Lake confided that Perry was "really angry" and was thinking of sending an aircraft carrier battle group into the Taiwan Strait. I said I thought Beijing would get the message if the U.S. Navy just "parked them off the east coast" of Taiwan.[169]

March 8 dawned clear and unusually cold. The Secret Service vans carrying Lake and his small delegation were delayed by ice and accidents on the rural roads to Middleburg. Willow Oaks, the Harriman estate, was well prepared for the informal discussions between the Chinese and Americans. Elegantly appointed but simple and rustic, the home was warm and intimate, with a fire in the living room fireplace. Liu and his small party arrived at about 10:00 a.m. and positioned themselves in comfortable couches and armchairs, rather than across from their counterparts at a formal table. The atmosphere may have helped take the edge off some very tough talk.

Lake had prepared thoroughly for the meeting. Besides the background papers from the NSC and the State Department on the context of the meeting and a lengthy set of talking points, he had received personal briefings from intelligence analysts on Chinese positions on the issues. He began with a lengthy introduction to American policy goals and strategic intentions, taking note of where the Chinese had misconstrued it. He sketched out U.S. Asia policy, then went into some detail about what role China and the U.S.-China relationship played in American plans. He raised four problems that he thought were important to managing the development of the bilateral relationship over the next few months: Taiwan, intellectual property rights, nonproliferation, and human rights. Much of the early part of the discussion focused on Taiwan, and Lake carefully discussed the Lee Teng-hui visit, what it meant and what it did not mean for U.S.-PRC relations. He warned Liu explicitly that China should not misinterpret the delicate and nuanced language of diplomacy: "grave consequences" were grave indeed. He urged China to cease provocative missile testing, break the cycle of competing military exercises, stop vilifying Lee Teng-hui, and return to the cross-Strait dialogue as a means of resolving problems.

Liu's response was harsh, delivered without notes, making exactly the points expected. Lee Teng-hui was at fault for "promoting Taiwan independence," and the United States had "hurt the feelings of the Chinese people" by allowing him to visit Cornell. Now it was up to Washington to take steps to improve the bilateral relationship, Taiwan was a part of China and the resolution of the problem "brooks no foreign interference," the military exercises were normal and no threat to the United States, but the situation was dangerous and could be "explosive" if not handled properly.

The same dynamic held for the other issues: Lake defining the problem and U.S. goals, making explicit recommendations for Chinese behavior; Liu responding aggressively but defensively, laying out China's standard positions, blaming the United States for the difficulties. The lunch break provided an opportunity for discussion of other topics, such as Russia and the Middle East, and the atmosphere lightened somewhat. But arguments resumed in the afternoon and continued until the talks wrapped up at 4:00 p.m. Both sides were satisfied with the outcome. Each had listened carefully to the other's positions and presented its views in detail. Nuances were discussed and common points identified. Though tough and occasionally heated, the discussions were bracing, respectful, and effective. At the Chinese embassy banquet that evening (which Lake did not attend), the Chinese were elated, saying the "Willow Oaks conference" would be seen as a turning point in the relationship.

Saturday, however, would stoke the confrontation higher. At breakfast, the key decisionmakers on security issues gathered at Secretary Perry's office in the Pentagon to consider how the United States should respond to China's missile tests. Besides Perry and Shalikashvili and some staff members, Secretary Christopher and Assistant Secretary Lord represented the State Department, and Lake and Berger attended for the NSC. Perry was still indignant about the missile tests and had given a great deal of thought to how the U.S. military forces should respond to show American commitment and resolve. He had discussed options with the Joint Chiefs on Friday, while Lake was in Middleburg, and wanted to develop a unified position to present to the president.[170]

Perry initially had favored an aggressive reaction, perhaps even sending one or more aircraft carrier battle groups through the Taiwan Strait to demonstrate that the United States could not be ignored or intimidated. Shalikashvili (with support from Pacific Command's admiral Joseph Prueher) had objected, on the grounds that it was unnecessarily provocative, and besides, U.S. carrier assets were already fully deployed. When Perry presented the options on Saturday, there was a ready consensus that the United States had to take some action to deter the Chinese from doing "something stupid" but without further aggravating the situation. Lake reviewed his meetings with Liu, while Christopher talked about the best means of conveying the messages to Beijing and Taipei. In the end, after some discussion, it was agreed that two carrier battle groups (CBGs) would be deployed in response to the Chinese exercises and missile tests: the USS *Independence*, which was already in the region, and the USS *Nimitz*, which would be moved from the Persian Gulf. Neither would deploy into the Taiwan Strait itself: *Independence* would relocate off the east coast of Taiwan, while *Nimitz* would proceed to the area as rapidly as possible and deploy west of the Philippines.[171] Although the two carrier battle groups comprised thirteen ships and more than 150 aircraft, the largest deployment of naval forces in the Pacific since the Vietnam War, it was the lowest-level option in the briefing Shalikashvili had provided the president in February. Later in the afternoon, the group briefed the president, who concurred with the decision.

Christopher appeared on NBC's *Meet the Press* on Sunday and very cautiously confirmed that the *Independence* would be moved closer to Taiwan. He did not, however, mention the redeployment of the *Nimitz*.[172] That announcement was made by the State Department on Monday, March 11, and was confirmed by Pentagon briefers the following day. Since the *Nimitz* was stationed in the Persian Gulf, enforcing the "no-fly zone" over Iraq, it would take some time to reach East Asia, and was expected about March 23, the date of Taiwan's presidential elections.[173]

With the NPC in session, China's reaction needed to be quick and public, but it was also careful. Foreign Ministry officials, including Qian Qichen and Liu Huaqiu (in Washington), denounced the deployment in some of the same terms the United States had used for the PRC missile tests. In an NPC press conference on March 11, Qian called the U.S. decision "reckless" and "erroneous." "Foreigners should not make irresponsible remarks and, still less, take some action to intervene in our internal affairs," Qian said. Asked about the carrier deployments, Qian replied, "It would be ridiculous for some people [in the United States] to call for an open intervention by the Seventh Fleet of the U.S. on this issue, and they even go so far as to call for the defense of Taiwan. I think these people must have forgotten the fact that Taiwan is part of Chinese territory, not a protectorate of the United States."[174] Jiang told PLA delegates that China's preference was for "peaceful reunification," but that it would not renounce the use of force.[175]

The PLA's reaction was rather more muscular but also contained an element of bluster—the *Nimitz* deployment had been a surprise. Live-fire exercises began as scheduled on March 12, with at least twenty ships, as well as high-performance fighters, including Soviet-built Su-27s, engaging in naval and aerial bombardment of shore areas thirty-five miles from Chin-men.[176] On March 13, one more M-9 was fired into the closure zone, although observers had been expecting more than that. No one was certain whether the curtailment was a sign of China's recognition that the tests were becoming counterproductive or resulted from technical problems. The PLA officers interviewed by pro-PRC newspapers in Hong Kong raised the symbolic ante, discounting American technical capabilities and courage and pledging in fierce terms to defend China's sovereignty and territorial integrity from the carriers. "If they interfere with China's internal affairs, we will smash them to smithereens!" one of them threatened.[177]

Officials in Washington tried first to reinforce a sense of calm, to ensure the Chinese understood the intent and limitations of the naval deployments. Shalikashvili told reporters that the Chinese exercises were a "dry run" intended to intimidate the people of Taiwan, but that he did not expect serious conflict. Winston Lord and others stressed the "precautionary" nature of the deployments and insisted, "We are not on the brink of war." He and Kurt Campbell, deputy assistant secretary of defense for East Asian and Pacific affairs, told a House hearing that chances of a deliberate attack on Taiwan by the PRC were "remote." American naval commanders, including Prueher and others, made clear without compromising operational orders that neither CBG was likely to go into the Taiwan Strait. "We will be very mindful of restricted airspace and territorial waters," a retired Seventh Fleet admiral told reporters. The U.S. Navy transported Taiwanese reporters to the *Independence,* where they filed stories about the readiness and proficiency of the American flight crews, but also made clear they were well off the east coast of Taiwan and not expecting combat.[178]

Privately, NSC and State Department officials were meeting with high-level officials from Taiwan. On March 11, Deputy Assistant to the President for National Security Affairs Sandy Berger and Undersecretary of State for Political Affairs Peter Tarnoff traveled to New York City, where they met secretly in a midtown hotel with Ding Mou-shih, secretary general of Taiwan's National Security Council. The meeting had been planned for some time, and Lake had informed Liu it would take place, though he provided no details. Like the March 8 meeting in Middleburg, the intention was to clarify U.S. goals and expectations in the region. Ensuring that the U.S. deployments were understood by the Taiwanese government and urging Taiwan not take advantage of the enhanced U.S. presence to provoke Beijing were also important. Neither TECRO nor the American Institute on Taiwan had been informed of the meeting, and Ding had taken such extraordinary precautions to avoid the relentless Taiwanese press that news of the meeting did not surface until seven weeks afterward.[179]

Ding presented a striking contrast to Liu Huaqiu. Tall, urbane, and soft-spoken, the former head of Taiwan's representative office in Washington conducted the entire meeting in impeccable English. Although not thought to be a member of Lee's innermost circle of advisers, he was well respected and could convey Washington's points directly to the president. After an intelligence briefing on the PRC exercises, Berger and Tarnoff went straight to the main points. The United States was deploying two CBGs to the region as a demonstration of the American commitment to the security and stability of the entire Asia-Pacific region. American support for Taiwan was dependable, and the growth of Taiwan's democracy—as demonstrated by the presidential elections—would strengthen the relationship. At the same time, the U.S.-PRC relationship was important and needed to be managed carefully. Taiwan's security was better served by stable U.S.-China relations than by instability and high tension. Both Taiwan and the PRC should avoid provocative military exercises and return to the bargaining table to resolve their differences. Ding assured Berger and Tarnoff that Taiwan had no wish to provoke Beijing, that it was most appreciative of U.S. support, and would cooperate with Washington fully in its efforts to ease tensions.[180]

As Taiwan's election day neared, U.S.-China tensions increased. Despite private Chinese assurances that the PLA exercises would be confined to Pingtan Island, rumors circulated that there might be an attack on one of the small, Taiwan-held offshore islands. Chinese officials seemed to feel driven to prove they were not intimidated by the U.S. naval presence, so they ratcheted up the threatening rhetoric even further. "If someone makes a show of force in the Taiwan Strait," Li Peng told NPC delegates on March 17, "that will not only be a futile act, but it also will make the situation all the more complicated . . . If armed strength is used to threaten China, history has proved long ago there will not be a good result."[181] American military officials countered by pointedly refusing to say whether the carriers would enter the Taiwan Strait. Rear Admiral James Ellis, commander of the *Independence* battle group, told reporters it was "possible" they would do so.[182]

Then Hong Kong's *Ta Kung Pao* made the quarrel personal, claiming that U.S. Secretary of Defense William Perry "deserve[d] a slap" for talking "nonsense" about American security interests in the region.[183] Stung, Perry told some members of Congress, "Beijing should know, and this [carrier deployment] will remind them, that while they are a great military power, the premier—the strongest—military power in the Western Pacific is the United States. America has the best damned navy in the world, and no one should ever forget that."[184] Perry's comments elicited the sharpest rhetoric from the Hong Kong *Wen Wei Po*, which quoted an authoritative "military observer" in Beijing, who warned, "Don't forget the Taiwan Straits . . . is within the combat range of Chinese planes and ships. Add the firepower of guided missiles and coordinated attacks from many units, form it into concentrated firepower and it will be enough to bury invading enemies in a sea of fire."[185] Two days later, Perry postponed indefinitely the visit of China's defense minister Chi Haotian, ostensibly out of concern about American reaction to China's insistence on full protocol treatment for Chi, as well as a meeting with the president. Belatedly, China claimed it had called off the visit, owing to Washington's support for Taiwan.[186]

That, in turn, led to sharper commentary and posturing in Washington. Congress, intent on showing the strongest support for Taiwan, passed H. Con. Res. 148 in the House, which asserted the "sense of Congress" that "the United States, in accordance with the Taiwan Relations Act and the constitutional process of the United States, and consistent with its friendship with and commitment to the democratic government and people of Taiwan, *should assist in defending them against invasion, missile attack, or blockade by the People's Republic of China.*"[187] The Senate passed a similar, but less provocative resolution by 97-0 two days later. Members also flooded the White House with letters calling on the president to demonstrate stronger support for Taiwan's threatened democracy. China's press spokesman demanded the United States "immediately stop its activities designed to interfere in China's internal affairs and to intensify the tension in the Taiwan Strait area."[188]

Part of the administration's difficulty in convincing Congress of its commitment to Taiwan's security was the widespread interpretation of American policy as a studied neutrality about Taiwan's future, which picked up the label "strategic ambiguity." Former assistant secretary of defense for international security affairs Joseph S. Nye Jr. had used the term in congressional testimony in October 1995 to describe the overall nature of the U.S.-China relationship, in which there were many strategic interests in common but also some major disagreements on important issues.[189] Unfortunately, the term came to be used by journalists and commentators as a shorthand way to describe the U.S. position on China and Taiwan—that Washington resisted specifying under what conditions it would invoke the Taiwan Relations Act and how it would respond to various types of PRC military pressure on Taiwan. The reluctance to provide a blanket guarantee of defensive support sprang from the absence of a treaty commitment and from concern that ambitious Taiwanese politicians might use such a guarantee to declare Taiwan an independent state and bring the United States into the resulting war.

Although Nye continued to say that "nobody knows" how the United States would react to a Chinese attack on Taiwan, other administration officials refrained from using the term "strategic ambiguity." It was never used in official policy documents. Lake declared it anathema in the NSC and Lord went to great lengths to disavow the term in public testimony and speeches.[190] During the brewing crisis in the Taiwan Straits, the administration tried to stress it was seeking clarity of policy, not ambiguity. The term, however, had staying power and was an easy catchphrase for critics to use as a characterization of Clinton's policy. Its incessant use put the administration on the defensive.

In the midst of the war of words between Beijing and Washington, the PLA started its large exercise on the island of Pingtan, off the Fujian coast at the northern end of the Taiwan Strait on March 18. Like the November 1995 exercise, this one was commanded by Zhang Wannian and involved artillery and air attacks, submarines and minesweepers, beach landings of soldiers and armored vehicles, heli-borne infantry assaults, and coordinated air force–navy–ground force operations, according to Chinese television and news accounts.[191] Although the total number of troops employed in the exercise is not known, estimates ran as high as 150,000.[192] Chinese military and civilian officials alike reassured their American counterparts that no military action was being planned against Taiwan.[193] None of the Chinese accounts revealed that heavy rains, fog, and high winds forced the exercises to start late and conclude early, although not before Chinese television turned the exercises into another propaganda special for viewers on the mainland and in Taiwan.

However successful the exercises were in preparing the PLA for combat on or against Taiwan, the political goals that animated them from the outset proved elusive. On March 23, Taiwanese voters went to the polls in the first direct popular election for president. The four main candidates were Lee Teng-hui of the ruling Kuomintang, Peng Ming-min of the Democratic Progressive Party, Lin Yang-kang of the New Party, and Chen Li-an, an independent favoring closer ties with the PRC. More than 75 percent of Taiwan's 14 million eligible voters turned out to cast their ballots. Lee won an unexpectedly large plurality of the votes, 54 percent, while Peng managed only 21 percent. Lin and Chen split the remaining 25 percent between them. Although it had been well understood for some months that Lee's position was unassailable, some elements of the PRC's propaganda apparatus continued to vilify him up until the day of the election, equating him with the DPP candidate as far as support for "Taiwan independence" was concerned. Lee had been defiant during the campaign, traveling to areas near closure zones, dismissing PRC exercises, and taunting Beijing about China's fear of democracy. By playing the military card so clumsily, Beijing probably added to Lee's mandate by several percentage points.[194]

Returning to Normal?

In the end, despite sharp rhetorical clashes, no "confrontation" between the United States and China ever took place. It was certainly tense, but there was no sense of imminent danger. No American aircraft came close to the Pingtan Island exercises, no ships sailed through the Taiwan Strait, no U.S. soldiers landed on Taiwan. No Chinese submarine or other vessel even came close to the *Independence* or the *Nimitz*. No blockades had to be broken, no small outposts were attacked. No further missiles were launched after March 13, no "sea of fire" materialized. Taiwan's presidential elections took place as scheduled on March 23, and Lee Teng-hui won handily. The PLA's vaunted exercises concluded ingloriously in dense fog and heavy rain. No further exercises were scheduled, and Taipei canceled its corresponding exercise at Washington's suggestion. The U.S. aircraft carriers returned to normal duty stations shortly after the election, and the crisis quietly came to a close.

It is impossible to know what the leadership in Beijing concluded from their exercise in coercive diplomacy against Taiwan and the United States. Beijing's propaganda organs, of course, hailed the military exercises as a great success, demonstrating the PLA's capabilities to carry out complex missions, loyalty to the Central Committee, and determination to prevent Taiwan from becoming independent. There were some who claimed that the exercises had foiled plots of those on Taiwan and in the United States who wanted Taiwan to become an independent state.[195] Some, including Jiang Zemin, claimed that the PLA had intimidated the United States from entering the Taiwan Strait during the crisis.[196] With perfect hindsight, Chinese strategic analysts have insisted to American interlocutors that China was successful in cutting back American support for Lee's independence drive, focusing U.S. policymakers' attention on the importance of the Taiwan issue, and establishing a "strategic" dialogue with Washington (through Tony Lake) that paid larger benefits over the longer run.[197] All that may be true, although it is difficult to argue those were among the goals that drove the PLA and its exercise in coercive diplomacy.

Objective observers in Beijing might have noted that China's reliance on the PLA for diplomacy had decidedly mixed results, however. Although the missile launches and robust exercises had opened up a possibility for a more substantive strategic dialogue via the Liu-Lake channel and sharpened the American focus on the centrality of the Taiwan issue to the relationship, the change in U.S. policy was not entirely for the better. The exercises had drawn the United States into a more explicit commitment to Taiwan's defense from both executive and legislative branches of the U.S. government, brought American military forces to China's shores to operate with virtual impunity, and reversed a general improvement in relations that had taken place in 1995. Beijing's perceived bellicosity had put China on the strategic map as "potential adversary" for more Americans than had been true for many years.

Political as well as economic relations with Taiwan were badly damaged by the military's efforts to intimidate Taiwan's voters. Clearly, some were swayed to vote for Lee Teng-hui rather than the pro-independence candidate. But the New Party candidate probably was hurt by association with the PRC's bullying and finished dead last in the voting. Combining Lee's total with the DPP's, 75 percent of Taiwan's voters had supported keeping the PRC at arms' length rather than moving toward reunification. Lee eased off on his anti-PRC rhetoric and indicated he did not plan any further trips to the United States. In his inauguration speech on May 20, he dismissed "Taiwan independence" as "totally unnecessary or impossible" and pledged to "embark on a journey of peace to mainland China." But he also belittled China's achievements in comparison with Taiwan's and promised to continue his "pragmatic diplomacy" to enhance the island's international standing.[198]

Various reports in the Hong Kong press suggested that the less-than-sterling success of the PLA intimidation campaign had heightened tensions in the Politburo and between civilians and military officers in the leadership.[199] There is little hard evidence available to support this contention, although there can be little doubt that leadership frictions and competition for power continued throughout the period, and may have intensified, given the high tension of the situation. Although the coercive diplomacy effort may have appeared feckless to outside observers, within the leadership, it apparently enjoyed considerable support. Jiang and Li Peng evidently shared a view that this was necessary to keep Taiwan from moving further away from the mainland's orbit. Qiao Shi, the chairman of the Standing Committee of the National People's Congress and widely viewed as Jiang's principal rival for power, appeared to be pushing Jiang toward an even tougher position on Taiwan issues, despite his reputation as a "reformer." And Li Ruihuan—also considered a reformer—frequently voiced stridently "hawkish" sentiments during this period.[200] But there was no visible fallout in the relationship between Jiang and Zhang Wannian, who if anything emerged from the exercises with his powers and reputation enhanced.

For the United States, the crisis marked something of a watershed. Several changes took place in the American policy toward China and Taiwan following the events of March 1996. Some were obvious and recognized by all. Others were subtle and have seldom been publicly noted.

—Substantively, there was a recognition by the administration and some in Congress that Taiwan and its relationship to the mainland was by far the most significant issue on the bilateral agenda. Developments in the cross-Strait relationship over which the United States had no control (that is, domestic politics in Taiwan and China) could have a major impact on U.S. relationships in the region.[201]

—The administration began in early 1996 an approach that focused on managing the U.S.-China relationship in coordination with Beijing—to ensure the leadership understood U.S. goals and intentions. It was broadly recognized that better communication with Taipei and Beijing was required, which entailed the maintenance of nonpublic channels of contact. Engagement was still the chosen policy approach, but it needed to be more carefully defined and better understood.

—Politically, the incident was viewed as a plus by the Clinton administration. The foreign policy and military experts had calculated that a minimal show of force in the region would work to reduce tensions, show American resolve, facilitate democracy on Taiwan, and leave room for making further improvements in U.S.-China relations. Despite the taunts of the critics, they were right.

—In the increasingly bitter partisan wrangling between the White House and the Gingrich-led Congress, politics no longer "stopped at the water's edge." Partisan attacks on Clinton's management of foreign policy were most rancorous on Bosnia but increasingly focused on China policy, too. Taiwan was the catalyst. Support in Congress for democratic Taiwan was enormous and susceptible to manipulation by the Taipei government.

—China policy in a crisis was more readily managed from the National Security Council than from the State Department, and the national security adviser could play a key role. Although Lake remained solicitous of Christopher's prerogatives in the implementation of American policy, he took the initiative for China policy more firmly into the White House.

CHAPTER SEVEN

Presidential Initiatives, 1996–97

With the Pingtan Island exercise completed, and new ones not planned, the role of the People's Liberation Army (PLA) in China's overall foreign policy decisionmaking appeared to diminish considerably in April 1996. Primacy was restored to the Ministry of Foreign Affairs (MFA) and Qian Qichen. With remarkable alacrity, Beijing moved to a less combative approach toward Taiwan once its elections were over. The decision to do so was probably made in mid-April in the Politburo Standing Committee on recommendations from the Taiwan Affairs Leading Small Group. In late April, the State Council's Taiwan Affairs Office held a three-day conference in Beijing, addressed by Qian Qichen and Wang Zhaoguo, who gave the appearance, at least, of a return to normal decisionmaking channels on Taiwan.

In his report to the meeting, Qian affirmed the correctness of the previous policy in "dealing a heavy blow to forces for 'Taiwan independence' and splittism on the island and fully revealing the Chinese people's strong determination and capability to safeguard national sovereignty and territorial integrity." He also, however, changed the tone and content of the PRC's public policy by pledging to "place [our] hopes on the people of Taiwan" rather than the Taiwan authorities, whom he continued to criticize, though in a milder tone. Qian and others focused on the need to "promote economic cooperation and exchanges between the two sides" and called on mainland officials to "more effectively implement the 'Law on Protecting Investments by Taiwan Compatriots' and protect [their] legitimate rights and interests."[1] Suisheng Zhao makes the case that coercive diplomacy and the effort to woo Taiwanese businessmen as part of a peaceful offensive are "two sides of the same policy coin," but China's less belligerent approach was welcomed by Taiwan's government and business leaders alike.[2]

Confrontation, Engagement, and Sanctions

Although the obvious tensions over Taiwan eased with the departure of U.S. aircraft carriers after Lee's election, Beijing's policy toward Washington remained tough and confrontational. The dialogue between Tony Lake and Liu Huaqiu began a process of improved communication and the building of mutual respect that eventually facilitated problem solving. But initially, it only served to identify the most urgent issues. The "American side" had raised three issues for special concern besides Taiwan in the Middleburg, Virginia, meetings, two of which involved the possible imposition of sanctions. The first was about nonproliferation, concerning a sale to Pakistan of "ring magnets"—used in gas centrifuges that enrich uranium for nuclear bombs. Second was China's failure to abide by a 1995 agreement on improving protection of American intellectual property, that is, not cracking down on massive piracy of U.S. computer software and music products in Chinese compact disk factories. Third was the lack of progress in China's human rights practices, documented in the State Department human rights report issued the day Liu arrived in Washington.

The State Department and the Office of the U.S. Trade Representative (USTR) had similar problems with the situation. Both had been making progress in their respective areas with Beijing bureaucrats. China's overall approach to international agreements on trade and the nonproliferation of weapons of mass destruction was clearly improving, and cooperation, while difficult, was tangible. Neither organization was under any illusions about the efficacy of sanctions, and each preferred engagement with Chinese counterparts to resolve problems. Both had used sanctions as policy instruments and credible threats. Both the State Department and USTR had to contend with strong lobbying groups that exerted pressure on senior bureaucrats and lawmakers and kept the media spotlight on their subjects of concern. Both relied on information collected by other organizations—the intelligence agencies for the State Department, and trade groups such as the Business Software Alliance for the USTR—and had no control over its dissemination. Both were also somewhat hemmed in by legislation that mandated sanctions in specified circumstances.

In 1996, both bureaucracies were fortunate to have highly competent midlevel officials to make engagement work. Robert Einhorn, austere and professorial, was deputy assistant secretary of state for politico-military affairs and had worked on nearly every proliferation issue for several years with a highly competent staff in his bureau and in the Bureau of Intelligence and Research. Assistant U.S. Trade Representative (AUSTR) Lee Sands, a former political and economic officer at the U.S. embassy in Beijing, was Mickey Kantor's point man on intellectual property rights, assisted by China desk director Deborah Lehr and a team of dedicated professionals from the USTR, the FBI, Customs, and the departments of Commerce and Agriculture. Sands and Einhorn enjoyed good contacts and cooperation with the National Security Council (NSC). Although the State Department and the USTR did not coordinate their approaches, at Principals Committee meetings in late February and early March their representatives agreed on proceeding cautiously during the height of the Taiwan Strait crisis, then moving to work out problems once China's post-crisis perspective on bilateral relations became clearer.

The State Department and Nonproliferation

Warren Christopher was dismayed. On top of all the other problems that afflicted U.S.-China relations in early 1996, there was now another nonproliferation issue, one that highlighted the complexity and inadequacy of trying to deal with the proliferation of weapons of mass destruction (WMD) and their associated technologies and components through embargoes and congressionally mandated sanctions. In late 1995, the Central Intelligence Agency had reported that the China National Nuclear Corporation (CNNC) developed and shipped to the A. Q. Khan Research Laboratory in Kahuta, Pakistan, some 5,000 "ring magnets," which the agency asserted would be used in the gas centrifuges that Pakistan operated to extract enriched uranium from uranium gas. The enriched uranium could then be used in the building of nuclear weapons.[3] Since the Khan Laboratory was a key part of Pakistan's "unsafeguarded" (that is, not subject to inspections by the International Atomic Energy Agency) nuclear program, the shipment, although valued at only about $70,000, was considered a violation of the Nuclear Proliferation Prevention Act of 1994.[4]

At first blush, the ring magnets seemed a minor matter. But because China had been accused for years of actively supporting Pakistan's rogue nuclear program, nonproliferation activists in the United States were eager to have China sanctioned. Beijing's initial response to the charges was typical: the Foreign Ministry denied them (as did Pakistan's foreign minister, who was visiting Beijing), discounted the information as "hearsay," and warned that sanctions would "seriously harm relations between the two countries."[5] It agreed, nonetheless, to a March visit by Deputy Assistant Secretary of State Robert Einhorn to confer on the case and to further discussions between

Foreign Minister Qian and Secretary Christopher in April. Its decisions were no doubt fostered by the State Department's public recommendation in late February that the U.S. Export-Import Bank should suspend consideration of $10 billion in new loan guarantees for American companies doing business in China.

The State Department had delivered a démarche to the Chinese about the issue, receiving denials and obfuscations in return. When the story broke in the *Washington Times* in February, members of Congress immediately weighed in with letters to the president and statements to the press, calling for the full imposition of sanctions against China. Although some officials evidently suggested the sanctions could be waived on the grounds of having a "serious effect on vital United States interests," Senator Arlen Specter (R-Pa.), chairman of the Senate Select Committee on Intelligence, wrote the president, saying a waiver would "make our national policy a laughingstock" and encourage the proliferation of nuclear weapons.[6] The issue was complicated by intelligence reports of other Chinese transgressions leaking into the press from various sources. China was suspected of selling to Iran the chemicals and the technology for producing "poison gas" weapons, in apparent violation of the Chemical Weapons Convention, which it had signed in January 1993.[7] Moreover, another report of the shipment of M-11 missile technology to Pakistan surfaced in the press in early March, as did reports of China selling the C-802 antiship cruise missile to Iran, a possible violation of a 1992 law prohibiting the sale of advanced conventional weapons to Iran or Iraq.[8] Principals Committee meetings were held in late February and again in March to discuss what the proper response should be to the new allegations.

Einhorn headed for Beijing in late March, just after Taiwan's election. He carried with him a draft statement for Beijing to sign that the State Department believed would provide a sufficient guarantee of China's commitment to nonproliferation so the imposition of sanctions could be averted. The statement involved a guarantee on China's part that it would not provide support of any kind to unsafeguarded nuclear programs of any country. Tony Lake had first given a copy of the statement to Liu Huaqiu as a "non-paper" at their meeting in Middleburg on March 8. Liu's "non-response" was not encouraging, but he did invite Einhorn to come to Beijing for further discussions, which was a good opening.

Preliminary discussions in Beijing of the State Department's proposed solution to the problem were not productive. Einhorn raised several issues, including the U.S. demand that China improve its export control regulations to ensure that even small sales of the "ring magnets" sort would be prevented. He also asked about the process of approving nuclear sales, to ascertain whether anyone at the upper levels of the Chinese regime might have been in the decision loop on the ring magnets deal. The Chinese stonewalled, and Einhorn returned to Washington.[9]

Einhorn's negative report went directly to a Principals Committee meeting on March 27, but the administration remained deadlocked on what kinds of sanctions should be applied: heavy penalties against the Pakistani and Chinese governments on the grounds that leaders must have known of the deal; light sanctions against only the corporations involved, CNNC and A. Q. Khan; no sanctions in exchange for a Chinese commitment to refrain from further support for unsafeguarded programs; or waived sanctions on grounds that U.S. interests would be better served by not imposing economic penalties for so minor an infraction (ring magnets, for example, are not on the official list of items prohibited from sale under the terms of the Non-Proliferation Treaty).[10]

The debate continued, however, and criticism of the administration's handling of the matter intensified. Conservatives like Charles Krauthammer accused the Clinton administration of "craven diplomacy" in not reacting to Chinese provocations on proliferation and other issues.[11] *New York Times* columnist A. M. Rosenthal charged Clinton with pursuing a "failed" policy of ignoring an evil dictatorship for the sake of American business interests.[12] Both called for tough sanctions in response to the ring magnets case. Numerous other scholars and pundits weighed in during the same period with conflicting and contradictory advice on how to deal with a China that appeared to many to be stubborn, hostile, aggressive, and spiteful. Conservative Republicans clearly hoped this issue of Clinton's irresolute policy toward China would become a major issue in the November presidential election.[13]

In mid-April, President Clinton paid a state visit to Japan—one that had been postponed when he stayed home from the 1995 Asia-Pacific Economic Cooperation (APEC) summit in Osaka because of budget problems. Aside from showcasing the renewed vitality of the U.S.-Japan relationship, which had been damaged by trade disputes in the first two years of the Clinton administration, the principal "deliverable" of the visit was a "Joint Declaration on Security—Alliance for the 21st Century." The document called for a review of the 1978 Guidelines for Japan-U.S. Defense Cooperation to enhance Japan's role in preserving the security of the Asia-Pacific region. It also focused on the need to "realign and reduce" U.S. forces in Okinawa, which had become a highly controversial issue in Japan.[14]

The Joint Declaration was immediately attacked by Beijing, which saw the agreement as an effort to contain China and a threat to its sovereignty over Taiwan. "The Japan-U.S. treaty is a bilateral defense treaty left over from history," Foreign Ministry spokesman Shen Guofang told a news conference. "It shouldn't go beyond its bilateral nature, otherwise there will be complications." If Japan's self-defense forces expand beyond their current scope, "that would cause concern among all other Asian nations."[15] Clinton administration officials were surprised by China's reaction. Deputy Assistant Secretary of Defense for Asian Affairs Kurt Campbell—who had been the principal negotiator on the U.S. side—observed later, "No one at any meeting—and I was in hundreds of meetings with the Japanese—conceptualized that the rationale for the U.S.-Japan revitalization had anything to do with the Taiwan Straits."[16] In hindsight, most officials admitted that more consideration should have been given to the possible Chinese reaction to the agreement, but it simply was not a factor at the time. The focus was on setting things right with Japan and on the Korean Peninsula.

Warren Christopher flew to meet with Qian Qichen in the Hague on April 20. After four hours of intensive discussions, the two men made considerable progress in narrowing differences on the shape of a final resolution of the ring magnets issue, but they could not reach full closure. In public, Qian continued to insist that China had not violated any nonproliferation agreements, so sanctions were not appropriate. On human rights, trade, and intellectual property rights, the two sides exchanged the usual talking points with the usual effect.

China's basic problem in the ring magnets case—as Qian doubtless knew—was the absence in legal or bureaucratic practice of a workable export control system for "dual-use" items, that is, products that could be used for the production of WMD but that could also have more benign purposes. In response to U.S. pressure and its participation in international control regimes, such as the International Atomic Energy Agency (which China joined in 1984), the Non-Proliferation Treaty (to which China acceded in 1992), and the Chemical Weapons Convention (agreed to in 1993), Beijing had sharply cut back on sales of WMD systems and components, at least compared with sales in the 1980s.[17] Dual-use items, however, were more problematic. Chinese laws and regulations lacked detail on what items were proscribed or required special export licenses. Regulatory jurisdiction was complicated by ongoing economic and bureaucratic reforms in China, which transformed into quasi-independent national corporations the State Council ministries that had previously overseen defense production.[18]

Five days after the Christopher-Qian meeting, the U.S. Export-Import Bank again froze loan guarantees for China, in response to a request from the State Department. The action, which delayed a $35 million loan guarantee for the Guangzhou metro-rail project, was probably intended as a warning, but Beijing had already decided to resolve the issue. Quietly, Beijing passed the word that if the United States would announce there would be no sanctions over ring magnets, China would issue a statement forswearing cooperation with unsafeguarded nuclear programs. Both sides bit the bullet. "There's no question that there was a ring magnet transfer to Pakistan on the part of the state entity in China," State Department spokesman Nicholas Burns said on May 10. "The Chinese, however, have assured us that the government in Beijing—the policymakers in Beijing—were not aware of this transfer." Therefore, "the Secretary of State has concluded that there is not a sufficient basis to warrant a determination that sanctionable activity occurred under Section 825 of the Nuclear Proliferation Prevention Act of 1994."[19]

"China strictly observes its obligations under the [Nuclear Non-Proliferation] treaty and is against the proliferation of nuclear weapons," Xinhua announced a few hours later. "China pursues the policy of not endorsing, encouraging or engaging in the proliferation of nuclear weapons, or assisting other countries in developing such weapons . . . China will not provide assistance to unsafeguarded and unsupervised nuclear facilities."[20]

Privately, Beijing also agreed to begin consultations with the United States on establishing a workable export control administration and to discipline the individuals responsible for the ring magnets transaction.[21]

The Clinton administration took a pounding from the press and Congress for the way the ring magnets issue was handled. One could make the case, however, that the facts did not really warrant the imposition of heavy sanctions: that the size and nature of the transaction made it highly unlikely that the Chinese government was, in fact, "knowing" of the deal. Moreover, the Chinese public pledge not to support unsafeguarded nuclear programs was an important step forward, one certainly worth the cost of forgoing sanctions that would punish American corporations doing business with China far more than the Chinese entity that sold the ring magnets. In testimony a year afterward, Einhorn insisted that the May 11 commitment was holding and that China had taken a more cooperative approach. "We have seen a greater willingness by the Chinese to scrutinize and restrain their nuclear exports and cooperative activities, to strengthen their national export controls, and to address more promptly and seriously the concerns we have raised," he told a Senate subcommittee.[22]

But the process of making the decision was messy. In the end, the State Department's careful, nuanced approach—trying to keep the larger issue of U.S.-China relations in perspective—failed to assuage the anger on Capitol Hill and in the press over China's seeming contempt for U.S. legislation, interests, and values. The president expressed satisfaction that the issue had been resolved satisfactorily, but accusations that he cared more about American business interests than American security would continue to dog his administration. "Beijing is a pathological proliferator, plain and simple," said Representative Edward J. Markey, a Democrat from Massachusetts. "I find it disturbing that the administration has decided to let one of the most eager vendors in the nuclear marketplace off the hook."[23]

USTR and Intellectual Property Rights

U.S. Trade Representative Mickey Kantor had been fuming for months. The Chinese were toying with him. The landmark agreement on intellectual property rights (IPR) he had signed in March 1995—after months of tough negotiations by his China trade team—was effectively a dead letter by the end of the summer. The American side, in accordance with the agreement, had provided training, equipment, consultations, and solid information about infringement to Ministry of Foreign Trade and Economic Cooperation (MOFTEC) officials and others in Beijing. They had written letters, held meetings in Beijing and Washington, cajoled, and pleaded with Chinese trade officials that China's implementation of the agreement was unsatisfactory by any standard. All to no avail. The U.S. negotiators believed the downturn in bilateral relations over Taiwan was affecting China's willingness to enforce the agreement.[24] But there were other problems, as well, having to do with corruption, excessive PLA involvement in business, and ineffective legal mechanisms and traditions in China.

The upshot was that most of the illegal CD factories closed down as part of the 1995 agreement were back in business, and new ones had been added. China claimed to have conducted "thousands" of police raids, netting millions of pirated disks, but nearly all were against small-scale retailers, not the producers. At the end of 1995, various U.S. industry sources reported that Chinese illicit CD production had cost the American music, book, and software industry as much as $2.3 billion that year.[25] And Kantor was aware that China's trade surplus with the United States had grown to nearly $34 billion.[26] He was determined to do something about it, and the something was sanctions. "We will not tolerate China ignoring its obligations under this agreement," he told reporters.[27]

Compared to the State Department's episodic conversations with Chinese Foreign Ministry officials about the misdeeds of China's National Nuclear Corporation, the USTR had a much more direct, intense, and detailed set of interactions with a broader range of Chinese officials about CD piracy. Like the Bush administration before it, the Clinton administration U.S. Trade Representative's Office, frustrated by China's unwillingness to take the steps necessary to curtail the growing IPR piracy, resorted to pressure and sanctions under special 301 provision of the Omnibus Trade and Competitiveness Act of 1988. The USTR negotiators—Lee Sands and Deborah Lehr—had decided to work with the various Chinese bureaucracies, involving them in finding a solution that met their needs and enforced their own law, rather than relying only on sanctions. Their hard work—plus the threat of 100 percent punitive tariffs on more than $1 billion in Chinese goods at the end of the negotiations to "get their attention," as Lehr put it—resulted in an agreement signed in February 1995 that provided for sweeping changes in the IPR law enforcement regime in China.[28]

The Chinese central government, however, was not able (or willing) to bring the pressures to bear on local officials to crack down hard, with the result that the piracy problem grew significantly worse in 1995. U.S. trade associations complained that the access to the Chinese market they had hoped would be part of the 1995 agreement was not happening. In the latter part of the year, with overall bilateral tensions rising, the USTR pressed its case aggressively. Sands and his team spent weeks in China, negotiating with trade, customs, public security, judicial, publishing, and local Communist Party officials about the importance of rigorous enforcement of China's relevant laws and the 1995 bilateral IPR agreement. The meetings were often acrimonious, and by the end of the year, Sands was being publicly criticized by MOFTEC for not showing sufficient courtesy to his Chinese hosts. Undeterred, Kantor sent him back in February 1996 with instructions to continue the negotiations.

The USTR levied four demands on the Chinese during this period, repeatedly and in detail: take action against more than thirty illegal CD production facilities, including seizures of goods and arrests of managers; crack down especially hard on Guangdong Province and its special economic zones, where most of the illegal CD producers were located; rigorously enforce customs regulations at China's borders, to prevent damage to non-Chinese markets of American IPR goods; and expand U.S. access to China's IP market, including establishment of joint ventures, licensing of American products, revenue-sharing projects, and other easing of government restrictions on legal sales of American entertainment and software products. MOFTEC argued that it had taken ample actions and provided voluminous documentation. Nonetheless, Kantor and his deputy, Charlene Barshefsky, escalated their warnings through February and March, telling the Chinese that they faced punitive tariffs on more than $1 billion of their exports to the United States unless the problem was resolved satisfactorily. Privately, some officials admitted that election-year politics and the president's need to look "tough" were significant factors in the USTR's approach.[29]

On April 30, after a trip to Beijing by Barshefsky failed to elicit better compliance, the USTR released its annual report on international trade performance, naming China as a "priority foreign country" under the special 301 section of the trade law. Barshefsky had given the Chinese to May 15 to come up with an "emergency action" plan to meet the four conditions, and Sands traveled to Beijing just before the deadline in hopes of striking a last-minute deal. On May 8, the Principals Committee recommended to the president that he authorize USTR to draw up a preliminary list of Chinese imports to be subjected to punitive duties to compensate for the estimated $2 billion that China's IPR piracy was costing the United States. Clinton—in a rare appearance at a foreign policy deliberation meeting—approved, knowing that congressional support for IPR sanctions was growing. He was also aware that his likely opponent in the 1996 presidential race, Senator Robert Dole, was planning to criticize his administration's "vacillation" in China policy. In light of the State Department's decision not to impose sanctions for the ring magnets case, the announcement of a plan to punish China was bound to be well received.[30]

After MOFTEC's refusal to budge in the face of the sanctions threat, USTR announced, on May 15, the list of goods that would be considered for countervailing sanctions, to be imposed in thirty days if negotiations failed. The USTR had done its research carefully and included many of China's most prominent exports to the United States, such as clothing, textiles, electronic goods, and other consumer items produced in Guangdong Province. Beijing reacted immediately, suspending approvals for U.S. joint ventures and promising punitive tariffs on a variety of American goods. Observers on both sides talked ominously of a "trade war."[31]

But Washington was in full communications mode—though indirect—during this period. The Principals and Deputies committee meetings of the preceding months had developed a more comprehensive China policy, and an eagerness to put it on the record, for domestic and foreign policy reasons. On May 17, Warren Christopher made his first public speech devoted entirely to China policy. In an address in New York to the Asia Society, Council on Foreign Policy, and the National Committee on U.S.-China Relations, he laid out a wide-ranging and nuanced approach to China that stressed three principles: a recognition that China's "development as a secure, open and successful nation is profoundly in the interest of the United States"; a goal of bringing about "China's full integration and its active participation in the international community"; and a "dialogue and engagement" approach to manage differences, but a willingness to use other methods, such as sanctions, when necessary. Included in Christopher's discussion was an open call for "regular summit meetings" between the two presidents.[32]

Three days later, President Clinton also stressed China policy heavily in a speech he gave to the Pacific Basin Economic Council, a business organization focused on Asia. "How China defines itself and its greatness as a nation in the future," Clinton said, coining an expression he would use throughout the rest of his presidency, "and how our relationship with China evolves will have as great an impact on the lives of our own people and, indeed, on global peace and security, as that of any other relationship we have." He pledged to continue an engagement approach "without illusion" and indicated he would not discard sanctions, if imposing them furthered U.S. interests. Most important, he announced—early—that he intended to extend unconditional MFN for the ensuing year.[33]

China appeared to get the message being conveyed by the administration, and its response was reflected in the end game for the IPR negotiations. American foreign policy commentators sometimes refer to complex and sometimes theatrical political interactions or negotiations that have a predetermined outcome as "Kabuki," after a stylized Japanese drama form. The IPR negotiations were more like Beijing opera—with loud, banging drums and cymbals, simulated combat, and discordant singing—but with an equally predetermined outcome. Despite dire threats from both sides that a trade war was looming if the other side did not back down, both were working quietly against the deadline to develop a package acceptable to both sides.

The AUSTR Lee Sands and his team had been in Beijing almost continuously since mid-May, exhorting, cajoling, educating, and warning the Chinese about the importance of the issue. They were accompanied, though not in negotiation sessions, by representatives of U.S. corporations with IPR equities in China, who also reminded their interlocutors of the benefits that would follow a successful agreement. What the Americans were looking for was some means of verifying that China was living up to the 1995 agreement and, more important, guarantees of better access to the Chinese intellectual property market, particularly in computer software. China was looking for an explicit lifting of the threat of sanctions as well as evidence that the American side understood how difficult it was for Beijing to enforce laws for which there was little public support. By June 12, five days before the deadline, they had gotten far enough along to bring in Deputy USTR Charlene Barshefsky to close the deal.

Barshefsky arrived on June 14, as the Chinese media were reporting a massive crackdown on illegal CD piracy, a tightening of customs enforcement in Guangdong, and the closure of bootleg CD factories in several cities. All were portrayed, of course, not as a result of U.S. pressure, but as part of China's legal reform. U.S. negotiators were skeptical but not dismissive. "It remains to be seen whether the Chinese effort . . . is sufficient to meet the terms of our [1995] agreement," read a USTR statement as they headed into the final weekend of discussions.[34] The final weekend was all too familiar to the American team: late snags over language and translations, protestations that Chinese negotiators were not empowered to make certain agreements, the passing of the deadline for imposing sanctions, last-minute haggling over petty details, the final June 17 meeting in the party-government leadership compound in Zhongnanhai with a beaming Jiang Zemin, and the announcement of the agreement not to impose sanctions or start a trade war. The USTR also dropped the designation of China as a "priority foreign country" in violation of IPR agreements.

In the end, USTR got much of what it wanted: the closure of fifteen illegal CD factories and confiscation of their production machinery, written commitments on enforcement of IPR laws by China's public security agencies, a title verification system for legally produced CDs, and improved market access for American corporations.[35] Not all of the problems were resolved, and USTR officials were frank in their judgments that problems remained and would take more time and effort to resolve. Like previous IPR agreements, this one was partly a face-saving arrangement, to avoid the sanctions both sides realized were not in their interest to impose. But both sides expressed satisfaction with it, as an example of working through a difficult issue by intense "engagement." Engagement—with clearly defined goals, intensive and respectful negotiations and discussions with a broad array of Chinese officials, obvious benefits for both sides, and the threat of sanctions as a last resort—proved workable and politically successful. And in fact, illegal CD production in China did drop significantly in the following years, enforcement of IPR regulations improved significantly, and China's software and computer industries flourished with improved access to American know-how and investment. "This proves that staying involved and engaged with China through the difficult times as well as the good ones is the right course of action," Clinton told reporters.[36]

Although the U.S. media did not give the agreement much notice, it clearly had a salutary effect on the House of Representative's consideration of China's MFN status, which came up for a vote less than two weeks later. The bill to overturn Clinton's decision to extend MFN—initiated, as usual, by Representative Gerald Solomon (R-N.Y.)—was defeated handily, 286-141, with more Republicans than Democrats supporting the president's recommendation. At the same time, however, the House passed by an overwhelming margin a bill calling for extensive hearings and legislation to deal with a lengthy list of Chinese failings in human rights, nonproliferation, Taiwan-related actions, and trade practices. It was a clear indication that the House, while not prepared to stake everything on the MFN vote, still was extremely dissatisfied with China's behavior on several issues and with the Clinton administration's policy toward China.

More Journeys to Beijing

Seven years and a week after National Security Adviser Brent Scowcroft's controversial trip to Beijing following Tiananmen, Tony Lake was flying to China on a comparable mission. There were, of course, plenty of differences: Lake was flying a commercial flight, one of many that catered to the growing number of business travelers between the United States and China, rather than a secretive U.S. Air Force plane. And while his trip had no accompanying press, it was not a secret visit. The U.S. embassy in Beijing was fully involved in its planning and execution. Assistant Secretary of State Winston Lord was a prominent participant and handled most of the press briefings and liaison for the trip. Lake brought two members of his personal staff, Sandy Kristoff and me from the Asia Directorate, and a small detail of Secret Service. One of the purposes of the visit—like Scowcroft's—was to try and improve strained relationships between the two governments. But while Scowcroft had hopes of eventually restoring the status quo pre-Tiananmen, Lake was hoping to start a dialogue that would take the relationship to a new and more productive level.

As he had before Liu Huaqiu's visit to Middleburg in March, Lake made extensive preparations for his meetings, tasking both written issue papers and oral briefings by intelligence community analysts and his own staff. On the fourteen-hour plane trip from Detroit to Beijing, he pored over thick briefing books, practiced pronouncing Jiang Zemin's sixteen-character slogan for improving the relationship, and rehearsed a global overview that he intended to use in his discussions with the Chinese.[37] Lake's strategic rap, "strat rap," as he characterized it, was intended as a counter to the classical, "multipolarism," balance-of-power notions of international politics that generally characterized Chinese presentations.

Lake's exposition was forthright: the United States was the single most powerful nation on the earth and was likely to stay so for some time. America had no desire to dominate the globe or destroy potential adversaries but could thrive in an era of contending great powers, if that is what it faced. American military deployments in Europe and Asia were not extensions of empire or hegemony but were intended to preserve stability and avert conflict. Washington's preference was for a world in which the "great powers"—the United States, European Union, Russia, Japan, and China—worked cooperatively to establish mechanisms and regulatory organizations that would minimize conflict and help raise the living standards of smaller nations.

On Monday, June 8, Lake and his party met for seven hours with Liu Huaqiu and numerous MFA and State Council note takers in China's official guesthouse complex, Diaoyutai. Although elaborate and well equipped, Diaoyutai lacked the informality of Willow Oaks, and the delegations were separated by a table and microphones. Despite the higher degree of officiality, discussions were still lively and occasionally contentious, as the long list of bilateral disagreements was reviewed in detail. During the lunch break, Lake invited Liu to take a "walk in the woods," a private one-on-one conversation outside, away from the rest of their respective delegations.[38] In their stroll around the grounds of Diaoyutai, Lake raised two issues, M-11 shipments to Pakistan and human rights, which were of particular concern to President Clinton. He had hopes that a private, off-the-record discussion might yield a path to progress. Liu was no more candid or forthcoming on either issue than in the larger sessions, although he did agree to have one of his staff accept what Lake called an "illustrative list" of prominent dissidents the United States hoped China would release.[39]

The following day, Lake met with Defense Minister Chi Haotian for a rather insipid discussion of strategic issues, and with Premier Li Peng, Vice Premier Qian Qichen, and finally with President Jiang Zemin. Most of the discussions were variations on the lengthy talks he had held with Liu Huaqiu the previous day. Jiang, however, demonstrated why so many of his American interlocutors found him quirky and strange. Ignoring Lake's efforts to raise substantive issues, Jiang talked about the water origins of both their surnames (Jiang means "river"), discussed computer chip technology, Chinese poetry, and philosophy, much of it in idiomatic English. Lake looked at his staff, shrugged, and put his talking points away, knowing that his ebullient host was going to take the conversation in his own direction, his own way.

Jiang's mood reflected the Chinese side's clear satisfaction with the conduct of the talks and with Lake's reiteration of the need for more regular summit meetings. He told them that a Jiang visit to the United States was being considered for the following year (that is, after the presidential election). Afterward, both sides briefed the press in an upbeat, positive manner. No diplomatic breakthroughs had been achieved, but none had been sought or expected. Lake and Lord tried to focus reporters' attention on the need for structure, process, and management of difficult problems. "Security and stability and predictability" were the words Lord used to describe American goals. "We're trying to be based on a little more . . . mutual expectation," Lord told reporters.[40] Both White House spokesman Mike McCurry and China's MFA spokesman Cui Tiankai credited Lake with improving "the overall climate of . . . bilateral relations,"[41] although both sides cautioned that there remained a long way to go before relations could be considered normalized.

In late July, Secretary of State Christopher met Qian again in Jakarta for the annual ASEAN ministerial conclave. Qian extended an invitation to Christopher to visit Beijing in November, which the secretary accepted, though with some misgivings. His previous trip, in 1994, had been a political disaster, and an objective appraisal of the relationship in the summer of 1996 would have had to conclude it had improved only a little since then.

The NSC, however, began developing an initiative in the one area of "engagement" in which there had been the least progress—human rights. Of the major issues on the Sino-American agenda of dispute, none was more difficult than China's human rights practices. From Beijing's perspective, human rights represented a problem with no positive elements, no "wins," no moral high ground, no advantage to be gained. The regime was not about to permit the kind of political reform that underlay most of the West's complaints about freedom of expression, press, and religious expression—that would simply be to cooperate in its own demise. It could not "reverse the verdict" on Tiananmen while Deng was alive or otherwise review the decisions made at the time without opening up a process of political accounting that would have tarnished the reputations of many of its topmost leaders. Certainly the PLA did not favor such a course, even though most of the officers who had carried out the crackdown or gained from it had already been retired or removed. No party review could be undertaken without raising the possibility of rehabilitating Zhao Ziyang, a course of action Jiang Zemin could never support.

Moreover, many Chinese—and not just within the Communist Party leadership—believed that foreign criticism of China's human rights record, demands for change, and advocacy of democratic reforms were simply a means of pressuring and subverting China, rendering it weak, and undermining its government. Thus despite continuing support inside China for opening up and further democratizing the political system, the government was able to play on patriotism to limit foreign and domestic pressures from joining forces. The regime was willing to negotiate for the lifting or averting of sanctions or the improvement of the atmospherics of foreign relationships, but only at the margins, on issues that did not require important changes in the party's rule. Its general approach on human rights was to stonewall on the large issues, engage in anodyne "dialogue" on a government-to-government basis, and negotiate for small-scale, marginal goals using its most fungible human rights asset—political prisoners. These it used cynically, in response to foreign pressures and in order to send the message to potential dissidents in China that foreign support was of little use. Beijing used Washington's concern for high-profile prisoner releases effectively to exile some of its most troublesome dissidents.

Beijing was vulnerable to international criticism of its human rights record, in the sense that it found public censure embarrassing and inconsistent with its aspirations for greater global influence. It therefore expended considerable political capital to prevent the adoption of resolutions faulting its human rights practices by the United Nations Human Rights Commission (UNHRC), which meets yearly in Geneva to consider international human rights conditions. By mobilizing "third world," socialist, and anti-American countries—which usually constituted a majority on the commission—China was able every year to block the resolution by passing a motion to take no action on it. Nonetheless, Beijing clearly was anxious to find some way to end the yearly struggle and was prepared to negotiate in order to do so.

On the premise that the administration's efforts and policies had done little for its own political constituencies or for the cause of human rights in China, I consulted with a few Washington-based representatives of major human rights organizations and with San Francisco businessman and human rights activist John Kamm, who had achieved notable success in gaining the release of Chinese political prisoners. I inquired what they thought the administration should try to achieve to replace the feckless approach pursued up until that point. They recommended focusing on getting China to sign and ratify two UN-sponsored human rights covenants—the International Covenant on Economic, Social, and Cultural Rights and the International Covenant on Civil and Political Rights—which would provide specific standards by which China's future actions could be judged. They also suggested pressing for the release of prominent dissidents, such as Wei Jingsheng and Wang Dan, and for getting Beijing to accept International Committee of the Red Cross (ICRC) protocols for visiting prisoners of conscience in China. They seemed somewhat more receptive to the idea of establishing a nongovernmental organization forum on human rights, a concept they had disparaged in 1994 on the grounds that China did not permit NGOs and would simply manipulate such a forum through quasi-official channels. Having seen how little the Clinton administration was prepared to use governmental leverage to pressure Beijing on human rights and how little had been achieved through the official dialogue, they seemed amenable to giving an NGO forum a chance.

Based on these discussions, I prepared a memorandum for Tony Lake to send to Warren Christopher with a proposition I knew much of the human rights community would not favor. I suggested that the United States consider dropping sponsorship of a resolution critical of China's human rights practices at the annual meeting of the UNHRC in exchange for Beijing agreeing to four conditions: releasing the prisoners on the list Lake had delivered in July; signing and ratifying the two covenants; permitting international visits to Chinese prisons under ICRC protocols; and establishing an NGO forum to discuss human rights. The United States had failed to get a resolution passed every year since 1990; it was generally a painful experience. China generally won the showdown but at considerable cost and loss of face. It might be willing to make some trade-offs. I believed that if the United States could get tangible results by forgoing the exercise, it was worth a try.

Lake was skeptical that the State Department would accept the proposal and doubtful the Chinese would agree to any of the conditions, but he was willing to pursue the idea quietly. He declined to send the memorandum to Christopher officially under his own signature but agreed to forward it under mine. Thus was born a singular document form, the NSC director-to-secretary of state memorandum, the sole example of which was sent over by the NSC executive secretary in late August 1996. Christopher also was dubious of the idea, but the head of his Policy Planning Office, James Steinberg, was intrigued, and the State Department posed no objections to the NSC pursuing it quietly.

On the pretext of supporting a USTR mission to follow up on the IPR agreement, I traveled to Beijing in mid-September to present the plan to department-level officials in the Ministry of Foreign Affairs. American and Oceanian Department counselor Liu Xiaoming listened politely and with interest to my careful presentation—I made no commitments or specific linkages, and I was not authorized to follow up. Two weeks later, however, Liu made a special effort to ensure we were seated together at a Chinese-American banquet in Washington to celebrate China's national day and grilled me for two hours on the details and authority of the proposal. That was deemed sufficient interest to enable Steinberg to further develop the proposal when he visited Beijing in late October to hold discussions with his MFA counterpart and advance the Christopher visit. Steinberg's discussions showed the Chinese were intrigued by the proposal and willing to discuss it at a higher level but were still uncertain whether it had top-level support within the Clinton administration.

By that time, the proposal had already generated controversy in the State Department. When Steinberg vetted it before making his trip, objections had been raised by Winston Lord, who found it too easy on the Chinese, and John Shattuck, assistant secretary for democracy, human rights, and labor. Shattuck was concerned, correctly, that the trade-off would not be accepted by the American human rights community and that the official bilateral human rights dialogue—though in suspension—might be eclipsed by an NGO forum. Christopher's doubts probably were deepened by the Chinese decision—just after Steinberg's trip—to put Wang Dan on trial for conspiracy to overthrow the government. In what had become all-too-typical a dissident trial, Wang was found guilty and sentenced to eleven years in prison on October 30. Not surprisingly, news of the human rights "package" leaked to the press before Christopher's trip.[42]

Christopher's November 20–23 trip to China was not nearly as disagreeable as his 1994 visit. Apart from the trial of Wang Dan, there were no further actions against the few remaining voices of dissent in China, and the secretary refrained from public commentary en route. Knowing that Christopher had already announced his intention to resign at the end of the year, the Chinese treated him with respect and cordiality. Even Li Peng was less testy than usual, although he was critical of U.S. human rights policies. In his meeting with Qian, Christopher reviewed the entire array of U.S.-China bilateral issues in standard terms. He laid out the basic agenda for the Clinton-Jiang summit at the Manila APEC leaders meeting, which would follow later in the week, and indicated that an exchange of state visits would be agreeable, beginning with a Jiang visit to Washington in 1997.

When he got to human rights issues, he protested the treatment of Wang Dan and reiterated the administration's desire for improvements in China's approach to political prisoners, freedom of speech, and Tibet, among other issues. With Shattuck and Lord in attendance, the secretary ran through the UNHRC "package" quickly and without detail. Qian's reply was noncommittal but not unresponsive. In my interpretation, he clearly wanted to hear more. But Christopher interpreted his reply as a rebuff and moved quickly off the subject, to Qian's apparent perplexity. That effectively ended the issue as a topic of bilateral discussion for the ensuing six months and more.

After his Beijing meetings, Christopher proceeded to Shanghai, where he saw the economic transformation that was changing the face of China dramatically. But even the nonofficial portion of his trip reflected the administration's ambivalence and uncertainty about China policy. To the delight of Shanghai's burgeoning community of foreign policy experts, Christopher had agreed to give a speech and answer questions at Fudan University's Center for American Studies. His address was initially entitled, "Building a Partnership for the 21st Century," and a large blue banner with those words was prepared and hung behind the makeshift podium. As Christopher put it in his book, he began to have "second thoughts" about the title on the way to China. There was also a sharp disagreement within his delegation on the subject, with the China experts in favor of leaving the text and the banner as they were, and his speechwriters and other political advisers suggesting changing the term "partnership" to "cooperation." Christopher decided in favor of the latter. As he put it, "The term 'partnership' described relations with our closest allies, states like Great Britain, Germany, and Japan. Although our relations with China had certainly improved—and I wanted to convey exactly that—'partnership' sounded a little too cozy. It was what we were aiming for, but we weren't there yet. 'Cooperation' seemed a more apt term, and we changed the text (and the banner) the night before I gave the speech."[43] Chinese students, of course, noticed the change and queried Christopher about it, but he dodged the issue skillfully. He did not know that the president—on a pre-APEC state visit to Australia—was using the term "partnership" to describe his aspirations for U.S.-China relations.[44]

Clinton Triumphant, and Immediately Challenged

On November 6, 1996, William Jefferson Clinton was re-elected to a second term as president of the United States, defeating Senator Robert J. Dole by a popular vote of more than 47 million votes to 39 million, with 8 million votes cast for Reform Party candidate H. Ross Perot. In the electoral college tally, Clinton won by a resounding 379 to 159 votes. He won 48 percent of the popular vote in an election with the lowest voter turnout in more than sixty years. In congressional elections, the Republican Party lost seats in the House of Representatives but maintained an easy majority of more than twenty seats, and increased its dominance in the Senate by two additional seats. That dampened the ardor of Clinton's supporters, and the president called for a new spirit of cooperation with Capitol Hill in doing the nation's business. But given the enormous setback he had suffered in the 1994 midterm elections, his easy win over Dole was a huge vindication for Clinton, and he clearly savored it.

Analysts adduced several reasons for Clinton's victory, focusing mostly on general contentment with the booming American economy, approval of Clinton's stewardship of the office of president (if not his character), wariness of the seemingly radical Republican agenda, and a certain ineptitude in the way Dole ran his campaign. There was also considerable attention paid to campaign finance and what role it played in the outcome of the election. By October, a month before the elections, both the Federal Election Commission—established after the Watergate scandal of 1972 to enforce new laws limiting donations to candidates—and independent political monitoring groups like Common Cause were criticizing the Dole and Clinton campaigns for massive abuses of campaign finance regulations. There were numerous appeals to the Justice Department to appoint a special prosecutor to investigate how much the two parties had spent much on television advertising.[45] Whether television advertisements were important in the outcome of the election is still open to debate, as Clinton maintained a significant lead in public opinion polling throughout the campaign. But political money, and how it was raised and spent, would be a dominant issue in Clinton's second term.

Foreign policy issues had played a minor role in the campaign, although Bosnia and Haiti still excited considerable partisan controversy. China policy did not become a prominent campaign issue, even though some segments of the Republican Party—particularly representatives of the "religious right" and those more committed to an anticommunist ideological approach, such as Patrick Buchanan—wanted to make it so. Dole had been an active supporter of George Bush's China policy, believed in engagement as the most appropriate approach to China, and consistently supported the extension of China's MFN privileges. He did try consistently to attack the implementation of Clinton's policy, focusing on vacillation, inconsistency, and a lack of clarity. But he did not press that theme very hard.

As he showed soon after the election, however, Clinton had enthusiastically adopted the idea of improving relations with China as one of the key foreign policy goals of his second term. He did not mince his words. "The emergence of a stable, an open, a prosperous China, a strong China confident of its place and willing to assume its responsibilities as a great nation is in our deepest interest," he told reporters in Australia shortly after his reelection. "What the United States wants is to sustain an engagement with China . . . in a way that will increase the chances that there will be more liberty and more prosperity and more genuine cooperation in the future."[46] At the beginning of his second term, then, Clinton was fully supportive of a positive engagement approach toward China, even some form of "partnership." Critics would later charge that his embracing of such an approach was purchased through campaign contributions.

Although he had grown more comfortable with foreign policy issues during his first term, Clinton still relied on the advice of others, particularly Lake and Berger, and made few decisions outside established channels of policymaking. With respect to China policy, by the end of 1996, the initiative for China policy had passed from the State Department to the National Security Council. Lake had become more enthusiastic about the possibilities of engagement with China in light of his own personal diplomacy during and after the Taiwan Strait crisis.

Sandy Berger had been consistent in support of an activist approach to China, although he kept a relatively low profile because of his position as deputy national security adviser and his knowledge of the complex domestic policy issues that took precedence on Clinton's agenda. He saw more clearly than others the advantages of focusing on an economic and trade agenda with China for advancing the president's domestic interests. The November

APEC trip—which Lake did not join—was something of a "tryout" for Berger's bid to become national security adviser, and he pressed the president to take a more activist approach to Asia, where he was convinced America's future economic prosperity lay.[47] Sandra Kristoff brought to the senior director of Asian affairs position a marked skill for organizing and directing interdepartmental teams and was able to greatly reduce bureaucratic squabbling over China policy. Last but not least, the president was aware that a high-pressure, negative approach to China had yielded few positive results, and he was prepared to try a more accommodating method. His electoral victory appeared to give him some additional flexibility.

It was an obviously self-assured Bill Clinton who met Jiang Zemin at the November 24 APEC leaders meeting in Manila. Buoyed by his victory and by a vigorous state visit and golf vacation in Australia, where he was warmly welcomed, Clinton held a one-hour-and-twenty-five-minute meeting with Jiang in the most genial atmosphere yet of their yearly meetings. Jiang had always put a high value on interpersonal relationships and recognized the need to establish a personal bond with Clinton before problem solving could be undertaken.[48] Clinton, more reluctantly, owing to political pressures on China policy, evidently came to the same conclusion. Manila, in a sense, represented a mutual recognition that their interpersonal association would set the tone for the larger bilateral relationship, and both men set about deliberately to improve their rapport, despite substantial differences in style, personality, age, culture, and background.

With a limited agenda already decided by the Christopher and Lake visits to Beijing, the two presidents exchanged views on several subjects, including human rights, China's bid to join the World Trade Organization, the impending handover of Hong Kong to Chinese sovereignty, and the four-party Korean Peninsula peace talks proposal that had been raised earlier in the year. Jiang brought news of an American bomber that had crashed in southern China during World War II and promised to turn over the remains of its crew. Most important, the two agreed on a schedule of state visits, including a trip to China by Vice President Al Gore in the spring, a Jiang visit to Washington in the summer or fall of 1997, and a Clinton return trip to China in 1998.[49]

Both sides hailed the meeting as an important breakthrough, although press reaction in the United States was skeptical, even hostile. "America today lacks a consensus on China," *Washington Post* columnist Jim Hoagland observed. "Americans lack a shared perspective strong enough and deep enough to support a consistent policy, either of hostility or of cooperation . . . But Clinton's Manila performance mandates a turning point in the war of words over China policy between the president and his critics. The urgent point now is the widening gulf between the president and his critics, who predictably greeted Clinton's words of comfort for Beijing with a fusillade of attacks."[50] The *Post* editorialized that Clinton's China policy was based on "misguided and potentially dangerous" assumptions, while the *New York Times* continued regular criticism of Clinton's China policy through several of its foreign affairs columnists.[51]

Countercurrents

In previous years, the determination of two chief executives to improve the tone of the bilateral relationship might have been enough to move the relationship in a positive direction. In 1996, however, strong countercurrents were operating in both countries. In China, policy began to be affected by popular nationalism in ways that had not been true before. In the United States, the dynamic of the political scandal took its toll on the implementation of Clinton's China policy.

China: Popular Nationalism

The rise of populist nationalism in the post-Tiananmen period has been documented by several commentators. It has been attributed to many causes, including that the regime deliberately substituted nationalism for failed Marxism-Leninism and Maoism as a unifying ideology, a more or less natural development of Chinese intellectuals' traditional hope for a strong country, disillusionment with the failure of liberal democracy to provide a stable social order, and resentment against "American triumphalism" and bullying, as demonstrated in the *Yin He* incident and the dispatch of American aircraft carriers to the region in 1996.[52] Whatever the origins of the phenomenon, the Taiwan Strait crisis was the catalyst for a remarkable upsurge in popular nationalism, mostly directed against the United States.

Taking advantage of loosened government controls and the commercialization of the publishing industry in China, five young writers hastily wrote a potent anti-American diatribe called "*China Can Say No* (*Zhongguo Keyi Shuo Bu*) in March-April 1996.[53] It was published in May and immediately began attracting public notice. Although suspicions that it was sponsored by the central government are unverifiable, there was no doubt that leaders in Beijing found the book's strident tone attractive. One member of the government's Human Rights Commission provided an epilogue for the book, and Xinhua publicized favorable reviews as early as June. Officials from the Ministry of Foreign Affairs nervously mentioned the book to American counterparts, admitting that it was "not very good, but everybody is reading it."

By midsummer, it was touted as China's "no. 1 best-seller," having sold more than 2 million copies.

China Can Say No is a remarkable book—acerbic, contentious, humorous, xenophobic, and occasionally nostalgic. Ferociously anti-American throughout, it reflected and propagated a distorted understanding of American society and culture. The product of "thirty-something" intellectuals, it demonstrated how deeply the Communist Party's paranoid view of the West had sunk in. "Westerners believe they can use their monopoly of financial and science and technology markets to constantly interfere in China's internal affairs and achieve their colonial goals. So on the one hand, they smilingly carry out economic trade, and on the other hand they use Western culture to carry out infiltration, trying to change our cultural values and modes of behavior."[54] At various points, it charged that the Hollywood movie industry and the Central Intelligence Agency were part of the same plot to subvert China.

Despite its unofficial origins, *China Can Say No* echoed China's official line on most of the bilateral issues of that time, including intellectual property and human rights issues, and especially the Taiwan question. Sarcastic and blunt, the authors rejected American criticism of China's human rights and domestic policies in terms that many officials no doubt wished they could use. But it also occasionally advocated a degree of active resistance to U.S. "bullying" that the Chinese government was not prepared to take. And the authors adopted an almost openly contemptuous attitude toward those they considered insufficiently bold in resisting Westernization. Moreover, their ambivalence about economic reform and the social and political costs of Western-style modernization was out of synch with the government's overall approach. For example, they advocated cutting back trade with the United States to minimize the prospects for dependency. After a period of nearly open admiration and support for the book, the regime adopted a more balanced approach beginning in the autumn. Qian Qichen remarked to a foreign reporter that the authors were "inexperienced" in foreign policy, while party-sponsored publications increasingly aired commentaries that were critical of the book's stridency.[55]

By that time, however, the sequels had already begun. The commercial success of *China Can Say No* soon led to: *Why China Says No; China Still Can Say No; Why Does China Say No? China Says No Nine Times;* and the more reasonable, government-approved *China Doesn't Just Say No*. None of these works were as fashionable as the original, but they generally shared the same populist and nationalist sentiments that animated the first volume. Cumulatively, the impact of these books is hard to gauge. Joseph Fewsmith argues that they contributed to several ongoing debates within the party at that time over the direction and pace of reform, the effect of foreign investment on China's overall economic development, the growth of corruption and economic inequality, the future of state-owned enterprises, and the political importance of China's growing "middle class."[56] In the end, however, the books contributed nothing positive but rather only aggravated the sense of victimization that underlies Chinese nationalism, incited a yearning for action that could not be met by the Chinese government, and provided a distorted perspective on Chinese public opinion.

United States: The Campaign Finance Scandal

On the U.S. side, the Clinton administration's approach to China in its second term was beset even before it got started by a combination of domestic political partisanship, the structural flaws of the U.S. election system, and the dynamic of political scandal. The fundamental problems were the financing of American political campaigns, which had grown inordinately expensive, and the intense antipathy that had bloomed between congressional Republicans and the Clinton White House in the wake of the 1994 elections. Believing Clinton was defeatable in 1996—despite the thriving American economy and their own embarrassment over the 1995 shutdown of the federal government—Republicans had set about a concerted campaign to undermine and discredit the president by exploiting and publicizing every available shortcoming.

Clinton was a "target-rich environment" for political snipers: his Vietnam-era draft record, reputation as a womanizer, and questionable real estate transactions when he was governor of Arkansas had created a cottage industry of investigative reporters and full-time critics in conservative media. It had also drawn the attention of a special prosecutor, Kenneth Starr, who exercised a broad mandate under congressional legislation to investigate the president's alleged misdeeds. First-term errors in judgment involving the White House travel office, FBI personnel files, and the tragic suicide of a key aide heightened media and public interest in Clinton's character and probity in office. But it was more than that. For a combination of reasons too complex to recount here, American politics in the mid-1990s had taken on a decidedly vicious tone. Partisanship had increased as both parties appealed to narrow constituencies, tolerance and harmony decreased among members of Congress, and the normal strains between the executive and legislative branches sharpened into barely concealed contempt and animosity.[57] And Clinton seemed to inspire more partisan hatred than any president since Richard Nixon.

Reeling from the loss of House and Senate in 1994, the president's closest domestic advisers believed that if they were to retain the presidency, they needed to raise an enormous amount of money to offset the Republican Party's usual advantage among corporate donors. It had become an article of faith among both politicians and political commentators in the 1990s that the more money one could raise, the more successful a politician one was likely to be. Issues, integrity, and party affiliation still mattered, but raising funds for media advertising, polling, rallies, mass mailings, and other campaign purposes became far more important, and they were expensive. Clinton pushed his staff—both inside the White House and in the Democratic National Committee—to devise new ways of raising soft political money, not subject to as many restrictions under federal campaign finance laws.[58] Clinton and Vice President Gore were direct participants in some of these methods, which included White House "coffees" organized by the DNC for generous contributors and direct telephone contacts with potential donors.

In late September 1996, and picking up through mid-October, stories began appearing about a fund-raising scandal involving President Clinton and some of his former associates and friends from Little Rock, Arkansas. One was an Indonesian-Chinese banker named Mochtar Riady, whose Lippo Bank—with an office in Little Rock—reportedly provided a large fee to presidential friend Webster Hubbell after he resigned as deputy attorney general in early 1996. The trail also led to John Huang, a Taiwan-born former executive of Lippo, who had served as deputy assistant secretary of commerce in 1994–95, then was hired by the DNC to raise funds from Asian Americans. The story grew more complicated when it was learned that the DNC had returned some of the donations Huang had raised during the summer because they appeared to have been acquired from Asians who were not American citizens, a violation of American law.[59]

Thus began a story that transfixed the U.S. media, generated several congressional investigations, damaged the Clinton second term, and significantly affected the course of U.S.-China relations. During the next three years, an array of charges would be leveled at China, President Clinton, members of his staff, Chinese Americans in general, and one nuclear researcher named Wen Ho Lee in particular. Many of these charges proved untrue—some of them wildly so. Most were overtaken politically by the larger and more controversial issue of Clinton's sexual improprieties with a White House intern named Monica Lewinsky and his ensuing impeachment by Congress. In the wake of the indeterminate outcome of the scandals, numerous questions have been left unanswered, and some of the accusations, while unproven, probably are believed by many to be true.

It is impossible to escape the conclusion, in light of subsequent convictions and plea bargains of various DNC fund-raising specialists, that there were major campaign finance law violations attributable to John Huang and several others during this period. A few examples:

—Huang solicited a $425,000 donation to the DNC by Arief and Soraya Wiriadinata, permanent resident aliens in the United States who happened to be related to Mochtar Riady, a noncitizen who was the likely source of the money;

—Huang and a Taiwan-born businesswoman named Maria Hsia organized a fund-raising luncheon for Vice President Al Gore at the Hsi Lai Temple—a Buddhist monastery in Hacienda Heights, California—at which $140,000 was donated to the DNC by monks and nuns who had taken vows of poverty and were later repaid for their "contributions";[60]

—Charlie Yah-lin Trie, a Taiwan-born restaurant owner from Little Rock, donated $640,000—much of it in cash—to the president's legal defense fund and solicited a $325,000 contribution to the DNC from Yogesh Gandhi, whose California foundation had failed to file tax forms. Trie was subsequently appointed by the White House to the Commission on United States–Pacific Trade and Investment Policy;[61]

—Johnny Chien Chuen Chung, a Taiwan-born owner of a struggling "blast fax" business in California, donated $366,000 to the DNC, after which he gained unusual access (forty-nine visits) to the White House for special events, photo opportunities with the president, vice president, and First Lady.[62]

Where did the money come from? That is what the Federal Election Commission, the Justice Department, several congressional committees, and a growing flock of investigative reporters wanted to know. The Lippo Group of Mochtar Riady—Huang's former employer—was an obvious suspect, with its international reach among Chinese communities throughout Asia and in the United States. Once on the "money trail," investigative reporters in Washington uncovered several other stories, and some of them pointed to Taiwan as the source of the money. These stories involved more members of Clinton's staff, including former aides Mark Middleton and Mark Grobmyer, and James C. Wood Jr.—then-director of the Washington office of the American Institute on Taiwan (as noted earlier, the U.S. unofficial organization responsible for maintaining day-to-day relations with the Taiwan government). They allegedly solicited contributions to the DNC from Taiwanese businessmen, including Kuomintang Enterprises chairman Liu Tai-ying, citing Clinton's dispatch of aircraft carriers to Taiwan in its hour of need as justification.[63] The "venerable master" of the Hsi Lai Temple, at which Gore's fund-raising lunch was held, was one Hsing Yun, a member of the Kuomintang Advisory Committee who later became a member of its Overseas Chinese Affairs Commission.[64] (I had warned the vice president's staff about Hsing Yun's Taiwan affiliation before the April 1996 event, but my concerns were glossed over.)

Although the DNC leadership was concerned enough about the legality of some of Huang's contributions to return them to the donors, it was not just

Taiwanese money that was brought into question. The People's Republic of China turned out to be involved as well, a fact that drove the story to a fever pitch. Charlie Trie had brought the head of the China International Trade and Investment Corporation, Wang Jun, to a coffee at the White House in February 1996. Wang, the son of China's former vice president, was also involved with a Chinese dealer of military equipment called Polytechnologies. The president later admitted that Wang's visit to the White House was "clearly inappropriate," although no evidence was ever presented that he had made any political contributions.[65] Johnny Chung also brought PRC business associates to various fund-raisers and White House events. It was the PRC-related contacts that would generate the most controversy and the most difficulty for the second-term foreign policy team.

Clinton's Second-Term Security Team

The Donorgate scandal continued to roil the political system in the weeks following the election, even though there was never any evidence presented to suggest that the donations had made a significant difference in the outcome of the election. It exacted its first political casualties during the president's emplacement of the "national security team" for his second term. Clinton announced the second-term team on December 5, 1996, focusing on the quality of its members and on the fact that he conceived of it as "a team that will rise above partisanship and rise to the challenges of meeting the opportunities, of dealing with the challenges that we all face."[66]

Replacing Warren Christopher as secretary of state was Madeleine Albright, who had served as ambassador to the United Nations in the first term. The daughter of Czech immigrants, Albright had taught at Georgetown University and had developed a reputation at the United Nations for tough talk and decisive action.

William S. Cohen was nominated to replace William Perry as secretary of defense. A three-term Republican senator from Maine, Cohen was experienced in defense matters (having served as chairman of the Senate Armed Services Committee) and well respected by his colleagues in the Senate and by the senior military leadership in the Pentagon.

National Security Adviser Anthony Lake was nominated to serve as director of Central Intelligence, replacing John Deutch, who had replaced James Woolsey as the director in 1994. Lake, while more intellectually oriented than most directors of CIA, had distinct ideas about the need to reform and reinvigorate the agency and a deep understanding of what the American policy agenda needed in intelligence support.

Samuel R. "Sandy" Berger was selected to replace Lake as national security adviser, formalizing his predominance as the president's closest and most influential foreign policy adviser. Experienced and incisive, Berger had been with Clinton for many years and was expected to make an easy transition. For his own deputy, he chose James B. Steinberg, who had served as Christopher's director of policy planning.

Between their nomination in early December and confirmation hearings after Clinton's second-term inauguration, the new team members were exposed to intense political scrutiny by an energized investigative press corps. Donorgate was "Issue A," and conservative commentators were quick to bring accusations. William Safire, a former Nixon speechwriter and columnist for the *New York Times*, suggested that the connections between John Huang and Lippo were not an employee-employer relationship or overzealous campaign fund-raising, but were an "economic intelligence penetration" by the PRC intelligence services.[67] The archconservative *American Spectator* magazine attacked Cohen for being indiscriminate in his acceptance of gifts and fees from foreign governments and for having contacts with some of the principals in the Donorgate scandal.[68]

While Lake prepared for tough hearings before the Senate Select Committee on Intelligence, Berger also instituted a search of National Security Council documents to turn up evidence that the NSC had not been simply a doormat for the DNC in gaining access to the president or on any policy issues. Those documents—148 pages, which included several e-mails and memos that I drafted—were released on February 14, 1997. They did not have the desired effect. Rather than cooling speculation about Chinese efforts to influence policy, they only fed the lust for details about Chinese visitors to the White House and what they wanted. Instead of showing the NSC effectively blocking DNC incursions into policymaking, they showed examples of sound advice ignored and warnings unheeded by Clinton and his domestic staff. And rather than demonstrating Lake's careful separation of policy and politics, the documents and follow-on newspaper commentaries led to new questions about his judgment, managerial style, and reliability.

In early February, after Lake's confirmation hearings were postponed, the *Washington Post*'s notable investigative reporter, Bob Woodward, reported that "representatives of the People's Republic of China sought to direct contributions from foreign sources to the Democratic National Committee before the 1996 presidential campaign."[69] The bombshell claim, based on vague statements from "officials familiar with the inquiry," was padded with innuendo, speculation, and rumors, drawing sinister conclusions from well-known aspects of John Huang's employment at the Commerce Department, phone calls he made to Lippo, and a $5 taxicab receipt indicating he may have visited the PRC embassy. The accusation, in conjunction with the released NSC material, heightened the political clamor on Capitol Hill, and led Senator Richard Shelby (R-Ala.), Senate Select Committee on Intelligence chairman, to postpone hearings on Lake's appointment for a second time. A media frenzy ensued, with reporters tracking down more data points and connecting them to construct a picture of a devious conspiracy.

In late February, Woodward wrote up another leak from the Justice Department task force investigating illegal campaign finance activities. This one indicated that the task force was trying to find out if "representatives of the People's Republic of China attempted to buy influence among members of Congress through illegal campaign contributions and payments from Chinese-controlled businesses." While the accusation was initially considered "less serious" than stories of illegal contributions to the president's reelection campaign, the *Washington Post* story also alleged that the FBI briefed two NSC staffers on the information in the summer of 1996, but they did not pass the information on to senior NSC officials or to the president.[70]

That kicked off a scrap within the White House and between the NSC and the Justice Department over whether the two staffers, Rand Beers and Ed Appel, were instructed not to pass the information on to more senior officials. White House spokesman Mike McCurry insisted that the two officials had been told by their FBI briefers not to pass the information on to anyone else. The FBI countered publicly, saying it had placed "no restrictions whatever" on the information, which led to McCurry insisting, "The White House considers the FBI's statement to be in error." Clinton, exasperated, told reporters, "Yes, I believe I should have known. No, I didn't know. If I had known, I would have asked the NSC and the chief of staff to look at the evidence and make whatever recommendations were appropriate . . . It would have provoked, at least to that extent, a red flag on my part."[71] The Justice Department tried to ease the rift by disavowing the FBI statement as "intemperate," while suggesting the NSC officials may have misunderstood the controls and restrictions placed on the evidence by the originating agency, the National Security Agency.[72]

At the same time as they were briefing the NSC, the FBI evidently had felt obligated to inform Congress of the information about Chinese plans to influence legislative elections and passed on "vague" warnings to several members of Congress, including Senators Diane Feinstein and Barbara Boxer of California, Representatives Nancy Pelosi and Tom Campbell of California, and Senator Daniel Moynihan of New York. While there was no specific evidence that the Chinese had targeted their campaigns, the FBI took it upon itself to brief them of the possibility, presumably on the basis of their involvement in China-related issues. Initially, the bureau had considered thirty members of Congress as potential recipients but narrowed the list down to six. None of them took the warning very seriously, although Feinstein eventually returned some $12,000 in donations she thought might have been from Lippo Bank employees.[73]

Feinstein's return of donations was just the tip of the iceberg, however. Panicked, the DNC announced on March 1 that it was returning an additional $1.5 million in donations—mostly associated with Huang, Trie, and Chung—because it could not determine if the donors acquired or donated the money legally. That was on top of the $1.5 million it had already returned by the end of 1996. The new DNC chairman, Roy Romer, announced strict new regulations limiting contributions, instituting a screening process for people attending fund-raisers, and prohibiting "perquisites" in exchange for donations.[74] Observers in both parties admitted that the fund-raising system was "broken." Editorialists in most major papers decried the excesses and called for a serious effort to institute campaign finance reform. That effort, focused through the Senate Committee on Government Reform, chaired by Senator Fred Thompson (R-Tenn.), eventually broke down in partisan haggling, and campaign reform legislation would eventually die.[75] But the damage to the Clinton presidency was immediate and serious—his approval rating dropped significantly in the first few months of 1997—and would get worse.

Lake was the first high-level casualty of the scandal. His long-delayed hearings, which began on March 11, turned quickly from a discussion of the CIA and the need for intelligence in a post–cold war world to an examination of more details of the NSC's involvement in campaign finance wrongdoing and of Lake's management style. Lake's response to the focus on campaign finance was called "anemic."[76] He was hampered by his reputation as a standoffish intellectual, and he had cultivated few friends on the Hill. After only three days of questioning, his nomination was viewed as being in trouble. Senator Robert Kerrey (D-Nebr.), the ranking Democrat on the Senate Select Committee, informed the White House by the weekend that he had developed strong reservations about the nomination on substantive grounds, particularly the access to NSC officials granted to a Lebanese American DNC donor with a "checkered background." Chairman Shelby suggested he might further delay the hearings so that all committee members could review extensive FBI files on Lake.[77]

Frustrated at the delays and the unprecedented probe of his personal life, Lake asked the president on March 18 to withdraw his nomination to be director of Central Intelligence. In a stinging withdrawal letter, he charged that his nomination had become "a political football in a game with constantly moving goalposts." After incessant delays, he saw "no end in sight" for the nomination, which had become a "political circus." "Washington has gone haywire," he concluded, and the political process had become distorted by partisanship and gamesmanship. He did not wish to see the CIA and NSC further damaged and politicized by such a process.[78] Reluctantly and angrily, Clinton accepted Lake's decision and nominated George Tenet—a former Senate Select Committee on Intelligence staff director and also an NSC senior director whom he had appointed as deputy director of Central Intelligence in 1995—to replace him. Tenet won easy confirmation and was sworn in as DCI in early July.

Donations and Policy

As an NSC director-level official at the time, I was not permitted to state publicly my views on the relationship between DNC campaign finance activities and the actual formulation of foreign policy and in particular China policy. But I had my own view at the time of the relationship between the president's political party, the campaign finance process, and the policy process, and it has remained consistent since then. It is a view perhaps different from the images held in the popular press, or even of other political scientists or commentators about the relationship between domestic politics and foreign policy. It is certainly different from the views of partisan polemicists like Kenneth Timmerman, Bill Triplett, and Edward Timperlake, who constructed elaborate arguments based on the idea that political contributions—in particular from the People's Republic of China—"led to concrete decisions by the Clinton administration that have harmed our national security."[79]

In my view, at least, campaign donations—no matter what the source—are given as an expression of unqualified support for a political party and candidate, or in the hope of gaining influence with them. The former is a donation, the latter a form of lobbying. Lobbying through contributions is an established practice in the United States, time-honored and deeply rooted. What the Asian DNC donors got, in some cases, was access: invitations to events where the president or vice president would be in attendance, a handshake in a receiving line, a photograph together, an opportunity to speak about issues over coffee, the courtesy of a reply to a letter, the opportunity to donate more, a flashy title. For some—Charlie Trie and Johnny Chung, for example—that was what they wanted. The perception of being influential gained them prestige and business opportunities overseas. They, in turn, were evidently taken advantage of by their PRC counterparts, who saw them as access agents.

But their access decidedly did *not* give them influence over policy. Were the views of Charlie Trie and Johnny Chung—or their alleged backers—factored into policy decisions at the presidential level? Did Wang Jun convince the president to extend MFN during a coffee? Did five Chinese executives persuade him during a two-minute Oval Office photo op to permit American satellites to be launched on Chinese rockets? Did a letter from Charlie Trie change the president's mind about support for Taiwan in 1996? Of course not. The foreign policy process did not work that way under Clinton or, one hopes, any other president. Decisions went through bureaucratic processes that involved many government officials of unchallengeable loyalty who were chosen for their foreign affairs experience, knowledge, and abilities. Papers and cables were written and circulated, meetings were held, issues were discussed, consensus reached, and options finally presented to the president for his decision. At no point was the DNC or any other political organization brought into the process.

Still less was the NSC—the president's foreign affairs staff—in any way beholden to the DNC. Contacts with the DNC were prohibited unless approved by the deputy national security adviser. In three and one-half years as an NSC staffer, I met with hundreds of people interested in having an influence on American policy: foreign and American diplomats, intelligence officers, soldiers, legislators, business leaders, academics, lobbyists, human rights activists, religious personages, people from every country and every political persuasion. Only a handful of them had any connection to the DNC, and they had no more, and probably less, influence on me than most of the others. It was my job to learn what people thought about Asia-related issues, what were the divisions and disagreements. I was also expected to explain and defend American policy and interests to concerned parties. They, in turn, brought information, opinions, reading materials, and knowledge that they hoped would be useful in the consideration of American policy.

As a policy process, it was a sensible and workable approach. But it was not visible to the public, and ultimately, it was misperceived. In September 1997, Sandy Berger—then the national security adviser—put the issue succinctly and encapsulated the experience of the NSC staff. "I did foreign policy, as did Mr. Lake in the last administration. I think there was no decision made by the president that we were not engaged in. And in no situation did I perceive, in any way, that any campaign contributor or campaign fundraising consideration had any influence on that policy. And I say that categorically."[80] That approach to the issue—professional insulation from domestic politics—was widely held in the foreign policy community and was both a strength and a liability as the campaign finance issue continued to dominate the political agenda. It enabled the NSC staff to continue working on the substantive issues without becoming completely distracted by the political maelstrom that swirled around them. But it also made them vulnerable to charges of naiveté and being manipulated.

"Chinagate": Policy Repercussions as the Scandal Intensifies

Tom Friedman, a highly respected foreign affairs reporter and columnist for the *New York Times,* was unusually forceful in his March 17 commentary on the campaign finance scandal and unusually prescient in setting out the foreign policy consequences of the ongoing scandal.

> Just when U.S. officials need to have a cool, clear head in thinking about China policy, just when it is critical that there be a broad domestic consensus on China policy, the Clinton team has made China policy radioactive by engaging in the most tawdry fund-raising from Chinese-Americans and overseas Chinese with dubious links to governments and business interests. Beyond shameful, this was breathtakingly stupid. Every major decision the Administration now makes on China is going to be scrutinized for links, real or imagined, to campaign donations. Administration China experts will be reluctant to take chances. And the prospects for bipartisanship on China will be diminished, since the China bashers in Congress are going to have a field day using China's own ham-fisted efforts at influence-peddling to discredit anyone who tries to engage Beijing on the urgent, serious agenda that needs addressing.[81]

The effects of the scandal soon began to be felt in the conduct of bilateral relations, which the Clinton administration was trying to improve. Secretary of State Madeleine Albright had asked the White House for a briefing on alleged Chinese efforts to influence congressional elections before her late February trip to Beijing to meet with Chinese leaders. FBI director Louis Freeh refused to allow the White House to have access to the material in question, and Albright had no choice but to raise the issue only briefly and in general terms. The Chinese leaders gave very general denials of complicity in response.[82] Shortly thereafter, Beijing began to complain about the coverage of the issue in the American press, calling in the chargé d'affaires, William McCahill, to protest the publication of "ill-intentioned fabrications" about Chinese efforts to donate money illegally to American political campaigns. Typically, China's Ministry of Foreign Affairs demanded the U.S. government put a stop to the stories. Publicly, Chinese press articles complained that mainstream U.S. newspapers were "waging a verbal war on China" because of China's pursuit of an independent foreign policy.[83]

Vice President Al Gore's trip to China in late March was intended to be a warm-up for the exchange of presidential summits and an expansion of bilateral cooperation into the realms of environmental cleanup and renewable energy. Gore's host, Premier Li Peng, had finally agreed to sponsor a joint "Forum on Environment and Development," after years of portraying American environmental policy as a tool for keeping the third world poor. The vice president was eager to establish a relationship and a precedent, knowing the more affable Zhu Rongji would succeed Li the following year. But the campaign finance scandal would cast a deep shadow over the trip from start to finish. Again, because of FBI and Justice Department concerns, no one in the vice president's party was given full access to pertinent information on China's alleged attempts to influence congressional elections.[84]

Reporters aboard the vice president's plane, of course, were primarily interested in the scandal, rather than environmental cooperation, and asked incessantly whether he would raise the issue with Chinese leaders. Gore responded, "In an appropriate and sensitive way, it'll be discussed, with every other matter that has potential for having some effect on our important relationship," reminding reporters that the issue was under a grand jury investigation, which limited what he could say.[85]

In their first bilateral meeting on March 25, it was Li Peng who brought up the allegations of Chinese interference in the American electoral process, denying the stories firmly and asking for a reassurance that the charges would not derail the hard-won progress in restoring bilateral relations. Gore responded that the administration was sincere in its efforts to improve relations through engagement, but that the charges were serious and would be treated seriously. He did not go into detail, however. In an evening backgrounder on the meetings, chargé McCahill told reporters that the vice president had reassured the Chinese that the investigations would not affect the overall relationship.

The following morning, seeing negative press comments about not appearing to take the issue seriously enough, Gore's national security adviser, Leon Fuerth, felt obligated to correct the record. The vice president, he told reporters, had "explicitly said that we take this very seriously, and if the allegations are true then, yes, it would be a serious matter."[86] Sensing some vulnerability and discomfort (Gore had been heavily criticized for the Hsi Lai Temple visit and for making fund-raising phone calls from his office), the press bore mercilessly on campaign finance for the rest of the visit. All other questions faded to irrelevance as they sought to pin down the vice president on what he did or did not tell the Chinese about the investigations and their impact on U.S.-China policy. In his press conference before departing for Xian and Shanghai, eight of the twelve questions asked were about campaign finance rather than the tougher substance of bilateral relations (which Gore had handled extremely well in his meetings with the Chinese).

Gore's discomfort was compounded by a protocol gaffe, courtesy of Li Peng. His domestic staff had agreed he would witness two trade deals while in Beijing, a $1.5 billion joint venture by General Motors for producing Buicks in China and a $685 million sale of wide-body jets by Boeing Aircraft. At the conclusion of the signing ceremony in the Great Hall of the People, waitresses brought out champagne to celebrate the deals. Before he realized what was happening, Gore was confronted by a smiling Li Peng—the "butcher of Beijing"—with glass in hand, expecting a toast. He handled it clumsily, but Chinese photographers were there to record the moment, and the American press had a field day. The vice president, who had managed to avoid a sensitive Tiananmen arrival ceremony by substituting one inside the Great Hall of the People and had a no-toast agreement for the welcoming banquet, was caught and embarrassed.

The crowning blow was for the vice president to be followed into Beijing—only two days later—by House Speaker Newt Gingrich and a group of eleven other members of Congress. Gingrich played almost entirely to the audience at home. According to his own account of his meeting with Zhu Rongji, he spoke bluntly about campaign finance. "I simply said that on the assumption that their Government statement that they were not involved is true, that meant there were apparently renegades that were violating both our law and Chinese government policy and that we would appreciate their help as we seek to determine who these renegades are."[87] He also spoke out about religious persecution, freedom, and American values in a direct way, which was inevitably contrasted with Gore's careful portrayal of issues. Gingrich, who was at that time also in political trouble over ethical issues, played on themes he knew would be popular back home, with little concern about the reaction in China. Again by his own account, Gingrich talked tough on Taiwan. "I said firmly, 'We want you to understand, we will defend Taiwan. Period.'"[88]

American commentators and reporters, of course, compared the two visits, and Gore came out the poorer. That is ironic, because from the perspective of restoring a working relationship between the United States and China, Gore's visit was far more effective and fruitful than Gingrich's. Gore's successes came in his private meetings—with Chinese leaders and with lower-level officials—which he carried out skillfully, because of his careful preparation and seriousness of purpose. They were closed to the American press, and he did not boast of them later. Gore impressed his hosts as thoughtful and considerate as well as knowledgeable and articulate. He was treated with respect and near head-of-state protocol. Gingrich was treated somewhat better than most congressional delegations (it was reported that nearly

20 percent of Congress had visited China during 1996–97).[89] But the Chinese had learned through experience that humoring and then ignoring visiting representatives was more practical than feuding openly with them. Gingrich's remarks about Taiwan thus were largely discounted, and Jiang Zemin described the state of bilateral relations as "sunshine after the rain" following their meeting.[90]

The Patriarch Passes, the Successor Succeeds

As the Clinton administration struggled with scandal and domestic political opposition at the beginning of its second term, Jiang Zemin was facing his most serious challenge as leader of China. In mid-January, Chinese television began broadcasting a twelve-part prime-time series on the life of Deng Xiaoping. Three years in the making, it was openly hagiographic but was widely viewed as a way of preparing people for Deng's death. It was timed to remind them of the regime's loyal implementation of the patriarch's policies, but also that the succession was complete, the new leadership in place, and that Deng's passage into history would be smooth and stable.[91] And yet the regime could not bring itself to admit publicly that Deng was gravely ill. "There has been no major change" in Deng's health, spokesmen said on January 7 and repeated regularly, even in mid-February.

On February 19, 1997, just after 9:00 p.m., Deng Xiaoping died in a Beijing military hospital from "failure of the respiration circulating functions," complicated by Parkinson's disease and other ailments.[92] He was ninety-three years old. Xinhua editors held the news, awaiting final Central Committee approval of the text of the death announcement. Because Deng's illness had been so extended and the final crisis so lengthy, the leadership was well prepared, and the delay in announcing the death was relatively short. At about 2:00 the following morning, Xinhua released the news in a bulletin, followed by an official obituary, which took the form of a 4,000-word letter to the people of China from the Communist Party, National People's Congress, State Council, and Military Commission.[93] Newspapers ran the full story in their morning editions.

Reaction to the news was subdued—none of the emotional outbursts that had followed the death of Mao Zedong or Zhou Enlai, none of the anger that had attended the death of Hu Yaobang. Deng was respected, even revered in some quarters. He was credited with starting China down the path to economic reform and prosperity. But his involvement with Tiananmen had diminished the restrained affection people had for him, so there was little overt grief. And post-Tiananmen indifference to politics, as well as the relatively smooth operation of the Jiang leadership, had dampened concerns about instability or a power struggle after his death. Rumors of Deng's death earlier in the month had caused sharp fluctuations in the volatile stock markets in Hong Kong, Shanghai, and Shenzhen, but the Beijing government responded to his actual passing by encouraging institutional buying. So although the markets dropped nearly 10 percent in early trading, they steadied throughout the day on February 20. As it became clear that the Beijing authorities had full control of the situation, the markets returned to normal, although investors still worried about longer-term political stability, according to market analysts.[94]

Jiang had been making active preparations for Deng's death for at least several months. Security and military support were, of course, the key to his plans. Deng's lengthy illness and incapacitation had given Jiang a three-year period in which to use his powers as Central Military Commission chairman to build a support base within the PLA. During that period, not only did he have the advantage over his potential civilian rivals of being able to make military appointments with virtually no need to consult them, but Deng was in no condition to exert significant influence, either. With the full cooperation of Zhang Wannian, Jiang began replacing senior officials appointed by Deng with ones he hoped would be loyal to him. In late 1996, the Central Military Commission had approved a structural change in its composition, enlarging its Standing Committee and probably weakening the command authority of Deng loyalists Zhang Zhen and Liu Huaqing.[95] Jiang and Zhang had replaced the air force and navy commanders, the head of the Commission on Science and Technology for National Defense, and several senior military region officers in December 1996. In December and January, both the General Staff Department and the Beijing Garrison—responsible for security in the capital—carried out high-profile political campaigns stressing their loyalty to the Central Committee "with Jiang Zemin as the core."[96] Other military units followed suit.

On February 24, Jiang led the official party mourners who came to the Beijing hospital to pay their last respects to the man who had dominated their lives for most of the past twenty years. As TV cameras provided a view for all of China, a somber and controlled Jiang led the Politburo and other leaders in making the ritual three bows before Deng's bier, then he spoke briefly with Deng's weeping wife and children. Only Zhu Rongji, of all the official mourners, showed any real emotion, seeming almost overwhelmed with grief. Afterward, a long procession of official vehicles followed Deng's hearse to Babaoshan Cemetery, final resting place of all of China's leaders. Thousands lined the streets in silent respect. In accordance with his explicit wish, Deng's remains were cremated at Babaoshan, and his ashes were later scattered at sea.

On February 24, 1997, the day Deng's remains were cremated, the day before his memorial service, one foreign guest was welcomed to Beijing, although not invited to the memorial. Madeleine Albright, newly appointed American secretary of state, had been midway through a nine-country tour when Deng's death was announced. Although it would have been easy to ask her to postpone until a less sensitive time, Chinese leaders requested she proceed with her visit. Albright's approach to China probably created some concern in Beijing. Strongly committed to the U.S. human rights agenda, she had promised to "tell it like it is" about China's human rights practices. Her department had just issued its annual human rights report, which criticized China for "widespread and well-documented human rights abuses," including the suppression of virtually all dissent.[97] Albright not only made no attempt to follow up on the four-point human rights proposal Christopher had raised the previous November, but she warned bluntly that the United States would cosponsor a resolution at the UNHRC meeting in Geneva if China did not make further "concessions" to U.S. demands. Nonetheless, she was received with courtesy and something approaching warmth by Qian Qichen and Jiang. Even Li Peng "appeared to be going out of his way to be charming," according to American officials.[98] For her part, Albright balanced blunt criticism of China's human rights practices with assurances that President Clinton wanted to continue gradually improving relations, including scheduling a summit in the fall.

Deng had asked that there be no public funeral, but with his family's concurrence, a memorial service was held in the Great Hall of the People the following day. Ten thousand of the party faithful were there, not only to pay respects to Deng but also to hear what Jiang had to say about a future that suddenly seemed less secure, less optimistic. Unlike Hu Yaobang's funeral, there were no throngs in Tiananmen. The security apparatus had done its work well, and the square was closed off. A few brave souls who tried to unfurl banners or place flowers at the Martyrs' Monument were quickly hustled away by police. Jiang's performance was appraised highly by Chinese and foreign observers alike.[99] Dramatically wiping away tears of sorrow at various points, Jiang delivered a fifty-minute eulogy forcefully and graciously, carefully setting down the party's evaluation of Deng's contributions, clearly articulating the leadership's intention to stay the course on reform and opening to the outside. It was a reassuring and carefully balanced message, avoiding past controversies, breaking no new ground.[100] It also was an opportunity for Jiang to display his leadership qualities, and he took full advantage of it.

But no Chinese leader would depend on charisma to ensure his succession, and Jiang was well prepared for the follow-up. The party propaganda apparatus kicked into high gear immediately, with countless articles extolling Deng's virtues, and special emphasis on how loyally and correctly his line was being carried out by "the Central Committee with Comrade Jiang Zemin at the core." Deng had designated Jiang as the "core" (*hexin*) of the leadership in 1989, and the term "Central Committee with Jiang Zemin at the core" had become a mantra for the collective leadership under Jiang. Now it became a touchstone for party loyalty. In its February 25 editorial commemorating Deng's life, for example, the *People's Daily* used the term no fewer than nine times.[101]

The following day, the PLA led the way in declaring its loyalty to Jiang. All three general departments, other central military headquarters, the People's Armed Police, and all seven military region headquarters held special rallies "to turn grief into strength and to rally more closely around the party Central Committee and CMC with Comrade Jiang Zemin as the core" and to obey Deng's "important political instruction," which was "to safeguard the authority of the party Central Committee and CMC with Comrade Jiang Zemin as the core."[102] The high command made study of Jiang's eulogy for Deng mandatory for all units. And while some observers noted that CMC vice chairmen Liu Huaqing and Zhang Zhen did not join in the chorus of support for Jiang—their disaffection for Jiang having become well known—their backing was no longer essential, as Zhang Wannian had effectively taken over leadership of the Central Military Commission and day-to-day operation of the armed forces.[103] Jiang subsequently reinforced his authority over the PLA by urging passage of a National Defense Law that placed the PLA under the command of the Communist Party and by setting out new ideological and educational campaigns for the armed forces.

Jiang had another advantage in succeeding Deng, which was the absence of the elders who had usurped the leadership of the Politburo in the crisis of 1989. Deng had won the "longevity contest." Of the "eight immortals" who had ousted Zhao and installed Jiang, four had predeceased Deng, including Chen Yun, Li Xiannian, Deng Yingchao, and Wang Zhen. Peng Zhen was mortally ill and could not even attend Deng's funeral (he died two months later), and Yang Shangkun had been politically neutralized in 1992. Bo Yibo was not politically active, either. Zhao Ziyang was still in political disgrace; his request to attend Deng's funeral had been denied. Other senior party and military leaders may have been unhappy with Jiang but were in no position to do anything about it. There was, in effect, no higher authority to whom anyone in the leadership could turn to undo the succession arrangements Deng had put in place. And although he had remained alive, Deng had been so ill as to have been no hindrance to Jiang in his management of party and military affairs since 1994. In other words, even Deng could not undo his succession arrangements.

Jiang did not lack for opposition within the party, however, and even strong army support and the absence of elders did not make his position unassailable. There were rivals on the Politburo Standing Committee. Premier Li Peng remained a formidable figure. Politically savvy and expert at manipulating power relations within the State Council, Li could have mounted a serious challenge to Jiang had he chosen to do so. But Li would have had to construct a justifiable rationale for overturning Deng's succession arrangements and would have faced serious opposition. Li's biggest problem was what American political strategists would have called his "strong negatives." He was still reviled by many, both inside and outside of China, for his role in Tiananmen. Acerbic, sarcastic, and temperamental, Li had the kind of personality that inspired respect—perhaps tinged with fear and loathing—but not admiration. Li had some health problems, although he appeared to have recovered well from his 1993 heart attack. There were rumors that his wife and children had obtained lucrative corporate positions through Li's influence.[104] But Li was no threat to Jiang. The two had established an understanding, a division of labor within the leadership that ostensibly kept Li satisfied with being number two. But the two-term limit on the premiership meant that another job had to be found for Li after he stepped down from that position. This created something of a dilemma for Jiang.

Li Ruihuan was also a potential rival but not a worrisome one. Vaulted to the Politburo Standing Committee by Deng in 1989, Li was a successful party functionary who rose through the ranks in Tianjin Municipality. One of the few Communist Party leaders with a real proletarian background (carpenter), Li was tough and outspoken, popular and by Politburo standards, relatively young at sixty-three. He was not college educated, however, and had not distinguished himself as head of the propaganda and media affairs leadership group. Li owed nothing to Jiang, but Li was not in a position to challenge him.

A more troublesome challenge for Jiang came from Qiao Shi, Politburo Standing Committee member and chairman of the Standing Committee of the National Peoples' Congress (NPC), a position he had held since 1993. Born in Zhejiang in 1924, Qiao came up through the East China party apparatus like Jiang and eventually was assigned to the party's International Liaison Department (responsible for relations with communist parties in other countries) in the early 1960s. In 1982, he was elevated to the Politburo and secretariat and also was made a vice premier. Qiao headed the "political and legal affairs" small group during that time, responsible for intelligence, public security, and judicial affairs. A shadowy and diffident figure, Qiao was considered a part of the "reformist" group under Hu and Zhao, but not an enthusiastic one. During the lead-up to June 4, he took a carefully neutral stance between Zhao and Deng, abstaining on the critical May 17 Politburo Standing Committee vote on imposing martial law.[105] Some accounts suggest Deng even offered him the general secretary position, but he turned it down.[106]

As NPC chairman, Qiao—along with his ardently reformist deputy Tian Jiyun—took an activist role, promoting the "rule of law"—even legislation that limited the party's powers and prerogatives—and expanding democracy at the village level. The NPC meetings under his guidance became more colorful and contentious, with delegates increasingly taking more seriously their responsibilities of overseeing government operations and representing their constituencies. The NPC occasionally showed flashes of independence, as for example, when 36 percent of NPC deputies voted against or abstained on the appointment of Jiang Chunyun as vice premier in 1995. Qiao became an outspoken advocate of enhancing the NPC's powers. In a March 1997 interview with a French newspaper, Qiao set out a clear distinction between party and legislative roles, reminiscent of reforms pushed by Hu Yaobang and Zhao Ziyang. He said the party should be responsible for decisions on the country's orientation, major issues, and high-level personnel, but that all of these "have to go through the legislative process at the NPC or its standing committee before becoming the state's will." Qiao also suggested that the chairman of the Central Military Commission, who is elected by the NPC, is "responsible to the NPC and its standing committee."[107]

Exactly when Qiao's disaffection for Jiang began is unknown, but by the time of Deng's death, it was being widely reported in the Hong Kong and Western press, and Qiao did little to discourage the speculation that he and Jiang were not on good personal terms. Qiao reportedly had been "openly critical" of Jiang's policies toward Taiwan in the 1995–96 crisis.[108] After Deng's death, he was noticeably late in extolling the "leadership of the Central Committee with Jiang Zemin at the core."[109] Qiao was the only Politburo Standing Committee member absent from a major ideological speech Jiang gave at the party school on May 29. While these subtle indicators may seem insignificant from a Western perspective in which open political opposition is common and accepted, they constitute important signals of dissent in China's political context.

The Berger Approach

Sandy Berger was a man more interested in solving problems than defining them, a pragmatist rather than a theorist. A graduate of Harvard Law School, Berger had alternated between work as a trade lawyer at the Washington law firm of Hogan and Hartson, a staffer at the State Department's Office of Policy Planning, and political activist for Democratic presidential candidates. He first met Clinton when they both worked on George McGovern's campaign in 1972, and the two developed a close friendship.

While he deferred to Lake's greater experience and academic credentials in the first term, by 1997, Berger was ready for the top job. Unpretentious and unkempt, Berger was known as an honest, generous, jovial, and cooperative person, at least when things were going smoothly. But he also was single-minded and determined to be the dominant player on the second-term foreign policy team. He continued Lake's custom of meeting for lunch weekly with the other key members and was diligent in consulting with Albright and Cohen regularly. He continued also the practice of having regular Principals and Deputies committee meetings to hash out issues and was credited with running them efficiently. But he made it very clear that the NSC would be the focal point for the important foreign policy issues.

Berger's assumption of the duties of national security adviser was relatively smooth, as he had worked closely with Lake and had very close relations with the president. He retained many of Lake's senior staff or replaced them gradually so as to cause no break in continuity. Within weeks of taking the position, however, Berger had a major staff problem to resolve, part of the fallout from the campaign finance scandal. Press revelations that NSC staffers had had some contacts with DNC donors, that the vetting system for foreign visitors was not working effectively, and that staffers had received sensitive intelligence briefings they did not share with the NSC front office led Berger to make some very public adjustments. He named James Steinberg the sole channel of communication between the DNC and the NSC. He established in writing a requirement for seventy-two-hour advance notice for NSC vetting of foreign visitors to the White House, and the appropriate channel for such requests, which focused on another deputy, Brigadier General Donald Kerrick. He instructed staff not to accept briefings that could not be passed up to superiors and asked them to limit outside contacts to those that would be seen as useful to making or explaining policy. But he also insisted, in public and private, that in no case had NSC staffers done anything wrong or illegal in the publicized cases, and he refused to take any disciplinary action against them.[110]

As a problem solver, Berger had no shortage of foreign policy issues on his plate in 1997. Middle East peace talks took on new impetus at the beginning of the second term, and the expansion of NATO to include former Soviet satellite states was still a major problem between Washington and Moscow. While the Dayton accords had eased the situation in Bosnia, tensions were spiraling in Kosovo, and conflict with Serbia seemed inevitable. North Korea was mulling the joint U.S.–South Korea proposal for "four-party" talks on settling the conflict on the peninsula. International economic issues were picking up, and the new U.S. Trade Representative, Charlene Barshefsky, was eager to press Congress to give the administration "fast-track" authority for signing trade agreements.

Few issues were more important to Berger, however, than the U.S.-China relationship, and he was determined to make it work, despite the problems besetting it. In an important speech at the Council on Foreign Relations in June 1997, Berger outlined his thinking on the importance of U.S.-China relations and established several of the principal themes and phrases that would be used throughout the rest of the Clinton administration. He also showed a clear awareness of how difficult it would be to make China policy work. "The emergence of China as a great power that is stable, open and nonaggressive; that embraces political pluralism and international rules of conduct; that works with us to build a secure international order—the emergence of that kind of China profoundly is in America's interest," Berger told a supportive audience in New York City. "The decisions we make will influence China's evolution. To wield our influence effectively requires sustained domestic support for a revitalized relationship with China and a clear-eyed approach based on our national interests. I am concerned that support is fracturing—and convinced that rebuilding it is vital to America's future."[111]

Berger insisted that pursuing a course of engagement, of developing a strategic dialogue with China, was the right course for three reasons: China was at a crossroads, and a turn inward toward nationalism and xenophobia would have disastrous consequences for Asia and the United States; the complex and multifaceted U.S.-China relationship could not be defined or dominated by one issue; and the "one-China" policy had worked in securing Taiwan's survival and democratization and should not be abandoned. He concluded his lengthy review of the problems and promise of engagement with a plea to Congress not to disapprove the extension of MFN treatment for China, which, he claimed, would undo virtually everything the United States had been trying to accomplish in years of relations with Beijing.[112] The speech was a tour de force—comprehensive, concise, and well ordered. It was the kind of speech China specialists and foreign policy mavens had been hoping to hear during the first term, and they welcomed it now.

In Washington, however, it fell on deaf ears, lost in the cacophony of variant voices and political posturing around Donorgate and other China-related issues, especially most favored nation status. Berger's speech was nearly ignored by the press, but there were plenty of reports suggesting that the MFN renewal was in serious trouble. Speaker of the House Gingrich called for reducing the MFN renewal period to six months, so as to monitor more carefully China's behavior, an idea echoed by Majority Leader Dick Armey. Minority Leader Richard Gephardt bitterly denounced both China and MFN shortly after President Clinton announced he was planning to renew it in late May. Berger, however, mobilized the forces available to push for approval. Not only his congressional liaison staff but Berger himself used telephone calls and personal visits to the Hill to impress on reluctant, often hostile, members of Congress that MFN was essential to sustaining U.S.-China relations. The president also met with members of Congress to persuade them that MFN was the right course. On June 25, House members voted their constituents' economic interests, rather than more ideological or political concerns, approving MFN by a vote of 259-173. It was the closest margin since 1990 but still a solid victory.[113]

Donorgate (or "Asiagate" or "Chinagate"—all press-bestowed names harking back to the Watergate scandal that brought down Richard Nixon) continued to generate juicy headlines that distracted the administration's attention. Investigative journalists discovered that one of the PRC nationals Johnny Chung brought into the president's company at a California fundraiser was a woman named Liu Chaoying—a PLA colonel, executive in a Chinese aerospace firm, and daughter of Liu Huaqing, one of China's most influential military leaders.[114] Charlie Trie had fled to China, refusing to return to testify before congressional committees or face Justice Department charges. John Huang also refused to testify, pleading his Fifth Amendment rights to avoid self-incrimination. One of his fellow donors and associates, Ted Sioeng—a California publisher of Chinese-Indonesian descent—was alleged to be an "agent of the Chinese government," reported the *Los Angeles Times*.[115]

Bob Woodward of the *Washington Post* received another FBI tip, this one claiming that unnamed "top" Chinese officials (Jiang and Li Peng were the implied culprits) had approved the campaign to "buy influence with American politicians."[116] This "amazing" evidence was briefed to the Senate Select Committee on Intelligence, but not to the White House or State Department, again on orders of FBI Director Freeh, even though Chinese vice premier Qian was coming to Washington and expected to raise the issue. Berger's complaint about that situation brought Freeh to the White House for what was called a "highly general overview" that did not satisfy anyone.[117]

China: Donorgate Complaints and Complications

As the American investigations of Donorgate continued, and the charges of Chinese improprieties grew more serious, Beijing could no longer afford to play the issue at a low key. The media and public furor in the United States focused intense interest and suspicion on nearly every aspect of U.S.-China relations. Members of Congress were threatening legislation to revoke MFN because of Chinese interference in electoral politics, the growth of China's trade surplus with the United States was under congressional attack, and concerns were growing that the Hong Kong turnover would go awry. American and European Union trade officials noted China's growing reticence on issues connected with its bid to join the World Trade Organization, out of fear, they surmised, that Beijing was worried that Congress would overturn any agreements reached in retaliation for the campaign finance abuses.[118]

With the stakes now clearly higher, China began to make its case more earnestly. Qian Qichen told a National Committee on U.S.-China Relations luncheon in April that the entire issue had "nothing to do with China" and accused American journalists of trying to "tarnish China's image."[119] In May, Jiang began his own presummit publicity campaign with the U.S. public, granting a television interview to CNN's Andrea Koppel. While he attempted a more casual and avuncular demeanor, talking about his musical and literary tastes, Jiang still came across as very stiff and uncomfortable, frequently looking down at notes to deliver stock answers to questions. After the interview, his staff provided a written answer from Jiang to a question about the campaign contribution issue. "My government has never been in or supported any political contribution. Some people in the U.S. even claim that the top leadership of China had approved of making political contributions. This has no base in fact."[120] In an interview later in the month with a *Newsweek* magazine editor, Zhu Rongji was more categorical, particularly about the idea of funneling money through the Chinese embassy. "Of course, I think this is totally untrue . . . This matter has been played up so much due to the political needs of some people in the United States. It has nothing to do with China."[121]

Once Clinton certified MFN renewal and Congress approved, Beijing's concern with the issue seemed to ease. But its stubbornness and suspicion did not. Of all the issues that roiled bilateral relations in the post-Tiananmen period, this was one of the most difficult for Chinese leaders to fathom. While there was plenty of evidence to support Zhu's assertion that it was all just domestic U.S. politics, there are many peculiar aspects to the Chinese side of the story. And quite likely, some fire behind a lot of smoke. Unfortunately, much of the information about China's activities comes from U.S. intelligence reporting, unavailable to the public but leaked selectively by sources unknown and possibly used selectively by reporters with their own agendas. China's reflexively secretive and suspicious government refused to cooperate with reporters, the FBI, or congressional investigators, leaving itself open to the most sinister explanations for its behavior. For their part, they assumed the most invidious explanation for what was going on in the United States, charging the stories were "malicious fabrications" by "ill-intentioned, anti-China elements." "Why does the *New York Times* hate China? Because China is an emerging power. China pursues an independent foreign policy and refuses to dance to the tune called by the United States," the *China Daily* huffed.[122]

One of the most troubling cases, which was revealed in full only in 1999, again involved Johnny Chung. The case was highly damaging to both China and the Clinton White House but must be viewed with great skepticism and caution. Virtually all the information available comes from Chung's testimony, which he dribbled out over a three-year period, as federal charges against him accumulated. According to Chung's account, he met privately in a Hong Kong restaurant on August 11, 1996, with the head of the Military Intelligence Department (or Second Department) of the PLA General Staff, General Ji Shengde.[123] The Taiwan-born entrepreneur had gained considerable attention by traveling in China, flashing around pictures of himself with the president of the United States, the First Lady, and various prominent American politicians. He also was involved in a questionable relationship with an American consular officer at Embassy Beijing, through which he helped arrange visas for Chinese businessmen.

These facts alone probably would have brought him to the attention of Chinese intelligence officials. Believing him to be influential as well as successful, Liu Chaoying, the daughter of Liu Huaqing (and probably also connected to the Second Department), had established a business relationship with Chung in June 1996 and acted as an intermediary in the meeting with Ji.[124] Two days later, Ji promised to send $300,000 to Chung through Liu, telling him, "We really like your president. We would like to see him reelected. I will give you 300,000 U.S. dollars and you give it to the president and the Democrat Party."[125] Chung eventually gave only $35,000 of the money to the Democratic Party, using the rest for his own business purposes, as well as to support Ji's son, who was "studying" in the United States and working for Chung's company.[126]

Although most American media accounts of this peculiar story focus on the effort to subvert the American political process or gain special favor for China's satellite launch industry (Liu Chaoying's employer, China Aerospace Group, was the firm responsible for launching foreign satellites on Chinese rockets), two other factors are more important to understanding this bizarre case. First is that Chung apparently was being set up by the PLA Military Intelligence Department as an access agent, someone who had influence and willingness to "do good things for China," as Liu put it to Chung. These included sponsoring visas, arranging meetings and photo opportunities, helping set up front corporations, and other things. The money paid to Chung probably was not intended for any particular purpose other than to enable him to remain well-connected enough to continue providing access services.

But in this case, there is another underlying issue: the growing venality and corruption of the sons and daughters of China's elite political and military leadership. Ji Shengde was the son of Ji Pengfei, formerly China's foreign minister and a state councillor, while Liu Chaoying's father was one of China's most powerful PLA leaders. They and many of their contemporaries had eschewed the high-profile political careers of their parents to take up privileged positions in China's semiprivate trading corporations or in government agencies with broad access to foreign goods. Using their exalted pedigrees and associated political *guanxi* networks, these children of privilege—often referred to as the "Princes' Party" (*taizidang*)—enjoyed easy access to government resources or at least were perceived by Hong Kong and Western businesses as having such access. This enabled them to broker numerous business deals that brought them great wealth and even greater influence. The misdeeds of several senior party officials' children—including Zhao Ziyang's sons—had been a factor underlying student discontent in 1989, and although Jiang and other party leaders had tried to discourage corrupt practices, the problem had grown significantly worse by 1996.

Both Liu and Ji sought out Chung under the auspices of their official or business positions, but both then made use of his "services" for private purposes. They solicited business favors of value only to themselves or their family members and lavished money on him with little concern for operational security or for China's larger interests. When Chung's improprieties in donating foreign funds to the Democratic National Committee and abusing his White House access to obtain Chinese business favors came to light in 1996–97, Liu's and Ji's escapades did serious damage to China's larger interests, at least in terms of improving relations with the United States and improving its overall international image.

And yet the party's reluctance to punish the "princelings" was evident even in so egregious a case. Although she was somewhat tethered in her foreign travel and contacts in the wake of the Chung affair, Liu suffered no apparent ill effects from her involvement in the Chung scandal, no doubt owing to her still-influential father. Ji Shengde was "transferred" as head of the Second Department within little more than a month of Chung's testimony implicating him, then was placed under house arrest two months later in connection with a massive corruption scandal in Fujian Province that involved scores of officials and millions of dollars. His trial and sentencing were carried out only after his father had died in February 2000, and Jiang Zemin is said to have personally decided on Ji's fifteen-year prison term, an unusually harsh sentence for a senior official.[127]

Building toward a State Visit

Despite domestic problems on both sides, there was a clear understanding in both the White House and Zhongnanhai that further improvement in the bilateral relationship was possible and would pay political dividends. Like Mao and Deng before him, Jiang as party head was expected to play a key role in directing China's international strategy and foreign policy, and as he expanded his influence, he became more active in foreign affairs, gradually encroaching on Li Peng's powers as head of the Foreign Affairs Leading Small Group. Shortly after Deng's death, it appears that Jiang had taken over leadership of the group, although most observers believe Li gave the position up only after he left the premiership in 1998. Although Jiang was not eager to develop a new world view for China (Mao had developed the "three worlds" theory, and Deng had promoted the "multipolar world" perspective and the "one country, two systems" approach to Hong Kong and Taiwan), he did have evident aspirations to make his mark, according to Hong Kong observers like Willy Lam. In October 1996, at the close of the Sixth Plenum of the Fourteenth Central Committee, Jiang delivered a strong speech that equated socialism and patriotism and spoke of a "greater China" that included Hong Kong and Taiwan.[128] Aside from his well-known affection for symbol and ceremony, Jiang wanted some high-profile successes in foreign affairs to improve his leadership credentials in China. He focused on Sino-American relations and on Hong Kong's reversion to the PRC.

With Jiang's evident approval, Chinese diplomats began making preliminary gestures to follow up on the human rights "bargain" that Christopher had introduced, even though Christopher's successor had shown little interest in pursuing it. In March 1997, China reopened discussions, after a two-year hiatus, with the International Committee of the Red Cross on granting unrestricted access to Chinese prisons. The Red Cross officials were hopeful that the discussions by "experts" on the technical aspects of compliance with its prisoner visit protocols might begin in April.[129] After announcing in late February that it was "considering" signing two UN covenants on human rights, Jiang told the French defense minister on April 9 that China would sign the Covenant on Economic, Social, and Cultural Rights by the end of the year.[130] In the UNHRC conclave in Geneva the following week, China won a vote to take no action on the U.S.-EU resolution criticizing China's human rights record. Its margin of victory, 27-17, was the largest ever in its seven-year battle against UNHRC condemnation.

Observers noted during this period that the nationalism tinged with anti-Americanism that had been so strong the previous year began to be toned down somewhat. The *Say No* books were no longer in vogue, replaced by more objective, less emotional books, such as *China Doesn't Just Say No*, and the surprisingly insightful *Studying in America* (Zai Meiguo Liuxue), by Qian Ning, son of China's vice premier and foreign minister Qian Qichen. Even the PLA was on its best behavior. General John Shalikashvili, chairman of the Joint Chiefs of Staff, visited China in May, making the rounds of tedious formal discussions with China's top brass. But besides the usual lectures about Taiwan, he also had Jiang's sixteen-character maxim on developing better bilateral relations quoted to him in every meeting. (Increase mutual trust, reduce troubles, develop cooperation, and avoid confrontation.) His speech at the PLA's National Defense University, where he made a strong pitch for improving military contacts and decreasing mutual suspicions, was well received, although little progress was made in persuading China to be more transparent in sharing information about its military budget and deployments.

Frustrated at the intensive politicking over Donorgate, Sandy Berger decided to press ahead with the president's substantive agenda on China. He encouraged his Asia Directorate staff to continue working toward resolving the numerous problems that beset the relationship, improve communication and trust, and realize the exchange of successful state visits that had been agreed to in 1996. The NSC senior director Sandy Kristoff took on the principal responsibility for putting together a package of "deliverables"—visible progress in areas important to the president—for the Jiang visit to the United States, which had been tentatively set for the autumn. She worked closely with Jeffrey Bader, deputy assistant secretary of state for East Asian and Pacific affairs, who replaced me on the NSC in August, and Alan Romberg, deputy director of policy planning.[131] Her predominance was facilitated by the late appointment of Stanley Roth as assistant secretary of state for East Asia and the Pacific in August. Roth, an acknowledged Berger protégé who had served on the NSC during Clinton's first term, recognized that China policy inevitably had to be run out of the White House and preferred working on other Asian issues. He was also given a political appointee to replace Bader as deputy assistant secretary for China, Taiwan, and Hong Kong. Susan Shirk, a knowledgeable China scholar from the University of California–San Diego, worked well with the NSC-led China team after she became accustomed to Washington bureaucratic politics.[132]

Berger had developed the concept of issue "baskets" into which presummit work could be divided and developed. There were essentially nine of them: nonproliferation; military-to-military relations; the general "security dialogue" (for example, Korean Peninsula, Southwest Asia); economic and commercial interests (including China's bid to enter the World Trade Organization); energy and the environment; human rights; rule-of-law issues; law enforcement cooperation (against illegal alien smuggling, drugs, terrorism); and science and technology.[133] During the summer, the NSC organized or delegated interagency meetings in each of these areas to summarize the bilateral state-of-play and identify and prioritize U.S. goals and what steps the Chinese might be able to take toward achieving them. Some of the findings were discussed at Deputies and Principals committee meetings.

Hong Kong Worries

Berger, Albright, and the president were sufficiently concerned about Hong Kong's reversion to Chinese sovereignty that they held back on decisions about the Jiang visit until it was resolved. In some ways, the American and Chinese perception of the Hong Kong issue was a classic example of how far apart the two governments were in their views of each other and of international affairs.

The return of Hong Kong to Chinese sovereignty was a long-awaited event fraught with enormous symbolic significance for all sides, and Jiang was determined to make the most of it. Although the island of Victoria (Hong Kong) was ceded to Britain in perpetuity after the First Opium War (1839–42) and Kowloon after the Second Opium War (1856–60), the New Territories—comprising most of the colony's territory and virtually all of its arable land—were only leased under the terms of the Convention of 1898. The ninety-nine-year lease was to expire at midnight, June 30, 1997. The government of Prime Minister Margaret Thatcher had attempted in 1982 to persuade Beijing to renew the lease, citing Hong Kong's obvious economic value to the mainland. Deng Xiaoping refused and took advantage of the opportunity to undo peaceably one of the hated and humiliating "unequal treaties" that had weakened China in the nineteenth century.

After difficult negotiations on how the handover was to be accomplished, a Joint Declaration on the Question of Hong Kong was signed by China and the United Kingdom in December 1984. Under the terms of the declaration, the entire colony of Hong Kong (including Kowloon and Victoria) would revert to Chinese sovereignty on July 1, 1997, as a "Special Administrative Region" of the PRC. Under the rubric of Deng's "one country, two systems" approach, Hong Kong was to have "a high degree of autonomy" (except in foreign and defense affairs); its own administrative authority, judiciary, legislature, and police; and a guarantee that its economic and social systems would not be changed by the PRC for at least fifty years.[134]

Negotiating Hong Kong's "Basic Law," codifying the declaration's promises in a constitutional format, proved difficult and controversial. Especially after June 4, 1989—when hundreds of thousands of Hong Kong citizens had poured into the streets in massive demonstrations of support for the democracy activists and opposition to the Beijing government—British, Hong Kong, and American observers grew more attentive to preserving the legal and democratic rights of the citizens of the future Hong Kong Special Administrative Region (HKSAR). London sent Christopher Patten as the colony's last governor in 1992, and he wasted little time in trying to expand the democratic rights of Hong Kong citizens. Beijing cut ties with him in November 1992 and resisted his efforts to strengthen Hong Kong's legislature in advance of the handover. Legislative elections in 1995 were ignored by Beijing, which installed its own hand-picked "provisional legislature" to oversee the transition. The provisional legislature then "elected" Tung Chee Hwa, a pro-Beijing shipping tycoon, as the chief executive of the HKSAR to replace Patten after the reversion. The Clinton administration became actively involved in promoting Hong Kong democracy and virtually replaced the United Kingdom as the principal proponent of preserving Hong Kong's democratic rights.

For democracy activists in the United States, Hong Kong's reversion was cause for great concern. They believed the democratic rights of Hong Kong's citizens were being trampled, or at least squeezed by Beijing's hand-picked government of tycoons and yes men, and the United States had become their last guarantor. Hong Kong's freedom of the press and its rule of law were at risk of sudden extinction. As *New York Times* editorialists put it, "The fate of this prosperous and freewheeling society of six million people as it comes under the authority of one of the world's last hard-line Communist dictatorships is a compelling human drama. Mr. Clinton's ability to influence it constructively will be a measure of his international leadership."[135] As the largest investor in Hong Kong and with more than 40,000 American citizens residing in Hong Kong, the U.S. government had a responsibility and right to make its views known.

Despite the controversy, the Beijing government pressed ahead with its plans for reversion. As the handover approached, Jiang and others used the issue to stoke Chinese patriotism in support of its successful and peaceful reversal of China's past humiliation. A huge clock went up in Tiananmen Square, counting down the seconds until midnight, June 30. Editorials and commentaries hailed the coming event as a testimony to Deng's wisdom, as proof of China's emergence as a world power, and as a model for eventual reunification with Taiwan. Tension mounted as plans for the high-profile handover ceremony were worked out, and concerns rose about whether a PLA garrison force might have to take action against Hong Kong demonstrators.

As the June 30 turnover date came closer, worries and anxieties increased in Washington, as the media and Hong Kong advocates mused about what could go wrong. Secretary of State Albright had been designated as the U.S. representative to the handover ceremony, and a number of "what if" scenarios were discussed. What if the Chinese snubbed her? What if the PLA moved in early? What if there were violent protests by democracy activists? Berger was particularly concerned about the possibility of violent protest, having been persuaded by Hong Kong Democratic Party activist Martin Lee that members of his party would countenance no diminution of their rights to express their views.

In the circumstances, the United States had virtually no means to influence events in Hong Kong. The agreement between the United Kingdom and China was legal and properly arrived at, the sovereignty issue was unassailable, and even issues pertaining to the selection of the chief executive and the legislature, while discomfiting, were scarcely less "democratic" than they had been under most of British colonial rule, when Hong Kong Chinese enjoyed few democratic rights at all. There were no sanctions to be applied, and U.S. "moral influence" was negligible in the face of rectifying 150 years of colonialism. The U.S. response was therefore reduced to pledges that it would watch over Hong Kong's democratic rights from afar and over time and rather fruitless symbolic words and gestures of displeasure with some of the events of the handover.

Jiang led the delegation that traveled to Hong Kong on June 30 to observe the transfer of sovereignty. Accompanying him were Li Peng, Qian Qichen, Zhang Wannian, Deng Xiaoping's widow and daughter, and numerous other dignitaries. At a grand Beijing send-off ceremony on June 29, Jiang pledged the delegation would "reflect the sense of glory and pride of the Chinese people . . . for Hong Kong's return to the motherland, . . . and reflect our diplomatic style, which is neither servile nor bumptious."[136] Jiang's style in Hong Kong was stiff and formal, aloof and insensitive, as the British saw it.[137] He arrived late in the afternoon with his delegation, skipped the British banquet, attended the formal handover ceremony at midnight, and made a brief speech. "The return of Hong Kong to the motherland after going through a century of vicissitudes indicates that from now on, the Hong Kong compatriots have become true masters of this Chinese land," he intoned, as Prince Charles, Prime Minister Anthony Blair, Madeleine Albright, and hundreds of Hong Kong dignitaries and guests stood by somberly. The following morning, he attended another ceremony marking the establishment of the HKSAR government and gave a longer speech, reiterating in detail the promises of autonomy, preservation of Hong Kong's economy and way of life, and even, eventually, election of the chief executive and legislature by universal suffrage.[138] He then returned immediately to Beijing, having spent less than twenty-four hours in Hong Kong.

Celebrations in Beijing were much more exuberant, if no less carefully scripted. On June 29, more than 500,000 people traveled to Tiananmen Square spontaneously to see the lights, have family pictures taken, and celebrate Hong Kong's impending restoration to Chinese sovereignty. Police watched carefully, but the largest crowd in Tiananmen since June 4, 1989, was well behaved and patriotic. On June 30, they were kept away from the square as about 100,000 carefully chosen representatives sat in neat rows of chairs to watch the midnight handover ceremony. As the giant countdown clock approached zero, they spontaneously broke into applause and congratulation while fireworks boomed overhead. The following afternoon, Jiang joined a slightly smaller crowd in a municipal stadium to watch thousands of singers and dancers and PLA soldiers celebrate the occasion in grand style, complete with balloons, fireworks, and Hong Kong entertainers, turning the celebrations into "an empire-sized karaoke session" that showcased China's national anthem.[139]

For the record, the handover in Hong Kong went smoothly and peacefully. Martin Lee and members of his party demonstrated in defiance of Hong Kong's new laws and were ignored by the police. There was no violence of any sort, and life in Hong Kong returned quickly to its normal, apolitical pace. Hong Kong suffered economically during the Asian financial crisis that began in 1997, and there were a few cases when it seemed that Beijing was wielding undue influence, particularly in some court-related issues. But the new Hong Kong government largely resembled the old one in its efficiency, honesty, and integrity; the markets maintained much of their vitality; and the press was little changed in its strengths and weaknesses under nominal PRC sovereignty. Legislative elections were held on schedule the following year. From a practical perspective, the issue dropped quickly off the bilateral agenda of U.S.-China relations.

After Albright returned from Hong Kong, preparations for Jiang Zemin's visit to the United States began in earnest. Putting together state visits—particularly after a hiatus of twelve years—is an extraordinarily complex and time-consuming task. Besides overseeing work on the issue baskets, Bader and Kristoff met regularly with the deputy chief of mission and political counselor of the Chinese embassy to exchange views on the overall context and expectations for the visit and to coordinate planning. They requested issues papers from both the State Department and the CIA. They prepared the agendas for Deputies and Principals committee meetings on China and wrote up the conclusions or findings afterward. They maintained regular contact by secure telephone with the U.S. embassy in Beijing to ensure Ambassador James R. Sasser and his staff knew what plans were being made and what was being asked of the Chinese. They coordinated with other NSC offices and with White House domestic policy offices—such as the chief of staff, congressional liaison, protocols and communications—on various aspects of the planning for Jiang's visit.[140]

Berger—along with Kristoff, Bader, and Assistant Secretary Roth—traveled to Beijing in mid-August to continue his regular strategic dialogue with Liu Huaqiu. His more important mission, however, was to exchange views and harmonize expectations on the Jiang visit to Washington. In that capacity, he was given an unusual "perk," a visit to the leadership retreat at Beidaihe, where Jiang and others were in the midst of final preparations for the Fourteenth Party Congress, which was to be held before Jiang's trip. Berger spoke there with Qian and Li Peng, as well as Jiang, focusing on nonproliferation, regional security, and environmental cooperation as items of common interest to the United States and China that could be developed in the context of a summit meeting.

As was usual in efforts to get specific commitments from Beijing, negotiations for making deposits in Berger's issue baskets were lengthy and difficult, as the Chinese were interested mainly in more symbolic and less binding agreements. Various American and Chinese officials shuttled back and forth over the ensuing two months, trying to focus on nonproliferation, regional security, human rights, and trade issues on which progress could be announced at the summit. The Chinese balked, looking for issues on which they, too, had something to gain. Early on, they pursued the Taiwan issue, and there were some forays on putting together a "fourth communiqué" to further define U.S.-Taiwan-PRC relations. Meeting unanimous resistance from the U.S. side, however, they backed away. Instead, they pressed for a general statement that would describe the broader Sino-American relationship. In keeping with agreements reached with France and Russia, the Chinese pushed for establishing a "strategic partnership." Washington was not ready to go quite that far. Negotiations continued as the agreed date for the week-long trip—October 27–November 3—neared. Sandy Kristoff went to Beijing in late September. Liu Huaqiu came to the United States two weeks before the Jiang visit.

As another "deliverable" of the summit, both sides also had agreed to focus on reviving a 1985 agreement on cooperation in the peaceful use of nuclear energy, which had been suspended in light of evidence of China's exporting nuclear-related material to Iran and Pakistan. At the time, China was rapidly expanding its power industry and was interested in nuclear power plants designed by American companies. American nuclear power companies, such as ABB, Bechtel, and Westinghouse, were eager to sell and lobbied in favor of lifting the hold on implementation. But under U.S. law, the president could not license nuclear power plant technology sales to China unless he could certify it was not providing assistance to unsafeguarded nuclear programs in other countries.[141]

The State Department's Robert Einhorn and the NSC senior director for arms control and nonproliferation, Gary Samore, were instructed by the Principals Committee to push for a cessation of Chinese nuclear assistance to Iran (even though it was provided under auspices of the International Atomic Energy Agency and its safeguards), as well as a cutoff of cruise missile sales to Iran (which had been highly controversial in Congress) and new guarantees on Chinese export controls as the price for reinstituting the agreement. Intensive negotiations took place in Beijing and Washington, as well as New York. Qian agreed to cut off exports of China's C-801 and C-802 cruise missiles in September. China issued new regulations on nuclear exports in early September, then publicly announced on October 16 that it would join the Zangger Committee—an international group to monitor nuclear exports. But the agreement to cut off all cooperation with Iran was more troublesome for Beijing, and it did not want the agreement publicized. The night before Jiang's arrival, the Chinese negotiator, He Yafei, was still working with Samore and Einhorn on details of a confidential letter Qian Qichen would send to Madeleine Albright forgoing further nuclear cooperation with Iran. Qian signed the letter on October 28, permitting the announcement of an overall agreement during the summit.[142]

Asia senior director Sandra Kristoff also negotiated with Assistant Minister of Foreign Affairs Yang Jiechi far into the night before Jiang's arrival to work out the language to be used to describe the overall bilateral relationship. In her own words:

> We went back and forth on a variety of different words, and we ended up with "building toward a constructive strategic partnership." And the "building toward" was important to us, and . . . it was "strategic partnership" that was important to them . . . And at the last minute, Yang and I went over to get a cup of coffee, and I said, "You know, we're down to this, why don't you give me 'building towards,' and I'll give you 'constructive strategic partnership.'" It says the same, it is the answer to both of our needs. So we went back, and I sold it to Berger, and he [Yang] had sold it as well. We reconfirmed that at the time that they were getting ready for the White House . . . arrival ceremony, and that's how it came to be.[143]

For all the hard work that went into preparing for the summit, the "deliverables" were rather meager, and the White House took pains to lower expectations in advance of Jiang's arrival. There would be no progress announced on getting China into the World Trade Organization, largely because of Beijing's failure to address the issue forthrightly with the USTR. There were renewed concerns reported in Beijing—fueled by the financial crisis then sweeping the rest of Asia—about the economic costs of opening its markets. Human rights issues were also pushed hard during discussions by NSC and State Department officials, but China was not willing to be seen as giving in to the United States, particularly in advance of a major party congress. So although the Chinese signed the International Covenant on Economic, Social, and Cultural Rights just before Jiang's visit and implemented revisions in China's civil criminal code in September, eliminating the "counterrevolutionary" category of crime altogether, there was no inclination to give Beijing credit for any improvement. Beijing also hinted—tacitly—that Wei Jingsheng would be released after the visit, but the details had not been finalized, and public discussion would have doomed the initiative.[144]

The "Triumphs" of Jiang Zemin—Fifteenth Party Congress and the Washington Summit

While planning for his Washington visit proceeded, Jiang was far more actively involved in preparations for the Fifteenth Party Congress of the Chinese Communist Party. In September, reports in the Hong Kong press suggested the contention between Jiang and Qiao Shi was intensifying. Personnel issues were becoming more urgent, as they generally do in the lead-up to a major party conclave. With positions and policy influence as the principal goals, Jiang had to try and balance competing individuals and interests. He wanted to bring some of his former subordinates from Shanghai to Beijing to serve in influential positions but needed support from others to do so. Li Peng was required to step down as premier the following year, having served the constitutional limit of two terms, but he was not yet at the mandatory retirement age (seventy) and expected to retain his due rank and position in the leadership. Zhu Rongji expected to replace Li as premier but had already begun to accumulate detractors for his peremptory nature and proposals for drastic change. Li Ruihuan and Hu Jintao were looking for evidence that they were to continue advancing as successors. Qiao Shi, at seventy-two, was past the generally accepted retirement age of seventy but wanted to stay on as chairman of the NPC Standing Committee. General Liu Huaqing was also retiring for age reasons, but decisions had to be made about whether the PLA would continue to be represented in the Politburo Standing Committee and who the representative would be.

The Fifteenth Congress of the Communist Party of China was held September 12–18 at the Great Hall of the People. Ordinarily, the party congress is the media and propaganda show that approves decisions already worked out in smaller work conferences. This time, however, various sources suggest that Beidaihe and other preparatory meetings had not completely resolved the question of what roles various senior Politburo members would play.[145] Jiang had to resort to some "sleight of hand" to force Qiao Shi and Liu Huaqing to retire from the Politburo Standing Committee without bringing about his own resignation (Jiang had turned seventy-one in August).[146] Qiao was abruptly dropped from the Politburo Standing Committee, with no formal explanation, but was not otherwise disgraced, and attended the entire conclave. Jiang also had to deal with yet another Zhao Ziyang letter to delegates, this one apparently genuine, calling on the Central Committee to "reverse the verdict" on Tiananmen.[147] It was not acted upon, of course, but did get broad publicity.

Aside from these challenges, most observers saw the congress as going very much Jiang's way. In sharp contrast to earlier assessments that he was a weak leader, and predictions that he was unlikely to survive long after Deng's death, Jiang emerged stronger than ever, more firmly in charge of China's domestic and foreign policies, and the clear "first among equals" in the Politburo Standing Committee. His power was not unchecked—several observers noted the obvious compromises he had to make to get his way in personnel matters.[148] But Jiang was the dominant figure at the congress from start to finish. He was the only top leader whose positions were unchanged. His three-hour speech emphasizing the need for further economic reform and active resistance to corruption dominated the substantive discussion at the meeting. And if he was not able to bring all his Shanghai protégés and associates into leadership positions, they still constituted the most significant "bloc" on the Politburo. Two military men added to the Politburo were Jiang appointees, not someone else's. Moreover, the entire "technocratic" cast of the new Central Committee (72 percent were college educated, 56 percent had experience in science, engineering, management, or financial work) suited Jiang's technocratic background and interests very well.[149] More than half of its members were "elected" for the first time.

The new Politburo was slightly larger than the previous one, although the Standing Committee remained the same size. Two new members were promoted to replace Qiao Shi and Liu Huaqing: Li Lanqing, a foreign trade specialist considered close to both Jiang and Li Peng; and Wei Jianxing, chairman of the party's Discipline Inspection Commission who was associated with Qiao. Jiang's strong military backers, Zhang Wannian and Chi Haotian, were added to the Politburo, although not to the Standing Committee. Other additions to the Politburo included two provincial party secretaries and Wen Jiabao, a staunch reformer considered closest to Zhu Rongji. Jiang's right-hand man and head of his personal office, Zeng Qinghong, was added only as an alternate (nonvoting) Politburo member, along with Minister of

Foreign Trade and Economic Cooperation (and the Politburo's only female) Wu Yi.

Overall, the congress was considered a strong boost for economic reform, especially authorizing the transformation of state-owned enterprises into "joint stock" corporations. In 1997, the state-owned sector remained the largest drag on the otherwise booming Chinese economy, with estimates that more than 70 percent of the largest 13,000 enterprises were losing money and that debt among the smaller ones had reached disturbingly high levels.[150] Plans and proposals for changing the woefully inefficient system had preoccupied many of China's most prominent economists for years. But plans for restructuring the massive industrial sector—which employed nearly two-thirds of China's urban labor force—had usually foundered on the ideological objections of conservative party ideologues or on the fears of urban officials about unrest among laid-off or unemployed workers. Others raised concerns about the cost of replacing the many social services being provided to workers by the enterprises—which included health care, education, and social security.

But of political reform there was virtually no sign at the congress. There was some discussion of the need for broadening democracy in China as part of a plan to defuse social tensions in the process of reforming the industrial sector. Jiang used the term often in his speech but meant it mainly in terms of the conduct of inner-party affairs. He praised democratic experiments at the village level and suggested they could be expanded, but he provided no details. But he also made clear the regime would continue to use repressive means to deal with dissent. There would be no reversal of verdict on Tiananmen. There would be no tolerance for mass expression of political or religious sentiment. There would be no adoption of "Western-style" pluralistic democracy.

Neither was there any hint of change in China's approach to foreign affairs. The foreign policy section of Jiang's speech was familiar territory, full of well-known positions. It affirmed "peace and development" as "the main theme of the present era," then followed with a bare-bones exposition of the emergence of a "multipolar" world, which was threatened principally by "hegemonism and power politics" (read the United States). Jiang reiterated that China would not interfere in the internal affairs of other nations nor allow them to interfere in China's; that it would join no bloc or alliance; that it would not attempt to impose its social system on other countries.[151] All stock terminology, and no doubt reassuring to the delegates, but curiously detached from reality, static and unchanging, nearly identical to his address to the 1992 congress.

Jiang's second "triumph" came at the end of October, when he departed Beijing for his long-desired state visit to the United States. It had been twelve years since China's president Li Xiannian visited Ronald Reagan's Washington; twelve years since China had enjoyed the pomp and circumstance of a state visit to the most powerful capital in the world; twelve years since China had stood in the international spotlight on an equal level with the United States. It had been eight years since Tiananmen, eight years of being castigated, isolated, and ignored. The trip was infused with enormous symbolic significance, and all eyes were on Jiang. He knew it, and he was ready. He had prepared diligently for the trip, practiced his English, read position papers, rehearsed press conferences. He met with more American dignitaries, including at least two senators and two Cabinet secretaries. He gave careful interviews to the American press and showed his personal side and even some spontaneity.

Jiang's staff continued working—until just before his arrival in Washington—to put together the "deliverables" for his visit. The itinerary and protocol events provided amply for the photo opportunities and symbolic statements that Jiang and others in China found appealing. The agreement to "build toward a constructive strategic partnership"[152] for the twenty-first century, while devoid of substantive commitments on either side, was useful to Jiang in fending off criticism from conservative military officers and party ideologues that the United States was determined to undermine or contain China. It also put the relationship in a longer-term perspective, making it easier to deal with some of the issues without appearing to be knuckling under to U.S. demands. As it was, the substantive agreements were not onerous.

—Beijing agreed to provide a written guarantee (in the form of a confidential letter from Qian to Secretary Albright) that it would provide no further assistance to Iran's nuclear program in exchange for the Clinton administration certifying to Congress that China was not in violation of the Non-Proliferation Treaty, enabling the 1985 U.S.-China agreement on peaceful nuclear energy to be implemented (that is, nuclear power reactor technology to be sold).

—The two sides agreed to establish a "hot line" between the White House and Zhongnanhai, so they could contact each other in emergency situations. They also agreed to a broader range of bilateral discussions of important international issues, such as the growing financial crisis then beginning to roil Asian stock markets.

—On the most sensitive issue, human rights, China officially signed the International Covenant on Economic, Social, and Cultural Rights just before Jiang's trip. He had pledged in April to do so, but it was finally accomplished so quietly in New York by China's UN ambassador that it went virtually unnoticed in the U.S. press. Jiang also agreed to meet with a delegation of American clerics to discuss religious freedom when they visited China. After the visit, Beijing released its most noted dissident, Wei Jingsheng, on "medical parole" and put him on an airplane for what amounted to exile in the United States. Jiang's ability to take this step was afforded by the death of Deng Xiaoping, who had been the principal target of Wei's sarcastic criticism. It was a clear indicator that he still was interested in negotiating further on the "deal" raised the previous year. China also reestablished contact with U.S. businessman and human rights activist John Kamm after the visit and resumed providing information to him on "obscure" Chinese prisoners, a dialogue that had been suspended in 1995.[153]

—As it had often done in the past, Beijing also made a major purchase of U.S. goods as a gesture of goodwill and means of strengthening its support within the American business community. In this instance, the big winner was Seattle aircraft manufacturer Boeing Corporation, which received an order for fifty commercial aircraft, worth about $3 billion.[154]

Jiang left for the United States on October 26. His entourage was relatively small (only about eighty), but included the government's top talent on matters relating to the United States: Foreign Minister Qian Qichen, Vice Minister and Minister in charge of the State Council Foreign Affairs Office Liu Huaqiu, Vice Minister Li Zhaoxing, Assistant Minister Yang Jiechi, Ambassador Li Daoyu, and various staff members of his embassy and the American and Oceanian Affairs Department of the Ministry. Jiang also brought several members of his personal staff: Zeng Qinghong, Teng Wensheng, and security chief You Xigui. There was also a substantial press contingent, as publicity back home was the key element of the trip.

Jiang's first stop was Honolulu, where he met with local officials and Commander in Chief of U.S. Forces in the Pacific admiral Joseph Prueher. Jiang placed a wreath at the Pearl Harbor Memorial, reminding all of the World War II alliance between China and the United States against Japan. He went for an hour-long swim in the Pacific off Waikiki, a deliberate gesture probably intended to reassure Chinese viewers about his health and to put him in symbolic company with Mao Zedong and Deng Xiaoping. At key points in their careers, both Mao and Deng had been photographed swimming. Mao swam in the Yangtze River in 1966 at the beginning of the Cultural Revolution. Deng took to the waters off Beidaihe in the mid-1980s, mainly to reassure people he was still vigorous and ready for challenges, despite his age.[155]

Jiang then flew to colonial Williamsburg before proceeding to Washington on October 28, where he was welcomed by Vice President Gore at Andrews Air Force Base, then taken to Blair House—"America's Official Guest House"—across from the White House, where Secretary of State Albright greeted him. That evening, Clinton invited Jiang, his wife, and a couple other members of his delegation (Qian and Liu Huaqiu) for a private get-together in the White House. The nearly two-hour meeting consisted of a tour of the residence, refreshments, and unstructured conversation, including a "long and probing" discussion of human rights and Tibet. Staff observers around the two men later said the private meeting was another high point in their personal relationship, in that they were able to discuss difficult issues calmly and in detail, had developed cordiality and ease with each other, and had achieved more understanding of each other's personal qualities.[156] It probably diminished any misunderstandings that might have arisen about events the following day, when they would disagree publicly about human rights and democracy. But it also contributed to a deeper sense of mutual respect and even something approaching friendship. Jeff Bader summed up what he saw as Clinton's attitude toward Jiang:

> I believe [Clinton] had very sensible views, and a pretty good understanding of China. Contrary to what many think, he liked and respected Jiang. He thought he was a savvy politician, likely to consolidate his position, not the buffoon that some saw in him. He had a good appreciation of the magnitude of the challenges facing China, the historic processes at play there, the ways in which social and economic change were influencing the political dynamics. He cared deeply about human rights, but had realistic expectations about what was achievable. He had a genuine commitment to engagement, and believed . . . that pushing things in through China's Open Door rather than preaching to them was the best way of affecting their behavior. He was uncomfortable lecturing Chinese leaders, seeing it as pointless. He approached them with great respect for Chinese culture and history.[157]

The next day was devoted largely to ceremony, with some substance. Jiang received the full protocol treatment on his formal arrival at the White House, including the welcome on the South Lawn, honor guard review, twenty-one-gun salute, national anthem, and ceremonial speeches. The two sides held a ninety-minute bilateral meeting, at which the "building toward a cooperative strategic partnership" was fleshed out in somewhat more detail—the two sides would take a more positive approach to each other and look for new areas in which to develop cooperation and agreement. In that sense, it was more of an attitudinal change than any alteration in either side's strategic outlook or perspective.

Jiang then had lunch at the State Department, hosted by the vice president, after which the two sides prepared for a joint press conference. The conference was a new experience for Jiang, who was more accustomed to the mild-mannered domestic press corps in Beijing. It was an opportunity for him to loosen his image a bit, but more important, to be on the stage with the most powerful leader in the world, holding his own and standing as an equal. He may not have realized that Clinton was also under some domestic pressure to stand up for American values and demonstrate serious resolve on critical issues. In the circumstances, it was only a matter of time before sparks flew.

A question about Tiananmen was the catalyst. Jiang was asked whether Beijing had any "regrets" about Tiananmen. He gave a stock reply, saying the party had drawn the "correct conclusion on this political disturbance," namely, that social and political stability were required for reform to continue. Clinton stepped on Jiang's answer, saying that intolerance for dissent, as demonstrated by the crackdown at Tiananmen, had prevented China from developing at the same pace as the rest of the world. He said America's reaction to that intolerance was to protest vigorously in various ways, including continuing the "Tiananmen sanctions."[158] Jiang replied that he had heard the protesters that had dogged him noisily at every stop, and understood what they were doing, but hoped it would not affect bilateral relations. Clinton shot back that on human rights, the Chinese government "is on the wrong side of history."[159]

It was a striking display of combativeness, even though brief and conducted without visible rancor, and reminded observers of Richard Nixon's "kitchen debate" with Russia's Nikita Khrushchev nearly forty years earlier. Neither man gained much from the exchange. Clinton got little credit from generally hostile editorial writers and pundits, who criticized virtually every aspect of Jiang's visit. Jiang's performance was not aired in China, probably because of the media's timorousness about showing controversy. Chinese viewers, in fact, got little news of the pro-Tibet protesters that greeted Jiang at every appearance, the harsh editorials, or the warmth of the private meetings. They missed the pointed remarks contrasting American freedom with Chinese repression. They learned only with difficulty about any of the substantive agreements reached between the two presidents. Instead, they saw the pomp and ceremony, the lavish banquets and toasts, the photo opportunities at famous American landmarks. They heard the grandiose words about strategic partnership, cooperation, and improving relations. Jiang was satisfied with the symbolic measures of success. Substantive achievements were far less important. In that respect, the White House banquet on the evening of October 30 was no doubt the highlight of the trip. Among the 234 guests were present and past political leaders from both executive and legislative branches, chief executive officers of some of America's largest corporations, and celebrities from various fields.

The following day, it was back to hard work. Jiang started with a flinty morning meeting with U.S. congressional leaders, who bombarded him with pointed questions about every human rights issue from abortion to religious persecution to transplanting the organs of executed Chinese prisoners. "A number of senators and House members really put it to him," said Representative Howard L. Berman (D-Calif.). "To his credit, he did not get defensive, he did not storm out."[160] Jiang of course repeated what by this time had become standard Chinese denials of any involvement in the Donorgate scandal. It was, in a way, another dialogue of the deaf, with neither side interested in hearing what the other had to say or giving it much credence.

Jiang then left Washington for Philadelphia, New York, Boston, and Los Angeles before returning home. The only notable point in the rest of the journey was his admission, in response to another question about Tiananmen at Harvard University, that China's leaders "have some shortcomings and even make mistakes in our work."[161] Again, Jiang's brief flirtation with candor was not reported in the Chinese press.

In the end, the trip was a success, if a modest one, for Jiang and for the relationship. There is no way to know how his performance was rated inside Zhongnanhai. Jiang's peers had access to the full transcripts and film footage of his visit, not the edited versions parceled out to the masses by Xinhua. They were no doubt offended by some of what they saw, but probably approved Jiang's forbearance in the face of protests and his spirited response to Clinton. After the visit, many Western observers credited him with being resilient and tolerant in the face of sometimes rude treatment, personable and relatively open-minded, tough without being hostile or harsh. Americans in general still disliked the Chinese government and most of its policies, but toward Jiang, at least, there was a sense of geniality and even some esteem. Although still not a figure with the bearing of a Zhou Enlai or Mao Zedong, Jiang demonstrated that he could hold his own and command respect.[162] He had added a foreign "triumph" to his domestic one and now seemed to have consolidated his position of "first among equals" within the Chinese leadership.

Moreover, in the opinions of many Chinese observers, the relationship seemed to cross an important divide with Jiang's trip. The Foreign Ministry's spokesman, Tang Guoqiang, observed that the visit marked "the end of the twists and turns in Chinese-U.S. relations over the past few years."[163] Other Chinese commentary spoke in far larger terms, hailing Jiang's trip as "entering a new stage of development" or "starting an historic new chapter" in bilateral relations.[164] In important ways, Chinese observers read too much significance into the journey, especially in light of the fact that they considered the United States had moved the greater distance in improving the relationship. It was, in a sense, as if they believed the United States had finally come to its senses, ceased its attempts to contain China, given up its constant badgering on minor issues, and recognized that the Chinese position on Taiwan-related questions was correct. "As a result of exchanges between the two nations, the United States has enhanced her understanding of China. The growing mainstream view in the United States recognizes that China's policy of reform and opening up has been successful, that China will keep growing in strength and will play a positive role in world peace and development," Hong Kong's PRC-controlled *Ta Kung Pao* asserted.[165] Wishful thinking, at best.

CHAPTER EIGHT

Scandals and Summits, 1997–98

Before Jiang's visit, both houses of Congress had made use of just about every legislative means available to reverse or adjust the Clinton administration's China policy. It was not a comprehensive effort or a unified one—but piecemeal, disaggregated, bipartisan, and issue oriented. Neither party in Congress had developed a wide-ranging approach that it wished to offer as an alternative to the administration's comprehensive engagement. Individual members had taken the lead on some aspects of policy. For example, in the House of Representatives, Nancy Pelosi and Frank Wolf headed what was called a Working Group on China, a congressional caucus that highlighted China issues—mostly pertaining to human rights and religious freedom abuses in China. They drafted letters, circulated information, and developed legislation designed to keep China from achieving what they perceived to be its goals with the United States unless significant improvements in its human rights practices were accomplished first. Representative Gerald Solomon usually sponsored legislation disapproving extension of most favored nation status for China. Other members focused on China's WMD proliferation practices, especially its dealings in nuclear materials to Pakistan and Iran, and transfer of ballistic missile technology to Pakistan. Prompted by active lobbying, many members sponsored legislation commending Taiwan or urging the administration to take certain actions favorable to Taiwan.

Congress and China Policy

For the most part, members were concerned with highlighting the misdeeds, falsehoods, and shortcomings of the PRC regime, faulting the president's policies for not being able to change China's behavior patterns, preventing significant improvement in bilateral ties without certain conditions being met, and forcing the administration's attention on Taiwan or Tibet. As far as actions were concerned, there were several different types of bills:

—Some were hortatory, "sense of the House/Senate/Congress" bills that had no binding authority. For example, S. Con. Res. 57, introduced in October 1997, declared several principles of U.S. policy toward China (such as promoting freedom and democracy) and urged the president to communicate them to Jiang "in the strongest possible terms" on his visit.[1]

—Others were intended to address a particular aspect of U.S.-China relations through the allocation of funds or tasking of reports. For example, H.R. 2195, the "Slave Labor Products Bill," introduced in July 1997, mandated a $2 million additional allocation to the U.S. Customs Service for monitoring forced labor products shipped to the United States from China, required a report from the U.S. Commissioner of Customs on the use of forced labor in manufactured products exported to the United States, and declared the "sense of Congress" that the 1994 U.S.-China Memorandum of Understanding on the issue should be renegotiated.[2]

—Others required punitive sanctions or other actions to be taken to redress specific problems. For example, H.R. 2570, the Forced Abortion Condemnation Act, required the secretary of state to deny a visa to visit the United States to any PRC government official who "has been involved in the establishment or enforcement of population control policies resulting in a woman being forced to undergo an abortion against her free choice."[3]

—Among the most effective means of affecting administration policy was to put amendments, or "riders," on important bills authorizing the appropriations for foreign affairs bureaucracies, such as the State or Defense departments. In 1997, for example, the State Department Authorization Bill (H.R. 1253) contained a section requiring the appointment of an ambassadorial-rank "special envoy for Tibet" within the State Department, an action the Clinton administration strongly opposed. Although the bill was not passed (a fate shared by several State Department authorization bills during the Clinton administration), Secretary Madeleine Albright nonetheless compromised by appointing a "special coordinator for Tibetan issues" without ambassadorial rank on October 31, 1997.[4]

Congressional pressure also was exerted through special committee hearings on aspects of the campaign finance scandal. In the Senate, the Committee on Governmental Affairs began televised hearings on July 8, 1997. Committee chair Fred Thompson (R-Tenn.) began with a dramatic opening statement, in which he said the committee had uncovered evidence of "a plan hatched during the last election cycle by the Chinese Government and designed to pour illegal money into American political campaigns. The plan had a goal: to buy access and influence in furtherance of Chinese Government interests." He charged the Chinese government attempted—through "individuals enlisted to assist in the effort"—to influence the congressional elections of 1996. But his most controversial claim was that "our investigations suggest it [the Chinese plan] *affected the 1996 Presidential race* and state elections as well."[5] Some of the means the Chinese used were illegal, although others were not. Democrats on the committee, notably senators John Glenn (D-Ohio) and Joseph Lieberman (D-Conn.), immediately challenged Thompson's claims, indicating the evidence shown the committee suggested that the Chinese government had decided to step up its lobbying efforts, but that there was no evidence of "direct funneling" of money into political campaigns by the PRC government, still less that it had affected the outcome of the election.[6]

The Thompson committee hearings degenerated into partisan bickering and stretched out for months. Although the committee called many witnesses and publicized a great deal of data, some of it classified, little new information was developed to substantiate Thompson's charges, much less some of the wilder interpretations of the doings of John Huang, Charlie Trie, Johnny Chung, and others that became staples on the Internet and on ultraconservative talk shows. In a late July private meeting with George Tenet, director of the Central Intelligence Agency, and Louis Freeh, director of the FBI, Thompson and his committee asked them directly if there was any evidence of Chinese involvement in the presidential election. Tenet said there was not, while Freeh said there were some reports to that effect. But neither would or could provide the committee with definitive evidence to back up Thompson's charges.[7] And because Majority Leader Trent Lott had refused to allow Thompson to enlarge his committee's mandate to cover the larger issue of campaign finance reform, the hearings, while occasionally interesting, were irrelevant.

The final committee report, while suggesting it was understating its case to protect intelligence sources, flatly declared Maria Hsia, Ted Sioeng, and James and Mochtar Riady to be "associated in some way with the Government of China" (some of them with Chinese intelligence agencies) and their DNC donations to be part of a larger "China Plan" to affect the outcome of the 1996 elections.[8] Democratic senators on the committee issued their own report at the end of the process, concluding that the "nonpublic information presented to the Committee . . . did not support the conclusion that the funds [donated to the DNC] from a variety of Asian countries were connected to the Chinese Government" or that "the so-called China Plan, or its implementation, was directed at, or affected, the 1996 presidential election."[9]

The House Committee on Government Reform and Oversight, chaired by Representative Dan Burton (R-Ind.), also conducted extensive investigations into the Donorgate affair. Unlike the Thompson Committee, its mandate was not limited, and the investigations stretched on well into 1999. But like its Senate counterpart, the Burton Committee's hearings, investigations, findings, and final report were characterized by bitter partisan disputes and diametrically opposite conclusions about the same evidence. Burton publicly denounced the White House for withholding evidence, attacked "anonymous Democratic agents" for "sleazy allegations" about his campaign finance actions, and cited Attorney General Janet Reno for contempt of Congress when she refused to turn over internal Justice Department memos on its investigation of campaign finance issues. Ranking minority member Henry Waxman (D-Calif.) repeatedly criticized Burton's handling of the inquiry and demanded his resignation as committee chair.

The proceedings hit bottom in April 1998, when Burton told the editorial board of the *Indianapolis Star,* "If I could prove 10 percent of what I believe happened, he'd [Clinton] be gone. This guy's a scumbag. That's why I'm after him."[10] By the time the committee issued its report in November 1998, the interparty rancor had far surpassed in newsworthiness any revelations about Chinese efforts to use political donations to buy influence either with Congress or the Clinton White House. By that time also, the case against Clinton—and China—had taken new turns, and questions about campaign finance were left unresolved and unremembered in their wake.

Zhu Rongji and the 1998 National People's Congress

Jiang's victory at the Fifteenth Party Congress was also a victory for Zhu Rongji in terms of his ability to manage economic reform in China. Although Zhu's formal assumption of the title of premier would not take place until the March 1998 National People's Congress, it was already clear by the close of the party congress that Zhu would replace Li Peng at the top of the government hierarchy. The promotion would cap the remarkable rise of a remarkable individual. Born in Changsha, Hunan Province, in 1928, Zhu Rongji overcame adversity and family hardship to gain admittance to Beijing's prestigious Qinghua University in the late 1940s. Assigned by the Communist Party leadership to do statistical work in northeast China, Zhu soon fell afoul of China's tumultuous politics. Never one to hide his opinions, Zhu was suspended from the Communist Party in 1958 during one of Mao Zedong's extreme campaigns to eliminate "anti-party rightists" he believed had sapped the party of its revolutionary will (that is, had opposed his preposterous policies and claims during the Great Leap Forward). Rehabilitated in 1962, Zhu was suspended again during the Cultural Revolution and was sent down to the countryside to clean latrines, raise animals, and tend fields. Zhu was not really restored to the bureaucratic level he had achieved in 1957 until 1978, when his party membership finally was restored. Thereafter, he rose rapidly within the State Economic Commission, becoming vice minister in 1983. In 1987, he was assigned to Shanghai as deputy secretary of the Municipal Party Committee, and eventually as mayor, succeeding Jiang Zemin, who was promoted to first secretary and a member of the Politburo.[11]

The relationship between Zhu and Jiang Zemin has been the object of great speculation among Western and Chinese observers alike. Although they were associates for several years in Shanghai, the two men were not considered close. Neither should they be considered rivals, however. They are very different personalities with different leadership styles. But despite their differences, the two men appeared to have established a symbiotic relationship in which Jiang carried the political and symbolic weight of party leadership, as well as its dominant authority, while Zhu shouldered the responsibility for steering the bureaucracy toward workable solutions to China's many problems, particularly the economic ones. Zhu did not aspire to be general secretary, and Jiang understood that and backed Zhu's programs—cautiously—with his own authority. Both had different constituencies within the party, Jiang's among the military and conservative rank and file, Zhu's with reformers once loyal to Zhao Ziyang and economic modernizers. Jiang recognized the importance of maintaining China's economic success, and Zhu's record was exemplary as vice premier and head of the State Commission on Economics and Trade and briefly as director of the Bank of China. With the strong support Jiang won for bold economic reform at the Fifteenth Party Congress, the way was opened for Zhu to accelerate the pace of change.

Unlike Zhao Ziyang, however, Zhu was not interested in political reform; nor was he attentive to the radical economic theories of the 1980s. Zhu was pragmatic and hardheaded about what needed to be done to fix the problems that had developed in the Chinese economy as it made the transition from a chronically inefficient planned economy to a market-driven economic dynamo. Zhu's principal concerns were with maintaining macroeconomic stability—growth without high inflation, industrial efficiency in the state-owned enterprises (SOEs) without mass layoffs and bankruptcies, gradual restructuring of the banking system, controlled development of capital markets, and continued opening of China to foreign trade and investment without undermining important domestic industries. Since his appointment as vice premier in 1993, Zhu had overseen the efforts to reform—more or less simultaneously—the banking and financial system, the state-owned enterprise system, and the tax and revenue system, all of which were stuck in a vicious circle of debt and unprofitability.[12]

As the economies of East Asia plunged into financial crisis beginning in July 1997, Zhu was increasingly concerned not only about the relationships between China's economy and the other economies of East Asia but also that China's debt-ridden banking system bore a strong resemblance to those that had already fallen victim to financial market breakdown and currency crashes. As the financial crisis spread and deepened in late 1997, Zhu frequently consulted other world financial leaders (including the U.S. Treasury secretary and his deputy). Most of them implored him to resist the temptation to depreciate China's currency, the *renminbi*, in an effort to remain competitive with other Asian economies, like South Korea and Thailand, where currency values against the U.S. dollar had dropped precipitously. Zhu promised China would not do so and held to the pledge, easing concerns that Asian currency devaluations would spin down out of control and earning great praise among international banker and finance ministers.[13]

In the wake of the Asian financial crisis, Zhu made some adjustments in plans for restructuring the Chinese economy. Earlier, for example, he had looked on South Korean industrial conglomerates, the *chaebol*, as possible models for the restructuring of China's thousand or so larger SOEs.[14] Once it became apparent in the autumn of 1997 that the inefficiencies and corruption of the *chaebol* were in part responsible for South Korea's calamitous economic downturn, however, Zhu altered his proposals accordingly. "We must not repeat Seoul's errors," he reportedly told a banking conference in November 1997.[15] He did not drop the plan to restructure the SOEs by consolidating large enterprises and having them absorb smaller, less efficient companies. But he did raise the priority of banking reform and urged banks not to focus solely on lending to the large enterprises.

Despite concerns about the Asian financial crisis, however, Zhu stuck to plans to accelerate the pace of economic reform. At the National People's Congress session held in March 1998, Zhu laid out surprising plans for sweeping economic and structural reform, despite concerns that some of them might prove destabilizing. They included three-year plans to restructure the SOEs, reform China's banking and financial system, cut staff in government organs by one-half, commercialize the housing market in China, reform the medical service system, and complete the reform of the tax system. All these had been discussed in the past, but Zhu made what amounted to open promises to achieve results at an unprecedented press conference on March 19. In some areas, such as cutting staff in central ministries, he pledged substantial progress by the end of 1998.[16]

Needless to say, Zhu's reforms faced serious opposition in China. Conservative ideological forces questioned the propriety of some of his more forward-leaning proposals, especially housing reform, which touched on the sensitive subject of private property. Midlevel officials in industrial ministries resisted his plans to cut staff and reduce the authority of their bureaucracies. Provincial officials sought to evade his tax reforms, as it would reduce the percentage of monies available to finance their pet projects. Enterprise managers questioned the efficacy of reform proposals that would reduce central control of China's industrial sector. At the upper levels of the leadership, Zhu's rapid and drastic reform initiatives, aggressive promotion of hand-picked subordinates, and impatient work-style did not win him many friends. Li Peng doubtless was concerned that many of the senior positions lost to Zhu's bureaucratic "streamlining" (he reduced the number of state ministries and commissions from forty to twenty-nine) were held by Li's protégés.

Zhu was soon faced with a serious problem from an unexpected source, the People's Liberation Army. In 1998, the involvement of the PLA in China's economy was beginning to have a negative overall effect on the entire system. That point had come about gradually but inexorably. As early as 1975, Deng Xiaoping had advised military officials that the PLA's hopes for modernizing its antiquated weapons depended on priority development of other sectors of the Chinese economy and that the army needed to remain patient. Central government budgetary support for the military would remain limited, as China—in a generally peaceful security environment—focused on other areas of its comprehensive modernization. This created some unhappiness among PLA leaders, but they had little alternative but to go along.

Military units were encouraged to compensate by, for one thing, developing and running their own business enterprises to generate income.[17] This they did on a massive scale and at every level. From the earliest days of the People's Republic, PLA units had always been responsible for producing many of their own supplies, so military farms and factories were commonplace throughout China. In the 1980s, they began to expand their operations to produce goods and services for the civilian economy. Some got into foreign trade, making increasing amounts of armaments and military matériel for external buyers. Companies like Norinco, Xinshidai, and Polytechnologies were formed to market China's weaponry abroad, sometimes with little regard for foreign policy implications. Chinese arms dealers, for example, made large quantities of conventional weapons available to both sides of the Iran-Iraq War. Chinese-origin weapons, including automatic and semiautomatic rifles and pistols began showing up increasingly in the U.S. market in the 1990s, sometimes in "sport" versions. Even more troubling to the United

States and other countries seeking to control the spread of weapons of mass destruction were Chinese sales of missiles (for example, CSS-2 intermediate-range missiles sold to Saudi Arabia in 1986), advanced conventional weapons like antiship missiles, and even nuclear and chemical weapons components and technology. External protests over such activity led to central government regulations to control military exports, but these were not always effective or stringently enforced.[18]

Domestically, some PLA industries switched production lines and began making consumer goods for the civilian economy, for example, going from building tanks and trucks to civilian vehicles, washing machines, and other durable goods. Military telecommunications plants easily made the transition into production of consumer electronics, such as radios and mobile telephones. Regional PLA headquarters and central military organizations, such as the General Logistics Department (GLD), formed large conglomerates of military enterprises to produce and market a broad range of consumer goods on a national scale. The GLD's Sanjiu Corporation, for example, sold wines and spirits, tobacco, medicines, nonmilitary uniforms, leather goods, and camping equipment. As China's economy developed further, PLA enterprises got into the services sector, building and operating hotels, restaurants, bars, and even brothels. With large amounts of capital and critical *guanxi* networks to support them, military entrepreneurs expanded into China's nascent stock and financial services market in Shanghai and Shenzhen. One of the most prominent and notorious was J and A Securities, operated jointly by PLA and Ministry of State Security officials (the initials standing for *jun*—military—and *an*—security). By 1997, some observers estimated that "PLA, Inc." operated more than 15,000 enterprises, employing more than 600,000 people, with annual sales of more than $18 billion.[19]

Not surprisingly, some PLA enterprises and military units were engaged in activity that was patently illegal. The most critical was smuggling of various foreign-made goods across China's borders to avoid customs tariffs. As early as the mid-1980s, U.S. intelligence analysts were amused and amazed to see PLA facilities on Hainan Island covered with thousands of Japanese automobiles, which subsequently made their way onto the mainland through elaborate smuggling networks run or protected by military units. Other high-tariff foreign goods, such as cigarettes, alcohol, computers and electronics, and petroleum products also came into China—mostly through Guangdong and Fujian Provinces—without passing through customs and circulated throughout China by way of the PLA's vast and independent transportation network. Over the years, the problem grew worse despite central and local government efforts to curb it, to the point that upward of $10 billion in customs revenue was being lost annually to smuggling. There were even reports of armed encounters between Customs Department units and PLA navy vessels smuggling foreign goods into China, with heavy casualties.[20]

Added to the growing smuggling problem, fraudulent activity in China's financial markets by PLA-backed firms like J and A Securities finally brought about a full-scale crackdown by Zhu Rongji. Details vary, but the Shenzhen-based company, with sixty branch offices and more than 3,000 employees, had been under suspicion for some time owing to reports of unusual wealth and lavish life-styles of its founding members—formerly officers in the Guangzhou Military Region. Civilian investigators from the State Auditing Administration were obstructed by military officials in their inquiries, and some reportedly were even manhandled and detained. They discovered not only huge amounts of money in personal bank accounts of senior officials but also that the firm had lost enormous sums, almost $1 billion, speculating in falling Asian stock markets.[21] Zhu, angry not only at the scale of the corruption but at the presumed immunity of PLA malefactors, sought Jiang's support for a clean-up and got it.[22]

In mid-July 1998, the Central Committee held a work conference to declare a "nation-wide attack on smuggling." On July 22, Jiang presided over a meeting of the entire PLA high command to propagate the Resolution by the Central Committee of the Chinese Communist Party on the Interdiction of Further Commercial Activities by the Military, Armed Police, and Government Agencies. In a speech to the assembled officers, Jiang ordered that "companies operated by units under the military and armed police forces must earnestly conduct housecleaning, and shall without exception no longer engage in commercial activities, effective immediately. The Central Committee has in addition determined that political and legal departments at the local level must earnestly conduct cleanup of various companies run by units under their direction, who shall without exception be prohibited from further commercial activities, effective immediately."[23]

Publicly, of course, the PLA's leadership enthusiastically supported the divestiture of the army's business operations. Some senior military leaders—notably former CMC vice chairman Zhang Zhen—had been warning for years that business activities by PLA units not only reduced the army's concentration on national defense responsibilities and deflated its "fighting spirit" but also lowered its reputation within society. Periodic anticorruption campaigns had taken down some of the more egregiously corrupt military officials, but the problem was so widespread that these efforts looked more like scapegoating than any serious effort to resolve the problem.[24] And with accusations of financial improprieties by leaders at the top of the Central Military Commission (or their children), and the PLA still dependent at all levels on extrabudgetary funding of military modernization, it is difficult to give full credence to news reports that soon began to appear about military units quickly turning over business assets to provincial and municipal governments. Typically, the process was more complicated and opaque than the propaganda stories recounted. Two years later, there was still ample evidence that military business enterprises were operating at various levels, domestically and internationally. Moreover, the PLA evidently sought and received pledges from the central government that its financial losses would be compensated by increased budgetary resources. Hong Kong media reported that more than 10 billion yuan would come out of central coffers, while local and regional governments would foot more bills for the enterprises and for providing the social services to demobilized veterans that were once covered by the PLA's business profits.[25]

Whatever the financial outcome of the divestiture, the scandals had clearly damaged the PLA's reputation. Aware of the loss of public esteem, Jiang and other senior military leaders pressed military units into active and visible flood control work during August, when summer flooding was said to be the worst since 1954. Stories of bravery and heroism by the some of the more than 250,000 soldiers called up to fight the floods seemed somewhat forced but were evidently considered necessary to restore the army's tattered reputation. Given the widespread abuse of military authority that had occurred, the campaign to get the army out of business surprisingly was not accompanied by any effort to weed out corrupt elements. Although there were some rumors that CMC vice chairman Zhang Wannian might be made answerable for the PLA's problems, that did not happen, and other accounts suggest Zhang was instrumental in slowing down the divestiture process and in "saying no to Zhu,"[26] who was impatient to complete the process by the end of the year.

The PLA was not the only Chinese bureaucracy to resist efforts to reform it, however. Zhu's ambitious plans to restructure the Chinese economy, especially the state-owned enterprise system and China's massive economic planning and management ministries, ran into difficulties at every stage. Many of these problems were simply practical—giant bureaucracies resist rapid change in every country, and China's institutional inertia was a longstanding problem. Difficulties were exacerbated by poor communications and information exchange systems and traditional localism that had reemerged with the weakening of central political and economic controls. Moreover, the SOE structure was so deeply rooted in China's economy and society that even minor changes were difficult to implement. State-owned enterprises had been the main source of government revenue for many years, they were at the heart of the social welfare system—providing health care, retirement benefits, and even primary and secondary education services for employees—and they were the primary training grounds for the party's economic managers and cadres. Most important, SOEs provided employment for more than 100 million people, an estimated 65 percent of China's urban work force, in 1995.[27] Reforms that increased unemployment or reduced benefits had the potential to generate significant social unrest and were viewed with great distrust.

But the system was an enormous burden to the continued success of China's economic modernization. In his study of China's financial and economic reform, *China's Unfinished Economic Revolution*, Nicholas Lardy documents the multiple burdens imposed on China's economy by the massive mismanagement of the SOEs. Many were woefully inefficient, turning out substandard products that were not salable, contributing to a waste of resources and inputs, and piling up useless inventory. They were increasingly unprofitable, especially compared to the growing number of private and foreign-invested firms in China. By 1996, the entire state-owned enterprise sector was in the red, with enterprise losses more than offsetting the profits of those firms that produced efficiently.[28] They therefore required central support to continue operating. While formerly supported directly by central budget allocations, early economic reforms had forced the SOEs to turn to China's banking institutions in hopes that would improve their efficiency and accountability. But the inadequacies of China's bankruptcy laws and procedures, the political incestuousness of local banking authorities and enterprise managers, and fears of social instability led to loose standards for bank lending, with the result that they became an "insatiable" draw on bank credit.[29] Essentially, their inefficiencies were simply passed on to the banking structure, which was not able to foreclose on outstanding debt. By 1995, the percentage of nonperforming loans held by China's four principal banking institutions reached 22 percent; by the end of 1997, it was 27 percent.[30]

Although Zhu and others had begun to institute well-planned reforms to privatize state-owned enterprises and commercialize the banking system, the Asian financial crisis of 1997–98 dealt a serious setback to those plans and exposed some of the fundamental institutional weaknesses of the Chinese economy. It reduced foreign investment capital available to China and increased pressure on the Chinese currency. It also, however, made the urgency of reforms of the banking system and the SOEs clear. Despite some of the advantages of the Chinese economy that distinguished it from others in Asia, many Chinese economists saw the financial near-collapse of South Korea and Thailand as a clear warning of what was to come for China if reforms were not instituted. Zhu had also come to the conclusion that one of the means necessary to force Chinese enterprises to reform themselves was to expose them to foreign competition in a controlled fashion. One way of doing so, which had additional political benefits in enhancing China's international reputation, was to join the World Trade Organization (WTO).[31]

Beijing had been negotiating entry into the General Agreement on Tariffs and Trade (GATT), the predecessor organization of the WTO, since 1986, although it was not a high priority for the leadership. Aside from the international prestige involved and the opportunity to contribute to the formulation of international trade policy, there were few obvious economic advantages for China in reducing tariffs on foreign goods, opening up its markets, or agreeing to the many other trade regulation and dispute adjudication mechanisms of the GATT/WTO. After 1989, China had sought to join as a means of normalizing its trade and political relationship with the United States, in particular to enjoy the automatic most favored nation trade status that members must accord one another. But the process of joining meant complex negotiations of detailed bilateral trade agreements with key members of GATT and the WTO, and Beijing was not willing to undo the complex web of tariffs and nontariff mechanisms protecting its domestic industries and agriculture. So the negotiations stalled, especially with Washington, as trade bureaucracies in both countries avoided serious efforts to come to an agreement.

Clinton under Siege

On January 21, 1998, the *Washington Post* published a story about the expansion of an investigation of President Clinton by Independent Counsel Kenneth Starr to include allegations that Clinton encouraged a former White House intern—Monica Lewinsky—to lie about her sexual relationship with him to lawyers for Paula Corbin Jones, who was suing Clinton for sexual harassment. The story also indicated that Clinton had given false testimony to the same lawyers, denying under oath that he had had a sexual relationship with Lewinsky.[32] What followed was a political scandal of epic proportions. Hundreds of media reporters wrote or filmed thousands of stories of illicit sex, broken marriage vows, betrayed friendships, legal shenanigans, public lies and private anguish, political cover-ups, personal feuds, and political vendettas—all swirling around the president of the United States. As the story moved agonizingly toward its seemingly inevitable culmination in an impeachment trial in Congress, foreign and domestic observers wondered aloud and often what effect the scandal would have on American global leadership and foreign policy.

Clinton's personality and attitudes helped him maintain his focus. Those around him were consistently struck by his ability to rise above the "feeding frenzy" atmosphere that characterized the Lewinsky scandal and work effectively on specific, often complex, policy issues. "I'm doing the job the American people elected me to do" was a refrain he used often and clearly believed. The scandal and movement toward impeachment, of course, diminished his ability to work closely with Congress, hamstringing much of his domestic agenda.[33] Thus it was that a president who seemed not to be interested in foreign policy during his first term began to pay a lot more attention and invest a good deal more political capital on international issues in his second.

In foreign policy, there was at least a veneer of bipartisanship and respect for the powers of the president to conduct the nation's international business. Clinton was also aided by a loyal and supportive national security team determined to prevent the domestic scandal from affecting American national interests. High-priority problems, such as Bosnia, Northern Ireland, NATO enlargement, and Middle East Peace efforts, absorbed much of the administration's attention. But China policy had also moved up the ladder of Clinton's priorities in his second term, driven in no small part by the success of Jiang's visit, the allure of China's rapidly growing economy, and the challenge of bringing Chinese behavior more in line with international standards. From an operational perspective, the main business of the China policy team (dominated by the National Security Council) in 1998 was making preparations for a successful return visit to China by President Clinton.

The work had begun shortly after Jiang departed. The dominant issue for the United States was human rights, as that was the issue on which the president consistently received the most criticism from the press and Capitol Hill. Before and during Jiang's visit, the Chinese had signaled they were still interested in the deal to avoid a resolution on China's human rights practices at the UN Human Rights Commission, signing one of the two international covenants and agreeing tacitly to organize a forum of nongovernmental organizations to discuss human rights issues. The release of Wei Jingsheng had been hinted at, and once the Jiang visit was completed, negotiations to complete Wei's release into U.S. custody moved forward. The administration needed a clear statement from Wei that he would be leaving voluntarily (not forced into exile), while China's Foreign Ministry wanted a commitment that the U.S. government would not "use" Wei against the PRC.

Because Wei's release was not an end in itself, but part of a larger process involving more dissidents and more concessions, the White House played Beijing's November 16, 1997, freeing of its most famous dissident on "medical parole" in a restrained manner. It issued a short statement welcoming the action and announcing Wei's departure for the United States but otherwise made no comment. Sandy Berger and Albright welcomed the news on weekend talk shows but provided no details of the complex and extended negotiations that had brought it about. As a result of the low-key treatment of the issue, the release was portrayed in most press accounts as a Chinese initiative. Wei was treated briefly in a Detroit hospital, but he soon moved on to New York, where he became an active critic of the PRC government and the Clinton administration. Clinton met with him privately in the White House on December 8, which drew a protest from Beijing even though the meeting was handled very quietly. Wei lectured Clinton not to be deceived by the communist leaders of China. As part of the vague pledge not to "use" Wei and out of concern for other dissidents not yet released from the 1996 list presented to the Chinese by Anthony Lake, the NSC sought to constrain an interview Wei was to hold with Voice of America later that month, but because of its statutory independence from executive branch control, the effort was not successful. The story was subsequently leaked to the press and became another source of criticism of the White House efforts to engage the Chinese on human rights.[34]

Early in 1998, Kristoff and Bader began to press harder for the release of more dissidents from the list, particularly Tiananmen leader Wang Dan, and for the signing of the International Covenant on Civil and Political Rights. They urged Beijing that visible action might bring a decision not to sponsor a resolution at the UN Commission on Human Rights (UNHRC). Their Ministry of Foreign Affairs counterparts balked. So did the U.S. secretary of state, who agreed with the argument of some within her department that the Chinese had not done enough to deserve a break on the annual resolution, even though the department's annual human rights report on China had noted some "positive steps" in legal reform and treatment of dissidents ("somewhat more tolerant"). Albright and others were also concerned that there would be a price to pay among human rights groups in the United States by appearing to back away from the issue. Sandy Berger had this point reinforced in a meeting of major human rights leaders in the White House, when he was told bluntly that forgoing the UNHRC resolution would be "morally appalling."[35]

Deputy National Security Adviser James Steinberg, however, argued strongly that the president's return trip to China might suffer if the United States again sponsored a resolution and that the Chinese might take some meaningful steps if the resolution were dropped. Again, it was a question of sequencing—which side would take the risky move first. Sandra Kristoff was dispatched to Beijing to seek a meeting with Qian, where she addressed the issue directly. The president, she told him, had decided in principle not to pursue a resolution at the UNHRC. To sustain the decision against political opposition, he needed to feel confident that the Chinese would release Wang Dan from prison and sign the second international covenant on civil and political rights. "He should have confidence," Qian replied.[36]

On March 11, the White House announced that the president was moving up his trip to China from the tentatively scheduled November date to the last week in June.[37] Qian announced on March 12 that China would sign the International Covenant on Civil and Political Rights. On March 14, the administration announced that it would not sponsor a resolution at the UNHRC criticizing China's human rights record. Slightly more than one month later, Wang Dan was released from prison on "medical parole" and put on an airplane for the United States. The four-point deal begun in 1996 had basically come to fruition, although two of the dissidents from the Lake list were not released until later.

Domestically, however, the administration received no credit for Wang's release, the signing of the covenants, or the visit of three American clerics to China to investigate the state of religious tolerance there. Human rights groups were dismissive. "By this act of forced exile [Wang Dan's medical parole], the Chinese government continues to show its contempt for human rights," remarked William F. Schulz, the director of Amnesty International United States.[38] "While we certainly support efforts to use the [President's] visit to secure concrete human rights improvements," said Sidney Jones, Asia director for Human Rights Watch, "we would much prefer that Chinese authorities released political detainees out of a realization that their arrest had been unfair and unjustified in the first place."[39] Despite what had by this time become the habitual scorn of the human rights community for any measure pertaining to China other than concerted criticism or feckless sanctions, the Clinton administration showed extraordinary sensitivity to human rights issues as it prepared for the president's visit. That was largely because the trip was shaping up to be high in symbolic significance but low on substantive progress, and because Congress—still in high dudgeon about China—was monitoring every aspect of the planning.

In late April, Secretary Albright visited China as part of preparations for the president's trip and to meet with Tang Jiaxuan, who had been appointed foreign minister at the National People's Congress session in March.[40] In a press conference at the end of her visit, Albright responded to a question on Taiwan policy with a formulation that reiterated the reassurances contained in the president's 1995 letter to Jiang Zemin, and which constituted the first public statement of what became known as the "three noes." "I made a point to [the Chinese] and I can make to you, is that we have no change in our China policy. (*sic*) Although we have a one-China policy—not a 'two China,' not a 'one China and one Taiwan' policy—and we do not support Taiwan independence or their membership in international organizations that are based on statehood."[41]

Administration staffers—Gary Samore, Sandra Kristoff, and Jeffrey Bader from NSC, Robert Einhorn, Susan Shirk, and Alan Romberg from the State Department—traveled frequently to Beijing to prepare the substantive agenda for the trip, the issue "baskets," the "deliverables." With the president's reputation in free fall, Berger was anxious to avoid a trip that seemed nothing more than a symbolic junket with no achievements, and he pushed his staff hard. Samore wanted to use the trip to bring China into closer formal compliance with the Missile Technology Control Regime (MTCR), perhaps with an agreement to be signed during the trip. Experts on "greenhouse gases" traveled to China to put together cooperative agreements in environmental areas. But progress was slow. As the date for the visit approached, NSC staffers, in particular, found themselves also being pushed by the president's domestic advisers—particularly Chief of Staff John Podesta—to negotiate some of the "formalities" of the visit. Principal among these was an earnest desire *not* to have the president welcomed on Tiananmen Square.

The need to avoid having the president of the United States be seen as in any way endorsing the 1989 crackdown became an obsession in April and early May. It generated furious arguments between domestic and foreign policy staff in the White House and nearly derailed the entire trip. Secretary of State Albright raised the issue quietly in her late April trip to Beijing and tried to get the public used to the idea that the president would visit Tiananmen, but the press and Congress weighed in heavily against it. At least 150 members of Congress wrote letters to the president urging him not to go at all if he had to be greeted in the square. Several nonbinding resolutions were drafted (one passed the House, 305-116, on June 4) enjoining the president either to cancel the visit altogether or to "reconsider" the Tiananmen welcome. Editorial opinion was scathing: Jim Hoagland of the *Washington Post* said the decision proved the presidency had reached "new depths in its continuing moral decline."[42] Former presidential adviser George Stephanopoulos charged it would be "shameful to go to the square . . . where people fighting for democracy were killed, and celebrate it." The president responded that canceling the trip because of the welcoming ceremony would be a mistake, but dispatched Sandy Berger to Beijing in a last-ditch effort to explain the situation and find an alternative.[43]

Berger arrived in Beijing on June 1 to raise the issue with Foreign Minister Tang Jiaxuan, Qian Qichen, and Jiang himself. "I tried to get them, among other things, to drop the Tiananmen arrival ceremony," Berger recalled. "I was unsuccessful. And I came back, and Clinton decided to go . . . He felt we should take the long view here, suck it up, go, take the criticism and find other ways of making sure the trip reflected our continuing concern for human rights."[44] Berger did that by pressing the Chinese hard to give the president live nationwide TV coverage for a speech he planned to make at Beijing University, as well as live coverage for the press conference that would follow the bilateral meeting. Not surprisingly, the Chinese resisted. There were no precedents; they would have no control. Negotiations dragged on.

Negotiations continued as well for progress in the other "baskets," and Deputy National Security Adviser James Steinberg and Sandra Kristoff were sent to Beijing to wrap up the final details. As usual, they were excruciating. Although the Chinese were willing to express interest in the MTCR, there was no movement toward signing up. The president had decided that an agreement by the two sides not to target each other with strategic missiles was a worthwhile agreement, even though China had less than two dozen intercontinental ballistic missiles that could reach the United States. It became clear as the talks continued that the Chinese had only one "basket" of issues: Taiwan. And they pushed hard for something in their "basket" in several other negotiations. In exchange for open press coverage of the president's speeches, for example, they asked for a public statement of the "three noes."

Clinton had prepared assiduously for the trip, and his staff had done all the right "spin doctoring" before his departure. He had given another major China policy speech on June 11, met with prominent China scholars, who publicly reaffirmed the strategic and economic significance of the visit, and had Sandy Berger and other administration officials speak in advance about the "achievements" of the visit. They sought to divert the focus of the media from the disagreements that still plagued the relationship, the lack of progress in resolving bilateral disputes, and China's still woeful behavior on human rights matters. They stressed instead the long-term importance of establishing predictable and cooperative relations with what would be one of the world's most important countries in the twenty-first century. Isolating China, they insisted, was unworkable. Only clear-eyed and realistic engagement with a rapidly modernizing China was in America's real interest.[45]

The Clinton Visit and Presidential Images

The return visit of President Clinton to reciprocate Jiang Zemin's tour of the United States came at the first anniversary of the Asian financial crisis and in the early stages of Zhu's renewed drive to restructure China's economy. The nine-day (June 25–July 3) grand tour—which took the president and his family to historic Xi'an, Beijing, Shanghai, Guilin, and Hong Kong and was given intensive media coverage in China—was considered the next step toward establishing the "constructive strategic partnership" the two presidents had agreed on the previous year. All in all, there was little substantive content to the summit; its main significance lay in the realm of the symbolic, although some of the symbolic elements would turn out to have important political repercussions. But it was politically important for both men, in their domestic and foreign policy responsibilities.

Jiang's main purpose appeared to be to demonstrate that China had achieved global status as an equal of the United States and that he was responsible for attaining that status through his relationship with Clinton. Even before Clinton's arrival, Jiang's role was being highlighted. Film footage of his swimming at Waikiki Beach was finally aired, contrasting his taking on the "wide Pacific Ocean" with Deng's bathing in the coastal waters off Beidaihe and Mao's swim in the internal waters of the Yangtze River.[46] Jiang took certain risks in order that the visit be considered a success. Most of them were in the area of human rights, which he knew would be one of Clinton's principal concerns. He permitted Tiananmen leader Wang Dan to be freed into U.S. exile in April and agreed that China would sign the second of two human rights covenants, the International Covenant on Civil and Political Rights, in the autumn. He also had to deal with yet another Zhao Ziyang letter—again leaked to the Western press—calling for an official review of the June 4, 1989, events. "President Clinton's visit to China marks a turn for the better in Sino-U.S. relations," Zhao wrote on the eve of the president's arrival. "But the United States and the whole of the West have again and again raised the issue of June 4 and the issue of human rights in China. Rather than let it become an obstacle to international relations, it would be better to resolve the issue of June 4 ourselves, voluntarily."[47] Needless to say, there was no official response to Zhao's entreaty, demonstrating again that the issue remained sensitive.

From the White House perspective, Clinton's nine-day trip to China was a public relations success, and to some degree, at least, a political one. Opinions of the trip, of course, varied widely before departure. Clinton had become one of the most controversial presidents in American history, and the scandal surrounding his personal behavior was growing. On top of that, the China policy issue had become very divisive on partisan and substantive grounds. The political forces opposed to the president's trip hit a crescendo the week before he left, and he was attacked from both left and right for everything from callous disregard for human rights to "appeasement" and "kowtowing" to Beijing over strategic issues, such as Taiwan's security. He was even charged with strategic miscalculation for avoiding stopovers in Japan and Korea en route to China. Letters of advice and protest flooded in from members of Congress.

Clinton, nonetheless, persisted on a trip designed to highlight for the Chinese the importance of human rights and freedom of expression as core American values. For the American public, he wanted to showcase the positive changes that had taken place in China—economic and political—and reinforce the importance of establishing a "partnership" with an enormous, complex, and rapidly growing power. The visit was a logistical extravaganza, involving hundreds of American support personnel, security, and staffers. Six cabinet members accompanied him, along with six members of Congress, nearly 50 senior staffers, and over 300 reporters. The presidential motorcade in Beijing consisted of sixty vehicles. Air Force One and its twin, as well as several other U.S. Air Force planes transported the delegation, the president's armored limousine, and tons of communications, transportation, and security equipment to several different Chinese airports.[48]

The "deliverables" of the summit were announced in advance, and they were numerous, reflecting the many "issue baskets" that Berger had developed. The United States and China agreed not to target each other with strategic missiles, and China agreed to give further consideration to joining the MTCR. The two sides endorsed the goals of the UN-sponsored Biological Weapons Convention, and China agreed to improving the process of verifying end users for American high-technology exports. The two countries approved a military-to-military consultative process designed to avoid "incidents" at sea—such as the *Kitty Hawk* incident of 1994—and to study cooperation in humanitarian and disaster relief operations. Although no progress had been made on China's application to join the WTO, a series of economic and trade negotiations were established, as well as consultative mechanisms on environmental issues, science and technology, law enforcement, education, and legal reform. Finally, the two sides agreed to a joint statement of mutual concern about tensions between India and Pakistan over nuclear testing.[49]

In response to U.S. demands, Jiang evidently forged a consensus—just before Clinton's arrival—within the Politburo Standing Committee that Clinton would have greater access than any previous American visitor to speak directly to the Chinese people through China's media. The first occasion was at a joint press conference held in the Great Hall of the People on June 27, after the two sides had held their first formal meeting. Chinese Central Television broadcast the event live, although the fact that it had not been announced in advance probably limited the audience somewhat.

As it had during their press conference in Washington the year before, human rights dominated the discussion, and both men seemed eager to score some public points. Clinton, who had braved enormous domestic opposition and endured a formal welcoming ceremony, complete with a review of PLA troops, in (or to be fair, near) Tiananmen Square, took pains to point out that the United States and China remained in fundamental disagreement about what had happened there in 1989. "I believe, and the American people believe, that the use of force and the tragic loss of lives was wrong. I believe, and the American people believe, that freedoms of speech, association, and religion are recognized by the UN Charter as the rights of people everywhere, and should be protected by their governments." He then pledged that "whatever our disagreements over past action, China and the United States must go forward on the right side of history for the future sake of the world" and to build a "partnership and honest friendship."[50] Jiang reiterated that the Chinese government had drawn the correct "historical conclusion" to Tiananmen and that China's current prosperity and stability could not have been achieved without the "resolute measures" taken in 1989. Clinton countered with a prediction that China would have to grant more freedoms to its people in the twenty-first century.

For his part, Jiang took the initiative to dismiss as "absurd and ridiculous" press stories about Chinese contributions to American political campaigns and to defend comprehensively China's policies toward Tibet. He set out the standard conditions for the Dalai Lama to meet in order to engage in a dialogue with Beijing, adding that he had to make a commitment that Tibet is an "inalienable" part of China and "recognize Taiwan as a province of China."[51] Clinton rejoined that the Dalai Lama was a spiritual leader and China's dialogue with him should reflect its tolerance of religious belief and practice. As in 1997, the two men disagreed firmly but decorously with each other, and both reaped political benefits with their home audiences. The American media credited Clinton with standing up for human rights, while Chinese observers—at least those willing to speak to foreign reporters—indicated Jiang had done well in articulating China's views and interests. But most of all, the Chinese were fascinated with the exchange of views on live television. They had never seen this kind of candor and open debate on television before. No one had provided an alternative interpretation of June 4, 1989, before.

Clinton then took his American message to Beijing University, where he spoke at length about the need for individual freedom and the free flow of information as China continued its modernization. Again, his speech was broadcast live, as was a tough question-and-answer session afterward, and although there were some difficulties with simultaneous translation, it was vivid political theater, with Clinton in the starring role. The *New York Times* said it was "a politician's dream. In two dramatic appearances, he talked directly to millions of people without those pesky reporters and producers getting into the act. . . . Reporters declared this trip a political success beyond the White House press office's wildest dreams."[52]

In Shanghai, Clinton was similarly accessible, making an appearance on a popular call-in radio program and several other well-publicized events. The bill for the relatively unhindered access to Chinese viewers and listeners came due on June 29, when Clinton reiterated American policy on Taiwan in an unusually forthright manner. In a meeting with Shanghai community leaders—broadcast live—Clinton responded to a comment from Fudan University professor Wu Xinbo that he had made a positive contribution to U.S.-China relations by talking about American policy toward Taiwan. "I had a chance [in meetings with President Jiang] to reiterate our Taiwan policy, which is that we don't support independence for Taiwan or two Chinas or one Taiwan, one China. And we don't believe that Taiwan should be in membership [*sic*] in any organization for which statehood is a requirement."[53] The statement was the most lasting remark of the entire trip and nullified much of the approbation his public speeches in Beijing had earned.

Administration spokespersons insisted that the statement did not represent a change in American policy. "It's merely a reiteration of longstanding U.S. policy that had previously been reiterated by the Secretary of State and by the National Security Advisor," said Mike McCurry to persistent journalists on June 30.[54] That was true. State Department spokesman Jamie Rubin had first used the formulation after the Jiang visit to Washington, Secretary Albright had said it in a press conference during her April visit to Beijing, and Sandy Berger had repeated the "three noes" policy during his visit in May. But the issue was highly sensitive to both Taipei and Beijing, as it presented a clear American position on critical questions of "Taiwan independence," the creation of two separate nation-states, and the entry of Taiwan into international organizations. Taipei had lobbied the Clinton administration and Congress hard to ensure the policy was not enshrined in a joint U.S.-PRC communiqué or official statement. Beijing had insisted, however, that a policy commitment made repeatedly in private should be made public. And although it was presented in a low-key manner far from Beijing, PRC media picked it up immediately. Taipei at first dismissed the statement, but after some consideration and consultation with the U.S. Congress, decided to decry it more openly.[55] Beijing made use of what it began publicly acclaiming as "the three noes" in propaganda directed at Taiwan, but Jiang also made use of the commitment as evidence that his approach to the United States could pay useful benefits. How much influence that had on other, more skeptical, voices in the leadership is not known.

In fact, however, the "three noes" of 1997–98 did represent a change in one aspect of U.S. policy toward Taiwan—support for its membership in international organizations. In the original formulation of the "three noes," Clinton's letter to Jiang in July 1995, he indicated the United States did not support Taiwan's efforts to gain admission to the United Nations (as it was then trying to do), making no reference to other international organizations. In the 1994 Taiwan policy review, the United States had pledged it *would* try to help Taiwan gain membership in international organizations that did not require statehood for membership. That was prompted by a hope that Taiwan could be brought into such organizations as the International Monetary Fund and the World Bank. Now the president was saying, in effect, that the United States would *not* support efforts by Taiwan to gain access to any international organizations whose membership was composed exclusively of sovereign states. It is perhaps an overly fine shade of difference, but fine points of rhetoric have often caused problems in U.S.-China-Taiwan relations in the past and did so again on this occasion.

Within a week of his return from China, Clinton was under heavy attack in Congress and the media for his Taiwan statements. Senator John Ashcroft (R-Mo.) accused the president of "stabbing a friend in the back," while Senator Frank Murkowski (R-Ala.) claimed the statement would "destabilize" Taiwan.[56] Senate Majority Leader Trent Lott called the statement a "grave mistake" and promised congressional investigation to clarify what Clinton meant and "repair the damage" he had done to Taiwan.[57] Leaders from both parties hastily prepared a resolution (S. Con. Res. 107) reaffirming the Taiwan Relations Act, particularly those clauses that stated American expectations that Taiwan's future would be determined by "peaceful means" and that maintained the right to sell arms to Taiwan. The resolution also enjoined the president to seek a public renunciation by Beijing of the use or threat of force.[58] It passed the Senate on July 10 by a vote of 92-0, with the House version passing ten days later by 390-1.

While Clinton was in Shanghai, Jiang made an unusual trip to Hong Kong to celebrate the first anniversary of the handover and to officiate at the opening of Hong Kong's spectacular new airport in Chek Lap Kok on Lantao Island. While there, he engaged in some of his own version of American-style politicking, stopping in a shopping mall to mingle with Hong Kong citizens and visiting the PLA garrison to praise the troops. Jiang had little chance of matching Clinton's easygoing style of communication, of course, but he did unbend somewhat, and Chinese audiences seemed to give him credit for it. Clinton praised Jiang at a press conference in Hong Kong on July 4: "I have a very high regard for his abilities . . . He's a man of extraordinary intellect, very high energy, a lot of vigor . . . He has vision. He can visualize. He can imagine a future that is different from the present."[59] High praise indeed, and Jiang no doubt appreciated it.

Jiang almost seemed to prove Clinton right in his foreign policy actions after the summit. With support from Zeng Qinghong—Jiang's protégé and head of his personal staff office—whom Jiang reportedly promoted to the Taiwan Affairs Leading Small Group in September, he proposed resuming unofficial talks with Taiwan, which had been broken off in 1995 after Lee Teng-hui's visit to the United States.[60] Uneasy about U.S. support in the wake of Clinton's "three noes," Taiwanese authorities agreed to take up discussions at a low level between Taiwan's Straits Exchange Foundation (SEF) and the mainland's Association for Relations across the Taiwan Strait (ARATS). Those talks culminated in a mid-October visit to Shanghai and Beijing by Koo Chen-fu, the wealthy Taipei businessman who headed SEF. Koo and his delegation met with their counterparts, including Jiang's mentor Wang Daohan, head of ARATS, and agreed to a four-point plan for gradually improving cross-Strait relations. Discussions then moved to Beijing, where Jiang played a major role in the discussions, extending his October 18 meeting with Koo and treating him to the full-scale charm offensive, including poetry and philosophical perorations. And although the two sides remained far apart on substantive issues, the agreement in principle that Wang Daohan would visit Taiwan the following year was considered a great step forward.

Jiang tried to capitalize on his foreign policy success after the APEC leaders meeting in November, traveling first to Russia to meet with an ailing Boris Yeltsin in a Moscow hospital, then to Japan for what he hoped would be an important symbolic visit. In both cases, he sought to repeat the formula that had worked with the American president—formal establishment of a "partnership" and agreement to isolate Taiwan. But even though Russia agreed in a communiqué to the same formulation Clinton had used in the "three noes" and reaffirmed the "strategic cooperative partnership" established in 1996, the meetings were generally lackluster.[61] The session with Yeltsin lasted only half an hour, and the Russian president appeared weak and dazed in the brief television coverage of the event.

Jiang then went to Japan, where he suffered a sharp setback in his efforts to present himself as a successful world statesman. Paying the first postwar visit to Japan by a Chinese head of state, Jiang had pressed his new foreign minister, Tang Jiaxuan, to obtain two "deliverables" for his meetings with Japanese government leaders: a formal written apology for Japan's occupation of parts of China during World War II, similar to that provided to South Korean president Kim Dae Jung in October; and a Japanese government concurrence with the "three noes." Prime Minister Keizo Obuchi, under pressure from conservative elements within his own party, refused to provide either item. Whereas the Japanese government had expressed "deep remorse" and a "heartfelt apology" to Kim for Japan's wartime occupation of Korea in a formal communiqué, the joint statement that followed Jiang's summit meetings in Tokyo fell well short of China's expectations: "The Japanese side

. . . keenly felt the responsibility for bringing serious disaster and damage to the Chinese people in its aggression to China in the past, and expressed deep retrospection for this."[62] No acknowledgement of "wartime atrocities," no apology. Obuchi expressed orally Japan's "remorse and apology" for its "unfortunate relationship" with China in the past but would not commit the words to paper, possibly out of concern it might generate endless legal claims by Chinese citizens. Jiang, angered, refused to sign the joint statement, then proceeded to lecture Japanese audiences sternly for the rest of his five-day trip on the importance of history, complete with anecdotes of his own student experiences at the hands of Japanese invaders. Having invested much in his ability to manage China's foreign relationships, Jiang's embarrassing trip to Japan did little good for the relationship or his reputation back home.

Missiles, Spies, and Donations—Again

At the same time as the Taiwan issue was taking on renewed significance, the stakes had risen to a very high level in congressional investigations of an older scandal and added disturbing national security allegations to the list of charges against the Clinton administration. To understand the significance of the new, more powerful Donorgate, it is necessary to take a closer look at the issue of satellite launches—American telecommunications satellites being launched on Chinese carrier rockets. Although the post-Tiananmen sanctions on exports of items from the Munitions List had prohibited the use of Chinese launch services, the president was afforded a waiver authority to permit American producers of telecommunications and weather satellites to contract with the China Great Wall Industry Corporation to place their satellites on Chinese launchers, which were far less expensive than American launch services. President George H. W. Bush had used the waiver twice after Tiananmen, and President Clinton used it nine times to permit American satellites to be placed aboard China's Long March rockets for placement in orbit.

The problem was that Chinese carrier rockets were not as reliable as American or European launchers. Three of these satellites—two manufactured by the Hughes Electronic Corporation launched in 1992 and 1995, and one made by Loral Space Systems launched in 1996—were destroyed when the Chinese rockets exploded shortly after launch. China blamed Hughes for the first two crashes, and although it admitted a Long March malfunction may have caused the failure of the 1996 Loral satellite launch, American insurance providers demanded an independent investigation.[63]

An independent review commission was established, composed of engineers from several American aerospace firms, and headed by a Chinese American scientist from Loral. In a report of more than 200 pages, the engineers concluded that the Loral failure was caused by a flaw in the electronic flight control system of the Long March 3B rocket, and they made general recommendations for improvements in design, quality control, testing, and launch safety procedures. The commission also discussed other aspects of the rocket's guidance and control systems during meetings held in China. Given the sensitivity of the subjects, post-Tiananmen regulations required that the company should have had a license authorizing participation in such a review and that the report should have been cleared by the Department of State before being shared with the Chinese. That was not done. The final report was faxed to China Great Wall Industry Corporation on May 10, 1996.[64]

Subsequently, on being informed that it may have violated the law in transmitting the report, Loral reported its actions to the State Department, which initiated an investigation, along with the Department of Defense and the CIA. The Defense Department analysts initially concluded that "moderate harm" had been done to American national security by Loral's giving the report to the Chinese, although the CIA concluded the Loral report "posed no proliferation concerns." The Defense Department's Defense Technology Security Administration, however, concluded in 1997 that the report had provided "significant benefit" to China's ballistic missile program "likely to lead to improvements in the overall reliability of their launch vehicles and ballistic missiles."[65] It recommended that the information be turned over to the Customs Service and the Justice Department to determine whether criminal activity had taken place.

While the case was still under review, another Loral satellite license was approved by the Clinton White House in February 1998, despite Justice Department concerns. According to later reports, the license application was hastened through the approval process out of concern for possible fines against Loral for nonperformance of contract obligations, because stringent safeguards were built into the contract to prevent unauthorized transfer of technology or information, and because it was not certain how long the investigation of Loral would take. During the approval process, which went from the Bureau of Politico-Military Affairs at State through the NSC (with inputs from other agencies through State), Justice Department lawyers complained the waiver compromised its investigation of Loral. But National Security Adviser Berger downplayed their concerns in his cover memorandum to the president recommending approval of the license.[66]

The story leaked to the press at about the same time Johnny Chung, the "hustler" who bought his way into the First Lady's office some forty-nine times, plea bargained with the Justice Department investigators in hopes of easing the judgment against him. Chung agreed to cooperate with Justice Department and congressional investigators pursuing other aspects of the case. According to leaks of his testimony to FBI investigators that appeared in a *New York Times* article by Jeff Gerth, Chung told the FBI that most of the money he provided to the Democratic National Committee (DNC) in 1996 (more than $100,000) came from Liu Chaoying, the PLA officer and China Aerospace Corporation executive Chung had escorted to see Clinton at a California fund-raiser in July.[67]

Gerth, an investigative reporter who had been following Clinton scandals for years, made a critical connection, which may have come from the FBI:

> It is not clear whether other Chinese officials or executives were involved in the purported payments by Ms. Liu, or what her motivation or the Chinese military's might have been. *At the time, President Clinton was making it easier for American civilian communication satellites to be launched by Chinese rockets, a key issue for the Chinese army and for Ms. Liu's company, which sells missiles for the military . . . The President's decision was valuable to Ms. Liu because it enabled her company to do more business with American companies, but it had also been sought by American aerospace corporations, including Loral Space and Communications and the Hughes Electronics Corporation . . . seeking to do more business in China.*[68]

Republican leaders in Congress, who had been looking for a link between DNC donations and issues of more serious policy concern, now had a trail to follow and an issue to press: the national security implications of American satellite launches aboard Chinese rockets. When added to the fact that Loral's chief executive officer, Bernard Schwartz, had given $632,000 to the DNC in 1996, and Hughes's CEO, C. Michael Armstrong, had also been a heavy donor, the scandal machinery kicked into high gear.[69] Conservative pundits and congressional Republicans vied with each other in sensationalizing the charges. "Was it treason? I hope not. I believe it was not," said Representative Dan Burton, who had chaired the House Committee that investigated the scandal in 1997. "Was it incompetence? Was it greed? Yes."[70]

Administration officials, including Berger and Steinberg, rushed to defend the process and the decisions, as did Loral's CEO Schwartz. But Congress moved quickly to take action. On May 21, it added amendments to the defense authorization bill (H.R. 3616) restricting space and missile technology transfer to China, prohibiting participation in launch failure investigations, and banning the export or re-export of missile technology and any satellites to China.[71] Acting on his own authority, House Speaker Newt Gingrich announced the establishment of a "select committee" to investigate the allegations that China had illegally obtained missile technology through companies that received favorable treatment from the administration. The "Select Committee on U.S. National Security and Military/Commercial Concerns With the People's Republic of China," consisting of five Republicans and three Democrats, was headed by Representative Christopher Cox (R-Calif.), and its mandate was established by H. Res. 463, which was passed on June 18. "This has nothing to do with campaign finance. This has to do with national security," Gingrich told reporters. "This is a profoundly deeper question than any other question that has arisen with this administration."[72]

Because the Cox Committee, as it came to be called, and the Senate Select Committee on Intelligence, which was investigating a similar set of issues, held most of their hearings in closed session, the new Donorgate issue had largely faded from public view by August 1998. Even the Burton Committee had "run out of fuel," with no new allegations or charges. Behind closed doors, however, the congressional committees were taking testimony and developing a story that would shock the development of U.S.-China relations yet again and bring a virtual halt to even the consideration of a "strategic partnership."

To close out the Donorgate issue, however, the Justice Department, however slowly, had continued investigating, bringing charges, and carrying them through to trial. All in all, twenty-six individuals and two corporations were charged in connection with campaign finance abuses. Among the most prominent cases:

—Johnny Chung, as noted, pled guilty to charges of bank fraud, tax evasion, and conspiracy to evade campaign finance limits and was sentenced to five years' probation.

—Yogesh Gandhi was convicted of mail fraud charges in 1999 and sentenced to one year in prison.

—Maria Hsia was convicted in March 2000 on charges of making false statements to the Federal Election Commission and was sentenced in March 2002 to three months' home detention and three years' probation.

—John Huang pled guilty in 1999 to a charge of illegally funneling funds from Lippo to the DNC and was sentenced to one year of probation and 500 hours of community service.

—Pauline Kanchanalak pled guilty to conspiracy and campaign finance violations and was sentenced in 2001 to three years' probation and six months of home confinement.

—James Riady pled guilty to conspiracy to defraud the U.S. government and paid a fine of $8.6 million. The Lippo Bank of California pled guilty to eighty-six misdemeanor counts of making illegal contributions.

—Charlie Trie returned to the United States in February 1998 and was charged with two counts of illegally funneling money into the Clinton campaign. He pled guilty in 1999 and was sentenced to three years' probation.[73]

By the end of the year, virtually all other U.S. government business came slowly to a stop, as the process of impeaching the president came to its wrenching conclusion. Other books have evaluated this story in all its detail, and more surely will be forthcoming. From the perspective of U.S.-China relations, the scandal seemed to have little effect, other than preventing the administration from taking any steps to counter the malaise that was setting in on both sides. It is not likely that more progress would have been made any sooner even if the president and Congress had not been distracted by the sordid details and legal intricacies of impeachment. China was going through a conservative swing of its own, and Jiang was not prepared to offer any concessions or changes of policy that would have made much difference. As far as the impeachment was concerned, Chinese media gave it little attention, although many more Chinese followed the details in nonofficial media.

American policy toward China was in flux for various reasons. Sandra Kristoff left the National Security Council for the private sector after Clinton's China trip and was replaced by Kenneth R. Lieberthal, a China specialist from the University of Michigan. Lieberthal brought extraordinary depth on China-related issues but had no bureaucratic, diplomatic, or broader Asia experience. He was viewed with distrust by Taiwan and many of its American supporters for his outspoken advocacy of an "interim solution" to cross-Strait problems. Jeff Bader was appointed to an ambassadorship in Africa and was replaced by Jim Keith, an experienced State Department China desk officer.

Honeymoon Over, Quarrels Resume

From Beijing's perspective, relations with Washington went downhill quickly. Although the Clinton visit had an overall positive impact on Chinese attitudes and approaches to several issues, including nonproliferation, human rights, and democracy, the positive atmospherics and promise of partnership did not last long. In Washington, Clinton's foreign travel—despite grudging acknowledgment that he had acquitted himself well—in no way diminished demands for his impeachment by Congress. Republican party critics sought to devalue the China trip's few accomplishments and to exaggerate its flaws.

Not surprisingly, they focused on Clinton's "three noes" remarks in Shanghai. Within days of his return to Washington, Senate and House Republicans had drafted "sense of the Congress" resolutions reaffirming American commitments to Taiwan's defense under the Taiwan Relations Act and countering what they believed to be Clinton's "mistake" in Shanghai. Both resolutions passed nearly unanimously. Beijing, of course, denounced the bills for infringing China's sovereignty and interfering in its domestic affairs. The Foreign Ministry spokesman also could not resist the opportunity to use Clinton's Shanghai statement to pressure Taiwan to "get a clear understanding of the situation, face reality and place importance on the national interest."[74] This statement was widely cited by China's detractors in Washington as evidence of the damage done to Taiwan's interests by the "three noes." Energized to "undo the damage," Congress, within weeks, took up more pro-Taiwan and "anti-China" legislation. Moreover, in August, the Pentagon announced the sale of $350 million of antiaircraft and antiship missiles to Taiwan. Added to the very public congressional investigations of China's purported campaign donations and alleged illicit acquisition of American missile technology, it appeared to be open season on China and Clinton's engagement policy.

Beijing's reaction to Clinton's political difficulties was cautious, as there was no wish to encourage corresponding American commentary about China's domestic politics. Xinhua reported sparingly but objectively on the Monica Lewinsky scandal, ascribing it primarily to partisan politics and noting that American public opinion still supported Clinton. Chinese authorities banned translation and public circulation of the report put out in October by Special Prosecutor Kenneth Starr on Clinton's affair with Lewinsky, finding its descriptions of sexual liaisons too graphic. They did not seek to suppress the story on the Internet, however, and many Chinese kept up with it in the many "chat rooms" that were increasingly free of government interference.[75] China, in other words, was not about to risk the relationship with the United States by taking sides on the outcome of a struggle between Clinton and congressional Republicans.

Toward its deteriorating repute in American opinion, however, the Chinese government took a strangely passive position. It routinely denied it had undertaken any effort to buy influence with either American political party, but it refused to cooperate with congressional efforts to investigate accusations of Chinese citizens. It belittled accusations of Chinese spying but made no effort to answer the many questions that arose within the American media and in Congress about the activities of Chinese attachés, business executives, and scientists in their interactions with American counterparts. This reticence seemed to American observers a sort of *omerta*, or silence of the guilty. In August 1998, for example, China's ambassador to the United States, Li Zhaoxing, agreed to talk to Congressman Christopher Smith (R-N.J.)—one of China's most virulent critics on the Hill—and his committee, but then balked when Smith portrayed his appearance as "testimony at a hearing." Li's refusal to appear in those circumstances tended to reinforce American impressions of Chinese culpability.[76] For its part, Beijing retreated into an easy but wrong-headed delusion that all its problems were caused by "a handful of anti-China elements," an explanation that had resonance in China but nowhere else.

U.S.-China relations took another downward turn over human rights issues in late 1998, as Beijing began a concerted effort to destroy the so-called China Democracy Party (CDP) that had sprung up in several locations during the year. Positive movement on human rights issues in the run-up to Clinton's visit had led to rumors in China of an overall political loosening and to a return of pressures for political reform. There were even preliminary indications that some local Communist Party officials acquiesced in CDP efforts to register itself as a political party in early 1998. Responding, perhaps, to reports that Clinton's forthright comments about human rights during his visit had re-energized the moribund dissident community in China, conservatives in the leadership, including Li Peng, called for a crackdown. Jiang, typically, agreed with them. Although the regime had begun harassing CDP leaders shortly after Clinton's visit, it took much stronger actions in the late autumn.[77] In November, Jiang made a speech to a party conclave, hardening the official position on political reform. China's one-party political system "must not be shaken, weakened or discarded at any time," he said, adding, "the Western mode of political systems must never be copied."[78]

Shortly afterward, prominent CDP leaders Xu Wenli, Qin Yongmin, and Wang Youcai were arrested, along with supporters in several cities, and charged with subversion of the Chinese state. Their arrest coincided with an announced tightening of restrictions on publications in China, an attempt to intimidate into silence several scholars pushing for legal reform, and the closure "for repairs" of Tiananmen Square.[79] International human rights groups condemned the arrests, pointing out the irony of China's having just signed the UN Covenant of Civil and Political Rights in October. On December 21, the regime announced jail terms of thirteen, twelve, and eleven years for Xu, Qin, and Wang, respectively—sentences considered harsh for their purported "crimes" of trying to establish an opposition party. None had been permitted to retain the services of defense lawyers, and their trials were closed to the public.[80] The Clinton administration criticized the sentences as "backward steps," terms much milder than those used by the media and Congress, some of whom declared yet again that the entire process of engagement with the Chinese regime had proven a failure and should be discarded. In part because of the action against the CDP, the Clinton administration decided the following spring to sponsor another resolution critical of China at the United Nations Human Rights Commission (UNHRC)—a measure it had dropped in 1998.

CHAPTER NINE

Back to the Cold, 1999–2000

By the end of 1998, it was broadly held that the U.S.-China relationship was in a serious downturn and needed concerted attention on both sides to avoid another showdown. Many foreign observers saw the entire process of engagement with China as being in jeopardy. Several Chinese commentators about the U.S.-China relationship have noted that even-numbered years tended to show progress and growth in relations, while odd-numbered years often brought strife and deterioration. The year 1999 offered credible evidence in support of this numerological fancy. For U.S.-China relations, it was a genuine *annus horribilis*.

The year began with the Clinton impeachment by the House of Representatives and trial in the Senate on charges that he had given "perjurious, false and misleading testimony" to a grand jury investigating the Paula Jones case and his relationship with Monica Lewinsky and had "obstructed justice" in trying to delay and impede the investigation of those cases.[1] The case was noisy, tawdry, and repellent, but there was neither strong public nor congressional support for removing the president from office, and the Senate votes on the counts of perjury and obstruction of justice both fell well short of the two-thirds majority needed to convict. Clinton set about the remainder of his term determined to establish a positive record and a worthwhile legacy. Still angry, congressional Republicans, embarrassed that their "all-or-nothing" strategy had netted them nothing, were determined to thwart him at every turn.

In the realm of foreign affairs, Clinton set out to make progress on several knotty and difficult issues, focusing on the Middle East peace effort and the escalating crisis in Kosovo. He appeared to have hoped that his trip to China had eased tensions sufficiently and engendered sufficient trust, that the relationship could coast for a while. But the sharp congressional backlash over Taiwan, a bubbling inquiry over China's technology acquisition, along with growing anger about Beijing's crackdown against the China Democracy Party led to a renewed sense of impending crisis.

Trade, Traitors, and Tradecraft—The Los Alamos Spy Scandal

By late October 1998, Kenneth Lieberthal, senior director at the National Security Council (NSC), was convinced it had become important to find a structural framework to facilitate China's western orientation and to undergird the U.S.-China relationship. He suggested to Sandy Berger that perhaps a renewed push for a World Trade Organization (WTO) agreement might suit the purpose. Berger agreed in principle but expressed doubt that it could be accomplished.[2] The president had discussed the prospect on several occasions with Jiang Zemin and had even hoped to announce progress toward the goal of a bilateral agreement during his trip to Beijing. But the Chinese were not ready to commit themselves to what they seemed to fear might be destabilizing economic changes while the region was still being rocked by the Asian financial crisis. They wanted some concessions on domestic market protection they believed they were entitled to as a "developing nation." And they were still suspicious that the United States was imposing more stringent conditions on China than it had on any other nation, perhaps for strategic reasons. In early November, the NSC drafted for Clinton's signature a letter to Jiang Zemin, suggesting both sides should try to put together a viable WTO package early in 1999.[3] In January 1999, Federal Reserve Chairman Alan Greenspan visited Beijing in connection with the Asian financial crisis and again raised the prospect of a WTO agreement, perhaps to be completed during Zhu's visit to Washington in the spring. Clinton sent another letter in early February, suggesting the same to Jiang.[4] During a visit by Deputy Treasury Secretary Larry Summers in late February, Zhu Rongji said China was prepared to make significant progress in the long-standing negotiation process. In an early March visit to China, U.S.Trade Representative (USTR) Charlene Barshefsky found that China's position was significantly changed and that concessions the United States had been seeking for years on issues such as agriculture, tariffs, market access for services, and many others were suddenly being offered by the Chinese side. Zhu had gotten serious about the WTO, and he wanted to know if the United States would say yes to a deal. Barshefsky could not give a clear answer.

The U.S. government was badly divided on China's WTO accession. Even within the USTR, views had varied for years about whether China could or would put together a "commercially viable" offer for a bilateral agreement. Some had suggested the Chinese, in order to justify concessions, needed mainly some reassurance that the United States was committed to signing a deal, while others insisted the Chinese system was simply unable to make the commitments that would be required. Barshefsky was ambivalent, knowing the business community's support for a solid agreement was strong, but congressional support was not. The NSC was in favor, largely for political reasons having to do with maintaining the momentum of bilateral relations and deepening China's involvement in international organizations; the Commerce Department also was supportive. The Treasury Department was hesitant, concerned that the U.S. business community would not lobby Congress to support an agreement. The State Department was in favor of a WTO agreement but was far more focused on human rights, particularly punishing China for the persecution of the China Democracy Party.[5]

In early March, a story broke in the *New York Times* that not only complicated the decision on WTO but sent the entire U.S. government into a bizarre and confusing tailspin and damaged badly any prospect of a significant improvement in U.S.-China relations. It also did great harm to the life and reputation of a Chinese American scientist and to relations between the U.S. government and the Asian American community. Like many of the issues that roiled U.S.-China ties since 1989, this one also had its origins in intelligence, espionage, and press leaks. Investigative reporters Jeff Gerth and James Risen based their March 6 front-page story on information from confidential sources and unnamed officials who spoke "on condition of anonymity."[6] Like most intelligence leaks, this one came from people with an alternative policy agenda or an axe to grind. It was incomplete, presenting only one side of the story, and it put the administration very much on the defensive, as it could not refute the stories without disclosing even more classified information.

The story emanated from the Senate Select Committee on Intelligence and Cox Committee hearings on China and its acquisition of American technology and know-how, which had continued through the end of 1998. An intelligence analyst assigned to the Department of Energy (DOE), Notra Trulock, told the Cox Committee late that year that analysis of a 1995 Chinese underground nuclear test strongly suggested the weapon was virtually identical to America's most sophisticated miniature nuclear warhead, the W-88. Further investigation—and a strange CIA report from a Chinese source who provided purported PRC documents on its nuclear weapons program[7]—indicated that the W-88 design information evidently had been stolen from one of the Department of Energy's national nuclear laboratories, probably the one at Los Alamos, New Mexico. The initial story acknowledged that there were disagreements within the intelligence community about the conclusions of the analysis, but these were imputed to be blocking efforts by the NSC. Members of the Cox Committee also charged about the same time that the administration was using protection of intelligence sources and methods as a pretext for holding up public release of the committee's report.[8]

The laboratories had been prime intelligence targets for the Chinese and the Russians for many years, and their administration by the University of California and the Energy Department made them easier targets for espionage. Risen and Gerth implied that the Clinton administration had ignored DOE and intelligence community warnings about the labs' vulnerabilities and had dismissed a 1997 DOE briefing on the apparent W-88 theft because it conflicted with the desire to improve relations with China in advance of Jiang's trip. Furthermore, the article charged, Trulock and his DOE investigators had identified a Chinese American suspect they believed had given the warhead data to the Chinese, but little action had been taken against him, mainly because of bureaucratic delays by the Federal Bureau of Investigation and Energy Department.[9]

The March story hit Washington hard, reviving allegations about Chinese campaign finance activities, the Clinton administration's blindness about China, and compromises of American security. Panicked into action, the executive branch began a series of steps (and missteps) to show it was vigilant and concerned. According to later accounts, FBI officials first asked the *Times* to hold the story for a day, then rushed to interview the principal suspect—a Taiwan-born scientist named Wen Ho Lee—over the weekend. Ill-prepared investigators confronted Lee harshly, threatening him with the death penalty for espionage. Lee—who had no lawyer present—strongly denied having stolen nuclear secrets on behalf of Beijing, but he then refused further cooperation. The DOE investigators searched Lee's office, discovering that he had evidently erased from his unclassified office computer improperly obtained classified files containing nuclear test data.[10]

Secretary of Energy Bill Richardson—a former congressman from New Mexico—fired Lee on March 9 for "failure to properly notify Energy Department and lab officials about contacts with people from a sensitive country, . . . failing to properly safeguard classified material and apparently attempting to deceive lab officials about security matters."[11] The FBI admitted, however, that it did not have enough hard evidence to bring espionage charges against Lee. Richardson subsequently tightened up security practices at all the labs and even closed down classified DOE computer systems out of concern they may have been compromised. As the story picked up steam, Trulock detailed and escalated his charges against certain individuals in the

Energy Department and against Gary Samore, NSC senior director for nonproliferation.[12]

Other parts of the administration reacted equally quickly and almost as clumsily. The NSC struggled to explain charges that it had ignored earlier reports of Chinese intelligence thefts of U.S. nuclear secrets, then claimed that the security problems at the nuclear labs had begun during the Reagan administration—which was true but sounded evasive. CIA Director George Tenet appointed an outside blue ribbon commission, headed by retired admiral David Jeremiah, to review the intelligence community's earlier finding that the Chinese had benefited from U.S. warhead research and design information but had not necessarily obtained it through espionage.[13]

Fed by unknown officials in the FBI, press stories revealed more details of the Wen Ho Lee case, and a sort of "Chinese spy mania" seemed to hit the country. Stories soon circulated about earlier Chinese efforts to get secrets out of the national labs and other facilities and about their success in obtaining other American high technology and military knowledge. Commentators compared the presumed loss of America's nuclear secrets to the Julius and Ethel Rosenberg case (American scientists executed for passing atomic bomb secrets to the Soviet Union) and other famous incidents of damaging espionage.[14] Elaborate theories were spun, linking fund-raising coffees, satellite launches, and nuclear tests, all on the theory that the Clinton administration had sacrificed American national security for a few thousand dollars of Chinese money.

For many members of Congress, this was the last straw, both for the administration and for its China policy. Even Senator Richard Lugar, a moderate Republican foreign affairs specialist from Indiana and supporter of engagement with China, chastised the Clinton administration for its unfocused approach to China. "The Clinton administration already had dug a very deep hole for itself on Capitol Hill with respect to China," he wrote in an op-ed article in the *Washington Post*. "That hole just got wider and deeper." Lugar called for more cooperation and dialogue between Congress and the White House on the overall direction and conduct of China policy.[15] Others were far less charitable, accusing the Clinton White House of "covering up" the espionage and calling for the resignation of National Security Adviser Sandy Berger. Several senators claimed the new revelations called into question the administration's entire policy toward China and insisted that it was not an appropriate time for the United States to be discussing WTO accession. Resolutions were drafted in the House and the Senate calling for prior congressional approval of any deal between the United States and China over WTO membership.

Mr. Zhu Goes to Washington

In the circumstances, China's reaction to Clinton's entreaty in early 1999 to step up efforts to craft a WTO agreement was one of understandable caution. Aside from the growing belief that the United States was tending toward "containment" of China rather than engagement and that Clinton was a politically damaged leader who could no longer deliver on his promises, Beijing remained divided on whether a WTO deal was even beneficial. With China's economy increasingly weakened by the Asian financial crisis, there were few who thought exposing it to increased foreign competition through enhanced market access was a good idea. Reform of state-owned enterprises was proceeding fitfully, sandbagged by local officials unwilling to make the sacrifices to restructure unproductive industries. Export growth had slowed, and foreign investment had leveled off, partly because of growing foreign anxieties about China's willingness to establish meaningful trade reciprocity.

Premier Zhu Rongji, however, had come around to firm support of WTO membership as a means of improving the competitiveness of Chinese industries, and he evidently decided to make completion of a bilateral WTO agreement with the United States the capstone of his planned April 1999 visit to Washington. Clinton had encouraged Jiang to accelerate the negotiations process and pledged that the Office of the U.S. Trade Representative would make every effort to achieve an early agreement. For China's part, Zhu informed visiting U.S. officials in early 1999 that China was prepared to make significant concessions on issues that had been in dispute for years and that he was substantially engaged in the process.[16] Negotiations intensified in February and March, and USTR Charlene Barshefsky agreed to visit Beijing in late March to try and finalize a deal before Zhu's trip to Washington, scheduled for April 8. Word leaked out in the U.S. press and among American business circles that a WTO deal was within reach and that the terms were good for the United States. Opposition to an agreement grew in both capitals, however, as it seemed that progress in crafting a trade agreement was not being matched by improvements in other areas or was causing other important subjects to be disregarded.

Of serious concern in China—and especially in the military—was the growing U.S. and NATO military activity in the Balkans. China had objected to American and NATO involvement in the dissolution of the Federal Republic of Yugoslavia (FRY) for years. Belgrade had been considered a staunch socialist ally by post-Mao Chinese leaders, and there was great interest in Yugoslavia's experimental approach to economic and political reforms. When the ethnic dissolution of the FRY began in the early 1980s, abetted (in China's view) by American and western European support for ethnic separatism, China expressed strong support for Belgrade's attempts to preserve its national integrity and criticized Western efforts to facilitate the breakup of a sovereign state. It did not take any steps to help Yugoslav president Slobodan Milosevic prevent the breaking away of Croatia, Slovenia, and Bosnia, however. As the situation in Kosovo heated up in 1998, exacerbated by Serbian repression of the ethnic Albanians who constituted the majority of Kosovo's population, China sided strongly with Milosevic. Chinese media ignored stories of Serbian atrocities and cruelty, focusing instead on Western "power politics" and "hegemonism" in pressuring Belgrade to negotiate a solution that would enhance Kosovo's autonomy. When NATO and the United States began threatening, then carrying out air attacks on Yugoslavia in October 1998, China's propaganda apparatus moved from criticizing the effort as ill-intended and ineffective to much stronger rhetoric.

China's position was not simply based on sympathy for Yugoslavia or even the secondary factor of providing support to its Russian "strategic partner" in opposition to NATO expansion. Beijing saw in the allied pressure against Serbia—done outside the context of the United Nations—a harbinger of what a "unipolar" world might bring to China, namely, a growing web of alliances that could take concerted military action against China under American leadership. It viewed Washington's justification for the Kosovo action, so-called humanitarian intervention, as an excuse to meddle in the internal affairs of other countries that might be applicable to China. And the People's Liberation Army (PLA) viewed the massive NATO use of air power and precision-guided munitions as the kind of attack that the United States might use against China in case of a conflict over Taiwan.[17]

China's concerns were no doubt heightened by congressional actions suggesting the United States was prepared to provide "theater missile defense" (TMD) equipment to Taiwan to counterbalance the growing threat of a PRC missile attack. Passage of the Defense Authorization Act of 1999 (H.R. 3616) authorized the secretary of defense to study a "theater ballistic missile defense system in the Asia-Pacific region that would have the capability to protect key regional allies of the United States."[18] Commentators made clear that, although not specified, Taiwan was included in the definition of "key regional ally." In February 1999, the PLA's newspaper, *Jiefangjun Bao,* demanded "that the United States abide by the three Sino-US communiqués and the relevant commitments, and that it does not extend its TMD system and the associated technology to Taiwan in any form."[19]

Growing disagreements over several international and bilateral issues, as well as the State Department's strong dissatisfaction with China's human rights practices in late 1998, contributed to yet another contentious meeting between a visiting U.S. secretary of state and her Beijing hosts. Madeleine Albright made a brief stop in Beijing in early March and had a series of what were called "forceful and tough" talks with Foreign Minister Tang Jiaxuan, as well as Premier Zhu. She was incensed by not only the reversal of China's policy on dissidents represented by the sentencing of China Democracy Party leaders in late 1998 but by further arrests and harassment of dissidents just before her arrival.[20] Both sides "let off steam" in the meetings, and Albright warned Zhu his trip to Washington would have to include progress on human rights or it would not be successful.[21]

Although the timing was coincidental, the fact that Jiang Zemin was visiting Italy on March 25, 1999, the date when NATO warplanes (some from Italian bases) began an intensified bombing campaign of Belgrade, added to Chinese anger over NATO actions. On his return to Beijing, Jiang convened a Politburo meeting to discuss growing opposition to Zhu's trip to Washington among senior officials, particularly in the PLA. Although some characterized the debate as intense, in the end it was decided that the potential benefits of Zhu's visit outweighed the drawbacks.[22] But it was also agreed that China's media would heighten its criticism of the United States and NATO at the same time. And military leaders began openly to advocate a change in China's overall "security concept"—from one that posited a world in which "peace and development" were the dominant aspirations of the major powers to one that viewed "hegemonism and power politics," as practiced by the United States, as seriously threatening to China's future. Deputy Chief of Staff Xiong Guangkai hosted one hundred prominent scholars at a forum on April 14 to discuss China's need to "protect itself from every angle," including economic defense, in light of the new situation.[23]

Despite the deterioration in public attitudes toward each other in both the United States and China, Clinton and Berger pressed for a WTO agreement, because they thought there might not be another opportunity to do so during the second term and because they hoped to show evidence of a positive dimension to the relationship.[24] The USTR, Charlene Barshefsky, traveled to Beijing one last time in late March in an effort to improve still further what already looked like a good deal. The Chinese balked at making more concessions, concerned that they were being too accommodating to a country whose strategic intentions—as demonstrated in the bombing of Yugoslavia—were so worrisome. Barshefsky departed after one day of consultations with Zhu Rongji and others, leaving the impression that the two sides were still far apart. Privately, however, USTR was leaking the information on Chinese concessions to business groups in hopes of enlisting their support. As

Barshefsky had put it, "Any deal that doesn't have the seal of approval of the business community isn't a deal worth doing."[25]

Within the administration, the debate over a WTO deal became extremely contentious in the week before Zhu's arrival. White House Chief of Staff John Podesta held meetings of the key players in his office, as Principals Committee meetings in the situation room had come to be considered too "leaky" on China policy issues. The leaks continued, however, straining interpersonal relations within the policymaking apparatus. But no decision was made. Sandy Berger and the president were increasingly preoccupied with U.S. military action in Yugoslavia and had little time for China.[26] Meanwhile, China's principal negotiator, Long Yongtu, was in town to try and hammer out the last details on such issues as agricultural inspection standards, foreign investment in Chinese telecommunications, the operations of American banks and brokerage firms in China, and continuing protection for the U.S. textile industry. The American side also wanted to maintain the right—considered important to Congress—to impose unilateral trade sanctions on China even after the WTO agreement was completed. But the Chinese refused to budge on the main issues.[27]

Before and during his trip, Zhu was candid in his comments to American interviewers, telling several that he did not really want to go to Washington, given the intensifying controversy over allegations of Chinese nuclear espionage. But he thought he could perhaps do some good in restoring momentum to the flagging movement toward a "constructive strategic partnership" and in presenting China's views and explanations of bilateral problems directly to the American audience.[28] He knew Americans responded well to his style of self-deprecating humor and blunt candor and that it was important for the first visit to the United States by the premier of China's State Council in nearly fifteen years to go well. He also knew that Chinese and U.S. negotiators had pieced together a bilateral agreement on China's accession to the WTO that both sides considered satisfactory. At his urging, the Ministry of Foreign Trade and Economic Cooperation (MOFTEC) had made what Zhu called "big concessions" on market access, telecommunications, agriculture, tariff levels, and other subjects in the run-up to his April visit. He was probably optimistic that he and President Clinton would formally sign a bilateral agreement in a White House ceremony on April 9, ending thirteen years of difficult and often bitter negotiations. It would be a signal accomplishment for China and a personal triumph for him. But he was still somewhat nervous and uncertain. "This visit won't be easy for me," Zhu told reporters.[29]

It was not easy for Clinton, either, and he appeared not to have made up his mind about the WTO agreement even as Zhu was arriving in Washington. The USTR and MOFTEC teams had been negotiating almost nonstop to get all the details arranged, but a few odds and ends were still missing. In a speech at the U. S. Institute for Peace on the morning of Zhu's arrival, Clinton waxed eloquent about the importance—and the complexities—of the bilateral relationship. He spoke perceptively about the bitter divisions China policy had engendered in the United States and reiterated his commitment to engagement. On WTO, he appeared to favor bringing the deal to closure. "The bottom line is this: If China is willing to play by the global rules of trade, it would be an inexplicable mistake for the United States to say no."[30]

In the afternoon, he consulted with key advisers, who provided conflicting counsel. Of special importance was Treasury Secretary Robert Rubin, who had headed the National Economic Council in Clinton's first term and for whom the president had great respect. He suggested the president take the deal right to the point of closure but not to close it. Congressional opposition, he said, was extremely strong, and business community support for the agreement was not sufficient to overcome it. With a bit more time and effort, a sustainable agreement might be achieved. But if Clinton were to reach an agreement now that Congress might subsequently overturn, the damage to bilateral relations would be even worse.[31]

So in the evening of April 7, Clinton did what in the morning he had called inexplicable—and said no to the agreement. Meeting privately with Zhu and a few advisers in the White House residence, Clinton tried to soften the blow in a peculiarly American fashion. He told Zhu the political atmospherics on Capitol Hill were such that Congress might disavow a WTO agreement or refuse to approve the granting of permanent normal trade relations that was an essential part of it. That would be catastrophic, he insisted. In a gesture common to American but not Chinese politicians, the president put his arm around Zhu's shoulders and said if he "really needed" an agreement back home in China, they could do it, even though it was a bad time in the United States. Zhu, unaccustomed to American political "body language," and unwilling to appear to be begging for an agreement, demurred.[32] The WTO agreement that had seemed so close slipped away in that moment; it would take six months to get to it again.

But worse was to come. In a nearly unseemly haste to try and "lock in" the concessions China had already made, officials at USTR compounded the problems for themselves and for Zhu. They prepared a document summarizing the agreements to date and put it on the USTR website on April 8. Unfortunately, they got some of the details wrong, claiming the Chinese had agreed on some issues when in fact the matters were still under negotiation.[33] Zhu disavowed the document publicly, and senior negotiators went into another marathon round of talks to try and agree on what they had agreed. In their joint statement on April 10, the president and premier agreed they would instruct their trade ministers to continue efforts to resolve the problems. "If you want too much too soon," Zhu warned in a speech to the America-China Society on April 9, "you might end up with nothing."[34]

Although Zhu may have been dismayed and put off by Clinton's approach to the WTO issue, and even more by the USTR list of China's "concessions," he was determined to make the best of the situation. At the joint press conference with President Clinton on April 8, Zhu refused to characterize the lack of an agreement as a failure, and he described the remaining points of disagreement as "not very significant." He said most of the problems were because of the "political atmosphere" of hostility toward China that was so pervasive in the United States.[35] Zhu confronted the political issues head-on, with a combination of candor, humor, sarcasm, and evasion:

—He dismissed stories of Ji Shengde giving $300,000 to Johnny Chung to buy political influence, insisting such a small amount was "too foolish" to be effective. But he also promised to cooperate with U.S. investigators.

—He denied that China had stolen nuclear technology from America's national labs, issuing a "solemn pledge" as premier that neither he nor President Jiang had any knowledge of such matters. He acknowledged that China had learned from foreign countries in developing its nuclear programs but advised Americans not to "underestimate the capability of the Chinese people to develop their own technology."

—Zhu acknowledged that China's human rights record had "room for improvement" but insisted that progress was being made steadily, and he objected to the United States and other countries criticizing China's record at the UNHRC meeting in Geneva.

—On Taiwan, he pledged fidelity to a "one country, two systems" deal for Taiwan, but he refused to rule out the use of force, citing Abraham Lincoln—whose bust he had seen in the Oval Office—as a model for bold action in preserving a nation's unity.[36]

Using that same combination of frankness, charm, and humor, Zhu continued his tour of the United States, focusing his attention on business groups and media outlets, telling them about the WTO "deal that wasn't," pointing out the significant advantages for American business. He also covered his domestic flanks by continuing to denounce as inaccurate the USTR list of Chinese concessions. The American business lobby, outraged at the administration's rejection of the Chinese offers, sent a torrent of protest to the Clinton administration and Congress. Concerned that he had turned down a deal that American business would encourage Congress to support, Clinton phoned Zhu as he left for Canada on April 14, offering to send Barshefsky to negotiate with Long even before the Chinese party departed North America for home.[37] Zhu—probably distrustful of Clinton's ability to deliver and well aware of divisions within the administration—demurred again, agreeing only that the two sides would engage in "intensive negotiation" to finish the WTO agreement. Those talks would take place, Zhu insisted, in Beijing.[38]

Zhu returned to Beijing to face a storm of criticism, although there was little evidence of it in any of China's official media. His failure to win an agreement on the WTO cost Zhu considerable "face" within the leadership, tarnished his reputation for skill with foreigners, and gave his numerous critics an issue on which to focus their wrath. Hong Kong media soon began reporting that Zhu had exceeded his instructions and was being charged with conceding too much to American demands. His offers to secure a "full package deal" were criticized as the "giveaway of the century." At least one Chinese minister reportedly tried to resign in protest, and the Internet chat rooms began attacking Zhu as a "traitor."[39] Some Chinese reportedly also charged that Zhu had not been sufficiently critical of the NATO bombing of Yugoslavia or of American support for Taiwan. Li Peng reportedly criticized Zhu at a late May Politburo meeting for misspeaking in the United States, for example, when he told American audiences he didn't really want to make the trip but came at Jiang's insistence.[40] Zhu's American trip, begun in such high expectations, had become a lightning rod, not only for various other discontents about Zhu and his headlong rush to economic reform but also for the growing dissatisfaction with the bilateral relationship.

The Belgrade Bombing

On May 7, thousands of miles away from both Beijing and Washington, the U.S.-China relationship suffered its most damaging blow since Tiananmen. At about midnight, over Belgrade, Yugoslavia, two U.S.-based B-2 "stealth" bombers released their loads of joint direct attack munitions (JDAMs)—2,000-pound conventional gravity bombs equipped with special guidance systems that enable them to strike within two to ten meters of their target points—at a variety of Serbian military installations. Among the targets was the Federal Directorate of Supply and Procurement at 2 Bulevar Umetnosti in New Belgrade, believed by CIA officials who selected the target to be involved in illicit proliferation of missile-related equipment to Iraq and Libya under the direction of close business associates of Slobodan Milosevic.[41] Unfortunately, owing to mistakes made in the targeting process and not corrected in premission reviews, the building identified as "target 493" was not the Directorate of Supply and Procurement—which was located about three hundred meters away—but the Embassy of the People's Republic of China, which had moved to this new location in 1997.

Of the five JDAMs dropped on the embassy, three struck their targets, destroying the Chinese military attaché's office at the south end of the building and badly damaging a residential section. The north side of the structure was undamaged. Three Chinese were killed and twenty injured in the explosions, which took place while most staff members were sleeping. The three killed were journalists: Shao Yunhuan, a female Xinhua correspondent; Xu Xinghu, a reporter for the *Guangming Ribao*; and his wife Zhu Ying, who worked for the same paper.[42] News of the bombing reached Beijing early in the morning of Saturday, May 8, precipitating a fast-paced series of events that nearly went out of control.

American ambassador James R. Sasser contacted Chinese counterparts in the Ministry of Foreign Affairs on the morning of Saturday, May 8, to apologize for what he characterized as a "terrible mistake" and offer condolences. But as the day wore on with no word from Washington (where it was the middle of the night), Chinese anger began to grow. By midmorning, news accounts of the bombing and the casualties provided gruesome details; television coverage of Yugoslav rescue workers sifting through the smoking rubble of the embassy and comforting bloodied, weeping survivors riveted Chinese viewers. The MFA denounced the bombing as a "barbarian act" and said that NATO would bear "full responsibility" for whatever happened, though it did not detail its intended response. It summoned Ambassador Sasser to the Foreign Ministry to hear China's "strongest protest against the U.S.-led NATO attack."[43]

Early Saturday afternoon, angry crowds of Beijing residents began milling around the U.S. embassy compound on North Xiushui Street, observed by growing numbers of police and PLA guards. Late in the afternoon, university students began arriving in buses provided by their schools, approved by the Beijing Municipal Party Committee. Well organized, with banners decrying American "Nazi murderers" and demanding "blood for blood," the students marched by the embassy in an orderly manner, shouting slogans in unison and presenting petitions to U.S. embassy officers. They seemed to Western reporters and other observers to be in a "controlled burn"—responding to the government's invitation to protest but clearly very emotional and angry that the United States would perpetrate such an act, which they had no doubt was deliberate.[44] As the day wore on, their actions became more threatening: rocks were thrown by some students, eliciting great cheers when they managed to break windows in the embassy building.

At dusk, the buses returned to the campuses, but the crowds swelled, becoming angrier and less controlled. Responding to calls on Internet chat rooms and mobile phones, as well as word of mouth, young Beijing residents flocked to the streets near the embassy to make their voices heard or simply to watch the fun. Joined by the same kinds of *liumang* that had made student demonstrations at Tiananmen so unpredictable and dangerous ten years before, the crowds turned decidedly ugly after nightfall. Rocks and paint bombs hurled from outside the fences—less than fifty feet from the embassy building—defaced the chancellery badly. Some Molotov cocktails were thrown, starting small fires that were quickly extinguished by the fourteen Americans—including the ambassador—who remained inside. Some Chinese attempted to scale the fences, but they were pulled back by police, whose numbers had swelled to more than 7,000. They made no efforts to disperse the crowds, however, but only prevented them from entering the compound or harming foreigners who happened to be in the vicinity.[45] Foreigners reported they were jostled and cursed by groups of young men who clearly were not students.

On Saturday morning, U.S. time, CIA Director George Tenet and Secretary of Defense William Cohen issued a joint statement, saying the bombing was an "error." "Those involved in targeting mistakenly believed that the Federal Directorate of Supply and Procurement was at the location that was hit. That military supply facility was the intended target, certainly not the Chinese Embassy. We deeply regret the loss of life and injuries from the bombing."[46] Later that afternoon, President Clinton, inspecting storm damage in Oklahoma, spoke briefly to reporters, calling the bombing a "tragic mistake" and expressing his "regrets and condolences" to China. But he also lashed out at those who had called the bombing "barbaric," insisting that it was Milosevic's "ethnic cleansing" policies that were barbaric.[47]

By early Sunday morning, May 9, the crowds outside the U.S. embassy had become sufficiently rowdy, and police lines sufficiently ragged, that the embassy staff began destroying sensitive documents, concerned that the police could not hold off the angry crowds much longer. "We thought the odds were 50-50 they were coming in," Sasser told reporters by phone.[48] Unable to reach any Foreign Ministry officials on the weekend to ask for additional protection, Sasser telephoned China's ambassador in Washington, Li Zhaoxing, to solicit his help, but to no avail. The mood of the crowds outside the embassy remained menacing, and more attempts were made to scale the fences and enter the compound. Failing that, demonstrators unfurled vulgar banners, burned American flags, and defaced effigies of Clinton, Secretary of State Albright, and the Statue of Liberty. But there was also a growing undertone of anger at the Chinese government's weakness in responding to the American attacks and a concern that, if the demonstrations were not brought under control, it could "lead to all sorts of unexpected consequences," including "great pressure" on Jiang and Zhu, observed Shanghai historian Xiao Gongqin.[49]

Clinton sent a letter to Jiang Zemin on May 9, expressing "apologies and sincere condolences for the pain and casualties brought about by the bombing of the Chinese embassy."[50] The previous evening, Secretary of State Albright hand-carried a letter of apology to Foreign Minister Tang Jiaxuan to the Chinese embassy, where she was jostled by Chinese reporters. Although they expressed their condolences and apologies several times, the president and other government spokespersons took pains to reiterate that the bombing campaign was justified and would continue. This only intensified Chinese anger.

On Sunday afternoon, the central government finally began applying the brakes. Chinese media broadcast a speech by Vice President Hu Jintao in which he repeated harsh criticism of the NATO attack and expressed approval of the "strong patriotism" of those who were protesting at various U.S. diplomatic establishments. But Hu warned protesters that they must obey the law. "We believe that the vast number of people will take into consideration the country's fundamental interests and act consciously to safeguard the interests of the whole so that these activities will proceed lawfully in an orderly fashion. We must guard against any overreactions, watch out for people who may take advantage of the opportunity to disrupt the normal social order, and take firm actions to safeguard social stability." He also assured foreign nationals that they would be protected under Chinese law.[51]

On Monday, May 10, the demonstrations began to take on a different character. Propaganda outlets that morning had stridently denounced America's "criminal acts" in Belgrade and pledged the Chinese people would prove they "cannot be bullied." While not perhaps an incitement to riot, the morning press coverage was designed to further heighten public anger over the incident. Security forces at the U.S. embassy were well prepared, however. As on Saturday, student protesters were transported to staging areas near the embassy, as were some government workers. But this time, they had to show proof of having secured permission to demonstrate from the Public Security Bureau. Near the embassy, they were organized into groups, given a designated route of march and a schedule for completion of their protest. Some were even given slogans to shout and banners to carry. Many sang the Chinese national anthem. Robed Buddhist monks marched with religious leaders of other faiths, denouncing American cruelty. Thousands marched past the embassy until well into the evening. By Tuesday, however, the numbers of protesters dwindled sharply—to only a few hundred—and the American embassy staff were able to return to their homes. By Wednesday the demonstrations were over.

As in the aftermath of the 1995 Lee Teng-hui incident, China cut off virtually all bilateral dialogues with the United States in the wake of the bombing.

On May 10, the Foreign Ministry conveyed a four-point demand to the U.S. government: a public and formal apology to the government and people of China and to the families of those who were harmed in the attack; a comprehensive and thorough investigation of the bombing of China's embassy in Yugoslavia; a prompt public disclosure of the details of the investigation; and severe punishment for those responsible for the incident.[52] It also formally suspended the military-to-military relations between the two countries, postponed consultations on human rights, nonproliferation, and other subjects, and canceled several high-level American visits to Beijing. Internationally, China called for a UN Security Council meeting to condemn the bombing and threatened to veto any UN peace plans for Yugoslavia unless NATO first stopped its bombing campaign.

On May 13, Jiang Zemin presided over a leadership rally welcoming the return of the bodies of the "revolutionary martyrs" killed in Belgrade. In a lengthy speech, Jiang used the opportunity to stress the continuity and consistency of China's domestic and foreign policies. He emphasized the need to continue working on economic reform and opening up, maintaining social stability, and upholding Deng Xiaoping's vision of "building socialism with Chinese characteristics." He did appear to take a compromise position on China's overall security strategy, which had been raised by conservative ideologues and PLA leaders the previous month. While affirming that "the lofty cause of peace and development" was still China's approach to international affairs, Jiang called on all countries to "jointly strive to oppose hegemonism and power politics, and give new impetus to building a just and reasonable new international order."[53]

Jiang's speech did not end the debate over policy toward the United States, however. In early June, *People's Daily* (*Renmin Ribao*) appeared to be publishing both sides of a virulent argument over what China's approach to the United States should be. On June 3, for example, it published an editorial entitled "Unswervingly Upholding the Independent Foreign Policy of Peace," in which it reminded readers that "establishing and developing healthy and stable relations between China and the United States, . . . not only are in the fundamental interests of the two countries, but also are in the interest of safeguarding world peace and stability."[54] The following day, however, it highlighted a "special commentary" by Zhang Dezhen, describing in vitriolic terms the American "Eurasian strategy," which included NATO expansion, the "partnership for peace" with former Soviet states, and a 1996 agreement with Japan on modernizing joint defense guidelines. Zhang claimed all these efforts were all part of the U.S. plan to "politically, economically, and militarily check . . . China's rise as a global power."[55] On June 7, another editorial exhorted people to turn their anger over Belgrade into unity and strength in working "to build a more prosperous state under the banner of Deng Xiaoping Theory and the leadership of the CPC Central Committee with Comrade Jiang Zemin at the core."[56]

In Washington, the finger pointing was just beginning. How could it have happened? NATO blamed an "intelligence error" for the bombing of the embassy, speculating that the CIA, which had "nominated" the Federal (Yugoslav) Directorate for Supply and Procurement as a target, had perhaps used an outdated map of Belgrade that had inaccurately located the directorate's location and had not noted the move of the Chinese embassy to Bulevar Umetnosti 2 in 1997. But the fact that the directorate was the only target nominated by the CIA in seventy-eight days of bombing raised questions about whether it was a mistake. The National Imagery and Mapping Agency—a joint CIA-DOD operation responsible for all military maps and satellite imagery—pointed out in its own defense that hard-copy maps are "neither intended, nor used, as the sole source for target identification and approval . . . Recent news reports regarding the accuracy of NIMA maps have been inaccurate or incomplete."[57]

The Clinton White House ordered a full-scale investigation of all aspects of the decisionmaking process that led to the bombing, and despite growing congressional anger at China over the riots outside the embassy, it decided to send a delegation to Beijing to present the results of its investigation to the Ministry of Foreign Affairs. Undersecretary of State for Political Affairs Thomas Pickering was chosen to head the delegation. He asked the CIA and the Department of Defense to provide senior officials to accompany him. The Defense Department declined to send a uniformed military officer and provided only grudging cooperation with Pickering's preparations. Susan Shirk, deputy assistant secretary of state for East Asian and Pacific Affairs, recalled the department's attitude as "completely unforthcoming, totally hostile to the whole approach [of the Pickering delegation]."[58]

Pickering had been prepared to travel in late May or early June, but the Chinese delayed the trip, explaining that "public opinion" was still too inflamed.[59] It is more likely that leadership meetings were still ongoing to prepare the official response. According to Hong Kong's *Cheng Ming* magazine—not always a reliable source—the debate was resolved with a resolution by the Politburo to maintain China's general course of peaceful development of its economy but to sharpen its vigilance against the United States and to prepare for future conflict. Although the notion of a "constructive strategic partnership" was not abandoned in public, it was deemed "unrealistic" by the Politburo. For Chinese military and civilian leaders alike, the Belgrade bombing proved that the United States had resolved to treat China as a strategic enemy. China's response was to "say no" to the United

States and prepare for a long-term hostility, possibly including war. For the short term, "whether or not Sino-US relations can be improved or eased depends on whether or not the United States will restrain itself in its strategy toward China."[60]

When he was finally allowed to deliver the explanation in Beijing, Pickering stressed the bombing was a result of a concatenation of errors:

—The original targeting work done by CIA analysts used inappropriate methods (namely U.S. Army land navigation techniques) to locate the Federal Directorate of Supply and Procurement and failed to consider the 1997 move of the Chinese embassy to the same area. They thus concluded the embassy building was the directorate.

—Intelligence community databases maintained to avoid targeting nonmilitary facilities (a "no-hit list") had not been updated to reflect the new location of the PRC embassy.

—Backup checks at the Joint Chiefs of Staff and NATO headquarters did not uncover the earlier errors (although one analyst questioned whether the targeted facility was the directorate, his concerns were not highlighted), and the mission bombing plan was approved.[61]

Pickering presented the report in a calm and businesslike meeting, but the Chinese rejected it, as he knew they would. "The explanations that the U.S. side has supplied so far for the cause of the incident are anything but convincing and . . . the ensuing conclusion of the so-called mistaken bombing is by no means acceptable to the Chinese Government and people," the Foreign Ministry announced the day after Pickering departed.[62] There were no further efforts to provide a fuller explanation, however.[63]

Four days later, *Renmin Ribao* published a commentary by an "observer" (*guanchajia*), a format usually indicative of an officially authorized but not approved minority view, which scathingly denounced American "hegemonism" in language that shocked both American and Chinese observers.[64] Entitled "Today's Hegemonism Should Look at the Mirror of History," the observer compared American foreign policy to that of Nazi Germany. "If we ask which country in the world wants to be the 'lords of the earth' like Nazi Germany did in the past, there is only one answer, namely the United States, which upholds hegemonism."[65] The article was noteworthy not only for the virulence of its anti-American rhetoric but also for its unmistakable deviation from the official line, which had been communicated earlier in *Renmin Ribao* editorials. Politburo member and Propaganda Department Director Ding Guan'gen—considered one of the leading "conservatives" in the leadership—probably was directly responsible for the article, one of the most obvious indicators at that time of the controversy surrounding China's policy toward the United States.[66]

China and the United States have never come to an agreement on what happened and whether the United States explained its actions appropriately. Although not an active dispute, the issue has been a major irritant in the relationship ever since, and as a result, most Chinese still believe the United States deliberately attacked their embassy for nefarious but unknown reasons. Some Western reporters have shared these suspicions. In October 1999, the London newspaper the *Observer* claimed the bombing was a deliberate act, undertaken because NATO had detected Chinese intelligence facilities providing "rebroadcast" support to the Yugoslav military after their own transmitters had been destroyed in the bombing.[67] Secretary Albright dismissed the *Observer* story as "balderdash," but the story fed Chinese suspicions, as did the CIA's customary unwillingness to comment on newspaper stories. Even when the agency took the unusual step in April 2000 of announcing the disciplinary firing of one (unnamed) employee and administrative disciplining of six others over the targeting mistakes, the Chinese still remained unconvinced.

In the circumstances, unanswered questions will persist and sustain Chinese suspicions. But whatever the cause and the unsolved mysteries of the Belgrade bombing, believing the bombing was something other than a mistake is far more difficult. Certainly no one at a senior level in the administration would have condoned an act so flagrantly in violation of international laws and conventions, no matter how desperate the situation in Kosovo. Neither could it have been a conspiracy by "rogue elements" in the CIA or the Defense Department—which would be impossible to carry out or cover up in the Defense Department or Central Intelligence Agency of the 1990s. An effort to undermine China? The idea bears no relationship whatsoever to American strategic thinking or policy process. As implausible as the official explanation may seem at points, all other "explanations" are far more implausible. To this day, China continues to demand a "satisfactory" explanation of what happened and punishment for those responsible. As so often in the past, the Chinese are carrying a grudge over an American action they do not fully understand.

Americans did little better in evaluating the Chinese reaction. After watching the well-organized marches on television, American politicians and pundits condemned the demonstrations as a sham, a cynical farce orchestrated by the government. "Barely disguised stage management of the riots and demonstrations displays the manipulative nature of the Chinese government," Representative Chris Cox told journalists.[68] Seizing on the fact that the Chinese media waited until Monday to publicize the apologies of President Clinton and Secretary Albright, some American observers dismissed the public demonstrations as political theater designed to distract people's attention from the tenth anniversary of the June 4 demonstrations.[69] Many seemed to believe that the incident would soon be forgotten, and other issues on the U.S.-PRC bilateral agenda would return to prominence. As they had been so often in the ten years since Tiananmen, the pundits were wrong.

The bombing of China's embassy in Belgrade was a watershed event for many Chinese, similar in emotional content, if not scale, to the effect of June 4, 1989, on many Americans. For Chinese students and urban elites, it represented the end of illusions about America's good intentions toward China. It was impossible to believe in a benevolent United States in the face of the deliberate bombing of an embassy, which caused the death of innocent men and women. Their reaction was one of confused and inchoate anger mixed with sadness. Images presented ironically in the United States—of Chinese students, dressed in jeans and Nike shoes, drinking Pepsi-Cola while they waited to throw stones at the American embassy—represented deep emotional trauma in China. So many young, modern Chinese had focused their hopes and aspirations on America—to wear American-style clothes, eat American-brand fast food, try to get an American education, learn American English, watch American movies and television, work in an American company in China, perhaps even emigrate to America. They felt betrayed and humiliated. Their rage was real, and the effects of it persisted. Educated elites knowledgeable about the United States bitterly agreed with conservative ideologues that the United States had "evil intentions" toward China. They even blamed the United States for sabotaging reform. "You were the ideal for so many of us," one official said. "And now your stupid bombs have killed our people. This is a perfect justification for slowing reforms. . . . And it's really your fault."[70]

Delivered Blows: The Cox Report

If the Belgrade bombing was a tragic mistake, the Cox Committee report was a direct attack on both China and President Clinton, and it did significant damage. The members of the Select Committee on U.S. National Security and Military/Commercial Concerns with the People's Republic of China had collected thousands of documents and taken thousands of hours of testimony from more than 150 witnesses, including many intelligence and military analysts, by the time they completed their classified report in January 1999. None of the government analysts had any control over how the eager, sharply partisan, and aggressive young staffers of the Select Committee—most of whom had little knowledge of China, nuclear weapons, or intelligence—wanted to use what they were given. Managers in the intelligence community had no mechanisms for reviewing the committee's work in progress or easing the burden on their own personnel of constantly attending to the Select Committee's demands. When the intelligence community was presented with the Select Committee's draft of its "unclassified" version, they were shocked to find great sections taken directly from the classified report, which had incorporated verbatim large amounts of raw intelligence reporting.

The Select Committee, eager to release the public report so it would factor into the planned impeachment of President Clinton, pressed the intelligence community and FBI for immediate approvals. The bureaucracies resisted. Weeks of wrangling over rewrites and redactions followed, during which members of the committee and others in the House Republican leadership accused the Clinton administration of covering up the scandal to protect itself and the Chinese. At the president's order, the CIA prepared its own "damage assessment" of Chinese spying and their nuclear program, which concluded that "China's technical advances have been made on the basis of classified and unclassified information derived from espionage, contact with U.S. and other countries' scientists, conferences and publications, unauthorized media disclosures, declassified U.S. weapons information, and Chinese indigenous development. The relative contribution of each cannot be determined." Those findings were reviewed by an independent commission and were confirmed in April.[71]

Finally, on May 25, the committee report was released. It was 874 pages long, in ten chapters, with a twenty-nine-page "overview." Although Cox lamented that rewrites had caused its conclusions to be weakened, the report made every effort to be categorical:

> The People's Republic of China (PRC) has stolen classified design information on the United States' most advanced thermonuclear weapons. The stolen U.S. nuclear secrets give the PRC design information on thermonuclear weapons *on a par with our own.*" (Overview)
>
> The PRC has used access to its markets to induce U.S. business interests to provide military-related technology. The PRC also uses access to its markets to induce U.S. businesses to lobby in behalf of common goals, such as liberalized export standards and practices. Agents tied to the PRC's military industries who have illegally provided political contributions may have used these contributions to gain access to U.S. military and commercial technology." [Overview]
>
> Almost every PRC citizen allowed to go to the United States as part of these [official] delegations [23,000 of them in 1996] likely receives some type of [intelligence] collection requirement. [Chapter 1]
>
> The stolen U.S. secrets have helped the PRC fabricate and successfully test modern strategic thermonuclear weapons. The stolen infor-

> mation includes classified information on seven U.S. thermonuclear warheads, including *every currently deployed thermonuclear warhead in the U.S. intercontinental ballistic missile arsenal.* [Chapter 2]
>
> Assistance from U.S. companies has improved the reliability of the PRC's military and civilian rockets, and the transfer of some of these improvements to its ballistic missiles is possible. [Chapter 4][72]

As political theater, the Cox Committee report was dramatic, bold, and effective. It portrayed the PRC as an "insatiable" thief of American secrets and weaponry and the Clinton administration as an appallingly inept, if not corrupt, steward of the "crown jewels" of American technological supremacy. Its release was accompanied by a call from eighty members of Congress (mostly Republicans) for the resignation of National Security Adviser Berger for "dereliction of duty" in not calling attention to the Chinese activities earlier and for the resignation of Attorney General Janet Reno for not authorizing the wiretapping of Wen Ho Lee on suspicion of espionage.[73]

The administration reacted with a combination of cooperation, defensiveness, and denial. The White House issued a lengthy statement agreeing with "the substance of nearly all the Committee's [38] recommendations" and claiming it was already implementing most of them.[74] Berger went on national television to defend his handling of the issue as well as the overall Clinton policy of engagement with China. Otherwise hapless candidates for the Republican Party nomination for president, Gary Bauer and Patrick Buchanan, as well as conservative stalwart columnist Robert Kagan declared China to be America's strategic adversary for the indefinite future.[75] Critics of Clinton's China policy made it clear that any disparagement by China specialists of the committee's report—which was, after all, bipartisan—would not be welcome.

But there were plenty of critics, and rightly so. As analysis, the Cox report was dreadful: poorly written, its conclusions were overdrawn and based on unseen (and some say, nonexistent) evidence. It was shot through with conditional language attached to alarmist conclusions. Members of the Select Committee admitted the report was written as a "worst case" assessment, intended to shake up the national labs and Department of Energy to tighten their security.[76] But its implications went far beyond the labs, extending to many other aspects of engagement with China, from government programs to trade to tourism. Even Notra Trulock, the investigator from the Department of Energy who broke open the Wen Ho Lee case, observed the report was too categorical, omitting some of the conditional language he had used in his testimony.[77] The Chinese, of course, issued an official critique of the report on July 15, but it was almost completely dismissed in the United States.

Nuclear weapons specialists belittled the Cox report, claiming it overstated China's capabilities significantly. In a stinging critique of security practices at the national laboratories carried out by a special advisory panel to the President's Foreign Intelligence Advisory Board, panel chair Warren Rudman criticized the Cox Committee for excessive analysis by innuendo: "possible damage has been minted as probable disaster; workaday delay and bureaucratic confusion have been cast as diabolical conspiracies. Enough is enough."[78] In December, four scholars at Stanford University would issue a blistering and lengthy critique of the numerous factual and analytical errors they found in the Select Committee's report.[79] Nonetheless, the report was treated in the media and Congress as something true and valuable, and efforts to rebut it were seen as politically motivated or worse.[80]

Another Taiwan Crisis

With U.S.-China relations reeling, the Taiwan issue re-emerged to do further damage. On July 9, Taiwanese president Lee Teng-hui met with radio reporters of the Voice of Germany (*Deutsche Welle*) in his office to respond to questions they had previously sent him. According to his autobiographical account, Lee had been planning for some time to adjust and clarify the definition of Taiwan's sovereignty in terms of international law and practice and had established a special committee of young scholars to study the issue in August 1998, shortly after the Clinton visit to China.[81] Responding to the reporters' first question about Taiwan being treated as a "renegade province" by the PRC, Lee launched into a well-prepared reply. Since 1949, he said, the PRC had never ruled Taiwan, never exercised sovereignty. Moreover, by virtue of amendments to the Taiwanese constitution adopted in 1991, Taiwan no longer claimed sovereignty over PRC-ruled territory. (Before that time, the Republic of China still claimed sovereignty over all of Chinese territory.) Therefore, Lee said, "The 1991 constitutional amendments have placed cross-Strait relations in the position of being *a state-to-state relationship, or at least a special state-to-state relationship*, and not like the relationship between a legal government and a renegade group, or like the relationship between the central government and a local government under 'One China.' And because cross-Strait relations are in the position of being special state-to-state relations, there is no longer any need to declare Taiwan independent."[82] Although seemingly innocuous and to many Americans a fitting and accurate description of the relationship between Taiwan and the mainland, Lee's statements hit the U.S.-China relationship, as well as the cross-Strait relationship, like another precision-guided bomb.

Even Lee's associates in Taiwan were caught by surprise, although the issue had been discussed in private. Straits Exchange Foundation Chairman Koo Chen-fu insisted that Lee's remarks represented no change in Taiwan's policy and expected it would not affect the planned October visit of Asociation for Relations across the Taiwan Strait Chairman Wang Daohan.[83] Su Ch'i, chairman of Taiwan's Mainland Affairs Committee, had been visiting the United States when Lee made his remarks. Hastily returning to brief the press, Su tried to explain that Lee was changing the language only because Taiwan had not been successful in getting Beijing to give Taiwan equal status in negotiations. He insisted Lee was not undertaking a major change of policy, but only that new terms were needed so that China and Taiwan could "end their convoluted 'one China' dispute of the past."[84]

In the highly esoteric world of cross-Strait relations, where language is more damaging and more frequently used than weapons, Lee's remarks and Su's "clarification" were a challenge the PRC leadership could not ignore, and they wasted little time in denouncing them in the harshest terms. A Xinhua commentator on July 12 criticized Lee's "naked separatist remarks" and accused him of "cheating Taiwan compatriots and the public, . . . poisoning cross-Strait relations and threatening stability . . . and dragging the Taiwanese into the mire of Taiwan independence."[85] Wang Daohan told reporters that same day he was "shocked" at Lee's comments and had demanded an explanation from Koo Chen-fu. On July 14, *Renmin Ribao* escalated the criticism of Lee, warning he would be "denounced by history and condemned by the nation" if he continued his efforts to undermine the "one China principle."[86] The PLA newspaper, *Jiefangjun Bao*, heightened the rhetoric the following day. Charging that Lee was "playing with fire," a commentator article claimed the army was "utterly infuriated by Li Teng-hui['s] criminal scheme of splitting the motherland" and warned in words reminiscent of 1996 that it would not "sit idly by" and allow it to happen. "He who plays with fire will certainly get burned! We warn Li Teng-hui not to be blinded by inordinate ambition and not to act arbitrarily. Anyone who attempts to split the motherland will certainly come to no good end," the article concluded.[87]

As usual, suspicions in China immediately turned to whether the United States had put Lee up to changing the language of cross-Strait relations. Officials in Washington took pains to reassure Beijing that this was not the case, responding in part to major press accounts that seem to have misinterpreted Su Ch'i's "explanation" of Lee's remarks. Although the Mainland Affairs Council chief's interpretation had focused narrowly on the fact that Taiwan no longer wished to use the term "one China," *Washington Post* reporter Michael Laris and others reported (from Beijing) that Taiwan intended to "scrap the 'one China' policy that had framed its relationship with

Beijing for years."[88] On July 13, State Department spokesman Jamie Rubin publicly reiterated that the United States maintained a "one China" policy and supported direct negotiations between Beijing and Taipei to resolve their differences. "We're concerned," he continued, "that it is not helpful for the Taiwanese authorities to make statements that would make it harder to have [cross-Strait] dialogue. We're also concerned that it's not helpful for Beijing to make statements that indicate that a dialogue is harder to achieve."[89] The White House spokesman weighed in with similar sentiments two days later.

As the crisis escalated during the week, with increasingly strident statements from Beijing, accompanied by threats of military action, Washington tried personal diplomacy. Darryl Johnson, director of the American Institute on Taiwan, met with President Lee, while Deputy National Security Adviser James Steinberg telephoned Lee's former national security director Ding Mou-shih, seeking clarification of Lee's statements and warning that Washington would not support unilateral changes in the overall status of PRC-Taiwan relations.[90] On July 19, Clinton used the "hot line" to call Jiang and counsel patience and calm, as well as reassure him that the United States did not support the kind of change Lee was proposing. In reply, Jiang warned Clinton that Lee had taken a "dangerous step." According to the account published in the Chinese press immediately afterward, Jiang told Clinton, "There are certain forces on the island of Taiwan and in the international community which aim to separate Taiwan from the motherland. We will not stand by and let this happen." He reaffirmed the PRC position that "peaceful reunification and one-country, two systems" remained the "main principle" for solving the dispute. But he also reminded the American president that ". . . we will not commit ourselves to renouncing the use of force on the Taiwan issue."[91]

The following week, Clinton ordered the postponement of a midlevel Defense Department delegation to Taiwan that was intended to make an assessment of Taiwan's air defense and missile defense needs. The president also sent Assistant Secretary of State Stanley Roth and Kenneth Lieberthal, NSC senior director, to Beijing to reiterate the U.S. position on "one China" and to counsel restraint.[92] The AIT Washington director, Richard Bush, went to Taiwan, where he met with Lee Teng-hui and the entire foreign policy establishment. In his book, Lee Teng-hui recounts the meetings with Bush and implies strongly that he was affronted by Bush's lower bureaucratic rank, which reinforced his grievance about Taiwan's lack of equal status with Beijing. He also describes his growing dissatisfaction with the Clinton administration, particularly after the appointment of Kenneth Lieberthal as NSC senior director, and his determination to use the U.S. Congress to press Taiwan's case.[93]

Congress needed no encouragement to challenge Clinton on Taiwan, which had been of consistent concern since 1994. Senate Foreign Relations Committee Chair Jesse Helms held hearings on the "Taiwan Security Enhancement Act" (S. 693) in early August and accused the administration of being "a bunch of nervous Nellies, afraid they will offend mainland China."[94] The act itself—along with similar legislation in the House (H.R. 1838)—proposed sharp increases in the quantity and quality of defensive weapons to be sold to Taiwan, including submarines, missile defense equipment, state-of-the-art antiaircraft missiles, and AEGIS-class destroyers, considered vital for a theater missile defense capability. The administration strongly opposed the legislation on the grounds that it would contribute to a heightening of tensions in the region; rather than dissuading Beijing from new military deployments in the Taiwan region, the legislation would likely spur Beijing to new deployments and new hostility.

As cross-Strait tensions mounted, nervous stock markets on both sides fell sharply, forcing Taipei to resort to market stabilization measures to offset the sharp decline in share prices. In a new twist to cross-Strait animosity, computer hackers on the mainland—some traced to government offices—mounted more than 72,000 attacks on Taiwanese websites by the end of August, including the legislative *Yuan* and numerous ministries.[95] Taiwanese hackers responded in kind, defacing PRC official websites to the point that the Communist Party and key State Council ministries were ordered to disconnect from the Internet in late August "to prevent the invasion and destruction by antagonistic elements."[96]

Unlike the 1996 situation, however, Beijing's bellicosity in 1999 was almost entirely rhetorical. It is difficult to tell how serious the "war fever" was in Beijing after Lee's remarks. Hong Kong press reports suggested senior PLA officers were pressuring Jiang heavily—during the leadership's summer retreat at Beidaihe—to authorize "resolute action," such as taking over Quemoy or Matsu islands. Younger officers—filled with patriotic fervor—supposedly were the principal proponents of such a course.[97] The Hong Kong press was filled with sensational stories of Chinese submarines lurking outside Taiwan's ports, of troops massing in Fujian Province, of planning for assaults on small offshore islands, of PLA leaders promising Taiwan would fall in five days. They were wildly inaccurate, probably planted for psychological effect against Taiwan. By contrast, PRC media basically ignored the presence of two U.S. carrier battle groups (*Kitty Hawk* and *Constellation*) exercising in the Western Pacific at the time, as well as the presence of the Seventh Fleet flagship *Blue Ridge* in Manila.[98]

Some military actions were taken. Beijing test launched its DF-31 ICBM—capable of hitting the United States—in early August, a move seen as a warning to the United States not to get involved in the Taiwan issue, even though the launch had probably been planned for some time.[99] The PRC fighter pilots flew unusually aggressively near the middle line of the Taiwan Strait, drawing Taiwanese fighters, and public complaints, in reaction. A Taiwanese resupply vessel was seized en route to one of the offshore islands, on the pretext that it had been engaged in smuggling. Small ground force training exercises were held in Guangdong, southwest of Taiwan, in August, and a larger exercise was hurriedly thrown together in the Zhoushan Islands far north of the Taiwan Strait in September. Zhang Wannian and other Politburo members reportedly observed the latter exercise, but it did not rival in scale or intensity the 1995–96 exercises at Dongshan and Pingtan islands.

Chinese diplomats took up the slack, however, regaling their contacts—particularly American China specialists—with tales of PLA outrage and a desire to "teach Lee Teng-hui a lesson." They fished for clues about how the United States might react to a PLA attack on one of the offshore islands and no doubt reported back accurately that their interlocutors counseled strongly against any military action.[100] The cold, hard facts, however, were that China was in no position to take serious military action against Taiwan in the summer of 1999, and the exaggerated outrage of diplomats and generals could not cover up its lack of preparedness.

In any event, Washington's efforts to smooth over the ill effects of Lee Teng-hui's provocative statement were effective in the short run, easing Beijing's suspicions that the United States had been behind Lee's "two states theory." There were no further threats of military action, air incidents over the Taiwan Strait decreased, and eventually, Washington and Beijing moved on to other issues. The Taiwan question, however, became even more a zero-sum issue—for Beijing, for Taipei, and for many in Washington. Along with many of the sacrifices to logic that a "strategic" relationship with China had entailed in earlier years, the sacrifices of Taiwan's dignity and esteem as a successful nation-state were no longer acceptable to many Americans. Beijing's perceived overreaction to Lee Teng-hui's remarks was simply proof of the unreasonableness of China's position. Efforts at neutrality from Washington did not prevent tensions from skyrocketing in ways similar to those in 1995–96. Both Beijing and Taipei hardened their rhetoric, with Lee gaining support from his own cabinet and from other politicians seeking to succeed him in the presidency.

At the Beidaihe leadership retreat in late July, how to respond to Lee Teng-hui (and his purported American supporters) was on the agenda, along with several other domestic issues. As was often the case at Beidaihe, economic policy was the principal focus of the beach-side leadership discussions, and Jiang evidently sided with the beleaguered Zhu Rongji in refocusing attention on the need to complete reform of the state-owned enterprise system.[101]

Taiwan reportedly was discussed at length, and critics were permitted to have their say. They did not prevail, but neither did they fail entirely.

One can speculate that Jiang may have argued at Beidaihe that his personal relationship with Clinton was an asset that could be used more effectively than military force in getting Lee to back down from his "two states theory." He might have cited as evidence that Washington had sent emissaries to reassure Beijing of its intention to maintain a "one China" policy and had agreed to provide $4.5 million to compensate the victims of the Belgrade bombing.[102] He may have taken note of Secretary of State Madeleine Albright's public criticism of Lee Teng-hui at an APEC meeting in late July, when she complained that Taiwan's explanation of Lee's comments "don't quite do it" in terms of reassuring Washington of his intentions, and her acquiescence in Tang Jiaxuan's characterization of Lee as a "troublemaker."[103] Critics would have noted, however, that Albright deflected Tang's demand that the United States commit not to sell theater missile defense to Taiwan, and that immediately after the APEC meeting, the Pentagon announced it had agreed to sell Taiwan $550 million in new aircraft and spare parts.[104]

In the end, the Beidaihe leadership meeting agreed on a nuanced but only slightly less militant approach to the Taiwan issue. Qian Qichen announced the position at a joint conference of the Central Committee and State Council Taiwan Affairs offices, held in Beijing on August 18. It was essentially a reiteration of existing policy, which, in the aftermath of Lee's comments, was a significant decision. The conference approved the condemnation of Lee and complete rejection of his "two states theory"; it reiterated the formulation of "peaceful reunification and one country two systems," while retaining the right to use military force; it placed special emphasis on promoting economic exchanges and guaranteeing "the legitimate rights and interests of Taiwan businessmen"; and it suspended quasi-official (SEF-ARATS) contact until and unless "the Taiwan authorities openly give up the 'two-state theory' and the 'special state-to-state relations' and genuinely return to the position of the one-China principle."[105]

Course Corrections

In the second half of the year, various changes took place that would alleviate some of the tensions and pressures that had built up in U.S.-China relations. Some were deliberate choices made by the Clinton administration, some were self-correctives brought about by bureaucratic review panels and inspectors general. They operated to temper the emotions that had risen in both countries over the way the "other side" was conducting the relationship, although they did not contribute to any easing of substantive disputes.

At Last, a WTO Agreement

In September 1999, President Clinton met again with President Jiang on the margins of the APEC leaders meeting, this time in Auckland, New Zealand. His goal was—yet again—to try to put a relationship that had gone awry back on a normal course, to recover a degree of communication and consensus on basic goals. Clinton let his frustration with Lee's July 9 press interview show through in the public discussion of the summit with Jiang. As Sandy Berger put it, the president told Jiang "that the statement by President Lee had made things more difficult for both China and the United States," but that the United States both reaffirmed a "one China policy" and warned China not to resort to military force.[106]

But Clinton's more urgent purpose was to restart the stalled negotiations on China's accession to the WTO, and he achieved some success. Despite doubts about the benefits of WTO membership, Jiang and Zhu Rongji were persuaded that Clinton was serious about reaching an agreement and that the overall course of the bilateral relationship would benefit from resuming the negotiations. But they were determined to play hard to get, and it took at least two phone calls after Auckland, and a special trip by Treasury Secretary Larry Summers to meet Zhu in Lanzhou, before the Chinese agreed to return to the table.[107] The table, of course, was in Beijing.

Charlene Barshefsky arrived on November 10, accompanied by the head of the National Economic Council, Gene Sperling (who had helped kill a WTO agreement in April); Ken Lieberthal; and an entourage of midlevel officials from various U.S. bureaucracies. They faced many disadvantages. The talks were in Beijing, making communication with Washington difficult; President Clinton seemed to want a successful agreement more than the Chinese did; Barshefsky, and particularly Sperling, could not afford to fail a second time, and they had to try and craft an agreement that would look better than the one they turned down in April, even though they knew full well that the Chinese had taken some of the earlier concessions off the table. There was still much resistance in Congress to the notion of granting permanent normal trade relations to China, and they were facing Long Yongtu, MOFTEC vice minister, a skillful and deft negotiator who had been involved in the GATT-WTO process from the earliest stages.

The discussions were long, detailed, and frustrating for both sides. Barshefsky fumed at the Chinese tactics of constantly going back over issues that were thought to have been agreed. Long Yongtu disparaged the U.S. delegation's penchant for histrionics, such as outbursts of anger, walking out of meetings, demanding to see senior Chinese leaders, and threatening to return home. Chinese tactics were not without an element of theatricality.

On November 12, for example, Barshefsky insisted on seeing Zhu Rongji to determine whether there was serious intent to reach an agreement. The Chinese woke Barshefsky at 3:15 a.m. on Saturday to tell her Zhu would meet her in Zhongnanhai later that morning. Magnanimously, Zhu encouraged the U.S. delegation with reassurances that an agreement was within sight, and they should press on to a successful conclusion.[108]

Optimistic that a deal was reachable, the delegation told President Clinton that he should plan to announce the agreement on Sunday morning, Washington time (November 14), before heading for a NATO meeting in Ankara, Turkey. But the follow-up negotiations went badly, with both sides blaming each other. Barshefsky spoke directly by phone to Clinton, who said she should come home if she could not turn the talks around. She told the Chinese on Sunday the delegation was packing its bags and would return home on a Monday morning flight. The Chinese invited her to the Ministry of Foreign Trade to wrap up the process with a brief statement for the press. She insisted on meeting before 4 a.m., leading the Chinese to believe she was leaving time for more discussions. They also noticed she had not confirmed her airline flight.[109]

As the final act in the drama, Zhu Rongji appeared at the ministry in midmorning to speak to the U.S. delegation one last time. By that point, the deal hinged on certain issues on which no further progress was deemed possible. These included the permissible foreign stake in Chinese telecommunications enterprises, the mechanism by which the United States could protect itself from Chinese "dumping" of low-cost goods, and matters related to insurance, banking, textiles, and audiovisual products introduced in China. Zhu offered concessions on two of the seven issues but said the U.S. side would have to compromise on the others. Barshefsky and Sperling withdrew to a women's bathroom and called Clinton, who was in Ankara. He readily agreed to the arrangements, and the U.S. delegation so informed the Chinese. As a final gesture of goodwill, Jiang Zemin escorted Barshefsky and her delegation through a seldom-seen pavilion in Zhongnanhai, the guarded leadership compound near the Forbidden City.[110]

Both sides were deliberately vague on the details of the final agreement, trying to avoid stirring new controversy by pointing out where the other side had given way. The USTR press release was a model of brevity and objectivity, with no hint of boasting or overstatement —Barshefsky had learned from the mistake in April. Both presidents stressed the important economic benefits for both sides of the trade agreement but also noted the positive impact it would have on the overall relationship. In an early morning statement in Ankara, Clinton said, "The agreement will create unprecedented opportunities for American farmers, workers and companies to compete successfully in

China's market, while bringing increased prosperity to the people of China. The trade agreement is part of a broader agreement, designed to bring China into global systems on issues from nonproliferation to regional security to environmental protection to human rights. With this agreement, the overall relationship between our countries is strengthened."[111] Clinton promised to move quickly to implement the most important commitment on the U.S. side, to grant China permanent normal trade relations (PNTR) status through an act of Congress.

The Trials of Wen Ho Lee

The final act in the "Clinton spy scandals" began with yet another administrative blunder by the FBI. On December 10, the FBI formally arrested Wen Ho Lee at his home in Los Alamos and transported him to Albuquerque, where he was indicted on fifty-nine counts of "gross negligence," mishandling classified information, and violating secrecy provisions of the Atomic Energy Act. Although the early press accounts and congressional inquiries implied Lee was suspected of having delivered all of America's top nuclear secrets directly to the People's Republic of China, the forty-four-page grand jury indictment made no mention of espionage, treason, or other capital crimes. Instead, the government charged Lee had improperly moved computer files from a classified system to an unclassified one, then made unauthorized copies of those files—which included both the physical properties of America's most sophisticated nuclear warheads and simulation codes for various nuclear explosions—onto several large-capacity computer tapes, which could not be accounted for.[112]

The indictment was the result of thousands of hours of work by more than 200 FBI agents, who probed millions of computer files, interviewed more than 1,000 witnesses, and surveilled Lee twenty-four hours a day for more than six months. After his arrest, Lee was placed in unusually restrictive custody, denied bail, and kept in solitary confinement for the following nine months. His family was not permitted to see him without a Chinese-fluent detention official present at all times. His phone calls were monitored. He was even forced to wear shackles during his daily exercise. The presiding judge justified these conditions on the grounds that Lee had not disclosed the whereabouts of the tape copies of classified information he had made. That was based on the government's insistence that it had a strong case against Lee and that national security demanded stringent treatment.[113] In fact, the government's case by the time of his indictment was hopelessly inadequate, which later reports indicated the FBI knew at the time.

Problems with the case had begun shortly after the FBI press leaks and the Cox Committee report had propelled the issue to national prominence in the spring of 1999. Aside from the usual difficulty of prosecuting an espionage case in open court, owing to the likely disclosures of intelligence sources and methods, prosecutors in the Lee case were hampered because at least some of the files Lee transferred were not classified in a formal sense but were merely considered "sensitive." Reports of other national lab researchers transferring sensitive files to unclassified computers made Lee's "crimes" seem less serious.[114] In the meantime, all the FBI's investigators could not find any solid leads tying Lee to China or its nuclear weapons program. It appeared that, if he had made any illicit transfers at all, they may have benefited Taiwan, not the PRC.[115]

In the summer, attention began to be focused on the quality of the investigation that led up to the accusations against Lee, as Energy Secretary Richardson struggled to assuage a growing legion of Capitol Hill critics. Richardson recommended disciplinary action against three security officers from Los Alamos in August. Two struck back almost immediately by informing the *Washington Post* that the investigation of the possible leak of warhead-related information was mismanaged by Notra Trulock—the "whistleblower" who had been a source of the February and March *New York Times* stories that cracked open the case to public scrutiny. They charged Trulock with focusing almost entirely on ethnicity in pursuing the source of the alleged compromises of information and that Lee was the principal suspect mainly because he was Chinese, not because the evidence pointed to him.[116] The inspector general of the Department of Energy released a report in September asserting there was no evidence to support Trulock's claim that he had been blocked from reporting on the espionage case in 1998. Trulock, whom Richardson had given a $10,000 award in April for exemplary service, resigned in protest.[117]

In early September, the *New York Times* published a lengthy assessment of China's nuclear weapons program and the Wen Ho Lee case by one of its science reporters, William J. Broad. In what was seen as an indirect critique and correction of the James Risen and Jeff Gerth stories that broke open the Lee case, Broad provided a balanced, objective assessment of China's nuclear weapons program and the likelihood that China had developed most of its programs indigenously, rather than by theft and espionage, and the growing doubts in the scientific community about the case against Lee.[118] That evidently encouraged other journalists to question openly the government's case against Lee and the ethics and the accuracy of the *Times* reporting on it. Commentators in several national newspapers then began to call into question some of the basic facts spread about the case through the media.[119]

The case that had been painted in such bold colors by congressional Republicans and some in the press now seemed more complex and undefined.

And with the issue of racial profiling that had been implicit in many of the assessments of both Donorgate and Spygate now out in the open, there was a sense of recoil and distrust of the accusations. Asian American groups, silenced but angered during the Donorgate scandals, openly voiced their dismay at the prosecution of Wen Ho Lee and the conditions under which he was held. Scientists offended by accusations of sloppiness or disloyalty pitched in to discredit the accusations and the accusers. The *Nation* charged the government investigation was started by "neo-McCarthyite Republicans who . . . hope to use the 'China threat' as a bludgeon against Democrats in the upcoming presidential election."[120] Seasoned investigative reporters like Vernon Loeb and Walter Pincus of the *Washington Post* and Bob Drogin of the *Los Angeles Times* filed numerous stories that highlighted more instances of FBI and DOE fumbling than of corroborating information in the case.

Despite the weakness of the case and a growing tide of controversy over how it was being handled, the Department of Justice proceeded with the indictment and incarceration of Lee. In the ensuing months, while the scientist languished in solitary confinement, lawyers wrangled over various aspects of the case, repeatedly delaying its being brought to court. Justice Department lawyers offered different "theories" of Lee's motives and continued to insist that he was a flight risk if bail were granted. Lee's lawyers accused the DOE and FBI of "racial profiling" and filed ever-widening requests for classified information from DOE, the FBI, and even the CIA.[121]

The government's case against Lee collapsed completely in mid-August 2000, when the FBI's chief investigator in the case, Robert Messemer, told a bail hearing before U.S. District Judge James A. Parker that he had provided "inaccurate testimony" about Lee and the case against him in earlier hearings. Despite government witnesses who swore the national security might be damaged and "hundreds of millions" of people might be killed if Lee were granted bail, Judge Parker ruled on August 24 that the government's case against him no longer had sufficient strength or focus to justify a denial of bail.[122] Although the conditions under which bail was granted were stringent, Parker's demands of the Justice Department lawyers were tougher. He demanded the prosecution turn over to his custody thousands of pages of documents, many classified, which defense lawyers charged would show a clear pattern of illegal racial profiling in Lee's case. Serious bargaining between federal prosecutors and Lee's lawyers began the following day.

Despite a last-minute stay from a federal appeals court in Denver on Lee's release on bail, the case moved rapidly toward an astonishing conclusion. On September 13, after furious negotiations between prosecution and defense lawyers, Wen Ho Lee pled guilty to one of the fifty-nine counts in his indictment—a felony charge of illegally copying files from a classified to an unclassified computer system at Los Alamos. All other charges were dropped by the government, and Lee walked out of the court a free man, sentenced to time already served. He agreed to drop his suit against the federal government for racial discrimination and to cooperate in determining what happened to the missing data tapes. In a closing statement to Lee and the assembled legal teams of both sides, Judge Parker apologized to Lee for the way he had been treated by the court and charged that "the top decision makers in the Executive Branch, especially the Department of Justice and the Department of Energy . . . have embarrassed our entire nation" by the way in which they handled the case.[123]

President Clinton did not criticize directly any of his Cabinet officials, but he told reporters he was "troubled" by the outcome of the case, particularly the inconsistency between the prosecution's strenuous arguments against bail for Lee, followed by dropping fifty-eight of fifty-nine charges.[124] Neither Attorney General Janet Reno nor FBI director Louis Freeh displayed any embarrassment, much less apology, in their testimony before Senate panels on September 26. Both insisted that their focus on Lee's wrongdoing was justifiable and that their acceptance of the plea-bargain arrangement was the best way to find out what had really happened to the data tapes.[125]

On the same day, the editors of the *New York Times* issued an explanation of their reportorial and editorial coverage of the Wen Ho Lee case. Responding to numerous charges that the "Gray Lady" of American journalism had published inaccurate and biased reporting, which had "stimulated a political frenzy amounting to a witch hunt," the editors allowed that, in retrospect, there were "some things we wish we had done differently." In tortured and nuanced language that would have made a government spokesman proud, the *Times* acknowledged that its journalistic standards had perhaps slipped, its tone had been somewhat alarmist, and it had failed to follow some important leads in the story.[126]

In retrospect, the Wen Ho Lee case was enormously destructive but completely inconclusive. The truth of what Wen Ho Lee did remains unknown. But the controversy ruined the careers of several government officials, cost millions of dollars to prosecute, and tarnished the reputations of the FBI, the Justice Department, the Department of Energy, the federal court system, and one of America's premier newspapers. In combination with the Donorgate fiasco, it alienated a large number of Asian Americans from both political parties. It generated extreme partisan controversy in Congress and exacerbated the strained ties between Congress and the Clinton administration. It sharply divided the academic and think tank "China watching" community, and in its indeterminate conclusion, heightened popular and official American attitudes of suspicion toward China, its leadership, intentions, and policies.

PNTR and "China Fatigue"

As he entered the last year of his presidency, Clinton had identified China, and establishing a constructive relationship with China, as one of his "legacy" issues, one he hoped would be seen as a singular foreign policy success. With the signing of the bilateral agreement between China and the United States on the conditions of its entry into the WTO, Clinton knew he had one more act to complete: the granting of permanent most favored nation status required by WTO norms (by 1998 statute, MFN was called "normal trade relations" to correct the impression that China would receive especially favorable treatment). That required congressional approval, but it was entirely a domestic policy issue, and Clinton set about it with deliberation and dedication. The challenge was not insignificant. Although the yearly renewal of MFN had been approved by the House of Representatives by sizable margins ever since 1993, China had become a major "inside-the-beltway" issue in 1999, and the president was taking no chances.

On January 10, 2000, Clinton announced his team and his plan for a full-scale campaign to win permanent normal trade relations (PNTR) status for China as part of the effort to bring it into the WTO. Chief of Staff John Podesta was put in overall charge, Cabinet members were to be active participants, and Secretary of Commerce William Daley and White House Deputy Chief of Staff Steve Ricchetti were designated to lead the congressional lobbying effort. Clinton tried to set a balanced tone, acknowledging there were many aspects of Chinese government behavior that were regrettable but insisting that the agreement was a step in the right direction for "reform and respect for the rule of law" in China. He affirmed the economic benefits for the United States—enhanced access to China's domestic markets and a significant lowering of tariffs on U.S. products exported to China, with no significant improvement of China's access to the American market.[127]

The process of granting PNTR to China was not especially complex, but it would be time consuming. The first step was to prepare legislation to submit to the Congress declaring Title IV of the Trade Act of 1974 (the Jackson-Vanik amendment) no longer applied to China and to recommend that nondiscriminatory trade treatment be extended to all products from China. Once China's accession was approved by the WTO itself, and the president reported to Congress that the terms of its accession were equal to or better than those reached in the U.S.-China bilateral agreement, the dates for the application of PNTR would be fixed. While USTR and legislative specialists worked to gather the documentation, Clinton and others began the publicity campaign, as well as the process of generating support for what would be a difficult legislative battle.

In his communications and speeches on the issue—and he made several major addresses on China in his final year in office—Clinton spoke from a strategic and a geopolitical perspective. The issues at stake in the debate, he insisted, were more than just trade benefits, although the trade benefits were substantial, and virtually all in America's favor. "China's entry into the WTO . . . is about more than our economic interests. It is clearly in our larger national interest. It represents the most significant opportunity that we have had to create positive change in China since the 1970s. . . . The path that China takes to the future is a choice China will make. We cannot control that choice, we can only influence it. . . . We can work to pull China in the right direction, or we can turn our backs and almost certainly push it in the wrong direction. The WTO agreement will move China in the right direction."[128]

Working in concert with NSC head Sandy Berger, deputy James Steinberg, and Asia senior director Ken Lieberthal, the White House developed a sophisticated message on China. It was realistic, unsentimental, and sensitive to the criticisms of China that had persisted in the United States ever since Tiananmen. China would enter the WTO in the near future, having completed most of the necessary bilateral trade agreements with other WTO members. If the United States chose not to grant PNTR, that would only deny Americans the access to China's trade and markets that the rest of the world would enjoy. China was in a dynamic process of change, with an uncertain outcome. There were many elements of the government's policies that were repugnant to the United States. WTO accession was part of a larger trend toward reform and opening, promoting the rule of law, and engaging China in international agreements that would, over time, make it a less authoritarian, more pluralistic society that recognized democratic and individual rights. Bringing China into the WTO would bring about economic, social, and political change in China, perhaps in a positive direction. Rejecting China's efforts to join the WTO would strengthen the hands of those in China who rejected globalization, reform, and opening up of China to international influence.[129]

The administration finally submitted draft legislation to Congress on March 8. Daley and others said they hoped for a House vote before the end of May, but they admitted they were uncertain of whether they could muster the 218 votes needed to pass the legislation. Senate passage was considered a safer bet but still not certain. Opposition began to jell almost immediately. To Clinton's dismay but not surprise, much of it came from within the Democratic Party and some of its main constituencies. The largest U.S. labor union, the American Federation of Labor and Congress of Industrial Organizations (AFL-CIO) declared its opposition almost immediately and vowed that defeating PNTR would be its principal legislative agenda item for the year. It was followed by the Teamsters Union, the United Auto Workers, the United Steelworkers of America, the American Federation of Teachers, the American Federation of State, County and Municipal Employees, the International Longshore and Warehouse Union, and numerous other labor organizations large and small. In rallies across the country, union leaders decried the absence of the right to organize independent unions in China, claimed that better trade with China would cost millions of American jobs, and pledged they would use their money and votes to defeat candidates who supported PNTR.

Human rights organizations, such as Human Rights Watch and Amnesty International, took a somewhat less forceful approach to WTO membership for China but made clear they believed the United States should not give up the option of using trade to pressure China into improving human rights. Their general perspective was that China's continuing poor record on human and civil rights demonstrated a systematic contempt for international norms. The administration should therefore condition China's entry into the WTO on achievement of certain human rights–related goals, such as opening up Tibet, releasing political prisoners, and dismantling the labor reform system.[130] Environmental groups, such as the Sierra Club, Friends of the Earth, the Humane Society, and others, opposed PNTR as part of their concern for Beijing's poor record on environmental issues and because they entertained doubts about the wisdom of the "globalization" policy that lay behind the agreement.

With key constituencies lining up strongly against PNTR, Democratic Party leaders in the Congress were under pressure to declare positions early. Several of them—notably House Minority Leader Richard Gephardt and Minority Whip David Bonior (D-Mich.)—had long been critics of China and opponents of MFN, so their opposition was expected, and was not long in coming. Members of the House "working group on China," such as Nancy Pelosi, pledged to work hard against the approval of the PNTR legislation. Democrats who favored the president's position—clearly in a minority—and those who were "on the fence" waited for the inevitable lobbying from various groups, colleagues, and administration officials. Some, such as California Democrat Robert Matsui, agreed to work with the administration to generate support among undecided and centrist members.[131]

Vice President Al Gore found himself in a political bind. As the front-runner to be the Democratic Party's candidate for president in the 2000 elections, Gore could not afford to alienate the party's labor base. In February, he had spoken privately to AFL-CIO head John Sweeney, expressing some reservations about the WTO agreement's lack of attention to labor and environmental issues. Sweeney told the press about Gore's remarks, which generated some concerns in the White House about whether Gore would support PNTR.[132] Gore finally wrote a letter to the president of the National Association of Manufacturers (NAM) supporting "the agreement reached by our Administration" on China's entry into the WTO.[133] Nonetheless, Gore would remain on the sidelines for much of the ensuing debate, and critics on both sides used his tepid position against him, both during the PNTR campaign and the presidential election.

Clinton knew he could count on strong support for PNTR from the American business community and somewhat less support from farmers, all of whom gained important benefits from the WTO agreement. Not unexpectedly, he focused attention early on business groups, such as the Business Roundtable, the U.S. Chamber of Commerce, NAM, the Business Software Alliance, the American Farm Bureau Federation, and prominent corporate executives. With the administration's tacit support, these groups undertook a "grassroots" campaign—comparable to the opposition effort—to publicize the benefits of PNTR. Clinton called on former presidents Gerald Ford, Jimmy Carter, and George Bush; former secretaries of state Henry Kissinger and Cyrus Vance; and numerous other political and economic luminaries to support WTO membership for China.

He also made full use of the persuasive power of the Oval Office to lobby undecided members of Congress directly, particularly Democrats and centrist Republicans. Inviting them in groups, often to the Yellow Oval Room in the White House residence, he listened to their concerns about losing labor support in an election year, about alienating key constituencies, then regaled them with facts and figures about the economic benefits for their states, and finally talked solemnly about the national interest and the importance of doing the right thing for America's future. In a few cases, he promised specific benefits or support for programs of individual members of Congress in exchange for PNTR support.[134]

What ensued over the next several months was an extraordinary and unprecedented public debate about China, its past and future, economy and political system, about Taiwan and Hong Kong, U.S.-China policy, American strategic security, globalization, and U.S. trade policy. It was not an organized debate, nor a clear one. It was emotional, divisive, and fueled by a lot of lobbying money. A good deal of the information made public was inaccurate, biased, or prejudicial. But issues were raised and ideas generated, and both the general public and political elites benefited in their understanding of the complexity and difficulty of China policy.

By early May, however, the vote counts in the House were still indeterminate. Although Republicans held a 222 to 211 advantage, many of their own number were opposed to China. Some were longtime critics of China—like

Frank Wolf and Benjamin Gilman—while others were opposed to China's behavior on specific constituency or personal concerns, such as nonproliferation, religious freedom, and abortion. Some were concerned China might use its WTO membership to block Taiwan's entry. Others were worried about the vagueness of some of the clauses in the bilateral agreement, particularly with regard to potential Chinese "dumping" of low-cost goods on the U.S. market. Finally, many were reluctant to give up the annual congressional review of China policy, believing it gave Congress important leverage over the administration and the Chinese.

With tacit administration approval, Congressmen Douglas Bereuter (R-Nebr.) and Sander Levin (D-Mich.) introduced "draft legislation for China/PNTR framework" on May 9. The proposal was designed to "address Congressional concerns about Chinese compliance with their WTO promises, human rights practices in China, and Taiwan's entry into the WTO" and included several recommendations:

—A Congressional-Executive Commission on China, which would report annually on China's human rights, labor, and democracy practices;

—A more detailed legislative road map for antidumping action;

—An annual report from the USTR on China's adherence to its WTO obligations;

—A task force to monitor China's exports of prison labor products;

—"Technical assistance" to develop the rule of law in China's commercial and labor markets; and

—Support for Taiwan's accession to the WTO at the same time as China's.[135]

Once these provisions were incorporated into the bill—increasing its length from one page to more than sixty—it moved through the House legislative process quickly. At the administration's request, Ways and Means Committee Chair Bill Archer (R-Tex.), a firm supporter of PNTR, introduced on May 15, 2000, H.R. 4444: "To authorize extension of nondiscriminatory treatment (normal trade relations treatment) to the People's Republic of China, and to establish a framework for relations between the United States and the People's Republic of China."[136] The Ways and Means Committee marked up the bill and reported it out of committee on May 17 by the remarkable margin of 34-4. It went to the House floor on May 23, where the House Rules Committee ordered it be considered with only three hours of general debate and with no amendments permitted other than to recommit the bill to committee.[137] The floor debate the following day, while short, was furious and highly emotional. Democrats cheered Republican opponents, while Republicans cheered Democrats for supporting the president. After defeating a recommit amendment, the House passed the measure on May 24 on a vote of

237-197. Republicans voted in favor of the bill by a margin of 164-57, while Democrats voted against by a margin of 138-73.

Senate approval of PNTR legislation was expected to follow in short order, but partisan politics again intervened. Two factors caused the president's schedule to be thrown off significantly. One was Senate rules, which would not impose the kind of debate limitation practiced by the House. The other was a desire on the part of Senate Republicans to stretch out the process as long as possible to maximize prospects for embarrassing Al Gore, who would be actively campaigning for president while at the same time ignoring labor's opposition to PNTR. Senator Fred Thompson persuaded Senate Majority Leader Trent Lott that his bill sanctioning violations of nonproliferation accords—clearly aimed at China—should be passed before PNTR was taken up. Senate Democrats, who were far more supportive of Clinton's position than their House colleagues, pushed for a quick vote. Compromises failed, bipartisanship broke down, and Lott had the vote postponed until after the summer recess, despite Democratic efforts to force it onto the agenda.

When the bill did come up in September, Lott ensured that it was not protected from amendments, and staunch opponents offered up nineteen of them in the ensuing ten days, on issues ranging from religious freedoms to forced abortions, nonproliferation, labor rights, trade deficits, and others. All but one were defeated or withdrawn, and the bill was finally passed on September 19 by a margin of 83 in favor to 15 against. Unlike the House, Senate Democrats supported PNTR by 38-7, while Republicans voted 45-8 in favor.[138]

While the politics of who voted for or against and why is extraordinarily complex, analysts agreed that President Clinton played the key role and demonstrated vision and skill in organizing a winning coalition for an unpopular cause; that domestic politicking was a more important consideration than international relations or even trade policy; and that U.S.-China relations would not necessarily see an improvement as a result of the vote.[139] China's reaction was surprisingly ungracious. The Foreign Ministry spokesman, Sun Yuxi, said the measure "serves the fundamental interests of the peoples of both China and the United States but is also of great significance to the healthy development of China-U.S. relations," and he thanked those who had made "vigorous and unremitting efforts" to secure its passage. But he registered the government's "firm opposition" to provisions on human rights monitoring, saying they "interfere in China's internal affairs."[140]

At the end of his term, Clinton would cite China's PNTR as one of the signal achievements of his administration. As he signed the bill, he said, "Today we take a major step toward . . . answering some of the central challenges of this new century. For trade with China will not only extend our nation's unprecedented economic growth, it offers us a chance to help to shape the future of the world's most populous nation, and to reaffirm our own global leadership for peace and prosperity."[141] Despite his hallmark hyperbole, history may prove Clinton right. The WTO membership and changes in China's approach toward foreign competition and market access will work untold changes on Chinese society and foreign relations.

But in the short run, the massive political effort to bring about PNTR had little effect, whether viewed in terms of bilateral relations, public attitudes toward China, or political support for Clinton. Bilateral relations stayed in the deep freeze they had entered after the Belgrade bombing. The Chinese government welcomed the legislation, lamented the fact that it had taken nearly fourteen years to bring WTO membership to fruition, and began preparing for the economic dislocations that would accompany it. The excited and highly vocal "debate" over China policy—as colorful and important as it was—mostly was ignored by the American public. Aside from a few "sound bites" and an occasional argument on public television, the major visual media paid little attention to the PNTR battle, its implications, or its drama. The debate changed few minds among political elites in Washington—it certainly did not achieve the national consensus on China policy that Sandy Berger and others had hoped for. If anything, the rancorous partisanship in both House and Senate during the PNTR process, and the numerous other challenges highlighted by the protagonists—nonproliferation, human rights, trade deficits, and other issues—sharpened the disagreements and laid the ground for future battles. In its formation of the Congressional-Executive Commission on China—and the subsequent establishment of the U.S.-China Security Commission—the potential remained for even more controversy and contention over China policy.[142]

In the presidential election of 2000, foreign policy again played a minor role. Whether Democratic candidate Al Gore lost some labor support because of his (reluctant) support of PNTR is a debatable point in what turned out to be America's closest election. China policy was scarcely mentioned during the campaign. The Republican candidate, George W. Bush, castigated the Clinton administration's "strategic partnership" with China, but openly supported PNTR. He did not dwell on China policy, or its related subject of relations with Taiwan, in any significant way. He referred to China as a "strategic competitor" on one occasion and promised more support for Taiwan's democracy but otherwise avoided the issue entirely, dwelling on restoring American values, integrity, and leadership to the White House.

At the end of the Clinton administration, the mythical court of American public opinion judged the bilateral relationship to be in nearly the same state as it had been following the Tiananmen tragedy of 1989. In various polls taken in the twelve intervening years, most Americans maintained an unfavorable view of China (36 percent favorable versus 57 percent unfavorable in November 2000, compared with 16 percent favorable and 78 percent unfavorable in 1989, after the Tiananmen events.)[143] A significant majority (77 percent) of Americans polled in 2000 saw China as an adversary or rival, not as a friend or strategic partner (12 percent). But views were more mixed on whether China was an enemy or threat to the United States.[144] Few recognized the positive changes brought about by China's transition to a market economy, and nearly half believed China would not live up to the economic agreements it had reached in acceding to the WTO. Only about one-third of Americans polled in 2001 thought U.S. policies would have a positive impact on China's development.[145] With a change in the presidency, public ambiguity, at best, about the importance of good relations, and continuing deep political animus toward China among many political actors, the bilateral relationship remained precariously balanced, volatile, and subject to political innuendo, misperception, and mistakes.

Taiwan Again—Beijing Fumbles, Taipei Recovers

After the August 1999 joint meeting to reiterate the leadership's overall policy line toward Taiwan, a special drafting committee was established in the Institute of Taiwan Studies of the Chinese Academy of Social Sciences to prepare a White Paper—for public release—on Taiwan , specifically refuting Lee Teng-hui's idea of "state to state relations." The paper went through numerous drafts, with different offices or ministries adding text to reflect their interests—a classic Chinese bureaucratic "paper chase." After review at the highest level, probably by Jiang and Qian and others within the Taiwan Affairs Leading Small Group, the White Paper was released to the public on February 22, 2000, by the State Council Information Office and the Taiwan Affairs Office. Entitled "The One-China Principle and the Taiwan Issue," the paper was long, somewhat dry, and academic, refuting the historical, legal, and political underpinnings of Lee's July 9 remarks. It contained little that was new or original and repeated what had become standard threats and incentives to persuade Taiwan's leaders to return to the "one China" principle. But it did contain one phrase that was considered new and threatening by Western news analysts: "If a grave turn of events occurs leading to the separation of Taiwan from China in any name, or if Taiwan is invaded and occupied by foreign countries, *or if the Taiwan authorities refuse, sine die, the peaceful settlement of cross-Straits reunification through negotiations*, then the Chinese Government will only be forced to adopt all drastic measures possible, including the use of force, to safeguard China's sovereignty and territorial integrity and fulfill the great cause of reunification."[146]

The purpose, evidently, was to increase slightly the pressure on Taiwan to return to negotiations, to refute Lee Teng-hui's ideas about a separate and equal political entity, and to halt what Beijing analysts saw as Lee's dangerous slide toward independence. But the execution of the document's release was clumsy. By the time it was completed and chopped by all the relevant agencies, the Taiwan presidential election was only weeks away, and Beijing was involved in another dispute with Washington over policy toward Taiwan. Because of an irreconcilable split within the Kuomintang between Lee Teng-hui and James Soong Chu-yu, which had caused Soong to run as an independent, the Taiwan presidential election was a three-way struggle among Lee's colorless vice president, Lien Chan; Soong; and DPP leader Chen Shui-bian. The White Paper probably was intended mainly for the Taiwan electorate, to warn of the dangers of voting for Chen Shui-bian, the candidate of the Democratic Progressive Party, which included in its party manifesto the goal of making Taiwan fully independent. But it had a more lasting effect on Washington, where its carefully balanced language was lost in the outrage over its timing and perceived threat to democracy in Taiwan. Adding insult to injury, the Ministry of Foreign Affairs evidently was not informed of the date the State Council had chosen to release the White Paper, and it failed to notify a visiting American delegation—headed by the deputy secretary of state, Strobe Talbott—of the impending policy pronouncement.

That diplomatic gaffe, whether deliberate or accidental, only magnified the public outcry that greeted the White Paper in Taiwan and in the United States. The addition of the third condition under which military force might be utilized was viewed as an ultimatum by the PRC to Taiwan: negotiate or suffer the consequences. Editorialists in Washington and New York competed with one another in denouncing Beijing for its threats and the Clinton administration for tolerating them. Members of Congress called the new formulation "unacceptable," the State Department called it "troubling," and the Undersecretary of Defense said it was "unfortunate and very, very unhelpful."[147] Whatever its original intent, the White Paper had the effect of strengthening the hand of those in the United States most eager to provide additional arms sales and defense assistance to Taiwan.

Qian and other Chinese diplomats seemed genuinely taken aback at the reaction of the Western press and the American government. In private, they tried to persuade their counterparts that the White Paper was neither new nor threatening but was intended to convey a message of encouragement for those on Taiwan who did not support the DPP position. Publicly, Qian denied that the White Paper represented any new policy initiative. "Some of the foreign media believed that there had been a major change in China's policy on resolving the Taiwan issue," Qian told the All-China Federation of Returned Overseas Chinese on February 29, "but this view is mistaken."[148] Jiang Zemin provided similar assurances two days later.

During the run-up to the Taiwan election, the United States took two steps that heightened the tension significantly. On February 2, the U.S. House of Representatives passed the Taiwan Security Enhancement Act (H.R. 1838), which directed the executive branch to strengthen cooperation in training and education with Taiwan's military and to expedite the process of making high-technology weapons available to meet Taiwan's needs.[149] Although the bill was much milder than earlier versions (which had specified inclusion of Taiwan in American missile defense development programs), faced further change in the Senate, and was likely to be vetoed by President Clinton, Beijing's reaction was disproportionate. Ambassador Joseph Prueher was called in to the Foreign Ministry to hear China's "utmost indignation and firm opposition," Xinhua and *Renmin Ribao* published rancorous commentaries, and various parliamentary committees in China expressed their outrage at American interference in China's domestic affairs. These responses were clearly for domestic consumption but were widely reported in the United States. If anything, they increased American support for the bill, although it died when it was not taken up by the Senate.

On March 1, just before the National People's Congress went into its annual session, and less than three weeks before Taiwan's elections, Taipei leaked the contents of its annual request for approval to buy U.S. weapons.[150] The list included additional batteries of Patriot antiaircraft (and antimissile) missiles, state-of-the-art AIM-120 long-range air-to-air missiles, submarines, and four Arleigh Burke–class destroyers equipped with the AEGIS air defense radar system, considered an essential building block for a theater missile defense shield for Taiwan.[151] Taipei also made clear it wished to be a part of any TMD programs the United States developed. Beijing's reaction was predictable—harsh criticism of both the United States and Taiwan—but in the context of its shrill rhetoric about Taiwan's independence in advance of the presidential election, it was little noted. On March 8, the United States announced a modest ($106 million) sale of Hawk antiaircraft missiles and improved air surveillance radars, which China promptly protested. Foreign Minister Tang Jiaxuan told a news conference the continued weapons sales "inflated the arrogance of the separatist forces in Taiwan" and therefore made the United States responsible for "the tension in the Taiwan Strait." He demanded the United States stop all arms sales to Taiwan and provide "unambiguous" guarantees it would not provide Taiwan with TMD.[152]

Confusion over whom to blame—the United States or various political leaders on Taiwan—for the PRC's declining influence over events on the island reached all the way to the top of the PRC leadership. Jiang Zemin reportedly briefed National People's Congress (NPC) leaders in early March on a lengthy policy paper he had prepared for the Politburo in January, in which he recommended increased preparations by the PLA for taking military action against Taiwan.[153] Jiang's continuing need for PLA support, while not as great as it had been in 1996, as well as his own conservative instincts left him somewhat passive in the face of the uncertain Taiwan situation. Central Military Commission Vice Chairman Zhang Wannian made the PLA's position very clear and very public. "'Taiwan independence' means war," he told NPC delegates and promised that the PLA "will take any necessary means to steadfastly smash the political gamble of splitting the motherland."[154]

Zhu Rongji appeared to focus mainly on the voters of Taiwan when he addressed the issue during a news conference on March 16, after the close of the NPC meeting. Speaking with uncharacteristic emotional intensity, Zhu responded to a question about Chen Shui-bian's chances of winning Taiwan's presidential election with a rambling diatribe that included references to China's painful history, lines from the PRC national anthem, and late news from Taiwan's stock market. Zhu implied that "villains" were plotting "to let Taiwan independence forces win." "At present, Taiwan people are facing an urgent historic moment. They have to decide what path to follow. They absolutely should not act impulsively. Otherwise, it will be too late for regrets. We believe in Taiwan compatriots' political wisdom. We believe Taiwan compatriots will make a wise historic decision. However, there are only three days left . . . Taiwan compatriots, you must be on your guard!"[155]

It was a curious performance, more nuanced and subtle than the response to it from Taipei and Washington, where it was viewed as another ultimatum. Zhu turned aside several follow-up questions and refused to link the Taiwan issue to overall Sino-American relations. He may have been concerned that unduly harsh rhetoric directed against the United States would jeopardize chances for U.S. congressional approval of the WTO agreement he had hammered out in November 1999. In any case, his statements were repeated in numerous commentaries in Taiwan and elsewhere and were explicitly rejected. All three major candidates expressed hope for stability and harmony, rather than continued tension, but reproached Beijing for interfering in the electoral process. The *Washington Post* was less charitable, comparing Zhu to a "Mafia kingpin."[156]

Whether the Communist Party leadership had a concerted but erroneous strategy or was in disarray in the face of the DPP's unexpected strength, the result of Taiwan's presidential election was another policy disaster for Beijing. On March 18, Taiwanese voters went to the polls in record numbers and elected as president the "pro-independence" candidate, Chen Shui-bian, who won just over 39 percent of more than 12.5 million votes cast. Independent candidate Soong Chu-yu finished second with 37 percent of the votes, while the ruling party candidate, Lien Chan, polled only 23 percent. Chen had downplayed his "Taiwan independence" credentials during the campaign and focused on corruption in the Kuomintang (KMT) and his own record of efficient government as Taipei's mayor. Observers judged he won primarily because of the Lee-Soong split of the ruling party, with additional support coming from endorsements by influential academics and businessmen.[157] Some noted that concerns about the tensions that Chen's party's independence platform might have caused were offset by a public backlash against Beijing's heavy-handed tactics.[158]

In his acceptance statement, Chen consciously sought to reach out to Beijing. "In order to maintain national security and the benefits of all the people [on Taiwan], we would like to immediately negotiate with China on the issues of direct links, direct commerce, investment and military confidence-building measures," he told supporters. He offered to go to China before his inauguration if it would help improve communication between the two sides, and he invited ARATS head Wang Daohan and even Zhu Rongji to visit Taiwan.[159] Beijing's response was an icy silence. Refusing even to print Chen's name after tersely announcing his victory, Xinhua first issued a pro forma statement from the Taiwan Affairs Office (TAO):

> The election of a new leader in the Taiwan area and its result cannot change the fact that Taiwan is part of Chinese territory. . . . We will absolutely not permit "Taiwan independence" in any form. We will judge Taiwan's new leader by his deeds, not just by his words. We will wait and see in which direction he will lead the cross-strait relations. We are willing to exchange views with all political parties, organizations, and public figures in Taiwan that endorse the one-China principle on cross-strait relations and peaceful reunification.[160]

The TAO held a two-day conference on March 22, at which the official line—probably hammered out in the Politburo—was enumerated by Qian Qichen. Qian maintained a hard-line position, threatening those who would push "Taiwan independence" but offering talks and exchanges with any Taiwanese leaders "so long as they recognize the one-China principle."[161] Privately, the leadership was taking an even harder position, according to Hong Kong reports. Chen Shui-bian's election tipped the balance of opinion within the Politburo even further toward so-called hawks, who favored taking military action against Taiwan sooner rather than later. The PLA leaders reportedly were the most demonstrative, sending petitions to Jiang and calling for higher-priority military modernization, particularly of the missile forces. But there seemed to be little opposition elsewhere within the leadership to making preparations to use military force against Taiwan. Chen Shui-bian was an unknown quantity, but he was uniformly distrusted because of the proindependence stance of his party. His vice presidential running mate, Annette Lu Hsiu-lien, was an outspoken advocate of independence. No credence was given to the notion that Chen had given up his aspirations for Taiwan's independence. Military pressure was increasingly perceived as inevitable.[162]

In the period between his election and his inauguration (May 20), Chen Shui-bian was subjected to a major pressure campaign by Beijing to see whether he would explicitly endorse some kind of "one China" formula. Besides low-level military maneuvers, Beijing kept the rhetorical pitch at a high level. The ARATS vice chairman, Tang Shubei, told Hong Kong reporters, "If they do not recognize the 'one China' principle, if they do not recognize that Taiwan is a part of China, then the result will not be peace but disaster, not harmony but conflict, not goodwill but enmity."[163] Still refusing to mention Chen's name, Beijing propagandists focused on Lee Teng-hui—taking grim satisfaction from his forced resignation as KMT chairman in the wake of the election—and on Vice President–elect Lu Hsiu-lien, whom they attacked relentlessly by name. Jiang and others issued statements to the effect that Taiwanese businesses could not support the DPP and "Taiwan independence" and expect to do business on the mainland—a position that was criticized even in Hong Kong.

Knowing that his narrow margin of victory did not include a mandate for independence and that his approach toward China would be seen as the most important facet of his new administration, Chen maneuvered adroitly and carefully. Although he refused to accept Beijing's definition of "one China," which he said "forced [Taiwan] into a corner" and was opposed by the majority of Taiwanese voters, Chen went out of his way to be conciliatory and to signal his desire to ease tensions. He pledged he would not declare Taiwan independent unless the PRC attacked, would not talk further of the "two states theory," would not hold a public referendum on independence, and would not change the name, "Republic of China"—statements that typically were dubbed "the four noes."[164] Beijing was obdurate. Nice words were not enough, said a Xinhua commentator just before Chen's inauguration, the "one China" principle was the touchstone.[165]

Having won the presidency despite Beijing's fierce opposition, Chen was not about to knuckle under on his first day in office. His inauguration speech on May 20 was entitled "Taiwan Has Stood Up"—a none-too-subtle evocation of Mao Zedong's October 1, 1949, address on the occasion of the founding of the People's Republic of China, "China Has Stood Up." The speech was devoted largely to domestic issues, and Chen pledged to be "president of all the people" and to continue cleaning up Taiwan's government apparatus. He promised to continue Taiwan's quest for "room for survival in the international arena," which was broadly supported in Taiwan but reviled in Beijing. On relations with China, Chen reiterated the "four noes" and invited Beijing "to create an era of reconciliation together." But he declined to accept Beijing's demand on the issue of "one China." He stated, "The people across the Taiwan Strait share the same ancestral, cultural, and historical background. While upholding the principles of democracy and parity, building upon the existing foundations, and constructing conditions for cooperation through goodwill, we believe that the leaders on both sides possess enough wisdom and creativity to jointly deal with the question of a future 'one China.'"[166]

Beijing, of course, did not rise to the challenge. After another high-level meeting late on May 20, the PRC leadership—which probably knew from Taiwanese press leaks most of the content of Chen's speech—chose to dismiss and criticize rather than explore his offers. A Xinhua commentary on May 21 laid out the official disappointment. "On the key issue of accepting the one-China principle, the new leader adopted an evasive and vague attitude, saying that one-China is an issue that will be dealt with 'in the future.' Evidently, his so-called goodwill reconciliation lacks sincerity . . . There are still unstable factors facing the development of relations across the Taiwan Straits."[167] Western observers noted an easing of Beijing's approach in the weeks following, with fewer military threats, more invitations to non-DPP Taiwanese politicians to visit Beijing, and a slight easing of the tone of threats to Taiwanese business executives. But there was also a sense of an opportunity having been missed, of Beijing returning to the tried and true, the same set of policies and rhetorical vapidity that had achieved so few of its Taiwan-related goals in the past.

Locked in Leninism

The lack of creativity or flexibility in Beijing's approach to Taiwan was symptomatic of a slowdown in innovation evident in other areas of policy. Relations with the United States were a prime example. Of course, the linkage of Sino-U.S. relations with cross-Strait ties had become, if anything, even tighter in the wake of the "two states theory" and the election of Chen Shui-bian. The support shown in the United States for Taiwan and its continued separation from the mainland—particularly on Capitol Hill and in the media—was no doubt disconcerting to Beijing and appeared to offset the efforts of the Clinton administration to clarify the executive branch's position and to ease cross-Strait tensions. After Lee's *Deutsche Welle* interview and after the Clinton-Jiang summit in September, Washington kept up a steady stream of high-level visits to Beijing. All carried a similar message: American policy on China and Taiwan had "three pillars:" a "one China" approach, support for cross-strait negotiations to resolve problems, and insistence on using peaceful means.[168] The Clinton administration spoke actively against a motion to review Taiwan's UN membership status in September (having previously remained silent). It took the initiative to settle the compensation for the Belgrade bombing and reopen negotiations on China's WTO accession.

Beijing's response varied from tepid to dismissive. In late July or early August 1999, Jiang had written a letter to Clinton demanding that the United States force Lee Teng-hui to retract his "two states theory," curb arms sales to Taiwan, and pressure Taiwan to engage in political discussions with the PRC.[169] At their summit meeting in September, he lectured Clinton on Taiwan, then presented him as a gift a book criticizing the Falun Gong movement in China, which some officials privately took as very bad taste, if not deliberately offensive. China continued to insist the U.S. explanation for Belgrade was unbelievable and unacceptable. During the ultimately successful WTO negotiations, the U.S. delegation was exposed to extraordinary psychological harassment and discourtesy by Chinese negotiators, with Zhu Rongji ultimately sealing a deal that was, in effect, virtually identical to the one the United States had rejected in April.[170] Chinese media reacted to the agreement, which was widely hailed in the United States, with comparative indifference.

Beijing's turn toward enmity in its relations with the United States did not come about suddenly. Even before the bombing of the PRC mission in Belgrade, Chinese "strategists," particularly in the PLA but also in academia, had been reviewing China's foreign policy posture in light of changing international conditions. The Belgrade bombing advanced and intensified the debate within the government and outside. Some of the positions presented, particularly by the military leadership, were fairly extreme, according to Hong Kong stories. Chief of General Staff Fu Quanyou, for example, was reported as exhorting the military to "be prepared mentally, organizationally, and in mobilization and strength to fight World War III" against the United States.[171] The strategic "debate" that ensued in the summer of 1999 was far more vigorous and open than usual. Security specialists and America experts in Chinese universities and think tanks were encouraged to offer their views candidly and in detail rather than simply to parrot the official line or write what they thought the authorities might want to hear. Their views may not have had much effect on Politburo deliberations, but they were available to the public in books, newspaper articles, television commentaries, and Internet postings.

The debate was ended, according to a study by David Finkelstein, at the time of the summer 1999 leadership conclave at Beidaihe. As was typical of both domestic and foreign policy compromises under Jiang's leadership, the consensus was a compromise between sharply differing positions, tending toward a more ideologically conservative, and not particularly realistic, position. The leadership decided that the fundamentals of their foreign policy line would not change: "peace and development" remained the principal trend in the world, economic globalization would continue, and all nations were seen to desire a reduction of world tensions. But they unmistakably identified the United States as the principal source of global instability, pointing out that "hegemonism and power politics" were on the rise, there was a tendency toward "intervention" in the sovereign affairs of other nations, and the preservation of economic inequality was deliberate.[172]

While nuance and balance may have been agreed to at Beidaihe, they did not last long. Chinese commentary and discussion of the United States declined steeply into propagandistic exaggeration and vilification in 2000. "The U.S. hegemonic ambition has rapidly expanded and the pace of establishing a [unipolar] world has quickened with each passing day," *Renmin Ribao* thundered in July 2000. "The behavior of the United States has undoubtedly aggravated the contradiction between the United States and other countries, . . . [and] has stimulated [a] new arms race." The influential weekly magazine *Outlook* (*Liaowang*) accused the U.S. political leadership of being driven by a "cold war mentality, a colonialist mentality, and a hegemonist mentality" in attempting to split Taiwan off from China and in other "anti-China activities."[173] It was tired, shopworn rhetoric, and while some observers believed it implanted assumptions of American hostility toward China deeply into popular consciousness, others saw signs it was not having a significant effect and that the Chinese, at least in the emerging middle class, were usually favorably disposed toward the United States.[174]

Probably no issue typified the regime's Leninist dilemma more than the campaign to destroy the Falun Gong spiritual movement, which began in 1999. Originally a variant of traditional Chinese *qigong* exercises, Falun Gong was begun in the early 1990s by Li Hongzhi, a native of Jilin province who attracted hundreds of thousands of adherents—mostly elderly retirees—to his unusual style of meditation and spiritual healing.[175] By 1998, his sect had begun to attract local government attention and harassment, and Li decided to move to New York, where he continued to guide his growing movement by means of the Internet. In reaction to local media reports criticizing the movement for practicing "superstition" and the arrest of sect leaders in Tianjin, organizers mobilized more than 10,000 faithful followers, ordering them to descend on Beijing on April 25, 1999. They arrived individually and in small groups at the appointed time, and they sat or stood for several hours in well-organized ranks outside the gates of the leadership compound at Zhongnanhai, openly defying the ban on demonstrations in Tiananmen. They were silent, waving no placards, shouting no slogans. They presented two demands: that Falun Gong be given proper recognition as a legal organization and that the practitioners arrested in Tianjin be released. Zhu Rongji reportedly received some of their number at the west gate of Zhongnanhai and promised a response to their petition in three days. Late in the evening, Beijing municipal authorities provided buses for the practitioners to return to the railway stations, and they disappeared, as silently and efficiently as they had arrived.[176]

Jiang Zemin and other central leaders were shocked and alarmed by the demonstration. There had been no warning from security authorities, no hint that thousands of loyal and disciplined people could be ordered through the Internet to disobey laws against demonstrations. But worse news was to come. As reports of Falun Gong's size and influence came belatedly forward, Jiang was appalled to discover that the movement had thousands of adherents within the Communist Party and the People's Liberation Army, and sympathizers had prevented the public security authorities from cracking down on Falun Gong for months. The leadership also discovered that Falun Gong differed from other *qigong* movements by virtue of its apocalyptic vision and mildly anti-party perspective. With the tenth anniversary of Tiananmen only weeks away, Jiang was in no mood to take chances. The Politburo Standing Committee, however, was not fully in agreement about the nature of the cult or what to do about it, so Jiang used his authority to order a renewed ban on demonstrations in Tiananmen Square, improved vigilance against religious organizations and their goals, and examinations of the "foreign connections" of Falun Gong and other similar groups.[177] Jiang took a special interest in the group and was the primary voice calling for a crackdown, according to various accounts. He used the group's prevalence within the party as an excuse for a party "purification" campaign, of the sort that had been common under Mao Zedong.[178]

Falun Gong refused to cave in to regime pressure, however, and actively resisted. The movement sent smaller numbers of activists to various public locations, particularly Tiananmen, to defy the government's criticisms. Some of these demonstrations turned violent. By July, after Falun Gong followers clashed with police in Tiananmen Square, the sect was formally outlawed, and police took preemptive action against its leaders. Thousands were arrested in sweeps of various provinces. The leadership—or at least Jiang—decided to publicize its actions, and the propaganda apparatus weighed in with books, pamphlets, and television "documentaries" denouncing the cult. News programs showed film clips of elderly women being pummeled to the ground by police and dragged off by their hair to police vans. The regime even published comic books depicting Falun Gong and Li Hongzhi as vicious evildoers of the same type as the "Gang of Four" and Lin Biao. But the campaign behind the comics was no laughing matter. By November, Hong Kong human rights monitors were reporting that more than 35,000 Falun Gong practitioners had been detained, and 2,000 had already been sent to labor camps.[179] Stories also proliferated, however, of resistance to the party's heavy-handed attack, of widespread party cadre disdain for what was perceived as Jiang's private vendetta, and of apathetic implementation of anti–Falun Gong directives.

Beyond the difficulties of persuading skeptical foreigners that Falun Gong presented a real threat to the government of China, the campaign refocused attention on some of Jiang's fundamental Leninist attitudes. It revealed a man—and a party—still frightened of its own population and convinced of the need to extirpate every organization or social movement capable of developing political alternatives to the Communist Party. It showed a party willing to use the coercive power of public security forces preemptively to attack a nonpolitical organization, even in the face of public apathy. It portrayed in stark definition a political party unprepared for political reform, unable to resist the temptation to view the world through ideological blinders. And it displayed the weakened authority of the party to work its will. Despite a concerted effort by the full force of the Communist Party to destroy its organizational structure, jail its leaders, and intimidate its practitioners, Falun Gong remained intact—though greatly reduced and weakened—nearly two years after the campaign against it had begun.

But the leadership seemed to accept the notion that Falun Gong was not a domestic phenomenon, not a reaction to the harsh changes brought about by China's rapid modernization, and not a search for a spiritual alternative to the party's vapid ideology. Rather, like the Tiananmen demonstrations of a decade before, it was a foreign-inspired conspiracy to undermine the communist regime, a deliberate interference in China's internal affairs for a nefarious and hostile purpose. Misunderstanding both its own political situation and international environment, the Jiang leadership showed, in a sense, that little had changed since June 4, 1989.

CHAPTER TEN

Epilogue and Conclusions

Nearly twelve years after the terrible events of Tiananmen Square, a book was published in the United States that purported to tell the whole story—the political story—in the words of the participants. The book, the *Tiananmen Papers,*[1] was the work of two well-known American China scholars, Andrew J. Nathan of Columbia University and E. Perry Link of Princeton University, who translated and edited a huge collection of Chinese-language documents, which had been copied, transcribed onto computer disks, and smuggled out of China by a man who called himself "Zhang Liang."[2] Prepared under unusually secretive procedures, the book was given a well-orchestrated debut with prepublication excerpts in the *New York Times,* an interview with Zhang Liang, "the compiler," on the CBS news program *60 Minutes*, and lengthy excerpts in an influential magazine, *Foreign Affairs.*

The book is a remarkable collection of documents supposedly from central Communist Party archives, covering the period from Hu Yaobang's heart attack on April 8 and death the following week through the People's Liberation Army's (PLA's) bloody seizure of Tiananmen Square seven weeks later to the mass arrests and crackdown that followed.[3] It includes what are claimed to be on-the-scene reports from Ministry of State Security operatives watching student demonstrations, written reports from provincial and municipal officials about demonstrations around China, meeting notes from Politburo Standing Committee meetings and informal meetings of "elders," transcripts of conversations between senior leaders, and much other original source material. It presents a compelling picture of indecision and disunity among the leadership, high-level confusion and misperception, and appalling self-delusion that what was done was necessary and right. Although many of the critical details of the story had been revealed in other publications, nowhere had they been presented in one place in such extraordinary detail and complete context. And the picture they presented of the leadership of the Communist Party—whether revered elders or hastily chosen successors—was anything but flattering.

Plenty of questions were raised in the United States about the documents, principally because of the way they were acquired. Zhang Liang, who implied in several interviews that he had help from other Chinese officials in collecting the materials—which could only have come from secret Central Committee archives—protected himself and his sources with great care. He disguised his face and voice in all interviews but also kept Chinese security officials off-guard by regularly accusing them of trying to hunt him down and silence him. His motives, as he explained them, were blatantly political. He wanted the party's verdict on the Tiananmen demonstrations to be reversed. Believing Jiang Zemin and Li Peng would never allow it, he wanted the next generation of leaders to do so and to have a basis of support within society and the international community to accomplish the task. "The pro-democracy faction in the Party is the key force for pushing political change in China. . . . What will replace the Chinese Communist Party will probably be a new force that emerges from within it, a group that regrets the errors of the Communist system more deeply than anyone else, a group deeply committed to establishing a healthy democratic system," Zhang told CNN's Mike Chinoy.[4]

Nathan and Link had their doubts about the authenticity of the materials Zhang brought them. The documents were not brought out on paper but were copied and transcribed into text files on computer disks. Thus they lacked the authenticating registration numbers and chops that distinguished hard copies of Central Committee documents. The two scholars had to balance a desire to consult with their China-watching colleagues with a recognition that security was essential for the safety of their source. Link and Nathan were well-known critics of the PRC (Link had accompanied dissident scientist Fang Lizhi on his attempt to attend a banquet hosted by George Bush, described in chapter 2) and were bound to be suspected of participating in a hoax to discredit the PRC government. But as Orville Schell described the situation in his appendix to the documents, they grew more confident in the authenticity of the documents as they brought their own experience, their investigation of the available public record, and their regular association with Zhang Liang to bear. In the end, while they could not vouch for the accuracy of the documents in any absolute way, they decided to go ahead. "The alternative to publication was to ignore this collection—in effect to yield to the Communist Party of China's protective shield of secrecy . . . and thereby engage in a form of passive suppression."[5]

Reaction to the appearance of the book varied sharply, as one would expect. In the United States, the book was acclaimed by critics of China as providing the "true story" of the events of 1989. But a lively discussion was carried out in various Western media over whether the documents were genuine. Some wondered at the objectivity of the editors—who were, in effect, "blacklisted" in China—and at the involvement of Human Rights Watch in the publication of the book. Veteran reporters and Sinologists noted inconsistencies and improbabilities in the documents, a few factual errors, and the likely distortions introduced by the highly partisan "compiler," Zhang Liang. Generally, they reviewed the book carefully, recalling numerous instances of famous forgeries of Chinese documents. The book sold fairly well in the United States and was translated into several European languages, but it did not generate much public excitement. Neither did the new George W. Bush administration—despite a tougher overall stance toward China—embrace the book or its findings in any public way.

China immediately denounced the book. "Any attempt to play up the matter again and disrupt China by the despicable means of fabricating materials and distorting facts will be futile," said Foreign Ministry spokesman Zhu Bangzao on January 8. Jiang Zemin—on a visit to Japan—said the *60 Minutes* account "distorted the facts" and gave an "incorrect judgment" about June 4.[6] But the early Chinese critiques were oddly equivocal, seeming almost careful not to deny completely the authenticity of the documents in the book. Equal stress was placed on defending the crackdown as "highly necessary."[7] Tiananmen-era dissidents, such as Bao Tong and others, told the Western reporters the documents were "plausible," while some families of Tiananmen victims publicly welcomed the publication and renewed their call for a full accounting of the events of June 4, 1989. Chinese authorities tried to prevent the book from reaching China, confiscating copies and threatening to arrest those who circulated the book through the Internet.

Jiang Zemin evidently grew more concerned as the April publication date of the Chinese-language version drew nearer. In mid-February, before the annual meeting of the National People's Congress, Jiang convened a Central Committee Work Conference in Beijing to discuss the *Tiananmen Papers* and the lethargic progress of the party campaign to extirpate the Falun Gong movement. During a three-day meeting intended to ensure there was no slippage of enthusiasm for Jiang's own vision of communism's future, each member of the Politburo Standing Committee (Jiang, Li Peng, Zhu Rongji, Li Ruihuan, Hu Jintao, Li Lanqing, and Wei Jianxing) was required to publicly "reveal his attitude" (*biaotai*) before the Central Committee on two questions. First, each was required to show support for Jiang's campaign against the "evil cult" of Falun Gong, which had flagged because of lack of public and official support. Second, each leader had to uphold publicly the correctness of the party's "verdict" on June 4, which had been delivered at the June 24, 1989, rump Central Committee plenum that had ousted General Secretary Zhao Ziyang and installed Jiang Zemin in his place. With television cameras rolling to record their words for posterity (and to ensure that none of them would lead a movement to "reverse the verdict" on Tiananmen), all of China's top leaders avowed that the decision to crack down on student demonstrators had been completely correct, and that had the "turmoil" not been checked, the ensuing stability and successful development of China's economy could not have been achieved.[8]

In addition, the work conference reportedly focused attention on policy toward the United States, linking the Falun Gong movement—whose spiritual leader, Li Hongzhi, had fled to the United States in 1998—and the *Tiananmen Papers* as two examples of the efforts of Western powers to divide the Communist Party. Jiang made clear his views that Falun Gong was a tool of the Central Intelligence Agency, which was also behind the Tiananmen book.[9] China took a series of actions, following the publication of the Chinese version of the papers, that seemed markedly tougher toward the United States, including the arrests of several Chinese Americans on charges of espionage and harassment of individuals (including some in the United States) suspected of being Zhang Liang. While probably unrelated to the discussions at the party work conference, China also took a more aggressive approach to American intelligence collection flights in the South China Sea. The latter change eventually resulted in a collision between a Chinese fighter jet and an American EP-3 reconnaissance aircraft, the loss of the Chinese pilot, detention of the American crew, and a significant—though temporary—deterioration of bilateral relations.

Concluding Observations

Although the publication of the *Tiananmen Papers* cannot be said to have done any damage to the U.S.-China relationship, the sharply contrasting viewpoints toward Tiananmen the book elicited in the early months of 2001 were a reminder of how differently the Chinese government and the American public viewed the June 4 tragedy.

The Prevalence of Old Ideas

For many in the United States, the Chinese leadership's reaction indicated that the regime remained frozen in time, still dedicated to preserving an unjust and repressive political system that defied most American values. Added to the unrelenting news of persecution of Chinese Christians, Falun Gong, dissident scholars, and others perceived as opponents by the regime, this unwillingness to confront the truth of Tiananmen acted as a reminder of how fundamentally alien "communist China" is for many Americans. For others, Tiananmen seemed a faded memory, irrelevant to an understanding of the dynamic change in today's China. People involved in business relations with China saw an energetic, enthusiastic, hard-working, increasingly open society eager to learn from the United States and work constructively with Americans. They saw that many of the leaders of China's economic elite are American trained and look to the United States for new technology, markets, and ideas. For these Americans, Tiananmen—and particularly the sanctions that were imposed in 1989 and remain in effect—seemed an impediment to developing a broader and more balanced relationship.

For some Chinese, at least in the government, publication of the *Tiananmen Papers* was proof the Americans were still dedicated to undermining China's legitimate socialist regime and looking for opportunities to embarrass China and hamper its progress. For others, the book was simply anachronistic. Many Chinese, including many Chinese students, had moved on to other interests and pursuits, such as finding good jobs and making money in China's increasingly westernized market. The Tiananmen issue was closed, and little good would come from reopening it. For still others, publication of the papers was a ray of hope, a reminder of the dark past of the current regime and of the need for genuine political reform if China is ever to break out of its authoritarian shackles.

But Tiananmen will endure as a subject of contention between the United States and China, at least as a subtext of other issues, particularly human rights. In a sense, neither side has gotten "beyond Tiananmen." Americans have not forgotten the hopes that were aroused for Chinese democracy, the admiration they experienced for the young man blocking the line of tanks, and the anger they felt at the brutality of the Chinese troops and police rounding up protestors. They remain offended that the Beijing government has never provided a full and honest account of what actually happened. Its explanations have been inadequate, to say the least, for a domestic or an international audience. It has failed to follow through on pledges to account for all casualties, or even, in its own defense, to provide the "real" documentation that might counter what it calls the "fabrications" contained in the *Tiananmen Papers*. The U.S. government cannot justify a "strategic partnership" or any other kind of forbearing approach to China if it requires Americans to ignore this issue.

For its part, the leadership of the Chinese Communist Party remains a product of Tiananmen. Few of them would have been in their current positions of power had not the events of twelve years ago taken place as they had. Admission of error and culpability would entail a great deal of political turmoil and blaming, retribution, and rectification of legal cases. The party is not prepared to undertake such a task and probably will not be for some time to come. Their legitimacy is tied to Tiananmen, and they insist that what happened there was right and necessary. The judgments made by Deng Xiaoping were the correct judgments. They could not have been in error. So the party leaders have punished with jail or exile or isolation all who have questioned those judgments, piling injustice on top of error.

Memory and anger are part of China's modern historical legacy as well. In the historiography of modern China, the West oppressed China for 150 years, defeating it in wars, pillaging its historical treasures, occupying its territory, mistreating and cheating its people, and forcing them to "eat bitterness." Chinese culture focuses heavily on demonstrations of respect and loyalty. Feelings are easily bruised and disrespect or insults are remembered for years. The Chinese Communist Party has successfully portrayed the actions of the West—and the United States in particular—as a continuation of that attitude of contempt for China. Affronts by the United States to the Chinese government since 1989 have been successfully portrayed by Beijing as examples of American disregard for the Chinese people and have fueled growth of anti-American nationalism. The boiling over of popular rage after the U.S. bombing of the Chinese embassy in Belgrade was in part manufactured but also in part a genuine reaction to accumulated and remembered instances of American disrespect.

U.S.-China relations since Tiananmen have been dominated by problems. The list of major problems has remained generally stable—human rights, nonproliferation, reciprocity in the trade relationship, and Taiwan. The period from 1989 to 2000 saw a constant series of disputes, wrangling, and tension over these four issues, occasionally interspersed with brief periods of relative amity and optimism as well as instances of tension and outright antagonism. There was no real norm, no status quo, but a constant effort was made to move the relationship into some other status, to "normalize" it. There seemed to be no consensus, however, on what a "normal" relationship could or should be. The touchstones and standards of the relationship—the "three joint communiqués" and on the American side, at least, the Taiwan Relations Act—were twenty to thirty years old, the product of a different global situation and far different domestic politics in both countries.

With the fall of the Soviet Union in 1991, the strategic basis for the U.S.-China relationship—tattered though it was—disappeared entirely. In the ensuing decade, the international situation has undergone enormous change. The East-West adversarial dynamic, the "cold war," has been replaced by an enlarged NATO, U.S.-Russian cooperation, the spread of democratic governments throughout eastern Europe, and now, the international campaign against terrorism. Economic prosperity and the revolution in telecommunications have sparked a new global economy, with changed patterns of interaction, trade, and investment. In Asia, the Korean Peninsula remains a dangerous and unpredictable standoff, and the Taiwan-PRC confrontation is of continuing increasing concern, but the rest of the region has enjoyed extraordinary prosperity and cooperation, facilitated by such international institutions as Asia-Pacific Economic Cooperation (APEC) and the Association of Southeast Asian Nations (ASEAN), among others.

Domestically, the United States and China have undergone remarkable changes since 1989, in both political and economic situations. Change in China is more striking and dynamic, altering the physical appearance of many of China's major cities, the life-styles of urban dwellers, and the attitudes and aspirations of millions of Chinese citizens. Most of the change is attributable to the remarkable growth that has taken place in the Chinese economy since Deng's *nanxun* in 1992. Whether measured by standard economic benchmarks or by less quantifiable standards, the bottom line is that China has grown far wealthier in the past decade than even Deng Xiaoping could have imagined. The statistics on China's growth tend to be controversial, generating more questions than illumination about the nature and success of China's economic policies during the past twelve years. But even the most cursory examination of some elementary numbers suggests trends that can hardly be denied. By some calculations, for example, China's GDP grew more than 500 percent between 1989 and 2000, while per capita income rose 400 percent between 1989 and 1997. China's total trade grew in value by more than 300 percent between 1992 and 2000, while some estimate that as much as $320 billion dollars in foreign investment flowed into China between 1991 to 2000.[10] Other indicators—such as the phenomenal growth in the number of private automobiles, televisions, personal computers (more than 10 million in 2001), or cellular telephones (from virtually none in 1989 to 130 million in 2001)—suggest a country where life-styles and values have undergone an extraordinary change in the past decade. But it is traveling to China and looking at the things and phenomena that were not present twelve years ago that can be most impressive—such as shopping malls, fashion shows, golf courses, private schools, upscale restaurants, call-in talk shows, children's television programming, new housing, domestic tourism, and environmental activism.

In the United States, the telecommunications and Internet boom of the 1990s changed the way Americans did nearly everything from communicating with friends to buying books (and writing them) to getting the news. Late 1980s concerns about the coming U.S. economic decline nearly disappeared in the face of extraordinary economic prosperity and growth. The Standard and Poor's 500 Stock Index grew from roughly 375 at the beginning of 1990 to more than 1,400 in 2000 (the Dow Jones industrial average went from 2,800 to 11,000), the country sustained an average annual GDP growth rate of more than 3.6 percent from 1992 to 2000, while inflation fell from 5 percent to less than 2 percent a year.[11]

The interlinkages between the two economies is a subject that gets too little attention. American direct investment in Chinese enterprises has been low in comparison with that of Hong Kong, Taiwan, and even Japan, but still represents a significant commitment to China's future by some of America's largest and wealthiest companies. But the impact of the United States is far larger and deeper than simple numbers suggest. Whether one looks at dress styles, music, television, legal reforms, product marketing, management models, banking and insurance reforms, stock market structuring, or other economic phenomena in China, it seems clear that many Chinese look to the United States as the model for their development, the standard against which their success will be judged. American consumers have welcomed goods produced in China—from shoes and textiles to garden tools, toys, furniture, and office equipment—contributing to an overall goods trade deficit of over $100 billion in 2002.

In neither country, however, has there been a commensurate change in the way U.S.-China relations are considered or in how the other country is viewed by their respective governments. Both sides have adopted general frameworks, or strategies, for the twenty-first century. But there is little agreement, and not much serious discussion between the two, on what the goals and parameters of the relationship should be. This book does not deal in any detail with events that took place after the end of the Clinton administration. As this book goes to press, there is considerable speculation that U.S.-China relations took a fundamental turn for the better after the September 11, 2001, terrorist attack on the United States, in that joint opposition to terrorism became the new strategic underpinning for U.S.-China cooperation. I do not subscribe to that view, although I recognize that some aspects of bilateral relations improved markedly, particularly in comparison to the tensions that followed the EP-3 incident of April 2001.[12] But in my opinion, the fundamentals of the relationship were little affected by the policy changes that took place on either side after "9-11." Suspicions, misperceptions, and miscommunication continue to mar the relationship and will limit the improvements that may ensue as the war against terrorism plays out.

The Clinton administration's efforts to build a "constructive, strategic partnership" with China fell flat, politically, and were quietly shelved, even by Vice President Al Gore as he ran for the presidency in 2000. The ultimately victorious campaign of Texas governor George W. Bush took a much harder line toward China, at least initially, denying that China was a strategic partner and declaring it a "competitor" or "strategic competitor" of the United States. In rhetoric reminiscent of the cold war approach to the Soviet Union, Bush cautioned Americans that China was investing in strategic nuclear weapons and other military might, that it constituted an "intelligence threat" to the United States, was "an enemy of religious freedom and a sponsor of forced abortion," and that it needed to be dealt with "without illusions."[13]

After gaining office, the Bush administration's policy toward China underwent a gradual change toward engagement of the sort practiced by the Clinton administration in its second term. Nonetheless, in its first published "National Security Strategy" paper in 2002, it took an ambivalent attitude toward China. "We welcome the emergence of a strong, peaceful, and prosperous China," it stated and highlighted several areas of cooperation. But it remained critical of China's domestic political situation: "The democratic development of China is crucial to [its] future. Yet, a quarter century after beginning the process of shedding the worst features of the Communist legacy, China's leaders have not yet made the next series of fundamental choices about the character of their state. . . . To make that nation truly accountable to its citizens' needs and aspirations, however, much work remains to be done. Only by allowing the Chinese people to think, assemble, and worship freely can China reach its full potential."[14]

In China, to judge by the official and quasi-official publications—*People's Daily* or any of the other government-sponsored newspapers and magazines, for example—there has been little development of China's view of the United States since the reiteration of the "peace and development/guard against hegemonism" line after Beidaihe in 1999, despite the changed circumstances since September 11. It was a tired approach even then. Jiang Zemin and other Chinese leaders continue to insist that China desires to maintain a constructive relationship with Washington, but their rhetoric is so stilted and formulaic that their statements carry little meaning or credibility. Jiang, for example, told *Washington Post* editors in March 2001: "China is the largest developing country. The United States is the most developed capitalist country in the world. And so there is a reason for our two countries to cooperate with each other and our two countries should seek common ground while putting aside differences and seek areas where joint cooperation is possible."[15]

Of course, the academic discourse on bilateral relations has been rich and varied in China and the United States. As China has opened up its media and book publishing business, more and more commentaries became available on foreign affairs in general and the United States in particular. Most academic articles and books are carefully calibrated by their authors to be well within the parameters of official policy guidelines, and few would dare to prescribe policies sharply at variance with those pursued by the regime. Among those willing to go beyond the orthodoxy, more tend to write about outright confrontation, even war, with the United States. Some of these works have been noted in the United States, where they are occasionally interpreted as representing the regime's "real" views. A few scholars are attempting to look at alternative options for policy toward the United States, downplaying the notion of "hegemonism" as a guiding principle of U.S. policy and focusing on the political realities of American policymaking.[16]

In the United States, the vigorous debate over China policy in the media and academia has continued, and American contemporary China scholarship provides a rich and varied literature. Since the campaign finance and spying scandals of 1998–99, a harsh tone has crept into some of the debate on China policy. Discussions took on a sharply partisan cast during the latter part of the Clinton administration, with Republicans moving away from the views of Henry Kissinger and George H. W. Bush toward a darker view of China, in part simply to define their differences with Clinton, who had adopted an "engagement" approach similar to that of his predecessors. Disagreements over the nature of the Chinese threat to the United States also sharpened, in light of China's increased wealth, rising military expenditures, and perceived enhanced threat to Taiwan. These had a decided effect on the China-watching community. A "blue team" organized itself, mostly among congressional staffers and ideological critics of China, and vigorously pressed its case for a more confrontational policy toward China.[17] This group occasionally attacked those who did not share its Manichaean view of China as the "red team," "panda-huggers," or other derogatory terms.[18] Others have taken even harder lines, suggesting that China indeed needed to be contained, that it was an aggressive, rising power similar to nineteenth-century Germany or early twentieth-century Japan. Again, while this debate moderated as the U.S. fight against terrorism dominated the nation's attention, its return is likely at some point.

In both countries, it is important to recognize that think tanks and academic discussions have only a limited and indirect impact on the thinking and decisions of key policymakers. Scholars may or may not have direct access to foreign policy officials, their articles may or may not be read, contradictory views may or may not cancel each other out. Generally, however, policy decisions have their own dynamic. Information flows and time horizons often do not accommodate dispassionate, lengthy, well-reasoned academic analysis.

The Dilemma of Strategic Thinking

Foreign affairs specialists in the United States and China highly value "strategic thinking" as an intellectual exercise, a perspective on international affairs, and a guide to policy. The U.S.-China relationship had its origins in the anti-Soviet strategic notions of Mao Zedong, Zhou Enlai, Richard M. Nixon, and Henry Kissinger, and both sides seem to harbor a nostalgia for the days when the relationship was focused on greater global goals and was more than the sum of its parts or its problems.

For the Chinese, grand strategy is the principal focus of much writing on global issues. Many commentators on American affairs structure their explanations of American actions in terms of the long-term strategic aspirations of the United States. They focus on domination, national aggrandizement, geopolitics, and energy sources. Mostly, however, they focus on power and particularly the unquenchable desire of the United States for power, which constitutes the motivating force of American "hegemonism."[19] As Yong Deng put it in a summary article in *Political Science Quarterly*, "China's mainstream strategy analysts . . . have overall perceived a consistent and malign U.S. strategy of global domination. . . . Chinese assessment sees the United States as a hegemon on the offensive for power aggrandizement."[20] Even those writers more familiar with the complexities of American policymaking are affected by traditional cultural predispositions toward "realism," Chinese style, and must occasionally alter their assessments to be congruent with the expectations of their readers.[21]

In the post–cold war world, American theorists have struggled with strategic formulations to encompass the relationship between the United States and a far more complex global situation. Before September 11, 2001, at least, there seemed to be no overriding security threat to the United States, but a broad array of other international issues called out for attention. It is beyond the scope of this book to review the literature or to conclude anything other than that there seems to be no consensus on what U.S. strategic aspirations or positions should be, the war on terrorism notwithstanding. It can probably be said, however, that even those who favor extending the so-called unipolar moment—America's unchallenged military supremacy—would find Chinese conclusions about U.S. goals and intentions overstated and inaccurate.

More important, the notion that American policy is directly driven by strategic considerations, or that explanations can be found for specific American policies in theoretical speculation about the actions of nation-states in certain circumstances, is grossly inaccurate. The American policy process is far more intricate and involved, more politicized and changeable than can be encompassed by even the most sophisticated theories of hegemonic behavior. As Robert Jervis put it in a paper called "Grand Strategy: Mission Impossible," in the post–cold war world, with the United States under no obvious or overwhelming threat, foreign policy will become more like domestic policy, in which "courses of action will be shaped less by a grand design than by the pulling and hauling of various interests, ideas, and political calculations," which he calls "pluralism with a vengeance."[22] Richard Betts makes a similar point, noting that too few scholars who focus on strategy "learn enough about the processes of decision-making or military operations to grasp how hard it is to implement strategic plans, and few focus on the conversion processes that open gaps between what government leaders decide to do and what government organizations implementing those decisions actually *do*."[23]

The White House publishes regularly a summary of its foreign policy plans, goals, and initiatives under the rubric of a "National Security Strategy." Defense Department planners also publish yearly reviews of global and regional issues, as well as forward-looking assessments of future international challenges. Chinese strategists routinely peruse these documents and discover the "true intention" of the United States, usually concluding, on the basis of their own preconceptions, that it is hostile to China's interests and is a strategy of containment, bullying, and division. "The United States may not have a global or overall strategy at all and may have too many strategic choices to form a grand master plan," observes Qin Yaqing of Beijing's Foreign Affairs College, "but in the eye of the Chinese, it does have one. It may not be called a grand strategy, but it is represented as a grand plan to deal with China. In this respect, whether or not the United States really has such a strategy is not important. What is important is that in the eye of the beholder there is one."[24]

There is considerable disagreement among American observers of China's strategy. Some take a lowest-common-denominator view of China's long-range goals, that is, that it seeks regime security, territorial integrity (especially the prevention of Taiwan's independence), and enhanced international influence.[25] Some posit further that China seeks the establishment of a global system of "multipolarity," which necessarily requires the reduction of American power, and the reestablishment of China's historically dominant role in East Asia, which would also entail a removal of U.S. forces from Japan and the Korean Peninsula.[26] At the extreme end of the spectrum are those who insist China has a plan for world domination and is carrying it out in the face of American apathy, or worse, with American complicity.[27]

Discussions of strategic relations often focus on intentions. Nations are assumed to have intentions, as if they were organic entities independent of their human leaders; or the intentions of the leaders are discerned and expanded to become national goals. Usually, intentions are used to describe the motivational forces for another nation's behavior; one's own nation is assumed to act on the basis of its interests and goals. Sometimes intentions are abstracted from the development of capabilities—on the understandable premise that if a country is developing a certain capability, it must intend to use it at some point. Sometimes they are more or less plainly stated, as in above-mentioned White House and Defense Department documents or Chinese "White Papers." Often, however, they are *ascribed* on the basis of analysis of events and actions. Thus some Chinese discerned the U.S. intention of "containing" China on the basis of the *Yin He* incident, while the Cox Committee perceived China's intention to build multiple independently targeted re-entry vehicles for their miniaturized warheads on the basis of the Loral-Hughes case in 1998. In many cases, ascribed intentions may have more to do with the one's own fears than with the reality of the other side's goals.

U.S.-China relations have not been well served by a general overconcentration on the "strategic" dimension of the relationship. First of all, the word itself has been deprived of substantive meaning over time and especially since the disappearance of a specific enemy or target for military action, such as the Soviet Union. Outside the context of a military campaign, the word "strategic" tends to get rather fuzzy in definition—sometimes meaning little more than "important in a larger context." The first Bush administration's expressed desire to restore a "strategic" relationship with China in the face of the collapse of communism in eastern Europe and Russia made little sense to the Congress or to the public. The Clinton administration's hope to build a "strategic partnership" with China was not well defined and created more confusion than clarity.

At the beginning of the twenty-first century, both sides have begun to use the term "strategic" more often with the other side as the adversary rather than as a partner. But since neither side is prepared to really treat the other as a strategic opponent, it might be wise to focus the relationship on other definitional terms. Until such time as the two sides can agree on what term should follow the word "strategic" in a definition of bilateral ties, and sell it to their respective domestic audiences, Washington and Beijing should accept the reality that they do not and will not have a strategic relationship. They can and do talk regularly about international events and trends and even about common interests, such as the Korean Peninsula and South Asia. But these do not constitute even a significant portion of a "strategic" relationship, and until the two countries can objectively define what role their military establishments play in relation to each other, the discussion of a "strategic relationship" might better be suspended.

Comity of Errors

Since 1989, the U.S.-China relationship has been shaped and buffeted by mistakes. American and Chinese policymakers have made many mistakes about each other: factual inaccuracies, poor intelligence, errors of judgment, sins of commission and omission, misperceptions, mistranslations, overestimates of knowledge, underestimates of sensitivity, misplaced confidence, misread intentions, unintended consequences, unreceived rewards, missed signals, ineffective bluffs, and violations of confidence, to name just a few. The term "mistake" is a subjective judgment and needs to be carefully defined. In a foreign policy context, it might be defined as an action that failed to bring about the desired results or that brought consequences that worsened the problem being addressed. But even in a narrowly defined sense, there is a perceptual difficulty in talking about mistakes—what one person might view as an error, another might consider a stroke of genius in solving an entirely different problem.

It is not my intent to break any new ground in the extensive literature of how mistakes are made in domestic or foreign policy. The work of Robert Jervis, among others, provides fascinating insights into how decisionmakers in international affairs misperceive one another, misunderstand signals, misread intentions, misinterpret actions (including the other side's mistakes), distort and deny information, project inaccurate images, and otherwise miscommunicate.[28] The reasons for doing so are many and varied and include the nature of the relationship, patterns and channels of communication, and the social psychology of the decisionmakers. Jervis sets out a series of hypotheses about how international actors interpret one another in different circumstances and concludes that decisionmakers "often not only have a limited understanding of the workings of others' arguments, they also do not know the structure of their own belief systems."[29] This leads individual decisionmakers into a psychological predisposition to misunderstand the actions and decisions of others.

In his seminal work on group decisionmaking dynamics, Irving Janis developed a concept called "groupthink," which helps account for some of the policy errors on both sides, particularly those made by small groups. Groupthink, according to Janis, is "a mode of thinking that people engage in when they are deeply involved in a cohesive group, when the members' strivings for unanimity override their motivation to realistically appraise alternative courses of action."[30] It manifests itself in three types, springing from overestimation of the group's power or morality, closed-mindedness toward outsiders, and pressure for uniformity. Although precise parallels are impossible in anything but a controlled experimental environment, Janis's hypotheses about how small groups can make completely erroneous judgments certainly ring true in some of the evident decisions of China's Politburo Standing Committee, Foreign Affairs Leading Small Group, or the U.S. Principals Committee.

But no theory ever encompasses complex reality. Every decision taken by Beijing or Washington had a complex and different train of information, analysis, deliberation, consultation, revision, determination, dissemination, and implementation. No two are alike, nor could be. Certain patterns might emerge from time to time, but identifying them with any precision would be misleading on the complexity of the process. Certainly one of the more notable patterns on both sides, but more on the American side, was the broadening of the domestic political audience involved in the decision process, at least in its early stages. In some cases, the broadening of the number of actors arguably contributed to decisions that turned out to be erroneous—for example, Clinton's linking of human rights standards and most favored nation status.

Equally notable as the mistakes and the damage they did to the relationship, however, is that the mistakes did not cause a complete breakdown in the relationship. Strains, certainly—some were serious and with long-lasting repercussions. But both Chinese and American decisionmakers, in the aftermath of errors and strains, usually took specific steps to correct the balance, sometimes in the face of opposition. There are probably several reasons, including the preference of the Chinese Ministry of Foreign Affairs and the U.S. State Department—key policy players—for stable, "normal" relations. Moreover, once invested with the authority and responsibility of foreign policy decisionmaking, most politicians, whether Chinese or American, recognize it is far easier to carry on a "normal" relationship, despite multiple problems, than to manage an active dispute or descent into hostility. Leaders on both sides, regardless of their background or familiarity with international relations, recognize that the relationship between the United States and China is going to be one of the most important in the world for some time to come. They understand instinctively that, however they may define their world views or strategic goals, long-term hostility and confrontation between the two countries cannot be justified as in their national interests, are not necessary, and not politically sustainable. Parochial interests in both countries may argue for more strain or confrontation, but at the end of the day, a certain comity can and must be maintained.

Domestic Politics and Foreign Affairs

As tempting as it might be to decry the encroachment of low domestic politics on the pristine world of high international relations and strategy, it would be unrealistic as to think it could or should be changed. Even in the wake of the September 11, 2001, terrorist attack on New York and Washington, D.C., and the ensuing Bush administration focus on a global war against terrorism, the foreign policy processes that have developed since the Vietnam War are not about to be changed to put exclusive power for foreign policy back in the hands of the president and his advisers. The suspension of criticism and debate between the executive and legislative branches that followed the attack was short lived, in part because the nature of the new strategic threat is not clear enough to produce a unanimity of purpose or policy. Arguments are sure to resume over many issues, eventually including China policy.

James Lindsay attributes the heightened level of partisan bickering over foreign policy to several societal factors as well as to the absence of a dominant security threat to the United States. American public opinion, he claims, has become apathetic and complacent about foreign policy; it is not a major issue in electoral politics. Politicians can therefore appeal to small constituencies with strongly held views on foreign policy without concern they will alienate moderate voters. "Anyone hoping that the . . . President will be able to restore a bipartisan foreign policy will be disappointed."[31]

In *Friends and Foes*, Rebecca Hersman points out that organizational reforms in Congress have weakened party discipline and the powers of committee chairs, creating a situation in which "issue loyalties" can become crucial in voting and the development of legislation. She also notes that congressional inputs into foreign policy are now more likely to be negative and intentionally disruptive, as various "issue leaders" cooperate to place their agendas in amendments to major budget authorization bills, which are less likely to be vetoed. The upshot is that individual members of Congress with single-issue agendas for China—human rights, nonproliferation, abortion, and religious freedom—may have significant influence on the larger policy agenda. This is done not simply by introducing legislation but also by writing letters to the president signed by many members (these are always answered by the president, thereby bringing the issue to his attention), holding hearings, mandating reports and notifications, withholding or "earmarking" funds, holding media events, and other actions.[32]

This situation results in a "nearly incoherent policy process," Hersman argues, and she recommends that Congress and the executive branch need to consider ways to manage the situation. Improving the informal consultation process is a must, she asserts, along with some procedural changes to restore party and committee discipline in Congress. Mostly, however, she stresses the need for clear articulation and backing of policies by the president and a willingness to use both the policy formulation authority of the executive branch and the persuasive powers of the White House to win support.[33] Both the Bush and Clinton administrations showed this was possible—on most favored nation and permanent normal trade relations—but it was a costly approach for China policy.

Post-Tiananmen congressional attitudes on China are likely to change only slowly and at the margins. They are determined by partisan politics and legislative-executive relations and not simply by lobbyists and policy trade-offs among "issue clusters." They are not simply the product of memories of Tiananmen or of ignorance of China's present-day realities. They are largely the result of and reaction to Chinese actions and behavior patterns, reinforced regularly by news and intelligence reporting on human rights violations, religious persecution, population control policy abuses, prison conditions, dissident arrests, nuclear and chemical weapons sales, theft of technology, advanced weapons research, military budget increases, trade imbalances, accumulation of U.S. currency, intellectual property piracy, dumping of cheap goods on Western markets, market access barriers, missile buildups along the Taiwan Strait, and crude pressure tactics against Taiwan. Until solid evidence appears that some of those troubling behavior patterns are changing, Congress—guardian of a values-based foreign policy—will continue to be tough on China.

Within the executive branch, interbureaucratic politicking has a huge impact on how China policy is developed and implemented. Despite periodic tensions and stress, the U.S.-China relationship has reached into virtually every arena of government interaction, from diplomacy to science, the environment, medicine, international finance, agriculture, military affairs, and many others. Just about every agency of the U.S. government has significant exchanges with counterparts in the People's Republic of China. While these contacts develop and enrich the relationship through multilayered cooperation, they also tend to fragment policy and make it difficult to focus. More or less normal divergences among bureaucracies with different interests and constituencies can easily be magnified by competing policy preferences related to China. Although the Department of State has traditionally guided and shaped American foreign policy, it is no longer in a position to direct the activities of other large bureaucracies, partly because it is often divided in its own regional and functional bureaus and partly because the scale of the bilateral relationship has become so large and complex.

I believe there is no substitute for leadership by the National Security Council on China policy. China policy is important enough in the broader scheme of American global policy that the president's perspective must predominate, and no other agency can speak so directly for the president. Obviously, the NSC must delegate and facilitate the policy formulation and implementation of other agencies and departments—its personnel resources are far too limited to do otherwise. NSC leadership must not dominate or exclude other executive branch departments from the policy process. Neither can the NSC become a policy implementation agency. The dangers of that were amply proven by the "Iran-gate" scandal during the Reagan administration. The Principals and Deputies committee processes—managed by the NSC—work well in coordinating and harmonizing policies within the executive branch. Moreover, only the NSC can promote the interbureaucratic cooperation and coordination needed to keep China policies moving in the same general direction.[34] The NSC can provide the necessary channels for candid and confidential communication with the Chinese (and Taiwan authorities) that are required to prevent misunderstanding and clarify policy positions. Finally, the NSC is structured to act speedily and efficiently as a crisis management center when that becomes necessary.

Other domestic political "policy actors" become increasingly prominent in a generally more "atomized" foreign policy process, but their effect on policy outcomes is manageable. Interest groups, for example, are often credited with having predominant influence over China policy in certain areas: business groups are credited or charged with pushing through "pro-China" policies, such as permanent normal trade relations; human rights groups are credited or charged with having had inordinate influence over certain State Department officials and members of Congress. Presidential campaign donors and "political action committees" often are accused of having directed policy decisions. Many of these charges are spurious, in my experience, with respect to foreign policy. Interest groups can provide effective and important inputs to the policy process. They may define or frame issues for public discussion and provide factual information to Congress and the executive branch, but they exert only minor influence in the actual deliberation and decision process for important policy matters. Regardless of sensational press charges, the policymaking process is well defined within any administration, the main players are established, and formal and informal processes materialize to facilitate decisionmaking. The influence of interest groups on important policy choices is marginal—and manageable—in comparison with bureaucratic interests, the actions of China and Taiwan, and the president's understanding of America's national interests.[35]

The power of the press and television is also limited, at least in "normal" times. Without doubt, both the legislative and executive branches of the U.S. government spend a good deal of time and energy on the care and feeding of various media. It is a dynamic relationship, and when it is operating smoothly, policymakers and the public are well informed, and competing ideas get appropriate attention. For foreign policy issues, the standard of journalism is rather high, particularly for some of the large urban newspapers and news services with the resources to station reporters in China. The *New York Times, Washington Post, Los Angeles Times,* Associated Press, and others provide objective, valuable information and insights to public and policymakers alike (most policymakers read the press carefully and early in the day).

Pundits, editorialists, and "news analysts" figure in the policy process, although not definitively. Often strongly partisan, they can affect the political atmospherics on Capitol Hill by bringing focused opinion to bear on specific issues. Administration figures may try to cultivate them in hopes they will support their policies but know they are not the only outlet available for elite opinion. Whatever their partisan affiliation, most journalistic opinionmakers are negative about China and critical of any administration that engages with it. Their reasons have principally to do with China's approach to human rights, religious freedom, or nonproliferation. Chinese who read the American press and complain about negative views and stereotypes they discern there are probably attaching more importance to such commentaries than they merit, however.

Policymakers usually get their information from written sources, which are more thorough than television news programs. They like to participate, however, in the Sunday talk shows and evening news analysis programs, such as the *Lehrer News Hour*, where they can expound and defend policies and rebut critics in somewhat more detail. This is done to shape elite, rather than public, opinion, as viewership of these programs is comparatively low. Americans do not learn much about foreign countries from television news, which generally concentrates on domestic stories with striking visual imagery or with high controversy. In 1997, for example, a year of considerable tension in U.S.-China relations, the main television news programs devoted sixty-four minutes of airtime to China news, most of which was negative in tone. By comparison, China had 881 minutes of news coverage in 1989, most of it devoted to the events of Tiananmen.[36]

When the foreign policy story takes on a domestic cast, the media can become significantly more influential, as witness the events that shook U.S.-China relations in the Donorgate and Spygate scandals of 1997–99. During those episodes, "investigative" reporting by the *New York Times,* the *Washington Post* and, to a lesser degree, the *Los Angeles Times,* and some other publications drove the policy agenda, limiting the president's flexibility on China and inflaming opinion in Congress against China. The results of the extensive Justice Department examination and prosecution of wrong-doing in these cases suggest that there was less to the early stories than the press initially suspected. John Huang, Ted Sioeng, Maria Hsia, Johnny Chung, and Charlie Trie clearly violated campaign finance laws and paid heavy costs for their misuse of the American political system. Some of them may have had relationships with Chinese intelligence, but they had no discernible influence on the policy process. Nor does it seem likely Beijing was involved in a complex and nefarious plot to undermine the U.S. electoral system. Neither the Justice Department nor Congress could find enough evidence to prove the allegations made by Senator Fred Thompson and others. But the impact of the stories on public opinion—and particularly the notion that China is a hostile power trying to use ethnic Chinese Americans to undermine the political system of the United States—has remained to this day.

The media's role in the Wen Ho Lee case is troubling. Dependent on leaks from biased sources and intelligence information they could not verify, several reporters manufactured a story of a massive theft of extremely sensitive information, which panicked the Department of Justice and the Department of Energy into taking precipitous actions against Lee. A climate of fear and suspicion of China and Chinese people was prevalent in the media, resulting from the Donorgate investigations, the closed nature of China's government, and perhaps the hostile activities of some of its intelligence and military organizations. Post-Watergate distrust of government, combined with a solicitude for the courageous "whistleblower," lent too much credence to a story with tantalizing elements of espionage and government "cover-up." In any case, too little attention was paid to information that would have exculpated Lee. Although subsequent reviews of how the case was handled did not reveal evidence of systematic racial bias, neither Lee nor many Asian Americans would agree. Chinese American scientists at the national laboratories and elsewhere have begun quietly to organize and monitor whether the suspicion that surrounded all of them during the Wen Ho Lee case has persisted and has led to slower promotions and clearances or other forms of job discrimination.[37]

Politics in Beijing is of a different character, and its impact on foreign policy is more muted, generally. It is still a highly centralized yet personalistic political system, with the preponderance of decisionmaking authority vested in the Communist Party's Politburo Standing Committee. Obviously, policy is affected by the outcome of interpersonal competition for power and position at that level. Given the great importance accorded to Sino-American ties throughout this period, responsibility for the relationship has been maintained by General Secretary and President Jiang Zemin as the "core" of the party's leadership. As he gradually solidified his hold on the levers of power within the party after 1989, and particularly after the Fifteenth Party Congress in 1997, Jiang steadily took charge of Sino-American relations, with the active support of former foreign minister and vice premier Qian Qichen, China's *éminence grise* in foreign affairs. Jiang's confidence increased visibly with each summit meeting, and the overall "character" of China's policy began more and more to reflect Jiang's personality and style: cautious, steady, suspicious, preoccupied with ceremony and symbolism rather than substance.

Interbureaucratic maneuvering has become more important to Chinese foreign policymaking as different ministries—such as foreign trade, health, science and technology, education, the People's Liberation Army (PLA), and others—developed their own equities in the bilateral relationship. But these departments are still generally held in check by the tilting of decisionmaking authority to the upper levels of the system. On major foreign policy questions, the record suggests that Jiang consults with other members of the Politburo Standing Committee, as well as the Politburo and the Foreign Affairs Leading Small Group, although it is not known how often the latter group meets or who prepares its agenda (one presumes Jiang's office does so). For foreign policy issues with an economic dimension, such as China's accession to the World Trade Organization, he is believed to solicit information from Premier Zhu Rongji, the Finance and Economic Leading Small Group (which Jiang heads), and key leaders at the Ministry of Foreign Trade and Economic Cooperation. For issues with a strategic or military component, such as the Taiwan crisis of 1995–96, Jiang has resources on the Military Commission he must consult, and he appears to have great confidence in Deputy Chief of the General Staff for Intelligence Xiong Guangkai.

There does not appear to be a formal policy coordination mechanism in China comparable to the National Security Council or the Principals Committee in the United States. Ministers are expected to work out differences privately or submit them through channels to the Politburo if they are unable to resolve disagreements. Information and policy guidelines are heavily "stovepiped" (not shared or coordinated with other ministries) in China. Below the level of minister, interministerial consultation is not authorized, although it takes place increasingly on an informal basis. Neither is there a fully operational crisis management system in place that can funnel information upward, focus expertise and policy guidance, and transmit orders downward in an emergency. Beijing has considered organizing a "national security small group," and Hong Kong and Japanese media reported one was set up in late 2000 to deal with emergencies. In composition, however, it looked very much like the Foreign Affairs Leading Small Group and still had to work under Politburo authority. Its existence has not been publicly acknowledged by Beijing.[38]

For advice on and implementation of general policy concerning the United States, Jiang has been advised by a group of America specialists that has remained fairly consistent over time. Fluent English speakers, they have moved up through the ranks of the Ministry of Foreign Affairs in the Information Department and the North American and Oceanian Affairs Department under the protection and tutelage of Qian Qichen and, to a lesser degree Foreign Affairs Office Director Liu Huaqiu. They include former ambassadors, assistant or vice ministers, and other department-level officials, most of whom have served one or more tours in the United States. But the group is comparatively small and seems to be composed largely of foreign ministry officials, reflecting the MFA's preponderant influence.[39] The ministry has also broadened somewhat its coordinating role, for example, by establishing departments that address principal topics of concern to the United States, such as arms control.

There is some disagreement in the China-watching field about the role of the PLA in China's overall decisionmaking apparatus. Since Tiananmen, there has been a decline in the number of military officers in the Politburo and its Standing Committee. Jiang Zemin has carefully cultivated the PLA leadership and maintained his role as chairman of the Central Military Commission, but the military's overall role is clearly subordinate to that of the party. But as the military has focused on professionalization and kept clear of politics, the party leadership has provided ample budgetary support for military programs and has attended to the PLA's concerns in policy areas that involve China's security.[40] Although there is no evidence to support the notion that the PLA has played a decisive role in major foreign policy decisions, earlier chapters have highlighted, however, the importance of the military in the overall conduct of China's relations with the United States. Whether one looks at standard military issues—such as missile deployments opposite Taiwan, patrolling along China's borders, the military budget and modernization of China's overall military capabilities—or at more esoteric topics, such as intelligence collection, sales and acquisition of military equipment and technology, and business practices of PLA-sponsored corporations, there is a notable pattern of PLA involvement in many of the "problem" issues in bilateral relations. Many of the "crises" in the relationship during the past twelve years have involved actions taken by the PLA, beginning with the suppression of democracy activists at Tiananmen and including the missile tests of 1996, the sales of technology for weapons of mass destruction to "states of concern," the illicit acquisition of U.S. technology, development of strategic doctrine hostile to the United States, and even the "EP-3 incident" of 2001. For their part, the Chinese have expressed concern about U.S. sales of advanced weaponry to Taiwan, the deployment of U.S. forces in Korea, Japan, and elsewhere, the operation of U.S. naval forces off the Chinese coast, and the development of theater missile defense in the Asia-Pacific region and national missile defense for the continental United States.

The nature of engagement between the PLA and U.S. military remains controversial on both sides. There is mutual recognition that the maintenance of a "normalized" U.S.-China relationship should include a full set of military-to-military exchanges on "strategic" and international issues, humanitarian relief operations under UN auspices, military education, and procedures to handle "incidents at sea" (such as the *Kitty Hawk* incident of 1994). But concerns about reciprocity and the maintenance of security about capabilities, along with uncertainty about the overall structure of the relationship (friendly, neutral, or adversarial), have made military-to-military relations one of the most sensitive and difficult issues to manage. The PLA's fundamental distrust of the United States and its focus on developing the capabilities to resolve the Taiwan issue by force and against U.S. opposition, if need be, have presented a substantial obstacle to maintaining a stable, predictable relationship.

China's National People's Congress, and even its Standing Committee, remain largely "rubber stamp" organizations, under the tight control of the central leadership. Although the NPC began to exercise some of its constitutional authority and independence under former Standing Committee chairman Qiao Shi, after 1998 it became less active as a political force under the leadership of Li Peng. It has, however, taken up some important issues that will affect China's foreign relations, particularly the expansion of the rule of law in China (of concern to human rights groups and the U.S. Congress) and the development of legislation to codify China's trade regulations in conjunction with its accession to the World Trade Organization. Besides its more active legislative functions, the NPC has begun to play something of a parliamentary role in questioning State Council ministers on their work. This function has not yet become as active as in other legislatures, but it can be expected to grow in importance. Furthermore, NPC delegates have become more serious about actually representing their constituents, which eventually will bring regional interests to bear on larger policy matters. While these have been mostly concerned with economic and welfare issues, it is not inconceivable that delegates may someday bring such perspectives to discussions of foreign and security policies as well. Insofar as the U.S. Congress and the NPC are gradually developing a more active program of exchanges, both legislatures can be expected to pay more attention to the conduct of bilateral relations by their respective executive bureaucracies.

The Communist Party has tried vigorously to ensure that the media in China remain under the tight control of central authorities, and for the most part, those efforts have succeeded. It would be difficult to argue that there is freedom of the press in China, in the sense that the media have a right to criticize or question the government. Certainly on major foreign policy issues, and especially relations with the United States, the regime has been successful in maintaining a generally unified public position. But it would be misleading to posit that the regime has anything close to the level of press control that it had immediately after Tiananmen. The number of press organs directly controlled by the Communist Party has shrunk to a handful, and they probably would not survive were it not for mandatory subscriptions for party branches. Hundreds, if not thousands, of new publications have emerged to test their appeal with China's hungry reading public. Most are not required to submit to prepublication censorship, although publishers understand that they will be closed down if they are seen to be challenging party authority, and so they practice self-censorship. But there is a constant sense of challenge presented by the fact that the regime cannot possibly keep up with all publications. China's press may not be free, but it is far less restricted than it was a decade ago.

Furthermore, the Internet has brought an enormous supply of additional news to China, much of it with foreign content. Again, the government makes a concerted effort through various technical mechanisms to control—or at least monitor—the information being made available to Chinese web users, but it is only partly successful, at best. And the trend is moving against the controllers as the number of Internet users grows each year by several million. China's enthusiastic adoption of all the newest forms of telecommunications—mobile phones, pagers, instant messaging—has transformed the world of communications in China, with far-reaching implications for the relationship between the government and the governed. Whatever powers the Propaganda Department (which now calls itself, in English, the "Publicity Department") may have regained in the wake of Tiananmen, it has lost far more control over the ideas that circulate within China.

The Internet has had one curious direct effect on the foreign policy process, however. It has made the Ministry of Foreign Affairs more accessible to Chinese surfers and web cranks. Semi-anonymous Internet users have, on occasion, flooded the MFA with unsolicited advice and criticism, some of it quite personal and insulting. Accustomed to working in anonymous privacy, MFA officials now find themselves exposed to the lash of a form of public opinion, and they do not necessarily enjoy it. The Internet also offers numerous chat rooms where readers can participate in discussions of various issues. Observers have been surprised to find that those who are willing to share their views about foreign policy issues in the chat rooms have often proved extremely nationalistic, even chauvinistic. Moreover, Chinese "hackers," some organized but most independent, have engaged in various network attacks on what they perceive as China's "enemies" in Taiwan, the United States, and Japan.

Some American observers have been surprised, even alarmed, at the direction and intensity of Chinese nationalism, as it has been expressed in various circumstances. And it has inspired varied commentaries, reflecting the range of American opinions about China. Some see China's nationalism as something new, anti-American, xenophobic, and threatening; others as varied, traditional, inchoate, even benign. There is a growing literature on the subject on both sides of the Pacific, which I will not attempt to summarize here.[41] But it makes clear that Chinese nationalism is an increasingly important factor in the formulation of Beijing's policy toward the United States. It is an outgrowth of the fact that China has progressed rapidly to become a leading nation in the world, and its citizens are in many ways justifiably proud of their country's accomplishments. There is also a "chip on the shoulder" aspect to some expressions of Chinese nationalism, which springs from its historical experience as a nation that has been downtrodden and disrespected. Resentment is easily ignited when foreign critics of China's government fail to distinguish their castigation of the Beijing government from condescension or affront to the Chinese people.

The Chinese government has occasionally appealed to national pride, even racial pride, in its efforts to maintain some semblance of legitimacy, fend off foreign pressure or criticism, or to generate consensus on problematic policies, such as coercive diplomacy toward Taiwan. For the most part, however, it has played the nationalism "card" carefully, knowing full well that it can slide out of control or even be used against the regime itself. The volatility of public opinion in China stems from the fact that it has few outlets for constructive expression. Until more outlets become available—through political parties, nongovernmental organizations, the free exchange of opinions, and elections—nationalism will remain an unpredictable element in China's domestic and foreign policy.

Event-Driven Relations, with Taiwan as the Main Event

With the fall of the Soviet Union having deprived U.S.-China relations of their strategic imperative, while Tiananmen and the Belgrade bombing took away illusions on both sides about liking the other, the relationship between the two governments has been without unifying principles or concord. It has become the sum of its disagreements and the product of mistakes and misperceptions. Without mutually agreed-on goals, it has become mostly event driven, subject to sharp swings of attitude or sentiment depending on the nature and outcome of the driving events. Some of the events are mutually planned, such as summit meetings, significant anniversaries, or the like. More often, they are unpleasant incidents that bring the two countries' contradictory interests into sharp relief or challenge the ability of political leaders to contain domestically driven emotions. The 1993 Olympics, the *Yin He*, "ring magnets," the Cornell speech, Donorgate, the "two states theory," the EP-3 incident—all are examples of the susceptibility of the larger relationship to political damage from unpredictable events.

In the past few years, Taiwan-related events or issues have become the most likely to create dangerous tensions in the U.S.-China relationship. There are several reasons for this situation. First, the incongruities of the so-called foundations of the relationship—the three joint communiqués—have become increasingly apparent. The key phrases that allowed the two sides to agree on the Shanghai communiqué in 1972—"The United States acknowledges that all Chinese on either side of the Taiwan Strait maintain there is but one China and that Taiwan is a part of China. The U.S. government does not challenge that position. It reaffirms its interest in a peaceful settlement of the Taiwan question by the Chinese themselves"—are no longer accurate.[42] Many in Taiwan, including its present president, Chen Shui-bian, and his ruling party, no longer are willing to maintain "there is only one China and Taiwan is a part of China." While they are not prepared to declare independence, they now seem unwilling to conceptualize a larger "China" that could encompass the PRC and Taiwan. Afraid to see Taiwan drift away into independence, Chinese leaders have raised the level of rhetorical and actual threat employed against Taiwan, which has prompted Taipei to seek more defense-related military equipment. The United States is obligated to provide that equipment under the terms of the Taiwan Relations Act of 1979. That has essentially mooted the August 17, 1982, communiqué, which pledged "that it intends to reduce gradually its sales of arms to Taiwan, leading over a period of time to a final resolution."[43]

Second, both Beijing and Taipei since 1995 now seem to see the United States as the main locus for the resolution of their disagreement. Neither side is satisfied with the status quo, nor does either accept American recommendations for a peaceful resolution brought about by dialogue. But rather than deal directly with each other, both seem to prefer trying to swing the weight of U.S. favor onto their side: Beijing to force Taiwanese authorities to negotiate the terms of their incorporation into "one China"; Taipei to induce the PRC leadership to renounce a military solution and deal with Taiwan as an equal. The cross-Strait dialogue has been effectively suspended, and the two sides are making little effort to communicate with each other. Both are determined to prevent the United States from "tilting" too far toward the other side. That increases the chances of provocation or miscalculation, with the United States caught in the middle.

Without a significant change in the overall attitude or structure of the PRC regime, it is unlikely that Beijing and Taipei will be able to reach agreement on a means of resolving their differences. The two governments seem united only in their propensity to see their relationship as zero sum: what one gains the other perceives as losing. In light of the increased importance of Taiwan-related issues in the U.S.-PRC relationship, this means that U.S.-China relations are, in the end, hostage to the condition of Taiwan-PRC relations. No matter what the state of the other dimensions of bilateral U.S.-PRC ties, the Taiwan issue can always create friction, if only on the basis of how Taiwan's leaders choose to "push the envelope" in terms of expanding Taiwan's international profile or purchasing the latest-generation U.S. weapons.

American officials have sometimes underestimated Taiwan as a bilateral concern, not realizing how intensely important the question has become in Chinese domestic politics. This was clearly true in 1995–96, for example, and probably also was true in 1998, in planning for President Clinton's trip to China. Americans may want to believe there is plenty of time to find a solution as the two sides converge politically and economically. Mao Zedong was once quoted as saying reunification with Taiwan might take as long as one hundred years to resolve. When he signed the normalization communiqué with the United States in 1978, Deng Xiaoping seemed to be saying China could be patient and wait for Taiwan—bereft of U.S. military support—gradually to become more isolated and persuaded by the combination of China's military superiority and what he thought would be an increasingly attractive offer of autonomy under the rubric of "one country two systems." Although the Taiwan Relations Act and continuing U.S. military arms sales to Taiwan were a profound shock to Deng and nearly caused a rupture in the relationship, the August 17, 1982, communiqué on limiting U.S. arms sales seemed to place the issue on the back burner.

The combination of Bush's decision to sell F-16s to Taiwan in 1992 (with delivery beginning in 1995) and Taiwanese president Lee Teng-hui's domestic reforms and international aspirations brought the issue back to a high pitch in 1995, and it has remained there. It salience is amplified by a combination of interpersonal politics, bureaucratic and budgetary maneuvering, and the growing importance of popular nationalism in Chinese foreign policy decisionmaking. In his quest for supremacy in the post-Deng leadership, and probably because he did not want to be accused of "losing" Taiwan, Jiang Zemin has taken reunification of Taiwan with China as one of his key "legacy" issues. Others in the leadership have used the issue on occasion to challenge his authority, for example, in 1995. The PLA leadership has used the issue to press its case for priority budgetary allocations for military modernization, which might otherwise be weakened by China's overall improved security in the wake of the dissolution of the Soviet Union. All these factors have increased the sense of urgency in Beijing for bringing about reunification, whether peaceably or by use of force. There have even been rumors that the leadership had established a timetable for the island's restoration to the "motherland."

In Washington, too, Taiwan has become a more important factor in domestic politics. Congress has taken a very activist approach to preserving Taiwan's security for a variety of reasons. Taiwan is now a full-fledged "values" issue, rather than a national security question, owing to the island's transformation into a thriving and colorful democracy. A "Taiwan caucus," organized in 2002, attracted more than 110 members. Taiwan is an issue in the multifaceted struggle between the executive and legislative branches of the U.S. government for control of the foreign affairs agenda. Congress insists that the Taiwan Relations Act, as the law of the land, supersedes any bilateral agreements, including the three U.S.-China joint communiqués. Increasingly, Congress has attached Taiwan-related measures to authorization bills, passed "sense of the Congress" resolutions recommending expanded support for Taiwan's international status, and demanded regular reports from the executive branch on Taiwan's security status in the face of China's buildup of missile forces across the Taiwan Strait. The issue has become rather partisan, with Republicans criticizing the Clinton administration for neglecting Taiwan's security in its efforts to build a "constructive strategic partnership" with China.

Repeated polls of American opinion suggest the general public has mixed views about the Taiwan issue and U.S. policy toward the feuding parties. Most Americans (62 percent in a 1996 Harris poll, for example) consider Taiwan "more like an independent country than as part of China," and 69 percent said it should be reunified with the mainland "only if the Taiwanese want to be."[44] Nonetheless, there is greater ambivalence about selling advanced weapons to Taiwan (about 50 percent in two 2001 polls opposed doing so), and strong opposition (more than 50 percent in several recent polls) to committing U.S. military forces to Taiwan's defense if it provokes a Chinese attack.[45]

Taiwan's democratization under former president Lee Teng-hui, ironically, has made the overall situation more volatile. Although Taiwan has become the democracy many Americans hoped China would become, its transformation from a monolithic one-party dictatorship—similar in appearance and attitudes to the PRC—to a vibrant and noisy multiparty system has made it more likely to provoke Beijing into taking precipitous military action. The triumph of the pro-independence Democratic Progressive Party candidate Chen Shui-bian in Taiwan's 2000 presidential election changed significantly the dynamics of the island's domestic politics. In and of itself, that heightened Beijing's concerns and lent support to those in China who favor a military solution to the problem. Although Chen has been careful with his policy pronouncements on cross-Strait issues, some of his DPP supporters have not, and Beijing's typically thin-skinned reactions to provocative statements from Taiwanese politicians have added a new feature to an already tense relationship.

Engagement, Communication, and Management

Ever since the earliest days of diplomatic relations, but especially since the events of June 4, 1989, American officials and diplomats have generally used the term "engagement" to describe the U.S. policy approach to China. Usually it is preceded by adjectives, such as "comprehensive, constructive, principled, enhanced, or broad," but that has not made the approach any clearer. "Engagement," when it is described at all, is usually defined by what it is not, namely, not containment, isolation, punishment, or military pressure. Usually, it implies the conduct of high-level meetings with Chinese officials. This absence of definitional clarity has led to problems on both sides. In the United States, it left an uncertain hierarchy of goals and enabled different bureaucracies to pursue their own sometimes conflicting agendas under the rubric of a single policy framework.[46] China's understanding of the U.S. approach was complicated by the fact that the Chinese language lacks a precise translation for the term "engagement," or an appreciation of its often implied nuance. But there is a more important difference. As put by Wang Jisi, one of China's most prominent America watchers, "Americans often regard high-ranking official engagements as opportunities to 'solve problems' that are otherwise difficult to discuss, whereas Chinese officials usually attach more 'symbolism' to such opportunities. In Chinese eyes, high-level consultations, if they are to take place, serve as a thermometer measuring the atmosphere in which substantive issues can be discussed, and as an indication of a spirit of equality and goodwill."[47]

But in either definition, the quality of communications is a serious problem in U.S.-Chinese relations. President George H. W. Bush had established good interpersonal relations with Deng Xiaoping and others in the Chinese leadership, but he was not able to reconnect after Tiananmen and Deng's retreat from active management of China's foreign relations. By the time Deng was back in full control, Bush had been defeated and replaced by a president who had little interest in personal communication with leaders he distrusted and disdained. President Clinton built a personal relationship with President Jiang only very slowly, taking more than five years to develop a modicum of trust and candor. That paid benefits briefly in 1997–98, but it could not be sustained in the face of domestic political pressures on both sides.

During the period after June 4, sterile, formalized conversations between foreign ministers became the norm for bilateral communications, even though both sides probably recognized they were not particularly effective. They were carefully staged and rehearsed, with each side presenting talking points fully cleared by the relevant bureaucracies. On James Baker's 1991 trip, Warren Christopher's trip in 1994, and Madeleine Albright's in 1999, the meetings became counterproductive, the venue for the symbolic venting of pent-up anger. Even when operating at their best, as in 1996 meetings between Qian and Christopher, for example, they seldom solved problems but rather clarified mutual complaints. At no point did U.S. secretaries of state and Chinese foreign ministers build the kind of interpersonal relations that could short-cut difficulties and find creative solutions to disagreements. As Tony Lake put it, "You'll never have serious, sort of personal conversations with [the Chinese] the way you can with the diplomats of most other nations. But you can have serious conversations . . . if you take the time and don't just read talking points to them, but try to build understanding."[48]

There needs to be routinized and informal exchanges between officials on both sides who are in a position to advise key decisionmakers. Ideally this would be at the level of senior director in the NSC and assistant secretary in the State Department, with counterparts at China's Foreign Ministry assistant or vice-ministerial level. If and as the Chinese establish the "national security small group" within the leadership to handle crisis management and other critical topics, it should ensure that it has regular and in-depth discussions with American counterparts. Meetings at this level already take place regularly, but they are often formalistic. The periods when frequent and candid communication has been operating in bilateral relations have been rare, but they have coincided with the most successful and cooperative periods in a troubled relationship. When such informal communications do not occur, it is extremely difficult to manage the complex politics of the bilateral relationship.

Looking Ahead

The record of U.S.-China relations in the fourteen years since Tiananmen does not give much cause for optimism. To be sure, both sides have recognized publicly and repeatedly that the relationship between the United States and China will be critical in shaping the course of the early twenty-first century. Both nations have acknowledged how important it is to develop the bilateral relationship. And it must be said that a certain equilibrium seems to have been achieved, as both sides seem willing to avoid the provocations that might do serious damage to the relationship. Particularly after the events of

September 11, 2001, there has been an important improvement in the tone and content of the official relationship, as reflected by three summit meetings between President Jiang Zemin and President George W. Bush within one year. But one does not discern a sense of permanence about the change. It does not seem to be grounded in a genuine strategic or political meeting of the minds. Chinese commentators, for example, tend to attribute the improvement to a belated recognition by the Bush administration of the importance of China, while American observers see a new pragmatism or maturity on the part of Chinese decisionmakers toward U.S. antiterrorist priorities. There is a perception of progress rather than a process to bring it about.

And on a deeper level, the sources of tension remain. In the United States, the anger, disappointment, mistrust, and antipathy that followed the tragic events of June 4, 1989, have persisted in popular views about China, despite a broad recognition that China has undergone great changes since that time. For various political reasons, hostility to the government of China has become nearly institutionalized in the U.S. Congress. Efforts by any administration to change the tone or substance of the bilateral relationship have to consider this atmosphere. Some U.S. strategic planners, looking beyond the war on terrorism, have focused on China as a potentially hostile strategic challenger to U.S. power and interests. But at the same time, sufficient goodwill, respect, and understanding of China's significance in the United States prevent a precipitous slide into confrontation and containment.

A similar ambivalence toward the United States has grown up in China during the past fourteen years, fostered by a succession of efforts undertaken by Washington to penalize, shame, or reprove China for its actions and attitudes or by political and ideological maneuvering among bureaucracies and individuals in a complex post-Deng China. While balanced by a broad recognition that China's economic progress remains tied to the United States, cultural and historical attitudes have left most Chinese unwilling to be seen as caving in to American pressure. American actions toward China—given particular emotional salience by the bombing of the Chinese embassy in Belgrade in 1999—are seen by the public and the government alike as bullying and presumptuous. Positive movement in the relationship often has been checked by actions or decisions made by Beijing out of concern for China's internal stability or because of sensitivity over Taiwan. American intentions toward Taiwan are widely misperceived as being part of some nefarious strategic plot to keep China weak and divided. And yet no country is more admired than the United States, no country has more influence.

It is tempting to conclude that only a regime change that brings to power a more democratic, representative, pluralistic government in China will provide the basis for a genuine and lasting improvement in bilateral relations. Yet at the same time, the process by which such a change might be accomplished is difficult to envision. A breakdown in political authority in China could just as easily bring about social destabilization, ultranationalism, or aggressive expansionism that would be even more challenging to U.S. interests in the region. In other words, while Americans may wish for a more democratic, less despotic regime in China, there is no course that could be taken to guarantee such an outcome. As odious as the Communist Party of China may be on occasion, that is the government with which the United States must deal.

The good news is that it is a government in transition to something different, a regime that is in the process of reforming itself. It is not seeking to become a more perfect Marxist state, although it retains—for social control purposes—heavy-handed instruments of propaganda, ideological education, and repression of heterodoxy. During the past fourteen years, China has fully embraced a vision for its future that is largely disconnected from its past Marxist ideals. In its quest for economic success that incorporates socialism and capitalism, the regime has assumed social, political, and ethical norms and goals more like those of the United States than of Mao's China. This ongoing process is by no means accepted by all nor guaranteed to succeed. The Communist Party of China is dedicated above all to its own survival in power. That survival dictates that it continue on the path of reform and opening up, of replacing the rule of men with the rule of law, of permitting its citizens to live, work, think, and communicate as they will. Economic progress has brought new challenges for the leaders of the Communist Party, including a more pluralistic society, a better-educated and informed populace, and greater awareness of the freedoms and privileges enjoyed by other modern societies. China's leaders may run what looks like a closed political system, and their decisions seem autocratic, but they are struggling to keep up with a society that is changing in a direction and at a speed they cannot fully control. American policymakers—and the general public—should never lose sight of the importance of that larger process of change.

Maintaining balanced, beneficial, and constructive relations between the United States and China will never be easy. There is no strategy, attitude, communications channel, or communiqué that can make it so; the relationship is simply too complex and multifaceted to allow for easy management. But management is the key—management of complex goals, multiple disagreements, sensitive emotions, cumbersome bureaucracies, countervailing pressures, unrealistic expectations, and imperfect information. Good management requires knowledge, patience, flexibility, planning, communication, dedication—all qualities not easy to develop in either government. But it is possible, providing both sides agree on the value of doing so. There have been periods during the past fourteen years when both sides have managed their role in the bilateral relationship well, though with difficulty. And certainly we have seen that the alternatives to managing the relationship are generally far worse and will only become more so.

Notes

Notes to Chapter 1

1. This book assumes a reader has a basic familiarity with the overall structure and functions of the Chinese and the American political systems. For a good introduction to the overall decisionmaking system in China, see Kenneth Lieberthal and Michel Oksenberg, *Policy Making in China—Leaders, Structures and Processes* (Princeton University Press, 1988).

2. These processes are described in more detail in various following chapters. See also Lu Ning, *The Dynamics of Foreign-Policy Decision-making in China* (Boulder, Colo.: Westview Press, 1997); and Carol Hamrin and Suisheng Zhao, eds., *Decision-Making in Deng's China: Perspectives from Insiders* (M. E. Sharpe, 1995).

3. Lu, *Dynamics,* pp. 26–30.

4. The Freedom of Information Act was passed by the U.S. Congress in 1966 and amended in 1974. Its purpose is to create processes by which the American public can gain access to the records of any and all agencies of the federal government, including intelligence agencies. Although the act has made it possible for some important U.S. policy documentation to become public, the approval process is cumbersome and time consuming, and still only provides partial, sometimes heavily redacted, versions of the documents that can mislead as often as inform. China's approach to secrecy is more comprehensive than that of the United States, and many routine procedural reports and articles are lightly classified as *neibu,* which means "internal." It is generally equivalent to U.S. government documents classified "for internal use only," meaning they may be sensitive in content but will not do damage to the government or its policies if divulged.

5. Many Western scholars have utilized unattributed quotes from unnamed officials or scholars in assessments of the Chinese political process, not identifying their interlocutors to provide them some protection from possible retribution. I have cho-

sen not to take that course, as I have found the anonymous officials seldom deviate significantly from the "official" line, are not particularly candid, and sometimes seem engaged in a form of "perception manipulation" that is of little objective value.

Notes to Chapter 2

1. MSNBC News, June 3, 1999.

2. See "The Truth about the Beijing Turmoil," a pamphlet sponsored by the Editorial Board of the Truth about the Beijing Turmoil (Beijing Publishing House, 1990), pp. 3–5. The board was a Beijing municipal party committee effort to counter foreign news accounts. See also Deng Xiaoping's June 9, 1989, address to Martial Law Units, broadcast by Beijing Domestic Television Service, June 27, 1989, in Foreign Broadcast Information Service (FBIS), China, June 27, 1989, pp. 8–10; and Chen Xitong, "Report to the National People's Congress on Quelling the Counter-Revolutionary Rebellion," in Michel Oksenberg, Lawrence R. Sullivan, and Marc Lambert, eds., *Beijing Spring, 1989: Confrontation and Conflict* (Armonk, N.Y.: M. E. Sharpe, 1990), p. 56.

3. In January 2001 a collection of documentary evidence purportedly smuggled out of Chinese archives and brought to the United States was published in a book called *The Tiananmen Papers*, Andrew J. Nathan and E. Perry Link, eds. (New York: Public Affairs, 2001). Compiled by a Chinese official who went by the pseudonym Zhang Liang, the papers constitute a very detailed and compelling account of leadership meetings, reports, telephone calls, and other materials from March to June 1989. Although the Chinese government dismissed them (rather obliquely) as "fabrications," they nonetheless strike me and many other observers as credible, if not complete, accounts of meetings, communications, and decisions made by China's Communist Party leaders during the "turmoil" of Tiananmen. I will refer to them frequently throughout this chapter, with the reservation that they are not absolutely reliable.

4. Deng Xiaoping's June 9, 1989, Address to Martial Law Units, Beijing Domestic Television Service, June 27, 1989; in Foreign Broadcast Information Service (FBIS), June 27, 1989, p. 8.

5. Hua Guofeng, Mao Zedong's chosen successor, remained chairman of the Communist Party for another year, but Deng had already marked him for replacement by his own protégé, Hu Yaobang, who subsequently became general secretary (the party chairman position was abolished in 1982).

6. Patrick Tyler, *A Great Wall: Six Presidents and China* (New York: Century Foundation, 1999), pp. 263, 267.

7. Big-character posters were a hallmark of the Cultural Revolution (1966–76), when they were used heavily to attack and vilify "class enemies, capitalist roaders," and other supposed opponents of Chairman Mao, many of them party leaders. Denunciation in a big-character poster often was followed by "dragging out" the individual for public criticism and, in many cases, by beating and expulsion from office. The practice of writing posters to protest government injustice—once guaranteed in

China's constitution—was generally not welcomed after 1976, given the revulsion many felt at the excesses of the Cultural Revolution. Press accounts of big-character posters often noted that security authorities would tear them down.

8. Merle Goldman, *Sowing the Seeds of Democracy in China: Political Reform in the Deng Xiaoping Era* (Harvard University Press, 1994), p. 42.

9. After Wei criticized China's February 1979 attack on Vietnam, he was arrested, subsequently charged with subversion and leaking classified information to foreigners, tried in October, and sentenced to fifteen years in prison.

10. Perry Link, *Evening Chats in Beijing: Probing China's Predicament* (W. W. Norton, 1992), p. 55.

11. Ibid., p. 157.

12. Dissatisfaction with Japanese imports helped spark student demonstrations in 1985 and 1986. See Goldman, *Sowing the Seeds*, p. 202.

13. Intellectuals were referred to as the "old, stinking ninth category" of class enemies by Mao and his radical followers during the Cultural Revolution and suffered enormous persecution and personal hardship. Hu lifted the stigma in 1978, on the premise that the modernization of China's economy would require the active participation of China's best minds.

14. Goldman, *Sowing the Seeds*, p. 125. "Spiritual pollution" was a code word for the adoption by Chinese of unhealthy Western influences, particularly in the realm of political values, ideology, philosophy, and other traits. Deng, along with other party elders and conservative ideologues, promoted the campaign in 1983, and again in 1985, under the guise of the milder term "bourgeois liberalization." Hu and then-premier Zhao Ziyang are credited with stopping it on both occasions.

15. Fang Lizhi was a professor of astrophysics at the Hefei (Anhui) Branch of the University of Science and Technology who publicly disputed the scientific validity of Marxism; Liu Binyan was a journalist who wrote daring exposés of party corruption; Wang Ruowang was a Shanghai essayist who satirized the party in his works.

16. Deng's views on these subjects can be seen in greater detail in *Selected Works of Deng Xiaoping*, vol. 2 *(1975–1982)* (Beijing: Foreign Languages Press, 1984). See, in particular, "Things Must Be Put in Order in All Fields," p. 47ff; "Emancipate the Mind, Seek Truth from Facts," p. 151ff; "Uphold the Four Cardinal Principles," p. 166ff; and "On the Reform of the System of Party and State Leadership," p. 302ff.

17. Lowell Dittmer, *China under Reform* (Boulder, Colo.: Westview Press, 1994), pp. 89–90.

18. The Central Military Commission is the Central Committee's long-established mechanism for maintaining control of the People's Liberation Army. Although the State Council technically has authority over the Ministry of Defense, the armed forces chain of command begins with the CMC. The Ministry of Defense itself is a ceremonial shell organization, responsible for maintaining China's international military relationships. Day-to-day operational control of the armed forces is maintained through the General Staff Department, political training and indoctrination through the General Political Department, and matériel support through the General Logistics Department, all of which are directly administered through the CMC. The Cen-

tral Military Commission itself consists of a chairman (usually the chairman or general secretary of the party), three or four vice chairmen (usually the most senior military leaders), sometimes a secretary general (usually the head of the General Political Department), and ordinary members consisting of the principal officers of the PLA service arms and military regions. The CMC meets in full session before or after Central Committee plenary meetings, although the chairman can call special meetings at any time.

19. Ruan Ming, a former subordinate of Hu, recounts a highly partisan but vivid and credible series of anecdotes about the struggle between party reformers and conservative elders in his book *Deng Xiaoping, Chronicle of an Empire*, trans. and eds. Nancy Liu, Peter Rand, and Lawrence R. Sullivan (Boulder, Colo.: Westview Press, 1992).

20. Goldman, *Sowing the Seeds,* p. 205; Dittmer, *China under Reform*, p. 98n; Ruan, *Deng Xiaoping,* p. 164.

21. Deng Xiaoping, "Remarks at the 6th Plenary Session of the Party's 12th Central Committee" (September 28, 1986), *Beijing Review,* no. 26 (June 29, 1987), p. 14, quoted in Goldman, *Sowing the Seeds*, pp. 188–89.

22. Goldman, *Sowing the Seeds,* p. 205.

23. Ibid., p. 202

24. Ruan, *Deng Xiaoping*, p. 168; Goldman, *Sowing the Seeds*, p. 204.

25. Ruan, *Deng Xiaoping*, p. 168.

26. Quoted in Nicholas D. Kristof, "Hu Yaobang, Ex-Party Chief in China, Dies at 73," *New York Times*, April 16, 1989, p. A38.

27. Goldman, *Sowing the Seeds,* pp. 208–09; Ruan, *Deng Xiaoping*, pp. 178–79. Ruan's claim that Zhao colluded with Deng to bring down Hu is not corroborated in detail by many reliable sources (Hong Kong media, notwithstanding). It is plausible, however, that Zhao would have seen it as being in his own interest to let Hu take the fall.

28. Goldman, *Sowing the Seeds*, pp. 236–37.

29. Ruan, *Deng Xiaoping,* p. 192.

30. Dittmer, *China under Reform*, p. 100; Ruan, *Deng Xiaoping,* p. 198.

31. Interviews with Brent Scowcroft, December 1999; Douglas Paal, December 1999; and Winston Lord, April 2000 .

32. See George Bush and Brent Scowcroft, *A World Transformed* (Knopf, 1998), pp. 22–23.

33. Interview with Douglas Paal.

34. Interview with Winston Lord.

35. Interview with J. Stapleton Roy, May 2000.

36. Goldman, *Sowing the Seeds*, pp. 196–99.

37. Deng Xiaoping, *Fundamental Issues in Present-Day China* (Beijing: Foreign Languages Press, 1987), p. 162.

38. Interview with Winston Lord.

39. Interview with Brent Scowcroft.

40. Link, *Evening Chats in Beijing*, pp. 30–32; Orville Schell, *Mandate of Heaven: A New Generation of Entrepreneurs, Dissidents, Bohemians, and Technocrats Lays*

Claim to China's Future (Simon and Schuster, 1994), pp. 39–41; Tyler, *A Great Wall*, pp. 346–47.

41. Daniel Southerland, "China Rebukes U.S. over Dissident," *Washington Post*, February 28, 1989, p. A1.

42. David Hoffman, "China's Objections to Dissident Didn't Reach Key Bush Officials, U.S. Says," *Washington Post*, March 3, 1989, p. A9; see also R. W. Apple, "'Blunder' at Beijing Dinner: U.S. Chides Embassy," *New York Times*, March 3, 1989, p. A3.

43. Interview with Winston Lord.

44. Interview with Brent Scowcroft.

45. Bush and Scowcroft, *A World Transformed*, pp. 93, 97.

46. Ibid., pp. 93–96.

47. Goldman, *Sowing the Seeds*, p. 301.

48. Sheryl WuDunn, "Hu's Death Is Stirring Unrest," *New York Times*, April 16, 1989, p. A38.

49. Schell, *Mandate of Heaven*, p. 45.

50. On May 4, 1919, more than 3,000 students from thirteen colleges in Beijing held a large-scale demonstration in Tiananmen against the decision of the Versailles Peace Conference to transfer former German concessions in Shandong Province to Japan—a decision to which the weak Republican government acquiesced. The demonstrations turned violent and spread to other cities in China, resulting in several student deaths and thousands of arrests. Merchants and citizens supported a student-led boycott of Japanese goods, and sympathy strikes were held in several major cities. Among the protesters were Mao Zedong and other early leaders of the Communist Party of China, which was formed two years later. May Fourth also set off a period of significant intellectual ferment and political activity.

51. Schell, *Mandate of Heaven*, p. 45.

52. The lack of consistency in student demands was due, in part, to the fact that they had not yet developed a coherent organizational structure. Some demands were somewhat extreme—such as one for a "collective resignation." See, for example, Nicholas D. Kristof, "Chinese Students March for Democracy," *New York Times*, April 18, 1989, p. A3.

53. Schell, *Mandate of Heaven*, p. 47; Nicholas D. Kristof, "Thousands Chant for Democracy within Earshot of China's Leaders," *New York Times*, April 19, 1989, p. A1; Mike Chinoy, *China Live: Two Decades in the Heart of the Dragon* (Atlanta: Turner Publishing, 1997), p. 187.

54. Sheryl WuDunn, "Thousands Again Protest in Beijing," *New York Times*, April 20, 1989, p. A8.

55. Schell, *Mandate of Heaven*, p. 49; Nathan and Link, *The Tiananmen Papers*, pp. 30–31; China Rights Forum, "Chronology of the 1989 Democracy Movement," special anniversary issue, June 1999 (http://iso.hrchina.org/iso/article.adp?article_id=120&subcategory_id=20).

56. Schell, *Mandate of Heaven*, p. 48.

57. Ibid., p. 49. In an April 20 report to the State Council, Ministry of State Security officials referred to the police action as "temporary martial law." See Nathan and Link, *The Tiananmen Papers*, p. 31.

58. Andrew J. Walder and Xiaoxia Gong, "Workers in the Tiananmen Protests: The Politics of the Beijing Autonomous Workers Federation," *Australian Journal of Chinese Affairs* (now *The China Journal*), no. 29 (January 1993), p. 1, reprinted on Gate of Heavenly Peace website (www.tsquare.tv/links/walder.html, accessed February 2003); see also China Rights Forum, "Chronology of the 1989 Democracy Movement."

59. China Rights Forum, "Chronology of the 1989 Democracy Movement." Actually, this might have been a provisional committee at Beishida alone. Nathan and Link cite Ministry of State Security documents on the formation of the Beida Autonomous Students Association on April 24. See Nathan and Link, *The Tiananmen Papers*, pp. 62–63.

60. Nathan and Link, *The Tiananmen Papers*, pp. 46–47. The China Rights Forum chronology indicates a Politburo meeting was held on April 20, at which Li Peng denounced the students, but the Nathan and Link volume does not substantiate it.

61. Nicholas D. Kristof, "100,000 Defy a Ban on Protests in Beijing to Demand Democracy," *New York Times*, April 22, 1989, p. A1.

62. Schell, *Mandate of Heaven*, pp. 50–51.

63. Nathan and Link, *The Tiananmen Papers,* p. 50.

64. See, for example, "The True Colors of the Federation of Autonomous Student Unions in Beijing Universities and Colleges," *People's Daily,* July 7, 1989, from Xinhua Overseas News Service, July 7, 1989 (www.freechina.net/pfdc/members/zhouxj.html, accessed February 13, 2000).

65. See, for example, Andrew Nathan, "Chinese Democracy in 1989: Continuity and Change," in *Problems of Communism* , October 1989, pp. 2–50 (www.tsquare.tv/themes/nathan.html, accessed February 2003).

66. Joan Shorenstein Barone Center on the Press, Politics, and Public Policy, "Turmoil at Tiananmen: A Study of U.S. Press Coverage of the Beijing Spring of 1989," John F. Kennedy School of Government, Harvard University, 1992 (hereafter Barone Center Study), p. 5 (www.tsquare.tv/themes/TatTcontent.html, accessed February 18, 2003).

67. Jackie Judd, quoted in the Barone Center Study, p. 3.

68. From a report sent by the Beijing Municipal Party Committee to Party Central on April 23, 1989, cited in Nathan and Link, *The Tiananmen Papers*, p. 53. The English "planned, organized turmoil" is translated from the Chinese *you zuzhi, you jihua de dongluan*. The term *dongluan* is more powerful in Chinese than the usual translation of "turmoil." Literally, *dongluan* means "to stir up chaos."

69. Nathan and Link, *The Tiananmen Papers,* pp. 59–61.

70. Ibid., pp. 71–73.

71. "A Document Circulated among Senior Party and Government Officials Earlier This Month (April 25, 1989)," originally leaked to the *South China Morning Post* (Hong Kong's principal English-language newspaper) and published on May 31, 1989, probably as a warning of the coming crackdown. Republished in Michel Oksenberg, Lawrence R. Sullivan, and Marc Lambert, eds., *Beijing Spring, 1989: Confrontation and Conflict* (Armonk, N.Y.: M. E. Sharpe, 1990), pp. 203–05. Nathan

and Link's version (see *The Tiananmen Papers,* p. 73.), based on party secretariat minutes of the meeting, has a briefer account of Deng's comments, and although the thrust is still the same, it does not contain Deng's comments on bloodshed. Both accounts agree the meeting decided to publish an editorial in *People's Daily*, based on Deng's criticism of the students.

72. "It Is Necessary to Take a Clear-Cut Stand against Disturbances," *People's Daily*, April 26, 1989, p. 1. Republished in Oksenberg, Sullivan, and Lambert, *Beijing Spring, 1989*, pp. 206–08.

73. Li Qiao, "Death or Rebirth? Tiananmen, the Soul of China," in Oksenberg, Sullivan, and Lambert, *Beijing Spring, 1989*, pp. 30–31.

74. Ibid., pp. 32–35; Schell, *Mandate of Heaven*, pp. 62–63; Chinoy, *China Live*, pp. 199–200; Nicholas D. Kristof, "150,000 March in Defiance of Beijing," *New York Times*, April 28, 1989, p. 1.

75. Kristof, "150,000 March."

76. Chinoy, *China Live*, p. 200.

77. Li Qiao, "Death or Rebirth?" in Oksenberg, Sullivan, and Lambert, *Beijing Spring, 1989*, pp. 39–41.

78. Chen Xitong, "Report to the National People's Congress on Quelling the Counter-Revolutionary Rebellion," in Oksenberg, Sullivan, and Lambert, *Beijing Spring, 1989,* pp. 65, 68.

79. See Nathan and Link, *The Tiananmen Papers*, pp. 86–90.

80. Oksenberg, Sullivan, and Lambert, *Beijing Spring, 1989*, p. 123.

81. See Lo Ping, "Li Xiannian Urges Changing the General Secretary," *Cheng Ming* magazine, no. 38, April 1, 1989, pp. 6–8, republished in Oksenberg, Sullivan, and Lambert, *Beijing Spring, 1989*, pp. 180–86. While open to question in terms of its factual accuracy, *Cheng Ming* is widely circulated and read in China. This story, published before Hu Yaobang's death, would have been well known throughout China, including among students.

82. Andrew J. Nathan, "Introduction: The Documents and Their Significance," in Nathan and Link, *The Tiananmen Papers,* p. xxvi.

83. Zhao Ziyang, "Make Further Efforts to Carry Forward the May Fourth Spirit in the New Age of Construction and Reform," in Oksenberg, Sullivan, and Lambert, *Beijing Spring, 1989*, pp. 244–51.

84. Xinhua coverage of Zhao's remarks, May 4, 1989, republished in Oksenberg, Sullivan, and Lambert, *Beijing Spring, 1989*, p. 255. The Party Central Office Secretariat excerpts of Zhao's speech in Nathan and Link, *The Tiananmen Papers,* pp. 115–16, are even more sympathetic to their cause and critical of party and government mistakes, particularly their failure to curb corruption.

85. Seth Faison of the *South China Morning Post*, quoted in Barone Center Study, p. 16.

86. Nathan and Link, *The Tiananmen Papers,* pp. 102–08.

87. Ibid., pp. 116–18.

88. Xu Jiatun, *Memoirs and Thoughts* (Mirror Books, 1998), chapter 14 ("The June 4th Storm—A Wave of Patriotic Anger"). Xu fled Hong Kong because of his

close ties to Zhao, and because he was to be held accountable for the enormous surge of sympathy for the student cause that was seen in Hong Kong's pro-PRC media during the period. See also Nathan and Link, *The Tiananmen Papers,* pp. 123–24, for notes of a private conversation between Zhao and Yang. The source for this document, however, is particularly obscure—a "friend" of Yang Shangkun, who cannot be further identified.

89. Nicholas D. Kristof, "Urging Chinese Democracy, 100,000 Surge Past Police," *New York Times*, May 5, 1989, p. A8.

90. Sheryl WuDunn, "Workers Joining Students in Beijing Demonstrations," *New York Times*, May 5, 1989, p. A8.

Notes to Chapter 3

1. Li Xiaowen, "A Chronicle of What Happened in Beijing from May 13 to 14, 1989: Efforts to Persuade Students to Leave Tiananmen Square," *China News Digest,* June 3, 1995, p. 2 (www.cnd.org/CND-Global/CND-Global.95.2nd/CND-Global.95-06-02.html, accessed August 27, 2001); Andrew J. Nathan and E. Perry Link, eds., *The Tiananmen Papers* (New York: Public Affairs, 2001), pp. 126–29, 131–38.

2. Orville Schell, *Mandate of Heaven: A New Generation of Entrepreneurs, Dissidents, Bohemians, and Technocrats Lays Claim to China's Future* (Simon and Schuster, 1994), pp. 78–79.

3. Li Qiao, "Death or Rebirth? Tiananmen, the Soul of China," in Michel Oksenberg, Lawrence R. Sullivan, and Marc Lambert, eds., *Beijing Spring, 1989: Confrontation and Conflict* (Armonk, N.Y.: M. E. Sharpe, 1990), p. 48.

4. Nathan and Link, *The Tiananmen Papers,* p. 149. The source for this information, again, is the "friend of Yang Shangkun," who took remarkably thorough notes of the three-way conversation between Yang, Deng, and Zhao. While the conversation reflects what most likely were the viewpoints of the three men, and it is certainly possible the three met at Deng's residence, the authenticity of the document, in my view, is questionable. It is just a bit too neat, too convenient, and too sympathetic to Zhao.

5. Li Xiaowen, "A Chronicle of What Happened in Beijing," p. 3.

6. Ibid. See also Nathan and Link, *The Tiananmen Papers,* pp. 168–69.

7. Joan Shorenstein Barone Center on the Press, Politics, and Public Policy, "Turmoil at Tiananmen: A Study of U.S. Press Coverage of the Beijing Spring of 1989," John F. Kennedy School of Government, Harvard University, 1992 (hereafter Barone Center Study), p. 23.

8. Schell, *Mandate of Heaven*, p. 88.

9. Mike Chinoy, *China Live: Two Decades in the Heart of the Dragon* (Atlanta: Turner Publishing, 1997), p. 210.

10. Jim Munson of Canadian TV, quoted in Barone Center Study, p. 21.

11. Mark Hertsgaard, "China Coverage—Strong on What, Weak on Why," *Rolling Stone* magazine, September 21, 1989 (republished at www.tsquare.tv/themes/hertsgaard.html, accessed February 18, 2003).

12. Chinoy, *China Live*, p. 207.

13. Nicholas D. Kristof, "China Update: How the Hardliners Won," *New York Times Magazine,* November 12, 1989, p. 39.

14. From Beijing Television Service, May 16, 1989, published by Foreign Broadcast Information Service (FBIS), republished in Oksenberg, Sullivan, and Lambert, *Beijing Spring, 1989*, p. 261.

15. Schell, *Mandate of Heaven,* p. 94.

16. Sheryl WuDunn, "150,000 Lift Their Voices for Change," *New York Times*, May 16, 1989, p. A12.

17. Nicholas D. Kristof, "Soviets and China Resuming Normal Ties after 30 Years; Beijing Pledges 'Democracy,'" *New York Times*, May 17, 1989, p. A1.

18. From "Minutes of the May 16 Politburo Standing Committee Meeting," prepared by the Party Central Office Secretariat, in Nathan and Link, *The Tiananmen Papers,* pp. 180–81.

19. From the "'Minutes of the May 17 Politburo Standing Committee Meeting" document supplied to Party Central Office Secretariat for its records by the Office of Deng Xiaoping, in Nathan and Link, *The Tiananmen Papers*, p. 185.

20. Ibid., pp. 188–89.

21. Ibid., pp. 192–93.

22. Ibid., pp. 200–01.

23. Ibid., pp. 204–11.

24. Beijing Television Service video report, "Li Peng and Others Meet Representatives of the Fasting Students," May 18, 1989, in FBIS, May 19, 1989, pp. 14–21; Schell, *Mandate of Heaven,* pp. 116–17.

25. Nicholas D. Kristof, "Crowds in Street Ask Deng's Ouster," *New York Times*, May 18, 1989, p. A1.

26. Andrew J. Walder and Xiaoxia Gong, "Workers in the Tiananmen Protests: The Politics of the Beijing Autonomous Workers Federation," *Australian Journal of Chinese Affairs* (now *The China Journal*), no. 29 (January 1993), pp. 3–4.

27. "Zhao Ziyang and Li Peng Visit Fasting Students at Tiananmen Square," Beijing Television Service, in Oksenberg, Sullivan, and Lambert, *Beijing Spring, 1989*, pp. 288–89; Nicholas D. Kristof, "Chinese Premier Issues a Warning to the Protesters," *New York Times,* May 19, 1989, p. A1.

28. Melanie Manion, "Reluctant Duelists: The Logic of the 1989 Protests and Massacre," introduction in Oksenberg, Sullivan, and Lambert, *Beijing Spring, 1989*, p. xxxvi.

29. "Li Peng Delivers Important Speech on Behalf of Party Central Committee and State Council," Beijing Television Service, May 19, 1989, in Oksenberg, Sullivan, and Lambert, eds., *Beijing Spring, 1989*, p. 309.

30. Geremie Barmé, "Beijing Days, Beijing Nights," excerpts from Jonathan Unger, ed., *The Pro-Democracy Protests in China: Reports from the Provinces* (Armonk, N.Y.: M. E. Sharpe, 1991) (reprinted at www.tsquare.tv/links/Beijing_Days.html, accessed February 16, 2003).

31. Press speculation on this issue was rife in U.S. media at the time and led to further misunderstandings later. Although General Xu may have checked himself into a hospital to avoid ordering the Thirty-Eighth into action against demonstrators, he

evidently was replaced by one who had no such compunctions. The Thirty-Eighth was one of the key units involved in the June 4 attack on unarmed demonstrators.

32. Tai-ming Cheung, "The PLA and Its Role between April–June 1989," in Richard L. Yang, ed., *China's Military: The PLA in 1990/1991* (Boulder, Colo.: Westview Press, 1991), p. 9. See also "Main Points of Yang Shangkun's Speech at Emergency Enlarged Meeting of the Central Military Commission," from *Ming Pao* article of May 29, 1989, in Oksenberg, Sullivan, and Lambert, *Beijing Spring, 1989*, pp. 320–27, especially p. 326.

33. Nathan and Link, *The Tiananmen Papers,* p. 212.

34. Nicholas D. Kristof, "Upheaval in China: Biggest Beijing Crowds So Far Keep Troops from City Center," *New York Times,* May 21, 1989, p. A1.

35. Chinoy, *China Live*, pp. 220–21.

36. Linda Jakobsen, "Lies in Ink, Truth in Blood: The Role and Impact of the Chinese Media during the Beijing Spring of '89," Discussion Paper, Joan Shorenstein Barone Center on the Press, Politics, and Public Policy, John F. Kennedy School of Government, Harvard University, August 1990 (republished at www.tsquare.tv/themes/liesink.html, accessed February 18, 2003).

37. One curious event, not yet fully explained, was the lifting of some restrictions on international news feeds via satellite on May 23. For less than a day, CCTV permitted foreign news agencies to broadcast live on its satellite. Coming at the same time as rumors that Zhao Ziyang was making a comeback and Li Peng was under attack, some reporters viewed the event as part of the power struggle at the top. One CNN executive told the *New York Times*, "Our feeling is that it means that the moderates in the party are winning the battle at the moment" (*New York Times*, May 24, 1989, p. A11). Just as unexpectedly, the service was terminated May 24. CBS broadcast the plug pulling live.

38. Merle Goldman, *Sowing the Seeds of Democracy in China: Political Reform in the Deng Xiaoping Era* (Harvard University Press, 1994), pp. 323–24.

39. Nicholas D. Kristof, "Chinese Update: How the Hardliners Won," *New York Times Magazine*, November 12, 1989, p. 71.

40. "Students Visit Marshals Nie Rongzhen and Xu Xiangqian," from Beijing Domestic Radio Service, May 21, 1989, republished in Oksenberg, Sullivan, and Lambert, *Beijing Spring, 1989*, pp. 316–17. Although long retired, Nie and Xu retained considerable influence and prestige within the active duty ranks of the PLA.

41. Nicholas D. Kristof, "Standoff Persists in Beijing; 7 Top Ex-Commanders Warn Army 'Must Not Enter City,'" *New York Times*, May 23, 1989, p. A1. Also Cheung, "The PLA and Its Role," pp. 8–9. The authenticity of the letter—supposedly signed by former defense minister Zhang Aiping and former chief of staff Yang Dezhi—is somewhat open to question, although it was published by one Xinhua-related agency. The letter was widely interpreted as being part of a counterattack against Li Peng. Other reports had cited open letters and petitions by large groups of PLA officers. Such reports made the rounds of protesters and the foreign journalists who relied on them for information, but they were never confirmed by official sources.

42. Cheung, "The PLA and Its Role," p. 6.

43. "Main Points of Yang Shangkun Speech at Emergency Enlarged Meeting of the Central Military Commission," in Oksenberg, Sullivan, and Lambert, *Beijing Spring, 1989*, p. 327.

44. Nathan and Link, *The Tiananmen Papers,* pp. 256–64.

45. Ibid., pp. 268–72.

46. Ibid., pp. 308–12.

47. Bruce Gilley, *Tiger on the Brink: Jiang Zemin and China's New Elite* (University of California Press, 1998), pp. 134–37.

48. Deng's speech to Li and Yao was widely circulated in China. See "'Full Text' of Speech to Li Peng and Yao Yilin [May 31, 1989]," published in *Tung Fang Jih Pao* (Eastern Daily), Hong Kong, July 14, 1989, in Oksenberg, Sullivan, and Lambert, *Beijing Spring, 1989,* pp. 333–38.

49. George Black and Robin Munro, *Black Hands of Beijing: Lives of Defiance in China's Democracy Movement* (John Wiley and Sons, 1993), pp. 216–20. Excerpts used here are from www.tsquare.tv/chronology/BlackHMay.html, accessed August 18, 2001.

50. Jan Wong, *Red China Blues* (Doubleday, 1996), p. 244.

51. Schell, *Mandate of Heaven*, p. 128.

52. Black and Munro, *Black Hands of Beijing*, pp. 216–20.

53. Patrick Tyler, "6 Years after the Tiananmen Massacre, Survivors Clash Anew on Tactics," *New York Times*, April 30, 1995, p. A12.

54. Chinoy, *China Live*, p. 245.

55. Nathan and Link, *The Tiananmen Papers,* p. 331, from a documentary report from the Beijing Municipal Party Committee and Government to the Politburo, entitled "On the True Nature of the Turmoil."

56. From the party secretariat minutes of "an important meeting, June 2, 1989," in Nathan and Link, *The Tiananmen Papers,* p. 357.

57. Ibid., pp. 361–62.

58. Many Western reporters were located in the Beijing Hotel, which is located nearly one-half mile from Tiananmen Square. Although they could certainly hear the noise of the action, even reporters in rooms closest to the square could not really see what was going on around the Martyrs' Monument.

59. *Webster's New Universal Unabridged Dictionary* (Simon and Schuster, 1983), p. 1106.

60. Schell, *Mandate of Heaven*, p. 135; Chinoy, *China Live*, p. 248.

61. Nathan and Link, *The Tiananmen Papers,* pp. 369–70 (emphasis added).

62. Schell, *Mandate of Heaven*, chaps. 13 and 14; Yi Mu and Mark V. Thompson, *Crisis at Tiananmen: Reform and Reality in Modern China* (San Francisco: China Books, 1989), pp. 82–83. The Twenty-Seventh group army is usually reported to have been the unit most involved in the use of excessive violence en route to Tiananmen, but accounts from State Security reporters cited in *The Tiananmen Papers* indicate it was the Thirty-Eighth.

63. Hou Dejian's own account of June 3–4, "Blame Me If You Want," appears in Mu and Thompson, *Crisis at Tiananmen*, pp. 239–49. See also Nathan and Link, *The Tiananmen Papers,* pp. 380–81; Schell, *Mandate of Heaven*, pp. 150–52.

64. See, for example, Chen Xitong, "Report to the NPC," in Oksenberg, Sullivan, and Lambert, *Beijing Spring, 1989*, p. 86.

65. Nicholas D. Kristof, "Artillery Firing in Suburbs Adds to Tensions in Beijing; Mystery on Leaders Grows," *New York Times*, June 7, 1989, p. A1.

66. Beijing television broadcast of June 6, 1989, in BBC Summary of World Broadcasts, FE/0476 B2/14, June 8, 1989. On June 6, State Council press spokesman Yuan Mu, Martial Law Command political commissar Zhang Gong, and two Beijing municipal officials gave a press conference for "domestic" journalists in Beijing. The casualty figures were provided at that time.

67. Casualty figures are discussed at several points in Nathan and Link, *The Tiananmen Papers*. Initial "State Security Ministry" figures are "about two hundred, with about two thousand wounded" (p. 376). In his report to the Politburo Standing Committee and the elders on June 6, Li Peng cited the following casualty figures: PLA and People's Armed Police—36 killed, 200 missing, 5,000 injured; civilian populace—approximately 200 killed, 2,000 wounded (p. 421). In an "official" report to the Politburo on June 19, Li Ximing claimed 23 soldiers and 218 civilians were killed, and about 5,000 soldiers and 2,000 civilians were wounded (p. 436).

68. From "Minutes of the Central Politburo Standing Committee Meeting, June 6, 1989," in Nathan and Link, *The Tiananmen Papers,* pp. 423–24.

69. Deng Xiaoping, "Address to Martial Law Units," in Oksenberg, Sullivan, and Lambert, *Beijing Spring, 1989*, pp. 377, 378–79.

70. Nicholas D. Kristof, "Deng Appears on Chinese TV, Surrounded by Hard-Liners," *New York Times*, June 10, 1989, p. A1.

71. Interview with Brent Scowcroft, December 1999.

72. George Bush and Brent Scowcroft, *A World Transformed* (Knopf, 1998), p. 90.

73. Ibid., p. 89.

74. Interview with Douglas Paal, December 1999; interview with Richard Solomon, January 2000.

75. Patrick Tyler, *A Great Wall: Six Presidents and China* (New York: Century Foundation, 1999), p. 348.

76. Interview with James Lilley, February 2000.

77. Robert Pear, "U.S. Voices Regret at Events in China," *New York Times*, May 20, 1989, p. A6.

78. Bernard Weinraub, "Bush Urges Protesters to 'Stand Up' for Beliefs," *New York Times*, May 22, 1989, p. A11.

79. Interview with Richard Solomon.

80. Interviews with James Lilley and Douglas Paal.

81. Interview with Douglas Paal.

82. "Resolution on Democracy in China (Senate—May 31, 1989)," in *Congressional Record*, p. S5791 (http:/thomas.loc.gov/cgi-bin/query/D?r101:1:./temp/~101YraOo6::, accessed February 18, 2003).

83. From the *Congressional Record* of May 24, 1989, cited in Eric Hyer, "United States' Response to the Tiananmen Massacre: Congressional Values and Executive Interests," *Conflict*, vol. 11 (1991), p. 172.

84. Robert Pear, "Crackdown in Beijing: President Assails Shootings in China," *New York Times*, June 4, 1989, p. A21; interview with William Clark Jr., March 2000.

85. Pear, "Crackdown in Beijing."

86. Thomas L. Friedman, "Administration Ponders Steps on China," *New York Times*, June 5, 1989, p. A12.

87. I was present at the meeting.

88. Interview with Carl Ford, April 2000.

89. Interviews with William Clark Jr. and Carl Ford. Nicholas D. Kristof, "Bush Bars Arms Sales to China," *New York Times*, June 6, 1989, p. A1. An additional program, the sale of Sikorsky Blackhawk helicopters to China for civilian use, was also suspended.

90. "The President's News Conference," June 5, 1989 (http://bushlibrary.tamu.edu/papers/1989/89060500.html, accessed January 21, 2003).

91. Bush and Scowcroft, *A World Transformed*, p. 98.

92. Bernard E. Trainor, "Bush Bars Normal Ties Now," *New York Times*, June 9, 1989, p. A1.

93. According to reports cited in the *Tiananmen Papers,* antigovernment demonstrations broke out in 181 Chinese cities after the Beijing operation. Most were nonviolent, but many required substantial police action. See Nathan and Link, *The Tiananmen Papers,* pp. 392–96, 398–416.

94. Manion, "Reluctant Duelists," in Oksenberg, Sullivan, and Lambert, *Beijing Spring, 1989*, p. xl.

95. Cheung, "The PLA and Its Role," p. 14.

96. Sheryl WuDunn, "Chinese Arrest 400 in Beijing amid Fears of a Wide Purge," *New York Times*, June 11, 1989, p. A1.

97. Interview with James Lilley.

98. Perry Link, *Evening Chats in Beijing: Probing China's Predicament* (W. W. Norton, 1992), pp. 46–47; James Mann, *About Face: A History of America's Curious Relationship with China, from Nixon to Clinton* (Alfred A. Knopf, 1999), pp. 201–04; interview with James Lilley.

99. Interview with William Clark Jr. In his book, *About Face*, James Mann credits Jeffrey Bader, deputy director of State's China Desk, working in conjunction with Kimmitt and others with reversing an earlier decision and offering refuge to Fang. Given the urgency of the situation, it is entirely possible that more than one phone call was made to the embassy. Baker's involvement is discussed in Thomas L. Friedman, "U.S. and Chinese Seek to Resolve Rift on Dissident," *New York Times*, June 13, 1989, p. A1.

100. Mann, *About Face*, pp. 201–04; interviews with James Lilley and William Clark Jr.

101. Nicholas D. Kristof, "China Seeks Arrest of Top Dissident, Now Living at U.S. Embassy," *New York Times*, June 12, 1989, p. A1.

102. "The President's News Conference, June 8, 1989," in Bush Presidential Library papers (http://bushlibrary.tamu.edu/papers/1989/89060803.html, accessed January 2003).

103. Kristof, "China Seeks Arrest of Top Dissident."

104. Lilley—a former CIA case officer—did in fact consider possible scenarios for exfiltrating Fang (he had secretly transported Fang Zhe out less than a week after his parents took up residence), but did not put them into effect. Chinese fears of such an attempt led them to increase armed surveillance of the embassy for months afterward. Interview with James Lilley.

105. Richard Bernstein, "A Precarious Mission: Restitching a Torn China," *New York Times*, June 25, 1989, p. A12.

106. Nathan and Link, *The Tiananmen Papers,* pp. 432–36. From party secretariat notes on the remarks of speakers at the Fourth Plenum.

107. Ibid.

108. "Victors in the Struggle among China's Leaders," *New York Times*, June 25, 1989, p. A10.

109. Ning Lu, *The Dynamics of Foreign Policy Decisionmaking in China* (Boulder, Colo.: Westview Press, 1997), p. 159.

110. The most thorough English-language biography of Jiang is Bruce Gilley's, *Tiger at the Brink: Jiang Zemin and China's New Elite* (University of California Press, 1998), pp. 8–24.

111. Ibid., pp. 47–48.

112. Ibid., pp. 63–64.

113. Ibid., p. 73.

114. Ibid., p. 94.

115. Ibid., pp. 126–27.

116. Ibid., pp. 128–30, 137–44.

117. Deng Xiaoping, "'Full Text' of Speech to Li Peng and Yao Yilin [May 31, 1989]," published in *Tung fang jih pao* (Eastern Daily), Hong Kong, July 14, 1989, in Oksenberg, Sullivan, and Lambert, *Beijing Spring, 1989,* p. 334. Also Gilley, *Tiger at the Brink*, pp. 132–35.

118. Daniel Southerland, "Deng Emerges, Says Reform to Go On," *Washington Post*, September 17, 1989, p. A33.

119. Bush and Scowcroft, *A World Transformed*, pp. 100–02.

120. Chen You-wei, *Zhonggong yu meiguo waijiao meimu (Inside Stories of the Diplomacy between Communist China and America)* Taipei: Cheng Chong Book Company, 1999), p. 137. Chen was a public relations consultant on the Chinese embassy staff at the time of Tiananmen.

121. Ibid, p. 138.

122. James A. Baker III (with Thomas M. Defrank*), The Politics of Diplomacy, Revolution, War and Peace, 1989–92* (G. P. Putnam's Sons, 1995), p. 109.

123. Mann, *About Face*, p. 206; interview with James Lilley.

124. Interview with James Lilley.

125. Bush and Scowcroft, *A World Transformed*, p. 106; Tyler, *A Great Wall*, p. 364; Mann, *About Face*, pp. 206–07; interview with Brent Scowcroft.

126. Bush and Scowcroft, *A World Transformed*, p. 107.

127. Ibid.

128. Ibid., p. 109.

129. Interview with Brent Scowcroft.

130. Bush and Scowcroft, *A World Transformed*, p. 110.

131. Baker, *Politics of Diplomacy*, p. 110.

132. Bush and Scowcroft, *A World Transformed*, pp. 110–11.

133. Interview with James Lilley.

134. Interview with Brent Scowcroft.

135. Baker, *Politics of Diplomacy*, p. 107.

136. Eric Hyer, "United States' Response to the Tiananmen Massacre: Congressional Values and Executive Interests," *Conflict*, vol. 11 (1991), p. 174; Thomas L. Friedman, "Congress, Angry at China, Moves to Impose Sanctions," *New York Times*, June 23, 1989, p. A5.

137. Don Oberdorfer, "House Plans New China Sanctions; Bipartisan Package Would Counter Bush's Caution," *Washington Post*, June 29, 1989, p. A1.

138. Don Oberdorfer, "House China Vote Shows Power of Domestic Politics," *Washington Post*, July 1, 1989, p. A1. As a group, these sanctions are generally called the "Tiananmen Sanctions," many of which are still in effect.

139. Richard Madsen, *China and the American Dream: A Moral Inquiry* (University of California Press, 1995), p. xvi.

140. Ibid., p. 4.

141. Barone Center Study, p. 38.

142. See "China's Untold Story: Who Died in the Crackdown?" *New York Times*, June 3, 1990, p. A20.

143. Barone Center Study, pp. 45–46.

Notes to Chapter 4

1. Beidaihe, a small town on the seacoast of Hebei Province about 170 miles east of Beijing, has long been a favorite retreat from the summertime heat of the capital. The resort area, originally built for Western businessmen in the nineteenth century, has been used since the early days of the People's Republic for senior leadership working vacations. Top leaders have large villas near the seashore and usually meet informally there to discuss important issues. Occasionally formal Central Committee meetings are held at Beidaihe, but more often, leaders prefer informal, smaller sessions, away from the demands of bureaucratic formality in Beijing. Deng no doubt used the facilities there both to recover his health and to meet privately with other senior leaders, including Yang Shangkun and Jiang Zemin.

2. Adi Ignatius and Walter S. Mossberg, "Deng Sends an Indirect Message to Bush Hinting China's Hard Line Is Softening," *Wall Street Journal*, October 26, 1989, p. 1.

3. Deng Xiaoping, "We Are Confident That We Can Handle China's Affairs Well," *Selected Works of Deng Xiaoping: Volume 3* (Beijing: Foreign Languages Press, 1994), p. 314. Also Bruce Gilley, *Tiger on the Brink: Jiang Zemin and China's New Elite* (University of California Press, 1998), p. 165.

4. Daniel Southerland, "Deng Resigns His Last Party Post," *Washington Post*, November 10, 1989, p. A1.

5. James A. R. Miles, *The Legacy of Tiananmen: China in Disarray* (University of Michigan Press, 1996), p. 59.

6. Private communications with John Kamm, July 1999.

7. "Deng Conciliatory over Crackdown," *New York Times*, October 19, 1989, p. A12.

8. Xinhua News Agency, no. 0625047, "Communiqué of Fourth Plenary Session of CPC Central Commission for Discipline Inspection," June 25, 1989.

9. Deng Xiaoping, "First Priority Should Always Be Given to National Sovereignty and Security," *Selected Works of Deng Xiaoping: Volume 3*, p. 335.

10. Ma Licheng and Ling Zhijun, *Jiao feng: dangdai zhongguo san ci sixiang jiefang shilu* (Crossed Swords: The Real Record of Three Efforts to Liberate Thought in Contemporary China) (Taipei: Commonwealth Publishing, 1998), pp. 117–18. *Crossed Swords* was written by two *People's Daily* reporters and constitutes a strikingly blunt discussion of the propaganda struggle over reform policy in 1978, 1990–92, and 1997.

11. Ibid., p. 119.

12. Willy Wo-Lap Lam, *China after Deng Xiaoping: The Power Struggle in Beijing since Tiananmen* (Hong Kong: P. A. Professional Consultants, 1995), pp. 56–57.

13. See Deng Xiaoping, "The International Situation and Economic Problems," *Selected Works of Deng Xiaoping: Volume 3*, pp. 341–43. Deng's remarks were made at a March 1990 meeting with unspecified Central Committee members.

14. Chen You-wei, *Zhonggong yu meiguo waijiao neimu* (Inside Stories of the Diplomacy between Communist China and America) (Taipei: Cheng Chong Book Company, 1999), pp. 99–100.

15. David Skidmore and William Gates, "After Tiananmen: The Struggle over U.S. Policy toward China in the Bush Administration," *Presidential Studies Quarterly*, vol. 27, no. 3 (Summer 1997). Available at www.drake.edu/artsci/PolSci/personalwebpage/tiananmen.html, accessed January 2003.

16. Bush news conference of June 27, 1989 (http://bushlibrary.tamu.edu/papers/1989/89062700.html, accessed January 2003).

17. George Bush and Brent Scowcroft, *A World Transformed* (Knopf, 1998), pp. 156–57.

18. Bush and Scowcroft, *A World Transformed*, p. 31.

19. Interview with Brent Scowcroft, December 1999.

20. See Summary and Status of H.R. 2712 (101st Congress) (http://thomas.loc.gov, accessed May 5, 2000).

21. Kenneth J. Cooper, "Chinese Students' Stays May Not Be Extended," *Washington Post*, November 23, 1989, p. A56.

22. Interview with Brent Scowcroft.

23. "Statement on the Disapproval of the Bill Providing Emergency Chinese Immigration Relief," November 30, 1989, Bush Presidential Library papers (http://bushlibrary.tamu.edu/papers/1989/89113003.html, accessed January 2003). Bush

vetoed the bill a week after Congress had adjourned for the Thanksgiving-Christmas holiday recess, probably in hopes that achievements planned for December would limit congressional anger.

24. "Memorandum of Disapproval for the Bill Providing Emergency Chinese Immigration Relief," November 30, 1989, Bush Presidential Library papers (http://bushlibrary.tamu.edu/papers/1989/89113002.html, accessed February 2003).

25. James A. Baker III (with Thomas M. Defrank), *The Politics of Diplomacy, Revolution, War and Peace, 1989–92* (G. P. Putnam's Sons, 1995), p. 111.

26. Interview with Michel Oksenberg, June 2000.

27. Richard M. Nixon, "The Crisis in Sino-American Relations," *Congressional Record*, November 21, 1989, p. S16553 (http:thomas.loc.gov, accessed February 2002). Oksenberg recalled that Nixon chose the descriptive adjectives for various leaders with great care.

28. Nicholas D. Kristof, "Better Relations Depend on U.S., Deng Tells Nixon," *New York Times*, November 1, 1989, p. A8. In *Selected Works of Deng Xiaoping: Volume 3* (see pp. 320–22), Deng's remarks are rendered slightly differently, but his denunciation of American involvement—and particularly of the role played by the VOA—is even more shrill.

29. Interview with Michel Oksenberg. Oksenberg maintains Nixon was unaware of the July Scowcroft-Eagleburger mission and presumably learned about plans for the December mission when Oksenberg was out of the room.

30. Sheryl WuDunn, "Kissinger, in Beijing, Seeks to Mend Fences," *New York Times*, November 9, 1989, p. A19.

31. Bush and Scowcroft, *A World Transformed*, p. 158.

32. Interviews with James Lilley, February 2000, and Douglas Paal, December 1999.

33. Interview with Douglas Paal.

34. Bush and Scowcroft, *A World Transformed*, p. 174.

35. Steven Erlanger, "Top Aides to Bush Are Visiting China to Mend Relations," *New York Times*, December 10, 1989, p. A1; Daniel Southerland, "U.S. Envoys Visit China to Improve Ties," *Washington Post*, December 10, 1989, p. A1.

36. *New York Times* editorial of December 12, 1989, p. A24.

37. Will comments cited in Haynes Johnson, "China and Double Standards," *Washington Post*, December 15, 1989, p. A2.

38. Winston Lord, "Misguided Mission," *Washington Post*, December 19, 1989, p. A23.

39. "Remarks and a Question-and-Answer Session with Newspaper Editors," December 11, 1989, Bush Presidential Library papers(http://bushlibrary.tamu.edu/papers/1989/89121103.html, accessed January 2003).

40. David Hoffman and Ann Devroy, "Bush Rejects New Sanctions for China, Clears Satellites," *Washington Post*, December 19, 1989, p. A1.

41. Maureen Dowd, "Two U.S. Officials Went to Beijing Secretly in July," *New York Times*, December 19, 1989, p. A1.

42. Don Oberdorfer, "U.S. Optimistic Dissident Fang Will Be Freed; Subject Taken up in Recent Talks," *Washington Post*, December 16, 1989, p. A28.

43. Don Oberdorfer and David Hoffman, "Scowcroft Warned China of New Hill Sanctions; U.S. Emissaries Stressed Need for Action by Beijing, Sources Say," *Washington Post*, December 15, 1989, p. A1.

44. Kerry Dumbaugh, "China: Current U.S. Sanctions," *Congressional Research Service Report 94-92 F*, updated April 14, 1995, p. 3.

45. David Hoffman and Hobart Rowen, "Quayle Sees 'Dividends' for U.S. China Policy," *Washington Post*, January 11, 1990, p. A26.

46. Ibid.

47. Daniel Southerland, "China Announces Release of 573 Detainees," *Washington Post*, January 19, 1990, p. A13.

48. David S. Broder, "Gingrich Opposes Bush on China Veto; GOP Backs Override, White House Is Told," *Washington Post*, January 19, 1990, p. A13.

49. Interview with Brent Scowcroft.

50. "The President's News Conference," January 25, 1990, Bush Presidential Library papers (http://bushlibrary.tamu.edu/papers/1990/90012504.html, accessed January 2003).

51. Thomas L. Friedman, "Senate, by 4 Votes, Fails to Override Bush's China Veto," *New York Times*, January 26, 1990, p. A1.

52. Helen Dewar, "Senate Narrowly Votes to Sustain Veto of Chinese Student Bill," *Washington Post*, January 26, 1990, p. A1.

53. Bush criticized the "legislatively-mandated sanctions" contained in the bill as "an unwise constraint upon the President's ability to conduct foreign policy," but nonetheless signed the bill with numerous reservations about some of its provisions. See "Statement on Signing the Foreign Relations Authorization Act, Fiscal Years 1990 and 1991," of February 16, 1990 (http://bushlibrary.tamu.edu/papers/1990/90021601.html, accessed January 2003).

54. Sheryl WuDunn, "Upheaval in the East, China Bitterly Protests Sanctions by Congress," *New York Times*, February 3, 1990, p. A9.

55. John M. Goshko, "Eagleburger Defends China Policy, Senators Unconvinced," *Washington Post*, February 8, 1990, p. A17.

56. "1989: Annus Mirabilis—Liberalization and Struggle in Communist Countries," *Encyclopaedia Britannica* (reprinted at www.britannica.com/eb/article?au=108371, accessed February 2003).

57. See Daniel Southerland, "Deng Said to Warn against Gorbachev's Ideas," *Washington Post,* November 23, 1989, p. A49.

58. Daniel Southerland, "Chinese Workers Seek Permission to Protest; Leadership Orders Security Forces to Crush Any Demonstrations," *Washington Post*, January 8, 1990, p. A1.

59. Gilley, *Tiger on the Brink,* p. 169.

60. Quoted in Lam, *China after Deng Xiaoping*, p. 4.

61. Interview with Brent Scowcroft.

62. Interview with Michel Oksenberg.

63. Robert Pear, "Bush Distressed as Policy Fails to Move China," *New York Times,* March 11, 1990, p. A1.

64. Interview with James Lilley.

65. Background information on MFN in the following paragraphs from Vladimir N. Pregelj, *Congressional Research Service Issue Brief 92094*, "Most-Favored-Nation Status of the People's Republic of China," updated version of December 6, 1996 (found at www.fas.org/man/crs/92-094.htm, p. 2, accessed January 2003); and Kerry Dumbaugh, "China's Most-Favored-Nation (MFN) Status: Congressional Consideration, 1989–1998," *CRS Report for Congress*, update August 1, 1998, p. 1.

66. Disapproval procedures are carefully stipulated and limit congressional flexibility. By statute, a disapproval resolution must be reported out of committee within 30 days of the June 3 (mid-year) deadline for extending MFN, it is not amendable, debate is limited to 20 hours, and the resolution must be approved by August 31.

67. James Mann, *About Face: A History of America's Curious Relationship with China, from Nixon to Clinton* (Alfred A. Knopf, 1999), pp. 230–31.

68. See *Congressional Record*, "Extension of Remarks," May 24, 1990, p. E1756, and "Summary of H.R. 4939" (http://thomas.loc.gov, accessed February 2003.)

69. Mann, *About Face*, p. 233.

70. *Congressional Record*, "Summary of H.R. 4939."

71. Lena H. Sun and David Hoffman, "President Is Ready to Renew China's Favored Trade Status," *Washington Post*, May 22, 1990, p. A1.

72. Daniel Southerland, "Leading Chinese Dissident Allowed to Leave Homeland," *Washington Post,* June 26, 1990, p. A1.

73. "Statement by Press Secretary Fitzwater on Fang Lizhi's Departure from China," June 25, 1990, from Bush Presidential Library (http://bushlibrary.tamu.edu/papers/1990/90062501.html, accessed February 2003).

74. David Hoffman, "Dissident Fang Criticizes U.S. China Policy; Professor Predicts Another Uprising," *Washington Post*, July 7, 1990, p. A14.

75. Interview with Richard Solomon, January 2000.

76. Information in this paragraph from Chen, *Zhonggong yu meiguo waijiao neimu* (Inside Stories of the Diplomacy between Communist China and America), pp. 280–83.

77. The terms "hegemon" (*ba*), "seeking hegemony" (*cheng ba*), and "hegemonism" (*baquan zhuyi*) are commonly used by Chinese commentators but not well understood in the West. The terms date from China's "Warring States" period (475–221 B.C.), when several small kingdoms fought bitterly and incessantly with each other for dominance, forging and breaking alliances, plotting and colluding to maximize their own power and prevent any of the others from achieving the goal of unifying China under their rule. Chinese understand the "hegemon" to be possessed of an insatiable lust for power and domination, modeled after the state of Qin, which destroyed the other kingdoms and unified all of China for the first time, establishing what was arguably its bloodiest, most tyrannical, and shortest dynasties. See Michael Pillsbury, *China Debates the Future Security Environment* (Washington: National Defense University Press, 2000), pp. xxxv–vi.

78. Lena H. Sun, "Chinese Foreign Minister Will Visit Middle East; Beijing Using Gulf Crisis to End Isolation," *Washington Post*, November 4, 1990, p. A32.

79. Baker, *Politics of Diplomacy*, p. 588.

80. David Hoffman, "China Signals Assent to UN Vote on Force," *Washington Post*, November 7, 1990, p. A7.

81. Interview with James Lilley.

82. Ibid. Chen You-wei gives a somewhat different account. See *Zhonggong yu meiguo waijiao neimu* (Inside Stories of the Diplomacy between Communist China and America), pp. 204–05.

83. Sheryl WuDunn, "Mideast Tensions, Chinese Official Leaves in Doubt How He Will Vote on Iraq at UN," *New York Times*, November 29, 1990, p. A15. Asked whether China would abstain, Qian replied, "You will know after I vote." It's hard to understand how Qian's statements were seen as ambiguous.

84. Chen, *Zhonggong yu meiguo waijiao neimu* (Inside Stories of the Diplomacy between Communist China and America), p. 205.

85. "Excerpts from U.S., Kuwaiti, Iraqi and Chinese Remarks on the Resolution," *New York Times*, November 30, 1990, p. A10.

86. Interviews with James Lilley and Douglas Paal.

87. Bush and Scowcroft, *A World Transformed*, pp. 414–15n.; Chen, *Zhonggong yu meiguo waijiao neimu* (Inside Stories of the Diplomacy between Communist China and America), p. 206; interviews with Douglas Paal and James Lilley.

88. Interview with James Lilley; Chen, *Zhonggong yu meiguo waijiao neimu* (Inside Stories of the Diplomacy between Communist China and America), p. 208. Chen claims Qian would have come to Washington regardless of whether he got a meeting with Bush, because Deng had ordered him to do so.

89. Nicholas D. Kristof, "Beijing Backs away from Full Support of the War," *New York Times,* February 1, 1991, p. A10; "China Skeptical of U.S. Gulf Role," *New York Times,* February 20, 1991, p. A14.

90. Interview with Carl Ford, April 2000.

91. Sheryl WuDunn, "War Astonishes Chinese and Stuns Their Military," *New York Times,* March 20, 1991, p. A13.

92. David Shambaugh, "China's Military: Real or Paper Tiger," *Washington Quarterly*, Spring 1996.

93. Lena H. Sun, "China Ending Trials of Dissidents," *Washington Post*, April 4, 1991, p. A29.

94. Lena H. Sun, "Chinese Leader Defends Crackdown," *Washington Post,* April 10, 1991, p. A29.

95. R. Jeffrey Smith, "China Aid on Algerian Reactor May Violate Pledges," *Washington Post,* April 20, 1991, p. A17.

96. John Burgess, "Bush Administration Includes China in List of Trade-Restriction Offenders; Beijing's Trade Surplus, Import Barriers Growing, Report Says," *Washington Post,* March 30, 1991, p. A14.

97. John W. Dietrich, "Interest Groups and Foreign Policy: Clinton and the China MFN Debates," *Presidential Studies Quarterly*, vol. 29, no. 2 (June 1999), pp. 295–96.

98. *Washington Post* editorial, "Message to China," May 19, 1991, p. D6.

99. Text of H.R. 2212, the United States–China Act of 1991, as sent to the President, Sec. 2 Findings and Policy (http://thomas.loc.gov).

100. Ibid., Sec. 3.

101. Don Oberdorfer and Ann Devroy, "Bush Seeks to Keep China Trade Status; Intense Debate on Benefits Expected," *Washington Post*, May 16, 1991, p. A1.

102. Ann Devroy and Helen Dewar, "White House Open to Conditions on China Trade; Mitchell Proposal Would Set 6-Month Review on Terms for Favored-Nation Extension," *Washington Post*, May 17, 1991, p. A21.

103. "Remarks at the Yale University Commencement Ceremony in New Haven, Connecticut," May 27, 1991 (http://bushlibrary.tamu.edu/papers/1991/91052700.html, accessed February 2003).

104. Don Oberdorfer, "President Plans Major Push on Renewal of Trade Status for China," *Washington Post*, May 29, 1991, p. A23.

105. Michael Weisskopf, "Hill Democrats to Fight Beijing Trade Benefits; Chinese Dissidents See Betrayal of Cause," *Washington Post*, May 28, 1991, p. A5.

106. That act gave the USTR authority to designate as "priority foreign countries" those that "deny adequate and effective protection" of U.S. patents, copyrights, and intellectual property rights. If negotiations failed to resolve the problem, the USTR was empowered to impose tariff increases of up to 100 percent on selected categories of the offending country's exports to the United States, up to and above the estimated amount of damage to U.S. trade by the piracy.

107. Thomas T. Moga, "A Journey into China—Notes from over the Wall," Part 2, *Intellectual Property Today* magazine, May 1997.

108. Clyde H. Farnsworth, "Bush Denies Satellite Parts to China," *New York Times*, May 1, 1991, p. A15. Information on the Algerian nuclear reactor—which turned out to be a small research reactor that Algeria eventually placed under International Atomic Energy Agency safeguards—was available as early as 1988, but no actions were taken to try and stop the project, much to the dismay of critics. See, for example, Elaine Sciolino and Eric Schmitt, "Algerian Reactor Came from China," *New York Times*, November 15, 1991. Rumors of possible M-9 missile sales also dated back several years, but the deal never was consummated. The post–Gulf War hunger for advanced weapons in the Middle East apparently led to a reopening of the bidding. The stories about M-11s to Pakistan began circulating in early 1991, when intelligence sources spotted M-11 transporter/launchers on the ground in Pakistan. See R. Jeffrey Smith, "Chinese Missile Launchers Sighted in Pakistan," *Washington Post,* April 6, 1991, p. A17.

109. Cited in David Hoffman, "Selling Missile Technology Would Risk U.S. Wrath, Baker Tells China," *Washington Post*, June 13, 1991, p. A36.

110. Lena H. Sun, "On MFN, China Sends Mixed Signals," *Washington Post*, July 7, 1991, p. A22. The Missile Technology Control Regime (MTCR), established in 1987, was an informal agreement among G-7 countries—subsequently expanded to include twenty-five others—that members would refrain from selling missiles or technology for missiles whose range exceeded 300 kilometers and whose payload exceeded 500 kilograms (considered to be the minimum range and payload for car-

rying a nuclear device). The so-called annexes to the MTCR agreement specified the technologies that members agreed to control, including guidance and stabilization systems, solid rocket fuel, and so on. China was not an original member of the MTCR—and was not invited to be one—but told the United States informally that it would abide by its guidelines in its missile sales. It insisted, however, that the provisions of the MTCR annexes only technically bound those countries that had formally joined.

111. The Treaty on the Non-Proliferation of Nuclear Weapons (more commonly, the Non-Proliferation Treaty, or NPT), signed in 1968 by the United States, the Soviet Union, and subsequently many other countries, committed its signatories not to assist any country not already in possession of nuclear weapons in obtaining or developing them. China had consistently refused to sign the treaty on the grounds that it was a plot by the two superpowers to monopolize both nuclear weapons and nuclear power.

112. Keith Bradsher, "A Hard Line from China on Trade," *New York Times*, May 13, 1991, p. D1.

113. Lena H. Sun, "China Warns against Ending MFN; Boeing Would Lose Plane Sales, Li Says," *Washington Post,* June 26, 1991, p. A9.

114. Chen, *Zhonggong yu meiguo waijiao neimu* (Inside Stories of the Diplomacy between Communist China and America), p. 236.

115. Ann Devroy and Guy Gugliotta, "White House Targets Senate on China Bill; Goal Is to Ward off Terms on Trade Status," *Washington Post*, June 23, 1991, p. A5.

116. Guy Gugliotta, "Bush Lists Ways of Moderating China's Policies," *Washington Post*, July 20, 1991, p. A24.

117. Lam, *China after Deng Xiaoping*, p. 59.

118. See Gavin Hewitt, "The Great Escape from China; How 'Operation Yellow Bird' Saved Scores of Dissidents from Beijing's Secret Police," *Washington Post,* June 2, 1991, p. D1.

119. David Kelly and Anthony Reid, "Weathering a Political Winter: The Chinese Academy of Social Sciences, 1990," *Australian Journal of Chinese Affairs*, no. 24 (July 1990), pp 347–55; Sheryl WuDunn, "Beijing Students Issue Leaflets on Democracy," *New York Times*, May 30, 1991, p. A8.

120. Lam, *China after Deng Xiaoping*, p. 156.

121. Lena H. Sun, "Chinese Battening Hatches; Beijing Misjudged Pre-Coup Moscow," *Washington Post,* September 11, 1991, p. A25.

122. Lam, *China after Deng Xiaoping*, p. 52.

123. Ibid., pp. 60–61.

124. Ma and Ling, *Jiao feng: dangdai zhongguo san ci sixiang jiefang shilu*, (Crossed Swords: The Real Record of Three Efforts to Liberate Thought in Contemporary China), p. 122.

125. Gilley, *Tiger on the Brink,* p. 175.

126. Ma and Ling, *Jiao feng: dangdai zhongguo san ci sixiang jiefang shilu*, (Crossed Swords: The Real Record of Three Efforts to Liberate Thought in Contemporary China), pp. 124–32.

127. Nicholas D. Kristof, "Chinese Advocates of Change Reportedly Make Small Gains," *New York Times*, May 23, 1991, p. A6.

128. Lena Sun, "Beijing Warns of Chaos in Wake of Soviet Coup," *Washington Post*, October 28, 1991, p. A14.

129. Lam, *China after Deng Xiaoping*, p. 6; Gilley, *Tiger on the Brink*, p. 177; Ma and Ling, *Jiao feng: dangdai zhongguo san ci sixiang jiefang shilu* (Crossed Swords: The Real Record of Three Efforts to Liberate Thought in Contemporary China), p. 136ff.

130. Deng's speeches were eventually collected, edited, and issued as Central Directives No. 2, 4, and 5 of 1992. The more abbreviated version cited here was also published openly—albeit more than a year later—by the Xinhua News Agency on November 5, 1993. It is found, among other places, in Lawrence R. Sullivan, ed., *China since Tiananmen—Political, Economic and Social Conflicts* (Armonk, N.Y.: M. E. Sharpe, 1995), pp. 151–54.

131. Lam, *China after Deng Xiaoping*, p. 20. In China's convoluted ideological lexicon, "leftism" has come to mean overemphasis on Maoist dogma and resistance to capitalistic ideas; "rightism" is equated with economic experimentation, reducing the state's control over the economy.

132. Gilley, *Tiger on the Brink*, p. 186; Lena H. Sun, "Beijing Backs Reforms for '100 Years'; Politburo Vote Seen as Victory for Deng," *Washington Post*, March 12, 1992, p. A20.

133. The term *nan xun* originally connoted an inspection of his southern domain by a Chinese emperor.

134. Lam, *China after Deng Xiaoping*, p. 15.

135. Tai Ming Cheung, "Following Orders," *Far Eastern Economic Review*, May 28, 1992, p. 24.

136. Nicholas D. Kristoff, "Chinese Wait for Deaths of Their Leaders, Who Just Get Older," *New York Times*, January 24, 1992, p. A9; Valerie Strauss, "Setting China's Future: Old Men at the Beach; Deng Aims to Beat Rivals by Outliving Them," *Washington Post*, August 1, 1992, p. A14.

137. There were rumors that Deng may have suffered a minor stroke in August 1992, but rumors about Deng's health problems were so common it is impossible to credit any one in particular. See Lam, *China after Deng Xiaoping*, p. 212.

138. Roy was selected directly by President Bush in February 1991, after having served as the State Department's executive secretary for two years. A consummate professional, he had served as ambassador to Singapore and deputy assistant secretary of state for East Asia. Born to missionary parents in China, Roy was fluent in Chinese (as well as Russian) and had been deputy chief of mission in Beijing during the normalization of relations.

139. Interview with Douglas Paal. See also David E. Sanger, "Nuclear Activity by North Koreans Worries the U.S.," *New York Times*, November 10, 1991, p. A1.

140. Baker, *Politics of Diplomacy*, p. 590.

141. Michael Wines, "Democrats Wary on Baker's Planned Trip to China," *New York Times*, November 5, 1991, p. A11.

142. Baker, *Politics of Diplomacy*, p. 590.

143. Don Oberdorfer and Lena H. Sun, "Baker, in Beijing, Holds Talks with Chinese Leaders," *Washington Post,* November 16, 1991, p. A21.

144. Interviews with Douglas Paal and J. Stapleton Roy, May 2000.

145. Baker, *Politics of Diplomacy*, p. 591.

146. Ibid., p. 593.

147. Thomas L. Friedman, "Baker's Trip Fails to Produce Pledge on Rights," *New York Times,* November 18, 1991, p. A1; Don Oberdorfer, "U.S. Seeks to Rescue China Ties," *Washington Post,* November 18, 1991, p. A1.

148. Keith Bradsher, "Chinese Goods Listed for Higher Tariffs in Trade Dispute," *New York Times,* November 28, 1991, p. D10.

149. Lena H. Sun, "China Says U.S. Must Show 'Sincerity' in Trade Talks; Beijing Blames Politics for Lack of Accord," *Washington Post*, January 6, 1992, p. A13.

150. Stuart Auerbach, "China, U.S. Reach Trade Accord; Beijing Agrees to Curb Piracy of Products, Safeguarded Material," *Washington Post*, January 17, 1992, p. A24.

151. Thomas Moga, for example, credits the USTR action for China's 1991 enactment of a copyright law and its accession in 1992 to the Berne Convention, the Universal Copyright Convention, and the Geneva Phonogram Convention. See Moga, "A Journey into China—Notes from over the Wall."

152. R. Jeffrey Smith, "U.S. Lifts Sanctions against Chinese Firms; Biden Seeks Session on Reported Violations," *Washington Post*, February 22, 1992, p. A15; Lena H. Sun, "20 Years of Changing Sino-U.S. Ties," *Washington Post,* February 23, 1992, p. A21.

153. Interview with Douglas Paal.

154. "Mr. Bush Meets Mr. Li," *Washington Post* editorial, January 31, 1992, p. A18.

155. Lam, *China after Deng Xiaoping,* p. 167.

156. "Message to the House of Representatives Returning without Approval the United States–China Act of 1991," March 2, 1992, at Bush Presidential Library (http://bushlibrary.tamu.edu/papers/1992/92030201.html, accessed February 2003).

157. Daniel Southerland, "Chinese Leader Has Surgery; President, 83, Reported Recovering from Acute Appendicitis," *Washington Post,* June 28, 1990, p. A34.

158. Tai Ming Cheung, "Back to the Front; Deng Seeks to Depoliticise the PLA," *Far Eastern Economic Review*, October 29, 1992, p. 15; Lam, *China after Deng Xiaoping*, p. 212 (Lam's account of Yang's secret meetings is based on unreliable Taiwan sources).

159. Lam, *China after Deng Xiaoping*, p. 214; Cheung, "Back to the Front; Deng Seeks to Depoliticise the PLA."

160. Lam, *China after Deng Xiaoping*, p. 24.

161. Lincoln Kaye, "Dengism Enshrined," *Far Eastern Economic Review*, October 22, 1992, p. 10.

162. Sheryl WuDunn, "Chinese Party Congress Replaces Nearly Half of Central Committee," *New York Times*, October 19, 1992, p. A7.

163. Kathy Chen, "China Signals Peril of Political Dissent by Upholding Decision against Zhao," *Wall Street Journal,* October 12, 1992, p. A7.

164. Jiang Zemin, "Accelerate the Pace of Reform and Opening and Modern Construction, Win New Victories for Socialism with Chinese Characteristics," report to the Fourteenth Congress of the Communist Party of China, October 12, 1992, available (Chinese version) (www.people.com.cn/GB/shizheng/252/5089/5106/5278/ 20010430/456848.html, accessed February 21, 2003).

165. William J. Clinton, Nomination Acceptance Speech to the Democratic National Convention, July 16, 1992; transcript in *New York Times*, July 16, 1992, p. A14.

166. Interview with Douglas Paal; Mann, *About Face*, p. 267.

167. Michael Wines, "The 1992 Campaign: $8 Billion Directed to Wheat Farmers and Arms Workers," *New York Times*, September 3, 1992, p. A1.

168. See Mann, *About Face*, chap. 14, pp. 254–73.

169. Jackson Diehl, "Bush Approves Sale of F-15s to Saudis; Israelis Said to Be Due Compensation," *Washington Post*, September 27, 1992, p. A1; "Strategic Plans Giving Way to Mideast Arms Flow; Israel, Saudi Arabia Appear to Prefer Military Hardware to U.S. Security Enhancements," *Washington Post*, October 4, 1992, p. A24.

170. Thomas L. Friedman, "The World, Selling Arms to Keep Jobs: The Signals It Sends Abroad," *New York Times*, September 20, 1992, p. A4.

171. The language of the communiqué is fairly explicit: "The United States Government states that it does not seek to carry out a long-term policy of arms sales to Taiwan, that its arms sales to Taiwan will not exceed, either in qualitative or in quantitative terms, the level of those supplied in recent years since the establishment of diplomatic relations between the United States and China, and that it intends to reduce gradually its sales of arms to Taiwan, leading over a period of time to a final resolution."

172. Interviews with William Clark Jr., March 2000; Carl Ford; and Douglas Paal. I also participated in the interagency meetings.

173. Thomas L. Friedman, "China Warns U.S. on Taiwan Jet Deal," *New York Times*, September 4, 1992, p. A3.

174. Interview with Douglas Paal.

175. Keith Bradsher, "U.S. Warns Chinese of Duties," *New York Times*, August 22, 1992, p. D33; James Sterngold, "U.S.-China Tensions over Trade," *New York Times*, September 14, 1992, p. D1.

176. *Renmin Ribao* (People's Daily), September 4, 1992, p. 1. Quoted in Su Ge, *Meiguo dui hua zhengce he Taiwan wenti* (U.S. China Policy and the Taiwan Problem) (Beijing: World Knowledge Press, 1998), p. 642.

177. Lena H. Sun, "Chinese Renew Criticism of U.S. Jet Deal," *Washington Post*, September 8, 1992, p. A15.

178. As part of the Peace Pearl program of upgrading Chinese aircraft, prototype models of F-8s were shipped to the United States for fitting out with American avionics packages. When the United States suspended the program after Tiananmen, the equipment was put in storage, and China was charged high storage fees, causing them eventually to cancel the program unilaterally, thus letting Grumman off the hook for failing to deliver on the contract.

179. Interview with William Clark Jr.

180. R. Jeffrey Smith, "China Said to Sell Arms to Pakistan; M-11 Missile Shipment May Break Vow to U.S.," *Washington Post,* December 4, 1992, p. A10; Mann, *About Face,* p. 271.

181. Interview with J. Stapleton Roy.

182. Patrick Tyler, *A Great Wall: Six Presidents and China* (New York Century Foundation, 1999), p. 378.

Notes to Chapter 5

1. In constant renminbi (RMB), not adjusted for inflation. GNP figures from the *1996 China State Statistical Bureau Yearbook*, available at the China Data Center of the University of Michigan (http://chinadatacenter.org/newcdc/, accessed February 2003). Economic statistics from China need to be used with caution, as they tend to vary widely due to the unreliability of Chinese accounting practices and standards of measurement. See Nicholas Lardy, *China and the World Economy* (Washington: Institute for International Economics, 1994), pp. 30, 51, 63. The figure for FDI is the amount actually used in China; that promised during the same period was up more than 800 percent.

2. See Barry Naughton, *Growing out of the Plan—Chinese Economic Reform, 1978–1993* (Cambridge University Press, 1995), p. 289ff; Willy Wo-Lap Lam, *China after Deng Xiaoping: The Power Struggle in Beijing since Tiananmen* (Hong Kong: P. A. Professional Consultants, 1995), pp. 82–90; Lardy, China and the World Economy, pp. 63–70.

3. There are many books about Deng, in Chinese and in English, that discuss his enormous impact on China's history, political system, and economy from a variety of perspectives. Perhaps nothing is more illuminating than his own words, even as edited and selected by Communist Party historians. See *Selected Works of Deng Xiaoping*, vol. 2 *(1975–1982)* (Beijing: Foreign Languages Press, 1984).

4. Steven Goldstein, "China in Transition: The Political Foundations of Incremental Reform," *The China Quarterly*, no. 144 (December 1995), p. 1106.

5. Lam, *China after Deng Xiaoping*, p. 77.

6. Lena H. Sun, "Chairman Mao's Thought: Chinese Prefer to Become Rich," *Washington Post,* October 29, 1992, p. A22. In a further ironic twist, Mou was indicted for bank fraud in 2000 and sentenced to life in prison.

7. Lena H. Sun, "Chinese Militant Swaps Protest for a Beeper; Making Money Seen as Step to Democracy," *Washington Post,* June 2, 1993, p. A21.

8. Nicholas D. Kristof, "Foreign Investment Pouring into China," *New York Times,* June 15, 1992, p. D1.

9. Steven Greenhouse, "New Tally of World's Economies Catapults China into Third Place," *New York Times,* May 20, 1993, p. A1. The new numbers were based on "purchasing power parity" assessments.

10. Nicholas D. Kristoff, "Entrepreneurial Energy Sets off a Chinese Boom," *New York Times,* February 14, 1993, p. A1.

11. Jiang also was elected to head the State Military Commission, the ceremonial front for the Party's CMC. When the State Military Commission was established in

the mid-1980s, it was expected eventually to replace the Party Commission. After Tiananmen, however, all such plans were dropped, and the PLA remained completely under the control of the Communist Party.

12. Lena H. Sun, "Leaders in Beijing Duck Sharp Press Questions; What Foreign Reporters Ask Is More Revealing than What Chinese Officials Answer," *Washington Post*, April 1, 1993, p. A32.

13. Lam, *China after Deng Xiaoping*, pp. 308–09.

14. Ibid., p. 299

15. See, for example, "China: The Mystery Deepens," *The Economist*, June 5, 1993, p. 41; Sheryl WuDunn, "Chinese Premier Reported to Be Ill," *New York Times*, May 13, 1993, p. A10. Lam claims Li had major heart surgery during his absence; see *China after Deng Xiaoping*, p. 351.

16. Associated Press, "After Long Presumed Illness, China Leader Is Back in View," *New York Times*, June 15, 1993, p. A18.

17. Lam, *China after Deng Xiaoping*, p. 330.

18. Some analysts believe that Zhu Rongji had been quietly given responsibility for all economic work after the Fourteenth Party Congress and that Li Peng's "illness" in fact was his own way of avoiding the blame for China's economic difficulties in early 1993. See Gao Xin and He Pin, *Zhu Rongji zhuan—cong fandang youpai dao deng xiaoping de jichengren* (The Story of Zhu Rongji—From Anti-Party Rightist to Deng Xiaoping's Successor) (Taipei: New News and Culture Publishing, 1996), pp. 273–74.

19. China Data Center Commodities Price Index (www.umich.edu/~iinet/chinadata/stat/ChinaStatistics /EconomyIndNation/Commodities.htm, accessed February 2003). Economic statistics for this period vary widely, depending on sources and analytical methods. All show consistent trends of retail inflation, sharp increases in the money supply, uncontrolled credit expansion, declining bank deposits, and a credit squeeze.

20. Lena H. Sun, "China's Output Growing at World's Fastest Rate; 13% Tops Goal, Fueling Inflation Concerns," *Washington Post*, April 25, 1993, p. A25; "China Tries to Chill Boiling Economy," *Washington Post,* July 3, 1993, p. A1; Sheryl WuDunn, "China Sells off Public Land to the Well-Connected," *New York Times,* May 8, 1993, p. A3; Minxin Pei, "The Political Economy of Banking Reforms in China," *Journal of Contemporary China*, vol. 7 (July 1998), pp. 321–50; David Malpass, "Counterpoint: The Man Who's Saving China from Soviet-Style Disaster," *Wall Street Journal*, July 29, 1993, p. A11. China's currency, the renminbi or yuan, is not freely convertible, but so-called swap markets were officially established where foreign currency trading was permitted under controlled circumstances. When Chinese authorities allowed the yuan to float in mid-1993, it immediately dropped in value from the official exchange rate of 5.7 to the dollar to more than 8 to the dollar. Black market rates reached 11 to the dollar.

21. Pei, "The Political Economy of Banking Reforms in China."

22. Nicholas D. Kristof, "China, Barreling along the Capitalist Road, Now Posts Strict Speed Limit," *New York Times,* July 23, 1993, p. A2; Lam, *China after Deng Xiaoping*, pp. 119–23; "China: Banking on Zhu," *The Economist,* July 3, 1993, p. 33.

23. See, for example, "China at Boiling Point," *The Economist*, July 10, 1993, p. 15.

24. Patrick E. Tyler, "Chinese End Austerity Drive in Favor of Yet More Growth," *New York Times*, November 23, 1993, p. A1.

25. Lam, *China after Deng Xiaoping*, p. 132. Although Lam's sources for this story are not clear, it is consistent with observations made by other reporters that Zhu's austerity program was being curtailed just as it was beginning to achieve results.

26. Quoted in Steven Greenhouse, "New Tally of World's Economies Catapults China into Third Place," *New York Times*, May 20, 1993, p. A1.

27. There is a substantial literature about Chinese nationalism and its curious duality, oscillating between xenophobia—the rejection of all things foreign—and radical anti-traditionalism, which has led many Chinese scholars to reject much of China's historical and cultural tradition. Suisheng Zhao summarizes this literature in "Chinese Nationalism and Its International Orientations," *Political Science Quarterly*, vol. 115, no. 1 (Spring 2000). Other thoughtful books and articles include Michael Swaine and Asheley Tellis, *Interpreting China's Grand Strategy—Past, Present and Future* (Santa Monica, Calif.: RAND, 2000); Allen Whiting, "Chinese Nationalism and Foreign Policy after Deng," *The China Quarterly*, no. 142 (June 1995), p. 295ff; Zi Zhongyun, "The Impact and Clash of Ideologies: Sino-U.S. Relations from a Historical Perspective," *Journal of Contemporary China*, vol. 6, no. 15 (November 1997); Jonathan Unger, ed., *Chinese Nationalism* (New York: M. E. Sharpe, 1996); Lowell Dittmer and Samuel S. Kim, eds., *China's Quest for National Identity* (Cornell University Press, 1993); and Michel Oksenberg, "China's Confident Nationalism," *Foreign Affairs*, vol. 65, no. 3 (1986–87).

28. Suisheng Zhao, "Chinese Nationalism and Its International Orientations," p. 4.

29. Suisheng Zhao, "'Chinese Intellectuals' Quest for National Greatness and Nationalistic Writing in the 1990s," *The China Quarterly*, no. 152 (December 1997), pp. 725–45; Joseph Fewsmith, "Neoconservatism and the End of the Dengist Era," *Asian Survey*, vol. 35, no. 7 (July 1995), pp. 635–51; Feng Chen, "Order and Stability in Social Transition: Neo-conservative Political Thought in Post-1989 China," *The China Quarterly*, no. 151 (September 1997), pp. 151–72.

30. Chen, "Order and Stability in Social Transition," p. 596.

31. Wang Shan, trans., *Luo yi ning ge er, disanzhi yanjing kan zhongguo* (Looking at China through a Third Eye) (Shanxi: People's Publishing House, 1994). Although ostensibly written by a German scholar, Wang Shan was clearly the author. He published a sequel in 1996. See Joseph Fewsmith, "The Impact of WTO/PNTR on Chinese Politics," National Bureau of Asian Research, *NBR Analysis*, vol. 11, no. 2 (1999) (www.nbr.org/publications/analysis/vol11no2/essay2.html, accessed February 2003).

32. Xinhua News Agency press release of July 19, 1995, quoted in Merle Goldman, "Politically-Engaged Intellectuals in the Deng-Jiang Era: A Changing Relationship with the Party-State," *The China Quarterly*, no. 145 (March 1996), p. 158.

33. Clinton first used the term "coddling tyrants"—a standard term for many members of Congress and some pundits to describe Bush's China policy—in his acceptance speech at the Democratic National Convention on July 16, 1992. At that point, it was rather cryptic, a slogan used to describe one of many parts of what he called a "New Covenant" for America. His "vision" for American foreign policy was "an America that will not coddle tyrants, from Baghdad to Beijing" (*New York Times*, July 17, 1992, p. 14). He expanded on it only a bit in a campaign that was nearly devoid of significant discussion of foreign policy issues. Although some of his supporters used the term "butchers of Beijing" to describe the Chinese leadership, Clinton himself used it sparingly, if at all. Nonetheless, the pairing of China with Iraq for alliterative purposes led imperceptibly to a tendency to pair the two as "rogue states" and as equals in terms of their hostility to democracy, human rights, and American values.

34. Quoted in Thomas L. Friedman, "Clinton's Foreign-Policy Agenda Reaches across Broad Spectrum," *New York Times,* October 4, 1992, p. 1.

35. It was actually Berger who introduced Lake to Clinton and brought him into the campaign in 1992. A trade lawyer and negotiator, Berger had headed the international trade practice of one of Washington's premier law offices, Hogan and Hartson, before joining the Clinton election effort.

36. The NEC was created by the president by Executive Order 12835 on January 25, 1993. Intended to be a counterpart of the National Security Council, it included eighteen senior officials in its formal makeup, including the president, vice president, and secretaries of state, treasury, commerce, agriculture, labor, housing and urban development, transportation, energy, the EPA, the USTR, and several others. It was in part the brainchild of a special bipartisan commission under the Carnegie Endowment for International Peace and the Institute for International Economics. The commission's report was published in *Foreign Affairs*, vol. 71, no. 5 (Winter 1992–93), beginning on p. 175. The commission envisioned the NEC as an "instrument for assuring that economic policy gets attention equal to traditional national security, working closely with the NSC and its staff when international economic issues are under consideration." Clinton enthusiastically supported the idea during the campaign, as it resonated with his focus on economic issues. Even as it was formally established, however, there was still ambiguity about the size and duties of its professional staff.

37. Thomas L. Friedman, "Clinton's Cabinet Choices Put Him at Center, Balancing Competing Factions," *New York Times,* December 27, 1992, p. A22.

38. Although senior Clinton officials have been adamant that the president was not uninterested in foreign policy, domestic advisers and press analysts painted a consistent picture. Controversial campaign adviser Dick Morris, for example, observed that Clinton "reacted, more or less reluctantly, to global concerns when they intruded so deeply into America's politics that he had to do something." Morris, *Behind the Oval Office—Winning the Presidency in the Nineties* (Random House, 1997), p. 245.

39. Nearly every incoming administration since the 1950s has chosen to change the names of its principal documents. Therefore, the Bush administration National

Security Review (NSR) series (comprehensive reviews of policy issues) became Clinton's Presidential Review Directives (PRD), and Bush's National Security Directives (NSD)—the actual decision documents on major policy issues—became Presidential Decision Directives, or PDDs, under Clinton. See Office of the Historian, Bureau of Public Affairs, Department of State, "History of the National Security Council, 1947–1997" (http://fas.org/irp/offdocs/NSChistory.htm, accessed February 2003).

40. By statute (P.L. 80-253, National Security Act of 1947), the National Security Council consists of the president, vice president, secretaries of state and of defense, advised by the director of central intelligence and the chairman of the Joint Chiefs of Staff, plus whomever else the president may "from time to time" designate. The expansion of the NSC was fully in keeping with the original statute, particularly in light of the fact that some of the originally stipulated positions (for example, secretary of the navy) had been quietly dropped.

41. By custom, the staff of the assistant to the president for national security affairs (APNSA) is also referred to as the National Security Council, which occasionally creates confusion with the statutory organization.

42. APNSA Lake tried to structure the IWGs so as to "revitalize the Assistant Secretary level" in the decisionmaking process, and therefore he established fewer permanent IWGs and encouraged more ad hoc ones. Interview with Anthony Lake, August 2000.

43. Gwen Ifill, "Security Official Guides U.S. Aims at Conference," *New York Times*, July 5, 1993, p. A5; interview with Anthony Lake.

44. Elizabeth Drew, *On the Edge—The Clinton Presidency* (Simon and Schuster, 1994), p. 336.

45. This problem was not unique to the Bush-Clinton transition but has been a source of frustration for every incoming administration. Several White House staffers interviewed for this book complained of the lack of a "paper trail" for policy issues, particularly on China, where previous private White House commitments were not completely known to successors and where continuity and precision of language on the Taiwan issue is so essential.

46. Federal News Service, "Press Conference with President Clinton and Thomas F. 'Mack' McLarty, White House Chief of Staff, Regarding Reorganization of White House Staff," February 9, 1993, p. 1 (Nexis-Lexis).

47. Interview with Anthony Lake.

48. See Anthony J. Eksterowicz and Glenn Hastedt, "Modern Presidential Transitions: Problems, Pitfalls, and Lessons for Success," *Presidential Studies Quarterly*, vol. 28, no. 2 (Spring 1998), pp. 299–319; also Matthew J. Dickinson, "No Place for Amateurs: Some Thoughts on the Clinton Administration and the Presidential Staff," *Presidential Studies Quarterly*, vol. 28, no. 4 (Fall 1998), pp. 768–72.

49. R. Jeffrey Smith, "Defense Policy Posts Restructured; Aspin Seeks to Focus More Attention on New Security Concerns," *Washington Post*, January 28, 1993, p. A4; Barton Gellman, "Rumblings of Discord Heard in Pentagon; Aspin's Civilian Leadership, Management Style and Agenda Irk Some Officers," *Washington Post*, June 20, 1993, p. 1; Drew, *On the Edge—the Clinton Presidency*, pp. 44–45, 141, 356–57; interview with Stanley Roth, August 2000.

50. Don Oberdorfer, "Balkans, Haiti, Iraq and Somalia Head NSC Policy Study List," *Washington Post,* January 31, 1993, p. A18.

51. Warren Strobel, "White House Disavows View of State Aide," *Washington Times,* May 27, 1993, p. A7.

52. Jim Hoagland, "Fumbling for a Foreign Policy," *Washington Post,* June 14, 1993, p. A19.

53. See, for example, Jonathan Clarke, "The Conceptual Poverty of U.S. Foreign Policy," *Atlantic Monthly* (September 1993); Michael Mandelbaum (Clinton campaign adviser), "Like It or Not, We Must Lead," *New York Times,* June 9, 1993, p. A21.

54. Warren Christopher, *In the Stream of History: Shaping Foreign Policy for a New Era* (Stanford University Press, 1998), p. 31 (emphasis added).

55. See, for example, his broadcast interview with Morton Kondracke on May 3, 1991, in Federal News Service, "American Interests" transcript, p. 4 (Lexis-Nexis).

56. Interviews with Winston Lord, April 2000, and Anthony Lake.

57. "Winston Lord, Assistant Secretary-designate for East Asian and Pacific Affairs. Statement before the Senate Foreign Relations Committee, Washington, D.C., March 31, 1993" (www.state.gov/www/regions/eap/930331.html, accessed February 2003).

58. Lord drew some criticism for putting too many "China hands" on his staff. See Don Oberdorfer, "Foreign Policy Arm Missing Japan Hand; Asia Team Picked by China Expert Winston Lord Draws Criticism," *Washington Post,* January 30, 1993, p. A11.

59. See 1992 Democratic Party Platform, IV. Preserving Our National Security, "China Trade Terms" (www.udel.edu/htr/American98/Texts/demoplat.html#5, accessed February 2003).

60. Interview with Winston Lord.

61. Federal News Service, "News Conference, Senator George Mitchell (D-Maine), Rep. Nancy Pelosi (D-California)," April 22, 1993, House Radio-TV Gallery (Nexis-Lexis).

62. "United States–China Act of 1993 Introduced in the House," H.R. 1835 (www.thomas.loc.gov, accessed February 2003 [emphasis added]).

63. In a section entitled, "Restoring American Economic Leadership," the platform called for "conditioning of favorable trade terms for China on respect for human rights in China and Tibet, greater market access for U.S. goods, and responsible conduct on weapons proliferation." See 1992 Democratic Party Platform, National Security section (www.udel.edu/htr/American98/Texts/demoplat.html, accessed February 2003).

64. Nicholas D. Kristof, "China Worried by Clinton's Linking of Trade to Human Rights," *New York Times,* October 9, 1992, p. A10; Gary Lee, "The Federal Page—Taking on the President over China's Trade Status," *Washington Post,* June 1, 1992, p. A17; John W. Dietrich, "Interest Groups and Foreign Policy: Clinton and the China MFN Debates," *Presidential Studies Quarterly,* vol. 29, no. 2 (June 1999), p. 286.

65. Interview with J. Stapleton Roy, May 2000.

66. Boren and Pell were refused visas to visit China in April 1992—it was "inconvenient" for them to come, PRC officials said. Their request to visit Tibet was considered to be the main problem.

67. *People's Daily* carried the slogan on its front page on November 30. Chen You-wei claims the sixteen-character slogan (with some minor variations) was first introduced by Deng Xiaoping in late 1991 but was not made public until Jiang's meeting with Schroeder. Chen You-wei, *Zhonggong yu meiguo waijiao neimu* (Inside Stories of the Diplomacy between Communist China and America) (Taipei: Cheng Chong Book Company, 1999), pp. 100, 183. American press commentaries read the phrase as a clear indication the Chinese were worried about Clinton's policies and wanted an improvement in relations. See, for example, Lena Sun, "China Works to Improve U.S. Relations; Rhetoric Toned down as Trade Status Viewed at Risk under Clinton," *Washington Post,* January 2, 1993, p. A1.

68. Lena H. Sun, "Congressional Democrats Tell China to Act on Rights or Face Stricture," *Washington Post,* December 1, 1992, p. A31.

69. Nicholas D. Kristof, "It's China against the World, with a Great Deal at Stake," *New York Times,* November 29, 1992, The Week in Review, p. 4. Observers also noted that Beijing appeared to have suspended the human rights dialogue with Washington sometime after the F-16 sale. Whether that was a reaction to the sale or a warning to the new administration cannot be determined.

70. Nicholas D. Kristof, "In a Nod to U.S., China Plans to Free 2 Dissidents," *New York Times,* February 2, 1993, p. A7.

71. Nicholas D. Kristof, "China Releasing Catholic Priests from Prison," *New York Times,* March 21, 1993, p. A19.

72. Geoffrey Crothall and Chris Yeung, "Top U.S. Aide Warns Beijing after Talks Fail to Reassure Clinton," *South China Morning Post* (Hong Kong), May 13, 1993, p. 1; Nicholas D. Kristof, "Clinton Aide Ends China Trip with No Sign of Accord," *New York Times,* May 13, 1993, p. A10.

73. "China 'Prepared for the Worst' after MFN Talks," *Ming Pao* (Hong Kong), May 13, 1993, p. 2; in BBC Summary of World Broadcasts, May 17, 1993, FE/1690/A1.

74. Lena H. Sun, "U.S. Warns China That Renewal of Trade Status Depends on Several Conditions," *Washington Post,* May 13, 1993, p. A19.

75. Allen Whiting, "Chinese Nationalism and Foreign Policy after Deng," *The China Quarterly,* no. 142 (June 1995), p. 307.

76. Interview with Samuel R. Berger, March 2001.

77. Interview with Winston Lord.

78. Jim Abrams, "Lawmakers Give Conditional Support as Clinton Moves toward China Policy," *Associated Press,* May 25, 1993.

79. "Statement by the President on Most Favored Nation Status for China," May 28, 1993 (www.ibiblio.org/pub/archives/whitehouse-papers/1993/May/Presidents-Statement-on-MFN-for-China, accessed February 2003).

80. Text of the Executive Order (http://www.archives.gov/federal_register/executive_orders/pdf/12850.pdf, accessed February 2003).

81. Quoted in Peter Passell, "A Cold War Weapon Isn't Used on China and May Never Be," *New York Times*, June 3, 1993, p. D2.

82. Interview with J. Stapleton Roy.

83. *People's Daily,* May 29, 1993, p. 1, quoted in Su Ge, *Meiguo duihua zhengce yu taiwan wenti* (American Policy toward China and the Taiwan Question) (Beijing: World Knowledge Publishing, 1999), pp. 673–74.

84. Daniel Southerland, "Clinton Sending First Trade Delegation to China," *Washington Post,* February 27, 1993, p. C1.

85. Paul Lewis, "UN Rights Group Cites Indonesia in Timor," *New York Times*, March 14, 1993, p. A9.

86. In what would become the norm for such meetings, the president "dropped by" a meeting between the Dalai Lama and Vice President Gore on April 27, avoiding the publicity of a formal meeting in the Oval Office. Although China protested that any meetings with the exiled spiritual leader of Tibet constituted support for "splittism," U.S. officials insisted they only met with him privately in his capacity as one of the world's most noted spiritual leaders.

87. Lo Ping and Li Tzu-ching, "One Hundred and Sixteen Generals Write to Deng Xiaoping on Policy toward United States," *Cheng Ming,* no. 188 (June 1, 1993), pp. 14–16, in Foreign Broadcast Information Service (FBIS)-CHI (June 2, 1993), pp. 33–36. Other accounts cited different numbers of generals and used different adjectives to describe American perfidy. There is considerable controversy among American sinologists as to how seriously to take this kind of story. Allen Whiting, in his excellent study of Chinese nationalism cited in note 75, takes the stories as being essentially accurate. So does John W. Garver, with reservations, in "The PLA as an Interest Group in Chinese Foreign Policy," in Dennison Lane, Mark Weisenbloom, and Dimon Liu, eds., *Chinese Military Modernization* (Washington: American Enterprise Institute Press, 1996), pp. 246–77. My own inclination is to treat them as "stories in circulation," or "news on the street" (*xiaodao xiaoxi*), rather than factually accurate accounts of events in Beijing. The "angry generals writing letters of protest" theme recurs regularly in post-Tiananmen China and was reported sufficiently often to be considered a factor in Chinese policymaking in the 1992–95 period.

88. Garver, "The PLA as an Interest Group in Chinese Foreign Policy," p. 260.

89. Andrew Nathan, "Human Rights in Chinese Foreign Policy," *The China Quarterly*, no. 139 (September 1994), p. 633.

90. Patrick E. Tyler, "Eye on Olympics, China Frees Top Dissident," *New York Times,* September 21, 1993, p. A6.

91. *The Economist*, August 21, 1993, p. 75.

92. Su Ge, *Meiguo duihua zhengce yu taiwan wenti* (American Policy toward China and the Taiwan Question), p. 675.

93. Suisheng Zhao, "'Chinese Intellectuals' Quest for National Greatness and Nationalistic Writing in the 1990s," *The China Quarterly*, no. 152 (December 1997), p. 731.

94. Joseph Fewsmith, "The Impact of WTO/PNTR on Chinese Politics," *NBR Analysis*, vol. 11, no. 2 (1999), National Bureau of Asian Research, p. 2.

95. Ann Devroy and R. Jeffrey Smith, "U.S. Evidence 'Suggests' China Breaks Arms Pact; Report Comes on Eve of Trade Status Debate," *Washington Post,* May 18, 1993, p. A9.

96. Bill Gertz, "Two Lawmakers Say Pakistan Has Missiles; Cite CIA Report on Chinese M-11s," *Washington Times,* June 21, 1993, p. A12 (Nexis-Lexis).

97. Under the terms of the "Helms amendment" to the Arms Control Export Act of 1990, "all activities . . . affecting the development or production of electronics, space systems or equipment, and military aircraft" are automatically sanctioned if a country is found to have violated the Missile Technology Control Regime. The law differentiates between "Category I" violations, which consist of items that make a "substantial contribution" to a missile program, and "Category II" violations, which involve shipping items and technology—listed in an annex to the MTCR agreement—"related to" the development of a non-MTCR-compliant missile system.

98. Lally Weymouth, "Chinese Take-out; Supplying Weapons to Rogue States," *Washington Post,* August 12, 1993, p. A27.

99. Lynn Davis, State Department Special Briefing, August 25, 1993; Lexis-Nexis. NSC Senior Director for Nonproliferation Daniel Poneman recalled that the NSC view differed with this interpretation somewhat. While the potential impact of sanctions on China or bilateral relations could have no bearing on the factual determination of *whether* sanctionable activity had occurred, that impact *was* relevant to deciding what conditions the U.S. should impose on China in order to justify the exercise of the national security waiver authority provided by the statute. Interview with Daniel Poneman, October 2000.

100. Interview with Daniel Poneman.

101. See Patrick Tyler, *A Great Wall: Six Presidents and China* (New York: Century Foundation, 1999), p. 396.

102. John Mintz, "The Satellite Makers' China Card; Martin Marietta and Hughes Warn U.S. Sales Ban Will Cause Massive Layoffs," *Washington Post,* October 20, 1993, p. C11.

103. Su Ge, *Meiguo duihua zhengce yu taiwan wenti* (American Policy toward China and the Taiwan Question), pp. 679–80; also Lena H. Sun, "Sino-U.S. Ties 'in Serious Jeopardy'; Beijing Says New Sanctions Will Force It to Halt Compliance with Missile Control Pact," *Washington Post,* August 28, 1993, p. A17.

104. R. Jeffrey Smith and Daniel Williams, "U.S. Offers to Waive China Trade Sanctions; Pledge Not to Export M-11 Missile Sought," *Washington Post*, November 11, 1993, p. A39.

105. The most complete account of the *Yin He* (also rendered *Yinhe*) incident is available in Patrick Tyler's *A Great Wall*, pp. 396–99. I was on the National Intelligence Council at the time, and although not directly involved in either the reporting or analysis of information pertaining to nonproliferation matters, I was aware of the main facts of the case. Tyler's reporting, based on interviews with several of the key participants, is consistent with my recollection of the incident.

106. Interviews with Daniel Poneman and J. Stapleton Roy.

107. Tyler, *A Great Wall*, pp. 396–98; R. Jeffrey Smith, "Mideast Allies Frustrate Ship Inspection by U.S.; Prohibited Chemicals May Be Bound for Iran," *Washington Post*, August 10, 1993, p. A6.

108. "China Lodges Protest against U.S. over Cargo-ship Incident," Xinhua News Agency, no. 0807153, August 7, 1993 (Lexis-Nexis).

109. Douglas Frantz, "Chemicals on Chinese Ship Usable for Arms, U.S. Says," *Los Angeles Times,* August 10, 1993, p. A6 (Lexis-Nexis).

110. Cable News Network, "Secretary Christopher Discusses the World's Hot Spots," August 12, 1993, Interview with Judy Woodruff, transcript no. 493–4.

111. Matt Forney, "U.S. Lawmakers Press China on Human Rights," United Press International, August 18, 1993 (Lexis-Nexis).

112. Interview with J. Stapleton Roy; Tyler, *A Great Wall,* p. 398.

113. Interviews with Daniel Poneman and Anthony Lake; Tyler, *Great Wall,* pp. 398–99.

114. Quoted in Lynne Duke, "China Seeks Apology in Ship Search; Poison Gas Material Not Found by U.S.," *Washington Post,* September 5, 1993, p. A43.

115. Patrick E. Tyler, "China Says Saudis Found No Arms Cargo on Ship," *New York Times,* September 3, 1993, p. 3; Associated Press, "Inspection Exonerates China but U.S. Doubts Finding," September 8, 1993 (Lexis-Nexis).

116. Terminology for describing the U.S. policy was somewhat difficult at first. "Enhanced engagement" gave way to "comprehensive engagement," with "constructive engagement" being discarded because it connoted policy toward South Africa. Despite becoming a shorthand term to describe an array of American policies, "comprehensive engagement" was not well defined within the government, nor well understood outside it. For further discussion of the problems of imprecise definition of engagement, see Robert L. Suettinger, "Tough Engagement: U.S.-China Relations," in Richard Haass and Meghan O'Sullivan, eds., *Honey and Vinegar: Incentives, Sanctions, and Foreign Policy* (Brookings, 2000).

117. Winston Lord, address to the United States Chamber of Commerce, March 29, 1994, Federal News Service (Nexis-Lexis).

118. Tyler, *A Great Wall,* p. 400; Don Oberdorfer, "Replaying the China Card: How Washington and Beijing Avoided Diplomatic Disaster," *Washington Post*, November 7, 1993, p. C7.

119. Oberdorfer, "Replaying the China Card.

120. Warren Christopher, "Building Peace in the Middle East," speech at Columbia University, September 20, 1993 (http://dosfan.lib.uic.edu/ERC/briefing/dossec/1993/9309/930920dossec.html, accessed February 2003).

121. Anthony Lake, "From Containment to Enlargement," speech at Johns Hopkins University School of Advanced International Studies, September 21, 1993 (www.mtholyoke.edu/acad/intrel/lakedoc.html, accessed February 2003).

122. Su Ge, for example, devotes twenty pages to an analysis of the new U.S. approach; see *Meiguo duihua Zhengce yu Taiwan wenti* (American Policy toward China and the Taiwan Question), pp. 645–64.

123. Barton Gellman, "Reappraisal Led to New China Policy," *Washington Post,* June 22, 1998, p. A1; interview with Anthony Lake.

124. Anthony Lake, "From Containment to Enlargement," speech delivered at Johns Hopkins University School of Advanced International Studies.

125. Jen Hui-wen, "Background to China's 'Four Nots' Policy towards the United States," *Xin Bao* (Hong Kong), September 17, 1993, p. 24, in FBIS-CHI, pp. 1–3.

126. Interview with J. Stapleton Roy.

127. Daniel Kwan, "Beijing Not Doing Enough for MFN—Envoy," *South China Morning Post,* October 21, 1993, p. 1 (Nexis-Lexis). Shattuck's judgment seemed to disregard the fact that some of China's most prominent dissidents, including Wang Xizhe, Wang Dan, Xu Wenli, and Wei Jingsheng, had been freed from prison in the first nine months of 1993.

128. R. Jeffrey Smith and Daniel Williams, "U.S. Offers to Waive China Trade Sanctions; Pledge Not to Export M-11 Missile Sought," *Washington Post*, November 11, 1993, p. A39.

129. Patrick E. Tyler, "China May Allow Red Cross to Visit Dissidents in Jail," *New York Times,* November 10, 1993, p. A1.

130. Quoted in Lena H. Sun, "China Hopes U.S. Talks Will Yield New Respect," *Washington Post*, November 18, 1993, p. A31.

131. Mary McGrory, "The Great Thrall of China," *Washington Post*, November 7, 1993, p. C1; Jim Hoagland, "Human Rights—On Balance," *Washington Post,* November 18, 1993, p. A23.

132. Wei Jingsheng, "The Wolf and the Lamb," *New York Times*, November 18, 1993, p. A27.

133. See Christopher testimony before the Senate Foreign Relations Committee, November 4, 1993, Federal Document Clearinghouse (Nexis-Lexis).

134. Jim Mann, "Executives Press Clinton to Smooth U.S.-China Ties," *Los Angeles Times*, November 19, 1993, p. A1.

135. Paul Quinn Judge, "Rights Issue Is Raised as China Leader Arrives in U.S.; Clinton Urged to Take Tough Line," *Boston Globe,* November 19, 1993, p. 1.

136. Interviews with Winston Lord and Stanley Roth. See also Daniel Williams, "Chinese Leader Plays to Audience at Home; Jiang, Who May Succeed Deng, Varies Little from Script," *Washington Post,* November 21, 1993, p. A34.

137. From Hong Kong's *Jing Pao* of January 5, 1994, p. 39. Bruce Gilley, *Tiger on the Brink: Jiang Zemin and China's New Elite* (University of California Press, 1998), p. 212.

138. David M. Lampton, "China Policy in Clinton's First Year," in James R. Lilley and Wendell L. Willkie II, eds., *Beyond MFN: Trade with China and American Interests* (Washington: American Enterprise Institute Press, 1994), pp. 22–23; also "America's China Policy in the Age of the Finance Minister: Clinton Ends Linkage," *The China Quarterly,* no. 139 (September 1994), pp. 609–10.

139. China's "reform through labor," or *laogai,* system operates in an extrajudicial fashion, enabling local authorities to send minor offenders off to labor reform camps for up to three years without any trial or approval by the court system. Over the years, the system became increasingly capricious and abusive. After Tiananmen, several thousand political dissidents were sent off to labor reform without trial. In 1992 an escapee from that system, Harry (Hongda) Wu, published an exposé called *Laogai: The Chinese Gulag*, in which he not only compared the labor reform system to Russian and Nazi concentration camps, but asserted that the products produced

by labor reform facilities were being exported to the United States in large quantities. The book—although considered dated and inaccurate by some experts—created a furor in the United States and led to both public opinion and legislative pressure to restrict "Chinese prison labor" exports. The Chinese government, of course, denounced the book, as well as its author, who would figure prominently in U.S.-China relations in 1995. In 1992 the Bush administration reached an agreement with the Chinese government to allow U.S. Customs officials to inspect suspected facilities to ascertain if they were run by the labor reform system. Differences soon appeared, however, over numbers of visits, notifications, reporting requirements, and other matters. Chinese officials reacted angrily when U.S. requests for information and inspections were based on Wu's book. By mid-1993 inspections had virtually ceased.

140. Patrick E. Tyler, "China Promises U.S. to Try to Improve Its Human Rights," *New York Times,* January 16, 1994, p. A1; "Beijing Will Take Steps on Rights, Bush Is Told," *New York Times,* January 17, 1994, p. A2.

141. Patrick E. Tyler, "Rights in China Improve, Envoy Says," *New York Times,* January 1, 1994, p. A5; Tyler, *A Great Wall,* p. 401.

142. Elaine Sciolino, "A Draft State Dept. Report Finds China's Rights Record Is Still Poor," *New York Times,* January 12, 1993, p. A1.

143. State Department briefing, January 14, 1994, Federal News Service (Lexis-Nexis).

144. Quoted in Tyler, *A Great Wall,* p. 403.

145. Thomas W. Lippman, "U.S. Says China Lagging on Human Rights Issue; Continuing Bilateral Talks Suggest Progress," *Washington Post,* January 24, 1994, p. A16.

146. The list of 235 political prisoners for whom the United States was demanding an accurate accounting was cobbled together by Shattuck's party at the last minute through telephone consultations with American NGOs. Many of the names were provided to Beijing without Chinese characters, while some were only a surname and a province where that person was believed to be incarcerated, such as "Zheng, Shaanxi Province."

147. See Patrick E. Tyler, "Discontent Mounts in China, Shaking the Leaders," *New York Times,* April 10, 1994, p. A3.

148. Lena H. Sun, "Chinese Rebuff Christopher on Human Rights; Dissident Movement Makes Comeback," *Washington Post,* March 13, 1994, p. A1.

149. Josh M. Goshko, "Annual State Department Report Calls Chinese Human Rights Efforts Weak," *Washington Post*, February 2, 1994, p. A15.

150. Patrick E. Tyler, "Beijing Is Warning Leading Dissident," *New York Times,* February 26, 1993, p. A4; Tyler, *A Great Wall,* pp. 405–06; James Mann, *About Face: A History of America's Curious Relationship with China, from Nixon to Clinton* (Alfred A. Knopf, 1999), pp. 297–300. Mann was told a cable was sent out before the meeting, but those who were traveling with Christopher insist they did not see it before he departed on March 4 for a lengthy trip to Asia.

151. See Tyler, *A Great Wall,* pp. 405–06, and Mann, *About Face,* pp. 298–99, for details of the Wei-Shattuck meeting. Tyler suggests the different surveillance teams assigned to Shattuck and Wei did not know whom their man was meeting, while Mann implies the leadership knew and used the incident to justify a crackdown they had been planning anyway. Although the facts are not clear, my own interpretation is that Wei's announcement forced Beijing's hand.

152. Patrick E. Tyler, "Highest U.S. Rights Official Meets with Leading Chinese Dissident," *New York Times,* February 28, 1994, p. A2; Daniel Southerland, "Chinese Dissident Asks U.S. to Get Tougher," *Washington Post,* March 1, 1994, p. A15.

153. Patrick E. Tyler, "Chinese Crackdown: Challenge Is Still Prohibited," *New York Times,* March 7, 1994, p. A8; "Chinese Dissident Appears; May Meet Christopher," *New York Times,* March 10, 1994, p. A11.

154. David Briscoe, "Christopher Heads for Asia under Cloud of Problems with China, Japan," Associated Press, March 4, 1994.

155. Interview with Winston Lord.

156. Interview with Stanley Roth; Elaine Sciolino, "U.S. Showing Frustration over China's Human Rights Policy," *New York Times,* March 9, 1994, p. A11.

157. MFA press spokesman, quoted in Daniel Williams, "China Trip Expectations Lowered; Christopher Concerned Beijing Is 'Going in Wrong Direction,'" *Washington Post,* March 10, 1994, p. A34.

158. Elaine Sciolino, "China Trip Begins on a Frosty Note for Christopher," *New York Times,* March 12, 1994, p. A1.

159. Daniel Williams, "Chinese Rebuff Christopher on Human Rights; Premier Says Beijing Is Willing to Forgo Trading with U.S.," *Washington Post,* March 13, 1994, p. A1.

160. Tyler, *A Great Wall,* p. 408; interview with J. Stapleton Roy; Elaine Sciolino, Thomas L. Friedman, and Patrick E. Tyler, "Clinton and China: How Promise Self-Destructed," *New York Times,* May 29, 1994, p. A1.

161. Quoted in Daniel Williams, "U.S. Softens Trade Stand with China; Human Rights Steps Would No Longer Be Spelled Out," *Washington Post,* March 14, 1994, p. A1.

162. Ibid.; Elaine Sciolino, "Christopher Ends Beijing Talks Citing Modest Gains," *New York Times*, March 14, 1994, p. A3.

163. Gilley, *Tiger on the Brink,* p. 228; Kathy Chen, "Chinese Politicians Jockey for Position—Reports of Deng's Ill Health Multiply as Top Officials Bolster Their Standing," *Wall Street Journal,* July 14, 1994, p. A6.

164. David Shambaugh, "China's Commander-in-Chief: Jiang Zemin and the PLA," in Lane Weisenbloom, and Liu, eds., *Chinese Military Modernization*, pp. 227–28.

165. I was present during Lake's conversation with Jiang on July 9, 1996.

166. Charles Krauthammer, "Mugged in Beijing," *Washington Post,* March 18, 1994, p. A29; Jim Hoagland, "Battered in Beijing," *Washington Post,* March 15, 1994, p. A19; Hobart Rowen, "Administration in Disarray on China Trade Policy," *Washington Post,* March 20, 1994, p. H1.

167. Elaine Sciolino, "Sourly, Christopher's Talks in Beijing Come to an End," *New York Times,* March 14, 1994, p. A3.

168. Interview with Winston Lord.

169. Warren Christopher, "My Trip to Beijing Was Necessary," *Washington Post,* March 22, 1994, p. A17.

170. Elaine Sciolino, "U.S. to Try a Conciliatory Tack with China," *New York Times,* March 23, 1994, p. A12.

171. Interview with Bowman Cutter, August 2000.

172. Quoted by Peter Behr, "Offering China a Carrot on Trade; In Exchange, U.S. Would Insist on Human Rights Improvements," *Washington Post,* January 29, 1994, p. C1.

173. Interview with Stanley Roth.

174. Patrick E. Tyler, "Beijing Says It Could Live Well Even if U.S. Trade Was Cut Off," *New York Times,* March 21, 1994, p. A1.

175. Wei would be held in these circumstances for the next eighteen months, a condition the Chinese called "depriving him of political rights" because he violated the conditions of his parole. It was a dubious procedure, even under Chinese law. Subsequently, the National People's Congress passed legislation to limit the time period in which someone could be held by the police without being charged. That did not help Wei, however.

176. In testimony before the Senate Foreign Relations Committee on May 4, for example, Mike Jendrzejczyk, Washington director of Human Rights Watch-Asia, said flatly, "At this stage, we cannot imagine how the Secretary of State could make a *credible* report to the President saying that China had fully met the conditions in the Executive Order." "Human Rights and MFN for China," testimony of Mike Jendrzejczyk before the Subcommittee on East Asia and Pacific Affairs of the Senate Foreign Relations Committee, May 4, 1994, Federal Document Clearing House (Lexis-Nexis).

177. Lord first raised the idea at the end of a speech to the Chamber of Commerce on March 30 as something that should be "looked at" to resolve the U.S. dilemma of wanting to punish China for its failure to improve human rights, but not wanting to punish private entrepreneurs in China or expose U.S. investors to retaliation. See Steven Greenhouse, "Aide Says U.S. May Scrap an Across-the-Board Penalty for China," *New York Times,* March 30, 1994, p. A10.

178. Qian expressed China's support for the declaration in a conversation with former UN secretary general Kurt Waldheim, who by that time had been accused widely of acquiescing in Nazi Germany's war crimes. The brief announcement of Qian's statement (Xinhua News Agency, no. 0406155, April 4, 1994) received almost no play from Western media.

179. Interview with Michael Armacost, April 2000.

180. Ibid. Armacost noted a contrast between White House and NSC attitudes on this issue and those at the State Department, where he found more uncertainty about how the decision would go.

181. Ibid.

182. In late April, Lord wrote and circulated widely within the Department of State a memo entitled "Emerging Malaise in Our Relations with Asia," in which he lamented the overall decline of U.S. influence in the region due to a series of "unilateral" actions that made the U.S. seem like a "nanny, if not bully." He also warned that Asians were critical of U.S. policies that seemed bent on "placating domestic interest groups" by using "tactics that destabilize relationships which are central to the region's peace and prosperity." The memo was leaked to the press in early May, and the full text appeared in *The Daily Yomiuri* (Tokyo) on May 17, 1994 (Lexis-Nexis).

183. Daniel Williams, "Christopher Cites Progress on Human Rights in China; Report Could Result in Lesser Trade Sanctions," *Washington Post,* May 24, 1994, p. A1.

184. Office of the Press Secretary, "Press Conference of the President," May 26, 1994 (www.ibiblio.org/pub/archives/whitehouse-papers/1994/May/1994-05-26-President-in-Press-Conference-on-China-MFN-Status, accessed February 2003).

185. Available online at www.ibiblio.org/pub/archives/whitehouse-papers/1994/May/1994-05-26-Briefing-by-Lake-et-al-on-MFN-Status-for-China (accessed February 2003).

186. Pelosi's bill, H.R. 4590, gathered 102 sponsors, but was watered down by a Hamilton amendment. It died in the Senate in August.

187. Interview with J. Stapleton Roy.

188. Xinhua News Agency, no. 0527070, May 27, 1994. Also Patrick E. Tyler, "China Welcomes U.S. Trade Policy," *New York Times,* May 28, 1994, p. A1; Lena H. Sun, "Trade Status Renewal Could Boost U.S.-China Relations, Analysts Say," *Washington Post,* May 28, 1994, p. A24. On a day when Russian prime minister Viktor Chernomyrdin was in town, this news was the last item in the evening newscast.

Notes to Chapter 6

1. The August 17, 1982, joint communiqué affirms specifically, "the United States Government states that it does not seek to carry out a long-term policy of arms sales to Taiwan, that its arms sales to Taiwan will not exceed, either in qualitative or in quantitative terms, the level of those supplied in recent years since the establishment of diplomatic relations between the United States and China, and that it intends to reduce gradually its sales of arms to Taiwan, leading over a period of time to a final resolution" (http://ait.org.tw/817.html, accessed February 2003).

2. "Historic 1993 China, Taiwan Talks Took Five Years of Groundwork," Agence France-Presse, July 19, 2000 (http://taiwansecurity.org/AFP/AFP-071900.htm, accessed February 2003); also "Lee Sent Secret Envoys to China," *Taipei Times*, July 20, 2000 (www.taipeitimes.com/news/2000/07/20/story/0000044446, accessed February 2003).

3. In late October 1992, the two sides, meeting in Hong Kong, worked to try and find common language on the meaning of "one China" as the guiding principle for negotiations. As evidence of the difficulty of cross-Strait talks, the two sides disagree to this day on whether they reached an agreement to disagree, that is, whether they

reached a consensus on "one China, respective interpretations." See, for example, Lin Cheng-yi, "The Security of Taiwan in the Year 2000: A Taiwanese Perspective" (www.dsis.org.tw/peaceforum/symposium/2000-12/121502.pdf, accessed February 2003).

4. China was eager, for example to establish the "three communications" (*san tong*)—direct shipping, mail, and air transport across the Taiwan Strait. Fearful of subversion, the Taiwan government held off agreeing to upgrade communications.

5. The scale of Taiwan's investment in Taiwan was difficult to measure in 1992–93. *The Economist* estimated total investment at $15 billion to 25 billion. "Twixt Handshake and Armlock," *The Economist,* May 22, 1993, p. 73 (UK ed.).

6. Rajiv Chandra, "Cautious Hands across the Strait," Inter Press Service, April 14, 1993 (Lexis-Nexis).

7. John Hughes, "Taiwan Seeks a Place at the UN," *Christian Science Monitor,* September 16, 1993, p. 18.

8. Lee made the public announcement of the UN bid in a wide-ranging press conference on May 20, 1993, during which he welcomed the Dalai Lama to visit Taiwan, dismissed the importance of meeting with PRC leaders, and offered to "teach" them about accounting and taxation. See "Lee Teng-Hui Holds Press Conference on Third Anniversary of His Presidency," PR Newswire, Coordination Council for North American Affairs, New York (de facto ROC consulate), May 20, 1993; "Taiwan President Rejects Meeting with Chinese Leaders," Agence France-Presse, May 20, 1993.

9. Suisheng Zhao, "Military Coercion and Peaceful Offence: Beijing's Strategy of National Reunification with Taiwan," *Pacific Affairs*, vol. 72, no. 4 (Winter 1999–2000), p. 496.

10. Although most Western analysts believe that Beijing's acquisition of Russian Su-27 high-performance fighter aircraft in 1991 led to the U.S. decision to upgrade Taiwan's fighter force with F-16s, the Chinese have never accepted that logic.

11. Taiwan Mainland Affairs Council, "Explanation of Relations across the Taiwan Straits," published in *Chung Kuo Shih Pao* (China Times), July 6, 1994, p. 2; English translation in BBC Summary of World Broadcasts, FE/2047/S1, July 14, 1994. The PRC White Paper, "The Taiwan Question and Reunification of China" (http://english.peopledaily.com.cn/whitepaper/7.html, accessed February 2003).

12. James Mann, *About Face: A History of America's Curious Relationship with China, from Nixon to Clinton* (Alfred A. Knopf, 1999), p. 317.

13. Ibid., p. 315.

14. Interview with Winston Lord, April 2000; Central News Agency (Taiwan), "U.S. Official Says Treatment of Lee in Hawaii Was 'Courteous,'" May 19, 1994 (Lexis-Nexis). Lord is most likely the official quoted anonymously in the story.

15. Full text of letter in U.S. Newswire, "In Blunt Letter to Clinton Sen. Simon Proposes Side Sanctions on China MFN," May 20, 1994 (Lexis-Nexis).

16. The defense authorization bill with a Brown amendment on Taiwan passed 86-14. See also Central News Agency (Taiwan), "Senate Approves Brown Amendment for Taiwan," August 6, 1994. House Foreign Affairs Committee Chairman Lee

Hamilton supported the administration's opposition to Brown's amendments. The defense authorization bill (S. 2182), sec. 1073, reads, "It is the sense of Congress that no visa should be denied for a high-level official of Taiwan to enter the United States unless the official is otherwise excludable under the immigration laws of the United States" (www.thomas.loc.gov).

17. "Statement by the President on Signing Visa Waiver Pilot Program," October 24, 1994, available online at www.ibiblio.org/pub/archives/whitehouse-papers/1994/Oct/1994-10-25-President-on-Signing-Visa-Waiver-Pilot-Program, accessed February 2003.

18. Consistent with the "unofficial" nature of the relationship with Taiwan, Winston Lord's press briefing on the details of the Taiwan policy review was off the record and not transcribed. His meeting with Ding Mou-shih was held in the State Plaza Hotel, a block away from the State Department. Points presented are from various press accounts and my own recollection.

19. Jim Mann, "U.S. Slightly Elevates Ties with Taiwan," *Los Angeles Times,* September 8, 1994, p. A4.

20. Su Ge, *Meiguo duihua zhengce yu taiwan wenti* (American Policy toward China and the Taiwan Question) (Beijing: World Knowledge Publishing, 1999), p. 731.

21. Patrick E. Tyler, "China Warns U.S. on Relations with Taiwan," *New York Times,* September 11, 1994, p. A14; Jen Hui-wen, "CCP Hierarchy Works out New Policy towards Taiwan," *Hsin Pao* (Hong Kong), September 16, 1994, p. 46, BBC Summary of World Broadcasts, FE/2121/G, October 8, 1994 (Lexis-Nexis). Jen—one of the more cautious and reliable of the China-watchers in Hong Kong, in my view—claimed the word "explosive" had not been used with regard to Taiwan in more than fifteen years.

22. Sheila Tefft, "China Fumes over Upgraded U.S.-Taiwan Ties," *Christian Science Monitor,* September 14, 1994, p. 2 (Lexis-Nexis).

23. Li Tzu-ching, "Leftists Are Active Again," *Cheng Ming,* no. 201, July 1, 1994, pp. 14–15, in Foreign Broadcast Information Service (FBIS)-CHI-94-129, July 1, 1994.

24. Chen Shao-pin, "Liu Huaqing Says China Will Oppose Hegemonism and Will Not Seek Hegemony," *Ching Pao,* May 5, 1994, p. 62, in BBC Summary of World Broadcasts, FE/1996/G, May 13, 1994 (Lexis-Nexis).

25. Lo Ping and Li Tzu-ching, "The Chinese Military Meddles in Policy towards United States," *Cheng Ming,* May 1, 1994, pp. 10–12, in BBC Summary of World Broadcasts, FE/1996/G, May 13, 1994 (Lexis-Nexis).

26. Willy Wo-lap Lam, "Army Boosts Diplomatic Role," *South China Morning Post* (Hong Kong), July 29, 1994, p. 12 (Lexis-Nexis).

27. Jen Hui-wen, "Beijing Political Situation" column in *Hsin Pao* (Hong Kong), July 8, 1994, p. 23, BBC Summary of World Broadcasts, FE/2050/G in July 18, 1994. In announcing the de-linkage of MFN and human rights on May 26, President Clinton extended the "Tiananmen sanctions on the PLA and added a prohibition on the import of Chinese-manufactured guns and ammunition—particularly automatic weapons configured as "sport" rifles—into the United States." Lo Ping, "CCP Mili-

tary Attacks Ministry of Foreign Affairs," *Cheng Ming,* July 25, 1994, in BBC Summary of World Broadcasts, FE/2058/G, July 27, 1994 (Lexis-Nexis).

28. Jen Hui-wen, "CCP Hierarchy Works out New Policy towards Taiwan," *Hsin Pao* (Hong Kong), September 16, 1994, p. 46, BBC Summary of World Broadcasts, FE/2121/G, October 8, 1994 (Lexis-Nexis).

29. Jen Hui-wen, "Measures Taken by Jiang Zemin to Remove Hidden Troubles in Army," *Hsin Pao* (Hong Kong), December 23, 1994, in BBC Summary of World Broadcasts, FE/2187/G, December 28, 1994 (Lexis-Nexis).

30. Although China had always insisted that the missile U.S. officials called the M-11 fell beneath the 500kg/300km-payload-range parameters of the MTCR, and never admitted it had sold M-11s to Pakistan, Qian implicitly accepted the American argument that the missile had the "inherent capability" of exceeding them by virtue of its size and fuel capacity. He therefore agreed not to sell the missiles to any other country. See "U.S., China Reach New Accords on MTCR, Fissile Cutoff Issues," *Arms Control Today,* vol. 24, no. 9 (November 1994).

31. Elaine Sciolino, "U.S. Offers China Deal to Resolve a Missile Dispute," *New York Times,* November 14, 1994, p. 1.

32. Steven Mufson, "U.S. to Help China Retool Arms Plants; Perry Received as 'Old Friend' in Quest of Military Ties; Human Rights Discussed," *Washington Post,* October 18, 1994, p. A28.

33. The most thorough published account of the incident is in Jim Mann and Art Pine, "Faceoff between U.S. Ship, Chinese Sub Is Revealed," *Los Angeles Times*, December 14, 1994, p. A1.

34. John F. Harris and Thomas W. Lippman, "Chinese Watched as U.S. Navy Tracked Sub; No Protest Has Been Lodged," *Washington Post*, December 15, 1994, p. A42; Patrick E. Tyler, "As Deng Fades, China's Leaders Tighten Grip on Power," *New York Times,* December 19, 1994, p. 3.

35. See Kathy Chen, "Chinese Communists Turn Cautious in Attempt to Bolster Party's Influence," *Wall Street Journal*, September 29, 1994, p. A9.

36. I was a note taker at the meeting. See also "Background Briefing on China Bilateral Talks," White House Office of the Press Secretary, November 14, 1994 (www.ibiblio.org/pub/archives/whitehouse-papers/1994/Nov/1994-11-14-Backgrounder-on-Bilateral-Talks-with-China, accessed February 2003).

37. See Xinhua News Agency, "Jiang Zemin and Clinton Discuss Human Rights, Sino-U.S. Ties," November 14, 1994, BBC Summary of World Broadcasts, FE/2153/S2, November 15, 1994.

38. Harris and Lippman, "Chinese Watched as U.S. Navy Tracked Sub; No Protest Has Been Lodged; Beijing Has Withdrawn Invitation for Visit by Peña," *Washington Post*, December 15, 1994, p. A49.

39. Jiang Zemin, "Continue to Promote the Reunification of the Motherland," Xinhua News Agency, January 30, 1995, in FBIS-CHI-95-019.

40. Agence France-Presse, "China Poses Greater Military Threat to Taiwan: Chief-of-Staff," February 24, 1995; "Military Official Says Chinese Denial of Moving

Missiles Totally Unbelievable," Central News Agency, Taipei, in English 0206 GMT 3 Mar 95, BBC Summary of World Broadcasts, March 8, 1995, FE/2246/F.

41. Dennis Engbarth, "Taipei Sets Six-Point Policy on Mainland," *South China Morning Post*, April 9, 1995, p. 7.

42. Beijing Central People's Radio commentator, "The Six-Point Response Lacks Sincerity," April 18, 1995, 2200 GMT, in FBIS-CHI-95-076.

43. See Elizabeth Drew, *Showdown: The Struggle between the Gingrich Congress and the Clinton White House* (Simon and Schuster, 1996), chaps. 1 and 2.

44. Mann, *About Face*, p. 320; Simon Beck, "Taiwan out from under Its Shell," *South China Morning Post*, February 16, 1995, p. 19.

45. Brett C. Lippencott, "Congress Should Chart a Steady Course in U.S.-ROC Relations," Heritage Backgrounder Update no. 238, January 27, 1995.

46. Slobodan Lekic, "House Speaker Gingrich Calls for Taiwan to Be Readmitted to UN," Associated Press, February 3, 1995.

47. See, for example, "U.S. Congress Pushes Recognition of Taiwan," United Press International dispatch of February 9, 1995 (Lexis-Nexis).

48. See S. Con. Res. 9, March 6, 1995, "Expressing the sense of the Congress regarding a private visit by President Lee Teng-hui of the Republic of China on Taiwan to the United States" (www.thomas.loc.gov).

49. "Senior Republican Calls on Clinton to Allow Visit by Taiwan's President," Agence France-Presse, March 15, 1995 (Lexis-Nexis).

50. Daniel Williams, "China Finds 'Comprehensive Engagement' Hard to Grasp," *Washington Post,* February 13, 1995, p. A17; David E. Sanger, "U.S. Threatens $2.8 Billion of Tariffs on China Exports, *New York Times*, January 1, 1995, p. A14.

51. See Patrick E. Tyler, "Chinese Aide Conciliatory Despite 'Foolish' U.S. Stand on Rights," *New York Times*, March 11, 1995, p. A5.

52. Interviews with Stanley Roth, August 2000, and J. Stapleton Roy, May 2000.

53. H.R. 1450, "To amend the Taiwan Relations Act to permit visits to the United States by the elected leaders of the people of Taiwan or their elected representatives," April 6, 1995 (http://thomas.loc.gov/cgi-bin/query/z?c104:H.R.1460, accessed February 2003).

54. Interview with Samuel R. Berger, March 2001.

55. Interviews with W. Anthony Lake, August 2000, and Stanley Roth; Jim Mann, "How Taipei Outwitted U.S. Policy," *Los Angeles Times*, June 8, 1995, p. A1; Don Oberdorfer, "Juggling the Two Chinas," *Washington Post*, October 23, 1995, p. C4.

56. Interview with Samuel R. Berger.

57. Without doubt, it was naive to think we would be able to keep the story under wraps for more than a day or two. The Taiwan press in Washington is extremely competent, well-connected, and nearly hyperactive on the issues of concern to Taipei. As I heard the story reconstructed later, the president himself told several senators after he had signed the decision memo, and one of them evidently passed the news on to the Taiwan press.

58. Federal News Service, State Department regular briefing, May 22, 1995 (Lexis-Nexis).

59. Christopher had used the phraseology in testimony before a Senate committee in February 1995. Although he used the term again in his meeting with Qian, he also warned the Chinese strongly about congressional determination to change the administration's Taiwan policy, as did others (including Winston Lord, Stanley Roth, and myself) during that period. Subsequent Chinese complaints that Christopher misled them seem quite disingenuous.

60. Patrick E. Tyler, "Chinese Leader Says 'Mistakes' by Government Fueled Inflation," *New York Times*, March 6, 1995, p. A1.

61. Patrick E. Tyler, "Deng's Daughter Opens a Long-Shut Door," *New York Times*, January 13, 1995, p. A1.

62. See Steven Mufson, "Chinese Congress Vote Shows Surprising Dissension," *Washington Post,* March 18, 1995, p. A21; Patrick E. Tyler, "Old Soldier May Take Deng's Mantle," *New York Times,* May 15, 1995, p. A6.

63. Willy Wo-lap Lam, "Cutting to the Core," *South China Morning Post*, April 19, 1995, p. 17.

64. Su Ge, *Meiguo duihua Zhengce yu Taiwan wenti* (American Policy toward China and the Taiwan Question), p. 739; Rone Tempest, "China Threatens U.S. over Taiwan Leader's Visit," *Los Angeles Times*, May 26, 1995, p. A6.

65. Taking a leaf from the PRC's book on developing influence in Washington, Taiwan tried to time the signing of letters of intent to buy eight Boeing 777s by two Taiwan airlines so that it would take place just before Lee's arrival and become a major media event. Ultimately the deal—which was preliminary, at best—was witnessed by Transportation Secretary Federico Peña the day after Lee departed. See *Journal of Commerce*, "Boeing Announces UPS, Taiwan Deals," June 13, 1995, p. 2B.

66. Lee Teng-hui, "Always in My Heart," Spencer T. and Ann W. Olin Lecture delivered at Cornell University alumni reunion (www.news.cornell.edu/campus/Lee/Lee_Speech.html, accessed February 2003).

67. Xinhua News Agency, "State Council Office Cancels 2nd Round of Wang-Koo Talks," June 16, 1995, in BBC Summary of World Broadcasts, FE/2333/G, June 19, 1995.

68. "Coercive diplomacy" is generally defined as an effort "to back a demand on an adversary with a threat of punishment for non-compliance that will be credible and potent enough to persuade him that it is in his interest to comply with the demand . . . [C]oercive diplomacy is essentially a diplomatic strategy, one that relies on the threat of force rather than the use of force to achieve the objective. If force must be used to strengthen diplomatic efforts at persuasion, it is employed in an exemplary manner . . . to demonstrate resolution and willingness to escalate to high levels of military action if necessary." See Alexander L. George and William E. Simon, *The Limits of Coercive Diplomacy* (Boulder, Colo.: Westview Press, 1994), p. 2.

69. Lo Ping, "There Are Serious Disputes among the Party, Government and Military on Policy towards United States and Taiwan," *Cheng Ming* (Hong Kong), July 1, 1995, p. 8, in BBC Summary of World Broadcasts, FE/2358/G, July 18, 1995.

See also Willy Wo-lap Lam, *The Era of Jiang Zemin* (Singapore: Prentice Hall, 1999), pp. 173–74.

70. Cheng Li and Lynn White, "The Army in the Succession to Deng Xiaoping: Familiar Fealties and Technocratic Trends," *Asian Survey*, vol. 33, no. 8 (August 1993), pp. 758–59.

71. China announces a defense budget figure every year as part of the report to the National People's Congress by the minister of finance. The numbers given are considered by most analysts to be only a fraction of actual military expenditures in China, although no methodology has been devised to provide a more accurate figure. The budget numbers are thought to be representative of overall trends in military expenditures, so if the figure is 12 percent higher than the previous year, it is generally accepted that PLA spending rose by that proportion.

72. David Shambaugh, "China's Commander-in-Chief: Jiang Zemin and the PLA," in Dennison Lane, Mark Weisenbloom, and Dimon Liu, eds., *Chinese Military Modernization* (Washington: American Enterprise Institute Press, 1996), p. 233.

73. At the risk of stereotyping and overgeneralizing, PLA officers who made it to the top ranks during Deng's generation and the succeeding one shared some character traits that affected how they operated politically. They were not well educated, valued bravery in battle and candor among peers, demonstrated and expected high degrees of personal loyalty, and were not highly rank conscious (ranks were introduced in the PLA in 1955, abolished during the Cultural Revolution, and restored in the mid-1970s). Politically, they tended to be conservative, valuing order and structure and holding fast to Maoist ideological tenets long after many others had abandoned them. They were strongly nationalistic, to the point of xenophobia. As the PLA has modernized and professionalized, the officer corps has become better educated and more sophisticated about a rapidly changing set of expectations and requirements. But to the degree that the PLA remains predominantly a ground-force army made up of conscripts from China's overwhelmingly rural population, some of these characteristics are still applicable.

74. Jen Hui-wen, "Measures Taken by Jiang Zemin to Remove Hidden Troubles in Army," *Hsin Pao* (Hong Kong), December 21, 1994, in BBC Summary of World Broadcasts, FE/2187/G, December 28, 1994; and Jen Hui-wen, "Jiang Zemin's Concept 'It Is First Necessary to Stabilize the Army in Order to Stabilize Political Power,'" *Hsin Pao* (Hong Kong), May 24, 1995, in BBC Summary of World Broadcasts, FE/2358/G, July 18, 1995.

75. Lam, *The Era of Jiang Zemin*, p. 173.

76. Lo Ping, "There Are Serious Disputes among the Party, Government and Military on Policy towards United States and Taiwan," *Cheng Ming* (Hong Kong), July 1, 1995, pp. 8–10, in BBC Summary of World Broadcasts, FE/2358/G, July 18, 1995.

77. The relationship between the Taiwan Affairs Leading Small Group (TALSG), the Central Committee's Taiwan Work Office (TWO), and the State Council's Taiwan Affairs Office (TAO) is not easy to describe, especially since the regime does not publicize the activities or membership of internal party work groups. Generally, au-

thority descends through the list, with the TALSG being under the Politburo Standing Committee, the TWO probably being under the Central Committee Secretariat, and the TAO being overseen by the premier of the State Council. Although staffs probably do not overlap, the leading member(s) of each subordinate organization belongs to the one above it.

78. Michael Swaine, "Chinese Decision-Making Regarding Taiwan, 1979–2000," in David M. Lampton, ed., *The Making of Chinese Foreign and Security Policy in the Era of Reform* (Stanford University Press, 2001), p. 300.

79. Lam, *The Era of Jiang Zemin*, p. 174; Willy Wo-lap Lam, "Army Takes over Policy," *South China Morning Post*, March 12, 1996, p. 11; Ken E. Gause, "China's Policy toward Taiwan," *Jane's Intelligence Review*, vol. 7, no. 12, (December 1995).

80. Swaine, "Chinese Decision-Making Regarding Taiwan," pp. 323–25; Wen Min, "Beijing's New Taiwan Policy: Use a Little Force if Necessary," *Apple Daily* (Hong Kong), July 19, 1995, p. 1, in BBC Summary of World Broadcasts, FE/2362/G, July 22, 1995; Lam, *The Era of Jiang Zemin*, p. 176.

81. Taiwan still garrisons and controls two small island groups just off the coast of Fujian Province. The largest is Chin-men (also rendered Jinmen, Kinmen, or Quemoy), one of twelve islands located off the PRC port of Xiamen, having a population of about 43,000, mostly Taiwan military forces and their dependents. The other major group is Matsu (also known as Mazu or Nankan), nineteen small islands just off the Min River estuary, with a total population of less than 5,000. Both the main islands are heavily fortified, but some of the small islands, such as Tung-chiu and Wu-chiu, have garrison forces of only a few hundred. China has threatened on a few occasions to recover these islands by force, particularly in 1958, when it began a major artillery bombardment of the garrisons at Chin-men and Matsu. Although the shelling and propaganda attacks have long since ceased, most military analysts view the larger islands as vulnerable to a determined PRC attack, and the smaller islands as indefensible.

82. Lu Te-yung, "Table of Mainland China's Group Army and Major Naval and Air Exercises since 1993," *Lien Ho Pao* (Hong Kong/Taiwan), July 3, 1995, p. 1, in BBC Summary of World Broadcasts, FE/2347/G, July 5, 1995. Xinhua acknowledged the exercise was going on but gave no details.

83. "PLA Announces Missile Launch Training on East China Sea," Xinhua News Agency, no. 0718139, July 18, 1995.

84. "Taiwan Appeals for Calm after China Announces Missile Exercise," Agence France-Presse, July 19, 1995 (Lexis-Nexis).

85. Press spokesman David Johnson, as quoted by Deutsche Presse-Agentur on July 21, 1995 (Lexis-Nexis).

86. David A. Fulghum and Michael Mecham, "Chinese Tests Stun Neighbors," *Aviation Week and Space Technology*, vol. 143, no. 5 (July 31, 1995), p. 23; "China Test-Fires Two More Missiles," Associated Press, July 25, 1995 (Lexis-Nexis).

87. Federal News Service, "Foreign Press Center Briefing with Winston Lord," July 24, 1995, p. 5. Critics would later charge this low-key response and reiteration of China's insistence that the tests were "normal" and not directed at Taiwan served to

encourage Beijing to undertake a more adventuresome course the following year. There is no particularly good reason to believe that a stronger U.S. response to the tests would have had any deterrent effect on Beijing's military exercise plans, however.

88. From Lee Teng-hui's "State of the Nation" address to the National Assembly, July 27, 1995, in BBC Summary of World Broadcasts, FE/2372/F, August 3, 1995; Willy Wo-lap Lam, "Lee Urges Military Buildup," *South China Morning Post*, July 28, 1995, p. 1.

89. "Second Wave of Exercise Fails to Attain Expected Objectives, Beijing Makes Follow-up Plans to Exert Pressure," *Lien Ho Pao* (Hong Kong), August 24, 1995, p. 1, in BBC Summary of World Broadcasts, EE/D2391/F, August 25, 1995.

90. Elaine Sciolino, "C.I.A. Report Says Chinese Sent Iran Arms Components," *New York Times*, June 22, 1995, p. A1.

91. R. Jeffrey Smith and David B. Ottaway, "Spy Photos Suggest China Missile Trade; Pressure for Sanctions Builds over Evidence That Pakistan Has M-11s," *Washington Post*, July 3, 1995, p. A1.

92. Martin Sieff, "U.S. Probes China on Missiles; Pakistan Sale May Trigger Sanctions," *Washington Times*, July 4, 1995, p. A1.

93. See Steven Mufson, "China Acknowledges Holding American," *Washington Post*, June 28, 1995, p. A25.

94. Harry (Hongda) Wu, *Laogai: The Chinese Gulag*, Ted Slingerland, trans. (Boulder, Colo.: Westview Press, 1992).

95. By 1994 the accuracy of Wu's charges was being called into question not only by the Chinese government, but also by some Western experts and analysts. U.S. Customs investigations of several facilities accused of being prison labor exporters found the charges to be unfounded. In my recollection, intelligence analysts advised privately that some of the information Wu cataloged in his book was outdated or inaccurate. Concerns were raised even by those who supported his work that Wu was exaggerating his information and taking unnecessary risks in order to prove ever more sensational charges. See Jonathan Spence, "The Risks of Witness," *New York Review of Books*, December 19, 1996, p. 50ff; Emily MacFarquhar, "Inside the Chinese Gulag," *New York Times Book Review*, November 10, 1996, p. 24.

96. Harry Wu, with George Vecsey, *Troublemaker: One Man's Crusade against China's Cruelty* (Times Books, 1996), p. 205; Elaine Sciolino, "U.S. Says It Warned Wu about Earlier Trip to China," *New York Times*, July 14, 1995, p. A6.

97. Wendy Koch, "U.S. Says China Misled It on Scholar's Whereabouts," *San Francisco Examiner*, July 4, 1995, p. A12.

98. Wu, *Troublemaker*, p. 44.

99. Xinhua News Agency, no. 0708066, July 8, 1995. It has become evident over the years that "espionage" *(jiandie)*, in China's perspective, does not necessarily entail working for a foreign government. Foreign news organizations, human rights organizations, and church groups can be the sponsors of the stealing of China's "state secrets."

100. Ministry of Foreign Affairs press spokesman Chen Jian, as quoted by Kyodo News International, "China Blasts U.S. for Diverting Attention," July 10, 1995 (Lexis-Nexis).

101. Xinhua News Agency, "U.S. Urged to Correct Its Mistakes, According to Chinese Premier," no. 0704233, July 4, 1995.

102. Federal News Service, Prepared Statement of the Honorable Henry A. Kissinger before the Senate Foreign Relations Committee, July 13, 1995 (Lexis-Nexis); Sid Balman Jr., "Kissinger: Wu Won't Be Freed Soon," United Press International, July 13, 1995.

103. From my own recollection of the July 13, 1995, meeting between Kissinger and Clinton, at which I was note taker.

104. These were confirmed publicly on October 2, 1995, by State Department spokesman Nicholas Burns. See Federal News Service, State Department briefing, October 2, 1995, transcript, p. 5 (Lexis-Nexis).

105. Presidential correspondence is an enormous undertaking that involves the coordinated efforts of several different offices within the White House. Routine correspondence with other foreign leaders—acknowledging national celebrations, anniversaries, advocating cooperation on international treaties, and more—usually is drafted by the State Department and routed through the NSC staff to the president's staff assistant for correspondence. Most such letters are autopenned, with an electronic version sent through the U.S. Embassy and the hard copy sent through the diplomatic pouch. More personal, issue-related correspondence is prepared by the NSC staff. Staffers may consult with other bureaucracies on the content of the message, but private presidential correspondence is carefully protected. The secretary of state will be shown copies of important correspondence, but copies are not routed through the department, largely out of concern for confidentiality. Final copies are generally signed by hand, and delivery may be through pouch, through the Washington embassy of the country concerned, or by personal courier. If speed is required, the White House Situation Room has electronic message capability and authority to transmit messages either through State Department or CIA channels.

106. See, for example, John W. Garver, *Face Off: China, the United States, and Taiwan's Democratization* (University of Washington Press, 1997), pp. 79–80; and Mann, *About Face*, p. 330.

107. The best resource on the terminological arcana of the U.S. "one China" policy—a source of considerable confusion—is Shirley A. Kan's Congressional Research Service Study RL30341, "China/Taiwan: Evolution of the 'One China' Policy—Key Statements from Washington, Beijing, and Taipei," March 12, 2001 (http://cnie.org/NLE/CRSreports/international/inter-71.cfm, accessed February 2003). She quotes Mann and Garver on the text of the July 1995 letter, however.

108. Xinhua version of Jiang's interview with Elizabeth Farnsworth of PBS, October 24, 1995, BBC Summary of World Broadcasts, EE/D2444/G, October 25, 1995 (emphasis added).

109. Warren Christopher, "U.S. National Interest in the Asia-Pacific Region," address to the National Press Club, July 28, 1995 (www.state.gov/www/regions/eap/950728.html, accessed February 2003).

110. Quoted by Martin Sieff, "Clinton Writes to Qian but Seeks No Summit," *Washington Times*, July 31, 1995, p. A17. The letter was to Jiang, delivered through Qian.

111. On Clinton's dislike of state visits, see Donnie Radcliffe, "Stomp on Pomp; Clinton Scuttles Lavish White House Affairs in Favor of 'Working' Visits," *Washington Post*, June 15, 1993, p. B1; interview with Stanley Roth.

112. See, for example, Todd S. Purdum, "Hard Choice for the White House on Hillary Clinton and China," *New York Times*, August 17, 1995, p. A1.

113. The e-mail was released to the public in connection with Anthony Lake's hearings on his nomination to be director of central intelligence. A full text is included in Stephen Labaton, "Clinton and Gore Received Warnings on Asian Donors," *New York Times*, February 15, 1997, p. A1.

114. Christopher Drew, "How Donor with Asian Ties Knitted Access and Success," *New York Times*, February 22, 1997, p. A1.

115. This memo was also released publicly in February 1997 and widely quoted in the press. See, for example, Nancy Gibbs, "Cash and Carry Diplomacy," *Time magazine*, February 17, 1997 (http://asia.cnn.com/ALLPOLITICS/1997/02/17/time/whitehousedonors.html, accessed February 2003).

116. William Rempel, "How Big Clinton Contributor Turned into Freelance Envoy," *Los Angeles Times*, March 2, 1997, p. A1; see also Federal Document Clearing House, "Johnny Chung Testifies before House Governmental Affairs Committee," May 11, 1999, transcript, p. 29. Although there is ample reason to distrust Chung, who dribbled out various pieces of his story as federal prosecutors closed in on him, his account of his involvement in the Harry Wu case, at least, seems credible.

117. "The China Policy Act of 1995," H.R. 2053(http://thomas.loc.gov/cgi-bin/query/z?c104:H.R.2053:, accessed February 2003).

118. Xinhua News Agency, "Cold War Thinking, Hegemonic Logic," unsigned commentary, no. 0823251, August 23, 1995 (Lexis-Nexis).

119. Xinhua domestic news, August 24, 1995, BBC Summary of World Broadcasts, EE/D/2391/G, August 25, 1995.

120. Michael Laris, "China Convicts American of Spying; Human Rights Activist Harry Wu Sentenced to 15 Years, Expulsion from Country," *Washington Post*, August 24, 1995, p. A1.

121. For Tarnoff's optimism, see Steven Mufson, "Clinton May Meet with Chinese Leader in U.S.," *Washington Post*, August 28, 1995, p. 20; for the Chinese reaction, see Xinhua's account of MFA press spokesman Chen Jian's remarks, August 29, 1995, in BBC Summary of World Broadcasts, EE/D2396/G, August 31, 1995 (Lexis-Nexis).

122. Most reporting on Beidaihe discussions comes from Hong Kong publications that are not always reliable reporters of political dynamics in China. Sources for the judgment on 1995 Beidaihe discussions include Hong Kong's *Ming Pao* and *Hsin Pao,* both of which generally are considered somewhat better informed.

123. Federal News Service, State Department briefing, September 18, 1995 (Lexis-Nexis).

124. "First Lady's Address to the UN Conference on Women in Beijing," Federal Documents Clearing House, September 5, 1995 (Lexis-Nexis).

125. "China Calls Hillary's Human Rights Criticisms 'Unwarranted,'" Deutsche Presse-Agentur, September 7, 1995.

126. Elaine Sciolino, "No Appetite in Washington for a State Dinner Now," *New York Times*, October 1, 1995, p. A10.

127. Kathy Wilhelm, "China Says United States Has Agreed to Limit Taiwan Visits," Associated Press wire report, October 2, 1995 (Lexis-Nexis).

128. Elaine Sciolino, "China Cancels a Sale to Iran, Pleasing U.S.," *New York Times*, September 28, 1995, p. A1; Christopher S. Wren, "Mixed Signals over Status of Iran Deal," *New York Times,* September 30, 1995, p. A4.

129. Nicholas Burns, State Department briefing, October 4, 1995, provided by Federal Information Systems Corporation (Lexis-Nexis).

130. "Communiqué of the Fifth Plenum of the Fourteenth Central Committee of the Communist Party of China," Xinhua News Agency, no. 0928131, September 28, 1995.

131. Willy Wo-lap Lam, "Triumph Tempered by Failure to Hasten Retirement of Generals Loyal to Patriarch," *South China Morning Post*, September 29, 1995, p. 10. Lam judged that Wang Ruilin had "crossed over" to Jiang's side.

132. "Jiang Appears at War Games," *Financial Times*, October 19, 1995, p. 6; Tan Tarn How, "Military Exercises 'Show China Would Use Force over Taiwan if Needed,'" *Straits Times* (Singapore), October 20, 1995, p. 1.

133. See "Press Briefing by Assistant Secretary of State for East Asian and Pacific Affairs Winston Lord and Director of Asian Affairs Robert Suettinger, October 24, 1995 (http://clinton6.nara.gov/1995/10/1995-10-24-briefing-by-winston-lord-and-bob-suettinger-nyc.html, accessed February 2003).

134. Steven Mufson, "Why Is China Taking on World by Trying Dissident?" *Washington Post*, December 12, 1995, p. A27; "China Sentences Democracy Advocate; 14-Year Prison Term Elicits Condemnation from U.S. and Human Rights Groups," *Washington Post,* December 14, 1995, p. A31.

135. David E. Sanger, "U.S. Again Tries a Trade Issue as a Carrot and Stick for Beijing," *New York Times*, December 14, 1995, p. A7.

136. "Press Briefing by Assistant Secretary of State for East Asian and Pacific Affairs Winston Lord and Director of Asian Affairs Robert Suettinger," October 24, 1995.

137. "Taiwan Holds Military Drill," United Press International, October 5, 1995.

138. Jen Hui-wen, "CCP Specially Sets up Headquarters to Plan Military Exercises Targeting Taiwan," *Hsin Pao* (Hong Kong), December 22, 1995, p. 9, in BBC Summary of World Broadcasts, FE/D2499/F, January 3, 1996; "Chinese Leaders 'More Pragmatic' towards Taiwan," *Hsin Pao* (Hong Kong), October 27, 1995, p. 18, in BBC Summary of World Broadcasts, EE/D2446/F, October 27, 1995; "Chinese Military Suggests Moderate Use of Force to Compel Taiwan to Give up Presidential Election Next Year," *Lien Ho Pao* (Hong Kong), November 5, 1995, p. 1, in BBC Summary of World Broadcasts, EE/D454/F, November 6, 1995; Fang Hsiao-yi, "Taiwan Experts Say Beijing Will Not Tolerate Expansion of Pro-Taiwan Indepen-

dence Forces," *Wen Wei Po* (Hong Kong pro-PRC journal), November 27, 1995, p. A1, BBC Summary of World Broadcasts, EE/D2473/G, November 28, 1995.

139. Patrick E. Tyler, "China Warns U.S. Again on Taiwan," *New York Times*, November 11, 1995, p. A6; "Chinese Defense Minister, U.S. Assistant Secretary Support Dialogue," Xinhua News Agency, November 17, 1995, BBC Summary of World Broadcasts, EE/D2465/G, November 19, 1995.

140. Nye's reference to what he told the Chinese quoted in R. Jeffrey Smith, "China Plans Maneuvers off Taiwan; Big Military Exercise Is Meant to Intimidate, U.S. Officials Say," *Washington Post*, February 5, 1996, p. A1.

141. "U.S. Warns against 'Serious Mistake' over Taiwan," Kyodo News Agency, November 17, 1995, Information Access Company, November 20, 1995 (Lexis-Nexis).

142. Clinton's last-minute decision not to attend the Osaka meeting was precipitated by the failure of congressional and administration leaders to come to agreement on various budget issues. Budget disputes were nothing new, and Congress usually passed "continuing resolutions" to keep the government running while negotiations proceeded. In 1995 the process broke down, largely because the Gingrich-led Republican majority in the House was trying to legislate through appropriation bills, adding riders and amendments that forced policies on the administration. Clinton chose to shut down the government in November rather than seek a new continuing resolution or compromise on his budget plans. See Elizabeth Drew, *Showdown: The Struggle between the Gingrich Congress and the Clinton White House* (Simon and Schuster, 1996), chap. 23.

143. See, for example, Fang Hsiao-yi, "Taiwan Experts Say Beijing Will Not Tolerate Expansion of Pro-Taiwan Independence Forces; Military Exercises Manifest Determination to Check Separatism," *Wen Wei Po* (a pro-PRC daily in Hong Kong), November 26, 1995, translated in BBC Summary of World Broadcasts, EE/D2473/G, November 28, 1995.

144. Agnes Cheung, "Taiwan Votes for Peace; KMT Retains Its Majority but the Breakaway New Party Capitalises on Rising Desire for Reconciliation with Beijing," *South China Morning Post*, December 3, 1995, p. 1; "Now, a Third Force; in a Key Election, China's Influence Boosts the New Party," *Asiaweek* magazine, December 15, 1995, p. 29.

145. The tenth Panchen Lama's death in 1989 had set in motion a process of searching for the successor, a boy who possessed the incarnated spirit of the deceased leader. By unwritten agreement, this process was supervised by Tibet's second-largest monastery, the Tashilhunpo Monastery in Shigatse, Qinghai Province, with the approval of both the Chinese government and the Dalai Lama. After a six-year search, the monastery selected its candidates and consulted first with the Dalai Lama secretly to get his approval. In May 1995 the Dalai Lama announced that a six-year-old boy named Gedhum Choekyi Nyima would be the eleventh Panchen Lama. Outraged at being cut out of the process, Beijing set aside the choice and detained the Tashilhunpo abbot in charge as well as the boy and his family. It then convened a large group of monks in November 1995, had them select from three other candi-

dates by lottery, and declared the winner, Gyancain Norbu, to be the eleventh Panchen Lama. The legitimacy of Beijing's choice and the fate of the Dalai Lama's choice have been extremely sensitive issues ever since, worsening already poor relations between the Beijing government and Tibet's government in exile in Dharmsala.

146. George Gedda, "U.S. Tells China of Its 'Grave Disappointment,'" Associated Press, December 14, 1995.

147. David E. Sanger, "U.S. Reopens Trade Dispute, Saying China Ignores Piracy," *New York Times*, December 1, 1995, p. D1.

148. See, for example, He Chong, "PRC Military Exercises 'Contain' Independence Forces," *Zhongguo Tongxun She* (China News Service, Hong Kong), March 24, 1996, in FBIS-CHI-96-058.

149. Robert Ross, "The 1995–1996 Taiwan Strait Confrontation: Coercion, Credibility, and the Use of Force" *International Security*, vol. 25 (Fall 2000), p. 89.

150. Suisheng Zhao, "Military Coercion and Peaceful Offence: Beijing's Strategy of National Reunification with Taiwan," *Pacific Affairs*, vol. 72, no 4 (Winter 1999/2000), p. 502.

151. See Yue Ren, "China's Dilemma in Cross-Strait Crisis Management," *Asian Affairs, An American Review*, vol. 24, no. 3 (Fall 1997), p. 135ff.

152. Interview with Charles W. Freeman Jr., October 2000.

153. Interview with Anthony Lake.

154. Ibid.; Barton Gellman, "Reappraisal Led to New China Policy," *Washington Post*, June 22, 1998, p. A1.

155. Interviews with Sandra J. Kristoff, September 2000, and Anthony Lake. There had been pressure for Lake to become more involved in China policy for some time, from within the NSC, from other segments of the foreign policy establishment unhappy with State's stewardship of the relationship, and from the academic community. Lake finally stopped resisting the pressure in late 1995 but was still highly sensitive to any appearance of trying to usurp Christopher's authority. For a general discussion of the topic of NSC's involvement in China policy, see "China Policy and the National Security Council," an Oral History Roundtable (Center for International and Security Studies, University of Maryland, and Brookings Institution, 2001), pp. 36–40.

156. Interview with Charles W. Freeman Jr.; Patrick Tyler, "As China Threatens Taiwan, It Makes Sure U.S. Listens," *New York Times*, January 24, 1996, p. A3.

157. Gellman, "Reappraisal Led to New China Policy."

158. Conversation with Admiral Joseph Prueher; interview with Kurt Campbell, November 2000.

159. Bill Gertz, "China Nuclear Transfer Exposed; Hill Expected to Urge Sanctions," *Washington Times*, February 5, 1996, p. A1.

160. R. Jeffrey Smith and Ann Devroy, "U.S. to Seek Closer Ties with China; More High-Level Talks Contemplated between Top Officials This Spring," *Washington Post*, February 21, 1996, p. A27.

161. Recollections of this meeting vary among participants, and I cannot even confirm its exact date, even though I attended it. Its content has been alluded to in

Patrick Tyler, *A Great Wall: Six Presidents and China* (New York: Century Foundation, 1999), pp. 21–22, who believed it took place in early March. Tyler's account has some inconsistencies, however, and conflates the outcome of several different meetings. Joint Chiefs' contingency planning for a Taiwan scenario was leaked to the *Washington Times* and published in a story by Bill Gertz, "Shalikashvili Doubts Invasion of Taiwan; China Can't Put Troops across Strait," February 16, 1996, p. A1.

162. "Ground-to-Ground Missile Test Coordinates Announced," Xinhua News Agency, March 5, 1996, in BBC Summary of World Broadcasts, EE/D2553/G, March 5, 1996.

163. Joyce Chiang, "Taiwan Bourse Reels under Chinese Missile Test Plan," Agence France-Presse, March 6, 1996.

164. Keith B. Richburg, "China Fires Missiles into Sea near Taiwan; Target Areas Are Close to Busy Port Cities," *Washington Post*, March 8, 1996, p. 23; Tan Tarn How, "Qian Tells Taiwan People Not to Panic While Some Others Are Concerned," *Straits Times* (Singapore), March 9, 1996, p. 1 (Lexis-Nexis).

165. Keith B. Richburg, "Of Missiles and Chinese Mind Games," *Washington Post*, March 7, 1996, p. A24.

166. See State Department and White House press briefings, March 5, 1996; Perry's comment quoted in Agence France-Presse, "Perry Says Beijing Makes a 'Very Bad Mistake' with Taiwan Maneuvers," March 5, 1996; GOP statement in congressional press release, "House GOP Unambiguous in Support for Defending Taiwan against Invasion Threat," Federal Document Clearing House, March 5, 1996.

167. *Jane's Defence Weekly*, vol. 25, no. 11 (March 13, 1996), p. 11.

168. Robert Burns, "Navy Ships, Air Force Spy Plane Monitor Chinese Missile Tests," Associated Press, March 9, 1996.

169. See Ashton B. Carter and William J. Perry, *Preventive Defense: A New Security Strategy for America* (Brookings, 1999), pp. 92–97; Tyler, *A Great Wall*, pp. 31–32; Barton Gellman, "U.S. and China Nearly Came to Blows in '96; Tension over Taiwan Prompted Repair of Ties," *Washington Post*, June 21, 1998, p. A1.

170. Carter and Perry, *Preventive Defense*, pp. 97–99; Tyler, *A Great Wall*, pp. 34–35; Gellman, "U.S. and China Nearly Came to Blows in '96"; interviews with Anthony Lake, Samuel R. Berger, Winston Lord, and Kurt Campbell.

171. Interviews in note 170.

172. Department of State press release, "March 10: Secretary Christopher Interview on 'Meet the Press'" (www.state.gov/www/current/debate/mar96_china_us_troops.html, accessed February 2003).

173. Captain Michael Doubleday, DOD news briefing, March 12, 1996, Federal Document Clearing House (Lexis-Nexis).

174. China Central Television, March 11, 1996, transcript in BBC Summary of World Broadcasts, EE/D2558/G, March 11, 1996. Qian's point about those calling for "defense of Taiwan" is a reference to H. Con. Res. 148, introduced on March 7, which proposed the United States should "assist in defending" Taiwan against "in-

vasion, missile attack, or blockade by the People's Republic of China" (www.thomas.loc.gov).

175. China Central Television, March 11, 1996, BBC Summary of World Broadcasts, EE/D2559/S1, March 11, 1996.

176. Richard Ingham, "China Doubles Numbers in Drill, Fires Missile; Taiwan Boosts Patrols," Agence France-Press, March 13, 1996 (Lexis-Nexis).

177. Liu Yue-ying, "Generals of Three Forces Comment on Movement of U.S. Aircraft Carriers," *Ta Kung Pao* (Hong Kong), March 13, 1996, p. A2, in FBIS-CHI-96-050, March 13, 1996.

178. Robert Burns, "Shalikashvili: Chinese War Games a Dry Run," Associated Press, March 12, 1996; Winston Lord on *The NewsHour with Jim Lehrer*, March 11, 1996, transcript 5481; Kurt Campbell testimony before the House International Relations Committee, March 12, 1996 (www.fas.org/news/taiwan/1996/960314-taiwan-usia2.htm, accessed February 2003); Ed Offley, "U.S. Navy Takes on a Delicate Role near Taiwan," *Seattle Post-Intelligencer*, March 14, 1996, p. A2.

179. The meeting was confirmed by the State Department spokesman on May 3, 1996, after it had been reported in the Taiwan press. Subsequent meetings, at the insistence of both the U.S. State Department and Taiwan's Ministry of Foreign Affairs, included participants from AIT and TECRO.

180. Principal points as I recall them.

181. China Central Television, March 17, 1996, in BBC Summary of World Broadcasts, EE/D2564/S1, March 18, 1996; Patrick E. Tyler, "China Warns U.S. to Keep away from Taiwan Strait," *New York Times*, March 18, 1996, p. A3.

182. Steven Mufson, "China Blasts U.S. for Dispatching Warship Groups; Beijing Resumes Maneuvers near Outlying Taiwanese Island," *Washington Post*, March 20, 1996, p. A21. The *Nimitz* had sailed through the Strait in December 1995 en route to Hong Kong, apparently without PRC military authorities realizing it had done so. Although the U.S. Navy had chosen that route for weather reasons, most observers, particularly in China and Taiwan, believed the passage was intended to be a show of force.

183. Tze Li, "Li Peng Issues a Warning; Perry Slaps His Own Face," *Ta Kung Pao*, March 19, 1996, p. A7, in FBIS-CHI-96-054, March 19, 1996.

184. Martin Sieff, "Verbal War Heats up over Taiwan; Perry Flaunts U.S. Naval Power," *Washington Times*, March 20, 1996, p. A1.

185. United Press International, "Invaders Face Chinese 'Sea of Fire,'" March 21, 1996 (Lexis-Nexis).

186. Elaine Sciolino, "White House Snubs China over Military Maneuvers," *New York Times*, March 23, 1996, p. A5.

187. H. Con. Res. 148, passed 369-14 on March 19, 1996 (http://thomas.loc.gov, accessed November 8, 2000 [emphasis added]).

188. Quoted in Tan Tarn How, "Beijing Tells U.S. to Stop Interfering 'Immediately,'" *Straits Times* (Singapore), March 20, 1996, p. 11 (Lexis-Nexis).

189. See his testimony before the East Asian and Pacific Subcommittee of the Senate Foreign Relations Committee, October 11, 1995, provided by Federal News Service (Lexis-Nexis).

190. See, for example, Defense Department briefing, "Remarks by Assistant Secretary of Defense Joseph Nye at Asia Society Washington Center," December 12, 1995, from Federal News Service (Lexis-Nexis); Winston Lord, "Testimony before House Subcommittee on Asia and the Pacific Hearing on 'Military Stability in the Taiwan Straits,'" March 12, 1996, from Federal News Service (Lexis-Nexis). Lord appealed to members of Congress to help him "stamp out" the use of the term.

191. Liu Huinian, Huang Qiusheng, and Cao Zhi, "Our Army Has Successfully Conducted Joint War Games of the Three Services in the Taiwan Strait," Xinhua News Agency, March 25, 1996, in BBC Summary of World Broadcasts, EE/D2571/F, March 26, 1996.

192. Steven Mufson, "China Plans Live-Ammunition Tests; Naval and Air Maneuvers Could Add Pressure before Taiwan's Vote," *Washington Post*, March 10, 1996, p. A20.

193. Sarah Jackson-Han, "Top Chinese Minister Gives Mixed Message on Taiwan," Agence France-Presse, March 11, 1996; Patrick E. Tyler, "China Signaling U.S. That It Will Not Invade Taiwan," *New York Times*, March 13, 1996, p. A3.

194. Patrick E. Tyler, "Taiwan's Leader Wins Its Elections and a Mandate," *New York Times*, March 24, 1996, p. A1.

195. See, for example, He Chong, "Chinese Military Exercises Contain 'Taiwan Independence' Forces," *Zhongguo Tongxun She* (China News Agency, Hong Kong), March 24, 1996, in FBIS-CHI-96-058, March 24, 1996.

196. Jiang told a group of visiting Japanese that the American carriers "lacked courage" to cross the centerline of the Taiwan Strait. "If the U.S. aircraft carriers come again, China will continue its military exercises," Jiang said, implying that the curtailment of the missile tests may have been related to the carrier deployment. See Kyodo News Service, "Jiang Tells Japanese Guests U.S. Lacks Courage," April 4, 1996 (Lexis-Nexis). Internally, Chinese officials subsequently spread the word that the carrier battle groups were deterred from entering the Strait by the activities of Chinese submarines. See Su Ge, *Meiguo duihua zhengce yu taiwan wenti* (American Policy toward China and the Taiwan Question), p. 750. In fact, the Pentagon had decided from the outset not to enter the Strait.

197. See, in particular, footnotes citing interviews with unnamed Chinese officials in Ross, "Coercion," pp. 92–95.

198. Vivian Pik-kwan Chan, "Lee Offers 'Journey of Peace' to Mainland," *South China Morning Post* (Hong Kong), May 20, 1996, p. 1.

199. See, for example, Willy Wo-lap Lam, "Diplomatic Folly," *South China Morning Post* (Hong Kong), March 27, 1996, p. 21; "Cadres Divided on Next Policy Move," *South China Morning Post* (Hong Kong), March 28, 1996, p. 10.

200. You Ji, "Changing Leadership Consensus: The Domestic Context of War Games," in Suisheng Zhao, ed., *Across the Taiwan Strait: Mainland China, Taiwan and the 1995–1996 Crisis* (London: Routledge, 1999), p. 79.

201. See Robert G. Sutter, "China Policy: Crisis over Taiwan, 1995—A Post-Mortem," Congressional Research Service Report for Congress, 95-1173 F, December 5, 1995 (www.fas.org/spp/starwars/crs/95-1173f.htm, accessed February 2003).

Notes to Chapter 7

1. "Chinese Work Conference on Taiwan Ends," *Zhongguo Xinwen She* (China News Agency, Hong Kong), April 29, 1996, BBC Summary of World Broadcasts, EE/D2600/F, April 30, 1996.

2. Suisheng Zhao, "Changing Leadership Perceptions: The Adoption of a Coercive Strategy," in Suisheng Zhao, ed., *Across the Taiwan Strait: Mainland China, Taiwan and the 1995–1996 Crisis* (London: Routledge, 1999), p. 99.

3. The deal, arranged in 1994 and delivered in 1995, was monitored by U.S. intelligence. The story was leaked to the *Washington Times*. See Bill Gertz, "China Nuclear Transfer Exposed; Hill Expected to Urge Sanctions," *Washington Times*, February 5, 1996, p. A1.

4. The act specifies sanctions against any person or country that contributes "materially and with requisite knowledge . . . any goods or technology . . . to the efforts by any individual, group, or non-nuclear-weapon state to acquire unsafeguarded special nuclear material or to use, develop, produce, stockpile, or otherwise acquire any nuclear explosive device." See H.R. 2333, the Foreign Relations Authorization Act of 1994–1995, Sec. 801, and the Nuclear Proliferation Prevention Act of 1994 (http://thomas.loc.gov, accessed February 2003).

5. Xinhua News Agency, "Spokesman Denies Alleged Export of Nuclear Weapons Technology, Equipment," February 15, 1996.

6. Bill Gertz, "Administration Weighs Sanctions over Nuclear Sale; Congress Seeks Punishment for China," *Washington Times*, February 9, 1996, p. A7.

7. R. Jeffrey Smith, "Chinese Exports Fuel Iran Effort on Poison Gas; U.S. Intelligence Officials Say Sales of Chemical Equipment May Violate Law," *International Herald Tribune*, March 9, 1996 (reprinted from the *Washington* Post). The Chemical Weapons Convention prohibits the development, production, stockpiling, and use of chemical weapons. After lengthy negotiations, it was opened for signature in January 1993 and entered into force in April 1997. China was one of the first to sign and last to ratify, as was the United States. See http://projects.sipri.se/cbw/docs/cw-cwc-mainpage.html (accessed February 2003) for more information on the convention.

8. Barry Schweid, "New Suspicions Beijing Sent Missile Technology to Pakistan," Associated Press, March 7, 1996.

9. R. Jeffrey Smith, "Chinese Rebuff U.S. Demand; Nuclear Shipments May Spur Penalty," *Washington Post*, March 24, 1996, p. A1.

10. R. Jeffrey Smith, "U.S. Officials Debate Role of Chinese Leaders in Illicit Sales to Pakistan," *Washington Post*, March 27, 1996, p. A25.

11. Charles Krauthammer, "China's Four Slaps and the United States' Craven Response," *Washington Post*, March 22, 1996, p. A25.

12. A. M. Rosenthal, "On My Mind; The Making of an Anti," *New York Times*, March 29, 1996, p. A21.

13. Jim Hoagland, "Now, a Clinton Doctrine," *Washington Post*, March 10, 1996, p. C7.

14. See "Text of Japan-U.S. Declaration on Security," Jiji Press Ticker Service, Tokyo, April 17, 1996.

15. Thom Beal, "China Warns U.S., Japan on Accord," United Press International, April 18, 1996.

16. Interview with Kurt Campbell, November 2000.

17. In the mid-1980s, Chinese military industries pursued something of an "open door" approach to foreign military sales, selling CSS-2 IRBMs to Saudi Arabia, nuclear materials and chemical weapons precursor reagents to a variety of countries in the Middle East and elsewhere, and conventional armaments to both sides in the Iran-Iraq conflict. After intense American pressure and negative international publicity, the Foreign Ministry was able to persuade the leadership that the political costs of continuing such activities outweighed the economic benefits. But in a declining defense budget situation, when military industries were encouraged to restructure and reform themselves to become profitable, the temptation to sidestep rudimentary regulations or unclear guidelines was strong.

18. See Bates Gill, "Twenty Years of Chinese Reform: The Case of Nonproliferation Policy" (www.future-china.org.tw/csipf/activity/19990408/mt9904_2-2.htm, accessed February 2003).

19. U.S. Department of State, Office of the Spokesman, "Special Briefing on U.S.-China Discussions on Non-Proliferation and Nuclear-Related Exports," May 10, 1996 (transcript at www.state.gov/www/current/debate/510spbrf.html, accessed February 2003).

20. Xinhua News Agency spokesman, May 11, 1996, BBC Summary of World Broadcasts, EE/D2610/G, May 12, 1996.

21. Robert Einhorn testimony at a hearing of the Subcommittee on International Security, Proliferation, and Federal Services of the Senate Committee on Governmental Affairs, April 10, 1997 (www.fas.org/spp/starwars/congress/1997_h/s-hrg-105-242.htm, accessed February 2003).

22. Robert J. Einhorn, "Engaging China on Nonproliferation," prepared testimony before the Subcommittee on International Security, Proliferation, and Federal Services, April 10, 1997, Federal News Service (Nexis-Lexis).

23. Quoted in R. Jeffrey Smith and Thomas W. Lippman, "U.S. Relents On Chinese Sanctions; Beijing Vows to End Nuclear Sales," *Washington Post,* May 11, 1996, p. A1.

24. Interview with Deborah M. Lehr, March 1999.

25. USTR Factsheet, "Intellectual Property Rights Enforcement in China" (www.ustr.gov/releases/1996/05/96-42/96-42.fact.html, accessed February 2003).

26. Wayne M. Morrison, CRS Issue Brief for Congress, "China-U.S. Trade Issues," updated April 13, 2001. Trade balance figures are a controversial subject in U.S.-China relations, in part because the two countries use different standards of measurement for goods re-exported through Hong Kong. The yearly American deficit with China, which had gone from $6.2 billion in 1989 to $33.8 billion in 1995, was a source of political difficulty rather than economic strain—principally because

China pursued a variety of protectionist and discriminatory trade policies designed to maximize its exports and minimize imports.

27. Gretchen Cook, "US Puts Business Loans on Hold over Row with China," Agence France-Presse, February 28, 1996.

28. Interview with Deborah M. Lehr. Among the actions China agreed to undertake: a six-month nationwide special enforcement period for IPR, closing or licensing twenty-nine illegal CD factories, implementation of new guidelines on trademark and copyright protection for computer software, and a gradual phaseout of illegal software on government computers. See USTR transcript of Deputy USTR Charlene Barshefsky press conference, February 26, 1995, p. 2.

29. David Sanger, "U.S. Warns China over Violations of Trade Accord," *New York Times,* February 4, 1996, p. A1; USTR Fact Sheet, "Intellectual Property Rights Enforcement in China," May 15, 1996 (www.ustr.gov/releases/1996/05/96-42/96-42.fact.html.)

30. R. Jeffrey Smith, "Clinton Renews Threat of Trade Sanctions on China," *Washington Post,* May 9, 1996, p. A18.

31. Paul Blustein and Steven Mufson, "U.S., China Take Risks in Threatening Tariffs," *Washington Post,* May 17, 1996, p. A29.

32. Warren Christopher, "American Interests and the U.S.-China Relationship," May 17, 1996 (www.state.gov/www/current/debate/96517qa.html, accessed February 2003).

33. William J. Clinton, "Remarks to the Pacific Basin Economic Council," May 20, 1996 (www.state.gov/www/regions/eap/960520.html, accessed February 2003).

34. Cited in Keith B. Richburg, "China's 'Get Tough' Publicity Doesn't Tell the Whole Story," *Washington Post,* June 14, 1996, p. A39.

35. China had resisted allowing more than a minimal number of U.S. films to be shown in Chinese theaters, both out of fear of competition from a more advanced U.S. movie industry and out of concern for "cultural infiltration" and "contamination" from Western ideas. For details of the agreement, see the press briefing by National Economic Adviser Laura Tyson and Secretary of Commerce Michael Kantor, June 18, 1996, M2 Presswire (Lexis-Nexis).

36. Quoted in Keith B. Richburg, "U.S. Withdraws Its Threat of Sanctions against China; Trade War Averted; Officials Cite Beijing Crackdown on Pirated Goods," *Washington Post,* June 18, 1996, p. C1.

37. See note 103 in this chapter. Lake remembered enough of his student study of Chinese to make a creditable attempt at reciting Jiang's aphorism. His purpose was to demonstrate respect and provide a pleasant, human touch to what might otherwise be sterile exchanges of talking points.

38. The "walk in the woods" metaphor originated in a 1982 discussion between U.S. arms control negotiator Paul Nitze and his Soviet counterpart, Yuli Kvitsinsky. Taking a break from formal and fruitless negotiations on arms control, the two men walked together by themselves in a park near Geneva, Switzerland, and worked out methods to get arms control discussions onto a more productive track. Both the U.S. and Soviet governments rejected the agreement, but it facilitated further progress later.

39. Interviews with Anthony Lake, August 2000, and Sandra J. Kristoff, September 2000. The list, which I had earlier drawn up in consultation with State Department China desk officials and John Kamm, included Wei Jingsheng, Wang Dan, Xi Yang, Liu Xiaobo, Zhou Guoqiang, Liu Nianchun, Bao Tong, and Ulanshuvo.

40. Quoted in Keith Richburg, "U.S., China Optimistic after Talks in Beijing; Lake Says Clinton, President Jiang Likely to Meet, Reaffirms Commitment to Human Rights," *Washington Post,* July 11, 1996, p. A21; Seth Faison, "Clinton Likely to Visit China in 1997 if He Is Re-Elected," *New York Times*, July 10, 1996, p. A3.

41. "Lake's China Visit Makes Positive, Useful Contribution: Spokesman," Xinhua News Agency, no. 0711175, July 11, 1996; Maggie Farley, "Top U.S. Envoy Tries to Repair Ties with China," *Los Angeles Times,* July 11, 1996, p. A4.

42. See Michael Dobbs, "Dissident's Long Prison Sentence Tangles Christopher's China Visit," *Washington Post,* November 3, 1996, p. A28; Steven Erlanger, "Christopher to Go Ahead with Visit to China," *New York Times,* October 31, 1996, p. A12.

43. Warren Christopher, *In the Stream of History: Shaping Foreign Policy for a New Era* (Stanford University Press, 1989), p. 514.

44. See, for example, "Transcript of Press Conference with President Clinton and Australian Prime Minister Howard," U.S. Newswire, November 20, 1996 (Lexis-Nexis); also Michael Dobbs, "Letter from Shanghai; When Is a Partnership Not Partnership? When It's 'Cooperation,'" *Washington Post,* November 23, 1996, p. A19.

45. Marcy Gordon, "Justice Department Reviewing Campaign Spending Allegations," Associated Press, October 10, 1996. Amendments to the Federal Election Campaign Act in 1974 set specific limits on how much an individual could give to a candidate and a political party, and in total. They also limited spending by candidates and by so-called political action committees. Many of those limitations were struck down in 1976 by the Supreme Court as inconsistent with First Amendment rights, although they did retain limits on individual contributions. Even these were evaded as distinctions were made between so-called hard money given directly to a candidate and soft money given to a political party or other organization for the purpose of developing or publicizing their issues. According to the Annenberg Center at the University of Pennsylvania, more than $150 million of such soft money was spent in 1996 on issue advertisements on television and radio, many of them "attack ads" on candidates. See Annelise Anderson, "Political Money: The New Prohibition," Hoover Essays in Public Policy, October 15, 1997 (http://andrsn.stanford.edu/Other/polmoney.html, accessed February 2003).

46. Quoted in John F. Harris, "Clinton Waxes Idyllic on Pacific Rim's Future; Optimistic Views Draw Cheers in Australia," *Washington Post,* November 21, 1996, p. A28.

47. Interview with Sandra J. Kristoff.

48. See Bruce Gilley, *Tiger on the Brink: Jiang Zemin and China's New Elite* (University of California Press, 1998), p. 71.

49. Charles Hutzler, "Deep Divisions Remain, but Manila Meeting Marks a Turning Point," Associated Press, November 24, 1996; John F. Harris, "Clinton, Chinese

Leader Meet; After 1½-Hour Talk, Presidents Agree to Exchange Visits," *Washington Post,* November 24, 1996, p. A1.

50. Jim Hoagland, "Mouseketeer Diplomacy," *Washington Post,* December 1, 1996, p. C7.

51. *Washington Post* editorial, "Selling Cheap in China," November 26, 1996, p. A14.

52. Geremie Barmé, "To Screw Foreigners Is Patriotic: China's Avant-Garde Nationalists," *The China Journal*, no. 34 (July 1995) (www.tsquare.tv/themes/toscrew.html, accessed February2003); Suisheng Zhao, "Chinese Intellectuals' Quest for National Greatness and Nationalistic Writing in the 1990s," *The China Quarterly*, no. 152 (December 1997), pp. 725–45; Feng Chen, "Order and Stability in Social Transition: Neo-Conservative Political Thought in Post-1989 China," *The China Quarterly,* no. 151 (September 1997), pp. 593–613; Joseph Fewsmith, *China since Tiananmen* (Cambridge University Press, 2001), especially chap. 5.

53. In the early 1990s, the central government ceased subsidizing most newspapers and magazines and made publishing houses responsible for their own profits and losses. By 1994, 540 publishing houses were turning out more than 90,000 titles per year (Xinhua News Agency, September 16, 1994) for increasingly affluent urban audiences with sophisticated tastes. This led to a boom in popular fiction and to the virtual abandonment of prepublication censorship for most publications. Song Qiang, Zhang Zangzang, Qiao Bian, and others, *Zhongguo keyi shuo bu* (China Can Say No) (Beijing: China Industrial and Commercial United Press, 1996). The title is adapted from a Japanese book, *The Japan That Can Say No*, by Shintaro Ishihara and Akio Morita, which caused a sensation in Japan in 1989 by questioning the benefits to Japan of American dominance of the alliance.

54. Song and others, *Zhongguo keyi shuo bu* (China Can Say No), p. 209.

55. Joseph Kahn, "Chinese Writers Increasingly Blast Anti-U.S. Bestseller," *Wall Street Journal*, September 19, 1996, p. A18.

56. Fewsmith, *China since Tiananmen,* chap. 6.

57. Elizabeth Drew, *The Corruption of American Politics—What Went Wrong and Why* (Secaucus, N.J.: Birch Lane Press, 1999), especially chap. 2.

58. Ibid., p. ix.

59. Ruth Marcus and Ira Chinoy, "A Fund-Raising 'Mistake'; DNC Held Event in Buddhist Temple," *Washington Post,* October 17, 1996, p. A1.

60. Ibid.

61. Ruth Marcus, "Oval Office Meeting Set DNC Asian Funds Network in Motion," *Washington Post,* December 29, 1996, p. A1.

62. Glenn F. Bunting, Alan C. Miller, and Rich Connell, "Donor Enjoyed Broad Access to White House," *Los Angeles Times,* November 28, 1996, p. A1.

63. Keith Richburg, "Taiwanese: Ex-Clinton Aide Said He Was Raising Money; No Direct Request Made, Political Scientist Says," *Washington Post,* October 30, 1996, p. A16. Wood was dismissed by Christopher.

64. See the "Investigation of Illegal or Improper Activities in Connection with 1996 Federal Election Campaigns," Final Report of the Committee on Governmen-

tal Affairs, Senate Rept. 105-167—105 Cong. 2 sess.—March 10, 1998 (www.fas.org/irp/congress/1998_rpt/sgo-sir/2-17.htm, accessed February 2003).

65. Susan Schmidt and Lena H. Sun, "Clinton Calls Wang Meeting 'Inappropriate,'" *Washington Post,* December 21, 1996, p. A1.

66. Public Papers of the Presidents, "Remarks Announcing the Second Term National Security Team and an Exchange with Reporters," December 5, 1996.

67. William Safire, "I Remember Larry," *New York Times,* January 2, 1997, p. A19.

68. Byron York, "Six Degrees of William Cohen," *American Spectator,* January 19, 1997, pp. 22–27.

69. Bob Woodward and Brian Duffy, "Chinese Embassy Role in Contributions Probed; Planning of Foreign Donations to DNC Indicated," *Washington Post,* February 13, 1997, p. A1.

70. Brian Duffy and Bob Woodward, "FBI Probes China-Linked Contributions; Task Force Examines Influence on Congress," *Washington Post,* February 28, 1997, p. A1.

71. Quoted in the Associated Press, "Clinton: Should Have Been Told of FBI Suspicions of Chinese," March 10, 1997; David G. Savage and Richard A. Serrano, "Clinton Not Told of China Donation Plan, Aides Insist," *Los Angeles Times,* March 10, 1997, p. A1; Warren P. Strobel and Jerry Seper, "FBI Opens Tiff with Clinton; Says Warning on Gifts Was Ignored," *Washington Times,* March 11, 1997, p. A1.

72. David Johnston, "U.S. Agency Secretly Monitored Chinese in '96 on Political Gifts," *New York Times,* March 13, 1997, p. A1. The involvement of the National Security Agency—responsible for collecting electronic and signals intelligence—as the originator of the reports helps explain why they were so sensitive. NSA reporting is always disseminated in an especially secure manner, with careful restrictions placed on those who are cleared to see it.

73. Robert Pear, "FBI Warned of Donations from China, Senator Says," *New York Times,* March 10, 1997, p. B8.

74. Sharon LaFraniere and Lena H. Sun, "DNC Returns Another $1.5 Million; Refunds to Include Donations from Foreigners and a Deceased Woman," *Washington Post,* March 1, 1997, p. A1.

75. See Drew, *The Corruption of American Politics*, for a comprehensive discussion of this complex and controversial issue.

76. "The Anthony Lake Nomination," *New York Times*, March 14, 1997, p. A32.

77. Elaine Sciolino, "Leading Democrat Tells of Doubts on C.I.A. Nominee," *New York Times,* March 19, 1997, p. A1; transcript of Jim Lehrer interview of Senators Shelby and Kerrey, *Online NewsHour*, March 19, 1997 (www.pbs.org/newshour/bb/fedagencies/march97/lake_3-18a.html, accessed February 2003).

78. Anthony Lake, "Letter to the President," March 18, 1997 (www.nytimes.com/library/politics/0318lake-cia-text.html., accessed February 2003).

79. Kenneth R. Timmerman, "Partners in Crime (What China Got for Its Money)," *American Spectator*, August 1999 (www.freerepublic.com/forum/a379758597e0b.htm, accessed February 2003); see also William C. Triplett II and

Edward Timperlake, *The Year of the Rat: How Bill Clinton Compromised American Security for Chinese Money* (Washington: Regnery Press, 1998). Works such as these, and there are many more of them, are so poorly researched and fraught with errors and misrepresentations that they scarcely bear mention as scholarship. They are more a testament to the extremes of partisanship and scare-mongering that ultimately became associated with this issue.

80. Samuel Berger's testimony at a hearing of the Governmental Affairs Committee, chaired by Sen. Fred Thompson, September 11, 1997, Federal News Service (Nexis-Lexis).

81. Thomas L. Friedman, "Beyond Stupid," *New York Times,* March 17, 1997, p. A15.

82. David Johnston, "FBI Denied Data the White House Sought on China," *New York Times,* March 25, 1997, p. A1.

83. Steven Mufson, "China Objects to Post's Coverage," *Washington Post,* March 11, 1997, p. A7.

84. As a member of Gore's delegation, I made one attempt to find out from the FBI liaison office in the NSC what had been in the intelligence briefing of the previous year, but was told I could not have access to it, as it was now the subject of a grand jury investigation.

85. James Bennet, "Gore to Raise Prickly Issue, Campaign Finance, in China," *New York Times,* March 23, 1997, p. A24.

86. Quoted in James Bennet, "Chinese Ask Gore about the Inquiry on Campaign Gifts," *New York Times,* March 26, 1997, p. A1.

87. Quoted in Patrick E. Tyler, "Now, Beijing Hears Another U.S. Voice: Gingrich's," *New York Times,* March 29, 1997, p. A3.

88. Cited by Seth Faison, "Gingrich Warns China That U.S. Would Step in to Defend Taiwan," *New York Times,* March 31, 1997, p. A1.

89. Steven Mufson, "Gingrich Presses Hot China Issues; Speaker, Following Gore, Brings His Own Agenda," *Washington Post,* March 29, 1997, p. A1.

90. "China, U.S. See Improved Relations," Xinhua News Agency, item 0328198, March 28, 1997.

91. Seth Faison, "Chinese Wonder if TV Documentary Means Deng Is Slipping," *New York Times,* January 9, 1997, p. A10.

92. "Deng Xiaoping Passes Away," Xinhua News Agency, no. 0219303 and no. 0219013, February 19, 1997.

93. "Chinese Media Given Early Notice of Deng Death," United Press International, February 19, 1997.

94. Leu Siew Ying, "China, Hong Kong, Taiwan Stocks Mixed after Deng's Death," Agence France-Presse, February 21, 1997 (Lexis-Nexis).

95. Wei Ming, "China's Top Military Body to Adjust Structure at Party Congress," *Ming Pao*, January 3, 1997, p. A10, BBC Summary of World Broadcasts, FE/D2808/G, January 4, 1997.

96. "Military Leader Stresses Awareness of Strategy, Politics," Xinhua News Agency, December 25, 1996; "Beijing Garrison Party Plenum Stresses 'Democratic Centralism,'" *Beijing Ribao,* January 10, 1997. Hong Kong's *Ping Kuo Jih Pao* (Apple

Daily) had reported in December that Jiang had ordered the strength of the Beijing Garrison augmented with 8,000 soldiers from other military regions, although this cannot be confirmed.

97. Thomas W. Lippman, "State Dept. Human Rights Report Chastises Several U.S. Allies," *Washington Post*, January 31, 1997, p. A16.

98. Michael Dobbs, "Albright Takes Balancing Act to Beijing," *Washington Post*, February 25, 1997, p. A12.

99. Foreign observers were restricted to watching on television, since no foreign dignitaries were invited to participate in the memorial service itself.

100. Xinhua News Agency, no. 0225055, February 25, 1997, contained excerpts of Jiang's memorial speech.

101. *People's Daily* editorial, "Recalling Contributions, Inheriting the Legacy, and Jointly Accomplishing the Great Cause," February 25, 1997, Xinhua News Agency, no. 0225007. See also Gilley, *Tiger on the Brink*, p. 295.

102. Xinhua News Agency, February 26, 1997, in BBC Summary of World Broadcasts, FE/D2854/G, February 27, 1997.

103. Willy Wo-lap Lam, "PLA General Consolidates Power Base," *South China Morning Post,* January 13, 1997, p. 6; "Generals Pledge Loyalty to Jiang," *South China Morning Post,* February 23, 1997, p. 7; "Old Guard Generals Snub Jiang," *South China Morning Post,* February 25, 1997, p. 1.

104. Steven Mufson, "Once the 'Butcher of Beijing,' Premier Li Takes Reconciler's Role," *Washington Post*, March 25, 1997, p. A13.

105. Andrew J. Nathan and E. Perry Link, eds., *The Tiananmen Papers* (New York: Public Affairs, 2001), p. 192.

106. *Ming Pao*, September 19, 1997, in BBC Summary of World Broadcasts, FE/D3030/S1, September 22, 1997.

107. Xinhua News Agency, English summary of Qiao's interview with Alain Peyrefitte, March 30, 1997, in BBC Summary of World Broadcasts, FE/D2882/G, April 2, 1997. Qiao was on perilous ground. Zhao Ziyang had advocated turning the PLA into a "state army" (*guojun*) in the mid-1980s and was strongly opposed by nearly the entire senior PLA leadership. Although a state military commission was established—and approved by the NPC—it was an empty shell, a carbon copy of the party's military commission, where the actual power rested. Qiao was careful to say that his idea "to fix . . . the status of the army within the state system . . . does not change the leadership of the party over the army." But it opened up questions of why he was proposing a restriction on Jiang Zemin's powers.

108. Bill Gertz, "Jiang's Control Shaky, CIA Says; Deng's Successor Faces Rivals," *Washington Times*, February 21, 1997, p. A1.

109. In a process called *biaotai*, or "stating one's position," the time elapsed between the announcement of a change in central policy or personnel and declarations of support by subordinates is carefully watched, as is the sincerity of the statement itself. Prior to his March 1 opening of the NPC, Qiao had passed up several opportunities to publicly support Jiang as the "core" of the leadership.

110. Alison Mitchell, "New Measures to Separate Foreign Policy from Politics," *New York Times,* April 21, 1997, p. A9.

111. Remarks by Samuel R. Berger, assistant to the president for national security affairs, "Building a New Consensus on China," at the Council on Foreign Relations, New York, released by the White House Office of the Press Secretary, June 6, 1997.

112. Ibid.

113. John E. Yang, "House Backs Clinton on China Trade Privileges," *Washington Post,* June 25, 1997, p. A1.

114. Michael Hirsch and Melinda Liu, "Beijing's Secret Wish List," *Newsweek,* April 21, 1997, p. 36.

115. James Risen, "FBI Said to Suspect Donor as Agent for China," *Los Angeles Times,* May 17, 1997, p. A1.

116. Bob Woodward, "Top Chinese Linked to Plan to Buy Favor," *Washington Post,* April 27, 1997, p. A1.

117. John F. Harris, "Freeh Briefs Clinton Adviser on China Probe; More Frequent Meetings Are Being Considered," *Washington Post,* May 1, 1997, p. A6.

118. David E. Sanger, "China, Wary on Mood of Congress, Balks at Opening Markets," *New York Times,* April 30, 1997, p. A13.

119. Xinhua News Agency coverage of Qian's speech, April 30, 1997, in BBC Summary of World Broadcasts, FE/D2908/G, May 2, 1997.

120. CNN interview with Jiang Zemin, transcript no. 97050910V18, May 9, 1997 (Lexis-Nexis).

121. "Asiagate' Is 'Just U.S. Politics,'" interview with Zhu Rongji, *Newsweek,* May 26, 1997, p. 34.

122. Quoted in Steven Mufson, "China Objects to Post's Coverage," *Washington Post,* March 11, 1997, p. A7.

123. Chinese intelligence agencies are organized and operate somewhat differently from those in the United States. The principal bureaucracies are the Ministry of State Security (MSS), the Military Intelligence Department (also known as the Second Department, responsible for human source intelligence) of the PLA General Staff Department, and the Third Department of the General Staff Department (responsible for technical intelligence collection), corresponding roughly with the Central Intelligence Agency, Defense Intelligence Agency, and National Security Agency, respectively. The Ministry of Public Security also conducts counterintelligence operations, and other bureaucracies have discrete intelligence-related responsibilities of a minor nature. See Nicholas Eftimiades, *Chinese Intelligence Operations* (Annapolis, Md.: Naval Institute Press, 1994) for a detailed, if somewhat sensationalized, study of the Chinese intelligence system.

124. Liu Chaoying was also a colonel in the PLA, as well as an official in a private Chinese company subsidiary to China Aerospace Group, the corporate entity that replaced China's Ministry of Aerospace Industry. The story of her involvement with Chung, which came out in 1998–99, has been widely covered in various American newspapers. See, for example, Francis X. Clines, "U.S. Inquiry Opens on the Military Elite of China," *New York Times,* May 16, 1998, p. A1.

125. Quoted in David Johnston, "Committee Told of Beijing Cash for Democrats," *New York Times*, May 12, 1999, p. A1. The *Los Angeles Times* first broke the story, using nearly the same quote, on April 4, 1999. See William Rempel, Henry

Weinstein, and Alan C. Miller, "Testimony Links Top China Official, Funds for Clinton; Ex-Democratic Fund-Raiser Chung Told U.S. Investigators That Military Intelligence Chief Secretly Directed $300,000 to Help President in '96; Embassy Spokesman Denies Beijing Was Involved in Elections," *Los Angeles Times*, April 4, 1999, p. A1.

126. See Chung testimony before the House of Representatives Government Reform and Oversight Committee, May 11, 1998, available through the Federal News Service on Lexis-Nexis.

127. Henry Chu and Jim Mann, "Chinese Reassign Intelligence Chief Implicated in Fund-Raising Scandal," *Los Angeles Times,* July 3, 1999, p. A4; Wu Zhong, "PRC Ex-Spy Chief Faces Court Martial in Graft Probe," *South China Morning Post* (Internet version), May 24, 2000; Erik Eckholm, "China Widening Crackdown on Corruption," *New York Times,* December 23, 2000, p. A10.

128. Willy Wo-lap Lam, "Jiang Theory Extols 'Greater Civilisation,'" *South China Morning Post,* October 17, 1996, p. 10.

129. Patrick E. Tyler, "China and Red Cross Agree to New Talks on Jail Visits," *New York Times,* March 2, 1997, p. A16.

130. American media paid almost no attention to the announcement, with the *New York Times* giving it only a brief note on April 9. The State Department spokesman said the announcement would not affect U.S. support for a resolution criticizing China's human rights at the annual UNHRC meeting.

131. My own involvement in China policy issues dropped off sharply after the vice president's visit to China and with the continuation of the "Donorgate" scandal. As the bureaucratic pieces were put in place to have Jeff Bader come to the NSC from State, it was proposed that I would return to the National Intelligence Council as national intelligence officer for East Asia. Much of my time in the last six months at the NSC (I left in October 1997) was taken up with testifying before various congressional committees investigating the scandal and dealing with non-China issues.

132. Interviews with Jeffrey Bader, July 2000; Stanley Roth, August 2000; and Susan Shirk, August 2000.

133. The term "baskets" was only used internally and informally. In public, they were generally referred to as "issue areas." See the unofficial transcript of Jeff Bader's briefing at the United States Information Agency's Foreign Press Center, October 22, 1997, where he identifies them (http://usinfo.org/sino/102303.htm, accessed February 2003).

134. For full text see http:/www.info.gov.hk/cab/topical/bottom1_2.htm, accessed February 2003.

135. "Speak Up for Hong Kong," *New York Times* editorial, April 18, 1997, p. A32.

136. Xinhua News Agency, June 29, 1997, in BBC Survey of World Broadcasts, FE/D2959/S1, July 1, 1997.

137. Teresa Poole, "Hong Kong Handover: China's New Top Brass Sweep in Like Emperors; There Were No Words of Thanks or Even Soft Words to the British for Their Stewardship," *The Independent* (London), July 1, 1997, p. 16 (Lexis-Nexis).

138. Agence France-Presse, "Jiang Zemin's Speech at Ceremony Marking Transfer of Rule," July 1, 1997 (Lexis-Nexis).

139. Jasper Becker, "The Sovereignty Song-Fest," *South China Morning Post*, June 29, 1997, p. 9; Xinhua News Agency, no. 0701251, July 1, 1997.

140. Interviews with Sandra J. Kristoff, Jeffrey Bader, and Susan Shirk.

141. The Peaceful Nuclear Energy Agreement of 1985 stipulated that the president would certify that China was not violating section 129 of the Atomic Energy Act of 1954, which "places restrictions on exports to nations that assist or encourage non-nuclear weapon states to acquire nuclear weapons." See Dianne E. Rennack, "Nuclear, Biological, Chemical, and Missile Proliferation Sanctions: Selected Current Law," Congressional Research Service Report 98-116, updated January 17, 2001, note 5 (www.ncseonline.org/NLE/CRSreports/international/inter-31.cfm?&CFID=6723979&CFTOKEN=46773367, accessed February 2003).

142. Wayne M. Morrison, "China's Proliferation of Weapons of Mass Destruction," Congressional Research Service Issue Brief 980717, updated July 15, 1998 (www.fas.org/spp/starwars/crs/980717CRSWeapons.htm, accessed October 11, 2000); Barton Gellman, "Reappraisal Led to New China Policy; Skeptics Abound, but U.S. 'Strategic Partnership' Yielding Results," *Washington Post,* June 22, 1998, p. A1.

143. Interview with Sandra J. Kristoff.

144. Interviews with Sandra J. Kristoff and Jeffrey Bader.

145. See "Beidaihe Meeting Ends, Seventh Plenary Session to Open in Early September," *Ming Pao*, August 16, 1997, p. A11, BBC Summary of World Broadcasts, FE/D3001/G, August 19, 1997; "Cross-Century Personnel Arrangements Reflect Stability," *Ming Pao,* September 15, 1997, p. A15, BBC Summary of World Broadcasts, FE/D3027/S1, September 18, 1997; Willy Wo-lap Lam, "Beidaihe Stalemate on Senior Party Positions," *South China Morning Post,* August 7, 1997, p. 9.

146. See Gilley, *Tiger on the Brink,* p. 306; Willy Wo-lap Lam, "Qiao 'Retired' by Scheming Party Veterans," *South China Morning Post*, September 20, 1997, p. 1; also Lam, *Era of Jiang,* pp. 335–36.

147. Seth Faison, "Ghost at China's Communist Banquet Recalls Tiananmen," *New York Times*, September 16, 1997, p. A3.

148. Richard Baum, "The Fifteenth National Party Congress: Jiang Takes Command?" *The China Quarterly*, no. 153 (March 1998), pp. 141–42; Li Cheng and Lynn White, "The Fifteenth Central Committee of the Chinese Communist Party: Full-Fledged Technocratic Leadership with Party Control by Jiang Zemin," *Asian Survey*, vol. 38, no. 3 (March 1998), p. 240; Willy Wo-lap Lam, "Jiang Holds Strength but Balance Tips," *South China Morning Post*, September 20, 1997, p. 10.

149. Baum, "The Fifteenth National Party Congress: Jiang Takes Command?" p. 150; Li and White, "The Fifteenth Central Committee of the Chinese Communist Party," pp. 248–51.

150. Wu Guoguang, "Normalizing Authoritarianism—The Meaning of the CCP's 15th Congress," *American Asian Review*, vol. 16, no. 2 (Summer 1998), p. 92; Seth Faison, "Major Shift for Communist China: Big State Industries Will Be Sold," *New York Times,* September 12, 1997, p. A1.

151. Jiang Zemin, "Hold High the Great Banner . . . Building Socialism with Chinese Characteristics to the Twenty-First Century," Political Report to the Fifteenth Congress of the Chinese Communist Party, sec. 9, September 12, 1997.

152. "Joint United States–China Statement," October 29, 1997, from *Public Papers of the Presidents*, 33 Weekly Comp. President. Doc 1680 (Lexis-Nexis).

153. China had revised its criminal code in March, eliminating the term "counterrevolutionary" from its catalog of criminal behavior. Rather than review the more than 2,000 cases of individuals imprisoned on charges of counterrevolutionary behavior, the Chinese government simply recategorized them all as "endangering [the] state security" and left them in jail. Kamm used his dialogue with Chinese Justice Ministry officials to press for a more rigorous review.

154. Elizabeth Shogren, "Jiang's State Visit . . .," *Los Angeles Times*, October 30, 1997, p. A12. China's propensity to conclude large commercial deals just before important bilateral events had ceased being an effective incentive and, in both press and official eyes, became more an embarrassment than a benefit to the relationship. Chinese motives for continuing the practice probably involved a desire to maintain leverage on American business as a means of influencing the U.S. government and to deflect the inevitable complaints about China's ever-growing trade surplus.

155. Curiously, the censors in Beijing decided not to show Jiang's swim, even though it received wide international publicity. (See Erik Eckholm, "At Home, Rosy News for Jiang's Trip," *New York Times,* October 31, 1997, p. A8.) They may have decided that the president—in pink and white swimming cap and goggles, his large swimming suit hiked up over his paunch—might have excited more mirth than admiration. Deng's and Mao's most famous photos pictured them in the water, mostly submerged. Or, as Eckholm speculates, they may have had in mind Li Peng's Beidaihe photos after his heart attack in 1993, which did not go over well with the public.

156. A review of the meeting was provided by a "senior administration official" (undoubtedly National Security Adviser Sandy Berger) the following day. See White House, Office of the Press Secretary, "Background Press Briefing," October 29, 1997 (http://clinton6.nara.gov/1997/10/1997-10-29-background-press-briefing-on-meetings-with-jiang-zemin.html, accessed February 2003); also interviews with Samuel R. Berger; Sandra J. Kristoff, March 2001; and Jeffrey Bader.

157. Interview with Jeffrey Bader.

158. The "Tiananmen sanctions" were restrictions on munitions list and other nuclear and high-technology exports to China, as well as blocking of various kinds of developmental assistance. See chap. 3, "American Reaction."

159. "Press Conference by President Clinton and President Jiang Zemin," October 29, 1997 (www.state.gov/www/regions/eap/971029_clinton_china2.html, accessed February 2003).

160. Helen Dewar and John E. Yang, "Jiang Vows Cooperation, but on China's Terms; Defiant Leader Gives No Ground on Rights," *Washington Post,* October 30, 1997, p. A1.

161. "Excerpts from Question-and-Answer Session after Chinese Pres Jiang Zemin's Speech at Harvard," *New York Times,* November 2, 1997, p. A14.

162. See, for example, John Pomfret, "Successful Visit Bolsters Jiang; Stronger Relationship Built with Clinton, Chinese in U.S.," *Washington Post,* November 3, 1997, p. A12; Seth Faison, "Beijing's New Face: Better Image for Jiang," *New York Times,* November 3, 1997, p. A1.

163. Steven Mufson, "Chinese Media Hail Jiang upon Return from U.S.; Image-Building Visit Called 'Highly Successful,'" *Washington Post,* November 5, 1997, p. A29; Seth Faison, "Beijing's New Face: Better Image for Jiang."

164. From an editorial in *Renmin Ribao* (People's Daily), "A New Stage of Development: Warmly Congratulating President Jiang Zemin on the All-Around Success of His Visit to the United States," November 5, 1997; and Xinhua News Agency, "A New Chapter in the History of Sino-American Relations," November 3, 1997. Both in Xing Hua, ed., *Jiegong jianshexing zhanlue huoban guanxi—zhongmei shounao hufang jishi* (Building a Constructive Strategic Partnership—A Record of Sino-American Summit Exchanges) (Beijing: Xinhua Publishing House, 1998), pp. 67–69, 70–71, respectively.

165. Xinhua News Agency, "Hong Kong Media on Jiang Zemin's Successful U.S. Visit," October 31, 1997, in FBIS-CHI-97-304, October 31, 1997.

Notes to Chapter 8

1. S. Con. Res. 57 IS was referred to the Senate Foreign Relations Committee, where it died (http://thomas.loc.gov, accessed February 2003).

2. H.R. 2195 EH passed the House by a vote of 419-2 on November 5, 1997, but it died in the Senate Finance Committee (http://thomas.loc.gov/cgi-bin/query/D?c105:3:./temp/~c1058yVAKm::, accessed February 2003).

3. H.R. 2570 passed the House by a vote of 415-1 on November 6, 1997, and was referred to the Senate Foreign Relations Committee, where hearings were held the following year. It was not referred out of that committee during the 105th Congress (http://thomas.loc.gov, accessed February 2003).

4. See section 306 of H.R. 1253 (http://thomas.loc.gov, accessed February 2003). See also press statement by spokesman James P. Rubin, "China: Special Coordinator for Tibetan Issues," on October 31, 1997 (http://secretary.state.gov/www/briefings/statements/971031a.html, accessed on February 2003). The appointee was concurrently the director of policy planning.

5. "Excerpts from Remarks on First Day of Campaign Finance Hearings," *New York Times,* July 9, 1997, p. B9 (emphasis added).

6. Edward Walsh and Guy Gugliotta, "Chinese Plan to Buy U.S. Influence Alleged," *Washington Post,* July 9, 1997, p. A1.

7. Elizabeth Drew, *The Corruption of American Politics—What Went Wrong and Why* (Secaucus, N.J.: Birch Lane Press, 1999), p. 103.

8. "Final Report of the Special Investigation," secs. 12–20 (www.senate.gov/~gov_affairs/sireport.htm, accessed February 2003).

9. Ibid., "Additional Views of the Minority on the Special Investigation," sec. 2, p. 2.

10. Quoted by Edward Walsh, "Panel Split over 'Scumbag' Comment," *Washington Post,* April 22, 1998, p. A6.

11. See Gao Xin and He Pin, *Zhu Rongji Zhuan—Cong Fandang Youpai dao Deng Xiaoping de Jichengren* (The Zhu Rongji Story—From Anti-Party Rightist to Deng Xiaoping's Heir) (Taipei: New News Books, 1993), pp. 13–60 passim.

12. See Nicholas Lardy, *China's Unfinished Economic Revolution* (Brookings, 1998), especially chap. 1, for a comprehensive review of economic reform efforts in the 1990s and the strategy used by the government to address its massive problems.

13. In light of the fact that China's currency was not internationally convertible, it did not face the same kinds of pressures that had weakened other Asian currencies. Nonetheless, there was some advocacy from coastal exporters for an easing of the currency against the dollar. Beijing ignored it.

14. Mark L. Clifford and others, "Can China Reform Its Economy?" *Business Week,* September 29, 1997, p. 116.

15. Antoaneta Bezlova, "China: Seoul's Woes Prompt Review of Homegrown 'Chaebol,'" Inter Press Service, February 19, 1998 (Lexis-Nexis).

16. Chinese Central Television, March 19, 1998, broadcast of press conference by Zhu Rongji and other State Council leaders, in BBC Summary of World Broadcasts, FD/D3180/S1, March 20, 1998.

17. For a comprehensive assessment of "PLA, Incorporated," see James Mulvenon, *Soldiers of Fortune: The Rise and Fall of the Chinese Military-Business Complex, 1978–1998* (Armonk, N.Y.: M. E. Sharpe, 2001).

18. Susan V. Lawrence and Bruce Gilley, "Bitter Harvest," *Far Eastern Economic Review,* April 29, 1999.

19. Dexter Roberts, Mark Clifford, and Stan Crock, "China's Army under Fire," *Business Week,* August 10, 1998, p. 18. Estimates of the size of "PLA, Inc.," vary considerably. Mulvenon points out that it is difficult to put a precise numerical estimate on the value of PLA industries, as many of them under-reported their earnings, particularly when acquired illegally. See Mulvenon, *Soldiers of Fortune,* chap. 7.

20. Michael Sheridan, "Army Runs China's Smuggling Boom," *Sunday Times* (London), September 2, 1998 (Lexis-Nexis). Hong Kong's *Apple Daily* reported in September 1998 that a pitched battle between twelve Customs Department vessels and seven PLA navy vessels protecting a smuggled oil shipment resulted in seventy-four casualties on the Customs' side, including thirteen killed. (*Ping Kuo Jih Pao* story of September 24, 1998, reported by BBC Summary of World Broadcasts, FE/D3342/G, September 26, 1998.) China admitted eight hundred law enforcement officers were killed fighting smugglers in 1997.

21. Roberts, Clifford, and Crock, "China's Army under Fire"; Lu Ning, "Zhu's Financial Clean-up Takes on PLA," *Business Times* (Singapore), July 18, 1998, p. 8; Willy Wo-lap Lam, "Army in Probe for Overseas Hoards," *South China Morning Post,* July 25, 1998, p. 7; David Evans and Patricia Lee, "J&A Denies Its HK Office Lost [Hong Kong] $6b on Speculation," *Hong Kong Standard,* July 17, 1998 (Nexis-Lexis).

22. See Mulvenon, *Soldiers of Fortune*, pp. 177–78, for yet another variation of the story.

23. Quoted in Financial Times Intelligence Wire, "PLA Business Activities Fraught with Abuses," November 1, 1998 (Lexis-Nexis); see also John Pomfret, "Jiang Tells Army to End Trade Role," *Washington Post,* July 23, 1998, p. A1.

24. See Mulvenon, *Soldiers of Fortune,* chap. 6. Also Tai-ming Cheung, "The Tainted Millions—Corruption Raises Its Ugly Head in the Army," *Far Eastern Economic Review,* August 12, 1993, p. 13; Yueh Shan, "General Zhou Keyu Dismissed," *Tung Hsiang* magazine, no. 137–138, January 15, 1997, pp. 19–20, BBC Summary of World Broadcasts, FE/D2825/G, January 24, 1997.

25. Mulvenon, *Soldiers of Fortune,* pp. 178–86. Also, "Government Reportedly Planning to Compensate Army Firms," *Ming Pao*, July 25, 1998, p. 12, in BBC Summary of World Broadcasts, FE/D3290/G, July 28, 1998; Willy Wo-lap Lam, "PLA Gets Payoff for Business Loss," *South China Morning Post,* August 3, 1998, p. 1.

26. Willy Wo-lap Lam, "Critics Besiege Great Rectifier," *South China Morning Post,* November 18, 1998, p. 18.

27. Lardy, *China's Unfinished Economic Revolution*, p. 27.

28. Ibid., p. 34.

29. Ibid., p. 137.

30. Ibid., p. 5, note 15. Although reliable statistics are scarce, Lardy makes the point that, by Western standards, China's four largest banks are all technically insolvent (see p. 119).

31. Joseph Fewsmith, "China and the WTO: The Politics behind the Agreement," National Bureau of Asian Research, November 1999 (www.nbr.org/publications/report.html, accessed February 2003).

32. Susan Schmidt and Peter Baker, "Clinton Accused of Urging Aide to Lie," *Washington Post,* January 21, 1998, p. A1; Ruth Marcus, "Allegations Could Lead to Impeachment," *Washington Post,* January 22, 1998, p. A12.

33. Helen Dewar and Barbara Vobejda, "Scandal Weakens Clinton's Leverage on Hill for Other Issues," *Washington Post,* September 16, 1998, p. A34.

34. Neil A. Lewis, "Voice of America Was Warned on China Interview," *New York Times,* December 18, 1997, p. A3.

35. See www.state.gov/www/global/human_rights/1997_hrp-report/china.html, accessed February 2003. Interview with Jeffrey Bader, July 2000.

36. Interviews with Sandra J. Kristoff, September 2000; and Jeffrey Bader.

37. Some newspaper accounts suggested the schedule change was made so that a high-profile foreign trip would distract attention from the late May trial of the president on sexual misconduct charges brought by Paula Jones. That rumor had no basis in fact. The president did prefer an earlier visit—as did the NSC—so as not to lose momentum in improving the relationship. Domestic political advisers to the president, in fact, preferred a visit later in the year, after the mid-term congressional elections.

38. William Branigan and Steven Mufson, "Chinese Dissident Arrives in U.S.; Release of Key Leader in '89 Protest Smooths Way for Clinton Visit," *Washington Post,* April 20, 1998, p. A1.

39. Human Rights Watch Bulletin, "Wang Dan's Release Welcome but Does Not Signify Improvement" (www.hrw.org/press98/aprl/wan-dan.htm, accessed February 2003).

40. Tang, a protégé of Vice Premier Qian Qichen, beat out U.S. specialist Liu Huaqiu, considered closer to Li Peng. Liu, who had evidently alienated Qian, was dismissed as vice foreign minister shortly afterward, although he still held the position of director of the State Council Foreign Affairs Office. Tang, experienced in Japanese and Asian affairs, was expected to help in particular with the summit meeting with Japanese prime minister Obuchi.

41. Secretary of State Madeleine Albright press conference at Beijing International Club Hotel, April 30, 1998 (http://secretary.state.gov/www/statements/1998/980430b.html, accessed February 2003).

42. Jim Hoagland, "Brazen Road to China," *Washington Post,* May 7, 1998, p. A23.

43. Peter Baker, "Calling off China Trip Bad Idea, Clinton Says; Avoiding Tiananmen Square a Possibility," *Washington Post,* May 27, 1998, p. A4.

44. Interview with Samuel R. Berger, March 2001.

45. See, for example, "Press Briefing by National Security Advisor Sandy Berger, Treasury Secretary Bob Rubin and Director of the National Economic Council Gene Sperling, June 17, 1998" (http://usinfo.state.gov/regional/ea/uschina/visitbrf.htm, accessed February 2003).

46. Erik Eckholm, "Movie before Clinton Visit Stars Jiang as the Statesman," *New York Times*, June 16, 1998, p. A10.

47. Excerpts of Zhao's letter taken from Seth Faison, "Ex-Chinese Leader Confronts Beijing on 1989 Massacre," *New York Times,* June 25, 1998, p. A1.

48. John F. Harris and Steven Mufson, "A Presidential Face in the Crowd; Throng of Aides and Journalists with Clinton in China Sets a Record," *Washington Post,* July 3, 1998, p. A30.

49. See White House Fact Sheet: "Achievements of U.S.-China Summit" (http://clinton4.nara.gov/textonly/WH/New/China/19980627-7898.html, accessed February 2003).

50. Chinese Central Television, June 27, 1998, transcript of Jiang-Clinton press conference, BBC Worldwide Monitoring, June 28, 1998 (Lexis-Nexis); also in *New York Times,* June 28, 1998, p. A1.

51. Ibid.

52. Caryn James, "Clinton's Dream Media Opportunity," *New York Times,* June 30, 1998, p. A9.

53. White House Briefing, "President and Mrs. Clinton's Discussion with Shanghai Community Leaders," June 29, 1998, provided by Federal Information Systems Corporation, transcript acquired through Nexis-Lexis.

54. Transcript of press briefing by Mike McCurry, Lael Brainard, and William Daley, June 30, 1998 (http://usinfo.state.gov/regional/ea/uschina/otrbrief.htm, accessed February 2003).

55. See John Pomfret, "Clinton Declaration on Independence Irks Taiwan," *Washington Post,* July 1, 1998, p. A26.

56. Cited by Tom Raum, "GOP Attacks Clinton's China Policy," Associated Press, July 7, 1998 (Lexis-Nexis).

57. Quoted in Herman Pan and Flor Wang, "Murkowski Charges Clinton with Making Compromise over Taiwan," Central News Agency (Taiwan), July 19, 1998 (Lexis-Nexis).

58. Text of resolution at http://thomas.loc.gov (accessed February 2003).

59. Excerpts from Clinton's news conference appeared in the *Washington Post* on July 4, 1998, under the headline, "We Can Build a Good, Positive Partnership," p. A20.

60. Willy Wo-lap Lam, "Key Jiang Aide 'to Run Taiwan Affairs Unit,'" *South China Morning Post,* September 16, 1998, p. 8.

61. From Xinhua's "tentative" translation of the "joint press communiqué" issued after the meeting: "Russia gives no backing to concepts of 'independence of Taiwan' in any form, supports the stand of the People's Republic of China against 'two Chinas' or 'one China, one Taiwan,' and opposes the admission of Taiwan into the United Nations and other international organizations that only sovereign states have the right to join." See Xinhua News Agency of November 24, 1998, supplied by BBC Worldwide Monitoring (Lexis-Nexis).

62. From a Xinhua report on the joint statement, November 26, 1998, supplied by BBC Worldwide Monitoring (Lexis-Nexis).

63. Jeff Gerth, "Satellite Maker Gave Report to China before Telling U.S.," *New York Times,* May 19, 1998, p. A19.

64. Jeff Gerth and Raymond Bonner, "Companies Are Investigated for Aid to China on Rockets," *New York Times,* April 4, 1998, p. A1; Jeff Gerth, "U.S. Business Role in Policy on China Is under Question," *New York Times,* April 13, 1998, p. A1. See also Final Report of the Select Committee on U.S. National Security and Military/Commercial Concerns with the People's Republic of China (Cox Committee), chap. 6 ("Satellite Launches in the PRC: Loral") (www.house.gov/coxreport/chapfs/ch6.html, accessed February 2003).

65. Cox Committee report, chap. 6.

66. Jeff Gerth and John M. Broder, "The White House Dismissed Warnings on China Satellite Deal," *New York Times,* June 1, 1998, p. A1.

67. Jeff Gerth, "Democrat Fund-Raiser Said to Detail China Tie," *New York Times,* May 15, 1998, p. A1.

68. Ibid (emphasis added).

69. Roberto Suro, Juliet Eilperin, and others, "Loral Denies Any Benefits in Return for Donations," *Washington Post,* May 19, 1998, p. A3.

70. Quoted in Marc Lacey, "House Votes to Restrict China Technology Deals," *Los Angeles Times,* May 21, 1998, p. A1.

71. See Shirley Kan, "China: Possible Missile Technology Transfers from U.S. Satellite Export Policy: Background and Chronology," Congressional Research Service Issue Brief 98-485 F, August 13, 1998. Kan's study is the most comprehensive and balanced work available on this complex topic.

72. Quoted by Juliet Eilperin, "Gingrich to Create Special Panel to Probe China Technology Deal," *Washington Post,* May 20, 1998, p. A4.

73. Department of Justice Bulletin, "Thai Businesswomen Sentenced on Campaign Financing Charges," April 20, 2001 (www.usdoj.gov/opa/pr/2001/April/182crm.htm, accessed February 2003).

74. John Pomfret, "China Tells Taiwan to 'Face Reality'; Call for Talks on Unification Follows Statement by Clinton," *International Herald Tribune,* July 10, 1998.

75. After being introduced to Chinese computer users in 1995, the Internet has grown enormously in China. As Chinese manufacturers increased their production of personal computers rapidly, the estimated number of Chinese using the World Wide Web grew from 50,000 in 1996 to nearly 9 million in 1999 to more than 22 million in 2000 (see Seth Faison, "Chinese Tiptoe into Internet, Wary of Watchdogs," *New York Times*, February 5, 1996, p. 3; "9 Million Switch on to Internet," *South China Morning Post*, January 19, 2000; "Survey on China's Internet Development," ChinaOnline, January 29, 2001 [www.chinaonline.com/internet_policy/NewsArchive/Secure/2001/January/C01011718.asp, accessed February 10, 2001]). The Communist Party has attempted to control Internet content and usage because of the Internet's ability to circulate information broadly and rapidly. While licensed Internet service providers, official portals, and control of the telecommunications network by the Ministry of Posts and Telecommunications have restricted information available on Chinese websites somewhat, the government's efforts to control it have not been entirely successful. See, for example, "China Sets up Office to Regulate Internet News," Reuters, April 21, 2000 (www.nytimes.com/library/tech/00/04/biztech/articles/22china-internet.html, accessed February 2003).

76. Simon Beck, "Diplomacy in Retreat," *South China Morning Post,* August 9, 1998, p. 7.

77. Willy Wo-lap Lam, "Jiang Goes Slow on Reforms," *South China Morning Post,* September 30, 1998, p. 19; Erik Eckholm, "Beijing Sends Potential Dissidents a Message: Don't," *New York Times,* December 25, 1998, p. A3; Elizabeth Rosenthal, "Spring Turns to Winter in Beijing," *New York Times,* December 27, 1998, p. D5.

78. Elizabeth Rosenthal, "Chinese Reminded: No Opposition Allowed," *New York Times*, December 19, 1998, p. A6.

79. Ostensibly part of the regime's efforts to beautify Beijing in advance of the fiftieth anniversary of its founding, the repairs were a convenient excuse to keep the square closed during the tenth anniversary of the June 4, 1989, uprising.

80. Erik Eckholm, "China Sentences 3 for Their Dissent," *New York Times,* December 22, 1998, p. A1.

Notes to Chapter 9

1. From the "Approved Articles of Impeachment," passed by the House of Representatives, December 19, 1998 (www.washingtonpost.com/wp-srv/politics/special/clinton/stories/articles122098.htm, accessed February 2003).

2. Interviews with Kenneth Lieberthal, November 2000, 2001; and Samuel R. Berger, March 2001.

3. Joseph Fewsmith, "China and the WTO: The Politics behind the Agreement," National Bureau of Asian Research, November 1999 (www.nbr.org/publications/report.html, accessed February 2003).

4. Ibid. Citing Chinese sources, Fewsmith claims a third letter was sent in early February, but this seems unlikely.

5. Interviews with Kenneth Lieberthal, Samuel R. Berger, and Susan Shirk, August 2000.

6. James Risen and Jeff Gerth, "China Stole Nuclear Secrets for Bombs, U.S. Aides Say," *New York Times,* March 6, 1999, p. A1.

7. Ibid. Subsequently, it was revealed that the Chinese source was a "walk-in" who appeared at the American Institute on Taiwan and volunteered to spy for the United States (see Bob Drogin, "Chinese Had Details of U.S. Nuclear Missiles," *Los Angeles Times,* May 11, 1999, p. A1). Walk-ins are traditionally treated with great skepticism by intelligence professionals, as they often have unknown personal agendas, have been directed to try and provoke an American reaction or uncover American intelligence officers, or have carried misleading and false information designed to obfuscate an issue or compromise other intelligence reporting.

8. Jeff Gerth and Eric Schmitt, "White House, Congress at Odds over Releasing China Spy Report," *New York Times,* March 10, 1999, p. A1.

9. Risen and Gerth, "China Stole Nuclear Secrets for Bombs, U.S. Aides Say."

10. Laurie P. Cohen and David S. Cloud, "How Federal Agents Bungled the Spy Case against Lee," *Wall Street Journal,* December 8, 2000, p. 1.

11. James Risen, "U.S. Fires Scientist Suspected of Giving China Bomb Data," *New York Times,* March 9, 1999, p. A1.

12. James Risen, "White House Said to Ignore Evidence of China's Spying," *New York Times,* March 13, 1999, p. A14.

13. Vernon Loeb, "CIA Probe Gets Outside Review; Retired Admiral to Examine Report on China Spy Case Damage," *Washington Post,* March 16, 1999, p. A16.

14. John F. Harris and Vernon Loeb, "Spy Case Tests U.S. Openness with China," *Washington Post,* March 14, 1999, p. A1.

15. Dick Lugar, "Threats from China," *Washington Post,* March 10, 1999, p. A23.

16. James Kynge, "Chinese PM Backs Effort to Join WTO," *Financial Times,* February 24, 1999, p. 5; James Mann, "U.S. and China Working to Get Beijing into WTO," *Los Angeles Times,* February 25, 1999, p. C1.

17. See Ellis Joffe, "China's Military Assesses Kosovo," *International Herald Tribune,* July 23, 1999; also Yossef Bodansky, "Beijing and the Kosovo Crisis," Defense and Foreign Affairs Strategy Policy, May–June 1999, p. 4 (Lexis-Nexis).

18. H.R. 3616, sec. 1533, "Report on Requirements for Response to Increased Missile Threat in Asia-Pacific Region" (http://thomas.loc.gov, accessed February 2003).

19. Zhang Zhaozhong, "Resurgence of the 'Star Wars' Programme," *Jiefangjun Bao* (Liberation Army Daily), February 4, 1999, translated by BBC Summary of World Broadcasts, FE/D3469/F, February 26, 1999 (Lexis-Nexis).

20. Matthew Lee, "Deep Rift over Human Rights Dominates Albright's China Talks," Agence France-Presse, March 1, 1999 (Lexis-Nexis).

21. Bob Drogin, "U.S., China 'Let off Steam' in Talks," *Los Angeles Times,* March 3, 1999, p. A4.

22. "Chinese Premier's U.S. Visit Reportedly Nearly Canceled Due to NATO Air Strikes," *Zhongguo Tongxun She* (Hong Kong), April 5, 1999 (Lexis-Nexis); Cary Huang, "Last-Minute Debate Gave Zhu Go-Ahead," *Hong Kong Standard,* April 6, 1999; Kyodo News Agency (Japan), "Jiang Called Top Secret Meeting to Save Zhu's U.S. Visit," April 8, 1999.

23. Xinhua News Agency, "China's Strategists Put Forward New Security Concept," April 14, 1999 (Lexis-Nexis). The "new security concept" was widely and actively debated throughout the remainder of the year and particularly after the U.S. bombing of China's embassy in Belgrade. See David M. Finkelstein, "China Reconsiders Its National Security: The Great Peace and Development Debate of 1999" Arlington, Va: CNA Corporation (December 2000), pp. 3–6.

24. Interview with Samuel R. Berger.

25. Quoted in David E. Sanger, "A China Trade Deal Is Now up to Clinton," *New York Times,* April 7, 1999, p. C1.

26. Interview with Kenneth Lieberthal.

27. Sanger, "A China Trade Deal Is Now up to Clinton."

28. See, for example, Zhu's April 2 interview with Peter Kann and several other members of the *Wall Street Journal* editorial board, published on April 6, 1999, p. A23, and reprinted by Xinhua on April 9, 1999.

29. Ibid.

30. White House Press Office, "President Clinton's 4/7 Speech on U.S. Policy toward China," Mayflower Hotel, April 7, 1999 (http://usinfo.state.gov/regional/ea/uschina/clint407.htm, accessed February 2003).

31. Interviews with Samuel R. Berger and Kenneth Lieberthal.

32. Steven Mufson and Bob Kaiser, "Missed U.S.-China Deal Looms Large," *Washington Post,* November 10, 1999, p. A1, citing an unidentified Chinese diplomat.

33. The document in question is entitled "Market Access and Protocol Commitments" (www.ustr.gov/releases/1999/04/Ch-Memo.html, accessed February 2003). No one has ever taken responsibility for posting it on the Internet.

34. Quoted in Steven Mufson, "U.S. Is Asking Too Much, Zhu Complains," *Washington Post,* April 10, 1999, p. A12.

35. Bob Drogin, "Trade Accord Eludes Clinton, China's Zhu," *Los Angeles Times,* April 9, 1999, p. A1; "Joint Press Conference of the President and Premier Zhu Rongji of the People's Republic of China," April 8, 1999 (www.state.gov/www/regions/eap/990408a_clinton_zhu_china.html, accessed February 2003).

36. "Joint Press Conference," April 8, 1999.

37. Interview with Kenneth Lieberthal. Chinese Central Television also mentioned the telephone call, though not its content, in its April 14 newscast.

38. Harvey Sicherman, "The Inscrutable Americans, Zhu Rongji, and the Deal That Wasn't," *Foreign Policy Research Institute E-Note*, April 23, 1999; Chinese

Central Television report of April 14, 1999, BBC Summary of World Broadcasts, FE/D3509/G, April 15, 1999 (Lexis-Nexis).

39. Willy Wo-lap Lam, "Zhu Goes for Broke," *South China Morning Post,* April 18, 1999, p. 10; "Zhu Deal Backlash," *South China Morning Post,* May 5, 1999, p. 19.

40. Joseph Fewsmith, "China and the WTO: The Politics behind the Agreement," National Bureau of Asian Research, November 1999, p. 8 (www.nbr.org/publications/report.html, accessed February 2003). The source for the account of Li's criticism of Zhu is unclear.

41. Of the many accounts of the events of May 7, 1999, the most authoritative is Steven Lee Myers's lengthy research article, "Chinese Embassy Bombing: A Wide Net of Blame," which appeared in the *New York Times* on April 17, 2000, p. A1 (www.nytimes.com/library/world/global/041700embassy-bombing.html, accessed February 2003).

42. Subsequent American accounts have observed that the three may have been involved in intelligence work, as China sometimes uses journalistic "cover" for overseas intelligence officers. While this has furthered speculation that the bombings were deliberate, there is no corroborating information available to support the allegations.

43. Text of MFA statement in Wang Shubai, ed., *Zhongguo buke qi* (China cannot be bullied) (Beijing: China Books Publishing House, 1999), pp. 161–62.

44. Elisabeth Rosenthal, "China Protesters Rage at America," *New York Times,* May 9, 1999, p. A1.

45. Similar protests were held outside U.S. consulates in Shenyang, Shanghai, Guangzhou, and Chengdu, with more than 10,000 protesters reported at each location. In Chengdu on Saturday night, the situation deteriorated sharply when protesters gained access to the consul general's residence and set it on fire. See Henry Chu, Maggie Farley, and Anthony Kuhn, "Crisis in Yugoslavia; Chinese Attack U.S. Missions as Protests Intensify," *Los Angeles Times,* May 10, 1999, p. A1.

46. "U.S. Deeply Regrets Bombing of Chinese Embassy," Joint Statement by Secretary of Defense William S. Cohen and CIA director George J. Tenet, May 8, 1999 (http://usinfo.state.gov/regional/ea/uschina/prccohn8.htm, accessed February 2003).

47. "Furor over Embassy Attack—CIA May Have Used Outdated Map," *Seattle Times,* May 9, 1999, p. 1 (Lexis-Nexis).

48. Elisabeth Rosenthal, "Envoy Says Stoning Will End, Ties Won't," *New York Times,* May 11, 1999, p. A11.

49. Quoted in Erik Eckholm, "After Protests Spill out, China May Find Sentiments Cannot Be Recorked," *New York Times*, May 11, 1999, p. A3.

50. Cited by Xinhua News Agency, May 10, 1999 (Lexis-Nexis).

51. Xinhua News Agency, "Televised Speech by Hu Jintao, Member of the Chinese Communist Party Central Committee Political Bureau Standing Committee and Vice-President of the State," May 9, 1999, transcribed by BBC Worldwide Monitoring (Lexis-Nexis).

52. Wang, *Zhongguo buke qi* (China Cannot Be Bullied), p. 168. Foreign Minister Tang Jiaxuan actually summoned U.S. ambassador Sasser to the Foreign Ministry, but he refused to go, citing demonstrations outside the embassy. Tang read the demands over the phone.

53. Text of Jiang's speech from Xinhua News Agency, May 13, 1999, in FBIS (OW1305175899), May 13, 1999.

54. "Unswervingly Upholding the Independent Policy of Peace," *Renmin Ribao,* June 3, 1999, p. 1, translated in FBIS-CHI-1999-0604, June 4, 1999.

55. "Special Commentary" by Zhang Dezhen, "On U.S. Eurasian Strategy," *Renmin Ribao*, June 4, 1999, p. 6, in FBIS-CHI-1999-0605, OW0506041699, June 4, 1999.

56. Xinhua News Agency, "'People's Daily' Editorial Urges Unity for Nation's Growth," June 7, 1999, in BBC Worldwide Monitoring, June 8, 1999 (Lexis-Nexis).

57. National Imagery and Mapping Agency (NIMA) press release no. 990516-2, May 16, 1999 (http://164.214.2.59/general/embassy.html, accessed November 22, 2001).

58. Interview with Susan Shirk.

59. I was in Beijing in early June and talked directly with Foreign Ministry officials, who made it clear that nothing Pickering said would be accepted by the Chinese government as a satisfactory explanation of the bombing. They indicated they would hear the undersecretary out but that his explanation would be rejected.

60. Lo Ping, "The Military Is Heating up Its Anti-Americanism Again," *Cheng Ming* magazine, no. 261, July 1, 1999, pp. 10–11, FBIS OW1907235499, July 19, 1999. *Cheng Ming*'s account of the Politburo meeting in late May cannot be corroborated, but its report on the meeting's conclusions are consistent with China's subsequent behavior.

61. Pickering's "talking points" for his briefing of Chinese officials, which took place on June 16, 1999, were released by the State Department spokesman on July 6, 1999 (http://usinfo.state.gov/regional/ea/uschina/bombrpt.htm, accessed February 2003). CIA Director George Tenet and Deputy Secretary of Defense John Hamre gave a similar account in testimony to the House Select Committee on Intelligence on July 22, 1999.

62. "U.S. President's Personal Envoy in China to Present the U.S. Government's Report on Its Investigation into the Bombing of the Chinese Embassy in the Federal Republic of Yugoslavia," Ministry of Foreign Affairs, June 18, 1999 (www.fas.org/news/china/1999/0622.htm, accessed February 2003).

63. Pickering had been authorized to raise the issue of compensation for victims and their families, and U.S. negotiators worked that issue diligently until December, when Beijing accepted a U.S. offer of $28 million for damage to the Belgrade Embassy, and China agreed to pay $2.87 million for damage to U.S. facilities in China. See "China-U.S. Agree on Compensation over Embassy Bombing," Agence France-Presse, December 15, 1999 (Lexis-Nexis).

64. Lyman Miller, formerly a Chinese media analyst with the Foreign Broadcast Information Service, communicated this interpretation of the significance of "ob-

server" articles in private correspondence. Nomenclature, authorship, and placement of opinion pieces in *Renmin Ribao* is a time-honored tool of China watching. For a detailed discussion, see Wu Guoguang, "Command Communication: The Politics of Editorial Formulation in the *People's Daily,*" *The China Quarterly,* no. 137 (March 1994), p. 194ff.

65. "Observer," *Renmin Ribao,* June 22, 1999, p. 6, in BBC Summary of World Broadcasts, FE/D3570/G, June 25, 1999.

66. Joseph Fewsmith, "The Impact of the Kosovo Conflict on China's Political Leaders and Prospects for WTO," National Bureau of Asian Research, July 1999, note 6 (www.nbr.org/publications/briefing/fewsmith99/index.html, accessed June 3, 1999).

67. John Sweeney, Jens Holsoe, and Ed Vulliamy, "NATO Bombed Chinese Deliberately," *The Observer,* October 17, 1999 (www.guardian.co.uk/Kosovo/Story/0,2763,203214,00.html, accessed February 2003).

68. Quoted by E. J. Dionne, "Blunder and Bluster," *Washington Post,* May 14, 1999, p. A33.

69. See, for example, "The Tempest in China," *New York Times* editorial, May 12, 1999, p. A24. Other newspapers were similarly dismissive.

70. Quoted in John Pomfret and Michael Laris, "Thousands Vent Anger in China's Cities," *Washington Post,* May 9, 1999, p. A1.

71. The full version of the damage assessment remains classified. The remarks of the review panel and the DCI's version of the document's key findings can be found at www.cia.gov/cia/public_affairs/press_ release/1999/0421kf.html, accessed February 2003.

72. Emphasis added. The online version of the Cox Committee report (www.house.gov/coxreport/, accessed February 2003).

73. Stephen I. Schwartz, "A Very Convenient Scandal," *Bulletin of the Atomic Scientists*, vol. 55, no. 4 (May–June 1999), available online (www.bullatomsci.org/issues/1999/mj99/mj99schwartz.html, accessed February 2003).

74. Office of the Press Secretary, "Clinton Administration's Response to Cox Committee Report on Chinese Espionage," May 25, 1999 (www.clw.org/coalition/whcox052599.htm, accessed February 2003).

75. Robert Kagan, "China's No. 1 Enemy," *New York Times,* May 11, 1999, p. A23.

76. Tim Weiner, "Nuclear Secrets: Questions; How Right Is the Report? Caveats by Experts," *New York Times,* May 26, 1999, p. A20.

77. William J. Broad, "Spies versus Sweat: The Debate over China's Nuclear Advance," *New York Times*, September 7, 1999 (www.nytimes.com/library/world/asia/090799china-nuke.html, accessed February 2003).

78. "Science at Its Best, Security at Its Worst," a special report by the President's Foreign Intelligence Advisory Board, June 1999 (www.fas.org/sgp/library/pfiab/foreword.html, accessed February 2003).

79. Alastair Iain Johnston, W. K. H. Panofsky, Marco Di Capua, and Lewis R. Franklin, "The Cox Committee Report: An Assessment," edited by M. M. May (www.ceip.org/files/projects/npp/pdg/coxfinal3.pdf, accessed February 2003).

80. See, for example, Frank Gaffney Jr., "The Empire Strikes Back," *Washington Times,* December 21, 1999.

81. Lee Teng-hui, with Tsou Ching-wen, *Li Tenghui chicheng kaopai shihlu* (A True Record of Lee Teng-hui in Power) (Taipei: INK Publishing, 2001), p. 223.

82. Ibid., p. 230, my own translation, emphasis added. Slightly different translated text also available at www.taiwandc.org/nws-9926.htm (accessed May 28, 2001).

83. "Lee's '2-Nation' Remark Sparks Mixed Reaction," *China Post* (from *Financial Times* News Global News Wire), July 11, 1999 (Lexis-Nexis).

84. Bear Lee, "No Major Change in China Mainland Policy: MAC Head," Central News Agency (Taiwan), July 12, 1999 (Lexis-Nexis). See also Lee, with Tsou, *Li Tenghui chicheng kaopai shihlu* (A True Record of Lee Teng-hui in Power), pp. 240–42. Lee is coy about his own intentions in using the term in the German radio interview and faults both the Western media for exaggerating the situation and Su Ch'i for not consulting enough with Lee's office before making follow-up statements.

85. Xinhua commentator, July 12, 1999, Xinhua News Agency, no. 0712013, July 12, 1999 (Lexis-Nexis).

86. Commentator's article, "Undermining the One China Principle Is the Crucial Issue," *Renmin Ribao,* July 14, 1999 (http://english.peopledaily.com.cn/other/archive.html, accessed February 2003).

87. Commentator, "Lee Teng-hui, Don't Play with Fire," *Jiefangjun Bao,* July 15, 1999, carried by Xinhua on July 14, 1999 (Lexis-Nexis).

88. Michael Laris, "Taiwan Jettisons 'One China' Formula; Irate Beijing Warns Step Is 'Dangerous,'" *Washington Post,* July 12, 1999, p. A14.

89. State Department daily briefing, July 13, 1999, from Federal News Service (Lexis-Nexis).

90. Jane Perlez, "U.S. Asking Taiwan to Explain Its Policy after Uproar," *New York Times,* July 14, 1999, p. A3.

91. "Clinton Reaffirms Commitment to 'One China,'" *China Daily,* July 19, 1999, from Financial Times Intelligence Wire (Lexis-Nexis).

92. Philip Shenon, "U.S. Cancels Military Aides' Visit to Taiwan," *New York Times,* July 22, 1999, p. A8.

93. Lee, with Tsou, *Li Tenghui chicheng kaopai shihlu* (A True Record of Lee Teng-hui in Power), pp. 239–45; 292–96.

94. Hearings of the Senate Foreign Relations Committee on S. 693, the Taiwan Security Enhancement Act, August 4, 1999, Federal News Service (Lexis-Nexis).

95. "Asia's Lethal Computers," *The Economist,* October 30, 1999.

96. Quoted in William J. McMahon, "Citing Security, China Unplugs Government Web Sites from Internet," *China Online,* August 25, 1999.

97. See Willy Wo-lap Lam, "PLA Elite Moved to Taiwan Region," *South China Morning Post,* August 10, 1999, p. 1; "Reality Ebbs from Beidaihe," *South China Morning Post,* August 11, 1999, p. 15.

98. Micool Brooke, "U.S. Navy Ready if Taiwan Crisis Explodes, Admiral Says," Associated Press, August 12, 1999; "U.S. 7th Fleet Monitors China-Taiwan Tension," Agence France-Presse dispatch, July 22, 1999 (Lexis-Nexis).

99. David A. Fulghum, "Words Will Fly, but Bombs Won't as China, Taiwan Huff and Bluff," *Aviation Week and Space Technology*, August 9, 1999, p. 83. As further evidence that the launch was part of a normal test cycle rather than a political signal, analysts noted that the target area was in western China rather than in the Pacific Ocean.

100. I attended one such session and spoke with others who held similar conversations. See also Michael Laris and Steven Mufson, "China Mulls Use of Force off Taiwan, Experts Say; Warnings Perceived as Effort to Gauge Likely U.S. Reaction," *Washington Post,* August 13, 1999, p. A1.

101. "Wavering, Not Drowning," *Financial Times,* August 12, 1999; Todd Crowell, "Time for Decisions," *Asiaweek,* August 20, 1999, p. 26; Steven Butler and Thomas Omestad, "Why Beijing's Grumpy Old Men Are So Grumpy," *U.S. News & World Report,* August 9, 1999, p. 31.

102. Seth Faison, "U.S. Agrees to Pay China for Embassy Bombing," *New York Times,* July 31, 1999, p. A5.

103. Michael Richardson, "Clinton Sets Talks with Jiang over Strained Ties," *International Herald Tribune,* July 26, 1999, p. 1 (Lexis-Nexis). Albright's views were mild compared to those of Commander in Chief of U.S. Forces in the Pacific admiral Dennis Blair, who, in remarks intended to be private, referred to Taiwan as the "turd in the punchbowl" of U.S.-China relations. See Bill Gertz and Rowan Scarborough, "Inside the Ring," *Washington Times,* July 30, 1999, p. A11.

104. Bill Gertz, "Pentagon to Sell 2 E-2 Planes, Radar Equipment to Taiwan," *Washington Times,* July 31, 1999, p. C5.

105. Xinhua News Agency, August 18, 1999, in BBC Summary of World Broadcasts, FE/D3618/F, August 20, 1999.

106. Press briefing by National Security Adviser Sandy Berger and National Economic Adviser Gene Sperling, September 11, 1999 (http://clinton3.nara.gov/WH/New/APEC1999/brief4.html, accessed February 2003).

107. Fewsmith, "China and the WTO: The Politics behind the Agreement," National Bureau of Asian Research, November 1999. China's chief negotiator, Long Yongtu, also provided an account of the last series of negotiations in the monthly magazine *Caijing* (November 5, 2001), making the point that the larger relationship was the principal reason for resuming talks.

108. David E. Sanger, "At the Last Hour, Down to the Last Trick, and It Worked," *New York Times,* November 17, 1999, p. A1; Hu Shuli, *Long Yongtu: Tanpan shi zheyang wancheng de* (Long Yongtu: This Is How the Negotiations Were Completed), *Caijing* (Finance) magazine, November 5, 2001 (www.caijing.com.cn/lbi-html/caijing/monthly/20011105/index.html, accessed December 12, 2001).

109. John F. Harris and Michael Laris, "'Roller-Coaster Ride' to an Off-Again, On-Again Trade Pact," *Washington Post,* November 16, 1999, p. A26; Hu Shuli, *Long Yongtu: Tanpan shi zheyang wancheng de* (Long Yongtu: This Is How the Negotiations Were Completed). Curiously, NSC Senior Director Lieberthal proceeded to the airport and boarded his flight for Washington, missing the final session and successful result.

110. Hu Shuli, *Long Yongtu: Tanpan shi zheyang wancheng de* (Long Yongtu: This Is How the Negotiations Were Completed); "Briefing by USTR Charlene Barshefsky and Economic Council Director Gene Sperling Following Negotiations with China on the WTO," Federal News Service, November 15, 1999 (Lexis-Nexis).

111. White House Press Office, "Remarks by the President to U.S. Embassy in Ankara," November 15, 1999 (www.state.gov/www/regions/eap/991115_clinton_china.html, accessed February 2003).

112. See Vernon Loeb, "Physicist Is Indicted in Nuclear Spy Probe; Wen Ho Lee Accused of Mishandling Secrets," *Washington Post,* December 11, 1999, p. A1; the text of the actual indictment can be found at www.fas.org/irp/ops/ci/docs/lee_indict.html (accessed February 2003).

113. Vernon Loeb, "No Bail in Atomic Data Case," *Washington Post,* December 30, 1999, p. A1.

114. Bill Mesler, "The Spy Who Wasn't: National Insecurity State," *The Nation,* August 9, 1999, p. 13.

115. See Walter Pincus, "Lee's Links to Taiwan Scrutinized," *Washington Post,* December 31, 1999, p. A1. A native of Taiwan, Lee in 1998 had visited the Chung Shan Institute in Taiwan—where much of the country's advanced weapons research is done—and may even have tried to access his classified computer from there.

116. Vernon Loeb, "Ex-Official: Bomb Lab Case Lacks Evidence; Suspect's Ethnicity 'a Major Factor' in China Spy Probe," *Washington Post*, August 17, 1999, p. A1.

117. Vernon Loeb, "Espionage Whistleblower Resigns; Energy's Trulock Cites Lack of Support as Debate about His Tactics Grows," *Washington Post,* August 24, 1999, p. A1.

118. William J. Broad, "Spies versus Sweat: The Debate over China's Nuclear Advance," *New York Times,* September 7, 1999 (www.nytimes.com/library/world/asia/090799china-nuke.html, accessed February 2003).

119. See, for example, Mesler, "The Spy Who Wasn't"; "What, No Smoking Gun?" *Village Voice,* September 21, 1999, p. 42; Robert Scheer, "Government Owes Wen Ho Lee an Apology," *Los Angeles Times,* October 6, 1999.

120. See Mesler, "The Spy Who Wasn't," p. 13.

121. Bob Drogin, "Nuke Secrets Deemed Vital to Scientist's Case," *Los Angeles Times,* June 16, 2000.

122. James Sterngold, "Agent Concedes Faulty Testimony in Secrets Case," *New York Times,* August 18, 2000, p. A1; "Accused Scientist to Go Free on Bail in Los Alamos Case," *New York Times,* August 25, 2000, p. A1; Bob Drogin, "Defense Shows Holes in Case against Scientist," *Los Angeles Times,* August 19, 2000, p. A1.

123. "Wen Ho Lee Freed after Pleading Guilty to One Count," Associated Press, September 13, 2000 (Lexis-Nexis).

124. See "The President's Remarks upon Departure on Patients Bill of Rights," September 14, 2000 (www.fas.org/irp/ops/ci/whl_clinton.html, accessed February 2003).

125. See their testimony before the Senate Judiciary Committee on September 26, 2000, Federal Document Clearing House Transcripts (Lexis-Nexis).

126. See "The Times and Wen Ho Lee," by the editors of the *New York Times,* September 26, 2000 (http://tms.physics.lsa.umich.edu/214/other/news/092600edno.html, accessed February 2003).

127. Office of the Press Secretary, "President Clinton on Trade Relations with China," January 10, 1999 (http://usinfo.state.gov/regional/ca/uschina/clin0110.htm, accessed February 2003).

128. Office of the Press Secretary, "Remarks by the President on China," at the Paul Nitze School of Advanced International Studies, March 8, 2000. See www.sais-jhu.edu/events/clinton.html, among other sites (accessed February 2003).

129. These themes recur in numerous speeches by the president, Sandy Berger, and others in early 2000. A full catalog of administration comments, speeches, and documents on China's entry into the WTO can be found at http://usinfo.state.gov/regional/ca/uschina/pntrpres.htm (accessed February 2003).

130. See the statement by Mike Jendrzejczyk, Washington director, Asia Division of Human Rights Watch at the HIRC hearing, May 10, 2000 (www.hrw.org/campaigns/china-99/china-testimony-051100.htm, accessed February 2003).

131. Charles Babington, "Clinton Softens Push for China Trade Bill," *Washington Post,* May 21, 2000, p. A6.

132. David E. Sanger, "Threat Seen to Trade Deal to Let China Join WTO," *New York Times,* February 24, 2000.

133. Gore's careful letter to NAM president Jerry Jasinowski was released by Senator Max Baucus (D-Mont.) in late February.

134. Interview with Samuel R. Berger; Babington, "Clinton Softens Push for China Trade Bill," p. A6.

135. See "Narrative of Draft Legislation for China/PNTR Framework," May 10, 2000 (http://info.state.gov/regional/ca/uschina/pntrbrtr.htm, accessed February 2003).

136. See the text of the H.R. 4444, as passed (http://thomas.loc.gov, accessed February 2003). For many Chinese, the bill number must have evoked deep foreboding, because the number "4" is homophonic with the word for "death" and is avoided, just as the number "13" is avoided by many Westerners.

137. See Overview and Action Summary of H.R. 4444 (http://thomas.loc.gov, accessed February 2003).

138. Ibid.

139. See James Gerstenzang, "In Vote, Clinton Wins a Laurel for His Legacy," *Los Angeles Times,* May 25, 2000; David E. Sanger, "Rounding out a Clear Clinton Legacy," *New York Times,* May 25, 2000.

140. "Remarks by Foreign Ministry Spokesperson Sun Yuxi on the Passage of the Bill on China's PNTR by U.S. Senate," September 21, 2000 (www.fmprc.gov.cn/eng/5153.html, accessed February 2003).

141. Office of the Press Secretary, "Remarks by the President . . . at Signing of China Permanent Normal Trade Relations," October 10, 2000 (www.usconsulate.org.hk/uscn/wh/2000/101001.htm, accessed December 15, 2001.) China

acceded to the WTO on November 11, 2001, followed immediately and without difficulty by Taiwan. President George W. Bush, who succeeded Clinton, certified in December 2001 that the terms of China's accession were equal to or better than the terms negotiated by the USTR in November 1999, then declared nondiscriminatory treatment would be offered permanently to products from the People's Republic of China, effective January 1, 2002.

142. Established via section 1238 of H.R. 4205, the National Defense Authorization Act of 2001, P.L. 106-398 of October 30, 2000 (http://frwebgate.access.gpo.gov/cgi-bin/getdoc.cgi?dbname=106_cong_public_laws&docid=f:publ398.106, accessed February 2003).

143. Different polls cited in the study had different percentages, but the overall results were that "public attitudes toward China changed [after 1989] from favorable to divided, leaning toward unfavorable—where they have stayed for over a decade. A majority has a negative view of China's human rights record. There is little optimism that the human rights record will improve or that China will become more democratic. Trust in China is fairly low." See Americans and the World: Public Opinion on International Affairs, "U.S. Relations with China," a database maintained by the Program on International Policy Attitudes, data at www.americans-world.org/digest/regional_issues/china/china1.cfm (accessed July 24, 2001).

144. See "U.S. Relations with China—Nature of the U.S.-China Relationship," at www.americans-world.org/digest/regional_issues/china/china2.cfm (accessed February 2003).

145. See "U.S. Relations with China—Trade with China," data at www.americans-world.org/digest/regional_issues/china/china5.cfm (accessed February 2003).

146. "The One China Principle and the Taiwan Issue," published by the State Council Information Office and the Taiwan Affairs Office, February 22, 2000 (emphasis added). The State Council English language version used the Latin term *sine die* (later rendered as "indefinitely") to translate the Chinese term *wu xianqi*, which means, literally, "without a limited time period."

147. Jane Perlez, "Warning by China to Taiwan Poses Problem to U.S.," *New York Times*, February 27, 2000, p. A1.

148. "Chinese Vice-Premier Qian Says Taiwan White Paper Not New Policy," Xinhua News Agency, February 29, 2000, BBC Summary of World Broadcasts, FE/D3778/F2, March 2, 2000.

149. Art Pine, "House Votes to Strengthen Military Ties with Taiwan," *Los Angeles Times,* February 2, 2000, p. A4.

150. Erik Eckholm and Steven Lee Myers, "Taiwan Asks U.S. to Let It Obtain Top-Flight Arms," *New York Times,* March 1, 2000 (www.nytimes.com/library/world/asia/030100china-us-taiwan.html, accessed February 2003).

151. The AEGIS Combat System (originally Advanced Surface Missile System, renamed in 1969 after the mythical shield of Zeus) is the U.S. state-of-the-art integrated radar tracking and missile launch system used aboard U.S. Navy Ticonderoga-class cruisers and Arleigh Burke–class destroyers. At its heart is a "multi-functional phased-array" radar system, capable of tracking more than 100 targets simultaneously.

It is computer linked to a variety of shipboard missile systems, including antiaircraft, antiship, antisubmarine, and land-attack cruise missiles. It is currently being upgraded to be capable of ballistic missile defense under the navy's area-wide and theater-wide programs. It is this missile defense capability—even though not yet fully developed—that makes the question of selling Arleigh Burke-class destroyers to Taiwan so controversial in a cross-Strait context. See *Jane's Information Group*, "AEGIS Weapon System MK-7" (www.janes.com/defence/naval_forces/ news/misc/aegis010425.shtml, accessed June 23, 2001).

152. Tang Jiaxuan press conference of March 10, 2000, *China Daily,* March 11, 2000, p. 1 (Lexis-Nexis).

153. Vivian Pik-kwan Chan, "Jiang Stresses Firm Stance on Taiwan," *South China Morning Post*, March 4, 2000.

154. From *Renmin Ribao*, "PLA General on Taiwan Issue," March 6, 2000 (http://english.peopledaily.com.cn/200003/06/print20000306N115.html, accessed February 2003).

155. Press conference transcript from CCTV, Beijing, March 15, 2000, provided by BBC Worldwide Monitoring, March 16, 2000 (Lexis-Nexis).

156. "Premier Zhu Don Corleone," *Washington Post* editorial, March 16, 2000, p. A26.

157. Nicholas D. Kristof, "Party Undone by Liberty It Nurtured," *New York Times,* March 18, 2000.

158. See Erik Eckholm, "After 50 Years, Nationalists Are Ousted in Taiwan Vote," *New York Times,* March 19, 2000.

159. Lin Chieh-yu and William Ide, "Chen Offers Peace, Sovereignty," March 19, 2000 (www.taipeitimes.com/news/2000/03/19/story/0000028411, accessed February 2003).

160. Xinhua News Agency, March 18, 2000, provided by BBC Worldwide Monitoring, March 22, 2000 (Lexis-Nexis).

161. Xinhua News Agency, March 24, 2000, from BBC Summary of World Broadcasts, FE/D3799/F2, March 27, 2000 (Lexis-Nexis).

162. Willy Wo-lap Lam, "Military Pressure Builds over Taiwan," *South China Morning Post,* March 29, 2000 (www.scmp.com/News/Columns/Article/Column_asp_NodeKey-IE2-2FChina-2FWilly.asp, accessed March 29, 2000). See also interview with Xin Qi, a research fellow at the China Peace and Development Study Center, in Hong Kong's *Ta Kung Pao*, April 27, 2000.

163. "Taiwan Threatened with Disaster," Reuters, April 28, 2000.

164. See Suzanne Ganz, "Chen Won't Yield to China Threats, Shelve Sovereignty Issue," *Kyodo*, Japan Economic Newswire, May 19, 2000; "Taiwan Forced into Corner, Says President-Elect," *South China Morning Post,* April 29, 2000.

165. "The Only Way Out for Relaxing the Cross-Straits Ties," Xinhua News Agency commentary, May 16, 2000.

166. Chen Shui-bian, "Taiwan Stands Up: Advancing to an Uplifting Era," speech delivered May 20, 2000 (http://th.gio.gov.tw/pi2000/dow_1.htm, accessed February 2003).

167. “The One China Principle Allows for No Evasion or Ambiguity,” Xinhua News Agency commentary, May 21, 2000.

168. President Clinton first used the “three pillars” phrase in a July 21, 1999, press conference.

169. Bill Gertz, “Jiang Pressed Clinton to Force Taiwan’s Hand,” *Washington Times,* August 20, 1999, p. A4.

170. Margaret M. Pearson, “The Case of China’s Accession to GATT/WTO,” in David M. Lampton, ed., *The Making of Chinese Foreign and Security Policy in the Era of Reform* (Stanford University Press, 2001), p. 345. Opinions vary on the subject of whether the WTO agreement reached in November 1999 was significantly better than what was available in April.

171. Lo Ping, “The Military Is Heating up Its Anti-Americanism Again,” *Cheng Ming* magazine, no. 261, July 1, 1999, pp. 10–11, translated by FBIS OW1907235499, published July 17, 1999. *Cheng Ming* is known occasionally to provide exaggerated news coverage of Chinese domestic politics.

172. See David M. Finkelstein, “China Reconsiders Its National Security: The Great Peace and Development Debate of 1999” (Arlington, Va.: CNA Corporation, December 2000), pp. 6–7, 21–23.

173. *Renmin Ribao* opinion, “Egoism, Overbearing Psychology,” July 7, 2000 (www.fpeng.peopledaily.com.cn/ 200007/07/eng20000707_44955.html, accessed May 13, 2001); Liu Jianfei, “Erroneous Areas of Mentality of U.S. Anti-China Forces,” *Liaowang,* June 5, 2000, p. 59, FBIS translation CPP20000612000039.

174. Joseph Fewsmith and Stanley Rosen, “The Domestic Context of Chinese Foreign Policy: Does Public Opinion Matter?” in David M. Lampton, ed., *The Making of Chinese Foreign and Security Policy in the Era of Reform* (Stanford University Press, 2001), p. 186; Alastair Iain Johnston, “Chinese Middle Class Attitudes toward International Affairs: Nascent Liberalization?” Unpublished manuscript, October 2001.

175. *Qigong* is a system of physical exercises, breathing, and meditation training, the purpose of which is to strengthen the body’s internal energy by controlling the circulation of *qi,* the breath or energy. Numerous schools of *qigong* have developed over many years, generally headed by a master who is often believed to have mystical powers. Some have become political opposition movements, such as the Boxer Movement of the late nineteenth century.

176. “Sect Members Deliver Their Demands to Beijing in Huge Petition,” *Ming Pao* (Hong Kong), April 26, 1999, p. A1, in BBC Summary of World Broadcasts, FE/D3519/G, April 27, 1999; John Pomfret and Michael Laris, “Silent Protest Draws Thousands to Beijing,” *Washington Post,* April 26, 1999, p. A11.

177. “Mainland Schools ‘Invaded’ by ‘Cult’ of Falun Gong,” *Ming Pao* (Hong Kong), April 27, 1999, p. A13, in BBC Summary of World Broadcasts, FE/D3520/G, April 28, 1999; John Pomfret, “Cracks in China’s Crackdown,” *Washington Post,* November 12, 1999, p. A1.

178. Susan V. Lawrence, “Jiang’s Two Faces,” *Far Eastern Economic Review,* December 2, 1999, available at www.feer.com/articles/1999/9912_02/p16china.html (accessed February 2003).

179. John Pomfret, "China Said to Detain 35,000 in Sect," *Washington Post,* November 30, 1999, p. A22.

Notes to Chapter 10

1. Andrew J. Nathan and E. Perry Link, eds., *The Tiananmen Papers*, compiled by Zhang Liang (pseudonym) (New York: Public Affairs, 2001).

2. In a review of the book, Yale University historian Jonathan Spence identified a historical antecedent for the pseudonym Zhang Liang: that being a third-century B.C. Han Dynasty official who "was a strategist of the highest order, a man whose subtlety at analyzing the nuances of political life, military realities and personal relationships was exceptional." See Jonathan Spence, "Inside the Forbidden City," *New York Times,* January 21, 2001 (www.nytimes.com/books/01/01/21/reviews/010121.21spencet.html, accessed February 2003).

3. A Chinese-language version, with more background material and a wider selection of documents, was published in April 2001 under the title *Liu-si zhen xiang* (June Fourth: The True Story) (Mirror Books, 2001).

4. Zhang Liang, "Reflections on June Fourth," in Nathan and Link, *Tiananmen Papers,* pp. xii–xiii. See also Zhang's interview with CNN's Mike Chinoy, June 3, 2001 (http://asia.cnn.com/SPECIALS/2001/tiananmen/papers.html, accessed January 8, 2002).

5. Orville Schell, "Reflections on Authentication,"in Nathan and Link, *The Tiananmen Papers*, p. 474.

6. "Jiang Zemin Refutes the Tiananmen Papers," *Ming Pao* (Hong Kong), January 8, 2001, p. 1.

7. Quoted in Allen T. Cheng and Tim Healy, "The Ghosts of Tiananmen," *Asiaweek,* January 19, 2001 (www.asiaweek.com/asiaweek/magazine/nations/0,8782,94722,00.html, accessed February 2003).

8. Erik Eckholm and Elizabeth Rosenthal, "China's Leadership Pushes for Unity," *New York Times,* March 8, 2001, p. A1; Vivien Pik-kwan Chan, "Film Used to Counter Tiananmen Papers," *South China Morning Post,* March 15, 2001 (www.special.scmp.com/june42001/tiananmen_papers/ZZZZEBRCFNC.html, accessed February 2003); "Greater Things to Come," *South China Morning Post,* March 17, 2001, p. 1.

9. Eckholm and Rosenthal, "China's Leadership Pushes for Unity."

10. Figures from *Business Week*, China's State Statistical Bureau, *People's Daily*, and the University of Michigan's China Data Center.

11. Data from Moore Research Center (www.mrci.com/pdf/stocks.pdf, accessed February 2003); Glencoe Economics Update (www.glencoe.com/sec/socialstudies/curevents/econupdate/2000/econ.html, accessed February 2003). Of course, the Internet and "dot-com" booms eventually collapsed, and the stock market and other economic indicators plummeted in 2001, but the economy generally remained healthy and the driving force for other world economies, including China's.

12. In April 2001 a U.S. EP-3 intelligence collection aircraft collided with a Chinese Air Force fighter patrol aircraft, destroying the fighter and causing damage to

the U.S. plane, which landed at a military airfield on Hainan Island. There the aircrew was held for eleven days, while the two governments argued vociferously over who was at fault and how the crew and aircraft were to be repatriated. The incident caused considerable strain between the newly elected administration of President George W. Bush and the PRC government.

13. Quotes from speech by then-governor George W. Bush, "A Distinctly American Internationalism," delivered at the Ronald Reagan Presidential Library, November 19, 1999.

14. From "The National Security Strategy of the United States," a report to Congress, published in the *New York Times,* September 20, 2002 (www.nytimes.com/2002/09/20/international/20STEXT_FULL.html?tntemail0, accessed February 2003).

15. "A Conversation with President Jiang Zemin," *Washington Post,* March 23, 2001.

16. See Phillip C. Saunders, "China's America Watchers: Changing Attitudes toward the United States," *China Quarterly* 161 (March 2000), pp. 41–65, for a more comprehensive review of the state of scholarship on the United States in contemporary China.

17. Terminology taken from standard war games and exercises, in which the American side, the defenders, are called the "blue team," while the aggressors are called the "red team."

18. See Robert G. Kaiser and Steven Mufson, "'Blue Team' Draws a Hard Line on Beijing," *Washington Post,* February 22, 2000, p. A1.

19. The lack of mutual understanding on this critical point of strategic thinking is aptly demonstrated by the fact that most English-language dictionaries carry no entry for "hegemonism." "Hegemony," from the Greek, is generally taken to mean "dominant or preponderant authority over others." Postmodern Marxist theory—especially that of Antonio Gramsci—has discussed "hegemony" as domination that does not rely entirely on force. Chinese terminology puts a completely negative spin on the term "hegemonism" (*baquan zhuyi*), which is defined as domination by force and rule by power rather than by virtue.

20. Yong Deng, "Hegemon on the Offensive: Chinese Perspectives on U.S. Global Strategy," *Political Science Quarterly*, vol. 116, no. 3 (Fall 2001), pp. 344, 352.

21. Saunders, "China's America Watchers," pp. 45–48; see also Thomas J. Christensen, "Chinese Realpolitik," *Foreign Affairs,* vol. 75, no. 5 (September–October 1996).

22. Robert Jervis, "Grand Strategy: Mission Impossible," *Navy War College Review*, Summer 1998, pp. 22–36 (www.nwc.navy.mil/press/Review/1998/summer/art2su98.htm, accessed February 2003).

23. Richard K. Betts, "Is Strategy an Illusion?" *International Security,* vol. 25, no. 2 (Fall 2000), p. 7.

24. Qin Yaqing, "Power, Perception and the Cultural Lens," paper presented at a Stanley Foundation Conference on the Global Role of the U.S. and Implications for the PRC, July 21–23, 2000; conference papers available at www.emergingfromconflict.org/china/voices00/report.html (accessed February 2003).

25. See, for example, Michael Swaine, *Interpreting China's Grand Strategy—Past, Present, and Future* (Santa Monica, Calif.: RAND, 2001), chap. 4, pp. 112 ff; Thomas J. Christensen, "China," in Richard J. Ellings and Aaron L. Friedberg, eds., *Strategic Asia 2001–2002—Power and Purpose* (Seattle: National Bureau of Asian Research, 2001), p. 30.

26. See Michael Pillsbury, *China Debates the Future Security Environment* (Washington: National Defense University Press, 2000), chap. 7.

27. Bill Gertz, *The China Threat—How the People's Republic Targets America* (Washington: Regnery Publishing, 2000).

28. See Robert Jervis, *Perception and Misperception in International Politics* (Princeton University Press, 1976).

29. Ibid., p. 410.

30. Irving L. Janis, *Groupthink: Psychological Studies of Policy Decision and Fiascoes*, 2d ed. (Houghton Mifflin College Press, 1982), p. 9.

31. James M. Lindsay, "The New Partisanship: The Changed Politics of American Foreign Policy," in *The American Agenda,* September 2000 (www.brookings.edu/views/articles/Lindsay/2000usfpa.htm, accessed February 2003).

32. Rebecca K. C. Hersman, *Friends and Foes: How Congress and the President Really Make Foreign Policy* (Brookings, 2000), pp. 11, 16, 43–44.

33. Ibid., pp. 110–16.

34. See "China Policy and the National Security Council," an Oral History Roundtable (Center for International and Security Studies of the University of Maryland and Brookings, 2001).

35. See John Dietrich, "Interest Groups and Foreign Policy: Clinton and the China MFN Debates," *Presidential Studies Quarterly,* vol. 29, no. 2 (June 1999), pp. 280–96.

36. Teresa Lawson, "U.S. Media Coverage of China," a conference report, National Committee on U.S.-China Relations, Policy Series no. 14, June 1998, p. 15 (www.ncuscr.org/Old%20website/Publications/conferen.htm, accessed February 2003).

37. See Murray Hiebert, "A New McCarthyism?" in *Far Eastern Economic Review,* January 13, 2000 (www.feer.com/0001_13/p19foreign2.html, accessed January 24, 2000); Fox Butterfield and Joseph Kahn, "Chinese Intellectuals in U.S. Say Spying Case Unfairly Casts Doubt on Their Loyalties," *New York Times,* May 16, 1999, p. A32; Robert Scheer, "No Defense: How the *New York Times* Convicted Wen Ho Lee," *Nation,* vol. 271 (October 2000), p. 11.

38. Lu Ning, *The Dynamics of Foreign-Policy Decisionmaking in China* (Boulder, Colo.: Westview Press, 1997), pp. 8–12, 16, 34; Vivien Pik-Kwan Chan, "National Security Group to React Rapidly to Crises," *South China Morning Post* (Internet edition), December 12, 2000.

39. Lu, *The Dynamics of Foreign-Policy Decisionmaking in China.*

40. See Ellis Joffe, "The Military and China's New Politics: Trends and Countertrends," in James Mulvenon and Richard H. Yang, eds., *The People's Liberation Army in the Information Age* (Santa Monica, Calif.: RAND, 1999), pp. 22–47; David

Shambaugh, *Modernizing China's Military: Progress, Problems, and Prospects* (University of California Press, Berkeley, 2003), pp. 11–55.

41. For varying perspectives, see Xiu Guangqiu, "The Chinese Anti-American Nationalism in the 1990s," *Asian Perspective,* vol. 22, no. 2 (1998), pp. 193–218; Zhao Suisheng, "Chinese Intellectuals' Quest for National Greatness and Nationalistic Writing in the 1990s," *The China Quarterly*, no. 152, December 1997, pp. 725–45; Suisheng Zhao, "Chinese Nationalism and Its International Orientations," *Political Science Quarterly,* vol. 115, no. 1 (Spring 2000), pp. 1–33; John Fitzgerald, "China and the Quest for Dignity," *The National Interest*, no. 55 (Spring 1999), pp. 47–59; Allen Whiting, "Chinese Nationalism and Foreign Policy after Deng," *The China Quarterly*, no. 142 (June 1995), p. 29ff.

42. Shanghai Communiqué, signed by President Richard M. Nixon and Premier Zhou Enlai, February 27, 1972.

43. U.S.-PRC Joint Communiqué, signed August 17, 1982.

44. Americans and the World: Public Opinion on International Affairs, "U.S. Relations with China" (www.americans-world.org/digest/regional_issues/china/china7.cfm, accessed February 2003), cites polls showing 62 percent of Americans think of Taiwan as an independent state, 69 percent believe it should not be forced into reunification, and 72 percent support its inclusion in various international organizations.

45. In several polls taken in 2001, for example, about half of respondents disagreed with making provocative arms sales to Taiwan, and a strong majority opposed committing U.S. troops to Taiwan's defense should it provoke a PRC attack. See Americans and the World: Public Opinion on International Affairs, "U.S. Relations with China—Defending Taiwan."

46. For a fuller discussion, see Robert L. Suettinger, "Tough Engagement: U.S.-China Relations," in Richard Haass and Meghan O'Sullivan, eds., *Honey and Vinegar: Incentives, Sanctions and Foreign Policy* (Brookings, 2000).

47. Wang Jisi and Wang Yong, "The Interaction of Policies: An Account of U.S.-China Relations since 1989," draft paper presented to the conference on "Forging a Policy Consensus: Making China Policy in the Bush and Clinton Administrations," held at the Miller Center of Public Affairs, University of Virginia, 1999.

48. Interview with Anthony Lake, August 2000.

Index

THE BROOKINGS INSTITUTION

The Brookings Institution is an independent organization devoted to nonpartisan research, education, and publication in economics, governance, foreign policy, and the social sciences generally. Its principal purposes are to aid in the development of sound public policies and to promote public understanding of issues of national importance. The Institution was founded on December 8, 1927, to merge the activities of the Institute for Government Research, founded in 1916, the Institute of Economics, founded in 1922, and the Robert Brookings Graduate School of Economics and Government, founded in 1924. The Institution maintains a position of neutrality on issues of public policy. Interpretations or conclusions in Brookings publications should be understood to be solely those of the authors.